Jan Weatherred
1978

Sociology Readings
FOR A NEW DAY

Thomas Ford Hoult

Arizona State University

RANDOM HOUSE
New York, N.Y.

First Edition
987654321
Copyright © 1974 by Random House, Inc.

All rights reserved under International and Pan-American Copyright Conventions. No part of this book may be reproduced in any form or by any means, electronic or mechanical, including photocopying, without permission in writing from the publisher. All inquiries should be addressed to Random House, Inc., 201 East 50th Street, New York, N.Y. 10022. Published in the United States by Random House, Inc., and simultaneously in Canada by Random House of Canada Limited, Toronto.

Library of Congress Cataloging in Publication Data

Hoult, Thomas Ford, comp.
   Sociology readings for a new day.

   1. Sociology—Addresses, essays, lectures.
I.   Title.
HM51.H68   301'.08   74-12256
ISBN 0-394-31885-4

Manufactured in the United States of America. Composed by Cherry Hill Composition, Pennsauken, N.J. Printed and bound by Halliday Lithograph, West Hanover, Mass.

CONTENTS

INTRODUCTION ix

PART I. THE INDIVIDUAL AND THE GROUP 1

1. Thomas S. Szasz, *"The Painted Bird"* 3
2. Stanley Karnow, *The Making of a Rebel* 6
3. Mary Wright, *Three Stories of Today* 18
4. Judd Marmor, *"Normal" and "Deviant" Sexual Behavior* 26

PART II. THE SOCIOLOGICAL POINT OF VIEW 37

5. Peter L. Berger and Brigitte Berger, *Postscript—Why Sociology?* 39
6. C. Wright Mills, *Personal Troubles and Public Issues* 45
7. Albert Szent-Györgyi, *Science, Ethics, and Politics* 50
8. John R. Howard, *Notes on the Radical Perspective in Sociology* 54
9. John F. Glass, *The Humanistic Challenge to Sociology* 60

PART III. SOCIOLOGY AND SCIENCE 73

10. Raymond W. Mack, *Science as a Frame of Reference* 75
11. Henry Anderson, *Toward a Sociology of Being* 78
12. Robert Redfield, *The Art of Social Science* 86
13. Gerard Piel, *Scientists and Other Citizens* 99
14. Norbert Wiener, *A Scientist Rebels* 107

PART IV. THE SOCIOCULTURAL ORDER 111

15. Howard S. Levy, *Chinese Footbinding* 113
16. Kenneth D. Kaunda, *A Humanist in Africa* 119

v

	17. Kathleen Kinkade, *Twin Oaks: A Commune*	123
	18. Clyde Kluckhohn, *The Meaning of Culture*	138

PART V.   SOCIAL DIFFERENTIATION — 151

19. Fletcher Knebel, *Anxiety Among the WASPs* — 153
20. Ann Doubilet, *A Woman's Place* — 161
21. Harry L. Gracey, *Learning the Student Role: Kindergarten as Academic Boot Camp* — 168
22. George Orwell, "*The Lower Classes Smell*" — 180

PART VI.   SOCIAL STRATIFICATION IN THE UNITED STATES — 187

23. Richard Sennett and Jonathan Cobb, *A Flawed Humanism* — 189
24. Peter Schrag, *The Forgotten American* — 193
25. Robert Coles, "*I'm the True Southerner*" — 206
26. John R. Howard, *The Making of a Black Muslim* — 213

PART VII.   SOCIAL INSTITUTIONS — 225

27. James Herndon, *Four- or Five-Minute Speech for a Symposium on American Institutions and Do They Need Changing or What?* — 227
28. Charles Lekberg, *The Tyranny of Qwerty* — 229
29. *NATAPROBU* — 234
30. Consumer Reports, Serc: *A Dizzying Story of Vertigo in the FDA* — 235
31. Mary Wright, *The Dusty Outskirts of Hope* — 239

PART VIII.   THREE MAJOR INSTITUTIONS: RELIGION, MARRIAGE AND THE FAMILY, EDUCATION — 245

32. Peter Marin, *Children of Yearning* — 247
33. William R. Catton, Jr., *What Kind of People Does a Religious Cult Attract?* — 255
34. Ira L. Reiss, *The Universality of the Family: A Conceptual Analysis* — 263
35. Lionel S. Lewis and Dennis Brissett, *Sex as Work* — 280
36. Marcia Seligson, *Weddings, Old and New* — 289
37. Samuel Bowles, *Unequal Education and the Reproduction of the Class Structure* — 300
38. Lee Stephenson, *Our Kept Universities* — 311

PART IX. POLITICO-ECONOMIC INSTITUTIONS 319

39. William Kornhauser, *"Power Elite" or "Veto Groups"?* 321
40. James Boyd, *Like Marrying a Rich Woman* 335
41. Gabriel Kolko, *The Concentration of Corporate Power* 336
42. Robert Coles and Harry Huge, *Peonage in Florida* 348
43. J. W. Fulbright, *The Starbird Memorandum* 355
44. David Halberstam, *The Vietnam Quagmire—How It All Began* 359
45. The New Yorker, *Terror Makes No Fine Distinctions* 366
46. Seymour Melman, *The Watergate Putsch* 368
47. William O. Douglas, *Civil Liberties: The Crucial Issue* 371
48. David McReynolds, *The American Myth is Dead* 380

PART X. DEMOGRAPHY AND ECOLOGY 383

49. Robert C. Cook, *Malthus in Retrospect: The Stork Visits Dorking—1766* 385
50. Harry M. Caudill, *Are Capitalism and the Conservation of a Decent Environment Compatible?* 390
51. Peter Schrag, *Is Main Street Still There?* 404
52. Barbara Ward and René Dubos, *Strategies for Survival* 416

PART XI. COLLECTIVE BEHAVIOR—SOCIOCULTURAL CHANGE 425

53. Margaret Nelson, *Prohibition: A Case Study of Societal Misguidance* 427
54. Daniel Walker, *A Police Riot* 441
55. David McReynolds, *We Have Been Invaded by the 21st Century* 449
56. Andrei D. Sakharov, *Change for Survival* 452

INTRODUCTION

This collection of readings has a dual purpose. First, it is intended to illustrate some of our most important sociological concepts. Second, it is meant to illuminate major aspects of sociology in the prophetic mode. This type of sociology freely criticizes social injustice and makes suggestions for remedies. The rationale for such activism is the realization that "social science" worthy of the name cannot exist in a repressive society. Furthermore, it has become painfully obvious that the old dream of building a social science free of ideological values more often leads to a nightmare, since such a discipline, with its benign neglect of practical politics, inadvertently gives comfort, if not aid, to the purveyors of totalitarianism. Would-be dictators find it advantageous when the most informed members of society say, in effect, "We do not make value judgments about affairs of the day."

Since it is impossible to be ideologically neutral (given the consequences of such "neutrality"), it is sensible to cast one's lot with those attempting to build a more humane society. Such a society would improve everyone's chance to lead a fulfilling life *and* maintain conditions necessary for the continuing practice of social science. Therefore, a number of sociologists in recent years have been attempting to build a humanistic sociology the primary aim of which is to develop sociological knowledge that will facilitate progressive social reform. It is with this aim in mind that the accompanying readings have been selected.

There are two reasons why humanistic sociology is accurately referred to as "sociology in the prophetic mode." Like prophecy of old, it emphasizes the denunciation of social shortcomings; but, also in the classic tradition, it is less certain when suggesting adequate reforms. This is so because knowledgeable people are aware that there are no simple ways to change complex situations. In society at large, as well as in individual societies, there is no Gordian knot to slice readily with socialism, religion, technology, and the like. Only demagogues claim otherwise.

The "way" of humanistic sociology is not, thus, the easy road to salvation promised by opportunistic politicians. Its way is the less glamorous, but surely more effective, gathering and analysis of accurate, representative knowledge of society. This, plus cooperative working arrangements between social scientists and those who initiate humane political and economic endeavors, will, we trust, help fulfill the fervent hope of an ancient prophet:

> ... let justice roll down as waters,
> and righteousness as a mighty stream.

The Individual and the Group

Part I

According to the "model of man" predominant in sociology, the most fundamental characteristic of human beings is their adaptability. This is a basic sociological principle. A vast variety of research data accumulated in the last sixty years has demonstrated that all people, provided they are born with physical attributes that fall within the rather broad range of what is considered "normal," have the potential to become almost anything, from mental retardates to prodigies. The crucial variable in practically all cases is the socialization process, with socialization being defined as all the procedures that influence a person's development. Obviously, such processes vary with sociocultural setting and with all the chance factors that form unique environments. A few facets of these fundamental sociological ideas about human personality are illustrated and explored in the four readings that follow.

1. "The Painted Bird"
THOMAS S. SZASZ

One of the reasons why people in any given society tend to act much alike—at least, in comparison with those native to other societies—is that most people fear variety among their fellows and, therefore, attack those regarded as "deviant." The result is that people are typically conformist; they soon observe that when they do not conform they are likely to become hated outcasts. This is the theme illustrated by Dr. Thomas Szasz in his discussion of, and quotation from, Jerzy Kosinski's The Painted Bird. Szasz speaks in part from personal experience. A psychiatrist and refugee from the present Hungarian government, he has aroused great controversy with his claim that there is no such category as "mental illness." He regards legal commitment to a mental institution as the modern equivalent of witch burning. His convictions on such matters have made him a "painted bird" in ordinary psychiatric circles.

To the right-thinking man, to be alone and to be wrong are one and the same . . .
—Jean-Paul Sartre[1]

The unifying theme of this book—running through and connecting a number of seemingly diverse topics discussed in it—is the idea of the scapegoat and his function in the moral metabolism of society. In particular, I have tried to show that social man fears the Other and tries to destroy him; but that, paradoxically, he needs the Other and, if need be, creates him, so that, by invalidating him as evil, he may confirm himself as good.

SOURCE: Thomas S. Szasz, *The Manufacture of Madness: A Comparative Study of the Inquisition and the Mental Health Movement* (New York: Harper & Row, 1970), pp. 290–292. Copyright © 1970 by Thomas S. Szasz, Trustee. Reprinted by permission of Harper & Row, Publishers, Inc.

These ideas are conveyed with consummate artistic skill by Jerzy Kosinski in his extraordinary book, *The Painted Bird*. The title alludes to this theme: "The Painted Bird" is the symbol of the persecuted Other, of "The Tainted Man."

The story is a harrowing tale of what happens to a six-year-old boy "from a large city in Eastern Europe [who] in the first weeks of World War II . . . was sent by his parents, like thousands of other children, to the shelter of a distant village."[2] To protect their son from the ravages of war in the capital, his middle-class parents entrust him to the care of a peasant woman. Within two months of his arrival, she dies. The parents do not know this, and the child has no way of making contact with them. He is adrift on a sea of humanity, sometimes indifferent, often hostile, rarely protective.

During his peregrinations through the countryside of war-torn Poland, the child lives, for a while, under the protection of Lekh, a huge, solitary, but decent young man, who makes his living as a trapper. It is this episode that so movingly portrays the theme that, to the tribe, the Other is a dangerous alien, the member of a hostile species that must be destroyed.

Lekh loves a woman, Ludmila, with whom he has passionate sexual relations. Ludmila had been raped as a young girl and, when we meet her, is crazed with sexual lust. The farmers call her "Stupid Ludmila." The episode that concerns us here occurs after a period of separation between Lekh and Ludmila. I shall quote it in full.

> Sometimes days passed and Stupid Ludmila did not appear in the forest. Lekh would become possessed by a silent rage. He would stare solemnly at the birds in the cages, mumbling something to himself. Finally, after prolonged scrutiny, he would choose the strongest bird, tie it to his wrist and prepare stinking paints of different colors which he mixed together from the most varied components. When the colors satisfied him, Lekh would turn the bird over and paint its wings, head, and breast in rainbow hues until it became more dappled and vivid than a bouquet of wildflowers.
>
> Then we would go into the thick of the forest. There Lekh took out the painted bird and ordered me to hold it in my hand and squeeze it lightly. The bird would begin to twitter and attract a flock of the same species which would fly nervously over our heads. Our prisoner, hearing them, strained toward them, warbling more loudly, its little heart, locked in its freshly painted breast, beating violently.
>
> When a sufficient number of birds gathered above our heads, Lekh would give me a sign to release the prisoner. It would soar, happy and free, a spot of rainbow against the backdrop of clouds, and then plunge into the waiting grown flock. For an instant the birds were confounded. The painted bird circled from one end of the flock to the other, vainly trying to convince its kin that it was one of them. But, dazzled by its brilliant colors, they flew around it unconvinced. The painted bird would be forced farther and farther away as it zealously tried to enter the ranks of the flock. We saw soon afterwards how one bird after another would peel off in a fierce attack. Shortly the many-hued shape lost its place in the sky and dropped to the ground. These incidents happened often. When we finally found the painted birds they were usually dead. Lekh

keenly examined the number of blows which the birds had received. Blood seeped through their colored wings, diluting the paint and soiling Lekh's hands.[3]

Still, Stupid Ludmila does not return. To vent his frustrated rage, Lekh prepares another bird-sacrifice. This is how Kosinski describes it:

> One day he trapped a large raven, whose wings he painted red, the breast green, and the tail blue. When a flock of ravens appeared over our hut, Lekh freed the painted bird. As soon as it joined the flock a desperate battle began. The changeling was attacked from all sides. Black, red, green, blue feathers began to drop at our feet. The ravens ran amuck in the skies, and suddenly the painted raven plummeted to the freshly-plowed soil. It was still alive, opening its beak and vainly trying to move its wings. Its eyes had been pecked out, and fresh blood streamed over its painted feathers. It made yet another attempt to flutter up from the sticky earth, but its strength was gone.[4]

The Painted Bird is the perfect symbol of the Other, the Stranger, the Scapegoat. With inimitable skill, Kosinski shows us both faces of this phenomenon: if the Other is unlike the members of the herd, he is cast out of the group and destroyed; if he is like them, man intervenes and makes him appear different, so that he may be cast out of the group and destroyed. As Lekh paints his raven, so psychiatrists discolor their patients, and society as a whole taints its citizens. This is the grand strategy of discrimination, invalidation, and scapegoating. Man searches for, creates, and imputes differences, the better to alienate the Other. By casting out the Other, Just Man aggrandizes himself and vents his frustrated anger in a manner approved by his fellows. To man, the herd animal, as to his nonhuman ancestors, safety lies in similarity. This is why conformity is good, and deviance evil. Emerson understood this well. "Society everywhere is in conspiracy against the manhood of every one of its members," he warned. "The virtue in most request is conformity. Self-reliance is its aversion."[5]

Anyone who values individual liberty, human diversity, and respect for persons can only be dismayed at this spectacle. To one who believes, as I do, that the physician ought to be a protector of the individual, even when the individual comes in conflict with society, it is especially dismaying that, in our day, the painting of birds has become an accepted medical activity, and that, among the colors used, psychiatric diagnoses are most in fashion.

NOTES

1. Jean-Paul Sartre, *Saint Genét: Actor and Martyr*, p. 24.
2. Jerzy Kosinski, *The Painted Bird*, p. 1.
3. Ibid., pp. 43–44.
4. Ibid., pp. 44–45.
5. Ralph Waldo Emerson, Self-reliance (1841), in Eduard C. Lindeman (Ed.), *Basic Selections from Emerson*, pp. 53–73; p. 55.

2. The Making of a Rebel
STANLEY KARNOW

The author of this selection, now a reporter of diplomatic news for the Washington Post, *was formerly an Asian correspondent for* Time *and* Life. *It was in the latter role that he became impressed with what now seems to be the "inevitability" of Mao Tse-tung's rise to power and the Communist revolution in China. Karnow shows clearly that, given China's historical development and Mao's individual experiences, the conversion of Mao to communism was as natural and expected as was musical interest among members of the Bach family. Chairman Mao is a living example of the principle that although most people conform to the standards set by powerful members of their society, the so-called "deviant" often plays a vital role in the processes that cause fundamental social change.*

In a very short time, in China's central, southern, and northern provinces, several hundred million peasants will rise like a mighty storm, like a hurricane, a force so swift and violent that no power, however great, will be able to hold it back.

—Mao Tse-Tung,
March 1927

Hunan Province, where Mao Tse-tung was born, is an area of hills, lakes, and fertile farmland that had served for centuries as a corridor linking north and south China. Insurgent and imperial armies recurrently passed through this corridor in their drives to conquer or defend dynasties, leaving a trail of destruction in their wake. During peaceful interludes, the province was not only an artery for commercial traffic but an avenue along which new ideas flowed. Hence the Hunanese, insular yet exposed to outside influences, developed the skills of soldiering and scholarship as well as a familiarity with civil strife. And perhaps, as Mao himself once noted, the red peppers in their diet also contributed to their vigor.

In sharp contrast to other Chinese classicists whose approach was largely academic, the scholars of Hunan tended to accentuate the political, economic, and social aspects of Confucian texts. Wang Fu-chih, the seventeenth-century Hunanese philosopher, laid the foundations of this pragmatism by expounding the view that political systems, economic structures, social customs, and man himself were all subject to change. Foreshadowing one of Mao's basic dogmas, Wang argued that "there is

SOURCE: Stanley Karnow, *Mao and China: From Revolution to Revolution* (New York: The Viking Press, 1972), pp. 28–42. Copyright © 1972 by Stanley Karnow. Reprinted by permission of The Viking Press, Inc.

not a single part of human nature already shaped that cannot be modified."[1]

The pragmatic tradition initiated by Wang inspired much of the advanced Chinese thinking in the nineteenth century, and many of the most persuasive works of the period were produced by Hunanese scholars such as Ho Chang-ling, who compiled an anthology of political and economic essays, and Wei Yuan, who wrote a treatise on world history and geography. Local Hunanese officials, moreover, were among the most enlightened in the country. In addition to encouraging educational reform and modern industries, they invited both native and outside progressives to address students and other educated elements of the provincial population. The brilliant Hunanese radical T'an Ssu-t'ung, executed by the dowager empress in 1898 for his role in the reform movement, based his patriotic Southern Study Society in the province. The first girls' school in China was opened in 1903 in Changsha, the provincial capital. One of the earliest American educational programs in China, sponsored by Yale, was established as well in Changsha.

Hunan was also the source from which the Ch'ing government drew many of its ablest civilian functionaries and military officers for posts in other provinces throughout the empire. In 1865, for instance, five of China's eight regional governors were Hunanese. The most effective Chinese general of his time was Tsèng Kuo-fan, a Hunanese scholar who finally defeated the Taiping and Nien rebels. Another eminent officer of the period, Tso Tsung-t'an, who consolidated Peking's hold over Central Asia, was also from Hunan. This background may account at least in part for the Hunanese predominance in the twentieth-century Communist hierarchy. With its progressive intellectual ferment, the Hunan environment was certainly significant in shaping Mao.

Located almost exactly in the geographical center of the province, the village of Shaoshan is some thirty miles west of Hsiangtan, a busy market town on the Hsiang River. It is an area of isolated farms lying among hills and a few peaks, one of them the site of an ancient Taoist hermitage in which, according to legend, a monk composed the *shao* style of music that gave the village its name. Here Mao was born on December 26, 1893, in a hillside farmhouse overlooking a lotus pond. He was the eldest of three sons and a daughter. His brothers and sister would later die violent deaths as political activists.

Mao's father, Mao Jen-shèng, had been a dispossessed peasant who joined the army to escape heavy debts and returned to his native village to become relatively rich. As Mao afterward recalled, his father had gradually managed to acquire more than three acres of land, from whose yield the family succeeded in saving one hundred forty bushels of rice per year. Mao Jen-shèng converted this modest grain surplus into cash, which he lent out at usurious rates of interest. He also began to expand into cereal trading, until he was a full-fledged merchant with a substantial amount of monetary capital.

From all accounts, including those of Mao himself, Mao Jen-shêng was a badly educated, bigoted, solitary man who demanded total obedience from his sons in conformity with the Confucian notion of filial piety. He compelled his children to work hard, beat them frequently, gave them no money, and often deprived them of food. Mao's mother, in contrast, was a devout Buddhist who exuded love, generosity, and gentleness, and she usually sided with her children against her husband. Relating his life to Edgar Snow in 1936, Mao humorously described the household as having been split into two "parties"—the Ruling Power personified by his father, and the Opposition "United Front" comprised of his mother, his brothers, and himself. "My mother advocated a policy of indirect attack," he recalled. "She criticized any overt display of emotion and attempts at open rebellion against the Ruling Power. She said it was not the Chinese way."[2]

Several Western writers using psychoanalytical techniques have sought to attribute Mao's revolutionary vocation to his avowed hatred for paternal authority. Mao himself has lent substance to this thesis. He told Snow that he learned in his disputes with his father that he could defend his rights only by "open rebellion."[3] But, as Jerome Ch'en has pointed out, the relationships in the Mao family were normal in China of that era. The father expected to be strict master of the house, and the children resisted or eluded his control in coalition with their mother.[4] But hints in the autobiographical account he gave to Snow suggest that Mao was not entirely lacking in sympathy for his father. Therefore, while his tender years were impressionable, Mao's longer-range outlook was undoubtedly molded by an assortment of other experiences.

Mao was only five years old when he started working on his father's land. Three years later, though continuing to lend a hand in the fields, he began to attend the local primary school in order to learn enough reading, writing, and arithmetic to keep the family ledgers. The school curriculum, unchanged for centuries, consisted of reciting incomprehensible Confucian classics. Despite Mao's later claim to have disliked this arid fare, the frequent references to the Chinese classics in his writing indicate that he absorbed a good deal of it. Like all Chinese schoolboys of his generation, he also devoured such traditional novels as *Romance of the Three Kingdoms, The Dream of the Red Chamber,* and *All Men Are Brothers,* with their tales of historical heroes and villains and daring bandits. Mao was especially captivated by *All Men Are Brothers*, which glorifies revolt, even though its rebels seek to rectify the abuses of the imperial system rather than alter the system itself.

Compelled by his father to quit primary school at the age of thirteen, Mao labored long hours in the fields by day and on the family ledgers at night. He grew into manhood and, in customary manner, acquiesced to an arranged marriage with a girl four years his senior. The marriage, later repudiated by Mao, was never consummated. During these years, meanwhile, Mao found time to continue reading. One of his favorite books was *Words of Warning to an Affluent Age,* by Cheng Kuan-ying, a Shanghai merchant and scholar who pleaded for technical and economic modernization and a constitutional monarchy. According to Mao, the book inspired him to resume his education. He ran away from home, first to study with an unemployed law student in the village, and afterward to enroll against the wishes of his father at the Tungshan Primary School, a progressive establishment in nearby Hsianghsiang, his mother's native district.

An incident occurred in Hunan about this time that, in Mao's later words, "influenced my whole life." There had been a severe famine in the province as a result of floods. When hungry peasants protested to government officials in Changsha, many were arrested and decapitated, and their heads were displayed on poles to discourage others. Though Mao heard the story from merchants returning from Changsha, the event scarred his mind. "I never forgot it," he told Edgar Snow thirty years afterward. "I felt that there with the rebels were ordinary people like my own family, and I deeply resented the injustice of the treatment given to them."[5]

Mao and his schoolmates were also fascinated in those days by an intermittent series of uprisings staged by a secret fraternity called the Society of Elder Brothers, which had many adherents among the peasants of Hunan. One of the leaders of the society, Huang Hsing, must have seemed to Mao to resemble a character out of *All Men Are Brothers.* After several thrilling exploits, Huang plotted to assassinate local dignitaries assembled to celebrate the birthday of the dowager empress in November 1904. The plan misfired. Helped by an Anglican missionary, he escaped to Japan, returning to China nine years later as a general in Dr. Sun Yat-sen's Kuomintang. Mao's imagination was also stirred by another attempted revolt by the Society of Elder Brothers against landlords in his own birthplace, Shaoshan. After defending a nearby mountain stronghold, the rebels were suppressed and their leader, known as P'ang the Millstone-Maker, was beheaded. Mao later recalled that he and his fellow students "all sympathized with the revolt" and regarded P'ang as a hero.[6]

At that stage, however, Mao understandably took a cautious attitude toward unrest that directly affected his family. During one period of serious food shortages in Hunan, his father ignored the pleas of starving peasants for aid until, in desperation, they seized a rice shipment he was transporting to the city. Mao recollected that he had been displeased by his father's selfishness. But, he added with unusual candor, "I thought the villagers' method was wrong also."[7]

Yet if Mao's social ideas at that time were ambiguous, his nationalistic sentiments were coming into sharper focus. He was aware of China's humiliating defeats by Japan and the European powers throughout the nineteenth century. Years later, he remembered that he first acquired "a certain amount of political consciousness" from reading a pamphlet deploring China's loss of suzerainty over Korea, Taiwan, Indochina,

Burma, and other territories and tributary states. "After I read this," he recalled, "I felt depressed about the future of my country and began to realize that it was the duty of all the people to help save it."[8]

By his own admission, Mao was then not opposed to the monarchy or the imperial bureaucratic system. Like many young, literate Chinese of the period, however, he gradually adopted the view that Western technology, institutions, and thought had much to offer China. The year he spent at the Tungshan Primary School, where he excelled as a student, was especially important in exposing him to contemporary Western trends. At the school he became acquainted with a teacher who had studied in Japan, deriving from that contact a vicarious pride in the Japanese defeat of Russia in 1905. There too he read about K'ang Yu-wei and Liang Ch'i-ch'ao, the Ch'ing government reformers he was later to repudiate—though he admitted to having "worshiped" them in his youth. His voracious reading during that year undoubtedly included as well some of Yen Fu's translations of Darwin, Spencer, and Mill. Another book, also translated by Yen Fu, was enormously popular among young Chinese at the time. Entitled *Principles of Western Civilization,* it was by an obscure English sociologist named Benjamin Kidd who argued that the individual must sacrifice himself for the sake of society in the struggle for progress. That belief would be echoed in Mao's credo more than a half-century afterward.

Another theme in Mao's thinking that had its origin in his schoolboy reading was his respect for martial strength and courage. He was impressed by George Washington and the American war for independence, about which he read in a now-forgotten volume called *Great Heroes of the World.* In 1964, he told a French delegation visiting China that he admired Napoleon the soldier more than Robespierre the revolutionary.[9] And his youthful imagination had been kindled by such ancient Chinese warriors as the legendary emperors Yao and Shun, and the king of Ch'in, who unified the empire in the third century B.C. In his first literary effort, published in 1917, Mao put forth a view that he continued to hold throughout his life: "The principal aim of physical education is military heroism."[10]

In the autumn of 1911, when he was nearly eighteen, Mao walked to Changsha in order to enroll in the secondary school there. He found the city bubbling with political excitement. Uprisings against the Ch'ing government had erupted at Canton to the south and in Wuhan to the north. The revolutionary effervescence spread to Changsha, where local radicals seized power. Mao was swept along in the ferment. Hardly had he arrived than he wrote a tract urging that Dr. Sun Yat-sen, the Kuomintang leader, return from Japan to head a new regime. Though he later described its thesis as having been "somewhat muddled," Mao remembered his tract as "my first expression of a political opinion." As a gesture of defiance against the Ch'ing dynasty, Mao also cut off his pigtail. And, about the same time, he quit school to enlist as a private in the new revolutionary army. His uneventful military career, which lasted only six months, gave him the leisure to read progressive newspapers and journals in which, he recalled later, he initially became acquainted with the notion of socialism.[11]

After leaving the army, Mao drifted until he entered the Hunan First Normal School in the spring of 1913, when he was almost twenty years old. His five years in this school, an institution for training teachers, constituted one of the most fruitful periods in his early life. For it was here that he laid the groundwork of his scholarship, began to shape his political ideas, and acquired his initial experiences in social action.

The curriculum and *ambiance* of the Normal School exposed Mao to a wide range of literature, both traditional and contemporary, Chinese and Western. One of his teachers, Yüan Liu-ch'i, persuaded him to discard his journalistic style in favor of the classical phraseology that would put sinews into his writing. Another professor, Yang Ch'ang-chi, was even more influential. Educated in Japan and England, he not only introduced his students to modern currents in European thought but inspired their devotion to China's national heritage. He also put them in touch with youth movements elsewhere in the country by encouraging them to read *New Youth*, the iconoclastic review then being published in Peking by Ch'en Tu-hsiu, later to become the first Secretary General of the Chinese Communist Party. Mao's first printed article, his appeal for physical fitness and military courage, appeared in *New Youth* in April 1917.

Faithful to his belief in a Spartan existence, Mao adhered to the rugged physical schedule he would observe for years to come. He took cold baths daily, swam as often as possible, walked tirelessly in all kinds of weather, climbed mountains, and even toyed with theories on nudism. During one summer vacation, he and a schoolmate hiked through the Hunan countryside with no money in their pockets, surviving on food given to them by peasants for whom, in exchange, Mao wrote scrolls in his bold calligraphy.

Meanwhile, plunging deeper into political activities, Mao became secretary of the Students' Society at the Normal School and initiated measures designed to break down its old-fashioned institutional regulations. Among other moves, he freed a student about to be forced into an arranged marriage, organized resistance to a levy on students to meet additional school expenditures, and created the Association for Student Self-Government, aimed at mobilizing opposition to unreasonable demands by the school authorities. In April 1918, a month before his graduation, he set up the New People's Study Society, a student discussion group, most of whose members were destined to join the Communist Party. By this time, Mao's opinions had grown increasingly radical. He decried religion, capitalism, autocracy, and Confucian morality as the "four evil demons of the empire." When his schoolmates discussed strategies to save China, he advised them to imitate the heroic rebels in his favorite novel, *All Men Are Brothers*, by taking to the hills to fight for equality and social justice.[12]

Exactly a decade later, Mao himself would ascend the misty heights of Chingkangshan to pursue a similar path.

The years at the Hunan Normal School gave Mao the solid erudition that he displayed throughout the rest of his life. His essays were adorned with learned footnotes and his poetry rivaled that of T. S. Eliot for its classical references. During the Cultural Revolution, when students were being exhorted to smash traditional vestiges, he betrayed surprise that the campaign had gone so far as to proscribe the literature he had loved as a young man. When his niece, defending the ban, asserted that the students should have a "precautionary injection" before reading T'ang dynasty poems and novels like *The Dream of the Red Chamber* in order to protect them against contamination by the classics, Mao replied impatiently: "You are being purely metaphysical."[13]

Later, however, Mao developed a strong bias against the excesses of formal education. He repeatedly cited such figures as Benjamin Franklin and Maxim Gorki as men who had succeeded without schooling. "One who goes to school for several years becomes more stupid as he reads more books," he said at a Communist Party conference in 1965.[14] About the same time, he addressed cadets at a military academy: "A little reading of books is all right, but a lot of it harms people—it really harms them. It is revolutionary war that rears cadres; the battlefield is the school."[15] Even his own education, Mao pretended, had been a waste of time. "I only learned something at the school for brigands," he told two of his closest comrades. "What I learned in thirteen years of study was not usable for making revolution...."[16]

For all their interest in Rousseau, Adam Smith, Darwin, Huxley, and other Western thinkers, Chinese intellectuals around the turn of the twentieth century paid virtually no attention to Karl Marx. The reason was simple: the Marxist concept of communism emerging in a highly developed industrial state bore no relevance to a society like China. Even so basic a document as the *Communist Manifesto*, issued by Marx and Engels in 1848, was not published in full translation in China until April 1920. By then, a cataclysmic event had occurred that gave communism a large measure of credibility. The event was the Russian Revolution. It struck many educated Chinese as a model to emulate in their own efforts to rise out of the dismal conditions that had overtaken China at the time.

The first Chinese Republic proclaimed by Dr. Sun Yat-sen in 1911 had disintegrated. The recognized Chinese ruler in Peking, Yüan Shih-k'ai, had died in 1916, leaving a vacuum that was quickly filled by warlords who fragmented the country as they built up their regional bases. Meanwhile, despite their rhetorical loyalty to President Wilson's principles of national self-determination enunciated at the close of World War I, the Western powers continued to carve up China. In particular, they secretly agreed to give Japan the special rights formerly held by Germany in the northern province of Shantung. This move ignited a student demonstration in Peking on May 4, 1919, that rapidly turned into a nationwide protest. Known as the May 4th Movement, it became the vehicle for a wide variety of political, economic, social, and nationalistic grievances that had been irritating Chinese intellectuals for years.

Within this context of discontent, ferment, and hope, then, the Russian Revolution had undeniable appeal. It was a welcome blow to the capitalist nations that were the cause of China's degradation. In addition, Lenin's seizure of power in Russia offered a lesson in the technique of staging a revolution that might serve progressive Chinese activists in their own attempts to bring about change in China. For those Chinese who still clung to the conviction that the methods of the West would save China, here was a Western "scientific" approach that could be imitated. Therefore, for many Chinese, the Bolshevik take-over in Russia was less the triumph of an alien and incomprehensible doctrine called Marxism than the victory of a system that could be employed to unify nationalism and eradicate imperialism in China. Indeed, the strategies that the Russians pursued in China were essentially aimed at eliminating the influence of their Western and Japanese rivals even more than establishing a Chinese brand of communism.

Significantly, the earliest enthusiasts for the Russian Revolution in China were two Peking University scholars who frankly admitted their ignorance of Marxism. One was Li Ta-chao, the university librarian and later history professor, who had evolved an abstract theory of man's relations with historic forces and the role of "the people" in society. The other was Ch'en Tu-hsiu, head of the University Literature Department and editor of *New Youth,* who had long believed that Western democracy and science could create a new order in China. In the spring of 1918, though not entirely convinced by communism despite their admiration for the Bolsheviks, they set up a Society for the Study of Marxism. It was the forerunner of the Chinese Communist Party, to be founded three years later. Among its members was Mao Tse-tung, who had just arrived in Peking and was employed as an assistant in Li's library.

Mao may have found the Marxist study sessions too tame. Perhaps he was troubled by his lowly status as a library assistant, which earned him rather humiliating treatment from the haughty university scholars. Sharing a bedroom with seven friends and trying to subsist on a monthly wage of eight dollars, he may have wanted to escape his miserable living conditions. Whatever the motive, he was restless. At one point, he considered going to France on a so-called "work and study" program—as did later Communist luminaries like Chou En-lai, Ch'en Yi, and Li Fu-ch'un —but evidently decided that he lacked the talent to learn foreign languages. Instead, he chose to return to Changsha as a primary-school teacher. There he began to read the translations of Marxist texts, then being circulated in China for the first time. There, too, he formed youth groups and even mobilized a student strike against a brutal provincial warlord. Defying the warlord's ban on his writing, Mao also contributed articles to local publications, including a magazine sponsored by the Yale University educational mission to China. One of these articles, hailing the Russian Revolution, stressed that the organization of people according to their social class was the key to unity and ultimate success.[17] That thesis, clearly inspired by Marx, lent substance to Mao's later disclosure that he had come to consider himself a Marxist "in theory and to some extent in action" by the summer of 1920.[18] Soon afterward, he claimed to head a Communist faction in Hunan—even though a national Communist Party had not yet been founded.

In Changsha, having repudiated the marriage arranged by his parents when he was fourteen, Mao wed Yang K'ai-hui, the daughter of the Hunanese professor who had befriended him during his first year at the Normal School. A decade later, Yang K'ai-hui and Mao's sister, Tse-hung, were arrested by the pro-Nationalist governor of Hunan and executed. In 1957, sending condolences to the wife of a comrade who had also died, Mao recalled Yang K'ai-hui in a sentimental poem:

> My proud poplar is lost to me,
>   and to you your willow;
> Poplar and willow
>   soar to the highest heaven.[19]

If Chinese radicals and reformers were infected by the messianic message of the Russian Revolution, the Bolsheviks were beginning to be fascinated by the possibilities of political action in China and elsewhere in the Far East. In a heated strategy debate at the Second Comintern Congress in July 1920, it was determined largely on Lenin's insistence that the International and local Communist groups should collaborate with "national revolutionary" movements in colonial areas, regardless of their ideological coloration. This decision was to have far-reaching consequences in China, for it laid the basis from which the Kremlin could, in the name of a "united front," subordinate the Chinese Communists to Chiang Kai-shek's Kuomintang whenever Soviet interests so demanded. Even at the outset, Comintern agents sent to the Orient seemed to play a deceptive game with their potential protégés as they sought to muster a wide spectrum of "nationalist" sympathy for the Soviet Union.

The first of these Comintern operatives, Gregory Voitinsky, reached China in the summer of 1920. He went straight to Li Ta-chao and Ch'en Tu-hsiu, the founders of the Society for the Study of Marxism, and proceeded to guide them in the establishment of a Chinese Communist Party. It was by no means an easy task. Among other things, an organization was difficult to shape since so many candidates for Party membership were undisciplined radicals with only the vaguest notions of Marxist-Leninist doctrine. Finally, in July 1921, the first Chinese Communist Party Congress assembled at a girls' school inside Shanghai's French Concession.

Among those present were two delegates from each of the six self-styled Communist factions of China, with Mao representing the Hunan contingent. Also attending were Voitinsky and a recently arrived Dutch agent, Henrik Sneevliet, alias Maring. The whole affair had a faintly comic character. Sniffed out by the police, the delegates fled the city and eventually, pretending to be taking a holiday excursion, completed their sessions on a boat in the middle of the famous lake near Hangchow, in nearby Chekiang province. The Congress announced the Party's intention to "overthrow the capitalist classes" while showing an "attitude of independence, aggression, and exclusion" that would "allow no relationship with other parties or groups." [20]

While the Comintern operatives had encouraged the Chinese Communist notion of exclusivity, they themselves had no such idea in mind for Soviet strategy. On the contrary, the Russian objective was to accept support wherever it could be found. Earlier, the Soviet Foreign Minister, G. V. Chicherin, had attempted a dual approach by simultaneously indicating a desire for normal diplomatic relations both with the recognized Chinese regime in Peking and with Sun Yat-sen's opposition Kuomintang based in Canton. Now, after the Congress of the new Chinese Communist Party had ended, Maring embarked upon a similar zigzag. Traveling south, he sounded out such figures as Wu P'ei-fu, the British-backed warlord of central China, and the governor of Hunan, Chao Heng-ti, later to become Mao's principal foe in the province. Eventually Maring met with Sun Yat-sen. The result of his mission, after lengthy negotiations, was an arrangement under which the Soviet Union would assist Sun's government with military aid and advisers, the most notable of whom would be Michael Borodin. In May 1924, the Kremlin broadened its options in China by establishing formal diplomatic ties with the very Peking regime that Sun was seeking to overthrow.

As for the Communists, they were directed by Moscow to cooperate by becoming a "bloc within" the Kuomintang—or, in effect, diluting their identity as a Party. When some Chinese Communists protested at a Comintern meeting held in Moscow in 1922, Karl Radek put them down with a blistering report: "Comrades, do not indulge in too rosy expectations, do not overestimate your strength. . . . You must understand, comrades, that neither the question of socialism nor of the Soviet Republic [in China] are the order of the day." [21] The Russians communicated virtually the same message in a different context to Sun Yat-sen when, seeking to allay his fears of Kremlin domination, they assured him that they did not regard China as suitable terrain for "the communistic order or even the soviet system."[22]

Several of the Chinese Communists who would prove to be most durable over the years were those who collaborated wholeheartedly with the Kuomintang during that period. The suave, skillful Chou En-lai, who had recently returned to China from four years in Paris, became chief of the Political Department of the Kuomintang's military academy at Whampoa, outside Canton, serving under Chiang Kai-shek. Mao also cooperated energetically with the Kuomintang, displaying such organizational talent that he was elevated to the movement's Executive Central Committee as an alternate member. This promotion brought him under attack from Communists who deplored the loss of their independence, and for a time, he was accused of having shifted to the right. Yet Mao evidently believed, as did the Kremlin, that the Chinese Communists would ultimately take over the Kuomintang from within through patient, prudent infiltration. The failure of that strategy later made him suspicious of "united front" arrangements he could not control. And, along with other experiences, it led him to doubt the wisdom of Soviet prescriptions for China.

It was in the mid-1920s that Mao, now operating as a professional political activist, began to perceive that tremendous revolutionary dynamism could be unleashed through the mobilization of China's vast, impoverished peasant population. The notion was neither so heretical as some students of communism have contended, nor so original as Mao's personal publicists have claimed. Both Lenin and Stalin had recognized that peasants could play a revolutionary role in underdeveloped areas. So had many early Chinese Communists, among them a landlord's son by the name of P'eng P'ai, who had created associations of discontented peasants in his native Kwangtung province in 1923. But in contrast and even in opposition to the Russians and many of his own comrades, who clung to the classical Marxist dogma that the urban proletariat must constitute the revolutionary vanguard, Mao introduced the proposition that the peasantry was potentially the backbone of the Chinese revolution. True to his dictum that theory is derived from direct observation, he first began to evolve this thesis from an examination of conditions in Hunan, his home province.

During the course of several visits to Hunan, Mao was impressed by the extent to which Hunanese peasants were rising in protest against local landlords and officials. This ferment accelerated in the autumn of 1926, when Chiang Kai-shek's Kuomintang legions, moving north from Canton in their expedition to eradicate warlords and unify China, inspired peasants in Hunan with the idea that a revolution had started that licensed them to overthrow their oppressive masters. Early in 1927, after a month spent investigating five counties in the province, Mao wrote a passionate report that laid the foundation for his lifelong conviction that rural rather than urban regions were the key centers of revolution not only in China but throughout the world. Predicting that the force of the peasants would "bury imperialism and militarism," he asserted that the value of any revolutionary party would be judged by its willingness to lead them. Further deviating from orthodox Marxism-Leninism, he neglected to affirm in his report that the peasants must be guided by the proletariat. Mao's report justified the "excesses" of peasant agitation in a celebrated passage expressing his doctrine that only "armed struggle" can bring about real change:

A revolution is not a dinner party, or writing an essay, or painting a picture, or doing embroidery; it cannot be so refined, so leisurely and gentle, so temperate, kind, courteous, restrained and magnanimous. A revolution is an insurrection, an act of violence by which one class overthrows another.[23]

NOTES

1. Quoted in Jerome Ch'en, *Mao* (Englewood Cliffs, N.J., 1969), p. 2.
2. Edgar Snow, *Red Star Over China* (New York, 1961), p. 125.
3. *Ibid.*, p. 126.
4. Jerome Ch'en, *Mao and the Chinese Revolution* (London, 1965), p. 19.
5. Snow, *op. cit.*, p. 130.
6. *Loc. cit.*
7. *Loc. cit.*
8. *Ibid.*, p. 131.
9. See Stuart Schram, *Mao Tse-tung* (London, 1966), p. 25.
10. Cited *ibid.*, p. 41.
11. Snow, *op. cit.*, p. 138.
12. Schram, *op. cit.*, p. 43.
13. "A Conversation between Mao Tse-tung and his Niece, Wang Hai-jung," Peking wall poster, February 1967.
14. Mao Tse-tung, "Talk at the Hangchow Conference," December 21, 1965, *Joint Publications Research Service*, No. 90 (February 12, 1970), p. 3.
15. Mao Tse-tung, speech delivered at the School for Military Affairs, February 20, 1967, quoted in wall poster of the 5th Middle School, Peking, February 21, 1967.
16. Mao Tse-tung, conversation with Comrades Ch'en Po-ta and K'ang Sheng (1965), in *Joint Publications Research Service*, No. 90, p. 26.
17. Ch'en, *Mao and the Chinese Revolution*, pp. 63ff.
18. Snow, *op. cit.*, pp. 155ff.
19. Mao Tse-tung, "The Immortals" (trans. Michael Bullock and Jerome Ch'en), in Ch'en, *Mao and the Chinese Revolution*, p. 347.
20. See Schram, *op. cit.*, p. 56.
21. Cited in Benjamin I. Schwartz, *Chinese Communism and the Rise of Mao* (Cambridge, Mass., 1951), p. 37.
22. Cited in John Fairbank, Edwin O. Reischauer, and Albert M. Craig, *East Asia, The Modern Transformation* (Boston, 1965), p. 678.
23. Mao Tse-tung, "Report on an Investigation of the Peasant Movement in Hunan," *Selected Works* (Peking, 1965), I, 23ff.

3. Three Stories of Today
MARY WRIGHT

This is the first of two selections by Mary Wright (see selection 31), a social worker who lives in the hill country of Kentucky. As indicated in her opening quotation, Ms. Wright is concerned with processes which, if unchecked, produce "a new generation of hopeless men." Far too many of the young people that social workers attempt to help are the hapless victims of a system that insures "the rich will get richer and the poor will get babies (at best)." As discouraging as the cases described by Wright may be, still more discouraging is the knowledge that, even though some individuals can be helped, the system that produced them still grinds out countless more who will not be saved and whose lives are realistically described as ones of constant desperation.

"We are raising a new generation of hopeless men, prepared for little more than their fathers' lives of grinding poverty, few jobs and little self-respect. At six they are bright-eyed, eager, inquisitive like six-year-olds everywhere; by eleven their gaze is empty and evasive, their minds dulled by lack of stimulation. Their period of mental growth has ended; their childhood is dead. The future of the region is dying with it."

—Report of the Appalachian Volunteers

Some folks I know would call them "lazy," "sorry," "no-'count good-for-nothings who would rather be shot than do a lick of work."

Maybe they're right. Maybe you and I would say the same thing if, as we passed, we happened to notice them, leaning on the jail-house bars or walking down the railroad tracks.

But before we name them, let me tell you about three I know. These three are only sixteen or seventeen years old, but it doesn't much matter. In a few years they'll be twenty-two or twenty-three, or forty or fifty. These three happen to come to mind because I've just been talking with them, but there are so many others. I wonder if you have noticed them as you passed by.

For instance, there's Ted. He's a school dropout like all the others, having spent from six to twelve years in school, depending on how you count it. He was in ninth grade when I knew him, though he had never got his eighth grade diploma and was on fifth grade level according to the tests.

SOURCE: Mary Wright, "Three Stories of Today," *Mountain Life and Work*, 1965 (The Council of the Southern Mountains, Inc., Box 2307, Berea, Kentucky, 40403, and Clintwood, Virginia. Reprinted by permission of author and publisher.)

Fifth grade. That's when his mother died. He had already had a rather rough time. His father was a drunkard, without a day of school in his life, and they lived in a cabin away up in a hollow. There wasn't much money, and when the snow was on the ground—since he had no boots—Teddy didn't get to school every day, though the teacher said he learned well when he did come. Also, his eyes were bad, but nobody really noticed, and when he copied things wrong they thought he was just being careless. But because of all these things, Teddy was already twelve years old when he got to the fifth, but he wasn't doing too badly, and actually he was a pretty nice little fellow. His mother thought a lot of him.

But then she died.

The uncles from Ohio came and took the younger ones, but Teddy was too old, they said; he might be hard to handle. So he and his father moved in with an old grandfather, and there were some wild times in that one-room shack.

When people saw Teddy hanging around in town late at night, they shook their heads and said, "Gonna be just like his old man. Just you wait and see."

Naturally, he was picked up by the police a number of times and questioned about different things (it was said he was an errand boy for a bootleg gang, though no one ever really knew) and of course, one night he and another boy were caught breaking into a store, picking up some candy and cigarettes. They came up before the Judge and the other boy was given a good lecturing and sent home with his mother, but Ted didn't have any mother and so he was "sent off" where they send boys like that.

They liked him at the Center. "Friendly, co-operative, wants to please," they said. "But timid and unsure of himself, also very homesick," they added. (He kept running away.) "And not much in his schoolwork."

There were one or two people at the Center who became very important to Teddy. One was an old man who worked around the place, who stopped and talked to him once in a while; the other, somebody's wife who used to give him cookies. He talked about them a great deal, though I suppose that by now they have forgotten who he was.

He spent two years of his life being "reformed" and then because he had nowhere to go, he was put in a children's home.

He was a big boy by now, five feet ten and fifteen years old. You can't put a boy like that in the fifth grade, and so they sat him in the ninth grade instead. There the teachers complained that he wouldn't do his work. Day after day he came without his homework, and he failed all the tests. One day one of them called him stupid.

And like a fool, he quit school.

We tried to tell him—about jobs and education and the way the world is these days—but all he could say was that he couldn't learn anything anyway and what did we want to trouble ourselves about him for and his father had never been to school and why didn't we just turn him loose and leave him alone?

After that, there was a lot of running away and coming back, while we tried to figure out what we could do for him. We even got him past the tests and the interviews into Vocational School, but that lasted just one day. They issued him some big books full of things he didn't know; he wandered into the wrong classroom; and the other guys made fun of him and picked a fight with him the very first day.

What would *you* do? He came home. Finally we had to admit that Teddy was right: We had nothing for him. And so we let him go, and him just sixteen.

He did pretty well for a while—he got a job killing chickens, 2,000 every day, chopped off their heads, week after bloody week, until I guess he got tired of that and one day just walked off. Later on, I heard he was digging graves, and he quit that too because he claimed you never knew how long it would be between people dying, and the days grew long and hungry while you were waiting around.

One evening—it was three months later—Ted came back to us, hungry, dirty, and ashamed. He wanted to go back to school. He said he'd sure found out the hard way, but he believed us now and knew you had to have schooling if you were going to make out in this world. He promised he'd work *so* hard. Please, he said.

Well, we doubted it, but we couldn't say no.

So he went back to school. But it was late in the year. "We don't have any more books," the principal said. "He's missed too much. He'll never make it anyway," his teachers said. "What do you expect *us* to do with him?" they said.

Two days later Ted ran away again.

I came across Ted the other day. He's in jail. He told me how he'd broken into a store and taken a whole bunch of nickels and dimes. When the police came snooping around, he gave himself up. "I had to have some place to stay," he said. He's been there three months, and nobody knows what to do with him.

Sammy is also seventeen. He's a good worker and a nice guy, friendly and helpful and good-natured. Everybody likes Sammy. He could really be somebody, we all kept telling each other.

The trouble with Sammy is that he doesn't know what kind of a somebody he wants to be. In fact, he doesn't really know who or what or if he is at all.

Sammy came along somewhere in the middle of a big bunch of kids. But he never knew what parents were, because his mother was crippled and took fits and his father drank too much and beat people up, and so Sammy went to stay with his grandfather, an old man who lived in a dirt-floored cabin away up in the woods. Sammy learned to hoe and dig and chop and build fires and he was a pretty good little worker. Moreover, his grandfather sent him to school almost every day—to the weather-beaten one-room schoolhouse on the ridge. And though he wasn't the brightest in the world, Sammy made out.

But one night, Gran'pa died, and Sammy was left alone.

It speaks something for a boy, to live a whole year on his own and never get picked up by the police. He slept in sheds and worked in people's cornfields when they would let him, and one family gave him one hot meal every day, though nobody would take him in, because they were poor people too, and after all he wasn't theirs.

And that's how we found him. Grimy, skinny, solemn, and all alone.

We never had a more grateful boy than Sammy was, or a heartier eater, or one that kept himself cleaner, after that first shower the night he came in. And you couldn't have called him lazy then. He was a good worker. He did his jobs well; he would do anything you asked him to do.

But there was one thing about him: he didn't like school. Of course, by now he was away behind, and our school had many rooms and many students and wasn't like the school he knew. He didn't understand the questions and didn't know the answers, and when I asked if he ever tried to get extra help from the teachers, he just shrugged his shoulders. The teachers are so busy, they don't have time, And so, although he got A's in conduct, Sammy didn't do too well in school.

Another thing about Sammy, whenever you asked him what he hoped to be, he never had any idea. A carpenter, a mechanic, a truck driver? He shrugged his shoulders and said he didn't know.

And what should he know? Had he ever really known a carpenter, a mechanic, a truck driver? All he knew was a little farming on the hill, and you don't have to go to school for that. His grandfather had a little farm, but his grandfather was dead. His father was a drunkard, but Sammy didn't want to be a drunkard.

Sammy didn't really mean to leave us. But school was coming hard and when he didn't pass and had to face the same grade over for the third time—well, Sammy tried for the Army. But he didn't make it. It's an eighth grade test, you know. You have to be able to tell what words like "lament" and "irreversible" mean, and fractions and decimals, and what all kinds of tools are for that he'd never seen in his life. He didn't make it, and although the recruiting officer was very nice and gave him a big fat cram book to study before he tried it again, the next day Sammy ran off.

I saw Sammy the other day. He was with his father and his little brother. It was a black and gritty house, with a coal fire on the hearth to keep them warm, two bare bedsteads, and one old chair, with stripped tires for lacing, which they gave me to sit on. Our Sammy was black, and his hair was long, and he wouldn't look at me, and I could scarcely get him to smile. I asked him what he was doing and he said, "Nothing." I asked him if he were going to school and he said, "No." I asked him if he were working and he said, "No." I asked him if he'd been looking for work and he said, "No." I asked him what he was going to do, and he stared at the ground and said he didn't know.

To move, you have to know where you are going. And if you have no place else to go, you go home. Even if your father's a drunkard and it's hungry and dirty and cold. You go home and wait and grow weary.

I believe Sammy was ashamed for me to see him so dirty.

There must be an answer. Special education. Individual attention. Custom-tailored material. With these surely you can catch the dropouts and make them learn.

But after sixteen years of defeat, even these don't always work.

It's hard to know who you are, when your father's not your father, and your own father's gone, and there's no one to claim you for his own.

Kenny had a mother and he loved his mother, but things were such that all the children were taken away and put in a "home" and after a while they were brought back, and then his sisters began having babies, and pretty soon there were twelve or thirteen people in their two-room shack. It was clean, and they papered the walls with old magazines, but oh, the racket!

There wasn't anything wrong with Kenny. Good-looking, quiet, bashful—he wasn't mean like some of them. It was just, as he put it, he "never could get interested" in school. It was something about the way he dressed, about having nothing to eat at dinner time, about the things the other kids said about his mother. Kenny had no friends at school. He rarely talked to anybody. He sat by himself and never raised his hand. And whenever the teacher asked him to do something, he said he couldn't, he didn't know how.

The funny thing is, he didn't stay home either. He was out on the street at all hours, he'd be gone for days at a time, sleeping on the railroad tracks, bumming food wherever he could get it. And though his mother pleaded with him, he began skipping school.

Finally, of course, he was picked up (he was found sleeping in an old man's house when the old man wasn't there: "breaking and entering" they called it) and "sent off" as a juvenile delinquent.

I guess that finished convincing him that he wasn't any good.

When Kenny came to us, he made it one week in school. Then he started running away, hiding in the woods. A dozen times we took him back. We put him in a special class. We bought him special books. We encouraged, cajoled, and reasoned with him. We showed him how, in three short months, he had advanced a whole year in his reading. But he didn't believe it. He couldn't believe it. He wouldn't believe it. And whether it was true or not, he still knew it was a fifth-grade reader he was using. And he slammed his book and tore up his papers and said he didn't know how. And the next day he spent in bed with the covers over his head.

Finally, we told Kenny he would have to work or he couldn't stay.

And because he would not be convinced that he was worth keeping, he chose to go.

He's at home now with his mother. Today there's just him and his mother and his sister, because all the rest of the children have been taken away again and put in a "home." I presume he's standing on a street corner or sleeping on the tracks. He's sixteen now. He doesn't have to go to school.

Maybe they *are* "lazy good-for-nothings." And it's probably true that they'd rather be shot than try to do what they've never learned how, and be laughed at and pushed aside. I would too.

But, defeated though they may be today, tomorrow is coming.

Do you know what Ted told me? "When I get out of here, I'll get me a *good* job. You wait and see, I'll make out. I'll be eighteen by then and things will be different."

Will the rest of us, I wonder, be ready by then to make things different?

[That is not the end of "Three Stories"—Ted's or Sammy's or Kenny's. It was only their stories up to three months ago. We asked Mary Wright to tell us what she could of the three boys since that time. She picks up the narrative at that point.—Ed., *Mountain Life and Work*]

Stories of today are never finished. They go on even as we are telling them. It is now three months from the time when I found Ted in jail and Sammy silent and ashamed at home, and when I left Kenny bumming along the railroad tracks.

What about them now?

Ted has gone again. The world with its favors and its impossible hopes was drawing too close. I came to him with Job Corps applications, and his keepers said, yes, they would let him go for something like that. He listened and seemed pleased, took the tests and passed them, although the fractions stumped him. "We should hear pretty soon," I said, to cheer him.

Two days later he broke out and ran away, and no one knows where he is. He *wants* to be a bum, some might say. But fear, I've found, takes strange forms and sometimes shies away even from the face of hope.

It was Christmas that brought me back to Sammy: a gaudy greeting card with a scrawly message I could scarcely read: "Can I talk to you?"

When I came, Sammy was walking along the railroad. He was in gray baggy work clothes and heavy boots, and his tousled blond hair curled over his collar. His shoulders stooped under an enormous sack of coal he had gathered along the way, for the black, gawky tipple stood just behind us. In his other hand he carried a gun and two tall dogs loped along at his heels. His legs—inches longer than I remembered them—took great long strides, and his head was bent low, intent upon thoughts of his own. An Appalachian hero straight from the pages of D. H. Lawrence, I thought, and for some reason, I wanted to cry.

I spoke to him from the car. The dogs growled and came sniffing around, and Sammy looked up in surprise.

We talked a bit. "You wanting to come back, Sammy?" "Uh-huh." That's all he would say. So I asked him: "Tell me, Sammy, have you heard anything about this Job Corps thing?" "Uh-uh," and he shook his shaggy head. "Well, it's like this. It's for kids about your age who are out of school and can't find a job. That's you, isn't it?" "Reckon so," he said. "They're opening up these camps where the guys work part-time—out in the woods, building roads, things like that—and they have some learning in reading and writing, and then they're taught a trade.... What do you think?" He shrugged his shoulders. "I don't know much about it myself," I went on, "since it's so new. I thought I'd go down to the Employment Office to ask about it today. Would you like to come along?" He nodded his head.

So Sammy took his gun and sack of coal and the dogs up the creek to the house. When he came back he had on a clean white shirt, his face was scrubbed and he really looked nice.

We drove the fifteen miles to town and found the Employment Office. Yes, the lady who took applications was in. Please sit down and wait. There was someone with her already.

There were other boys there: One little fellow sitting with his mother; three with sideburns and clicks on their heels, who stood outside on the sidewalk, cigarettes in their mouths, their fingers nervous; another came to sit by us and shattered the waiting-room hush with a loud: "You signing up for this job thing?" He picked up one of the brochures and thumbed through it. "Not bad ... How far you go in school? *I* just made it to the sixth. Got kicked out for fighting. They said I was the meanest kid they ever seen. How long you been out? I been out three years. I'm seventeen now. How old are you? You working? Neither am I. Nothin' to do ... Reckon you'll like it?"

Even some girls came in, one big-boned with a bush of hair and her jaws going fast on a wad of chewing gum. She never looked at all the boys' eyes watching her, but leaned over to the girl at the counter and whispered her question. "What did you say? ... You mean the Job Corps? Yes, there's to be one for girls, but it hasn't started yet. Come back in about a month." The girl stood there a moment and nodded her head, then with a quick, anxious glance at all of us sitting around, she turned and went out.

After a while another girl came in, small, pretty, with smart clothes and slim heels. She wanted to register for work, she said. How old? Seventeen. How much schooling? High school graduate. Any work experience? In the dime store over Christmas. Special skills? She had typing and shorthand and would like to be a secretary. The clerk made out some cards and pulled some papers from a file. She made a telephone call and gave the girl a couple of addresses. The girl thanked her and went out smiling.

After three hours of waiting, we finally got to see the Job Corps lady. Because it was already four o'clock, she took all the rest of us together. She explained the program at length, and asked the boys questions and had them sign their names on a card. I wondered if Sammy would sign. I hadn't even asked him yet if he wanted to join. But he signed, and gave my telephone number where he could be reached.

After all the talk—which took longer than it should have because of our friend with the loud mouth, who commented on this and then that and cracked raw jokes (We wondered if he would be chosen or, if chosen, how long he would be kept; perhaps even the Job Corps—like the school before it—might have its toleration limits.) After all that time the timid boy—the one with his mother—squirmed in his chair and with an apologetic grin his mother said to the lady, "I reckon we've come to the wrong place. We was after that there job training or something, like the boys are getting downtown. I can't let him go off from home; you know, he's all I got to depend on. This hain't what you're wantin' is it, Jimmy?" The boy shook his head, and so they got up and she whisked him out of there before anybody could get their hands on him.

Sammy signed up and took the tests (four right out of a dozen or so on the math test would pass you: add, subtract, multiply, divide. Fractions and decimals started getting hard.) We brought him back for his physical exam and signing the consents, and again to get his skin test read, and Sammy was put on the list.

The lady had mentioned a camp in Arizona, and all the way home that day he wondered if maybe they'd send him out to the cowboy country. Maybe they'd teach him to be a cowboy.

Sammy's been waiting a month now. I keep telling him to be patient, for after all, the whole thing is very new. They can't possibly take everybody at once, because, believe me, there are going to be a heck of a lot of these boys! He's staying with us till he gets his call, and he's not lost hope—yet. He's clean and neat now, and he eats like a horse. And best of all Sammy's smiling again.

How about Kenny?

I heard from his social worker the other day. She told me he wants to come back to us. It's no good, he says, the way things are at home. There's no work, and nothing to do, except argue all day, and feel bad. *Please* let him come back.

If Sammy gets in, maybe we'll try the Job Corps for Kenny too. If it's not too late for him . . .

In fact, I think I'll even hold Ted's papers a while longer, just in case . . .

4. "Normal" and "Deviant" Sexual Behavior
JUDD MARMOR

The impact of group life on personality development is rather spectacularly illustrated by the great range of sexual orientation that exists among us. Depending almost solely upon unique factors in particular socialization processes, people learn to be "turned on" by an incredible variety of situations. This is illustrated by psychiatrist Judd Marmor's discussion of so-called "normal" and "deviant" behavior. In The Journal of the American Medical Association *Dr. Marmor presents the weighty evidence supporting the view that even seemingly biological aspects of personality, such as femininity, masculinity, and sex preference, are properly attributed to social organization and cultural values. It seems particularly significant that this sociological view has penetrated the ranks of professionals whose work has traditionally stressed biological factors alone. (Readers might wish to skip ahead here and look at selection 15, which shows how Chinese men were once socialized to believe that the smell of rotted flesh is sexually exciting—and so it was, to them.)*

It is difficult to approach the topic of human sexuality with the same kind of dispassionate scientific objectivity that can be applied to functions such as speech, digestion, or locomotion. Sexual behavior is so intimately entwined with moral issues, religious and cultural value systems, and even aesthetic reactions, that those who attempt to deal with it too open-mindedly are likely to be charged by their contemporaries with being immoral or amoral, if not illegal. Sigmund Freud's efforts at the turn of the 19th century to bring the "problems of the bedroom" under scientific scrutiny caused both colleagues and friends to turn away from him in embarrassment, and even sixty years later, in the relatively enlightened second half of the 20th century, the meticulous physiological studies of Masters and Johnson stimulated cries of outrage in many quarters and titters of embarrassment in others.

Nevertheless, no discussion of human sexual behavior can be truly objective if one does not attempt to stand outside of the narrow framework of one's own cultural bias to see how the raw data of human sexual biology are shaped by and shape the infinitely varied mosaics of human experience in different places and at different times.

SOURCE: Judd Marmor, "'Normal' and 'Deviant' Sexual Behavior," *The Journal of the American Medical Association* 217 (July 12, 1971), 165–170. Reprinted by permission of the author and publisher.

HISTORICAL CONSIDERATIONS

Even a cursory look at the recorded history of human sexuality makes it abundantly clear that patterns of sexual behavior and morality have taken many diverse forms over the centuries. Far from being "natural" and inevitable, our contemporary sexual codes and mores, seen in historical perspective, would appear no less grotesque to people of other eras than theirs appear to us. Our attitudes concerning nudity, virginity, fidelity, love, marriage, and "proper" sexual behavior are meaningful only within the context of our own cultural and religious mores. Thus, in the first millennium of the Christian era, in many parts of what is now Europe, public nudity was no cause for shame (as is still true in some aboriginal settings), virginity was not prized, marriage was usually a temporary arrangement, and extramarital relations were taken for granted. Frank and open sexuality was the rule, and incest was frequent. Women were open aggressors in inviting sexual intercourse. Bastardy was a mark of distinction because it often implied that some important person had slept with one's mother. In early feudal times new brides were usually deflowered by the feudal lord (jus primae noctis). In other early societies all the wedding guests would copulate with the bride. Far from being considered a source of concern to the husband, these practices were considered a way of strengthening the marriage in that the pain of the initial coitus would not be associated with the husband.

It was not until the Medieval Church was able to strengthen and extend its control over the peoples of Europe that guilt about sexuality began to be a cardinal feature of Western life. Even the early Hebraic laws against adultery had nothing to do with fidelity but were primarily concerned with protecting the property rights of another man (the wife being considered property). Married men were free to maintain concubines or, if they preferred, multiple wives; also, there was no ban in the Old Testament on premarital sex. The Medieval Church, however, exalted celibacy and virginity. In its efforts to make license in sexual intercourse as difficult as possible, it sanctioned it only for procreative purposes and ordained laws against abortion—laws that had not existed among the Greeks, Romans, or Jews. At one time it went so far as to make sexual intercourse between married couples illegal on Sundays, Wednesdays, and Fridays, as well as for forty days before Easter and forty days before Christmas, and also from the time of conception to forty days after parturition. (By contrast, Mohammedan law considered it grounds for divorce if intercourse did not take place at least once a week.)

Moreover, when the sexual taboos of the Medieval Church began to be widely enforced by cruel sanctions, a veritable epidemic of sexual pathology ensued—sodomy, flagellation, hysterical "possession" by witches and devils, incubi, succubi, phantom pregnancies, stigmata, and the like. In contrast, it is worth noting that in societies in which access to sexuality was open and guilt-free—the early Greeks, Europe prior to the Middle Ages and most "primitive" societies—the so-called sexual perversions tended not to be present. The homosexuality of the early Greeks, incidentally, was not an exclusive homosexuality, but part of a pattern of bisexuality in which homosexual feelings were considered to be as natural as heterosexual ones.

The ideals of romantic love and marriage for love which are taken for granted today are a relatively late development in Western history and did not make their appearance until the 12th century AD.[1] Clearly, there is nothing about our current sexual attitudes and practices that can be assumed to be either sacrosanct or immutable. They have been subject to much change and evolution in the past, and they will undoubtedly be different in the future.

BIOLOGICAL AND CULTURAL CONSIDERATIONS

Before we can proceed, it is necessary to clarify certain fundamental questions about the nature of human sexuality that have a bearing on the problem of sexual deviation. What is the biological core of human sexuality? Is it exclusively heterosexual, or does it have a bisexual composition? Is man "naturally" polygamous? Is woman naturally monoandrous? Are most "perversions" "unnatural"? What form does natural sexuality take in children?

Zoological and cross-cultural studies in recent years clearly demonstrate that the issue of sexual behavior goes far beyond its reproductive functions. Caspari's definition of the sexual process as "the exchange of nuclear material between cells of mating types or sexes" may have validity for relatively primitive forms of life, but as we ascend the phylogenetic scale this definition becomes manifestly inadequate. Patterns of sexual behavior evolve with the species, and at higher mammalian levels there is an increasing emphasis on various sex-related activities rather than on purely reproductive ones.

Sex in human beings is usually spoken of as being an "instinct." By this we mean that it is a fundamental behavioral pattern dependent on internal biological factors but capable of being triggered by external cues. Either may create a state of disequilibrium experienced as urgency or tension; this tension then leads to behavior that has the effect of restoring the previous state of balance, with an accompanying sense of subjective gratification. It is important to remember, however, that such a reaction takes quite a different form in human beings than it does in lower animals, even though the term instinct is used equally for both. The lower in the scale of evolution an animal is, the more totally developed and less modifiable are such instinctual patterns; but as one moves up the evolutionary scale inherited instinctual patterns tend to become less preformed and more subject to modification by learning. This development reaches its highest point in man, whose instinctual patterns at birth tend to be relatively unfocused biological drives, subject to enormous modifiability by learning and experience. This is a major factor in the extraordinary range of human adaptability.

This essentially unfocused quality of man's sexual drive in infancy is what Hampson and Hampson[2] have referred to as man's inherent "psychosexual neutrality" at birth—a neutrality that "permits the development and perpetuation of diverse patterns of psychosexual orientation and functioning in accordance with the life experiences each individual may encounter and transact." This concept of psychosexual neutrality does not, as some have mistakenly inferred, mean a "driveless" state, but rather an inborn biological drive with no specific inborn object, but with the potential for adapting its gratifactory needs to whatever objects the environment makes available to it. The term "psychosexual multipotentiality" probably expresses this more adequately than psychosexual neutrality.

In human sexual behavior, situational and learning factors are of major importance in arousal and response. In the absence of heterosexual objects, human beings (as well as many lower animals) may ultimately seek gratification in homosexual objects, or if no human object is available, in relations with animals of other species, or even by contact with inanimate objects. Even the physiological route of gratification, whether through the genitals or some other erogenous zone, or via patterns of behavior which seem to have no inherent elements of erogenicity in them at all, are subject to conditioning by specific experiences or associations. Other factors in sexual responsiveness include age, health, fatigue, nutritional state, and recency of drive fulfillment.

Freud believed that the bisexual anlage which can be observed in the human embryo is subsequently reflected in a universal bisexual tendency at a psychological level. The evidences of such psychic bisexuality, in this view, are seen in "latent homosexual" manifestations such as affectionate feelings for members of one's own sex and in patterns of behavior or interest that are usually (in our culture) considered to be characteristic of the opposite sex. Examples of these would be artistic or culinary interests or "passive" attitudes in males, or athletic or scientific interests or "aggressive" attitudes in females.

This hypothesis was first challenged in the psychoanalytic literature by Rado[3] who pointed out that "in the final shaping of the normal individual the double embryological origin of the genital system does not result in any physiological duality of reproductive functioning." More than this, we now know that with the exception of the relatively uncommon individuals with sexual chromosome abnormalities, in almost all human beings, biological sex is clearly differentiated at the moment of conception by the XX and XY chromosomal patterns. Nevertheless, the theory of psychic bisexuality is sometimes still defended on the basis that both "male" and "female" sex hormones—androgens and estrogens—can be found in the blood of both sexes. However, although the biological activity of these hormones is essential for the growth and maturation of the primary genital apparatus in both sexes and for the development of secondary sexual characteristics, there is no evidence in humans that these hormones affect the direction of human sexuality or that they determine psychological "masculinity" or "femininity."[4] As Money has put it:

> There is no primary genetic or other innate mechanism to preordain the masculinity or femininity of psychosexual differentiation. . . . The analogy is with language. Genetics and innate determinants ordain only that language can develop . . . but not whether the language will be Nahuatl, Arabic, English, or any other.[5]

Psychological and behavioral patterns of masculinity or femininity constitute what is meant by "gender role," and are not necessarily synonymous with an individual's biological sex. As the Hampsons have pointed out:

> The psychologic phenomenon which we have termed gender role, or psycho-sexual orientation, evolves gradually in the course of growing up and cannot be assigned or discarded at will. The components of gender role are neither static nor universal. They change with the times and are an integral part of each culture and subculture. Thus one may expect important differences in what is to be considered typical and appropriate masculine or feminine gender roles as displayed by a native of Thailand and a native of Maryland . . .[6]

Opler, in the same vein, comments that

> a Navajo Indian may be a he-man, or gambler, and a philanderer while dressing in bright blouses adorned with jeweled belts, necklaces, and bracelets. French courtiers in the retinues of effete monarchs were equally philanderers, though rouged, powdered, and bedecked with fine lace. The Andaman Islanders like to have the man sit on his wife's lap in fond greetings, and friends and relatives, of the same or opposite sex, greet one another in the same manner after absences, crying in the affected manner of the mid-Victorian woman. . . . Obviously, the style of social and sexual behavior is something of an amalgam and is culturally influenced.

> The fact is that the patterning of human sexual behavior begins at birth. From the moment a child is identified as either boy or girl, it begins to be shaped by multitudinous cues which communicate certain gender role expectations to it over the succeeding years. This results in a "core gender identity" of either maleness or femaleness, which becomes so profoundly fixed by the age of three, that efforts to reverse this identity after that time are almost always doomed to failure.[7]

Within every society, the process of acculturation that takes place during these critical years begins to condition the child's behavior so as to enable it to conform to the mores of its environment—how and what it should eat, where and when it may urinate and defecate, what and whom it may play with, how it should think and express itself, and how and toward whom it may express its sexual needs. The so-called "polymorphous-perverse" sexual behavior of young children described by Freud in his *Three Contributions to the Theory of Sex* constitutes the normal behavior of children before the acculturation processes of our society have funneled their sexual patterns into "proper channels." From it we can infer what form the "natural sexuality" of man would probably take if no cultural taboos or restrictions at all existed in this sphere. Freud obviously was not unaware of this when he wrote that "it is absolutely impossible not to recognize in the uniform predisposition to all perversions . . . a universal and primitive human tendency.[8]

DEVELOPMENTAL FACTORS

In his libido theory, Freud hypothesized that the sexual instinct followed a phylogenetically predestined evolutionary pathway. In the first year of life, the primary erotogenic focus was the oral zone, in the second and third years, the anal zone, and in the fourth and fifth years, the phallic zone. From the sixth year to puberty, the sexual drive then underwent an involutional process—the "latency period"—during which the "sexual energy" was deflected from sexual goals and "sublimated." With puberty, the sexual drive was again unleashed and now directed toward the ultimate adult goal of full genital gratification.

With the shift in psychoanalytic theory from an instinct-psychology to an ego-psychology, the unfolding of human sexuality may be viewed in a somewhat different light. The infant's sexual needs are seen as rather primitive and undifferentiated at birth. Such as they are, they find expression in the exercise of the child's relatively underdeveloped ego functions—in sucking, in body movements, and in experiencing cutaneous and kinesthetic sensations. In the course of its adaptive development the child discovers sucking its thumb and handling its genitals as special sources of somatic pleasure, and if not discouraged, will utilize these as accessory sources of gratification. Indeed, infantile masturbation may be regarded as one of the earliest experiences of autonomy in normal development. When the child discovers erogenous zones within himself that he can stimulate to give himself pleasure, he has achieved a significant step in ego mastery. Such masturbation is analogous to the behavioral patterns described by Olds[9] in his experimental rats when they discovered their ability to stimulate a "pleasure area" in their hypothalamus.

This author has never been convinced that the shift to "anal erogenicity" during the second year is either as clear-cut or as inevitable as Freud believed. Where it does seem to occur, it may well be the consequence of the emphasis on bowel training which takes place at this time in our culture, and which often becomes the locus for an emotionally laden transaction between child and mother. Moreover, the struggle at this point is not so much over the issue of the child's wish for anal-zone pleasure per se, as it is over the child's wish to move its bowels whenever and wherever it wishes. Thus the issue is not anality, but the broader one of the pleasure-principle versus the reality-principle—the basic battleground of every acculturation process.

It is probably not accidental also that phallic-zone interest develops when it does. The third year of life corresponds with the shift in cultural emphasis from bowel sphincter training to the development of urinary control. Simultaneously, the developing and intrusive ego of the child at this age begins to perceive, and concern itself with, the shame-ridden issues of the anatomical differences between the sexes, where babies come from, and how much fun it is to play with forbidden genitals. This is the period of the "polymorphous-perverse."

That a latency period should occur in our culture after this kind of behavior should not come as a surprise. Freud believed this period to be "organically determined," but the absence of such a reaction of latency in cultures where there are no prohibitions to the free expression of sexuality in children, clearly indicates that this is not so. Sexual latency, when it occurs, is obviously the result of repression in a culture that strongly indoctrinates the child with the conviction that its "polymorphous and perverse" sexual interests are dirty, shameful, and sinful. Under this pressure with threats of physical punishment and loss of love (both "castration" threats), many children in our society repress their sexuality until the imperative thrust of puberty brings it to the fore again. It is worth noting, however, that there has been evidence in recent years that increasing numbers of children in their prepubertal years continue to be sexually active and interested. This is a reflection of the more accepting attitudes toward sexuality that have been emerging in our culture in recent decades.

The subsequent vicissitudes of adult sexuality also take many forms. Monogamy as a compulsory pattern of mateship, for example, occurs in only a minority of human societies—only 16% of 185 societies studied by Ford and Beach.[10] (Even in that 16%, less than one-third wholly disapproved of both premarital and extramarital liaisons.) Strict monogamy, however, is not necessarily a mark of advanced civilization—some extremely primitive societies are strongly monogamous.

Patterns of monogamy and polygamy (or polyandry) are usually dependent on economic factors. Even in societies where multiple mateships are permitted, only the well-to-do usually are able to exercise this option, and single mateships, although not required, are the rule.

Rules governing premarital and extramarital relations also vary widely in different cultures. There are numerous societies in which extramarital sex is permitted and expected, and in which there is no censure of adultery. Indeed, among the polyandrous Toda of India, there is no word in their language for adultery, and moral opprobrium is attached to the man who begrudges his wife to another! It is interesting to note also that in societies that have no double standard in sexual matters and in which liaisons are freely permitted, women avail themselves of their opportunities as eagerly as men, a fact that casts serious doubts on the popular assumption that females are, by nature, less sexually assertive than males.

DEFINITION OF SEXUAL DEVIATION

How then can one define sexual deviations? It is clear from our preceding discussion that an adequate definition cannot be based on any assumption of the biological "naturalness" of any particular pattern of sexual behavior in man. What is evaluated as psychologically healthy in one era or culture may not be so in another. The normal sexual behavior of an adolescent girl among the Marquesans or Trobrianders would be considered nymphomanic or delinquent in our society. Homosexual behavior is regarded as deviant in many cultures, including our own, but was not so adjudged in ancient Greece and pre-Meiji Japan, or among the Tanalans of Madagascar, the Siwanis of Africa, the Aranda of Australia, the Keraki of New Guinea, and many others.

It is sometimes argued that this kind of culture-oriented relativistic concept of normalcy is fallacious because it fails to recognize that there is an "optimal" conception of health that transcends all cultural norms. The difficulty with this argument is that the concept of optimal itself is culture-bound. Even granting that within any culture a concept such as personality homeostasis or self-realization has validity, the content of such concepts still vary in different times and places. A definition of psychological health in psychoanalytic terms implies the ability of the "ego" to effectively handle and integrate its relationships with the "id," the "superego," and the outer world. Such a definition could undoubtedly be used cross-culturally. But again, its content will vary in different cultural contexts since the nature of the "normal" superego and of the outer world are culture-dependent.

COMMENT

It seems to this author, therefore, that there is no way in which the concepts of normal and deviant sexual behavior can be divorced from the value systems of our society; and since such value systems are always in the process of evolution and change, we must be prepared to face the possibility that some patterns currently considered deviant may not always be so regarded. The fact that we now refer to sexual "deviations" rather than to "perversions" already represents an evolutionary change within our culture toward a more objective and scientific approach to these problems, in contrast to the highly moralistic and pejorative approach of the previous generation. Perhaps some day we shall talk simply of "variations" in sexual object choice.

Such a relativistic approach to normalcy should not, however, be mistaken for a nihilistic one. We are all products of our culture, and within the context of our current Western cultural value system there are indeed certain patterns that can be regarded as psychologically optimal and healthy.

Although there is a wide spectrum of variations in human sexual motivation and behavior—most human beings, in the privacy of their bedrooms, in one way or another, and at one time or another, violate the rigid conventional standards of "proper" sexual behavior—there are nevertheless certain more widely deviant patterns of sexual behavior that in all likelihood would be considered abnormal in every society. For example, practices that involve serious injury to one of the participants in the sexual relationship could hardly be considered adaptive in any society since they would ultimately jeopardize its survival.

One way of defining a large category of sexual practices that is considered deviant in our culture is that they involve the habitual and preferential use of nongenital outlets for sexual release. The emphasis in this definition is on the terms "habitual" and "preferential," since extragenital gratification may be a part of normal sexual foreplay, or of variations in sexual experiences between perfectly normal adults. When, however, such variant activity becomes an habitual end in itself, it almost always, in the context of our culture, means some disturbance in personality functioning.

It should be noted that the above definition is a psychiatric not a legal one. Statutes in most of the United States regard any use of nongenital outlets for sexual release as illegal. Kinsey and his coworkers, after their extensive surveys of sexual practices of males and females, concluded that there are probably very few adults who have not technically violated such statutes at one time or another.

Other major forms of sexual behavior that are defined as deviant in our society involve activity that is homosexual, or sexual activity with immature partners of either sex (pedophilia), animals (bestiality), dead people (necrophilia), or inanimate objects (fetishism).

Although sexual deviations are commonly separated in terms of their outstanding clinical manifestations, in actuality they are far from discrete phenomena. There is frequent overlapping among them and it is not uncommon for an individual to present simultaneous evidence of more than one of these manifestations. Thus, a fetishist may also be an exhibitionist and a voyeur; a transvestite may also be involved in sadomasochistic practices; incest and pedophilia may be associated in the same person, and so forth.

. . .

The choice of deviant pattern, like the choice of symptom in neurosis, is dependent on complex determinants which have to be ferreted out by a painstaking history and psychodynamic evaluation in each individual case. Disturbances in core family relationships, impairment in gender identity development, poor ego development, and specific conditioning experiences are all involved.

Apart from such clearly definable deviant patterns, human sexual relationships are often complicated by unconscious motivations of fear, hate, or guilt, which leave their stamps on the quality of the sexual transactions between partners. In our culture, a key distinguishing factor between what is regarded as healthy or unhealthy sexual behavior is whether such behavior is motivated by feelings of love or whether it becomes a vehicle for the discharge of anxiety, hostility, or guilt. Healthy sexuality seeks erotic pleasure in the context of tenderness and affection; pathologic sexuality is motivated by needs for reassurance or relief from nonsexual sources of tension. Healthy sexuality seeks both to give and receive pleasure; neurotic forms are unbalanced toward excessive giving or taking. Healthy sexuality is discriminating as to partner; neurotic patterns often tend to be nondiscriminating. The periodicity of healthy sexuality is determined primarily by recurrent erotic tensions in the context of affection. Neurotic sexual drives, on the other hand, are triggered less by erotic needs than by non-erotic tensions and are therefore more apt to be compulsive in their patterns of occurrence.

A sharp line of distinction, however, cannot always be drawn between healthy and neurotic sexuality. Since patterns of sexual behavior always reflect personality patterns and problems, and since no one in our complex society is totally exempt from individual idiosyncracies, tensions, and anxieties, these will be manifested in sexual patterns no less than in other areas of interpersonal transactions. No human being is perfect, and nowhere is the humanity of man more transparent than in the varied patterns of his sexual relationships.

NOTES

1. G. R. Taylor, *Sex in History* (New York: Vanguard Press, 1954).
2. J. L. Hampson, Joan G. Hampson, "The ontogenesis of sexual behavior in man," in W. C. Young, ed., *Sex and Internal Secretions* (Baltimore: Williams & Wilkins, 1961), vol. 2, ed. 3.
3. S. Rado, *Psychoanalysis of Behavior* (New York: Grune & Stratton, 1956), vol. 1.
4. W. H. Perloff, "Hormones and homosexuality," in J. Marmor, ed., *Sexual Inversion: The Multiple Roots of Homosexuality* (New York: Basic Books, 1965) pp. 44–69.
5. J. Money, "Developmental differentiation of femininity and masculinity compared," in S. M. Farber, R. H. L. Wilson, eds., *Man and Civilization* (New York: McGraw-Hill Book Co., 1963), pp. 56–57.
6. Hampson and Hampson, *op. cit.*
7. M. K. Opler, "Anthropological and cross-cultural aspects of homosexuality," in J. Marmor ed., *Sexual Inversion: The Multiple Roots of Homosexuality* (New York: Basic Books, 1965), pp. 108–23.

8. S. Freud, *Three Essays on the Theory of Sexuality*. J. Strachey (trans., 1905), (New York: Basic Books, 1962).
9. J. Olds, "Self stimulation of the brain," *Science* 127:315–24, 1958.
10. C. S. Ford, F. A. Beach, *Patterns of Sexual Behavior* (New York: Harper & Bros., 1952).

The Sociological Point of View

Part II

The sociological point of view is one which, in any given situation, examines phenomena with this question in mind: What are the human relationship factors involved? Thus, sociologists are not concerned with personality per se; they are concerned with how personality is affected by human interaction. For example, sociologists are not interested in leadership in and of itself; rather, they focus attention on the relationships, between groups and individuals, that apparently make particular leaders effective. Such an emphasis on human interaction and its consequences is one product of a long developmental process that continues unabated, as illustrated in the following readings.

5. Postscript—Why Sociology?
PETER L. BERGER AND BRIGITTE BERGER

During the last 150 years, sociology has developed into the most generally inclusive of all the social sciences concerned with human relationships. As it evolved, sociology's practitioners commonly put more and more emphasis on "hard science" by acknowledging the importance of purely empirical data, employing technically impressive analysis techniques, and eschewing some value judgments. Certain aspects of this type of sociology have, however, been severely criticized in recent years. Among the critics, Peter and Brigitte Berger are two of the most effective (perhaps because of their gentleness and scholarly thoroughness). Peter Berger is beyond doubt the best known and most widely read of the new breed known as "humanist sociologists." In the following selection taken from their introductory text, the authors suggest some important shifts sociology has made toward a more humane emphasis and away from the abstract empiricism that has traditionally prevailed.

There are, of course, different reasons why students take an introductory course or read an introductory book on sociology. These range all the way from earnest career plans to the tactical requirements of seduction, not to mention the campus reputation and grading habits of sociology instructors. We have no objections to the less than earnest motives. But, optimists by inclination, we assume that having finished the course, and (needless to say) having read this book, at least some students will be more rather than less interested in sociology. In that case the question, "Why sociology?" will also be more interesting to them than it was at the outset.

SOURCE: Peter L. Berger and Brigitte Berger, *Sociology: A Biographical Approach* (New York: Basic Books, 1972), pp. 357–364. Copyright © 1972 by Peter L. Berger and Brigitte Berger. Reprinted by permission of Basic Books, Inc., Publishers, New York.

The question can be asked with two different senses: "What can one actually do with sociology?" And, more searchingly: "Is sociology worthwhile?"

MAKING A LIVING IN THE "KNOWLEDGE INDUSTRY"

One thing that one can obviously do with sociology is to become a sociologist. Only a very small fraction of those who take sociology courses as undergraduates take this direction. For those considering this awesome option, a few words on its practical implications are in order here.

The discipline of sociology is today a well-established and well-organized profession in America. As of late 1969, the membership of the American Sociological Association, the major professional organization of the discipline, was 12,903 if one includes student members and 8,461 if one only counts the fully certified brethren—in either case, a number not to be sneezed at.[1] The association has an impressive headquarters in Washington and holds conventions in enormous hotels.

The visible output of American sociologists is impressive, too. Large numbers of books are published in sociology every year. There are dozens of journals in the field, more than anyone can possibly read and do anything else besides, so that there is now (as in other disciplines) a journal *about* journals, *Sociological Abstracts,* which classifies and summarizes this vast and rapidly growing body of professional lore.

Sociology constitutes a significant division of what Fritz Machlup, an economist, has called the American "knowledge industry." What is probably more important, sociology occupies, and has occupied for a considerable period of time, a respected place on the American intellectual scene. Naturally, there are also detractors, like the sardonic commentator who said some years ago that a sociologist is a man who will spend ten thousand dollars to discover the local house of ill repute. By and large, though, statements about society by sociologists exercising their professional judgment widely command authority or at least gain a serious hearing. This is true in the mass media, in political debate over current issues, among decision-makers in government and business, and in broad segments of the general public. We would not be sociologists if we did not agree that, much of the time, this intellectual status of the discipline is merited. To mention only some of the problems currently troubling American society, sociologists have contributed both important information and clarifying insights to the public discussion of urbanism, of the racial situation, of education, of government measures against crime and against poverty.

American sociology continues to hold a pre-eminent position in the discipline, comparable, say, to the position held by German philosophy and German historical scholarship in the nineteenth century. Sociology in no other country compares with American sociology in terms of academic and intellectual status, the variety and sophistication of theoretical approaches and research technology, both the quantity and quality of output, and the sheer size of the professional establishment. American books and journals throughout the field are necessary reading for foreign sociologists, while the reverse is only true for limited aspects of sociology (as, for example, for sociological theory). Foreign sociology students, if at all possible practically, seek to spend at least some portion of their studies in an American university's sociology department. Not surprisingly, English (one is tempted to add, especially if one looks at the writings of British sociologists, *American* English) has become the lingua franca of sociologists everywhere.

All the same, there has been quite a remarkable upsurge of sociology abroad over the last two decades. Sizable sociological establishments have grown up in Western Europe, particularly in Germany, France, Britain, Holland and the Scandinavian countries. Although the attitude toward sociology by Communist regimes has vacillated between condemning it as a "bourgeois ideology" and gingerly accepting it as a useful instrument in social planning, sociology is now a going concern in the Soviet Union and in the socialist countries of Eastern Europe. The holding of the 1970 World Congress of Sociology in Bulgaria symbolized this new acceptability of the discipline in the "socialist camp" (at least the part of it that is within the Soviet orbit). In the countries of the Third World, sociology is very widely regarded as an important aid for development planning and policy.[2]

What are American sociologists actually doing? The very great majority are engaged in teaching at colleges and universities.[3] This means, quite simply, that anyone planning to become a professional sociologist should reckon with the fact that most jobs in the field are teaching jobs, and that teaching is very probably what he will be doing at least much of the time. The most important other activity of sociologists is research, though for many this is not a source of continuous employment but rather something that they do besides teaching or on occasional leaves from teaching jobs. All the same, there are a good number of full-time research jobs, some connected with university research programs, others in agencies or research institutes of the government, business, labor or other organizations (such as churches) with an interest in discerning societal trends. Thirdly, there is a scattering of sociologists in jobs of the most different sorts, ranging from advertising and personnel management to community action in this country or abroad. Whether interested in teaching or one of the other options, the aspiring sociologist should realize that graduate study, increasingly up to and including the doctorate, is a prerequisite for jobs that carry professional status (not to mention the pay that one associates with such status). Different graduate programs emphasize different aspects of the field and some thought ought to be given to the choice of school, especially since the American academic system does not encourage easy transfers from one school to another.[4]

"ESTABLISHMENT" AND "RADICAL" SOCIOLOGY

There has recently been much debate within the profession about its present condition, the directions it has been taking and the directions that it should take in the future. There are strong differences of opinion among American sociologists both as to diagnosis and prescription.[5] Political radicals in the field have attacked what they consider to be "establishment sociology" as an ideological tool of the status quo and have demanded a new conception of sociology as a discipline standing in the service of radical or even revolutionary politics. Black sociologists have called for sociological work designed to serve the interests of the black community, sometimes meaning by this nothing more than work that would be more sensitive to the black experience in America than that of (or so they claim) the work of many white sociologists, sometimes going much further by demanding a distinctively black sociology that would be part of and ideologically attuned to "black consciousness." Various movements concerned with "liberation," most recently (and very audibly so) the Women's Liberation movement, have sought to enroll sociologists and sociology in their ranks. Whatever one may think of these critiques and redefinitions of the field, they have greatly enlivened sociological discourse in recent years. All of this has taken place against the background of a much broader feeling that intellectuals and their disciplines should be involved in the agonies of our time and concerned with the solutions of our most agonizing problems. It is understandable that this feeling has been particularly strong among sociologists, proponents of a discipline that explicitly takes society as its object of inquiry.

Since only a small minority of those who take undergraduate courses in sociology goes on to professional work in the field, a rationale for these courses as nothing but pre-professional education (comparable, say, to a pre-medical curriculum) is hardly persuasive. There ought to be other things that one can do with sociology.

DEALING WITH MEN DIRECTLY: THE HUMAN SCIENCES AND THE HUMANITIES

Information and perspectives provided by sociology have wide applicability to other fields. This is obvious in a variety of practical fields that, in one way or another, must take cognizance of social structures. These range all the way from social work to the law. Sociology, by its very nature, has relevance for most other sciences dealing with man (those that the French, very aptly, call "human sciences"). In many places in this book we have seen the relation of sociology to other social sciences—political science, economics, cultural anthropology and social psychology, to name the major ones. But even in the humanities, where there has been a strongly ingrained animus against sociologists and their "barbarian" incursions into territory where they have no business, the recognition of the usefulness of sociological insights has grown. This is especially true among historians, but it may also be found today among scholars of religion and literature.[6]

But what about the individual who has none of these professional or scholarly ambitions? Is sociology worthwhile for him? We think so. Anyone who wants to live with his eyes open will profit from a better understanding of his society and his own situation in it. But perhaps even more important is the ability to understand the situations and the social worlds of others. Contemporary society needs this ability more than ever.

A PLURALISTIC SOCIETY: IS LOVE REALLY ALL YOU NEED?

Good will is not enough. Let us take just one example out of many possible ones. A few years ago a group of white upper-middle-class young people from the New York suburban area decided that, in order to show their concern for the "ghetto" and its people, they would go into some of the black neighborhoods of the city and help in fixing them up. They did so, on one fine weekend, the first and the last of the experiment. They came in full of enthusiasm and started to paint houses, sweep the streets, clean up piles of garbage and engage in other "obviously" desirable activities. Before long they were surrounded by angry black teenagers, and a good many angry black adults, who yelled obscenities at them, threw disagreeable objects and generally interfered with the progress of operation uplift. There is no reason to impugn the good will of the young whites. At worst, they were guilty of naïveté, slightly spiced with self-righteousness. Even a whiff of sociological insight on their part, however, would have avoided the entire debacle. It hardly needs emphasizing that better insight into the social situation, and therefore the motives and meanings, of others can be very useful for blacks as well.

Contemporary society, as we have seen, is becoming increasingly complex and variegated. This is what is commonly called "pluralism." What is more, contemporary society, or any conceivable variation of its present structure, will break down into howling chaos unless a plurality of social groups and social worlds succeeds in existing together with a measure of mutual understanding. Under these circumstances, the insights of sociology are anything but an intellectual luxury. This is especially so if there is a future for democracy in this society. Sociology, as the application of critical intelligence to society, has a particular affinity to democracy, that political form that is based on the assumption that social conflicts can be resolved and social problems alleviated by means of rational persuasion and without recourse to violence. Non-democratic regimes, whether of the "right" or "left," have an instinctive aversion to sociology. Conversely, sociology has developed best in situations where the political structure had some real relationship to democratic ideas.

AWARENESS EXPANSION: A SENSE OF ONE'S POSSIBILITIES

If sociology has a particular affinity for democratic types of government, it has another, more personal relation to liberty.[7] Anyone who seriously immerses himself in the perspective of sociology will find that his awareness of society, and thus his awareness of himself, will have changed considerably. This changed awareness is not always or one-sidedly "liberating," in the sense of expanding the individual's sense of being free and being himself. Sociological insight may lead to a recognition of limitations that one was previously unaware of, and it may further lead to the sad conclusion that courses of action that one had previously regarded as capable of realization are, in fact, illusions and fantasies. Working hard in one's vocation is *not* the sure way to wealth and fame. Participating in a campus riot is *not* a step toward the revolutionary overthrow of the capitalist system. And so on and so forth. Also, sociological insight may lead to an understanding of the great fragility of all the things one holds dear, including one's notions as to who one is, because sociology shows their ongoing dependence on social processes of definition and redefinition. This understanding, more than any other provided by sociology, can be deeply upsetting, as it seems to shake the very ground on which one is standing.

Thus the relation of sociology to the individual's sense of his own liberty is not a simple or easy matter. Still, when all is said and done, the perspective of sociology, correctly understood, leads to a deepening of the sense of liberty. Long ago the Stoics declared that wisdom consists in knowing what I can and what I cannot do, and that freedom is only possible on the basis of such wisdom. There is something of this wisdom in sociologically formed awareness. Precisely because sociology teaches the limitations and the fragility of what the individual can do and be in society, it also gives him a better sense of his possibilities. And, leaving aside philosophical sophistication, perhaps this is as good an operational definition of liberty as any—having a sense of one's possibilities. Politics has been described as the art of the possible. If so, in all modesty, sociology might be described as a *science of the possible.*

It is for these reasons, we think, that sociology has a place in a "liberal arts" curriculum. Whatever may be its uses for professional training or scholarly enterprises, sociology has a bearing on the growth of personal awareness of the world, of others and of self. There is much controversy today over the future of college and university education. Whatever this future may turn out to be, we hope that it will have a place for this "liberal" conception of education, and thus for the peculiarly "liberal" discipline of sociology.

NOTES

1. American Sociological Association, *Directory of Members* (Washington, D.C., 1970).
2. A good way to obtain an idea of the international scope of recent sociology is to look at the *Proceedings* of, respectively, the 1966 (Evian, France) and 1970 (Varna, Bulgaria) World Congresses of Sociology, published by the International Sociological Association. For an interesting discussion of sociology in the Soviet Union, see George Fischer (ed.), *Science and Ideology in Soviet Society* (New York: Atherton, 1967). For an overview of the place of sociology in development planning, see Gayl Ness (ed.), *The Sociology of Economic Development* (New York: Harper & Row, 1970).
3. For an excellent overview of the various applications of sociology in America, see Paul Lazarsfeld et al., *The Uses of Sociology* (New York: Basic Books, 1967).
4. For the student thinking of graduate study in sociology, a logical first step is to discuss this with a sociology instructor at his undergraduate college. Most college libraries have a fair collection of university catalogues, and it pays to study their graduate sociology offerings with some care. The American Sociological Association publishes an annual *Guide to Graduate Departments of Sociology*, covering the United States and Canada; although professors do a lot of job-hopping, this gives a general idea of who teaches where at a given time.
5. For a broad view of this, see Robert Friedrichs, *A Sociology of Sociology* (New York: Free Press, 1970). For sharply critical views, see Irving Horowitz, *Professing Sociology* (Chicago: Aldine, 1968), and Alvin Gouldner, *The Coming Crisis in Western Sociology* (New York: Basic Books, 1970). A good source for what goes on within the profession, in these debates as in other things, is *The American Sociologist*, one of the journals published by the American Sociological Association.
6. See Lazarsfeld, *op. cit.*, pp. 3ff.
7. For a recent, more detailed discussion of this, see Peter Berger, "Sociology and Freedom," *The American Sociologist*, VI(1971):1.

6. Personal Troubles and Public Issues
C. WRIGHT MILLS

Among the critics of "establishment sociology," the late C. Wright Mills is best known for his caustic criticisms of trends that prevailed up to the time of his death in 1962. It is every sociologist's prime duty, Mills felt, to show that the roots of a multitude of serious difficulties for individuals lie in general social conditions over which the individual, however talented, has no control whatsoever. In

SOURCE: C. Wright Mills, *The Sociological Imagination* (New York: Oxford University Press, 1959), pp. 8–13. Copyright © 1959 by Oxford University Press, Inc. Reprinted by permission.

addition, in the following selection Mills maintains that there are purely personal troubles largely unrelated to the nature of the social system. A well-developed "sociological imagination" is one which readily differentiates between the two types of problems. Teaching people the difference between the two is the primary political task of the social scientist, Mills asserts; if the politically aware social scientist does his work well, there is a chance that there will be a turn away from the traditional (and largely useless) emphasis on individual character, and a turn toward the only tactics—political and economic—whereby social problems can be effectively countered.

Perhaps the most fruitful distinction with which the sociological imagination works is between "the personal troubles of milieu" and "the public issues of social structure." This distinction is an essential tool of the sociological imagination and a feature of all classic work in social science.

Troubles occur within the character of the individual and within the range of his immediate relations with others; they have to do with his self and with those limited areas of social life of which he is directly and personally aware. Accordingly, the statement and the resolution of troubles properly lie within the individual as a biographical entity and within the scope of his immediate milieu—the social setting that is directly open to his personal experience and to some extent his willful activity. A trouble is a private matter: values cherished by an individual are felt by him to be threatened.

Issues have to do with matters that transcend these local environments of the individual and the range of his inner life. They have to do with the organization of many such milieux into the institutions of an historical society as a whole, with the ways in which various milieux overlap and interpenetrate to form the larger structure of social and historical life. An issue is a public matter: some value cherished by publics is felt to be threatened. Often there is a debate about what that value really is and about what it is that really threatens it. This debate is often without focus if only because it is the very nature of an issue, unlike even widespread trouble, that it cannot very well be defined in terms of the immediate and everyday environments of ordinary men. An issue, in fact, often involves a crisis in institutional arrangements, and often too it involves what Marxists call "contradictions" or "antagonisms."

In these terms, consider unemployment. When, in a city of 100,000, only one man is unemployed, that is his personal trouble, and for its relief we properly look to the character of the man, his skills, and his immediate opportunities. But when in a nation of 50 million employees, 15 million men are unemployed, that is an issue, and we may not hope to find its solution within the range of opportunities open to any one individual. The very structure of opportunities has collapsed. Both the correct statement of the problem and the range of possible solutions require us to consider the economic and political institutions of the society, and not merely the personal situation and character of a scatter of individuals.

Consider war. The personal problem of war, when it occurs, may be how to survive it or how to die in it with honor; how to make money out of it; how to climb into the higher safety of the military apparatus; or how to contribute to the war's termination. In short, according to one's values, to find a set of milieux and within it to survive the war or make one's death in it meaningful. But the structural issues of war have to do with its causes; with what types of men it throws up into command; with its effects upon economic and political, family and religious institutions, with the unorganized irresponsibility of a world of nation-states.

Consider marriage. Inside a marriage a man and a woman may experience personal troubles, but when the divorce rate during the first four years of marriage is 250 out of every 1,000 attempts, this is an indication of a structural issue having to do with the institutions of marriage and the family and other institutions that bear upon them.

Or consider the metropolis—the horrible, beautiful, ugly, magnificent sprawl of the great city. For many upper-class people, the personal solution to "the problem of the city" is to have an apartment with private garage under it in the heart of the city, and forty miles out, a house by Henry Hill, garden by Garrett Eckbo, on a hundred acres of private land. In these two controlled environments—with a small staff at each end and a private helicopter connection—most people could solve many of the problems of personal milieux caused by the facts of the city. But all this, however splendid, does not solve the public issues that the structural fact of the city poses. What should be done with this wonderful monstrosity? Break it all up into scattered units, combining residence and work? Refurbish it as it stands? Or, after evacuation, dynamite it and build new cities according to new plans in new places? What should those plans be? And who is to decide and to accomplish whatever choice is made? These are structural issues; to confront them and to solve them requires us to consider political and economic issues that affect innumerable milieux.

In so far as an economy is so arranged that slumps occur, the problem of unemployment becomes incapable of personal solution. In so far as war is inherent in the nation-state system and in the uneven industrialization of the world, the ordinary individual in his restricted milieu will be powerless—with or without psychiatric aid—to solve the troubles this system or lack of system imposes upon him. In so far as the family as an institution turns women into darling little slaves and men into their chief providers and unweaned dependents, the problem of a satisfactory marriage remains incapable of purely private solution. In so far as the overdeveloped megalopolis and the overdeveloped automobile are built-in features of the overdeveloped society, the issues of urban living will not be solved by personal ingenuity and private wealth.

What we experience in various and specific milieux, I have noted, is often caused by structural changes. Accordingly, to understand the changes of many personal milieux we are required to look beyond them. And the number and variety of such structural changes increase as the institutions within which we live become more embracing and more intricately connected with one another. To be aware of the idea of social structure and to use it with sensibility is to be capable of tracing such linkages among a great variety of milieux. To be able to do that is to possess the sociological imagination.

What are the major issues for publics and the key troubles of private individuals in our time? To formulate issues and troubles, we must ask what values are cherished yet threatened, and what values are cherished and supported, by the characterizing trends of our period. In the case both of threat and of support we must ask what salient contradictions of structure may be involved.

When people cherish some set of values and do not feel any threat to them, they experience *well-being*. When they cherish values but *do* feel them to be threatened, they experience a crisis—either as a personal trouble or as a public issue. And if all their values seem involved, they feel the total threat of panic.

But suppose people are neither aware of any cherished values nor experience any threat? That is the experience of *indifference*, which, if it seems to involve all their values, becomes apathy. Suppose, finally, they are unaware of any cherished values, but still are very much aware of a threat? That is the experience of *uneasiness*, of anxiety, which, if it is total enough, becomes a deadly unspecified malaise.

Ours is a time of uneasiness and indifference—not yet formulated in such ways as to permit the work of reason and the play of sensibility. Instead of troubles—defined in terms of values and threats—there is often the misery of vague uneasiness; instead of explicit issues there is often merely the beat feeling that all is somehow not right. Neither the values threatened nor whatever threatens them has been stated; in short, they have not been carried to the point of decision. Much less have they been formulated as problems of social science.

In the thirties there was little doubt—except among certain deluded business circles that there was an economic issue which was also a pack of personal troubles. In these arguments about "the crisis of capitalism," the formulations of Marx and the many unacknowledged re-formulations of his work probably set the leading terms of the issue, and some men came to understand their personal troubles in these terms. The values threatened were plain to see and cherished by all; the structural contradictions that threatened them also seemed plain. Both were widely and deeply experienced. It was a political age.

But the values threatened in the era after World War Two are often neither widely acknowledged as values nor widely felt to be threatened.

Much private uneasiness goes unformulated; much public malaise and many decisions of enormous structural relevance never become public issues. For those who accept such inherited values as reason and freedom, it is the uneasiness itself that is the trouble; it is the indifference itself that is the issue. And it is this condition, of uneasiness and indifference, that is the signal feature of our period.

All this is so striking that it is often interpreted by observers as a shift in the very kinds of problems that need now to be formulated. We are frequently told that the problems of our decade, or even the crises of our period, have shifted from the external realm of economics and now have to do with the quality of individual life—in fact with the question of whether there is soon going to be anything that can properly be called individual life. Not child labor but comic books, not poverty but mass leisure, are at the center of concern. Many great public issues as well as many private troubles are described in terms of "the psychiatric"—often, it seems, in a pathetic attempt to avoid the large issues and problems of modern society. Often this statement seems to rest upon a provincial narrowing of interest to the Western societies, or even to the United States—thus ignoring two-thirds of mankind; often, too, it arbitrarily divorces the individual life from the larger institutions within which that life is enacted, and which on occasion bear upon it more grievously than do the intimate environments of childhood.

Problems of leisure, for example, cannot even be stated without considering problems of work. Family troubles over comic books cannot be formulated as problems without considering the plight of the contemporary family in its new relations with the newer institutions of the social structure. Neither leisure nor its debilitating uses can be understood as problems without recognition of the extent to which malaise and indifference now form the social and personal climate of contemporary American society. In this climate, no problems of "the private life" can be stated and solved without recognition of the crisis of ambition that is part of the very career of men at work in the incorporated economy.

It is true, as psychoanalysts continually point out, that people do often have "the increasing sense of being moved by obscure forces within themselves which they are unable to define." But it it *not* true, as Ernest Jones asserted, that "man's chief enemy and danger is his own unruly nature and the dark forces pent up within him." On the contrary: "Man's chief danger" today lies in the unruly forces of contemporary society itself, with its alienating methods of production, its enveloping techniques of political domination, its international anarchy—in a word, its pervasive transformations of the very "nature" of man and the conditions and aims of his life.

It is now the social scientist's foremost political and intellectual task— for here the two coincide—to make clear the elements of contemporary uneasiness and indifference. It is the central demand made upon him by other cultural workmen—by physical scientists and artists, by the intellectual community in general. It is because of this task and these demands, I believe, that the social sciences are becoming the common denominator of our cultural period, and the sociological imagination our most needed quality of mind.

7. Science, Ethics, and Politics
ALBERT SZENT-GYÖRGYI

The humanistic trends that have been developing in sociology are also found in other disciplines, including even the "purest of the pure" sciences such as physics and chemistry. The reasons underlying this new orientation are discussed by Nobel prize winner Albert Szent-Györgyi. A biochemist now living in the United States, Szent-Györgyi is a native of Hungary. This background accounts for his mention of the Hungarian revolutionary leaders who fell victim to the "salami technique." The reference is to the revolutionists who, in 1956, overturned the authoritarian Hungarian government and were, in turn, imprisoned by extremists who obtained help from the Soviet Union.

We are often told that science has no moral content. Certainly, if I measure the respiration of a tissue, I have little to do with morals or ethics, but on the same ground one could deny a religious content to the Holy Communion, drinking wine and eating bread not being, in themselves, religious acts. If there should be a Creator, then scientific research would be tantamount to worship, there being no greater compliment to a creative artist than an effort to understand his work.

The scientist is searching for truth, for truth's sake, and, if it is found, he processes it without fear of consequences. This demands the highest ethical standards and brings him into line with the religious and moral leaders of mankind. What the scientist really wants to know are the internal laws that hold the universe together with all that is in it. Morals are

SOURCE: Albert Szent-Györgyi, "Science, Ethics, and Politics," *Science* 125 (February 8, 1957), 225–226. Reprinted by permission of the author and the American Association for the Advancement of Science.

the laws that hold human societies together. So science is not devoid of relations to ethics and morals.

MORAL LAW

Morals are practical prescriptions that tell us how to live to be able to live together. The moral outlook of a scientist has to be wider than that of the average, simply because his society is wider, not being limited by time or space. The community in which I live has Galileo, Newton, and Lavoisier as its active members, and I cannot help feeling more affinity to Chinese or Indian scientists than I do to my own milkman.

As to politics, up till lately, there was no need for the scientist to take cognizance of its existence. However, lately, politics has penetrated not only into science but also into the private lives of individuals, forcing the scientist, too, to make a stand. That science, in certain countries, is dictated by political dictators is so crude a matter that it demands no discussion.

A subtler question may be asked about the aims of science. The main driving force of researchers is mostly some sort of a curiosity, the gratification of a mental need, which makes research a selfish occupation. However, from a higher point of view, scientific research is one of the human efforts aimed at elevating man. Within the last decade, science has created the most powerful tools, which, like any tools, can be used for construction or destruction. The scientist cannot remain a neutral spectator and refuse all moral responsibility when he sees the politician run away with these and turn them into tools of destruction.

We all have the bad luck to be born in an age of a moral crisis, and according to Dante, the hottest places in Hell are reserved for those who remained neutral at times of a moral crisis. So we all have to take a stand, simply as human beings. Humanity has its well-established moral code on which human relations are based. It is these moral laws that enable man to live in a society, and the problem is whether these morals apply only to the individual or also to groups of men, whether crimes which are punished by death in one country should be suffered to be practiced on a big scale as a routine by governments in another country, being "internal affairs." This is more than an ethical problem. As a society could not exist without a moral convention among its members, so countries cannot exist, side by side in peace, without a moral code. I am deeply convinced that this is the simple root of all our political troubles, the whole political superstructure being but a "pseudo-problem."

ONE MORAL CODE

I also believe that there cannot be two moral codes, an individual one and a political one. There is but one, and this one is very deeply written into our minds by our education. It is so deeply engraved that we see no need to restate it every time we make any agreement, and we tacitly suppose all written agreements to be based on this unwritten moral code. For instance, if we make an alliance, we see no need to state explicitly that it is made so that we may help one another and not to enable us to stab our ally in the back, as we were advised to do by Lenin.

It is natural that any system can achieve a great temporary advantage by rejecting the moral code that is written so deeply in its adversary's mind that he will believe and fall, over and over again. How often the world believed, *ad nauseam*, when Hitler called every demand his last one. The Hungarians fell for the famous "salami technique" (one slice at a time). We saw just the other day, how, with a boring repetition, all leaders of a revolution could be trapped and marched to jail by an invitation to a "discussion."

There is but one moral code, and, if any government rejects it inside its borders, it will reject it in its international relations as well and create disorder. The question is whether any deviation from moral convention should be suffered by the rest of mankind. There are international laws to control pestilence, for fear that that pestilence may spread across borders. Why not the same for moral pestilence?

POLITICAL QUESTIONS AND THE INDIVIDUAL

For most of my colleagues, these questions may seem so crude, and the answers so self-evident, that discussion of them is superfluous. But, political questions can come into the scientist's life also in subtler forms, making decisions more difficult. Let me illustrate from my own experience.

Before the war, in Hungary, my home country, the government often invited from abroad scientists whom I was glad to receive, until I found that the invitations followed a political pattern and were thus a part of a political plot, of which I was made an instrument. After the war I was treated by the Soviet Government with utmost kindness and distinction, which obliged me to the deepest gratitude. What was I to do later, when I found the methods of the Soviet rule based on moral principles contrary to my own? Was I to trade morals for gratitude? A difficult choice, indeed, for gratitude itself has its moral aspect. And finally, should I follow the invitation to see my colleagues and discuss, say, the origins of life and accept the hospitality of a government when I know that it will make out of that conference political capital, and when the dealings of that government recall not colonialism, but the darkest days of African slave trade?

These are subtle and difficult questions, but we have to make order in our minds, make a stand to avoid being made into tools of politics with which we may disagree. Everyone will have to answer these questions for himself. What I wish to do here is to call the attention to three psychological factors that may make the choice difficult and obscure the issue unless we have recognized them.

The first of these can be summed up by the saying, "things are not as we see them, but we are as we see things." An honest man will think the world honest; a dishonest man, or government, will think that the rest of the world is made of criminals or warmongers. This is natural. We really know only our own mental machine and are likely to suppose that it represents *the* mental machine of man. So, if honest people hear and read about crimes committed in other countries, they just do not believe it, or may believe it with their minds only, not with their hearts. How far this is true is shown by the Communist trials in which Stalin had most of his comrades executed. The whole world listened to the confessions of guilt, and it occurred to nobody that all this may be just the result of a new invention, brainwashing.

Another peculiarity of the mind is that man likes to commit his crimes and gratify his animal instincts, or craving for power, in the name of high-sounding principles. So, we cook up such principles and appoint ourselves their defenders. Men of good will thus are sidetracked, giving their honest consideration to the principles instead of to the crimes. Even good ends do not justify bad means, so I keep myself to the advice, "watch deeds, not words." In politics, I observe "acts" and lend a deaf ear to "principles" until my moral standards have been satisfied by the former.

My third, and last, remark concerns the fact that the brain is not an organ of thinking, but an organ of survival, like claws and fangs. It is made in such a way as to make us accept as truth that which is only advantage. It is an exceptional, almost pathological constitution one has if one follows thoughts logically through, regardless of consequences. Such people make martyrs, apostles, or scientists, and mostly end on the stake or in a chair, electric or academic.

In my home country, in the turmoil of the last decades, it was almost impossible for anyone who followed thoughts through to their bitter end to survive. Those, for instance, who took Christian doctrine seriously and refused to kill were themselves killed. I myself had the great honor to be declared a traitor by my Government twice—in opposite directions— within one decade. I have seen men of good faith believe the craziest *nonsense* once it brought jobs. So the scientist, when trying to make up his mind, should not give too much credence to the words *faith* or *creed*, either in himself, or in others.

Another difficulty may lie in the fact that moral laws are not always unequivocal. If morals are the rules which make living together possible, then they may change according to the conditions under which we have to live together. Bigamy is regarded as a crime in one country, while in another it may be the rule for any self-respecting gentleman. Even the most basic rule, "Thou shalt not kill," may change from time to time. At the dawn of mankind it might have read, "Thou shalt not kill inhabitants of your own cave." Politicians would like to keep it at this level.

So, what is really needed is an international "bureau of moral standards," passing out "weights and measures." If these were generally enforced or accepted, we would march toward a more hopeful future and would not have to find consolation in the fact that, after all, our globe is but a second-rate planet and so its blowing up does not really matter.

8. Notes on the Radical Perspective in Sociology
JOHN R. HOWARD

Professor Howard's "radical" sociology is the same variety of sociology which we have heretofore referred to as "humanist." That he prefers the term "radical" over "humanist" has little significance. What is significant is the burgeoning of a new sociology whose practitioners—people such as John Howard—feel that their prime task is to play an active part in using their discipline to help make a better world for all.

Contemporary American sociology is probably viewed by many persons as being a radical discipline. In an article in *The New York Times Sunday Magazine,* Irving Kristol suggested that much of the unrest on college campuses across the nation during the Fall of 1968 had been inspired by sociologists—graduate students and faculty;[1] and even Vice President Spiro Agnew was quoted during the 1968 election campaign as stating that policy with regard to urban problems should be guided by the hardheaded knowledge of the businessman and the engineer rather than the dubious nostrums of the sociologist.

In truth, sociology's reputation for daring is hardly deserved. Like the fake priest played by Humphrey Bogart in the movie *The Left Hand of God,* the discipline is not what most people think it is. It has neither posed a radical analysis of the society nor consistently concerned itself with alternatives and change.

In the last few years an increasing number of sociologists have begun to question the orientation of the discipline. In a piece appearing in *Trans-action* magazine Herbert Gans criticized his colleagues for not

SOURCE: John R. Howard, "Notes on the Radical Perspective in Sociology," in Steven E. Deutsch and John Howard, eds., *Where It's At: Radical Perspectives in Sociology* (New York: Harper & Row, 1970), pp. 1–8. Copyright © 1970 by Steven E. Deutsch and John R. Howard. Reprinted by permission of Harper & Row, Publishers, Inc.

choosing to do research having greater relevance for policy—particularly with regard to poverty.

> Sociology has long limited itself to describing and explaining human behavior, using methods and concepts not easily adapted to the needs of policy. As a result, sociologists find it easier to catalogue behavior (and misbehavior) of the poor than to suggest experiments that would test ways of eliminating poverty.[2]

Many published studies, Gans commented, "are still small and narrow, often intended more for colleagues than for application to current social problems."

Alvin Gouldner,[3] Maurice Stein,[4] and Thomas Hoult[5] have also questioned some of the basic dicta of the discipline, particularly the principle of "ethical neutrality."

Discontent is to be found among graduate students as well as faculty. The November, 1968, issue of *The Human Factor*, the journal of the Graduate Students Union at Columbia University, was devoted to a self-proclaimed radical critique of the discipline. We quote from the conclusion of Albert Syzmanski's "Toward a Radical Sociology." Whatever the dismay felt by the elders of the sociological tribe, Syzmanski's article represents the thinking of at least some of the people who will play a role in shaping the future of the discipline.

> We maintain that radical sociologists must have an integral conception of their role as radical-sociologists, and avoid the schizophrenic dissociation of their academic and political activities. Radical sociology should not mean contributing money to radical causes, nor should it mean dropping out to organize slum dwellers, draft resisters, or guerrillas. The goal of radical sociologists should be above all the formulation and propagation of a sociology relevant to the practical problems facing man. We must conceive of our contribution to the building of a decent society in terms of (1) the development of an understanding of the organization and dynamics of our society; (2) the development of an understanding of how that society can be changed and a human social organization substituted; and (3) the dissemination of these understandings to our fellow social scientists, our students, and to men in general.[6]

The elders of the discipline probably view sentiments of this sort as the aberrations of youth, or as an expression of outrage at the multiple indignities of graduate student life—some academic equivalent of the Freudian drama of the slaying of the father. It is possible, however, that they bespeak more than momentary madness or infantile leftism.

This book forms a part of the dissent from the discipline as traditionally constituted. In this brief essay we shall explore the meaning of the term "radical sociology." Is it possible, in any scholarly sense, to speak of a radical sociology? Some might argue that it makes no sense to link words such as these: that on one level it is verbal magic, while on another level, it is like speaking of "Baptist sociology" or "Stalinist sociology"—that is, it connotes an ideological bias which precludes the objective analysis of behavior.

In the remainder of this essay we shall attend to these questions.

RADICAL SOCIOLOGY: NOTES FOR A DEFINITION

Radical sociology rests upon a certain conception of the social role of the sociologist. We are in accord with Thomas Hoult's observation that "it is both logical and necessary for sociologists to become involved in at least certain aspects of building the 'good society.'" That

> It is appropriate for sociologists *acting as such*, to "take sides" relative to those controversial social issues which are functionally related to conditions that seem likely to enhance or undermine the development of the social sciences.[7]

Hoult argues that a sociology having any degree of integrity cannot exist except in a society with libertarian values. Therefore, involvement in the actions and passions of the times, in the continuing struggle to maintain and extend those values should be part of the professional role of the sociologist.

In this sense, radical sociology tends to focus on what might loosely be termed "social problems." It is not the case, however, that all sociology dealing with social problems is per se radical. A number of attributes identify the radical perspective.

First, it is assumed that certain of the questions with which sociologists concern themselves are more important than others. Certain questions bear on deep and enduring cleavages in the society and on complexes of values which have great portent in terms of its character. Thus, issues and questions of class, race, and generation, of the distribution of power, and the management of dissent bear on what kind of society now exists and what kind of society it will become.

Second, even when important phenomena are studied, the manner in which questions are put may preclude radical analysis. Put somewhat differently, attendance to important issues it not per se radical; it is also, in part, a matter of how one asks one's questions. C. Wright Mills in "The Professional Ideology of Social Pathologists" indicated that many sociologists and social workers tended to view the difficulties of people as personal and psychological in nature rather than as consequences of social structure.[8] The radical raises questions with regard to social structure and whether it generates and sustains the problems of individuals.

There is an extensive literature in sociology which acknowledges the existence of certain kinds of social problems—poverty, racism, powerlessness—but often there is the accompanying assumption that these problems can be understood in terms of the characteristics of their bearers rather than in terms of system defects. For example,

—Regarding education, a vast literature attempts to account for the inferior performance of slum children in the public schools in terms of their "cultural deprivation," "impoverished home lives," "lower aspiration levels," and the like. The radical would at least raise questions as to whether the school system itself generates failure. Are there systematic differences in the quality of physical plant between slum and nonslum schools?[9] Do teachers expect lower-class children and nonwhite children to be stupid and therefore react to them as if they were in fact stupid?[10]

—Regarding the disproportionately high percentage of households among blacks headed by a female, does one seek an explanation in terms of the "self-image of the Negro male" and the "historical legacy of slavery" or in the persistent exclusion of blacks from the job market by employers and trade unions?[11]

The radical perspective has important consequences for the formulation of policy. It is not simply a matter of preference or prejudice, but a question of how one accurately accounts for certain problems. Explanation governs the formulation of policy. Some of the work of E. White Bakke on unemployed whites during the depression revealed the same kind of family breakdown that the Moynihan report indicated for blacks.[12] The disintegration of the family among whites was directly and clearly a consequence of the breakdown of the economy and of course had nothing to do with "self-image" or "historical legacies." The radical perspective suggests that system analysis not only is likely to generate sounder explanations for the phenomena in question, but also holds more promising possibilities for the formulation of effective policy.

In short, then, radical sociology has recourse to the distinction which C. Wright Mills made between "the personal troubles of milieu and the public issues of social structure."[13] In other words, if a few people are poor, one may look to "case factors." If masses are poor, one has grounds for asking questions about social structure.

Radical sociology asks whether the problems generated by social structure are inherent within it (a consequence of "internal contradictions," if one will) or simply "mistakes" or unintended consequences? Poverty, for example, can be seen as simply a residual category, i.e., the poor are these people who have *not yet* been raised up in standard of living by the dynamic of an expanding economy. Alternatively, it may be viewed as an inevitable consequence of a certain kind of economy. The policy implications of these alternatives are quite profound. If problems are seen simply as accidents, then one poses policies which leave the fundamental structure of the system intact (in terms of education, for example, bonus pay for teachers willing to work in slum schools). On the other hand, if defects are discerned to be an integral part of the way the system normally operates, then policy calling for more fundamental kinds of restructuring becomes necessary (again, in terms of education, something such as "community control" of schools by ghetto people).

Further, the radical perspective generates its own definition of problems and system defects. It deals in an area where there is broad consensus—poverty and inequality, for example—but it does not assume that conventional definitions exhaustively identify what is. As John Seeley indicated in "The Making and Taking of Social Problems," one needs to ask who is doing the defining. Seeley commented on the inadequacy of conventional definitions.

> ... the table of contents of almost any "social problems" text shows a notable bias in the predictable direction. The text I have momentarily at hand lists among "Deviant Behavior" only Crime, Juvenile Delinquency, Mental Disorders, Drug Addiction, Suicide, and Prostitution; and among "Social Disorganization" Population Crisis, Race and Ethnic Relations, Family, Work, Military, Community and Traffic Disorganization and Disaster. The presence of the military chapter is unusual and somewhat happenstantial, but otherwise this pretty well is the "mix as usual," representing our study of categories of persons sufficiently powerless to offer small resistance to violation by enquiry.
> ... on the Social Disorganization side also we have a more or less customary collection of relatively unresistant units that could be disorganized and could be enquired into. Note no business disorganization, religious disorganization, intellectual anomie, political breakdown, or disorganization, debasement and degradation of the most eminent candidate: post primary education.
> Safe. Safe. Safe.[14]

Radical sociology generates its own definition of social problems partly by asking questions about system defects and about the possible role of social structure in perpetuating problems and defeating the intentions of meliorative policy.

Lest it be said that the radical perspective involves the sociologist in making judgments which are properly foreign to any science, let us point out that there is no such thing as being "above the battle." A number of persons have indicated that the social scientist who refuses to take sides opts by default for the status quo. Beyond this, there is a respected body of theory in sociology which rationalizes and justifies the status quo. One need only mention Talcott Parsons's "Revised Analytic Theory of Social Stratification"[15] or the Davis-Moore theory of stratification.[16] The logical shortcomings and analytic insufficiencies of the functionalist approach to stratification and inequality have already been commented upon at length in other places, and there is no need to discuss them here. As Howard Becker suggested, no matter how one approaches it, ultimately it is a question of "Whose Side Are We On?"[17]

Finally, radical sociology is a sociology of *engagement*. Traditionally the role of the sociologist in the field has been that of observer. He has confined himself to watching others do their thing. The radical perspective suggests that it is legitimate (in a scholarly sense) for the sociologist to play a vigorous role in the situations and organizations which he studies. Etzkowitz and Schaflander in their article "A Manifesto for Sociologists" gave several illustrations of engaged social science.

One social scientist who has gone beyond the non-involved, observer-participant category is Robert Coles, a psychiatrist. He went to study the Student Non-Violent Coordinating Committee in Mississippi during the Summer of 1964. Once down there he found that no one in SNCC was interested in talking to him. To them he seemed to be just another social scientist asking what they thought were irrelevant questions. But instead of just asking his questions and getting "put on" answers, he decided to stay for the summer and offered to become their doctor. Gradually he came to be trusted by them enough to begin group psychotherapy.

Coles came to occupy a key position in their organization. As part of the inner circle, he helped to make decisions and then participated in the action they took. He thus knew what was going on from the inside. The insight and knowledge he gained thereby was far greater than that of the sociologist who flies down on the "Civil Rights Special" to ask Stokely Carmichael "How's it going, baby?" over a one-night scotch-and-steak quiz session.

SNCC trusted Coles and he was able to tape record and take notes without having to ask any questions. He was interacting in a real life situation. His resources and materials were drawn from his daily life. He learned more about what was happening that summer than any sociologist could learn by any other sociological method. No outside observer, no one coming in with a questionnaire, or sending a questionnaire down, or coming down there to do depth interviewing, could learn as much as he did as part of the decision making apparatus. Like any other social scientist, when he returned North he scientifically checked and evaluated his research.[18]

It can be questioned, then, whether the purposes of scholarship are necessarily served by lack of involvement. Indeed, under some circumstances scholarly purposes may be properly attended to *only* if the sociologist becomes involved.

Etzkowitz and Schaflander go beyond this; they suggest that the sociologist should play a positive role in the creation of institutions which embody humanist and libertarian values. They suggest that this is necessary both in terms of the professional obligation of the sociologist to use his skills in the alleviation of social ills, and in terms of the superior quality of the data which emerges when the sociologist has been deeply involved in a situation rather than riding the coattails of people who are involved.

. . .

NOTES

1. Irving Kristol, "A Different Way to Restructure the University," *The New York Times Sunday Magazine*, 4, No. 13:3, 50–53, 162–180, December 8, 1968.
2. Herbert Gans, "Where Sociologists Have Failed," *Trans-action*, October 1967, p. 2.
3. Alvin W. Gouldner, "Anti-Minotaur: The Myth of a Value-Free Sociology," *Social Problems*, 9, No. 3:199–213, Winter, 1962.
4. Maurice R. Stein, "Value Sterility, Value Neutrality, or Value Advocacy: The Choice Before Us," *The Human Factor*, 8, No. 1, November 1968.
5. Thomas Ford Hoult, ". . . who Shall Prepare Himself to the Battle?" *The American Sociologist*, 1, No. 1:3–7, February 1968.

6. Albert Szymanski, "Toward a Radical Sociology," *The Human Factor*, 8, No. 1:21, November 1968.
7. Hoult, *op. cit.*, p. 3.
8. C. Wright Mills, "The Professional Ideology of Social Pathologists," in Irving Louis Horowitz (ed.), *Power, Politics, and People* (New York: Oxford University Press, 1967).
9. Patricia Sexton, *Education and Income* (New York: Viking Press, 1961).
10. See for example, Robert Rosenthal and Lenore Jacobson, *Pygmalion in the Classroom: Teacher Expectation and Pupils' Intellectual Development* (New York: Holt, Rinehart & Winston, 1968).
11. Steven E. Deutsch and John Howard, *Where It's at: Radical Perspectives in Sociology* (New York: Harper & Row, 1970), p. 283.
12. E. White Bakke, *Citizens Without Work* (London: Oxford University Press, 1940).
13. C. Wright Mills, *The Sociological Imagination* (New York: Oxford University Press, 1959), pp. 8–13.
14. John Seeley, "The Making and Taking of Social Problems: Toward an Ethical Stance," *Social Problems*, 14, No. 4:382–389, Spring 1967.
15. Talcott Parsons, "Revised Analytic Approach to the Theory of Social Stratification," in Reinhard Bendix and Seymour Lipset (eds.), *Class, Status, and Power* (Glencoe, Ill.: Free Press, 1953).
16. Kingsley Davis and Wilbert Moore, "Some Principles of Stratification," *American Sociological Review*, 10:242–249, 1945.
17. Howard S. Becker, "Whose Side Are We On?," *Social Problems*, 14, No. 3:239–248, 1967.
18. Henry Etzkowitz and Gerald M. Schaflander, "A Manifesto for Sociologist Institution Formation—A New Sociology," *Social Problems*, 15, No. 4:399–408, 1968.

9. The Humanistic Challenge to Sociology
JOHN F. GLASS

Professor Glass, like Professor Howard (the author of Selection 8), is a representative of the new sociology that evaluates and criticizes and attempts to play a significant part in furthering human potential and liberating humankind from exploitation. Glass' particular emphasis is on the limitations and superficialities inherent in applying purely empirical methods to the study of human behavior. As an alternative to such methods, Glass suggests the use of an approach that permits the researcher to become a part of what he

SOURCE: John F. Glass, "The Humanistic Challenge to Sociology," *Journal of Humanistic Psychology* 11 (Fall 1971), 170–183. Reprinted by permission of the author and the Journal of Humanistic Psychology.

> *studies, thus giving him a chance for thorough understanding without treating the study object as an "it." It is bitterly ironic that, for taking such a stance, Glass was refused tenure at one of the California state universities. (His chairman claimed that humanistic sociology is a "phantom movement" and, therefore, people committed to it are not making worthwhile contributions to sociology as a discipline.) At present, Professor Glass is a faculty member and Coordinator of the Culture and Society Series at the California School of Professional Psychology in Los Angeles.*

When I began graduate study in sociology at UCLA in 1962, I discovered the then emerging humanistic psychology movement, became involved with the Sensitivity Training program at UCLA, and read two books which had just been published, Abraham Maslow's *Toward a Psychology of Being*, and Carl Rogers' *On Becoming a Person*. While my career as a sociologist was profoundly altered from that time on, I quickly discovered that almost no sociologists were aware of this movement or the manifestations of it (Maslow called it the Unnoticed Revolution) because it is still almost completely overlooked by much of the intellectual community. I did find it flourishing at UCLA among a small group of professors in the business school. The Human Relations Research Group, later becoming the Division of Behavioral Science at UCLA's Graduate School of Business Administration, did some of the early groundwork in T-group theory and organizational development and influenced a considerable number of behavioral scientists who came in contact with them, including Abraham Maslow (see his book *Eupsychian Management*, 1965), Carl Rogers, and J. F. T. Bugental (Bugental, 1967). While I pursued the requirements for a Ph.D. in sociology, I moonlighted in the business school and was greatly enriched both personally and professionally.

In the last several years there have been a number of developments that I see as related to humanistic psychology. The rapid increase in popularity of T-groups (encounter groups, sensitivity training, etc.) and the emergence of more than a hundred growth centers and other manifestations of what is known as the human potential movement have been nothing short of phenomenal. The development of a counterculture (Roszak, 1969) and New Left Movement among youth on a scale never before witnessed, the appearance of radical caucuses in sociology, political science, and economics, Women's Liberation, and more, are all signs of social change with humanistic aspects.

In psychology, this movement has gone the farthest. Maslow (1968) wrote in the introduction to the second edition of *Toward a Psychology of Being* that humanistic psychology is now quite solidly established as:

> a viable third alternative to objectivistic, behavioristic (mechanomorphic) psychology and to orthodox Freudianism. It is beginning to be *used* espe-

cially in education, industry, religion, organization and management, therapy, and self-improvement. . . .

I must confess that I have come to think of this humanist trend in psychology as a revolution in the truest, oldest sense of the word, the sense in which Galileo, Darwin, Einstein, Freud, and Marx made revolutions, i.e., new ways of perceiving and thinking, new images of man and of society, new conceptions of ethics and of values, new directions in which to move.... . .

This psychology is *not* purely descriptive or academic, it suggests action and implies consequences. It helps to generate a way of life not only for the person himself within his own private psyche, but also for the same person as a social being, a member of society (p. iii).

What does this revolution mean for sociology? In this article I would like to give an account of where sociology is *at*, and where it converges with some of the developments mentioned above.

A CRITIQUE OF FUNCTIONALISM

The dominant approach in sociology today, that of functionalism—best personified by the work of Talcott Parsons—is being attacked from many sides. Basically, the functionalist views society as a set of institutions serving its functional needs, ignores historical perspective, and sees change and conflict as deviations rather than as inherent social processes. The dominant concern of functionalism is with order in society—an order based on man's conformity to shared values, and one in which joy, freedom, self-fulfillment, and other aspects of man stressed by the humanistic psychologist usually don't appear. The model of man, often not explicit in such theories, frequently resembles McGregor's Theory X and the behaviorist-psychoanalytic models for which humanistic psychology is providing an alternative. Although it is acknowledged that social order is a function of shared values, the values themselves are seldom considered and are thought of not so much as man-*made*, man-*transmitted*, or man-*received*.

Analogous to those psychologies which emphasize the body-mind dualism, functionalism hardly acknowledges that men have bodies:

> Modern Sociological Functionalism focuses on "social systems" that are seen primarily as systems of symbolic interaction, not between embodied men but between disembodied "role players"; between psychic "selves" who communicate-from-a-distance but who never seem to touch, to hold, to feed, to strike, to caress (Gouldner, 1970, p. 431).

Criticisms of the structural-functional school and mainstream sociology are not new (Lynd, 1939; Sorokin, 1956; Mills, 1959; Black, 1961; Stein & Vidich, 1963; Horowitz, 1964; Reynolds & Reynolds, 1970), but have steadily increased and culminated in Alvin Gouldner's critique, *The Coming Crisis of Western Sociology* (1970).

The critique of functionalism is not so much that it does not allow for a humanistic model of man, but that it is, both implicitly and explicitly, conservative and justifies the status quo:

> A theory is conservative to the extent that it: treats . . . institutions as given and unchangeable in essentials; proposes remedies for them so that they may work better, rather than devising alternatives to them; foresees no future that can be essentially better than the present, the conditions that already exist; and, explicitly or implicitly, counsels acceptance of or resignation to what exists, rather than struggling against it (Gouldner, 1970, p. 332).

The model of man that sociology uses too often reflects the same despairing view of other social sciences:

> The premise that man acts so as to satisfy needs presupposes a negative conception of the good as amelioration or the correction of an undesirable state. According to this view, man acts to relieve tension; good is the removal of evil and welfare the correction of ills; satisfaction is the meeting of a need . . . peace is the resolution of conflict; fear of the supernatural or of adverse public opinion is the incentive to good conduct . . . (Lee, 1948, p. 392).

Social science today focuses on man's adjustment to society, on conformity and adaptation, on man as a controlled product of society and culture rather than as a determiner of his own fate. Sociology's view of man is reflected in the subfield known as "deviant behavior" which deals exclusively with pathological deviations: poverty, crime, delinquency, mental illness, alcoholism, etc. What about deviance in the other (healthy) direction? There are almost no studies of creativity, joy, self-fulfillment, or of social institutions and organizations that facilitate these!

Can we not learn as much about human nature and behavior by looking at alternatives, at the positive side of man, as we can by repeated documentation of our ills, a path which has had unintended consequences—that of making the pathological appear inevitable or "normal"?

Shortly before his death, Maslow became increasingly irritated at this subculture of despair. Many sociologists deserve his characterization of despairing debunkers who deny the possibility of improving human nature and society, or of discovering intrinsic human values, or of being life-loving in general (Maslow, 1970, p.x.).

SOME ALTERNATIVES TO FUNCTIONALISM

A number of newer sociological theories are prominent today, in addition to functionalism: the interactionist perspective—best known through the work of Erving Goffman (1959, 1967), the exchange theories of Peter Blau (1964) and George Homans (1961) and the ethnomethodology of Harold Garfinkel (1967). Goffman's dramaturgical approach deals with appearances—how people manage situations and impressions in everyday interpersonal relationships. Garfinkel's ethnomethodology, while similar in its focus on everyday interactions, is more interested theoretically in the tacit understandings and assumptions that underlie social life. Exchange theories come closest to behavioristic psychology.

What all these theories have in common is an active view of men as builders and users of social structure, not simply as receivers or transmitters (Gouldner, 1970, pp. 378ff.). Their focus is on social interaction; they are ahistorical and social-psychological in nature.

What is interesting is that the view of man implicit in these newer theories is not much different from the functionalist view. Goffman deals almost exclusively with deception, deceit, stigma, and the effects of repressive institutions on the individual. His work, as well as that of Garfinkel, is full of the embarrassments, discomforts, intrigues, and other "deviant" behavior that persons carry on in their encounters with each other and in making out with the institutions of their society. Coercion, despair, and pessimism abound in Goffman's books, and part of his popularity probably comes from the fact that he makes a sort of hero out of the underdog.

There is much of value in the work of these theorists; they are masters at direct, qualitative observation, but they do not deal with the healthy side of man and society any more than the functionalists do.

The Radicalization of Sociology. A radical movement has emerged in sociology and several other social sciences (see "The New Sociology," *Time*, 5 January 1970, for a journalistic overview). Many of the younger sociologists active in this movement were graduate students in the sixties, the period when functionalism came under increasing attack, and they experienced the reemergence of social concern which had been dormant in the fifties.

Gouldner sees the failure of functionalism as a theory closely tied to the failure of our welfare state to deal with some of our most urgent social, political, and economic problems. He predicts the growth of a "radical sociology," which, while it will not become the dominant perspective of academic sociology, will grow in influence, particularly among the younger generation.

Deutsch and Howard's *Where It's At* (1970), and Deutsch [The latter reference cites Steven E. Deutsch, "The Radical Perspective in Sociology," *Sociological Inquiry* 40 (Winter 1970): 85–93.—Ed.] give comprehensive introductions to the radical perspective in sociology. Radical critiques principally revolve around the enormous dependence of sociology and sociologists on government-sponsored research, and more generally, on the whole nature of the sociological enterprise as supporting and being supported by the establishment. Sociological research is seen as serving corporate needs: the value focus is on stability and the maintenance of the system, and the socialization of its members into the system as it is, rather than as it might be. Radicals see the proper role of sociology as providing a structural analysis of society exposing repression, alienation, racism, inequality, and war as resulting from established value systems and power structures. Manipulation, oppression, control, and dehumanization of man are not proper functions of sociological research according to this viewpoint.

Closely allied in some respects to the radical movement in sociology is an increasing interest in a "sociology of sociology," or a reflexive sociology, as Gouldner calls it. A reflexive sociology transcends sociology as it now exists. It is also a radical sociology, in Gouldner's (1970) opinion:

> Radical, because it would recognize that knowledge of this world cannot be advanced apart from the sociologist's knowledge of himself and his position in the social world, or apart from his efforts to change these. Radical, because it seeks to transform as well as to know the alien world outside the sociologist as well as the alien world inside of him. Radical, because it would accept the fact that the roots of sociology pass through the sociologist as a total man, and that the question he must confront, therefore, is not merely how to *work* but how to *live* (p. 489).

TOWARD A HUMANISTIC SOCIOLOGY

Basically, I see the criticisms of sociology today and the possibilities for a humanistic sociology in a broader context than the radical critiques that have recently come from within sociology. Nor should a liberal-radical debate among humanists divide us.[1] Rather, I see humanistic sociology as a perspective, not an ideology or prescription for social change, that has relevance for many areas of sociology, especially methodology, applied sociology, and the very nature of the sociological enterprise itself.

New Directions in Methodology. A growing number of sociologists (Cicourel, 1964; Bruyn, 1966; Strauss, 1967; Blumer, 1969; Filstead, 1970; Staude, 1971) are concerned with developing a methodology for sociology that is more appropriate for the study of human behavior than the positivistic methods which were borrowed from the natural sciences via the assumption that the social sciences should be approached with the same methods and objectives. Under various names—existential or phenomenological sociology, ethnomethodology, symbolic interactionism, participant observation—a number of sociologists are taking as their point of departure the world as the individual or group studied sees it and constructs it, rather than how the researchers themselves predefine or categorize it. They recognize that man is a thinking, feeling, experiencing, intentional being, and that he should not be studied as an object, thing, or subject detached from the researcher who gathers "information" about him. Rather, the proper study of human behavior requires an intuition, an empathy, an awareness of the other as a person who places meanings on his behavior and who cannot really be understood without an awareness of the relationship between the researcher and the subject and self-awareness on the part of the researcher (Argyris, 1968; Glass & Frankiel, 1968).

Humanistic sociology allows and even welcomes speculation, predictions, and theorizing about the future and unrealized possibilities for man and society. This prediction is very different from the predictions currently dominant, which are mainly extrapolations. Nettl (1968) emphasizes this clearly:

> Prediction in modern sociology no longer has anything to do with the counterposing of alternatives which might be attained by conscious action, but consists merely of extrapolating existing trends on the assumption that the future is simply more of the present. American sociology is thus exceedingly supportive of the here and now which it characterizes as modernity (p. 303).

Sociologists preoccupied with realism and scientism are reluctant to delve into areas where empirical verification is impossible. Yet, as Lynd (1958, p. 219) has pointed out so well: "Realism that excludes the longer, enduring purposes of men and men's unrealized dreams is less than full realism . . . the utopianism of one era has repeatedly become the basic norm of decency for the next." If we assume that man has some control over his environment and that change is not a predetermined or mechanical process, then biased theories (Bierstedt, 1960) and speculation about the future are worthy activities for social scientists.

The humanistic social scientist's highest commitment is not a worship of science but a concern for man. What is argued for is an enlarged view of science, beyond the narrow goals of control and prediction, of studying only what is quantifiable or measurable, away from the behavioristic, positivistic, and technicist ethos borrowed from the hard sciences. In an interview, Michael Polanyi, chemist, philosopher, and one of the great sociological thinkers of our time said: "Sociologists set aside the motive of belief in freedom because it is intangible. They claim that they can explain all human activities in society without being concerned with right or wrong. They want to consider only things that can be handled by what they think are the methods of physics."[2]

Objectivity is to be sought, not through studied indifference to meanings, but through heightened awareness of the assumptions used and values involved, making them clear and open to examination (Lynd, 1958, p. 114). This can be achieved, according to Maslow, by enlarging our conception of objectivity to include not only "spectator-knowledge" (laissez-faire, uninvolved knowledge, knowledge about, knowledge from the outside), but also experiential knowledge and what he calls love-knowledge or Taoistic knowledge. Just as love can be so complete and accepting that it becomes non-interfering, liking someone just as he is with no impulse or need to change him, Maslow holds that we can love truth the same way. It takes great love to let something alone, to let it be and become:

... it is possible to love the truth yet to come, to trust it, to be happy and to marvel as its nature reveals itself. One can believe that the uncontaminated, unmanipulated, unforced, undemanded truth will be more beautiful, more pure, more *truly* true than that same truth would have been had we forced it to conform to a priori expectations or hopes or plans or current political needs (Maslow, 1970, p. xxxv).

Applied Sociology. A humanistic approach to science does not necessarily mean that the scientist seeks to change or alter what he studies. I feel strongly, however, that applied social science has a central and rightful place in any social science that seeks to be humanistic.

Maslow (1970) also believes that normative zeal (to do good, to help mankind, to better the world) is quite compatible with scientific objectivity and makes conceivable a better science with a far wider jurisdiction than it now has when it tries to be value-neutral (leaving values to be arbitrarily affirmed by non-scientists on nonfactual grounds).

Applied social science and "action" research (Sanford, 1970) are misunderstood by many and are often in disfavor with those on the far left as well as with traditional academics. The radicals point to the fact that most money for social science research comes from the government and thus inextricably involves the researcher with the Establishment: traditionalists often question the appropriateness of applied research in a "pure" academic discipline. I agree with Warren Bennis, who stated in a recent book review: "It may be that applied social sciences may revitalize their parent disciplines and that the line between "pure" and "applied" social science is illusory. The harsh confrontation between theory and practice may bring about newer models, not only capable of solving problems, but of substantially augmenting social theory."[3]

Sociologists and psychologists, even many humanistically oriented ones, have been astonishingly unaware of the literature and developments in what Maslow calls normative social psychology—more commonly known as applied behavioral science, human relations, or organizational development.[4] In the field of applied behavioral science, men such as Chris Argyris, Warren Bennis, and Robert Tannenbaum can be characterized as liberal humanists—liberal because they seek change within the system, and humanists because their underlying values, methods, and assumptions about human nature (McGregor's Theory Y) are very similar to those of the humanistic psychologists. Indeed, there is some overlap in membership between the two groups.

Much of applied behavioral science is more applied sociology than applied psychology especially where change is sought in social institutions, systems, and organizations, but sociologists have already given up by default their influence in such efforts.

POSSIBILITIES FOR A HUMANISTIC SOCIOLOGY

Sociology needs an alternative to the "despairing debunkers" who focus exclusively on the dark side of man and the repressive nature of society, and who ignore human possibilities and potentials in their preoccupation with pathology, cynicism, and hopelessness. And sociology, I contend, is essential to an understanding of man from a holistic and humanistic perspective.

Psychologists must remember that man is inescapably a *social* being; he becomes human only through interaction with others and the world he finds himself in. This is the flaw of "pure" existentialism and of *intra*personal psychology, which considers man in a vacuum, the individual apart from the society he lives in. To believe that the individual can achieve fulfillment as an isolated person is sheer folly, but some humanistic psychologists appear to take this view. Creation of the self is a process, something that is developed through interaction and contact with society, and this is a lifelong process. Symbolic interactionists (e.g., Blumer, 1969) are quite clear on this.

Yet there is indecision in sociological theory over the relationship between the individual and society. Functional theories tend to define the nature of man by his cultural and social world. The fulfillment of the self is seen as no more than the satisfactory internalization of that culture, which needs only adequate opportunities to express its possibilities. Winter (1966) poses the question squarely:

> The problem is essentially whether society determines the content of the self or furnishes the cultural and social milieu in which the self actualizes its freedom and fulfillment. If society provides the substance of the self, then freedom is basically found through conformity to the possibilities made available by society. If the self is more than an expression of social process, then freedom is the pre-supposition of culture, even as culture is the actualization and enrichment of human freedom and sociality (p. 32).

This problem is not an academic one—it was raised recently by John Holt in a letter to *Commentary* (Aug. 1970, p. 6): "Most people define education as sculpture, making children what we want them to be. I and others . . . define it as gardening, helping children to grow and to find what they want to be."

Maslow and most humanistic psychologists hold the "gardening" theory and Maslow has carried the issue a step farther by his study of healthy individuals:

> Practically every serious description of the "authentic" person extant implies that such a person, by virtue of what he has become, assumes a new relation to his society, and indeed to society in general. He not only transcends himself in various ways; he also transcends his culture. He resists enculturation. He becomes a little more a member of his species and a little less a member of his local group. My feeling is that most sociologists and anthropologists will take this hard. I therefore confidently expect controversy in this area (Maslow, 1968, p. 11).[5]

A central task of humanistic sociology, then, would be to ask which institutions and social arrangements, supported by which values and norms, promote the capacity and ability of groups and individuals to make free and responsible choices in light of their needs to grow, to explore new possibilities, and to do more than simply survive. Man is more than a player of preexisting roles, he is a meaning maker and value chooser. He chooses his existence within a social and cultural context. This is not solely a psychological or interpersonal phenomenon but one that is greatly influenced by the interaction of the individual with society, interaction that has consequences both for society and the individual.

Humanistically inclined sociologists might ask what the social correlates of trust, interdependency, autonomy, and other individual characteristics are in terms of groups, associations, and other social structures—from the family to the giant corporation.

A study of the values and ideologies by which men and societies live is as fundamental an issue in sociological analysis of a humanistic nature as it is to the humanistic psychologist concerned with individual behavior.[6] A humanistic sociology would study the degree to which specific values, and institutions based on those values, facilitate or hinder the "good" society. We need to study the social and personal consequences of the values held in our society, not only as preached, but as practiced.

CONCLUSION

I am somewhat troubled by the nagging thought that perhaps the most important issues to which we need to address ourselves have not received the emphasis they should. The debates over applied vs. pure research, the similarities and differences between humanistic psychology and sociology seem to be overshadowed by the following:

1. The crisis our society seems headed for—an impending clash between two cultures. These are not the two cultures of C. P. Snow, but the new and the old, the emerging counterculture based on the joy and the fulfillment of human needs and potentialities and the established culture with its scarcity psychology and blind subservience to technology. The pressures for change and the possibilities for repressive reaction seem enormous. Slater (1970) provides a brilliant analysis of this crisis.

2. The traditional faith of humanists in science and technology to solve all our problems must be tempered with the reality that the desired outcome is by no means certain, without furthering the mistaken notion that humanistic social scientists are anti-intellectual and anti-science.

3. There is a deeply felt ambivalence over the individualism vs. social commitment issue. There is a danger that some of our emphasis on ex-

istentialism and the subjective side of man will lead us to a further separation from nature, history, and community—a danger well captured by Paul Shepard:

> The proponents of this fanatic individualism retreat from a hostile and absurd world to an inner life where the only values are personal and subjective. By valuing only the unique and the individual, they rightly oppose mass man and the treatment of human beings as replaceable machines—at the price of ecological nihilism (as quoted in Means, 1969, p. 258).

Slater (1970) also poses the dilemma accurately:

> On the one hand there is increasing experimentation with communes and communal arrangements, and a serious awareness of the Nuremburg Trials and their proclamation of man's personal responsibility to all men. On the other hand, there is a great fascination with the concept of anarchy—with the attempt to eliminate coercion and commitment in any form from human life (p. 148).

Wrestling with these issues may yet provide humanists from all the sciences with their greatest challenges and opportunities.

NOTES

This is a revision of a paper presented at the 8th Annual Meeting, Association for Humanistic Psychology, Miami Beach, Florida, September, 1970. I wish to thank Judith Glass, Steven Deutsch, James Elden, and Charles Hampden-Turner for their helpful comments on the earlier versions of this paper.

1. I do not wish to use the terms "humanist" and "radical" interchangeably even though there is overlap between the two. Humanists can be radical, liberal or conservative, the sociologist Peter Berger being an outstanding example of the latter. See his chapter "On Conservative Humanism" in Berger and Neuhaus (1970), and also Berger (1963).
2. As quoted in *Psychology Today*, May 1968, p. 20.
3. As quoted in *American Journal of Sociology*, January 1969, p. 430.
4. This growing movement largely originated from the work of Kurt Lewin and the founding of the National Training Laboratories (now NTL Institute for Applied Behavioral Science) over 20 years ago (see Tannenbaum, Weschler, and Massarik, 1961; Maslow, 1965; Bennis, Benne, and Chin, 1969; and Schmidt, 1970).
5. The new "fourth force" in psychology, Transpersonal, might be matched by a Transcultural sociology dealing with values, social structures, and social behavior that seems to be universal, culture free, and transcendental from a sociological perspective.
6. Richard Means' excellent work, *The Ethical Imperative* (1969), makes a persuasive case for the need to make the study of values and their consequences a central focus in sociology.

REFERENCES

Argyris, C. "Some Unintended Consequences of Rigorous Research." *Psychological Bulletin* 70 (1968), 185–97.

Bennis, W.; Benne, K.; and Chin, R., eds. *The Planning Change*, 2d ed. New York: Holt, Rinehart, and Winston, 1969.

Berger, P. L. *Invitation to Sociology*. New York: Doubleday Anchor, 1963.

Berger, P. L., and Neuhaus, R. *Movement and Revolution*. New York: Doubleday Anchor, 1970.

Bierstedt, R. "Sociology and Humane Learning." *American Sociological Review* 25 (1960): 3–9.

Black, M. ed. *The Social Theories of Talcott Parsons*. Englewood Cliffs, N.J.: Prentice-Hall, 1961.

Blau, P. *Exchange and Power in Social Life*. New York: John Wiley & Sons, 1964.

Blumer, H. *Symbolic Interactionism: Perspective and Method*. Englewood Cliffs, N.J.: Prentice-Hall, 1969.

Bruyn, S. T. *The Human Perspective in Sociology: The Methodology of Participant Observation*. Englewood Cliffs, N.J.: Prentice-Hall, 1966.

Bugental, J. F. T. *Challenges of Humanistic Psychology*. New York: McGraw-Hill, 1967.

Cicourel, A. V. *Method and Measurement in Sociology*. New York: Free Press, 1964.

Deutsch, S. E. "The Radical Perspective in Sociology." *Sociological Inquiry* 40 (1970): 85–93.

Deutsch, S. E., and Howard, J. *Where It's At: Radical Perspectives in Sociology*. New York: Harper & Row, 1970.

Filstead, W. ed. *Qualitative Methodology*. Chicago: Markham, 1970.

Friedrichs, R. W. *A Sociology of Sociology*. New York: Free Press, 1970.

Garfinkel, H. *Studies in Ethnomethodology*. Englewood Cliffs, N.J.: Prentice-Hall, 1967.

Glass, J. "The Presentation of Self and the Encounter Culture: Notes on the Sociology of T-Groups." *Comparative Group Studies* 3, No. 4 (November 1972): forthcoming.

―――. "Toward a Humanistic Sociology." *Association for Humanistic Psychology Newsletter* 6 (April 1970): 1–2.

Glass, J. and Frankiel, H. "The Influence of Subjects on the Researcher: A Problem in Observing Social Interaction." *Pacific Sociological Review* 11 (1968): 75–80.

Goffman, E. *Interaction Ritual*. New York: Doubleday Anchor, 1967.

―――. *Presentation of Self in Everyday Life*. New York: Doubleday Anchor, 1959.

Gouldner, A. W. *The Coming Crisis of Western Sociology*. New York: Basic Books, 1970.

Hampden-Turner, C. *Radical Man: The Process of Psycho-social Development*. New York: Doubleday Anchor, 1971.

Homans, G. *Social Behavior: Its Elementary Forms.* New York: Harcourt Brace Jovanovich, 1961.

Horowitz, I. L. ed. *The New Sociology.* New York: Oxford University Press, 1964.

Lee, D. "Are Basic Needs Ultimate?" *Journal of Abnormal and Social Psychology* 43 (1948): 391–95.

Lynd, H. M. *On Shame and the Search for Identity.* New York: Science Edition, 1958.

Lynd, R. S. *Knowledge for What?* Princeton, N.J.: Princeton University Press, 1939.

Maslow, A. H. *Eupsychian Management.* Homewood, Ill.: Richard D. Irwin, 1965.

———. *Motivation and Personality.* 2d ed. New York: Harper & Row, 1970.

———. *Toward a Psychology of Being.* 2d ed. New York: Van Nostrand, 1968.

Means, R. L. *The Ethical Imperative: The Crisis in American Values.* New York: Doubleday, 1969.

Mills, C. W. *The Sociological Imagination.* New York: Oxford University Press, 1959.

Nettl, J. P. "Are Intellectuals Obsolete?" *Nation,* 4 March 1968, pp. 300–305.

Reynolds, L. T. and Reynolds, J. M. eds. *The Sociology of Sociology.* New York: McKay, 1970.

Rogers, C. R. *On Becoming a Person.* Boston: Houghton Mifflin, 1961.

Roszak, T. *The Making of a Counter Culture.* New York: Doubleday Anchor, 1969.

Sanford, N. "Whatever Happened to Action Research?" *Journal of Social Issues* 26 (1970): 3–23.

Schmidt, W. H. *Organizational Frontiers and Human Values.* Belmont, Calif.: Wadsworth, 1970.

Slater, P. E. *The Pursuit of Loneliness: American Culture at the Breaking Point.* Boston: Beacon Press, 1970.

Sorokin, P. *Fads and Foibles in Modern Sociology.* Chicago: Regnery, 1956.

Staude, J. R. "Theoretical Foundations for a Humanistic Sociology." Paper presented at the American Sociological Association Annual Meetings, September 1971 at Denver, Colorado.

Stein, M., and Vidich, A. *Sociology on Trial.* Englewood Cliffs, N.J.: Prentice-Hall, 1963.

Strauss, A. L. and Glaser, B. G. *The Discovery of Grounded Theory: Strategies for Qualitative Research.* Chicago: Aldine, 1967.

Tannenbaum, R.; Weschler, I.; and Massarik, F. *Leadership and Organization.* New York: McGraw-Hill, 1961.

Winter, G. *Elements for a Social Ethic: Scientific and Ethical Perspectives on Social Process.* New York: Macmillan, 1966.

Sociology and Science

Part III

In this section the focus of attention is on various aspects of research, with particular reference to sociology. Some humanistic sociologists are convinced that the use of scientific methods for research in the field should be eschewed by those who are genuinely concerned with the human condition. They feel that the empirical methods of science are potentially dangerous when applied to human society, because such methods necessarily treat the subjects under study as "things." As editor of this collection of readings, I share only a part of this concern. I agree fully with the conviction that there is great danger in applying the "hard science" approach to the study of human beings, because it can so very easily become a viciously manipulative technique. In addition, pure empiricism, when applied to human affairs, often produces results that are trivial in the extreme. At the same time, however, I am convinced that properly controlled science is an important vehicle for achieving social reforms. Through science, correctly applied, we can obtain thorough and widely agreed-upon diagnoses of the human condition. Without science, we are thrown back on methods—intuitive and personalized —the findings of which are impossible to evaluate carefully. Note, however, that when I opt for "science" I do not mean to decry the insights and guidance we can glean from the arts, aspects of religion, and purely personal experience.

10. Science as a Frame of Reference

RAYMOND W. MACK

In the first of our science selections Raymond Mack, Northwestern University professor of sociology, presents a traditional view that is best compared and contrasted with that of Professor Anderson, author of selection 11. Dr. Mack opts for empiricism—defined as the belief that our most certain knowledge comes through the senses alone—as the most efficient method for gathering data. His view is shared by many in the social sciences, and it almost totally dominated the sociological fraternity up to about 1960. It is impossible to say what is dominant now; it is certain, however, that the view held by Professor Mack is less pervasive and less aggressively asserted than was once the case.

"A social scientist is a man who, if he has two little boys, sends one to Sunday School every Sunday and keeps the other one home as an experimental control group." So runs one of our bits of occupational in-group humor. Would that we more often knew such precision!

The scientific *method* in social science is the same scientific method which underlies the work done in the chemist's laboratory, the zoologist's dissecting room, and the astronomer's observatory. But the *techniques* of gathering information vary from discipline to discipline: the chemist has his Bunsen burner and his watch glass, the zoologist his scalpel and his microscope, the astronomer his radio telescope and his charts. The social scientist has his interview schedule and his questionnaire. For each, the

SOURCE: Raymond W. Mack, "Science as a Frame of Reference," *Trans-action*, vol. 2, no. 1 (November/December 1964), 24–25. Copyright © 1964 by Transaction, Inc. and reprinted by permission.

controlled experiment is an ideal seldom achieved but often approximated. For all, the canons of the scientific method are identical.

The unity of the sciences lies in their method. The scientific method is a way of trying to make sense out of the booming, buzzing confusion of the universe. It is an intellectual stance toward information. The scientific method is a set of assumptions about when a fact is a fact. The method provides scientists with a set of guideposts for gathering information and for bringing order to congeries of data.

Persons using the scientific method as a frame of reference operate under three assumptions: (1) that the human senses are the most reliable medium for gathering data; (2) that human reason is the most valid tool for organizing data; and (3) that agreement among a number of competent observers is the best check on the efficiency of the data gathering and organizing process called for in the first two assumptions.

Knowledge is scientific, then, when (1) an observer gathers information through one or more of his senses—sight, hearing, touch, taste, or smell—and (2) uses logic to interpret his information, that is, to relate one fact to another, and (3) other scientists sufficiently well-trained in the observer's specialty to understand what he has done use their sense experience and human reason on the information and arrive at the same conclusion.

When one of these criteria is violated in the search for knowledge, the conclusions are not scientific. Science does not provide us with knowledge about God because, by definition, the supernatural cannot be experienced through human senses. A random collection of facts does not constitute a science because facts do not speak for themselves; human reason must be employed to explain the relationships among facts and among sets of facts.

Scientists often use instruments for collecting information: thermometers, stethoscopes, tape recorders, questionnaires. These are the techniques which vary from discipline to discipline. They are simply aids to implementing the scientific method, which is unvarying. These devices are auxiliaries to the human senses. Scientists use them to bring greater precision to their own sense experience.

But the most refined gauge does not measure anything. A human being does the measuring. The instrument extends the range and sharpens the precision of his observations. A yardstick does not measure, and a Geiger counter does not count: a man does. It is the eye and the ear of the scientist using them that translate their sensitive markings and murmurings into scientific facts.

It is hardly correct, then, to speak of facts as being more or less scientific. A set of observations may be more or less precise, but if they are the product of sense experience logically interpreted and independently verified, they are scientific.

While the method of science is unvarying, the bodies of knowledge accumulated via the scientific method are ever-changing. The scientific method does not change, but the content of a scientific discipline does.

This does not necessarily mean that a set of facts is disproved, but often that the gaining of additional information leads to a reinterpretation of what is known. Einstein's theory of relativity does not disprove Newton's scientific facts; it explains more by adding to and reinterpreting Newton's observations.

When a man accepts science as a frame of reference, and uses it in his daily work life, it is bound to have some impact upon his frame of mind. The stereotype which nonscientists hold of the scientist offers a clue to that frame of mind. Laymen often see scientists as cold-blooded skeptics, uninvolved in the values of their culture or the issues of their society, and hard to convince of anything. Like most stereotypes, this one is organized around elements of truth. The scientist is neither as bad as some people think in his lack of capacity for emotional conviction, nor as good as others think in his ability to separate his personal preferences from his objective scholarly conclusions.

But his training and practice do lead a scientist to attempt to separate his own wishes and convictions from the process of observing and interpreting data. The scientific method, with its commitment to sense experience and independent verification, is an attempt to assure complete objectivity. A social scientist, even more than others, should be aware that his own experience and cultural conditioning will influence his choice of research problems. He has learned in his own society a set of rules and preferences and even a way of thinking. That is why he uses the scientific method: as a guard against confusing what he would like to find with what is actually there.

He may not be able to bring his scientific frame of mind to every problem he addresses as a Republican, as a Baptist, as a father, or as a friend, but when he is working, his commitment to the method helps him to get outside himself and his milieu and to see his physical and social environment objectively. In this sense, too, the stereotype is founded on fact: the scientist *at work* is a man alienated from his society. As a citizen, the bacteriologist may loathe the ravages of tuberculosis and want passionately to find a means of preventing the disease. As a citizen, a sociologist may love democratic concepts of justice and deplore the ways in which poverty and racial discrimination cause his society to fall short of its own ideals. But at work, the bacteriologist must measure, not curse, the virulence of the bacillus; the sociologist must invest his work time in analyzing the effectiveness of special interest groups, not in cheerleading.

Calling something science does not make it scientific, of course. Astrology remains more popular than astronomy. Alchemy preceded chemistry, and there were hosts of economic and political philosophers eager to turn the lead of their opinions into the gold of truth long before there were many economists and political scientists using the scientific method to further their understanding of human behavior. There are still people who call themselves social scientists, but who evidence little inclination to subject their pet theories to the hazards of empirical test.

Nonetheless, this century has seen a larger and larger proportion of scholars using the scientific method as a means to the end of learning more about human social behavior. Every year, more students are exposed to science as a frame of reference. The mass media report and comment upon information gathered by observation, interviews, and questionnaires. Political leaders, educators, businessmen, church administrators make policy decisions based upon data gathered by social scientists. The growing acceptance of science as a frame of reference can encourage belief that decision makers may come to feel more at home with science as a frame of mind.

11. Toward a Sociology of Being
HENRY ANDERSON

Although the author of this article has an advanced degree in sociology, he has become disenchanted with formal aspects of the discipline and works full time for the California Department of Health. At present, he is engaged in a study of the effect of pesticides on the physical well-being of farm workers. As is evident in the accompanying article, Mr. Anderson takes the very opposite stance from that of Professor Mack in selection 10. Anderson speaks disparagingly of "mechanistic sociology," behaviorism, and survey research. Sociology, he says, ". . . continues to lag in its grasp of the nature of human nature. . . ." He concludes that only by turning away from the old, established methods of knowing do we have even a prayer of developing the only kind of sociology worth having: "a sociology of human becoming."

The questions to be studied, the ways they are to be studied, and everything else that passes under the rubric of "sociology" depend on assumptions which are usually not articulated at all, and which most sociologists appear to avoid as "insusceptible of proof": assumptions about the nature of man. Sociologists usually do not openly utilize the terminology of behavioristic psychology. But without examining or acknowledging their debt, they commonly rest everything they do on these premises borrowed unwittingly and whole: that man is by nature a collection of conditioned responses to situational stimuli. It is difficult otherwise to account

SOURCE: Henry Anderson, "Toward a Sociology of Being," *Manas* 21 (January 17, 1968), 1–2, 7–8. Reprinted by permission.

for the orthodox sociological conception of man as a creature whose behavior is so patterned that one may sum up each person in terms of his roles and statuses; and, indeed, that one may abstract from the behavior of large numbers of persons such regularities that roles and statuses are often spoken of as though they were entities with an existence of their own.

Sociology has been able to survive as long as it has with this worldview because people do indeed act in a fairly predictable way much of the time. This enables one, after interviewing a sample with a standardized questionnaire, to say, with an appropriate number of weasel words, that the people who live in Piedmont will more likely vote Republican than the people who live in East Oakland, and so forth. For some limited kinds of purposes such findings are doubtless meaningful. None of these is a particularly "sociological" application, however. Statistical methods are inherently unable to shed much light on most of the important questions about what is going on in society. The important questions are the ones that are hard to answer, and they are hard to answer precisely because man is not just a creature who acts out a series of social roles. Man is also a creative and cantankerous creature who sometimes kicks over the traces. Babbitts try their hand at abstract expressionism; crooks become honest men, and honest men sell out for the right price; ministers desert their wives and run off with organists, or leave the organists and return to their wives. And this kind of latent indeterminacy is not just individual. Sometimes substantial numbers of people kick over the traces in the same way at the same time. People get swept away by a demagogue; welfare recipients rise up in protest against being degraded; young people drop out to become hippies.

The entire range of social movements, fads, fashions, booms, panics, crazes, mobs, riots, revolutions, is incomprehensible in terms of man "programmed" to act and talk and think in a certain socially acceptable and predictable way. The sociology of the survey research method says almost nothing, and can say almost nothing, about this whole vast area of human behavior. Gagged by the consequences of its conception of the nature of man, it is virtually mute on the subject of social change—the area which should constitute the growing edge of sociology. Societies are obviously changing, and changing at an accelerating rate. They are changing primarily in the above mentioned ways—the "unacceptable" ways which lie outside the competence of polls and interviews.

The behavior of human beings—not only when they are running outside of established channels, but, for that matter, when they are acting more "stably"—is adequately accounted for only in terms of a radically different conception of the nature of man. Man is a creature, the only creature, with a sense of self. Given this sense of self, he is able to carry on internal dialogues with himself, and he does so during practically every waking moment. Some of the exchanges in this dialogue are more common than others, and in these cases the internal conversation may flow back and forth almost instantaneously and unreflectively. Shall I turn off the alarm clock? Yes. Shall I put on a clean pair of socks? Yes. Right foot first? Yes. Now left foot? Yes. White shirt next? No. Undershirt? Yes.

Repetition may cut down the transaction times of such dialogues to tenths or even perhaps hundredths of seconds, but the process never becomes purely "automatic." And the moment anything slightly out of the ordinary occurs—and there are hundreds of such moments in every human being's existence, every day—the internal communication slows down, blooms and proliferates in all manner of new directions. This razor blade is getting dull. Shall I change it or make do one more time? What's the matter with these blades, anyway? Should I pick up a box of that other brand today? Say, has my wife been shaving her legs with my razor again? How many times do I have to ask her not to? Is this a sign that she is growing away from me? Am I being unreasonable? And so forth. These sequences cannot be accounted for by behavioristic theory.

A human life is built up of such rich, blooming, variegated give-and-take. It is "social" to the extent that the internal images which pass in review as one is thinking, speaking, or acting are derived from experiences one has had with others. This is a very great extent indeed. But "the others"—i.e., society—can never completely control the content of the images, the sequences in which they will pass in review in the individual's private dialogue, or the selections which the individual will make on a particular occasion.

There is nothing esoteric about this conception of man's nature. Nor is it a sentimental view of the way one might like human beings to be. It is the way human beings are, and cannot help being. Whoever you are, you may verify this conception of the nature of your own nature by looking into yourself (your Self) during any waking minute. You cannot stop the flood of images and subvocal conversation even if you try—and the harder you try, the more will flood in through the back door. For example, as you have been reading this piece, hundreds of reactions, recollections, propositions, and possibilities have passed fleetingly in review within your perpetual dialogue.

Human behavior, then, is the outcome of dialogue, rather than any fixed stimulus-response arcs, instincts, or metaphysical imperatives such as "role" or "status." To account for human behavior, there is no substitute for "getting in on the dialogue." This is another way of saying that, for anything more than the most superficial kinds of understandings, sociology requires a conception of the nature of man which is humanistic rather than mechanistic.

Let us consider a few examples of how orthodox, mechanistic sociology and a new humanistic sociology might differ in their approaches to the same problems. Let us say we are interested in the question of employee morale or job satisfaction. If we happen to be survey research sociologists, we prepare a battery of questions, and after a number of pre-tests, we select, say, a dozen questions which provide a "scalable" basis for ranking informants from very low job-satisfaction to very high job-satisfaction. We find, say, that 5 per cent rank in what we call a very low satisfaction category, 5 per cent in a very high satisfaction category, with other percentages distributed in a "normal curve" in whatever categories we have ordained between the two extremes.

Like the strictly objective scientists that we aspire to be, we let these statistics speak for themselves—but they speak neither very loudly nor very accurately about what is really going on in the job situations of our society. They cannot. For one thing, many informants are not in close enough touch with themselves and their internal dialogues to be aware of how they honestly feel toward their jobs. For another thing, many would not tell an interviewer the truth even if they were in touch with it. For example, it is commonplace for people to feel resentful toward bureaucracies for homogenizing them, and to "fight back" by subtle forms of sabotage, by boondoggling, by taking a whole day to do a task that might take no more than an hour if their morale were good. To observe these things is crucial to any serious understanding of what is happening in American working life, and will happen increasingly as more jobs become bureaucratized.

People are unlikely to admit to an interviewer—even an interviewer highly skilled at manipulating their privacy—that they have been boondoggling. They usually do not openly admit it to themselves. It is probably not so much a matter of their fearing that they will be fired if the truth is known, as fear of a loss of esteem: self-esteem, and esteem by another. Most people crave the good opinion even of an interviewer they have never seen before and know they will never see again. The crucial understandings are a closed door as long as the researcher has a questionnaire in his hand. The door begins to open only as he grows sensitive to the *sub rosa* dialogues that lie behind overt dialogues—for example, what people are really saying as they engage in idle office gossip during coffee breaks. Or, perhaps even better, the researcher may work at a white-collar job himself, and tune in on his own internal communication, moment by moment.

Another example, from among many which could be given, of the way a humanistic sociology, as distinguished from a mechanistic sociology, might operate in a given area: Traditional sociology collects data on divorces and classifies them by age of the principals, length of marriage, number of children, etc. These statistics usually appear in courses and sections of tests entitled "social pathology," "social disorganization," and the like. Such a perspective conceals more than it reveals. Behind the statistical curtain, a tremendous ferment is taking place, moving in the direction of redefining the relationships between men and women in our society—redefining love, sexuality, the family, maternity, paternity, masculinity, femininity. Some of this ferment, to be sure, is rebellion without a cause, and many people are being badly hurt to no constructive purpose. But much of what is going on might better be thought of as social reorganization than as social disorganization. The family is not going to be tomorrow what it was yesterday or is today. If sociology is to make a useful contribution to the understanding of this deep tide, it must have almost totally new methods of observation.

The *reductio ad absurdum* of the survey research method was the census of orgasms conducted by Kinsey, who was, of course, a biologist, but was ever afterward called a "sociologist" because he used the orthodox sociological method of asking people some simple questions and adding up the simple answers. Any number of sociologists promptly went out to conduct similar censuses, and then quibbled over whose sampling technique was the best. All of it was so irrelevant to what is really happening in the relationships between the sexes that it was tantamount to outright falsification. If there is any one thing of which we may be sure about the present process of redefinition, it is that, amid all the fitful starts and blind alleys, it points in the direction of quality of relationship rather than quantity. Women are demanding that they be perceived not as sexual objects, or housekeepers, or nursemaids, but as full persons in their very own right. And so are men, a little more slowly perhaps, and in their own ways.

How does a researcher apprehend these things? He becomes attuned to the conversation of gestures. He learns what is meant by silences as well as by words. He learns what is meant by the sighs, frowns, giggles, tears. He has to get behind masks, to where the gropings, the agonies, the intimacies are. He cannot possibly do this in an interview. The instant he knocks at the door of a couple in the midst of a quarrel, or an act of love, or any other kind of authentic revelation, the authenticity ceases, and he gets answers from masks, not from the real people behind. His findings may be "true" in the sense that most people prefer to wear masks in the presence of interviewers and other strangers. But his findings will be false in the sense that there were critical dialogues taking place behind the masks, dialogues by definition inaccessible to strangers.

The survey research method is helpless in the face of most significant social questions because of a kind of Heisenberg effect which is far more serious than anything in the physical or biological sciences: the very act of observation distorts that which is being observed. But whereas the natural sciences accept the "uncertainty principle" with an appropriate humility, sociology tries to nullify it by investing more time and talent in sharpening the very methods that are trivializing human social life, cutting back its true boundaries, betraying it, falsifying it.

It is difficult to think of a precedent for this: a would-be science busily engaged in denying and eroding the character of its subject-matter. Sociology, as the study of human relationships should, before anything else, have a clear conception of what genuine human relationships are, as distinguished from ersatz varieties.

If two people act like automatons toward one another—one consistently subordinate, one consistently superordinate, let us say, or one consistently aggressive, the other consistently passive—they are the beau ideal of orthodox sociological research. And if you multiply them by a million, you have the beau ideal of a stable, predictable, quantifiable society. But can they be said to have a human relationship? It would be more accurate to say that they have an inhuman relationship.

Sociology is going to fall farther and farther behind in its comprehension of what is actually happening in society, and what is going to happen, because people are growing more and more dissatisfied with inhuman relationships. What is taking place behind the masks is growing richer all the time. Social roles are not what they may have been. People are building their interior castles stronger, getting in touch with themselves better. That is the root reason why our society is growing increasingly dynamic: men are increasingly demanding that their essential human nature be recognized and fulfilled. All kinds of people are mounting this demand in one way or another, from the millionaire business executive who joins an "encounter group," to the man with the hoe who no longer dumbly accepts the blowing out of the light in his brain but is joining a union or asking for land of his own. It is dawning on vast numbers of people that they are real and that they are individuals, unique in all the world, not just a bundle of projections of what their parents, teachers, employers, and others think they ought to be. It is dawning on people that they are entitled to demand that they be allowed to function and grow as authentic persons. This is the greatest revolution among all the revolutions of our time, and it is bound to spread. For after all the other revolutions are consummated—computerization, the guaranteed annual income, "black power," land reform, or whatever—the most basic of hungers will remain to be satisfied: the hunger to be a truly human being.

If sociologists devoted themselves to sensitivity rather than methodological rigor—if they spent more time looking behind social roles and less time at the façades (including a great deal of time looking behind their own roles and searching for their own selves)—would this be the abandonment of sociology as a "science"? It all depends on what one means by science. Yes, if science is the accumulation of numbers representing observations which can later be duplicated more or less exactly by some other observer. No, if science is the accretion of wisdom, insight, and understanding of the subject-matter by means which are most appropriate to the nature of the subject itself.

The question of "subjectivity" and "objectivity" is a bugbear in any such discussion. The process envisaged here does not require that sociology take to the hustings and plump for the humanization of man, mount shot and shell against the dehumanization of man, or even to use the naughty words that one is "good" and the other is "bad." Man's nature is his nature, no matter what sociology says, and man is going to struggle toward the fulfillment of his nature no matter what sociology does or does not do. What is envisaged here would not involve "taking sides," losing scholarly dignity, or whatever other red herrings the sociological establishment might try to draw across the trail. All that is suggested here is that, for the sake of its own survival if for no other reason, sociology begin asking the right kinds of questions—those which really get at the things which hold groups of human beings together, tear them apart, and enable them to reassemble themselves in some coherent way. These are the legitimate sociological questions. All questions which assume that human beings are mechanical are unrealistic, unsociological, and in the truest sense of the word "unscientific."

It is entirely proper that a work of literature—a novel by Dickens or Zola, for example—be considered also a work of sociology, quite possibly a greater work of sociology than a statistical study of nineteenth-century England or France could have been if there had been survey research sociologists at large in those days. It is entirely possible that more might be learned about family life in modern Mexico from five families telling their stories honestly than from any number of stilted interviews with any size sample.

The *sine qua non* of human science is not numbers; it is insights, and the power of prediction which insights confer. If plays by Ionesco announce to those who have ears to listen amidst the laughter, that communication between husbands and wives, teachers and pupils, has become absurd, and that people are growing restive with absurd communication, then these are major sociological statements, and may be said to have forecast such developments as the Free Speech Movement better than any academic sociological statements. If plays by LeRoi Jones anticipated, before Watts, that there was going to be violence between "black" and "white" in the North, they should be counted as better sociology than any of the surveys.

The best sociology is not usually by sociologists, but by those who are free from any obsession with statistical methods: anthropologists, existential psychologists, theologians, philosophers, novelists, playwrights. For example, Buber is most often thought of as a philosopher—the founder of the "philosophy of dialogue." But he was as much a sociologist as anything else, and he gave us the conceptual tools for a "sociology of dialogue," or what we have here called "humanistic sociology."

One of the most significant features of the survey method is that it precludes any dialogue between the interviewer and interviewee. The interviewer is carefully trained to stifle all his normal human impulses—to take from the informant, but to give nothing of himself in return. This cannot but perplex the informant, throw him off stride, render the entire situation counterfeit. In real life, people do not function without cues from others.

Without dialogue, there is no such thing as society. Without listening to this dialogue, tactfully, attentively, lovingly, there is no such thing as an adequate sociology.

If sociology continues to lag in its grasp of the nature of human nature, and what this nature implies for research problems and methods, it will increasingly be cast into the intellectual penumbras of our time. It will be overshadowed by the philosophers of being, psychologists of being, and others who are in touch and in sympathy with the great contemporary revolution in man's understanding of his own nature.

It does not strain the imagination excessively to visualize institutions of higher learning, twenty years or so from now, in which sociology departments occupy approximately the same kind of place that classics departments do today. Since the Academy changes cautiously, a corner will be reserved for the present crop of bright, young, mathematically-oriented assistant professors of sociology, by then grown into full professors. They will still get grants from the National Institutes of Health and other federal agencies. They will be given a computer for their very own, and they may command a somewhat distant admiration from their less mathematically-inclined colleagues who do not know how to write a computer program. But their version of sociology will be regarded as an anachronism by most students, and without students any academic field grows old, sere, crotchety, quaint, and irrelevant. Students will gravitate toward the promise of greater wisdom, which will lie in such areas as the psychology of Maslow, the philosophy of Kierkegaard, the theology of Tillich, and even more, in areas we can presently only vaguely foresee: creative combinations of "talking about" the psychology, philosophy, theology, anthropology of Being, and actually Being through body movement, sensory awareness, self-revelation, painting, whatever.

It does not exhaust the imagination to visualize "courses" and perhaps even a whole "curriculum" in which "students" and "professors" begin by learning to shuck their masks by dance, improvisatory theater, and the like, and then go on simply to share their life-stories. More might be learned about sociology, and a score of other "subjects," in these ways, than from any number of formal lectures.

If this is the trend, why trouble to protest against the shortcomings of contemporary sociology? Why not let events take their course, and let sociology go into eclipse? What difference does it make where the insights come from, as long as they come?

It does make a difference whether the emphasis is on the dialogue of John and Mary Smith, or whether the question is, how are all the other Smiths doing with their dialogue, empathy, sharing, genuineness, joy, love, and other aspects of humanness? Are they going forward, by and large; are they going backward; or are they standing still? Why are some people moving more than others? What are the processes by which a fledgling human being, necessarily dependent on those around him for his images, identity, and very survival, grows beyond this dependency and becomes a unique person? How can people pass along the necessary continuities to the fledgling human beings who are born to them, and then, in due time, help those beings become less conforming and more fully human? What are the environmental influences which tend to assist this process? What influences hinder it? What can be done to encourage the influences which foster human development? What can be done to minimize the influences which retard it?

With exemplary modesty, most humanistic psychologists and others who are in the vanguard of the revolution in Being focus on the individual, and do not attempt to address the sweeping broad-gauge questions. But somebody must be so immodest as to do so, for these questions will determine whether society itself lives or dies. These questions constitute the province of what might be called a "sociology of dialogue" or "humanistic sociology." Since the word "humanistic" is subject to various misinterpretations, perhaps it would be preferable to say that what is advocated here is an ushering out of the old sociology of seeming, and an ushering in of a sociology of human becoming and of being.

12. The Art of Social Science
ROBERT REDFIELD

The late Robert Redfield was for many years a widely popular and immensely productive anthropologist at the University of Chicago. We turn to him now because of his belief that social science, when properly applied, is art as well as science. In his approach, Redfield in effect borrows gracefully from the views represented in the preceding two articles by Mack and Anderson, respectively. It is appropriate that such a mediating role should be assigned to an anthropologist, because sociocultural anthropologists have long been committed to research methods that stress intuitive insight along with external understanding. Professor Redfield, in particular, battled throughout his career against the possibility that the manipulative techniques of "pure science" might become established in his discipline as they had in other social sciences.

A dozen years ago I was a member of a committee of social scientists on social science method charged to appraise some outstanding published works of social science research. Our task was to find some good publica-

SOURCE: Robert Redfield, "The Art of Social Science," *The American Journal of Sociology* 54 (November 1948), 181–190. Copyright © 1948 by The University of Chicago Press and reproduced by permission.

tions of social science research and then to discover in what their methodological virtue consisted. The first part of our task we passed on to the communities of social scientists themselves. We asked economists to name some outstanding work in their field, sociologists to pick a work in sociology, etc. We limited the choice to publications by living social scientists. Of the books or monographs that received the greatest number of nominations, three were then subjected to analysis and discussion. I participated in the study of the methodological virtues of *The Polish Peasant* by Thomas and Znaniecki and of Webb's *The Great Plains*. These were books nominated by sociologists and historians, respectively, as outstanding in merit.

A curious thing happened. Herbert Blumer, who analyzed *The Polish Peasant* for the committee, came to the conclusion that the method in that book was really unsuccessful because the general propositions set forth in the work could not be established by the particular facts adduced. The committee had to agree. Yet it remained with the impression that this was a very distinguished and important work. Webb's history of cultural transformation in the American West fared no better at the hands of the young historian who analyzed that work. He pointed out many undeniable failures of the author of *The Great Plains* to use and to interpret fully some of the evidence. And yet again a majority of the committee persisted in the impression that Webb's book was truly stimulating, original, and praiseworthy.

Of course one does not conclude from this experience that the failure of facts to support hypotheses, in whole or in part, is a virtue in social science or is to be recommended. No doubt these books would have been more highly praised had these defects been proved to be absent. But does not the experience suggest that there is something in social science which is good, perhaps essential, apart from success with formal method; that these works have virtues not wholly dependent on the degree of success demonstrated in performing specified and formalized operations on restricted and precisely identified data?

I recall a comment I heard made by a distinguished social scientist whom I shall call A, about another distinguished social scientist whom I shall call B. A said of B: "He is very successful in spite of his method." Now, A was one who laid great stress on the obedience of the research worker to precise methods of operation with limited data, whereas B was much less so concerned. Yet A admired B, and the success he recognized in B was not worldly success but success in advancing our understanding and our control of man in society. Perhaps A felt that B's success was troubling to A's own views as to the importance of formal method. But A, a generous and able man, recognized something of virtue in B as a great student of man in society—a something other than methodological excellence.

What is that something? In attempting an answer here, I do not propose a separation between two ways of working in the scientific study of society. Nor do I deny that social science is dependent upon formal method. I seek rather to direct attention to an aspect of fruitful work in social science which is called for, in addition to formal method, if social science is to be most productive.

Let us here try to find out something about the nature of this nonformal aspect of social science through a consideration of three books about society that have long been recognized as important, influential, and meritorious: De Tocqueville's *Democracy in America,* Sumner's *Folkways,* and Veblen's *The Theory of the Leisure Class.* For from almost fifty to a hundred years these books have interested and have influenced many kinds of social scientists. Veblen and Sumner were economists, but the books they wrote are important for sociologists, anthropologists, historians, and other kinds of social scientists. De Tocqueville's book is a work interesting to political scientists as well as to historians of America, but it is quite as much a work in sociology, for De Tocqueville was concerned not so much in reporting what went on in the United States in 1830 as he was in defining a sort of natural societal type: the democratic society, including in the type not merely its political institutions but also its moral, familial, and "cultural" institutions and attitudes, treated as a single whole.

None of these books tells very much about research method, in the sense of teaching special procedures of operation with certain kinds of data. There is nothing in any of them about kinship genealogies, or sampling, or guided interviews, or margins of error. There is nowhere in them any procedure, any kind of operation upon facts to reach conclusions which might not occur to any intelligent and generally educated person. Sumner made notes on the customs of exotic peoples as he read about them. Veblen's methods, as represented in *The Theory of the Leisure Class,* are no more formal than Sumner's. The factual substance of De Tocqueville's book is the record of his own observations as he traveled about America looking at what there was about him and talking to the people he met. If these books have merit, it is not by reason of any inventions or devices of method, for they exhibit none. Yet these are books which have for many years profoundly affected the course of social science and have contributed to our understanding of man in society. They might be even more important if they also made contributions to or through formal method, but, as they do not, something may be learned from them about that part of the study of society which is not formal method.

Perhaps these are not works of research. Perhaps for some "research" always means special procedures of operation which have to be learned or means analysis of some small set of facts or very limited problem. If this is your view of research, I shall not dispute it. Then the three books are not works of research. But what is there in them that is admired and that is valuable in the study of man in society that is not dependent upon formal method?

If these three classic books are not books in social science, what are they? They are surely not novels, or journalism, or yet belles-lettres. That they have qualities of literary style is true—and is not to be deplored—even Sumner's book impresses with the effective iteration of its terse, stark sentences. But the value of these books for the student of society lies not in any appeal they make to aesthetic sensibilities but for the illumination they throw upon man's nature or upon the nature of society. It is true that great novels do that too. But there are, of course, important differences between the books named, on the one hand, and, let us say, *War and Peace* and *The Remembrance of Things Past*, on the other. These last are works for social scientists to know about and to learn from, but they are not works of social science. They are not because neither Proust's book nor Tolstoi's is a generalized description of the nature of society stated at some remove from the personal experiences of the writer. De Tocqueville made his own observations, but he stated his results objectively in generalized and analytical terms making comparisons with other observations and conclusions easy. Tolstoi wrote about a real Russia during the real Napoleonic Wars, but his Pierres and Natashas are imagined, individual, personal, intimate, and ungeneralized. It is not difficult to distinguish the great analyses of society, as objectively studied and presented in generalized conclusions, from the works of personal record and of freely creative imagination.

Are the three books "objective" descriptions of society? In varying degree, but all three to some degree. Probably De Tocqueville, who of the three writers was least a professional social scientist, impresses one most with an air of severe detachment, of willingness to look at this social being, a democratic society, without blame or praise. De Tocqueville's work seems as objective as a social scientist might wish. Sumner, too, is describing, not evaluating, yet there is in the *Folkways* an undertone of patient scorn for the irrationality of man, for man's obedience to whatever folly his tradition may decree. Veblen seems the least objective. Below the forms of scientific analysis lies, urbanely and ironically disguised, the condemnation of a moralist. As a recent writer on Veblen has put it, he used "the realistic paraphernalia of scholarship" to attack the morality of capitalistic society.[1] Nevertheless, even Veblen's book presents a fresh description of a part of modern society, and the description is not that of a creative artist but of one who is responsible to facts studied and facts verifiable.

The three books are works which are not novels, which do not have much to say about formal procedures of research, and which, nevertheless, throw light upon man in society through the more or less objective presentation of generalized conclusions from the study of particular societies. In these respects they correspond with what is by at least some people called "scientific." What did the authors do that constitutes their contribution to the understanding of man in society?

It is surely not that these writers have been proved to be invariably right. Indeed, in each case there are points in which in the later days they have been found wrong. Veblen's account overemphasizes competitiveness in terms of consumption and accepts a good deal of what was then current as to race and as to stages of social evolution which is not unacceptable today. Sumner's conception of the mores, immensely stimulating as it was, exaggerates the helplessness of men before tradition and is especially inadequate as a concept for understanding modern societies—as Myrdal has recently shown. And, although De Tocqueville's account of early American society is perceptive and revealing to a degree that is almost miraculous, there is certainly confusion in it between what is necessarily democratic and what is characteristic of the frontier and between what must be characteristic of any democracy and what happened to be in the Anglo-American tradition.

In three respects these books, which have nothing to teach about formal methods, make great contributions to the understanding of man in society.

In the first place, each is an expression of some perception of human nature. In each case the writer has looked at people in a society, or in many societies, and has directly apprehended something about their ways of thinking and feeling which are characteristic of the human race under those particular circumstances. His central concern has not been some second- or third-hand index or sign of human nature, some check marks on a schedule or some numbered quantities of anything. He has looked at people with the vision of his own humanity.

Not all of what is called social science is concerned with human nature. The study of population is not concerned with it until matters of population policy are reached. Marginal analysis in economics is concerned with such a slender sliver of human nature, so artificially severed from the rest, that it, too, is unrepresentative of studies of human nature. And this is also of necessity true of much of the archeology of the North American Indian.

These last-mentioned kinds of investigation, worthy as they are, are the special or marginal cases that mark the outskirts of the study of man in society. The essential nature of man in society is his human nature and the expressions of that human nature in particular institutions. To find out the nature and significance of human nature there is no substitute for the human nature of the student himself. He must use his own humanity to understand humanity. To understand alien institutions, he must try to see in them the correspondences and the divergences they exhibit in relation to the institutions with which he is more closely familiar. To understand an alien culture, it is not, first of all, necessary to learn how to interview or how to make schedules for a house-to-house canvass, useful as these skills are. It is first needful to have experienced some culture—some culture which will serve as the touchstone in apprehending this new one.

One aspect of the great merit of the three works mentioned lies in the central attention directed by Sumner, Veblen, and De Tocqueville to the humanity of their subject matter and in the success each had in apprehending the particular facet of that humanity as it was shaped and conditioned by the surrounding circumstances. Sumner, looking especially at small, long-isolated societies or at the later little-changing societies derived from primitive conditions, saw the resulting creation, in each individual there born and reared, of motives and designs of life that were there, in the customs of that society, before him. He saw in human nature the extraordinary malleability of human nature and the precedence of custom over habit. Veblen looked freshly at the behavior of consumers, saw them as people who actually do buy and consume, in their families and their communities, and recognized theretofore insufficiently recognized aspects of human nature in society. De Tocqueville touched Americans in their age of self-confidence and in a great number of true perceptions saw what their behavior meant to them and why. Just compare his success in using his own humanity with imagination, and yet with detachment, with Mrs. Trollope's failure to achieve understanding of these same people.

It is at this point that the methods of the social sciences—now using "method" in its broadest sense to include all the ways of thinking and even feeling about subject matter—approach the methods of the creative artist. Like the novelist, the scientific student of society must project the sympathetic understanding which he has of people with motives, desires, and moral judgments into the subject he is treating. Neither the one nor the other can get along without this gift, this means of understanding. But whereas the novelist may let his imagination run freely, once it is stimulated by personal experience and reading, the scientific student must constantly return to the particular men, the particular societies, he has chosen to investigate, test his insights by these, and report these particular facts with such specificity that his successor may repeat the testing. In spite of this all-important difference, the territories of the humanities and of the scientific study of man in society are in part the same. The subject matter of both is, centrally, man as a human being. Human beings are not the subject matter of physics and chemistry. So it would be error to build a social science upon the image of physics or chemistry. Social science is neither the same as the humanities nor the same as the physical sciences. It is a way of learning about man in society which uses the precise procedures and the objectivity characteristic of physics as far as these will helpfully go in studying human beings but no further; and which uses, indispensably, that personal direct apprehension of the human qualities of behavior and of institutions which is shared by the novelist.

A second observation may be made about the three books chosen. Each brings forward significant generalizations. In the case of Veblen's book, the general conceptions that are known by the phrases "pecuniary emulation," "vicarious consumption," etc., are, like the concepts in *Folkways*, names for new insights into persistent and widely inclusive aspects of man's nature in society. In reading these books, we catch a glimpse of the eternal in the light of the ephemeral. We see ourselves as exemplifications of patterns in nature. Social science is concerned with uniformities. The uniformities are exaggerated; they transcend the particularity of real experience and historic event; they claim more than each fact by itself would allow; they say: "If it were really like this, this would be the pattern." De Tocqueville, too, offers such patterns that go beyond the particular facts. Indeed, the case of De Tocqueville is particularly plain in this connection, for so interested is he in presenting a system of coherent generalizations as to the necessary nature of democratic society that in many passages he makes no reference at all to what he saw in the United States but derives one generalization as to the democratic society he conceives from some other generalization already brought forward. He is not, therefore, to be rejected as a contributor to the scientific understanding of society, for these deductions are tied to generalizations that in turn rest upon many particular observations of many particular men and events. The concept, like the novel, is a work of creative imagination but a work more closely and publicly bound to particular facts of observation and record.

Like the apprehension of the humanly significant, the making of the generalization is a work of imagination. Sumner did not find out that there is such a thing as the mores by learning and applying some method of research. He discovered it by watching the people around him and by using the observations recorded by other men and then by making a leap of thought across many diversities to apprehend the degree of uniformity that deserves the term "mores." In the reaching of a significant generalization as to man in society there is an exercise of a gift of apprehension so personal and so subtly creative that it cannot be expected to result merely from application of some formal method of research.

The three books show thinkers about man in society who have had some new and generalized apprehension of human nature or of human institutions. They have succeeded in communicating this apprehension in such a way as to show it to be both important and true. It is true in the sense that there are facts accessible that support it. It is not, of course, all the truth, and it may be that some other apprehension will come to appear "more true," that is, even more illuminating, as applied to some set of circumstances.

There is another quality in the thinking and the creating of the three writers that deserves recognition by itself: the freshness and independence of viewpoint with which each looked at his subject matter. One feels, in reading any one of the three books, how the writer saw what he saw with his own eyes, as if the previous views of it were suspect, just because they were previous. One feels in the case of each writer a discontent with the way some aspect of man in society was then being regarded, a clear-headed wilfulness to take another look for himself. There is a disposition to make the thing looked at a true part of the viewer's own being, to go beyond obedience to the existing writings on the subject. De Tocqueville was dissatisfied with the views of democracy current in his time: the passionate condemnations or the equally passionate espousals. He would go to the country where the angel or the monster was actually in course of development, and he would, he resolved coolly, look for neither monster nor angel; he would look at what he should find, and grasp it, in its whole and natural condition, as one would look at a newly arrived class of animal. He could weigh the good and the bad, then, after he had come to understand the natural circumstances that would produce the creature. Sumner's book is in one way a reaffirmation of a viewpoint then current and in another way a reaction against it. As the folkways come about by no man's planning but through the accidental interactions of men and the competition of alternative solutions, they are consistent with that conception of unrestrained individualistic competition which Sumner supported in the economic sphere. On the other hand, the *Folkways* reads as a reaction against the Age of Reason. It seems to say that men do not, after all, solve their problems by rational calculation of utilities. Looked at anew, the ways of men appear not reasonable but unreasonable and determined by preexisting customs and moral judgments which make the calculation of utilities seem absurd. From this point of view the book is an act of rebellion. An economist looks for himself at the whole human scene and says, too emphatically, no doubt, what needs to be said to correct the preceding vision. Something not so different could be said about the fresh look that Veblen took.

It may be objected that the qualities in these three works are qualities one may expect to find only in an occasional book written by some unusual mind. These books have passed beyond social science, or they fall short of it; and the humbler toiler in the vineyard cannot expect to learn from them anything that would help him in tending the vines of his more limited hypotheses or in pressing the wine of his more restricted conclusions.

Yet all three of the qualities found in these works may be emulated by the student of any human aspect of man in society. It is not only in good major works that there is found that human sympathy which is needful in apprehending a human reality. The exercise of this capacity is demanded in every study of a community; it is exacted in every consideration of an institution in which men with motives and desires like our own fulfil the roles and offices that make it up; it is required in every interview. One may be taught how to pursue a course of questioning, how to map a neighborhood, or how to tabulate and treat statistically the votes cast in an election; but to know how to do these things is not to be assured of meaningful conclusions. Besides these skills, one needs also the ability to enter imaginatively, boldly, and, at the same time, self-critically into that little fraction of the human comedy with which one has become scientifically concerned. One must become a part of the human relations one studies, while holding one's self also a little to one side, so as to suspend judgment as to the worth of one's first insight. Then one looks at the scene again; perhaps, guided by something one has known or read of human beings in some comparable situation, in some other place or age, one may get a second insight that better withstands reexamination and the test of particular observations. This procedure, call it method, nonmethod, or what you will, is an essential part of most of social science, great and small.

As for the exercise of the ability to see the general in the particular, is this not also demanded of anyone who takes a scientific attitude toward anything in human nature or society? We are not freed from the obligation to look for what may be widely true by the narrowness, in time and space, of the facts before us. Surely Sumner did not wait to conceive of the mores until he had piled up those five hundred pages of examples. Malinowski provided a clearer understanding of the nature of myth, in its resemblance to and its difference from folk tale, from the view he had of the stories told and the ways they were told in a small community in the South Seas. Webb, a historian rather than one of those students of society who more easily announce generalizations thought to be widely applicable, does not, in his *The Great Plains*, announce any; but the value of the work lies for many in the fact that it is easily read as an exemplification of the tendency of institutions adjusted to one environment to undergo change when imported into a new and of the effects of changes in technology upon human relations. The social scientist is always called upon to use his imagination as to the general that may lie within the immediate particulars. The formal method may lead him to these generalizations; after he has added up the cases, or completed the tests, he may for the first time see some corespondences that suggest a generalization. But it happens at least as often that he sees the generalization long before the formal methods have been carried out; the exercise of the formal method may then test the worth of his insight. And a significant generalization may appear without formal method. The conceptions of marginal utility in economics and of the marginal man in sociology perhaps illustrate the development of a concept, on the one hand, with close dependence upon formal method and, on the other, without such dependence. In the latter case Park was struck by resemblances in the conduct of particular men and women whom he met, American Negroes, mission-educated Orientals, and second-generation immigrants: humane insight, guided by scientific imagination, then created the concept.

The third quality of good social science in its less formal aspects is freshness of vision. It is the looking at what one is studying as if the world's comprehension of it depended solely on one's own look. In taking such a look, one does not ignore the views that other men have taken of the subject matter or of similar subject matter. But these earlier views are challenged. Maybe, one says, it is not as my teachers told me I should find it. I will look for myself. One has perhaps heard something about folk society. But at this particular society with which I am concerned I will look for myself. Perhaps there is no folk society there. Perhaps there is something else, much nearer the truth.

It is difficult for teachers who have expounded their own views of some aspect of man in society to teach their successors to take some other view of it. Perhaps it cannot be taught. Yet somehow each generation of social scientists must rear a following generation of rebels. Now rebellion is not well inculcated in the teaching of formal procedure. Indeed, an exclusive emphasis on formal procedure may cause atrophy of the scientific imagination. To train a man to perform a technique may result in making him satisfied with mastery of the technique. Having learned so much about field procedure, or statistics, or the situations in which interviews are held and recorded, or the criticism of documents, the new social scientist may come to feel that he has accomplished all the learning he needs. He may rest content in proficiency. Proficiency is excellent, but it must be combined with an imaginative dissatisfaction. In little investigations as in large ones, the situation studied demands a whole look and a free look.

It is equally doubtful whether one can give instruction in the exercise of humane insight or in recognizing the general in the particular when the generality is not thrust upon the student by a marked statistical predominance. These are qualities of the social science investigator that perhaps depend upon the accidents of natural endowment. Humane insight is a gift. The concept is a work of creative imagination; apprehension is a gift. In stressing the necessity, in good social science, for the investigator to think and to speculate independently and freely, in emphasizing the reliance of good social science upon the personal and human qualities of the investigator, one seems to be talking not about a science but about an art and to be saying that social science is also an art. It is an art in that the social scientist creates imaginatively out of his own human qualities brought into connection with the facts before him. It is an art in degree much greater than that in which physics and chemistry are arts, for the student of the atom or of the element is not required, when he confronts his subject matter, to become a person among persons, a creature of tradition and attitude in a community that exists in tradition and in attitude. With half his being the socal scientist approaches his subject matter with a detachment he shares with the physicist. With the other half he approaches it with a human sympathy which he shares with the novelist. And it is an art to a greater degree than is physics or chemistry for the further reason that the relationships among the parts of a person or of a society are, as compared with physical relationships, much less susceptible of definitions, clear and machine-precise. In spite of the great advances in formal method in social science, much of the understanding of persisting and general relationships depends upon a grasp that is intuitive and that is independent of or not fully dependent on some formal method. In advancing social science, we invent and practice techniques, and we also cultivate a humanistic art.

The nature of social science is double. In the circle of learning, its place adjoins the natural sciences, on the one hand, and the humanities, on the other. It is not a result of exceptional political ambition that political scientists and anthropologists are to be found included both in the Social Science Research Council and in the American Council of Learned Societies; it is a recognition of the double nature of social science. On the one hand, the student of society is called upon to apprehend the significant general characteristics of human beings with something of the same human insight which is practiced by a novelist or a dramatist. On the other hand, he is obliged to make his observations and his inferences as precise and as testable, and his generalizations as explicit and as compendent, as the examples of the natural sciences suggest and as his own different materials allow.

It is the example of the natural sciences which social scientists have on the whole striven to imitate. In the short history of social science its practitioners have turned their admiring gazes toward their neighbors on the scientific side. They have looked that way, perhaps, because the natural sciences were the current success. They have looked that way, surely, because when the students of human nature in society came to think of themselves as representing one or more disciplines, with professors and places in universities and in national councils, social science was not very scientific: it was speculative and imprecise. To achieve identity, it had to grow away from the making of personally conceived systems of abstract thought. It had to learn to build, a brick at a time, and to develop procedures that would make the building public and subject to testing.

But now the invention and the teaching of special procedures have received too exclusive an emphasis in the doing of social science and in the making of social scientists. In places the invention and the teaching of special procedures have gone ahead of the possibility of finding out anything very significant with their aid. It is certainly desirable to be precise, but it is quite as needful to be precise about something worth knowing. It is good to teach men and women who are to be social scientists how to use the instruments of observation and analysis that have been developed in their disciplines. But it is not good to neglect that other equally important side of social science.

To identify social science very closely with the physical sciences is to take one view of the education of social scientists: to think of that education chiefly in terms of formal method and formal knowledge of society already achieved and to be taught. Then programs for making social scientists will be made up of training in techniques and the opportunity to take part in some kind of research in which the procedures are already determined and the problems set by some established master. Then the holder of a fellowship will go to a school, where a way of working is well known and well fixed, and he will acquire the procedural competences taught at that school.

If this is all we do for young students of society, we are likely to have proficient technicians, but we are not likely to have great social scientists or to have many books written that are as illuminating and as influential as those by Sumner, Veblen, and De Tocqueville.

It would be well to give some attention to the humanistic aspect of social science. Part of the preparation of good social scientists is humanistic education. As what is called general education, or liberal education, is largely humanistic, it follows that the social scientist has two interests in liberal education. Like the physicist, like everybody else, the social scientist needs liberal education in his role as a citizen. But, in addition, he needs liberal humanistic education in his role as a social scientist.

The art of social science cannot be inculcated, but, like other arts, it can be encouraged to develop. The exercise of that art can be favored by humanistic education. If the social scientist is to apprehend, deeply and widely and correctly, persons and societies and cultures, then he needs experience, direct or vicarious, with persons, societies, and cultures. This experience is partly had through acquaintance with history, literature, biography, and ethnography. And if philosophy gives some experience in the art of formulating and in thinking about widely inclusive generalizations, then the social scientist needs acquaintance with philosophy. There is no longer any need to be fearful about philosophy. The time when young social science was struggling to make itself something different from philosophy is past. Now social science is something different. Now social scientists need to learn from philosophy, not to become philosophers, but to become better social scientists. The acquaintance with literature, biography, ethnography, and philosophy which is gained in that general education given in high schools and colleges is probably not rich enough or deep enough for some of those who are to become social scientists. The opportunities for advanced education given to some who appear to have exceptional gifts as students of man in society may well consist of the study of Chinese or East Indian culture, or of the novel in Western literature, or of the history of democracy.

The humanistic aspect of social science is the aspect of it that is today not well appreciated. Social science is essentially scientific in that its propositions describe, in general terms, natural phenomena; in that it returns again and again to special experience to verify and to modify these propositions. It tells what is, not what ought to be. It investigates nature. It strives for objectivity, accuracy, compendency. It employs hypotheses and formal evidence; it values negative cases; and, when it finds a hypothesis to be unsupported by the facts, it drops it for some other which is. But these are all aspects of social science so well known that it is tedious to list them again. What is less familiar, but equally true, is that to create the hypothesis, to reach the conclusion, to get, often, the very first real datum as to what are A's motives or what is the meaning of this odd custom or that too-familiar institution, requires on the part of one who studies persons and societies, and not rocks or proteins, a truly humanistic and freely imaginative insight into people, their conventions and interests and motives, and that this requirement in the social scientist calls for gifts and for a kind of education different from that required of any physicist and very similar to what is called for in a creative artist.

If this be seen, it may also be seen that the function of social science in our society is a double function. Social science is customarily explained and justified by reason of what social science contributes to the solution of particular problems that arise in the management of our society, as a help in getting particular things done. As social scientists we take satisfaction in the fact that today, as compared with thirty years ago, social scientists are employed because their employers think that their social science is applicable to some practical necessity. Some knowledge of techniques developed in social science may be used: to select taxicab drivers that are not likely to have accidents; to give vocational guidance; to discover why one business enterprise has labor troubles while a similar enterprise does not; to make more effective some governmental program carried into farming communities; to help the War Relocation Authority carry out its difficult task with Japanese-Americans.

All these contributions to efficiency and adjustment may be claimed with justice by social scientists. What is also to be claimed, and is less commonly stressed, is that social science contributes to that general understanding of the world around us which, as we say, "liberalizes," or "enriches." The relation of social science to humanistic learning is reciprocal. Social scientists need humanistic learning the better to be social scientists. And the understanding of society, personality, and human nature which is achieved by scientific methods returns to enrich that humanistic understanding without which none can become human and with which some few may become wise. Because its subject matter is humanity, the contribution of social science to general, liberal education is greater than is the contribution of those sciences with subject matter that is physical. In this respect also, creative artist and social scientist find themselves side by side. The artist may reveal something of universal human or social nature. So too may the social scientist. No one has ever applied, as a key to a lock, Sumner's *Folkways* or Tawney's *Religion and the Rise of Capitalism* or James's *The Varieties of Religious Experience*. These are not the works of social science that can be directly consulted and applied when a government office or a business concern has an immediate problem. But they are the books of lasting influence. Besides what influence they have upon those social scientists who come to work in the government office, or the business concern, in so far as they are read and understood and thought about by men and women who are not social scientists, or even as they are communicated indirectly by those who have read them to others, they are part of humanistic education, in the broad sense. Releasing us from our imprisonment in the particular, we are freed by seeing how we are exemplifications of the general. For how many young people has not Sumner's book, or Veblen's book, or some work by Freud, come as a swift widening of the doors of vision, truly a liberation, a seeing of one's self, perhaps for the first time, as sharing the experiences, the nature, of many other men and women? So I say that social science, as practiced, is something of an art and that, as its best works are communicated, it has something of the personal and social values of all the arts.

NOTES

1. Daniel Aaron, "Thorstein Veblen—Moralist," *Antioch Review*, VII, No. 3 (fall, 1947), 390.

13. Scientists and Other Citizens
GERARD PIEL

The "pure science" recommended by traditional sociologists is both a philosophical impossibility and a political anomaly, according to the following analysis by Gerard Piel, long the editor of Scientific American. Mr. Piel describes issues facing the American Association for the Advancement of Science, but his points apply to all the specialty sciences; and they apply in some ways more today than they did when he wrote in the 1950s, considering the recent widespread assaults on the job tenure that has long been the major protector of academic freedom. Perhaps the most important point is that so far as potential political consequences are concerned, there is no such phenomenon as "pure research." The implication is that those who claim scientific organizations should always refrain from taking political positions are giving public testimony that they are either philosophically naive or politically dangerous.

The American Association for the Advancement of Science is the peak organization of science in the United States, a holding company to which all other scientific societies and some 40,000 individual members adhere. When the A.A.A.S. was founded in 1848, it was the forum to which scientists reported their work. Over the century, as scientists became biologists, physicists, chemists, anthropologists, and specialists in the ever narrower subdisciplines of these fields, the A.A.A.S. has yielded this substantive function to its member societies. It still assembles 5,000 to 7,000 scientists at its annual convention in Christmas week. As these meetings

SOURCE: Gerard Piel, *Science in the Cause of Man*, Second Edition, Revised and Enlarged. (New York: Alfred A. Knopf, 1962), pp. 29–40. Copyright © 1951, 1952 by Gerard Piel. Reprinted by permission of Alfred A. Knopf, Inc.

have been emptied of formal scientific content, they have become increasingly preoccupied with the relations of science and society.

In 1953, when the A.A.A.S. gathered in Boston, the question of academic freedom, the subject of this essay, was at the top of the agenda. The subcommittee of the Committee on Government Operations of the U.S. Senate, headed by Joseph McCarthy, had joined the Un-American Activities Committee of the House in disturbing the peace on the campus and especially in the laboratories of the universities. The A.A.A.S. had responded to attacks upon a succession of its distinguished members by electing them to its presidency. The chairman of our symposium on the evening of December 29, 1953, was Edward U. Condon, then president of the A.A.A.S. and a scientist who had endured the attentions of the committees for nearly a decade.

Curiously, my holding on this occasion that "academic freedom is not a different kind of freedom, nor a special privilege for a pressure group," was to be overruled by Mr. Justice Frankfurter. In *Sweezey* v. *Wyman*, he wrote pages of eloquent dicta in praise of academic freedom as distinguished from the ordinary elector's freedom and as a special privilege of scholars.

But neither the weight nor the grace of his prose was to hold down the scales for academic or any other kind of freedom when the U.S. Supreme Court, in later opinions with Frankfurter concurring, proceeded to apply the Frankfurter "balancing" doctrine and sent college professors off to jail impartially with other citizens convicted of contempt of Congress. In his dissent in the Wilkinson case, Mr. Justice Black declares:

> The result of all this is that from now on anyone who takes a public position contrary to that being urged by the House Un-American Activities Committee should realize that he runs the risk of being subpoenaed to appear at a hearing in some far-off place, of being questioned with regard to every minute detail of his past life, of being asked to repeat all the gossip he may have heard about any of his friends and acquaintances, of being accused by the Committee of membership in the Communist Party, of being held up to the public as a subversive and a traitor, of being jailed for contempt if he refuses to cooperate with the Committee in its probe of his mind and associations, and of being branded by his neighbors, employer and erstwhile friends as a menace to society *regardless of the outcome of that hearing.*

The universities have been less troubled by congressional visiting committees during the past few years. One must, however, await the next cycle of campus hearings with trepidation. Academic freedom, having now, for sure, no reality inscribed on fading parchment, will exist only to the degree that it is asserted by the action of men.

We may take heart in the fact that almost every recent meeting of the A.A.A.S. has featured a symposium on the double heading of science and society. One heavy price we have had to pay for the advancement of science is specialization. Scientists and other citizens have hitherto been content to live in separate worlds, almost in separate societies, to the detriment and hazard of both. It may not be too late now to discover that science is a social activity which involves other citizens as well as scientists. The fact is, science today in America is a largely socialized activity that is bringing scientists into new and not always comfortable association with their fellow citizens.

American science was never really demobilized at the end of the Second World War. This year expenditures on research in our universities will exceed $50 million, more than twelve times prewar expenditures. Nearly nine tenths of this money comes from government and industry. The bulk of it is for military research, and almost all of it, no matter how pious the protestations of the sponsors and the scientists involved, must be credited to the support of applied, as contrasted with basic, research.

This flood of money has profoundly altered the conditions of scientific work and the lives of scientists in our country. As Curt Richter, of The Johns Hopkins University, said in a recent issue of *Science*: "Large funds encourage great enterprises, great experimental designs. They encourage 'great teams of workers'; they take good research men away from their workbenches to direct many technicians." Worse yet, they set up pressures that divert scientists from their own work to devote their energies to the projects of others. Especially in war-motivated grants, says Professor Richter, "it is the project, the design that counts. Who does the work is often relatively unimportant."

This subordination of the scientist to the status of employee, even in an executive capacity, heavily conditions his independence. All too often it means loss of independence from within as well as from without. Unquestionably it has a role in encouraging the preoccupation with little questions and the soft-pedaling of fruitful controversy about which scientists in every field may be heard complaining. One wonders what effect it must have upon the quality of teaching, since students traditionally take aspiration from their masters.

Their new and closer relationship to their fellow citizens thus faces scientists with a host of problems. But there is none more serious, because it compromises the possibility of action on all others, than that which confronts scientists in the realm of civil liberties. The present erosion of their academic and personal freedoms is in itself a measure of the decline of the scientist's traditional status as an independent scholar. The public record shows an increasing frequency of affronts to the integrity of scientists as citizens. In secret proceedings, many more scientists have suffered humiliation and jeopardy as the result of invasion of their freedom and privacy.

The situation must be deeply disturbing to anyone who senses the crucial relationship between the ethics and law of a free society and the conditions that are essential to the work of science. Freedom of conscience, speech, publication, and assembly are required alike by the advancement of science and the self-government of a democracy. Due process in the law has its analogue in the tests of logic and evidence observed in research, and both have the purpose of arriving at the truth by induction. No scientist can surrender his freedom as a citizen without resigning his independence as a scientist. No society that muzzles political dissent will long delay the clamping of restraints upon science. In any discussion of the relationship between science and society today, these issues must come to the top of the agenda. They are the topic of legitimate professional concern, not only because they affect colleagues who have been wronged but because they ultimately involve the freedom of every scientist to carry on his work.

Taking a broader view of this situation, two observations force themselves upon us. The first is that scientists are not alone in their plight. The constriction of the freedom of scientists is part of a general pattern that involves the freedom of people in every department of intellectual activity. The same indignities have been visited upon writers, actors, scholars, government administrators, teachers, lawyers, and ministers. The present movement differs from similar episodes in the American past in that it favors intellectuals as its target.

The second observation is that this movement has its origins deep in the structure and condition of American society today. It is no mere case of democracy fumbling, as has been said, with the difficult reconciliation of security and freedom in a dangerous world. Espionage, sabotage, and treason are familiar perils to the existence of national states. Our people long ago equipped the federal government to deal with them by methods that accord with the institutions and ideals we want to protect. The spectacle we have been witnessing is not only repugnant to the spirit of our society but largely irrelevant to national security. In fact, according to Senator Herbert H. Lehman, this "full-scale assault on the Government service, the schools, the stage, the publishing world and even the churches has done more harm to the national security than disclosure of all the nation's defense secrets could have done."

Nor is this the first time that conscienceless politicians have undertaken to exploit popular apprehension in a time of world unrest. They have ample precedent in our history from the XYZ papers to the Palmer raids. But the present crop of demagogues and their ignoble collaborators have been spared for too long the wrath that should spring from the sense of fair play innate in the American tradition. That is why we are moved to see these events as symptomatic of some serious malaise in our culture, of grave disturbance in our social order.

Though they are not really looking for the causes of these deeper troubles, our contemporary inquisitors seem to sense that the hunt is warmer when they have a scientist in the dock. It is, after all, quite widely understood that science does have something to do with the amenities and the troubles of living in our time.

In an address before a similar gathering of the British Association for the Advancement of Science last year, Alexander Macbeath, professor of logic and metaphysics at The Queen's University in Belfast, described the situation thus:

> ... it is to the power over his environment which it placed at man's disposal, that science mainly owes its present prestige. The miracles of the modern world—motorcars and airplanes, radio and television—all derive from science; and for the mass of mankind, they constitute its justification. ... But the dangers and discomforts which have come in their train have been equally great—high explosives and atom bombs, the squalor of urbanization, the exploitation of man by man—and it is of these that men have become painfully conscious during the 20th century. ... After learning by bitter experience that [the knowledge and power that science brings] are not always used wisely, men have reacted not only against freedom to misuse them, but against freedom in general.

In fear and insecurity, the people seek the reassurance of conformity and thereby create the market for our latter-day revivalists and promoters of authoritarianism. The intellectual who disturbs their uneasy peace with doubting questions comes to be regarded as a heretic, a revolutionary, and worse. Hence the apathy, if not the approbation, with which the public has thus far permitted the stifling of our civil liberties to advance.

That advance is already considerable. There is not enough time here to catalogue the grievances. Suffice it to say that they include practices which recall the obnoxious test oath, bills of attainder, search and seizure without warrant, Star Chamber prosecutions, and other abuses to the relief of which our Declaration of Independence and Constitution were addressed.

Many of these practices have unfortunately been found to be, as Supreme Court Justice William O. Douglas recently observed, "within the letter of the law." "But," says Justice Douglas, "even when lawyers and judges justify them, they violate the ideals of freedom we profess." In formal opinions from the bench, he and other judges have observed that the courts, too, may be swayed by the tides of emotional majorityism that have swamped the executive and legislative departments.

With great wisdom Alexander Meiklejohn has observed that our Constitution provides for a fourth independent branch of the government, co-equal with the executive, legislative, and judicial. This fourth branch in the division of power is the sovereign citizenry, acting in its capacity as the electorate. Clearly, if our system is to work, each elector must be protected from intimidation and coercion, especially with regard to his political action, by public officials who become infected with the insolence of office. That protection is provided by the secrecy of the ballot box and by the right of privacy that shelters the freedom of conscience, speech, and association.

Now, as we have been told so often in the past few years, a citizen has no right to a job on the public payroll. But he is nonetheless entitled to protection against harassment and deprivation of livelihood by executive department loyalty procedures that violate the essence of his constitutional rights. The independence of the elector draws the same clear boundary around the matters that may be legitimately inquired into by legislative committees. Officials and legislators who overstep this boundary are guilty of invading the integrity of the fourth branch of our government and stand in contempt of the electorate.

There is a disturbing tendency for these inquisitorial procedures to spread outside the government into private business, labor unions, and civic organizations. Pressures in this regard are especially heavy upon educational institutions. The president of Harvard, for example, was recently reminded that only a legal fiction insulates privately endowed institutions from supervision by a congressional committee. They could be stripped of their tax exemption for failing to meet some congressional standard in faculty appointments.

In view of the pronounced tendency of this movement to persist and increase in intensity, the following description by Leo Szilard of parallel events in Germany may be taken as a warning of where we might go from here:

> The German learned societies did not raise their voices in protest against these early dismissals. . . . It seemed much more important at that moment to fight for the established rights of those who had tenure, and this could be done much more successfully, so they thought, if they made concessions on minor points. In a sense, the German government kept its word with respect to those who had tenure. It is true that before long most professors who were considered 'undesirable' were retired; but they were given pensions adequate for their maintenances. And these pensions were faithfully paid to them until the very day they were put into concentration camps, beyond which time it did not seem practicable to pay them pensions. Later many of these professors were put to death, but this was no longer, strictly speaking, an academic matter with which the learned societies needed to concern themselves.

Fortunately, there are signs of a willingness and a resolve on the part of the academic community to get defensive counteraction going before it is too late. Not all these efforts, however, are wisely conceived. Many betray an utter failure to understand the nature of the challenge. Among them are resolutions and declarations that speak on the topic of civil liberties with great warmth and erudition. But they have a common flaw that vitiates their impact. This is the plea of "not guilty." The plea is entered, of course, against the charge of communism. By now it should be clear that no person or institution can be completely cleared of the stigma attaching to this charge. This is because it relates not to acts but to the private realm of conviction and belief.

By its very nature, therefore, the charge tends inevitably to become ever more vague and meaningless. In this condition, it serves even more admirably the purposes of those who use it as a weapon. The less precise and meaningful it is, the less does it need to be proved and the more impossible does it become to disprove. For the objectives of the demagogue, it must be capable of infinite expansion, ultimately to compromise every position and every conformity except the demagogue's own. The label of communism has served this purpose well; it embraces not only all shades of Marxism and socialism but New Dealers, Fair Dealers, and Democrats, and now includes even Republicans.

The real charge here, of course, is not communism at all, but heresy. This is an imaginary crime in the most literal sense of the term, since it is one that a man is supposed to commit inside his own head. To plead "not guilty" to such a charge is to permit it to be lodged and thereby to resign the dignity of citizenship that rules such inquiry out of order in the first place. This is the point on which the American Association of University Professors has stood fast since 1915. It is the point that the Association of American Universities regrettably failed to make in its declaration early this year on the problems raised by the self-appointed visiting committees from Congress.

The issue is complicated by the fuzzing out of the legal concept of conspiracy to comprise another new crime—crime by association. Like heresy, this chimera, too, is dissipated by the clear test of action. It is basic to our sense of justice that a man can be charged only for his own personal acts and cannot be held responsible for the behavior of associates. The charge of guilt by association must be met on the same grounds as that of guilt by thinking: its admissibility as a charge must be denied at the outset.

The charge of heresy is a hoax. But it takes a party of the second part to bring it off. Like the emperor's new clothes, the crime of heresy derives its principal substance from the consent of those who are willing to be hoaxed.

No defense of academic freedom can compromise on this issue of the admission of the crime of heresy to our law and ethics. To do so is to surrender the day to the demagogues and to lend the sanction of scholarship and science to the promotion of fraud. On the contrary, it is what Robert Redfield has called "the dangerous duty of our universities" to defend the heretic and provide sanctuary where heresies may thrive.

It is not only that freedom for somebody else's wrong idea secures my freedom to advance my right idea. Error is essential to the determination of truth itself. Heresy has the same role in scholarly inquiry and in politics as "noise" in communication theory. The theory adapts the powerful concept of entropy, from thermodynamics, to permit us to measure information quantitatively. In information theory noise plays the role of entropy and is equated with maximum disorder. Noise thus assumes a critical relationship to information. As Warren Weaver has explained: "Information . . . is a measure of one's freedom in selecting a message. The greater this freedom of choice, the greater is the uncertainty. . . Thus greater freedom of choice, greater uncertainty and greater information go hand in hand." In the context of a concern with human freedom, this idea takes on a significance transcending its importance in communications engineering. It states, in effect, that what we know depends equally upon knowing what *is* the case and what is *not* the case.

Hence the paradox and the futility of enforced orthodoxy. It is not only that the received view of any subject whatsoever may be in error. It may be in the right. But we can know this with assurance only to the extent that we are informed on all the known alternative views. To the degree that alternative views are either not recognized or are suppressed, our information and, hence, our capacity for rational thought and action are reduced. To our peril, we expose ourselves to an increased risk of believing and acting mistakenly.

In the end, civil liberties cannot merely be defended. They must be exercised. They have no reality inscribed on fading parchment; they are sustained by no brooding omnipresence in the sky. They exist only to the degree that they are asserted by the action of men. Academic freedom is the most vital area of human freedom because it comprises the frontier. It is not a different kind of freedom, nor a special privilege for a pressure group. It includes and is continuous with the freedom of other citizens. The scholar and the scientist, however, require the widest range of freedom. When they exploit their liberty and advance its boundaries, they enrich and increase the liberty of all.

Here is the connection between the narrowing freedom of American scientists and the condition of our scientific enterprise as a whole. If the objectives of science in America have been subordinated to the demands of technology, this is in part because American scientists have failed to advance to their fellow citizens the case for science in its true role in our culture. Now that the taxpayer has assumed the burden of the financing of science, his well-known enthusiasm for its mere utility must be offset by a deeper understanding of what science is. The people must be shown that science is concerned with the ends as well as with the means of human life; that through increased understanding of himself and the world around him, man may expect to set himself free from the residues of superstition and ignorance which still darken his existence; that in the expanding horizons of knowledge he will find motivations and objectives for his actions which are worthy of his natural endowment.

Such an undertaking is essential if the National Science Foundation is not to become a poorhouse for American science, a catch basin for the overflow of design and development projects from other departments of the federal government. We may hope that the public education campaign projected for the A.A.A.S. at Arden House will be directed to this end and that it will secure the backing of all who have the welfare of science at heart.

The same considerations give added force to the recent statement issued by the Society for Social Responsibility in Science, calling on scientists to "maintain and strengthen the spirit of free enquiry by clear and courageous public expression of considered opinions concerning the relation of science and society." The statement declares: ". . . each person has the individual and moral responsibility to consider the end results of his work as far as he can see them. This is a responsibility to society and implies a strong insistence on public expression of opinion."

Finally, the present situation calls upon scientists to take an unequivocal and unbudging stand on civil liberties. That stand is simple to define: There shall be no compromise whatever with the freedom of the mind. But it is a position that is difficult and dangerous to maintain in practice. It means professors must often be braver than their universities. It means defending persons and ideas that may be obnoxious as well as unpopular. It means individual risk that no man can ask of another. But this is the example of tolerance and courage that distinguishes the contribution of scientists to the history of liberty. It is the example of freedom that our country needs in this hour of danger.

14. A Scientist Rebels
NORBERT WIENER

In this brief selection Norbert Wiener "wraps it all up" in his assertion that providing ". . . scientific information is not a necessarily innocent act, and may entail the gravest consequences." This being the case, it seems logical and wise to consciously choose service in the cause of humanitarian ends. If we can't escape political involvement, we had best be reasonably sure of precisely which political goals we are serving. The fact that this point is suggested by the late Norbert Wiener seems particularly significant because he made his reputation as the physicist-mathematician-genius who was the prime mover in developing machines—computers—which aim to duplicate the powers of the human mind. Here, thus, we find a representative of "hard science" who does not hesitate to take the humanistic stance—in contrast to some social scientists who hesitate to become involved in political issues lest their science be "contaminated."

SIR:

I have received from you a note in which you state that you are engaged in a project concerning missiles, and in which you request a copy of a paper which I wrote for the National Defense Research Committee during the war.

As the paper is the property of a government organization, you are of

SOURCE: Norbert Wiener, "A Scientist Rebels," *The Atlantic Monthly* 179 (January 1947), 46. Copyright © 1947 by The Atlantic Monthly Company, Boston, Mass. Reprinted with permission.

course at complete liberty to turn to that government organization for such information as I could give you. If it is out of print as you say, and they desire to make it available for you, there are doubtless proper avenues of approach to them.

When, however, you turn to me for information concerning controlled missiles, there are several considerations which determine my reply. In the past, the comity of scholars has made it a custom to furnish scientific information to any person seriously seeking it. However, we must face these facts: The policy of the government itself during and after the war, say in the bombing of Hiroshima and Nagasaki, has made it clear that to provide scientific information is not a necessarily innocent act, and may entail the gravest consequences. One therefore cannot escape reconsidering the established custom of the scientist to give information to every person who may inquire of him. The interchange of ideas which is one of the great traditions of science must of course receive certain limitations when the scientist becomes an arbiter of life and death.

For the sake, however, of the scientist and the public, these limitations should be as intelligent as possible. The measures taken during the war by our military agencies, in restricting the free intercourse among scientists on related projects or even on the same project, have gone so far that it is clear that if continued in time of peace this policy will lead to the total irresponsibility of the scientist, and ultimately to the death of science. Both of these are disastrous for our civilization, and entail grave and immediate peril for the public.

I realize, of course, that I am acting as the censor of my own ideas, and it may sound arbitrary, but I will not accept a censorship in which I do not participate. The experience of the scientists who have worked on the atomic bomb has indicated that in any investigation of this kind the scientist ends by putting unlimited powers in the hands of the people whom he is least inclined to trust with their use. It is perfectly clear also that to disseminate information about a weapon in the present state of our civilization is to make it practically certain that that weapon will be used. In that respect the controlled missile represents the still imperfect supplement to the atom bomb and to bacterial warfare.

The practical use of guided missiles can only be to kill foreign civilians indiscriminately, and it furnishes no protection whatsoever to civilians in this country. I cannot conceive a situation in which such weapons can produce any effect other than extending the kamikaze way of fighting to whole nations. Their possession can do nothing but endanger us by encouraging the tragic insolence of the military mind.

If therefore I do not desire to participate in the bombing or poisoning of defenseless peoples—and I most certainly do not—I must take a serious responsibility as to those to whom I disclose my scientific ideas. Since it is obvious that with sufficient effort you can obtain my material, even though it is out of print, I can only protest *pro forma* in refusing to give you any information concerning my past work. However, I rejoice at the fact that my material is not readily available, inasmuch as it gives me the opportunity to raise this serious moral issue. I do not expect to publish any future work of mine which may do damage in the hands of irresponsible militarists.

I am taking the liberty of calling this letter to the attention of other people in scientific work. I believe it is only proper that they should know of it in order to make their own independent decisions, if similar situations should confront them.

The Sociocultural Order

Part IV

The following selections illustrate some important aspects of two basic concepts: culture and society. Culture is usually defined as the total way of life of a given group of people. Society is defined as a group of people who maintain their own way of life in terms of a culture that is relatively unique. The fact that we illustrate these two concepts with only four readings should not be taken as an indication that they are of minor importance. Indeed, if we had to salvage only two concepts from the entire fields of sociology and anthropology, surely "society" and "culture" would be chosen by an overwhelming number of professionals. Thus, in the four readings that follow, we touch upon only a tiny fraction of the multifaceted nature of sociocultural systems, and we touch not at all on the multitude of concepts that represent important fragments of the all-embracing social and cultural features of human life.

15. Chinese Footbinding
HOWARD S. LEVY

The vital importance of culture to human relationships is demonstrated by Howard Levy's description of ancient Chinese footbinding. This practice has no current significance, of course, but it shows dramatically that cultural practices shape individual attitudes about even the most fundamental things, such as sexual excitation (a point made earlier by Dr. Judd Marmor in selection 4). This selection is comprised of various parts taken from Levy's book. Interested readers may well want to read the entire work, for it is fascinating from beginning to end. Mr. Levy is knowledgeable about oriental matters in general. He is the author of Biography of Hugan Ch'ao, *and has been director of the U.S. Department of Foreign Service Institute Japanese Language School, located in Tokyo.*

There are aged Chinese gentlemen today who still consider bound feet more attractive than natural ones, but they are usually reticent on the subject, hesitant to express opinions which seem inconsonant with the present age. They may also be embarrassed to try to justify footbinding to an unsympathetic and hostile Western audience.

The tiny foot was a popular theme in poetry, fiction, and essay as late as the first third of the twentieth century. The lotus enthusiast generally avoided foreign confrontation, but presented an eloquent defense of footbinding to the domestic audience:

> There are many good points about tiny feet, but I will talk only about the best ones. A tiny foot is proof of feminine goodness. Women who don't bind their feet look like men, for the tiny foot serves to show the differentiation. It is also an instrument for secretly conveying love feel-

SOURCE: Howard S. Levy, *Chinese Footbinding: The History of a Curious Erotic Custom* (New York: Walton H. Rawls, 1966), pp. 181–227 passim. Copyright © 1966 by Howard S. Levy. Reprinted by permission.

ings. The tiny foot is soft and when rubbed, leads to great excitement. If it is touched under the coverlet, love feelings of the woman are immediately aroused. The graceful walk gives the beholder a mixed feeling of compassion and pity. Natural feet are heavy and ponderous as they get into bed, but tiny feet lightly steal under the coverlets. The large-footed woman is careless about adornment, but the tinyfooted frequently wash and apply a variety of perfumed fragrances, enchanting all who come into their presence. The tiny shoe is inexpensive and uses much less material, while the large foot by way of contrast is called a lotus boat. The really tiny foot is easy to walk on, but the large tiny foot is painful and inconvenient. The natural foot looks much less aesthetic in walking. Everyone welcomes the tiny foot, regarding its smallness as precious. Men formerly so craved it that its possessor achieved harmonious matrimony. Because of its diminutiveness, it gives rise to a variety of sensual pleasures and love feelings.

There were also stories about smelling the tiny foot, generally favorable in tone. Whether the odor pleased or offended depended on whether the individual was an impartial observer or a lotus enthusiast. A Japanese visitor to Shanghai in 1919, for example, said that bound feet, usually washed only once every two weeks, smelled most unpleasant. But he admitted that the Chinese male was pleased rather than offended by the aroma. During his student days in Kwangtung, a Chinese writer made a similar observation. He met a studious scholar there named Kuan, who lived with his wife in perfect harmony. When they slept together, Kuan placed his head by his wife's feet, so that the couple resembled two steamed and salted fish. Kuan slept this way in order to smell the aroma of his wife's bound feet, for only then was he able to sleep soundly.

. . .

Chinese storytellers commonly created fiction from a basis of fact by building their plots around famous historical figures. They depicted charms of the tiny foot by conjuring up suggestive and mildly erotic bedroom scenes. Nan-kung Po, a master of this technique, is a well-known contemporary Chinese historical novelist. He once wrote a fictional adaptation of Sung dynastic episodes called *The Lady of An County* and included incidental remarks about the sensual delights of footbinding. A few of these passages have been translated below because of their relevance to our study, as they indicate how the attractions of the tiny foot were described in widely-read popular works. The plot centered about the love affair of Han Shih-chung, a Southern Sung general, and a courtesan with the art-name of Carmine Jade. The first scene describes how they met:

> It was an early hour, with few guests present. More than ten courtesans were seated at tables, idly chatting. Shih-chung's army friend nudged him with his elbow:

"Look how tiny their feet are! They must be only an inch long!"

"An inch? You silly fool, the smallest golden lotus is three inches; I've never heard of one an inch long."

"I was really referring to their width."

While the courtesans couldn't hear what was being said, they seemed to have guessed the topic of conversation. They displayed their tiny feet, forming a sort of Bound Foot Exhibition.

"Look," said Shih-chung in embarrassment, "they seem to know what we're talking about."

"They're all purchasable, so why shouldn't we first look over the goods?"

Shih-chung failed to reply, for he was staring at a pair of tiny feet in startled appreciation. They were the most beautiful he had ever seen. Though the shoes were not pretty, being an ordinary black color and lacking ornamentation, the foot itself was slightly over four inches long and about three fingers in width. Viewed in its over-all dimensions, the foot was unusually lovable. It narrowed from heel to toe, and about halfway towards the tip narrowed so suddenly that it was as slender as a long pepper. The tip curled upwards slightly.

A foot that long was a common sight in the capital, but it was rare to see one which narrowed as this one did. Most feet were unavoidably puffed up at the ankle, with the instep shaped like a dumpling, looking very much like a horse's hoof. Such types, no matter how small, were not aesthetic in the slightest.

Only this pair of bound feet led the viewer to think of rubbing them in his palms. Han Shih-chung imagined that her feet must be as soft as a ball of flour; otherwise, how could they be so delicate and tender? Shih-chung suddenly resolved to take them in the palms of his hands and knead them furiously with his fingers.

"Ouch!" The lovable pair of bound feet suddenly jumped up. Shih-chung was startled, thinking that he must have hurt her by the very thought of kneading her feet. This of course was not true, but "lovely feet" had cried out in actual pain. There had been a glass of boiling water at her table. When she turned to look at Shih-chung, the courtesan beside her deliberately spilled it over her and accused her of having done it herself. The women quarreled, spurred on by the words of the other courtesans, who were envious of "lovely feet," and began fighting furiously. This alarmed Shih-chung, who realized the tiny feet of the courtesan whom he admired were the object of widespread jealousy. A ponderous five-inch foot suddenly stamped down on "lovely feet." Shih-chung bellowed out in rage and rushed to her side, causing her adversaries to flee in panic.

"It must be very painful: I hope that you did not suffer serious injury."

"They tried to break my feet," she murmured, pressing her tiny feet with both hands."

"What is your name?"

"Carmine Jade . . . and your name, sir?"

For the general and the courtesan, it was love at first sight. In the bedroom scenes which follow, the ways in which the tiny foot enhanced sensation are clearly suggested:

Carmine Jade's bed was spotless; Shih-chung threw himself on it, stretched out, and beckoned to her:

"Why don't you come closer?"

She blushed, but slowly approached the bed and sat down, leaning on the bedpost. Shih-chung looked her over greedily, from tip to toe, until he felt satiated. He finally fixed his glance upon her thighs and raised her skirt in order to inspect her tiny feet.

Carmine Jade felt giddy; she reclined, extending her feet. Shih-chung, who was very strong, placed her foot in his palm, where it fitted perfectly. He pressed the foot with his fingers, causing her to cry out involuntarily.

"You press my foot till it hurts, without feeling tenderly toward me," complained Carmine Jade, struggling to free herself . . .

A pair of tiny feet, encased in red sleeping slippers, was outlined by the bedcovers. Her legs were crossed and entangled under a single coverlet, with the curve of her thighs enticingly revealed. Shih-chung was amazed that her thighs were so voluptuous and large. He stared at them thinking: "How hard it must be for tiny feet to support those thighs!" He couldn't help feeling compassion for her lower extremities. Compressing the feet in order to thicken the thighs must have been the invention of a genius. And of course the inventor must have been a woman . . .

She felt at ease with him and, without thinking, extended her feet across his stomach. Shih-chung was just then reflecting on other matters, but when she placed her feet there he conveniently grasped them and rubbed them in his palms. He had very powerful hands and grasped and rubbed her feet so that she became more excited with each passing moment. For her it was a mixture of suffering and pleasure. The more it hurt, the more intense became her feelings of delight; she moaned, unable to bear the excitement any longer . . .

She usually felt pain in her little feet, bound so tightly, whenever she walked around. But when her feet were held in Shih-chung's palms and powerfully rubbed, though she cried out, this pain was really delightful. Not only was she unafraid, but she hoped that he would apply even greater pressure . . .

He rubbed her feet as usual; she cried out as usual. She thought: "If I hadn't made my feet so tiny through binding, perhaps Shih-chung couldn't enclose them in his palms so tightly." . . . Shih-chung had previously doubted that women's bound feet were of any use. Now he understood for the first time that they were for the convenience of a man to knead, and in addition made the flesh of the thighs especially sensual. "This was certainly the invention of an unknown genius!"

. . .

Footbinding achieved its greatest popularity towards the end of the Ch'ing dynasty, but the seeds of destruction were already evident. The frequent dynastic prohibitions against it increased awareness of its shortcomings, and an abolition movement came to be supported by liberal Chinese critics and Western missionaries. These diverse elements worked together closely as time went on; after the Revolution, the attack gathered increasing momentum and wider scope.

. . .

Wives who had formerly bound their feet now found themselves deserted or divorced. They had been forced into binding by their mothers to enhance their marital prospects, but the result was the reverse. When women heard of wives being rejected because of tiny feet, they tried everything to make the foot revert to normal size. To accelerate the process they would soak their feet in cold water nightly, suffering as much as in early childhood. No matter how hard they tried, there was really no way to keep up with the changing times. Women who had let out their feet in middle age could be seen plodding through the streets in visible discomfort. Footbinding was dictated by male preference and submitted to because the male view of aesthetics demanded it. Women who were born in the traditional age but reached maturity during or after the Revolution were the tragic figures of the period. Some recorded their experiences in the nineteen-thirties, at a time when memories were still fresh and events were vividly recalled. The motive may have been to further the cause of emancipation; whatever it was, the accounts have a ring of truth to them and obviously were the result of firsthand experience.

. . .

[For example:]

THE TWIN-HOOKED MAID
by Lotus-Loving Scholar

Two years ago, my wife hired a maid servant named Chang. She had twin hooks under her skirt, slender and not enough to grasp in one's hand. This is what *Tun-fang yu-chi* meant in saying that they could be placed in a glass; such words were true. Though the maid was middle-aged, she still had an air of elegance about her. But she walked in a rather forlorn manner and could barely fulfill household tasks. My wife encouraged her to let her feet out, but this so increased her pain that she decided against it. She was of a gentle nature, and our family greatly enjoyed conversing with her. My wife was especially fond of her and always rendered a helping hand. One day, the maid unexpectedly spoke in great detail about footbinding experiences:

> I was born in a certain district in western Honan Province, at the end of the Manchu dynasty. In accordance with custom, at the age of seven I began binding. I had witnessed the pain of my cousins, and in the year it was to begin was very much frightened. That autumn, distress befell me. One day prior my mother told me: "You are now seven, just at the right age for binding. If we wait, your foot will harden, increasing the pain. You should have started in the spring, but because you were weak we waited till now. Girls in other families have already completed the process. We start tomorrow. I will do this for you lightly and so that it won't hurt; what daughter doesn't go through this difficulty?" She then gave me fruit to eat, showed me a new pair of phoenix-tip shoes, and beguiled me with these words: "Only with bound feet can you wear such beautiful shoes. Otherwise, you'll become a large-footed barbarian and everyone will laugh at and feel ashamed of you." I felt moved by a desire to be beautiful and became steadfast in determination, staying awake all night.

I got up early the next morning. Everything had already been prepared. Mother had me sit on a stool by the bed. She threaded a needle and placed it in my hair, cut off a piece of alum and put it alongside the binding cloth and the flowered shoes. She then turned and closed the bedroom door. She first soaked my feet in a pan of hot water, then wiped them, and cut the toenails with a small scissors. She then took my right foot in her hands and repeatedly massaged it in the direction of the plantar. She also sprinkled alum between my toes. She gave me a pen point to hold in my hands because of the belief that my feet might then become as pointed as it was. Later she took a cloth three feet long and two inches wide, grasped my right foot, and pressed down the four smaller toes in the direction of the plantar. She joined them together, bound them once, and passed the binding from the heel to the foot surface and then to the plantar. She did this five times and then sewed the binding together with thread. To prevent it from getting loosened, she tied a slender cotton thread from the tip of the foot to its center.

She did the same thing with the left foot and forced my feet into flowered shoes which were slightly smaller than the feet were. The tips of the shoes were adorned with threads in the shape of grain. There was a ribbon affixed to the mouth of the shoe and fastened on the heel. She ordered me to get down from the bed and walk, saying that if I didn't the crooked-shaped foot would be seriously injured. When I first touched the ground, I felt complete loss of movement; after a few trials, only the toes hurt greatly. Both feet became feverish at night and hurt from the swelling. Except for walking, I sat by the *k'ang*. Mother rebound my feet weekly, each time more tightly than the last. I became more and more afraid. I tried to avoid the binding by hiding in a neighbor's house. If I loosened the bandage, mother would scold me for not wanting to look nice. After half a year, the tightly bound toes began to uniformly face the plantar. The foot became more pointed daily; after a year, the toes began to putrefy. Corns began to appear and thicken, and for a long time no improvement was visible. Mother would remove the bindings and lance the corns with a needle to get rid of the hard core. I feared this, but mother grasped my legs so that I couldn't move. Father betrothed me at the age of nine to a neighbor named Chao, and I went to their house to serve as a daughter-in-law in the home of my future husband. My mother-in-law bound my feet much more tightly than mother ever had, saying that I still hadn't achieved the standard. She beat me severely if I cried; if I unloosened the binding, I was beaten until my body was covered with bruises. Also, because my feet were somewhat fleshy, my mother-in-law insisted that the foot must become inflamed to get the proper results. Day and night, my feet were washed in a medicinal water; within a few washings I felt special pain. Looking down, I saw that every toe but the big one was inflamed and deteriorated. Mother-in-law said that this was all to the good. I had to be beaten with fists before I could bear to remove the bindings, which were congealed with pus and blood. To get them loose, such force had to be used that the skin often peeled off, causing further bleeding. The stench was hard to bear, while I felt the pain in my very insides. My body trembled with agitation. Mother-in-law was not only unmoved but she placed tiles inside the binding in order to hasten the inflammation process. She was deaf to my childish cries. Every other day, the binding was made tighter and sewn up, and each time slightly smaller shoes had to be worn. The sides of the shoes were hard, and I could only get into them by using force. I was compelled to walk on them in the courtyard; they were called distance-walking shoes. I strove to cling to life, suffering indescribable pain. Being in an average family, I had to go to the well and pound the mortar unaided. Faulty blood circulation caused my feet to become insensible in winter. At night, I tried to warm them by the *k'ang*, but this caused extreme pain. The alternation between frost and thawing caused me to lose one toe on my right foot. Deterioration of the flesh was such that within a year my feet had become as pointed as new bamboo shoots, pointing upwards like a red chestnut. The foot surface was slightly convex, while the four bean-sized toes were deeply imbedded in the plantar like a string of cowry shells. They were only a slight distance from the heel of the foot. The plantar was so deep that several coins could be placed in it without difficulty. The large toes faced upwards, while the place on the right foot where the little toe had deteriorated away pained at irregular intervals. It left an ineffacable scar.

My feet were only three inches long, at the most. Relatives and friends praised them, little realizing the cisterns of tears and blood which they had caused. My husband was delighted with them, but two years ago he departed this world. The family wealth was dissipated, and I had to wander about looking for work. That was how I came down to my present circumstances. I envy the modern woman. If I too had been born just a decade or so later, all of this pain could have been avoided. The lot of the natural-footed woman and mine is like that of heaven and hell.

Love of the lotus disappeared when I heard her words; my wife was also similarly affected. I have recorded this in order to warn the young girls of today against binding their feet.

16. A Humanist in Africa
KENNETH D. KAUNDA

In this letter to a friend, the president of Zambia, a new African republic, contrasts tribal (communal) and national (associational) societies. He suggests that the former have advantages most Westerners do not appreciate. This selection by President Kaunda is but one small section of his book. From the book, it is clear that Kenneth Kaunda is a remarkable man, truly a philosopher-king if ever there has been one.

You ask me to expand my statement that Africa may be the last place where Man can still be Man. I think that two elements have gone to make up what might be called the African philosophy of Man. These are

SOURCE: Kenneth D. Kaunda, *A Humanist in Africa* (Nashville, Tennessee: Abingdon Press, 1966), pp. 22–27. Copyright © 1966 by Kenneth D. Kaunda and Colin Morris. Reprinted by permission of Abingdon Press and Longman Group Limited.

the African's relationship with Nature and the psychological impact upon him of centuries of existence within tribal society.

I believe that the Universe is basically good and that throughout it great forces are at work striving to bring about a greater unity of all living things. It is through cooperation with these forces that Man will achieve all of which he is capable. Those people who are dependent upon and live in closest relationship with Nature are most conscious of the operation of these forces: the pulse of their lives beats in harmony with the pulse of the Universe. They may be simple and unlettered people and their physical horizons may be strictly limited, yet I believe that they inhabit a larger world than the sophisticated Westerner who has magnified his physical senses through invented gadgets at the price, all too often, of cutting out the dimension of the spiritual.

Only the other evening I was reading in the Book of Psalms. I came across a verse in which the Psalmist is praising God for having 'set his feet in a large room'. Now David came from a pastoral people dependent upon Nature, and though I find some of his ideas about God crude and mistaken there is a sort of bold sweep to his thinking which comes from inhabiting the "large room" of Nature rather than the machine-packed workshop of industrial society. The Psalmist can make a declaration linking God and the Universe in one verse of fifty words. Scientifically-orientated modern Man often requires a hundred thousand words to state a thesis concerning some tiny, specialised aspect of truth. Now I know, of course, that these two approaches are not contradictory and I am not denying the importance of the scientific method. But my point is that people in close relationship with Nature are forced to ask *big* questions however crude their answers might be. I could entertain you for hours retelling the traditional stories of my people I first heard in my childhood, many of which offer ingenious if somewhat fanciful explanations of the great riddles of life to which the world's great thinkers have sought solutions.

It is easy, of course, to romanticise Nature, but this is an error more likely to be made by those comfortably protected from it than people like myself who have experienced its cruellest moods in disease, blight, famine and drought. To be exposed to Nature and to have to live your life at its rhythm develops humility as a human characteristic rather than arrogance. Men are more companionable and take the trouble to live harmoniously together because they know that only by acting together can they reap the benefits and try to overcome the hardships of Nature.

Was it not the Luddites in England who went around smashing the new machines of the Industrial Revolution because they could not face the future? I am no Luddite! I welcome all the advantages which Western science and technology have brought to Africa. I even welcome the fact that technology reduces our dependence upon the uncertainties of Nature, in spite of all that I have said. Yet my question is this. Is there any way that my people can have the blessings of technology without being eaten away by materialism and losing the spiritual dimension from their lives? I suppose the answer is that however intensely we industrialise, the vast majority of the peoples of Africa will still live in close contact with Nature and so keep alive this element in our culture.

The second element in African humanism stems from the structure of the traditional society and its effects upon African psychology. The devoted work of anthropologists has now borne fruit and only the bigot would dismiss tribal society as primitive and chaotic. It is widely recognised that these societies were, in fact, highly organised and delicately balanced in the network of relationships which held their members together. I need not go into great detail since the characteristics of the tribal community are well known. Let me draw attention only to three key factors which reinforce the humanist outlook.

The tribal community was a *mutual* society. It was organised to satisfy the basic human needs of all its members and, therefore, individualism was discouraged. Most resources such as land and cattle might be communally owned and administered by chiefs and village headmen for the benefit of everyone. If, for example, a villager required a new hut, all the men would turn to and cut the trees to erect the frame and bring grass for thatching. The women might be responsible for making the mud-plaster for the walls and two or three of them would undoubtedly brew some beer so that all the workers would be refreshed after a hot but satisfying day's work. In the same spirit, the able-bodied would accept responsibility for tending and harvesting the gardens of the sick and infirm.

Human need was the supreme criterion of behaviour. The hungry stranger, could, without penalty, enter the garden of a village and take, say, a bunch of bananas or a mealie cob to satisfy his hunger. His action only became theft if he took more than was necessary to satisfy his needs. For then he was depriving others.

Obviously, social harmony was a vital necessity in such a community where almost every activity was a matter of team work. Hence, chiefs and tribal elders had an important judicial and reconciliatory function. They adjudicated between conflicting parties, admonished the quarrelsome and anti-social and took whatever action was necessary to strengthen the fabric of social life. I should emphasise that this way of life was not a kind of idealised social experiment such as may be found in Europe where groups of people take themselves off into pleasant rural surroundings in order to avoid the tensions of industrial society. Life in the bush is hard and dangerous and a high degree of social cohesion is necessary for survival. The basic unit of life is not the individual or immediate family (as in industrial societies) but the community. This means that there must be fundamental agreement upon goals and all must act together.

In the second place, the tribal community was an *accepting* community. It did not take account of failure in an absolute sense. The slow, the inept and incapable were accepted as a valid element in community life provided they were socially amenable. Social qualities weighed much heavier in the balance than individual achievement. The success-failure complex seems to me to be a disease of the age of individualism—the result of a society conditioned by the diploma, the examination and the selection procedure. In the best tribal society people were valued not for what they could achieve but because they were *there*. Their contribution, however limited, to the material welfare of the village was acceptable, but it was their *presence* not their *achievement* which was appreciated.

Take, for instance, the traditional Africa attitude to old people. I remember being horrified on the first occasion I made the acquaintance of that Western phenomenon, the Old People's Home. The idea that the State or some voluntary agency should care for the aged was anathema to me, for it almost seems to imply that old people are a nuisance who must be kept out of the way so that children can live their lives unhampered by their presence. In traditional societies, old people are venerated and it is regarded as a privilege to look after them. Their counsel is sought on many matters and however infirm they might be they have a valued and constructive role to play in teaching and instructing their grandchildren. Indeed, to deny a grandparent the joy of the company of his grandchildren is a heinous sin. The fact that old people can no longer work, or are not alert as they used to be, or even have developed the handicaps of senility in no way affects our regard for them. We cannot do enough to repay them for all they have done for us. They are embodied wisdom; living symbols of our continuity with the past.

No doubt a defender of the Western way of life might retort that institutions for the care of old people are inevitable in large-scale societies and that but for the efforts of the State and voluntary agencies many old people would starve. This is undoubtedly true but it merely serves to underline my point that in a society which regards person to person relationships as supremely important no one can be so isolated that responsibility for his welfare cannot be determined and assigned.

The experts have all kinds of standards by which they judge the degree of civilisation of a people. My own test is this. How does that society treat its old people, and, indeed, all its members who are not useful and productive in the narrowest sense? Judged by this standard, the so-called advanced societies have a lot to learn which the so-called backward societies could teach them.

In the third place, the tribal community was an *inclusive* society. By this I mean that the web of relationships which involved some degree of mutual responsibility was widely spread. I would describe industrial society as an *exclusive* society because its members' responsibilities are often confined to the immediate family, and I have noted that the family circle may be a self-entire little universe, preventing the acceptance of wider commitments.

Let me give you an example of the inclusiveness of the traditional society. I do not restrict the title "father" to my male parent. I also address my father's brothers as "father." And I call my mother's sisters "mother" also. Only my father's sisters would I address as "aunt" and my mother's brothers as "uncle." My "brothers" would include not only the male children of my father but also certain cousins and even members of the same clan who have no blood relationship to me at all. Now this, to the Western mind, very confusing state of affairs, is not merely a matter of terminology. These are not just courtesy titles. With the title "father" for example, goes all the responsibility of parenthood and in return all my "fathers" receive my filial devotion. Hence, no child in a traditional society is likely to be orphaned. Should his literal parents die then others automatically assume the responsibility for his upbringing. By the same token, no old person is likely to end his days outside a family circle. If his own offspring cannot care for him then other "children" will accept the duty and privilege.

17. Twin Oaks: A Commune
KATHLEEN KINKADE

In selection 16 it was shown that most Westerners do not appreciate the psychic and social advantages to be derived from communal settings. That some Westerners do appreciate communal life is illustrated by the young people who have recently attempted, sometimes successfully, to develop communes. One such commune, Twin Oaks, is described here by Kathleen Kinkade. The unique feature of Twin Oaks is its attempt to put into practice the ideas expressed by behaviorist B. F. Skinner in his book Walden Two. *As described in the following pages, behavioral principles are used to "shape equality behavior" among those who live at Twin Oaks.*

You drive to Twin Oaks through farm country. It is red and gray clay, poor land, worn out by tobacco crops long ago. Most of it grows grass now, for the small herds of Angus and Hereford cattle that look up at you

SOURCE: Kathleen Kinkade, *A Walden Two Experiment: The First Five Years of Twin Oaks Community* (New York: William Morrow & Company, 1973), pp. 36–58. Copyright © 1972, 1973 by Twin Oaks Community, Inc. Reprinted by permission of William Morrow & Company, Inc.

as you drive past. There are no large farms here, just small ones of about a hundred acres. Twin Oaks is one of these. As you turn in the driveway marked by a mailbox with the Community's name, you notice a typical white farmhouse and a row of weathered oak barns. Different from the rest of the countryside are two large buildings, one black and green, one stained brown. They could be anything—factories, barns, warehouses. They are dormitories and workshops, you find out later.

Five dogs rush out to greet your car as you pull up beside the other parked vehicles. You see several people working or sitting around talking. They glance at you but continue their conversation. Someone yells, "Hey, Maggie—visitor!" A girl in a red and white striped turtleneck and patched jeans comes out of the farmhouse and approaches you. She introduces herself, asks how long you are staying, and shows you around.

The farmhouse has been converted into three dining rooms and a kitchen. A closet contains a stereo turntable, which is playing. There are two large speakers in one of the dining rooms. Several people are sitting quietly around the table in that room, listening. The other dining rooms are empty, except for a man sweeping the floor. There is a speaker in the kitchen, too, and two girls and a man are singing along with the record while they prepare the next meal. They smile at you as you pass through but do not stop singing. Maggie shows you the Community's only bathroom, and you ask leave to use it. There are two towels on the floor, slightly wet, and three more towels thrown carelessly over a towel rack. The bathroom does not look as clean as you would like. Perhaps the man with the broom hasn't got to it yet. Later you will notice that some parts of the buildings are freshly cleaned and organized, others gathering dust, cobwebs, and dirty laundry. The longer you stay, the more you will notice this—the clean, sparkling areas getting dirtier, and the messy spots being cleaned up, giving the overall effect of a household caught in mid-spring cleaning and not at all prepared for visitors.

The big green-and-black building contains an auto shop, wood shop, print shop, and hammock-weaving shop, as well as several private rooms and the community clothes area. The community clothes are housed in a large room and are evidently much used. You see boxes marked "good turtleneck shirts," and "grubby turtleneck shirts," "black socks," "white socks," "matched socks." Rack upon rack of blouses, shirts, and dresses present a variety of clothing for the members. Your guide tells you that you are welcome to use community clothes if you like.

Your room is in the brown building. It contains four bunks, evidently made on the premises by the members. Two of the bunks are already taken by other visitors. You put your sleeping bag on a lower bunk and follow Maggie out into the hall for a look at the library. The Community's books line the walls of the two hallways and the living room. This building contains the bedrooms of the members.

Maggie tells you a little about the Community's history and institutions and then leaves you to do as you please. You step outside and look around. The fields are a pleasing bright green. A man is clearing away piles of mulch from what he tells you is a strawberry bed. Two others are making some rows for the spring planting of peas. Three or four people are lounging in hammocks which have been hung in a group underneath the apple trees. The man who was sweeping comes out of the farmhouse, his arm around a girl. They stop and kiss each other without self-consciousness, then continue their walk.

Someone steps out of the farmhouse and strikes a large metal disc with a horseshoe. The resultant clanging is evidently the lunch bell. You follow the others back into the farmhouse and stand in line. There is a blackboard with the menu for the meal printed on it. Today's offering says "Onion soup; toasted cheese sandwiches; various yummy leftovers; lemon pudding." Someone turns off the record player for the meal, and members and visitors carry their full plates to one of the dining tables. You seat yourself and are tasting the leftovers (not too yummy, but edible) when you are spotted by a young girl with a sheaf of papers. "Aha!" she says. "A visitor. How would you like to help with lunch dishes?" You say you would be glad to, and she beams at you with satisfaction. "I knew there must be a visitor around here someplace," she says.

Thus you begin your first job on Twin Oaks's labor credit system. If you stay as long as a week, you may wash dishes several times. You will probably also do some gardening, learn to weave a hammock, and perhaps help to put up the hay. Visitors' work assignments are fairly predictable, since there are many jobs they cannot do without training. The same is not true for members.

There is no such thing as a typical day at Twin Oaks. I will have to describe several people's days in order to give a realistic picture.

My day today, for example, is set aside entirely for writing this book. In fact, I am taking several consecutive weeks for that purpose, being interrupted only occasionally to do a little manual labor that the labor people found hard to fit into somebody else's schedule.

That doesn't make me a special person. Any member who has demonstrated the ability to interest a publisher in his writing could do the same. I get paid a standard one credit an hour for my actual writing time. If the book doesn't sell or isn't ultimately accepted, it is the Community that has taken the risk—I don't have to make up the lost labor. On the other hand, if it sells well and brings in a fat check, I still get only one credit an hour. The profit, if any, goes to the Community.

Gideon's day is quite different. He put in a 9:30–11:00 typing shift (one of our little businesses, addressing envelopes for a local concern), then drove the tractor over to a neighbor's farm to borrow their scraper-blade attachment. By the time he returned, it was lunch time. This afternoon he will probably scrape the cow yard and level the new volleyball court with the borrowed scraper. He might take time out for a bath before supper, and quite possibly work in the automobile shop for a while afterward, unless there is a meeting of some kind. The only part of the day which is actually scheduled for Gideon by the labor people is the morning typing shift. The rest is simply written "20 hours auto maintenance during the week" and "level cow yard." Gideon prefers a loose schedule of this kind. He works out his own hours, and he generally gets everything done, sometimes doing unscheduled things that come up midweek.

Naomi, on the other hand, is likely to have a tight schedule with precise hours. This is because she likes cooking and kitchen work, and this work must be done at specific times. Today, for instance, she did "Morning Kitchen Clean," fixed supper, and will do the late night dishes shift. In addition, Naomi is signed up for several "during the week" jobs like food inventory and cleaning out the freezer. Since she is also our bookkeeper, she is scheduled to spend one afternoon paying the bills and balancing the checkbook, as well as overseeing the bookkeeping, which is being done by other members, recently trained.

Phil takes a daily shopping trip to nearby Louisa as part of his labor quota, and makes up most of the rest of it in dishwashing or hammock weaving. He is Library Manager, so he schedules some managerial time for himself each week to keep the library in usable shape.

Rod spends almost his full time in farm and garden work. Yesterday he supervised the planting of 150 fruit trees; this afternoon he is disking up some land for the garden. Farming is his specialty. Other than an occasional shift of dishwashing, he virtually lives out-of-doors.

Members of Twin Oaks are required to do a full, equal share of the necessary work. Within that limit, they are free to choose whatever work they like. The system makes that freedom possible and practical.

Community members work about forty hours a week, usually spread over the full seven days. This work includes all the farming, housework, cooking, shopping, businesses and industries, office work, and anything else that is necessary for the group's survival and progress.

In the book *Walden Two* there is a labor system hinted at but not described. The basic theme of it is that, while all work is equally honorable, not all is equally desirable, and that those who do the nastiest jobs should get the shortest hours. We were gung-ho Walden Twoers even from the beginning, but we did not invent a labor system until we had been on the land for three weeks. I think that we wanted to have a free, unstructured time of just doing what we pleased. So we did as we pleased, and there were some gross inequalities, but it didn't matter a lot in those first days of excitement.

Carrie did almost all the cooking and housework. Perhaps once a day someone would help wash the dishes at one of the meals, but she carried the brunt of it. I was still in the city, trying to untangle myself from some financial problems, and went to the land only on weekends for the first two months of the Community's existence. So the only other female on the premises was my daughter, Jenny, aged fourteen, who wasn't interested in housework. The men worked at projects that appealed to them. They built a work table and put up some shelves in a storage barn. They experimented with rammed earth. They built a swimming dock.

The first request for a labor structure came from Carrie, who simply wanted to know why Jenny didn't help out with the housework. Jenny, who has understood women's liberation from her crib, replied that she would rather help build shelves and experiment with rammed earth. The men backed her up but also agreed with Carrie that if the housework had become a chore, it was time to share it. It was evidently time to begin the intriguing task of structuring the distribution of labor. The initially difficult problem was defining work. Everybody agreed that there were tasks which, though useful to the group, were so much fun to do that they couldn't really compare to housework. Finally it was settled that the group would divide that work which the members did not enjoy doing but leave creative work off the system to be done when we felt like it.

The line between creative and unpleasant moved steadily toward the unpleasant as the weeks progressed. At first there was nothing on the system except housework. Then hoeing the garden lost its savor and was added. Tending the tobacco crop quickly became part of the system, then blackberry picking. Within a month we were going by the concept that every kind of work that was useful to the group (except thinking, talking, reading, and research) belonged on the labor credit system. This served two purposes—making sure everyone did a fair share of the work, and making sure that everyone got a chance to do the more interesting parts of it.

Deciding who worked at what was a more complicated task. The first system was a card game. On 3" x 5" cards we wrote the names of the jobs and the lengths of time estimated to complete them. One card said, "Tuesday fix lunch, ½ hour," and another said, "Blackberry picking Wednesday, 1 hour." Then we sat in a circle and dealt out the hand. Each of us examined the hand we had been dealt and determined which jobs we might like to keep and which to pass on. Then we started passing cards to the right, each discarding jobs which seemed to us most disagreeable. The person on my left passed cards to me, and I selected one or two of them and passed the rest on. When I had acquired by this means a full hand (my fair share of hours, previously calculated and announced), my part of the game was over, and the others continued until each person was satisfied that he had done as well for himself as he could. Everybody got stuck with something he didn't like, and everybody got something he preferred, and all of us got a lot of things in the middle range of desirability. From there we made out our own schedules.

This system was fun, but it took too long. Brian kept saying that we couldn't seriously think of a community of one thousand people (our theoretical goal) sitting in a circle and passing cards every week.

After a few weeks we moved on to a signup system, whereby the jobs were all described on cards in a file box, and we each took turns placing our initials on the job cards of our choice. Then a clerical person took the data, tossed coins to determine who among competitors got a desirable job, and assigned the losers to jobs that nobody wanted. We adjusted the credit value of the jobs at this time. If you competed for a job, the credit value went down (and stayed down for succeeding weeks); if it had to be assigned to someone who didn't want it, the credit value went up. We used the increment of 10 percent per week, an arbitrary figure that controlled inflation. The average credit is always worth one hour.

A further variant on this system, called simultaneous signup, allowed each person to sign up on a separate sheet, not knowing who else was signing up for what. This eliminated some logrolling and general manipulation.

The clerical part of the labor credit system rapidly became systematized. Two people working together complete it each week, using the better part of two days to do the work. This may seem a high clerical cost, but we don't find it too high. From it come (1) individual labor schedules—every member has his own sheet to refer to at any time; (2) general schedules posted where everyone can find out who is scheduled for what; and (3) bookkeeping in which members' surplus credits or deficits are recorded. All jobs are covered with assigned workers; all members have a fair share of the work.

We are willing to pay the price in clerical work, because the alternative is role assignment. No serious community of our size and complexity (forty members plus about ten working visitors) can just let the work go from day to day on the assumption that someone will do it. Meals must be fixed on time and the kitchen cleaned. The cows have to be milked. The garden does not thrive on haphazard labor, and nobody would even propose trying to run a business or industry without a labor system of some kind. The anarchistic commune may be therapeutic, but it is not serious about proposing an alternative societal structure.

Since the work must be done, it must either be assigned (as we do it) in a carefully worked-out jigsaw of moving pieces, or it must be handled by professional workers—the kitchen people always doing kitchen work, the cow people always doing cow work, and the hammock workers making all the hammocks, etc. This is the way it is handled in every other serious commune that we know of or have read about. We are willing to conduct our work lives by role assignment if it turns out to be necessary. But our members do not want it. They want not only to choose their work but to choose it anew from week to week or even from day to day. This fiercely defended desire to try everything has created and maintains our complex labor system. A lot of visitors shake their heads over it and tell us it isn't worth the bother of the clerical work and weekly signup. But the critics are not members, and the members are not the critics. We like it.

We like it so much, in fact, that at one time it was difficult to make any changes in it. After the development of simultaneous signup, we worked for two years with no changes in the system. It worked smoothly, and minor complaints were handled by saying; "Well, somebody has to do it, and you were assigned by a random-number table," which was true.

In 1970 a combination of sudden population growth and fresh minds applying themselves to old problems brought about another revolution in the labor credit system. The new people could see what some of us longer-term people had overlooked—that with forty people on the system it is possible to do away with random assignment of aversive tasks. The chances are that in a group as large as this, we can almost always find somebody who doesn't mind a particular job as much as somebody else. It might literally be possible for us all to work just at those things we like—or at least didn't hate. With this exciting possibility in mind, it became important to know the degree of desirability each job had for each person.

Our current system asks each member to take a list of all the available jobs and place them in the order of his personal preference. After that, he doesn't have to sign up at all. The labor clerical people take over and work for two days filling out everyone's schedule as close to their personal preferences as possible. These days one gets high credits for doing work which one finds *personally* disagreeable. Two people might be shoveling manure side by side, and the person who enjoys the work is getting less credit for it than the person who doesn't. Most of us these days don't have to do a lot of unpleasant work. One dishwashing shift a week perhaps, or a shift of hay baling, might fall to each member. This system works even better than the one we had for two years.

But this is not the end. There are still problems to be worked out, and we will undoubtedly find that fundamental changes in the labor system will be necessary from time to time. We may even lose our resistance to specialization and find some of our members preferring and requesting role-assignment jobs. There is already some evidence of this. What will probably not change is the basic idea of the labor credit—all work is equally honorable. But the less pleasant the work, the less time one should have to put into it.

Since early in our history we have had to adjust the labor credit system to make it possible for members to take vacations. We do that by working longer hours than we are assigned and accumulating a surplus of credits. Most members have fairly large surpluses and can take a vacation whenever they choose. Money for traveling is provided by the Community in very small amounts, and members are allowed to accept travel money from their parents or to work for their own spending money on their own vacation time.

"What would you do if a member didn't do his work?" asked Burris of Frazier in *Walden Two*. "I can't imagine it," said Frazier. "We'd think of something." We are often asked the same question, but our answer is a little more definite, probably because our techniques of behavioral engineering aren't worked out quite so well as they were in the book. "We would ask him to leave," is what we reply. The problem of laziness and willingness to sponge off the labor of others is not a serious one here at Twin Oaks. We try to make it obvious that leaving one's work undone is equivalent to asking other members to do it for you, and not many people are so lacking in conscience that they are willing to do that on a regular basis. All of us goof off from time to time, and minor infractions of work equality are largely ignored by the group. There have been very few occasions when we have had to implement our rule that allows us to expel members who don't do their share. There are a lot of things we can try before resorting to such extremes.

The first step would be for the Labor Manager to talk to the member who is getting behind. The chances are pretty good that the member will be worried about it, anyway, and it will be a relief to him to have the problem in the open. Together the two will look at the kinds of work that the member has been signing up for (but not doing) and talk about ways of overcoming the specific behavior problems that get in his way. Perhaps he has trouble getting up in the morning. The Community can, at his request, have someone wake him. Changing to scheduled work, like cooking, milking, or dishwashing, might solve the problem, or at least help him catch up. The Labor Manager will arrange a schedule with the member whereby he makes up his labor deficit a little at a time. The group would never expel a member who made a real effort to change his behavior, no matter how lazy he might have been or how many credits he had to make up.

Occasionally there is a case of work undone that is not caused by bad habits or carelessness but is a deliberate attempt to avoid work entirely. It is rare, but it happens. It has happened twice in our history.

The first one was Charlie, in the fall of 1967. Charlie didn't say to himself, "I don't like work much, but I'm going to have to do my share here, so I may as well face it." If he had admitted that much to himself, he might have been able to adjust to Twin Oaks. What he said to himself was that he was a philosopher and a poet. He spent a good deal of time practicing his guitar, and he said that a decent society ought to be able to support its philosophers, poets, and musicians. He was aware, of course, that society at large had not arrived at that utopian stage. Charlie had spent most of his adult life (he was twenty-eight) being supported by women who fell in love with him, including a wife who had borne several children by him. He had never in his life faced and solved the problem of doing something for which society was willing to support him in return. Even the women in his life left him after a while. Charlie's view of all this was that society was all messed up and that he had won a spiritual independence of the system by not depending on money. "I don't use money," he told us with pride.

It turned out that he didn't use labor credits either. He did, however, use other people. Marie, a woman who joined the Community about the same time Charlie did, fell in love with him immediately and understood his need to be free to devote himself to poetry. She made out his labor sheet for him (he refused to touch it) and kept track of what he was supposed to be doing. She signed both of them up for cooking or washing dishes together, quietly did the work alone, and awarded the credits to him. We were only twelve people then, and we could not help noticing that Charlie had a great deal more free time than the rest of us. Brian, as Labor Manager, intervened. It was then that we made the policy which is still fundamental to our system: "The person who does the work gets the credit," Brian told Charlie. "Regardless of who signs up for the job, the credit goes to the worker." This made it impossible for Marie to make a gift of her labor to her lover. Marie was as angry and frustrated as Charlie. "Why can't I work for him?" she asked. "That's what I want to do. He needs to be free of work, and I can carry his share. The group isn't losing anything. What business is it of yours if I do his work? I love him." It was difficult to answer this question, coming from Marie. When someone demands the right to be exploited, the designers of an equalitarian society feel muddled, to say the least. But we stuck to our principles, and insisted that Charlie support himself with his own labor. We felt that our society could not stand a precedent that would permit work to be laid on the altar of love.

Charlie next circumvented the system by signing up for long hours of hammock weaving at no specal hour. That gave him time to procrastinate. He did some work, when he felt inspired, so it was four weeks before the group became sufficiently annoyed to take any action. We had a brief meeting at which we decided that the principle was more important than the member in this case, and that Charlie should be faced with a clear alternative—work or leave. Dwight was appointed to bear the message. All Dwight said to Charlie was, "You are seventy-five credits in deficit, and the group feels that you should be making some progress toward making that up." He was going to go on to suggest a program whereby Charlie could do this a little at a time, but Charlie did not care to listen to it. "Well, to be frank," he said, "I was thinking of leaving anyway. My only problem is getting enough money for a bus ticket back to Indiana. If you people would be interested in buying my wrecked VW in exchange for the bus ticket . . ." The bargain was sealed in short order.

Two years later another member tried to live here without working. But Henry didn't mind dirtying his hands with labor credit sheets. He was a college graduate and very intelligent. He understood the system very well, and he turned in all his sheets clearly marked with the credits he claimed. Unfortunately, the truthfulness of these records was less pronounced than their neatness. If Henry had done fifteen hours of hammock weaving, no one, least of all the Hammock Manager, had seen him. Yet the sheet was clearly marked as if he had done the work. His sheet said he had done four hours of food processing; the Kitchen Manager remembered that he had worked for less than an hour, taken off for a cigarette break, and not returned to the job. Cheating of this magnitude went beyond our willingness to overlook. The Labor Manager asked him to explain the discrepancy. Henry replied with a barrage of verbal abuse and ended by beating up the Labor Manager. There is more to Henry's story than his laziness. In his case even being a good worker would not have made it possible for him to get along in community. In both his case and Charlie's, the refusal to work was combined with an extreme hostility to the Community, a continuous sarcastic commentary on our institutions and approaches to problems, and a sneering disdain of the "power structure." Both members, before they left, thoroughly alienated not only the power structure but every individual in the Community. It may be the case that only people who feel such hostility would openly refuse to do their work in an equalitarian society. Certainly such attitudes have been very rare. Most members bog down in their work from time to time, but perk up again after a vacation or a fresh approach or a change of job. Occasional members have taken refuge in questionable "sick leave," but even this is uncommon.

Neither is there any truth in the classic assertion that there is no incentive to work without personal financial gain. We have members who have the same intense dedication to their work that characterizes happy professionals in the competitive outside world. Their involvement is with the work itself and with building the Community. The credits are beside the point, as the money would be beside the point if they were working for wages. They want to get a good hammock brochure printed, or an engine rebuilt, or a new labor system perfected, or an orchard properly planted, or the kitchen remodeled. The reinforcement comes from the finished product, the purr of the new engine, the neat rows of baby trees—and from the appreciation of the other members of the Community.

Equality in labor is a large step toward social justice, but it is not the only step Twin Oaks has taken toward equality. Our financial and property policies reflect our determination to avoid a privileged class. Members get no cash income except a very small allowance which has ranged between twenty-five cents and a dollar a week. Any money which they might have owned before joining simply stays in the bank for their first three years unless they want to donate it to the Community. In any case, Twin Oaks receives the interest on it, as well as dividends on any stocks and bonds, rents from any real property, or any continuing income of any kind. It is not common for incoming members to own much property beyond their clothing and a few records and books, and we have had scant experience with stocks and bonds. Nevertheless the principle is clear: no member should enjoy financial privileges that are denied the rest of us. The three-year delay in making all property communal is meant to be a protection for the individual member, in case he changes his mind about being a communitarian. We have yet to collect any money from this provision. The Community is only four years old, and members who have been here for that length of time have long ago donated what property they owned.

Twin Oaks's government, unlike the rest of its systems, is not left to rotation, coin tosses, or personal choice. It is one area where we feel it necessary to choose people for their ability.

The overall direction of the Community is in the hands of a three-person board of planners (a name derived from *Walden Two*). Their job is to appoint and replace managers, settle conflicts between managers, decide touchy questions having to do with ideology, and replace themselves when their eighteen-month terms expire. Most of the authority of the Community, most of the important decision-making that affects the daily lives of the members, belongs not to the planners but to a group of managers, members who are in charge of various areas of work. Managerial positions are continually being created, and are awarded on the basis of interest and work.

The Visitor Managership, when Maggie took it over, was simply a job of telling people whether they could visit or not. Maggie took a real interest in it and began to keep good records on the visitors. She also got a room in our newest building set aside for guests, saw to it that it was painted and furnished with sturdy bunks, and bought matching fitted sheets for them. She decides how many guests we can accept at one time, and which ones to turn down. She deals with visiting psychology classes, prospective members, and local drunks. On those rare occasions when a visitor's behavior is such that he isn't welcome here, it is Maggie's job to ask him to leave. Maggie is eighteen.

If someone else had been Visitor Manager, the job might have been entirely different. There might be six bunks in the room, or visitors might be sleeping on the floor on mattresses. The room decor would be different, and there might be more (or fewer) than ten at a time. Thus, Maggie has a great deal of authority in her area.

We pair authority with responsibility, and we are usually short of managers. There are more areas of community work to be expanded than there are people interested in getting involved in them.

We have been told from time to time that the word "manager" really turns people off. There is something about it that reminds one of the word "authority" or "boss." All I can say is that after you have lived a while at Twin Oaks, it loses those connotations. The actual job comes closer to "servant" than "boss," as in the commonly heard "Where's the Animal Manager—the cows are out again," or, "Nobody has showed up to wash supper dishes—where's the Labor Manager?" What the term means here is "person responsible." Anybody willing to take responsibility can get it. The more time and thought a member puts into his particular job, the bigger that job gets.

It seemed to us when we started the Community that eight people didn't need much government. On the first day of our communal lives, we called a meeting to discuss decision-making. Our first problem was that

Carrie did not want to come to the meeting. She wanted to take a nap. Carrie was fond of country living, and she was willing to go along with communal principles up to a point, but at the beginning, at least, she didn't want to have to think about it any more than necessary, and meetings constituted more than necessary. So we gathered without her and talked about how to make decisions. Sandy proposed that we should meet each week as a group and make decisions by consensus. He explained that consensus procedure consisted of discussing problems and possible solutions until everybody agreed. I thought the idea absurd, but I did not want to break the harmony of the first afternoon by saying so. I just asked Sandy what we were supposed to do if someone remained unconvinced, and we still disagreed at the end of a meeting. He said it was an experiment, and that if it didn't work, we could change the government. Even a decision to change the government, I pointed out, would have to be made by consensus, and anyone who was benefiting by a breakdown of consensus procedure might not be willing to go along with a different system. But Sandy kept saying that it was an experiment and that he knew of groups that had made it work. Finally I shrugged my shoulders and went along with it. By consensus that first day we made decisions to have community of property and to open a group bank account. We drew straws to determine who would be signers on the account.

But most decisions were really made by individuals who just thought of doing something and did it. Sandy opened up a cash record book, and Carrie decorated a cash box, which was kept in a public room. Any member took money for whatever he deemed necessary but wrote it down, together with what it was spent on, in the cash book. Incoming money was entered in the same book. It wasn't an efficient system, but we do have records, of a sort, even from those early days.

Consensus government was sorely tested on the issue of buying cattle. It had been suggested to us by our neighbors that we purchase a few head of beef cattle and let them graze our pastures during the summer, then sell them in the fall. We were supposed to make a profit on their increased weight, and at the same time keep our pastures under control. I was in favor of this plan, and so was Fred. Sandy was dead set against it. He didn't approve of agriculture as a community activity. The more we talked about it, the angrier we got. I found myself shouting and shaking, and Sandy just talked slower and slower and got stubborner and stubborner. Unable to come to a "yes, buy the cows" decision by consensus, we were automatically left at the end of an exhausting meeting with a "no, we won't buy the cows" decision. It was clear to me that consensus was operating as a one-person veto. I was ready to go to a voting system, or anything else that would get a decision based on something besides one person's stubbornness. But Brian, outside of meeting time, talked to Sandy and persuaded him to go along with the cattle plan. Brian didn't really care one way or the other. He just wanted to keep peace. So we bought the cattle and kept consensus procedure for a while. But Carrie never would come to meetings, and Jenny to fewer than half of them. The decision-making group became defined as simply those people who were willing to put up with the slowness of consensus procedure. Arguments could go on for hours, and there were other things to do. We needed managers—people who would take responsibility for one area of work or another and make sure it was taken care of. A few managerships arose spontaneously, like Fred and auto maintenance. I found myself in charge of canning and freezing the garden produce, just because I had seen my mother do it years before and had confidence that I could follow a cookbook. Brian had already begun to invent labor systems, and that was the issue that caused the conflict that precipitated our getting a formal government after five weeks without one.

Quincy liked everything to be precise and carried out according to the rules. He could not deal with Norms, Understandings, or Assumptions. He could not function with gray areas. He liked precision and order. In addition, he had a hankering for leadership. So when Brian began inventing labor systems and the rest of us started referring to Brian as "Labor Manager," Quincy protested. "Who elected him?" he demanded. "Since when does a labor manager appoint himself?" I mumbled something about its being generally understood that Brian would be Labor Manager. Quincy said it wasn't understood by *him*. That I believed. I didn't want to argue against Quincy's position, because in theory I agreed with it. Formally designated leadership has advantages. For a group of eight it seemed superfluous. If Quincy had not been one of us, I believe we could have gone up to a group of ten or twelve without formal government. But not even a group of three could have functioned informally if Quincy was one of them. I talked the matter over with Dwight. I suggested that we could best deal wth Quincy's absurdities and his ambitions by voting in a set of officers. Once the rules were set up, Quincy would obey them to the letter. Didn't we intend to have a system of government eventually? What would be the harm of starting now? Dwight was worried lest the wrong people be put into office. He thought Brian our most capable leader, and he didn't want to submit to a democratic election that might by some fluke omit Brian from the board. This worry sounded almost as silly to me as Quincy's protests. I told him there was no way in the world for the group not to have noticed Brian's talents, and that he would of course be elected. Dwight's distrust of democracy was deep, but he submitted to the election process. The others were not difficult to persuade. Sandy was disappointed to see consensus procedure abandoned after such a short trial, but he recognized that our particular group was not really interested in making it work, and he gave his consent to the election. Brian, Dwight, and I were elected planners. Our first task was to organize the community work into managerships. We immediately appointed Brian Labor Manager, and Quincy made no protest. The rest of the managerships were divided as best we could among the members, by asking all the members what areas they felt capable of directing.

Our bylaws leave us free to change our form of government any time two-thirds of the group wants it different. I personally think Twin Oaks would survive under a variety of governmental systems, including consensus or even democracy, as long as the managerial system was left intact. The important decisions are made at this level. It is the Construction Manager who researches sewage systems and building designs and presents them to the Community with his recommendations. The garden and food managers between them determine our diet. The Clothing Manager decides whether we buy new clothes or make do with old ones, and the Health Manager makes doctor's and dentist's appointments on the basis of need. Any of these people can be overruled by the board of planners, and the board in its turn can be overruled by the membership as a whole, but such occasions are exceptional. Managers use their best judgment in making decisions that benefit the group as a whole. They have nothing to gain by doing otherwise.

What keeps our system from turning into a tiresome bureaucracy is its simplicity—that decisions can be made swiftly by at most three people, and usually by a single manager, using his or her own judgment. What keeps it from being a dictatorship is that there is nothing to gain from being dictatorial. All decisions that are of interest to the group as a whole are discussed with the group as a whole. No legislation can be put across unless members are willing to go along with it. There is no police force here to carry out anybody's will. Our only technique is persuasion.

In spite of our hierarchical-sounding governmental setup, we are antiauthoritarian in both principle and practice. Bossiness quickly dies out as a personal trait, because the group does not reward it with obedience. Bossy people are simply avoided; bossy managers can't get people to work with them. We like having managers in charge of things, because we need to feel that someone has done some research and knows what should be done, but managers simply do not give orders. They point out things, make suggestions, define the job, and occasionally disqualify a sloppy worker. Once in a while we have as a group asked a manager to get tough in a troublesome area like kitchen cleanliness, in order to make sure that the dishwashers do a thorough job. All such requests have been refused. Managers may try it for a day, but no longer. "I would rather resign," they say, or, "I would rather leave the kitchen dirty. It isn't worth it."

I remember one summer we were having trouble getting stretcher work done. Stretchers are the wood part of our hammocks. Stretcher work is machine work, drilling holes with the drill press and sanding with an electric sander. It is boring and noisy. Also, the machinery kept breaking down, and the whole operation used to take place out-of-doors with no protection from the heat at certain hours of the day. The need for stretchers was great, and we had people scheduled for the machinery all during the daylight hours. The work was extremely unpopular, and the credit value skyrocketed without effect. Fewer than half the scheduled work hours were actually being done. People simply skipped their shifts and went swimming instead. As a possible solution, the hammock manager added the job of foreman to the system. It was to be the foreman's job to go around to all the people signed up for stretchers each day and ask them if they had done their work for the day, thus giving a small reminder and making it more difficult to skip out on the work. The job of foreman fell by lot (no one volunteered for it) to Naomi, seventeen years old. She tried to do her job, but the replies she got left her in tears. People were not accustomed to being reminded, did not want to be reminded, and also did not want to do stretcher work. The foreman idea was discarded.

Actually, we should have known better. In the end we solved the problem the Walden Two way. As soon as we got a little money, we brought the job indoors and bought a better drill press.

In general our approach to systems has been to take first the ones proposed in *Walden Two* and stick to them as long as they work well. As we find fault with them, we then make changes to correct the faults and make the systems fit our situation better. Skinner's book has been of immense service to us in giving us a point of general agreement for a starting place. Because we have *Walden Two*, we do not need a leader or teacher. Cooperation is possible because we have all, before we even joined, agreed upon the general principles of the community described in that book. Enormous ground is covered in that general agreement—including such items as the scientific, experimental approach to problem solving, the community of property, the dissolution of the nuclear family, and the willingness to be deliberate about the molding of character and personality. The debt we owe Dr. Skinner is enormous, but there is nothing sacred about the institutions we derived from his book. All of our systems are subject to change, and most of them have changed even over the few years that we have been a community.

We are a long way from Walden Two, not only in our modest physical plant and substandard per capita income, but even in its fundamental goal of creating a society where every member does what he ought just because he wants to. We believe in that, but we don't know how to do it yet, and we still use some of the traditional props of government—rules, systems, pep-talks—as substitutes for more "natural" reinforcers. Part of the reason for this is sheer poverty. Just as we couldn't get good work behavior for making stretchers until we improved the working conditions, just so we can't really run our entire community on positive reinforcement until a higher degree of affluence makes it possible for us to get rid of some of the rules.

If it weren't for shortages, equality wouldn't be very important. Nobody worries about getting an equal plateful of food here. There is plenty of it, and we each eat according to our desires. It is perfectly reasonable to predict that machinery and automation will some day put desirable work in the same class as food. Not too far in the future we shouldn't have to do any work we don't like, because the machines will do it for us.

With only a little money for construction, all our head-scratching over the distribution of living space will be a thing of the past. The principle has a very general application: first provide an adequate supply; then let everybody take what he wants. The need for rules and propaganda falls away by itself.

There is one other important factor, too. In order to make even an adequate supply of anything go around, it is necessary for everyone to have simple and modest tastes and desires. That means the creation of an entirely new culture—noncompetitive, nonconsumerist. Twin Oaks is tackling both these problems at once, and both of them are difficult. First there is the problem of making a decent supply of desirable things available. That's economics. Then there's the necessity of keeping people's desires within bounds, so that the economic problem doesn't keep multiplying. That's cultural planning. All of Twin Oaks's group activities fall under one or another of these goals. Until both of these states are achieved, it will be necessary for us to continue to legislate a rough equality, knowing full well that equality is just a halfway house on the road to the good life.

18. The Meaning of Culture
CLYDE KLUCKHOHN

The late Clyde Kluckhohn, Harvard anthropologist, was director of the university's Russian Research Institute. He was a prolific author; his works include To the Foot of the Rainbow *and* Mirror for Man, *the latter being the source of this reading. In his discussion of culture, Kluckhohn clarifies the unique way anthropologists and sociologists use the term "culture." His description, if properly understood, indicates the futility and illogic of looking askance at particular culture patterns simply because they vary from those to which one is accustomed. However, this does not mean that simply because what others do is a part of their culture, one must accept and even like every jot or tittle of their behavior. It does mean that the people themselves, however seemingly unique, deserve respect and acceptance (even though selected items of their behavior, if harmful to "outsiders," must be rejected or even countered).*

SOURCE: Clyde Kluckhohn, *Mirror for Man: The Relation of Anthropology to Modern Life* (New York: McGraw-Hill Book Company, 1949), pp. 17–36. Copyright 1949 by McGraw-Hill, Inc. Used with permission of McGraw-Hill Book Company.

Why do the Chinese dislike milk and milk products? Why would the Japanese die willingly in a Banzai charge that seemed senseless to Americans? Why do some nations trace descent through the father, others through the mother, still others through both parents? Not because different peoples have different instincts, not because they were destined by God or Fate to different habits, not because the weather is different in China and Japan and the United States. Sometimes shrewd common sense has an answer that is close to that of the anthropologist: "because they were brought up that way." By "culture" anthropology means the total life way of a people, the social legacy the individual acquires from his group. Or culture can be regarded as that part of the environment that is the creation of man.

This technical term has a wider meaning than the "culture" of history and literature. A humble cooking pot is as much a culture product as is a Beethoven sonata. In ordinary speech a man of culture is a man who can speak languages other than his own, who is familiar with history, literature, philosophy, or the fine arts. In some cliques that definition is still narrower. The cultured person is one who can talk about James Joyce, Scarlatti, and Picasso. To the anthropologist, however, to be human is to be cultured. There is culture in general, and then there are the specific cultures such as Russian, American, British, Hottentot, Inca. The general abstract notion serves to remind us that we cannot explain acts solely in terms of the biological properties of the people concerned, their individual past experience, and the immediate situation. The past experience of other men in the form of culture enters into almost every event. Each specific culture constitutes a kind of blueprint for all of life's activities.

One of the interesting things about human beings is that they try to understand themselves and their own behavior. While this has been particularly true of Europeans in recent times, there is no group which has not developed a scheme or schemes to explain man's actions. To the insistent human query "why?" the most exciting illumination anthropology has to offer is that of the concept of culture. Its explanatory importance is comparable to categories such as evolution in biology, gravity in physics, disease in medicine. A good deal of human behavior can be understood, and indeed predicted, if we know a people's design for living. Many acts are neither accidental nor due to personal peculiarities nor caused by supernatural forces nor simply mysterious. Even those of us who pride ourselves on our individualism follow most of the time a pattern not of our own making. We brush our teeth on arising. We put on pants—not a loincloth or a grass skirt. We eat three meals a day—not four or five or two. We sleep in a bed—not in a hammock or on a sheep pelt. I do not have to know the individual and his life history to be able to predict these and countless other regularities, including many in the thinking process, of all Americans who are not incarcerated in jails or hospitals for the insane.

To the American woman a system of plural wives seems "instinctively" abhorrent. She cannot understand how any woman can fail to be jealous and uncomfortable if she must share her husband with other women. She feels it "unnatural" to accept such a situation. On the other hand, a Koryak woman of Siberia, for example, would find it hard to understand how a woman could be so selfish and so undesirous of feminine companionship in the home as to wish to restrict her husband to one mate.

Some years ago I met in New York City a young man who did not speak a word of English and was obviously bewildered by American ways. By "blood" he was as American as you or I, for his parents had gone from Indiana to China as missionaries. Orphaned in infancy, he was reared by a Chinese family in a remote village. All who met him found him more Chinese than American. The facts of his blue eyes and light hair were less impressive than a Chinese style of gait, Chinese arm and hand movements, Chinese facial expression, and Chinese modes of thought. The biological heritage was American, but the cultural training had been Chinese. He returned to China.

Another example of another kind: I once knew a trader's wife in Arizona who took a somewhat devilish interest in producing a cultural reaction. Guests who came her way were often served delicious sandwiches filled with a meat that seemed to be neither chicken nor tuna fish yet was reminiscent of both. To queries she gave no reply until each had eaten his fill. She then explained that what they had eaten was not chicken, not tuna fish, but the rich, white flesh of freshly killed rattlesnakes. The response was instantaneous—vomiting, often violent vomiting. A biological process is caught in a cultural web.

A highly intelligent teacher with long and successful experience in the public schools of Chicago was finishing her first year in an Indian school. When asked how her Navaho pupils compared in intelligence with Chicago youngsters, she replied, "Well, I just don't know. Sometimes the Indians seem just as bright. At other times they just act like dumb animals. The other night we had a dance in the high school. I saw a boy who is one of the best students in my English class standing off by himself. So I took him over to a pretty girl and told them to dance. But they just stood there with their heads down. They wouldn't even say anything." I inquired if she knew whether or not they were members of the same clan. "What difference would that make?"

"How would you feel about getting into bed with your brother?" The teacher walked off in a huff, but, actually, the two cases were quite comparable in principle. To the Indian the type of bodily contact involved in our social dancing has a directly sexual connotation. The incest taboos between members of the same clan are as severe as between true brothers and sisters. The shame of the Indians at the suggestion that a clan brother and sister should dance and the indignation of the white teacher at the idea that she should share a bed with an adult brother represent equally nonrational responses, culturally standardized unreason.

All this does not mean that there is no such thing as raw human nature.

The very fact that certain of the same institutions are found in all known societies indicates that at bottom all human beings are very much alike. The files of the Cross-Cultural Survey at Yale University are organized according to categories such as "marriage ceremonies," "life crisis rites," "incest taboos." At least seventy-five of these categories are represented in every single one of the hundreds of cultures analyzed. This is hardly surprising. The members of all human groups have about the same biological equipment. All men undergo the same poignant life experiences such as birth, helplessness, illness, old age, and death. The biological potentialities of the species are the blocks with which cultures are built. Some patterns of every culture crystallize around focuses provided by the inevitables of biology: the difference between the sexes, the presence of persons of different ages, the varying physical strength and skill of individuals. The facts of nature also limit culture forms. No culture provides patterns for jumping over trees or for eating iron ore.

There is thus no "either-or" between nature and that special form of nurture called culture. Culture determinism is as onesided as biological determinism. The two factors are interdependent. Culture arises out of human nature, and its forms are restricted both by man's biology and by natural laws. It is equally true that culture channels biological processes —vomiting, weeping, fainting, sneezing, the daily habits of food intake and waste elimination. When a man eats, he is reacting to an internal "drive," namely, hunger contractions consequent upon the lowering of blood sugar, but his precise reaction to these internal stimuli cannot be predicted by physiological knowledge alone. Whether a healthy adult feels hungry twice, three times, or four times a day and the hours at which this feeling recurs is a question of culture. What he eats is of course limited by availability, but is also partly regulated by culture. It is a biological fact that some types of berries are poisonous; it is a cultural fact that, a few generations ago, most Americans considered tomatoes to be poisonous and refused to eat them. Such selective, discriminative use of the environment is characteristically cultural. In a still more general sense, too, the process of eating is channeled by culture. Whether a man eats to live, lives to eat, or merely eats and lives is only in part an individual matter, for there are also cultural trends. Emotions are physiological events. Certain situations will evoke fear in people from any culture. But sensations of pleasure, anger, and lust may be stimulated by cultural cues that would leave unmoved someone who has been reared in a different social tradition.

Except in the case of newborn babies and of individuals born with clear-cut structural or functional abnormalities we can observe innate endowments only as modified by cultural training. In a hospital in New Mexico where Zuñi Indian, Navaho Indian, and white American babies are born, it is possible to classify the newly arrived infants as unusually active, average, and quiet. Some babies from each "racial" group will fall into each category, though a higher proportion of the white babies will fall into the unusually active class. But if a Navaho baby, a Zuñi baby, and a white baby—all classified as unusually active at birth—are again observed at the age of two years, the Zuñi baby will no longer seem given to quick and restless activity—*as compared with the white child*—though he may seem so as compared with the other Zuñis of the same age. The Navaho child is likely to fall in between as contrasted with the Zuñi and the white, though he will probably still seem more active than the average Navaho youngster.

It was remarked by many observers in the Japanese relocation centers that Japanese who were born and brought up in this country, especially those who were reared apart from any large colony of Japanese, resemble in behavior their white neighbors much more closely than they do their own parents who were educated in Japan.

I have said "culture channels biological processes." It is more accurate to say "the biological functioning of individuals is modified if they have been trained in certain ways and not in others." Culture is not a disembodied force. It is created and transmitted by people. However, culture, like well-known concepts of the physical sciences, is a convenient abstraction. One never sees gravity. One sees bodies falling in regular ways. One never sees an electromagnetic field. Yet certain happenings that can be seen may be given a neat abstract formulation by assuming that the electromagnetic field exists. Similarly, one never sees culture as such. What is seen are regularities in the behavior or artifacts of a group that has adhered to a common tradition. The regularities in style and technique of ancient Inca tapestries or stone axes from Melanesian islands are due to the existence of mental blueprints for the group.

Culture is a *way* of thinking, feeling, believing. It is the group's knowledge stored up (in memories of men; in books and objects) for future use. We study the products of this "mental" activity: the overt behavior, the speech and gestures and activities of people, and the tangible results of these things such as tools, houses, cornfields, and what not. It has been customary in lists of "culture traits" to include such things as watches or lawbooks. This is a convenient way of thinking about them, but in the solution of any important problem we must remember that they, in themselves, are nothing but metals, paper, and ink. What is important is that some men know how to make them, others set a value on them, are unhappy without them, direct their activities in relation to them, or disregard them.

It is only a helpful shorthand when we say "The cultural patterns of the Zulu were resistant to Christianization." In the directly observable world of course, it was individual Zulus who resisted. Nevertheless, if we do not forget that we are speaking at a high level of abstraction, it is justifiable to speak of culture as a cause. One may compare the practice of saying "syphilis caused the extinction of the native population of the island." Was it "syphilis" or "syphilis germs" or "human beings who were carriers of syphilis?"

"Culture," then, is "a theory." But if a theory is not contradicted by any relevant fact and if it helps us to understand a mass of otherwise chaotic facts, it is useful. Darwin's contribution was much less the accumulation of new knowledge than the creation of a theory which put in order data already known. An accumulation of facts, however large, is no more a science than a pile of bricks is a house. Anthropology's demonstration that the most weird set of customs has a consistency and an order is comparable to modern psychiatry's showing that there is meaning and purpose in the apparently incoherent talk of the insane. In fact, the inability of the older psychologies and philosophies to account for the strange behavior of madmen and heathens was the principal factor that forced psychiatry and anthropology to develop theories of the unconscious and of culture.

Since culture is an abstraction, it is important not to confuse culture with society. A "society" refers to a group of people who interact more with each other than they do with other individuals—who cooperate with each other for the attainment of certain ends. You can see and indeed count the individuals who make up a society. A "culture" refers to the distinctive ways of life of such a group of people. Not all social events are culturally patterned. New types of circumstances arise for which no cultural solutions have as yet been devised.

A culture constitutes a storehouse of the pooled learning of the group. A rabbit starts life with some innate responses. He can learn from his own experience and perhaps from observing other rabbits. A human infant is born with fewer instincts and greater plasticity. His main task is to learn the answers that persons he will never see, persons long dead, have worked out. Once he has learned the formulas supplied by the culture of his group, most of his behavior becomes almost as automatic and unthinking as if it were instinctive. There is a tremendous amount of intelligence behind the making of a radio, but not much is required to learn to turn it on.

The members of all human societies face some of the same unavoidable dilemmas, posed by biology and other facts of the human situation. This is why the basic categories of all cultures are so similar. Human culture without language is unthinkable. No culture fails to provide for aesthetic expression and aesthetic delight. Every culture supplies standardized orientations toward the deeper problems, such as death. Every culture is designed to perpetuate the group and its solidarity, to meet the demands of individuals for an orderly way of life and for satisfaction of biological needs.

However, the variations on these basic themes are numberless. Some languages are built up out of twenty basic sounds, others out of forty. Nose plugs were considered beautiful by the predynastic Egyptians but are not by the modern French. Puberty is a biological fact. But one culture ignores it, another prescribes informal instructions about sex but no ceremony, a third has impressive rites for girls only, a fourth for boys and girls. In this culture, the first menstruation is welcomed as a happy, natural event; in that culture the atmosphere is full of dread and supernatural threat. Each culture dissects nature according to its own system of categories. The Navaho Indians apply the same word to the color of a robin's egg and to that of grass. A psychologist once assumed that this meant a difference in the sense organs, that Navahos didn't have the physiological equipment to distinguish "green" from "blue." However, when he showed them objects of the two colors and asked them if they were exactly the same colors, they looked at him with astonishment. His dream of discovering a new type of color blindness was shattered.

Every culture must deal with the sexual instinct. Some, however, seek to deny all sexual expression before marriage, whereas a Polynesian adolescent who was not promiscuous would be distinctly abnormal. Some cultures enforce lifelong monogamy, others, like our own, tolerate serial monogamy; in still other cultures, two or more women may be joined to one man or several men to a single woman. Homosexuality has been a permitted pattern in the Greco-Roman world, in parts of Islam, and in various primitive tribes. Large portions of the population of Tibet, and of Christendom at some places and periods, have practiced completely celibacy. To us marriage is first and foremost an arrangement between two individuals. In many more societies marriage is merely one facet of a complicated set of reciprocities, economic and otherwise, between two families or two clans.

The essence of the cultural process is selectivity. The selection is only exceptionally conscious and rational. Cultures are like Topsy. They just grew. Once, however, a way of handling a situation becomes institutionalized, there is ordinarily great resistance to change or deviation. When we speak of "our sacred beliefs," we mean of course that they are beyond criticism and that the person who suggests modification or abandonment must be punished. No person is emotionally indifferent to his culture. Certain cultural premises may become totally out of accord with a new factual situation. Leaders may recognize this and reject the old ways in theory. Yet their emotional loyalty continues in the face of reason because of the intimate conditionings of early childhood.

A culture is learned by individuals as the result of belonging to some particular group, and it constitutes that part of learned behavior which is shared with others. It is our social legacy, as contrasted with our organic heredity. It is one of the important factors which permits us to live together in an organized society, giving us ready-made solutions to our problems, helping us to predict the behavior of others, and permitting others to know what to expect of us.

Culture regulates our lives at every turn. From the moment we are born until we die there is, whether we are conscious of it or not, constant pressure upon us to follow certain types of behavior that other men have created for us. Some paths we follow willingly, others we follow because we know no other way, still others we deviate from or go back to most unwillingly. Mothers of small children know how unnaturally most of this comes to us—how little regard we have, until we are "culturalized," for the "proper" place, time, and manner for certain acts such as eating, excreting, sleeping, getting dirty, and making loud noises. But by more or less adhering to a system of related designs for carrying out all the acts of living, a group of men and women feel themselves linked together by a powerful chain of sentiments. Ruth Benedict gave an almost complete definition of the concept when she said, "Culture is that which binds men together."

It is true any culture is a set of techniques for adjusting both to the external environment and to other men. However, cultures create problems as well as solve them. If the lore of a people states that frogs are dangerous creatures, or that it is not safe to go about at night because of witches or ghosts, threats are posed which do not arise out of the inexorable facts of the external world. Cultures produce needs as well as provide a means of fulfilling them. There exists for every group culturally defined, acquired drives that may be more powerful in ordinary daily life than the biologically inborn drives. Many Americans, for example, will work harder for "success" than they will for sexual satisfaction.

Most groups elaborate certain aspects of their culture far beyond maximum utility or survival value. In other words, not all culture promotes physical survival. At times, indeed, it does exactly the opposite. Aspects of culture which once were adaptive may persist long after they have ceased to be useful. An analysis of any culture will disclose many features which cannot possibly be construed as adaptations to the total environment in which the group now finds itself. However, it is altogether likely that these apparently useless features represent survivals, with modifications through time, of cultural forms which were adaptive in one or another previous situation.

Any cultural practice must be functional or it will disappear before long. That is, it must somehow contribute to the survival of the society or to the adjustment of the individual. However, many cultural functions are not manifest but latent. A cowboy will walk three miles to catch a horse which he then rides one mile to the store. From the point of view of manifest function this is positively irrational. But the act has the latent function of maintaining the cowboy's prestige in the terms of his own subculture. One can instance the buttons on the sleeve of a man's coat, our absurd English spelling, the use of capital letters, and a host of other apparently nonfunctional customs. They serve mainly the latent function of assisting individuals to maintain their security by preserving continuity with the past and by making certain sectors of life familiar and predictable.

Every culture is a precipitate of history. In more than one sense history is a sieve. Each culture embraces those aspect of the past which, usually in altered form and with altered meanings, live on in the present. Discoveries and inventions, both material and ideological, are constantly being made available to a group through its historical contacts with other peoples or being created by its own members. However, only those that fit the total immediate situation in meeting the group's needs for survival or in promoting the psychological adjustment of individuals will become part of the culture. The process of culture building may be regarded as an addition to man's innate biological capacities, an addition providing instruments which enlarge, or may even substitute for, biological functions, and to a degree compensating for biological limitations—as in ensuring that death does not always result in the loss to humanity of what the deceased has learned.

Culture is like a map. Just as a map isn't the territory but an abstract representation of a particular area, so also a culture is an abstract description of trends toward uniformity in the words, deeds, and artifacts of a human group. If a map is accurate and you can read it, you won't get lost; if you know a culture, you will know your way around in the life of a society.

Many educated people have the notion that culture applies only to exotic ways of life or to societies where relative simplicity and relative homogeneity prevail. Some sophisticated missionaries, for example, will use the anthropological conception in discussing the special modes of living of South Sea Islanders, but seem amazed at the idea that it could be applied equally to inhabitants of New York City. And social workers in Boston will talk about the culture of a colorful and well-knit immigrant group but boggle at applying it to the behavior of staff members in the social-service agency itself.

In the primitive society the correspondence between the habits of individuals and the customs of the community is ordinarily greater. There is probably some truth in what an old Indian once said, "In the old days there was no law; everybody did what was right." The primitive tends to find happiness in the fulfillment of intricately involuted cultural patterns; the modern more often tends to feel the pattern as repressive to his individuality. It is also true that in a complex stratified society there are numerous exceptions to generalizations made about the culture as a whole. It is necessary to study regional, class, and occupational subcultures. Primitive cultures have greater stability than modern cultures; they change—but less rapidly.

However, modern men also are creators and carriers of culture. Only in some respects are they influenced differently from primitives by culture. Moreover, there are such wide variations in primitive cultures that any black-and-white contrast between the primitive and the civilized is altogether fictitious. The distinction which is most generally true lies in the field of conscious philosophy.

The publication of Paul Radin's *Primitive Man as a Philosopher* did much toward destroying the myth that an abstract analysis of experience was a peculiarity of literate societies. Speculation and reflection upon the nature of the universe and of man's place in the total scheme of things have been carried out in every known culture. Every people has its characteristic set of "primitive postulates." It remains true that critical examination of basic premises and fully explicit systematization of philosophical concepts are seldom found at the nonliterate level. The written word is an almost essential condition for free and extended discussion of fundamental philosophic issues. Where dependence on memory exists, there seems to be an inevitable tendency to emphasize the correct perpetuation of the precious oral tradition. Similarly, while it is all too easy to underestimate the extent to which ideas spread without books, it is in general true that tribal or folk societies do not possess competing philosophical systems. The major exception to this statement is, of course, the case where part of the tribe becomes converted to one of the great proselytizing religions such as Christianity or Mohammedanism. Before contact with rich and powerful civilizations, primitive peoples seem to have absorbed new ideas piecemeal, slowly integrating them with the previously existing ideology. The abstract thought of nonliterate societies is ordinarily less self-critical, less systematic, nor so intricately elaborated in purely logical dimensions. Primitive thinking is more concrete, more implicit—perhaps more completely coherent than the philosophy of most individuals in large societies which have been influenced over long periods by disparate intellectual currents.

No participant in any culture knows all the details of the cultural map. The statement frequently heard that St. Thomas Aquinas was the last man to master all the knowledge of his society is intrinsically absurd. St. Thomas would have been hard put to make a pane of cathedral glass or to act as a midwife. In every culture there are what Ralph Linton has called "universals, alternatives, and specialties." Every Christian in the thirteenth century knew that it was necessary to attend mass, to go to confession, to ask the Mother of God to intercede with her Son. There were many other universals in the Christian culture of Western Europe. However, there were also alternative cultural patterns even in the realm of religion. Each individual had his own patron saint, and different towns developed the cults of different saints. The thirteenth-century anthropologist could have discovered the rudiments of Christian practice by questioning and observing whomever he happened to meet in Germany, France, Italy, or England. But to find out the details of the ceremonials honoring St. Hubert or St. Bridget he would have had to seek out certain individuals or special localities where these alternative patterns were practiced. Similarly, he could not learn about weaving from a professional soldier or about canon law from a farmer. Such cultural knowledge belongs in the realm of the specialties, voluntarily chosen by the individual or ascribed to him by birth. Thus, part of a culture must be learned by everyone, part may be selected from alternative patterns, part applies only to those who perform the roles in the society for which these patterns are designed.

Many aspects of a culture are explicit. The explicit culture consists in those regularities in word and deed that may be generalized straight from the evidence of the ear and the eye. The recognition of these is like the recognition of style in the art of a particular place and epoch. If we have examined twenty specimens of the wooden saints' images made in the Taos valley of New Mexico in the late eighteenth century, we can predict that any new images from the same locality and period will in most respects exhibit the same techniques of carving, about the same use of colors and choice of woods, a similar quality of artistic conception. Similarly, if, in a society of 2,000 members, we record 100 marriages at random and find that in 30 cases a man has married the sister of his brother's wife, we can anticipate that an additional sample of 100 marriages will show roughly the same number of cases of this pattern.

The above is an instance of what anthropologists call a behavioral pattern, the practices as opposed to the rules of the culture. There are also, however, regularities in what people say they do or should do. They do tend in fact to prefer to marry into a family already connected with their own by marriage, but this is not necessarily part of the official code of conduct. No disapproval whatsoever is attached to those who make another sort of marriage. On the other hand, it is explicitly forbidden to marry a member of one's own clan even though no biological relationship is traceable. This is a regulatory pattern—a Thou Shalt or a Thou Shalt Not. Such patterns may be violated often, but their existence is nevertheless important. A people's standards for conduct and belief define the socially approved aims and the acceptable means of attaining them. When the discrepancy between the theory and the practice of a culture is exceptionally great, this indicates that the culture is undergoing rapid change. It does not prove that ideals are unimportant, for ideals are but one of a number of factors determining action.

Cultures do not manifest themselves solely in observable customs and artifacts. No amount of questioning of any save the most articulate in the most self-conscious cultures will bring out some of the basic attitudes common to the members of the group. This is because these basic assumptions are taken so for granted that they normally do not enter into consciousness. This part of the cultural map must be inferred by the observer on the basis of consistencies in thought and action. Missionaries in various societies are often disturbed or puzzled because the natives do not regard "morals" and "sex code" as almost synonymous. The natives seem to feel that morals are concerned with sex just about as much as with eating— no less and no more. No society fails to have some restrictions on sexual behavior, but sex activity outside of marriage need not necessarily be furtive or attended with guilt. The Christian tradition has tended to assume that sex is inherently nasty as well as dangerous. Other cultures assume that sex in itself is not only natural but one of the good things of life, even though sex acts with certain persons under certain circumstances are forbidden. This is implicit culture, for the natives do not announce their premises. The missionaries would get further if they said, in effect,

"Look, our morality starts from different assumptions. Let's talk about those assumptions," rather than ranting about "immorality."

A factor implicit in a variety of diverse phenomena may be generalized as an underlying cultural principle. For example, the Navaho Indians always leave part of the design in a pot, a basket, or a blanket unfinished. When a medicine man instructs an apprentice he always leaves a little bit of the story untold. This "fear of closure" is a recurrent theme in Navaho culture. Its influence may be detected in many contexts that have no explicit connection.

If the observed cultural behavior is to be correctly understood, the categories and presuppositions constituting the implicit culture must be worked out. The "strain toward consistency" which Sumner noted in the folkways and mores of all groups cannot be accounted for unless one grants a set of systematically interrelated implicit themes. For example, in American culture the themes of "effort and optimism," "the common man," "technology," and "virtuous materialism" have a functional interdependence, the origin of which is historically known. The relationship between themes may be that of conflict. One may instance the competition between Jefferson's theory of democracy and Hamilton's "government by the rich, the wellborn, and the able." In other cases most themes may be integrated under a single dominant theme. In Negro cultures of West Africa the mainspring of social life is religion; in East Africa almost all cultural behavior seems to be oriented toward certain premises and categories centered on the cattle economy. If there be one master principle in the implicit culture, this is often called the "ethos" or *Zeitgeist*.

Every culture has organization as well as content. There is nothing mystical about this statement. One may compare ordinary experience. If I know that Smith, working alone, can shovel 10 cubic yards of dirt a day, Jones 12, and Brown 14, I would be foolish to predict that the three working together would move 36. The total might well be considerably more; it might be less. A whole is different from the sum of its parts. The same principle is familiar in athletic teams. A brilliant pitcher added to a nine may mean a pennant or may mean the cellar; it depends on how he fits in.

And so it is with cultures. A mere list of the behavioral and regulatory patterns of the implicit themes and categories would be like a map on which all mountains, lakes, and rivers were included—but not in their actual relationship to one another. Two cultures could have almost identical inventories and still be extremely different. The full significance of any single element in a culture design will be seen only when that element is viewed in the total matrix of its relationship to other elements. Naturally, this includes accent or emphasis, as well as position. Accent is manifested sometimes through frequency, sometimes through intensity. The indispensable importance of these questions of arrangement and emphasis may be driven home by an analogy. Consider a musical sequence made up of three notes. If we are told that the three notes in question are *A, B,* and *G,* we receive information which is fundamental. But it will not enable us to predict the type of sensation which the playing of this sequence is likely to evoke. We need many different sorts of relationship data. Are the notes to be played in that or some other order? What duration will each receive? How will the emphasis, if any, be distributed? We also need, of course, to know whether the instrument used is to be a piano or an accordion.

Cultures vary greatly in their degree of integration. Synthesis is achieved partly through the overt statement of the dominant conceptions, assumptions, and aspirations of the group in its religious lore, secular thought, and ethical code; partly through habitual but unconscious ways of looking at the stream of events, ways of begging certain questions. To the naïve participant in the culture these modes of categorizing, of dissecting experience along these planes and not others, are as much "given" as the regular sequence of daylight and darkness or the necessity of air, water, and food for life. Had Americans not thought in terms of money and the market system during the depression they would have distributed unsalable goods rather than destroyed them.

Every group's way of life, then, is a structure—not a haphazard collection of all the different physically possible and functionally effective patterns of belief and action. A culture is an interdependent system based upon linked premises and categories whose influence is greater, rather than less, because they are seldom put in words. Some degree of internal coherence which is felt rather than rationally constructed seems to be demanded by most of the participants in any culture. As Whitehead has remarked, "Human life is driven forward by its dim apprehension of notions too general for its existing language."

In sum, the distinctive way of life that is handed down as the social heritage of a people does more than supply a set of skills for making a living and a set of blueprints for human relations. Each different way of life makes its own assumptions about the ends and purposes of human existence, about what human beings have a right to expect from each other and the gods, about what constitutes a fulfillment or frustration. Some of these assumptions are made explicit in the lore of the folk; others are tacit premises which the observer must infer by finding consistent trends in word and deed.

Social Differentiation

Part V

The next four selections focus on some features of *social differentiation*, which is defined as the process whereby individuals and groups acquire unique characteristics and are thus set off from one another. Differences in role and status set people apart, as do special interests and beliefs. One of the most important differentiation processes is termed *social stratification*. This denotes all of the ways in which societies become divided into groupings, each of which is made up of members with roughly similar amounts of the three basic elements of social differentiation: power, privilege, and prestige.

19. Anxiety Among the WASPs
FLETCHER KNEBEL

It is obvious that white Anglo-Saxon Protestants have long dominated American society. Their dominance, however, is waning, according to author Fletcher Knebel. "Tremors of anxiety" rattle the "snug hive" of the WASPs. Knebel's colorful account is what one would expect from a journalist who has become an immensely successful novelist. As an artist, he knows just where to put the right emphasis.

Tremors of anxiety are rattling the snug hives of the WASPs—White Anglo-Saxon Protestants. In the nearby Negro ghettos can be heard that husky, insistent growl: "Bread or burn." Leaders of the nation's six million Jews, electrified by the swift martial triumph of Israel last year, are demanding: "Make room at the top in America." In New York City, Puerto Ricans clamor for more and better jobs. In the great Southwest, Mexican-Americans apply political and labor-union pressure for a larger cut of the economic pie. Meanwhile, those vast Catholic minorities, the Irish and the Italians, surge upward at a pace that bests that of the Dow-Jones averages.

The prospect of economic siege is not all that agitates the WASP. He finds new cause for alarm in Dr. Christiaan Barnard's heart transplants. For, if a mulatto heart can be snugly anchored beneath a white chest, might not the day arrive when an aging proper Bostonian would lunch at his Somerset Club with a Negro kidney, a Jewish left auricle, a Catholic liver, 12 feet of healthy intestine donated by an American Indian and a cornea from the eye of a Japanese-American airline stewardess? And what would the late George Apley say to that?

But the WASP is, above all, an economic animal, and whatever the future

SOURCE: Fletcher Knebel, "The WASPs: 1968," *Look* 32 (July 23, 1968), 69–70, 72, 76. Copyright © 1968 by Cowles Communications, Inc. and reprinted by permission.

pedigree of his organs, it is his dollar that seems to be in imminent jeopardy. Everywhere, it appears to the harried WASP, the Negroes, the Jews, the Irish, the Italians, the Hungarians, the Puerto Ricans, the Poles and the Mexicans are stampeding the corridors that debouch on the executive suite, and—pity be—hardly a one of the invaders is a communicant at the Episcopalian altar.

The whole business has the smell of an uprising, albeit not a conspiratorial one. Tremors are said to stir such innermost retreats of the WASP as the Links Club (New York), Pacific Union Club (San Francisco), the President and Fellows of Harvard College (Cambridge), the Duquesne Club (Pittsburgh) and the whole swatch of country clubs, Union League clubs, country day schools, hunt breakfasts, charity dances, racquet clubs and resorts where Cleveland Amory's WASP elite is reported to hole up in times of stress.

Writer Stewart Alsop recently described the WASPs as a "dwindling minority" in America. Dwindling they may be in repute and allure, but minority they decidedly are not—unless Alsop refers to the in-WASP, a special category to which he and his brother, the columnist, presumably belong.

No matter how you slice the figures, the White Anglo-Saxon Protestant is still the majority in the United States, numbering roughly 116,000,000 souls—pardon—people, or about 53 percent of the population. To arrive at this figure, you start with our 200,000,000 inhabitants and, dealing in round numbers, subtract about 50,000,000 Roman Catholics, 22,000,000 Negroes, almost 6,000,000 Jews, more than 4,000,000 Eastern Orthodox, about a million people of Oriental and Polynesian descent, about 550,000 American Indians and some 650,000 others, including Eskimos, Muslims and Bhutanese. There are more exact, if tortured, methods of depicting the American mosaic, but none of them nudges the WASP from his majority posture—for remember always that the WASP does not have to attend church to retain his standing, prejudices or behavior patterns. He can be agnostic, atheist or lazy.

The WASP culture is divided into two main hives, the in-WASP and the out-WASP. The in-WASP is the person whose vintage ancestors ventured—or were chased—to America from England, Scotland, Wales and Northern Ireland. The out-WASP's progenitors came from Northwestern Europe—Germany, Holland, Belgium, Denmark, Norway, Sweden and, occasionally, Finland and Switzerland.

The in- and out-WASPs have much in common. They intermarry freely, they seek shelter in the same clubs, do first-name business on the telephone. But the in-WASP prefers the Episcopalian ritual, while the out-WASP fills up the Lutheran pews. Presbyterians, Methodists and Baptists harbor both breeds. Boston is the capital and the historic shrine of the in-WASP, while Minnesota is the most beautiful of the out-WASP provinces. Its capital is the Minneapolis Club.

Although he seldom mentions it, the in-WASP's bloodlines are as tangled as the out-WASP's, and far more so than those of the Irish-Catholic, the Italian, the Jew, the Negro or the American Indian. For little England, long before the United States, was history's melting pot. First to conquer the native savages were the Iberians, a dark-complexioned people from the rims of the Mediterranean. Later came the Celts in three great waves, then the Romans, who ruled and spawned for four centuries, then the Saxons, Frisians, Jutes and Angles from Northwest Europe. Still later came the Vikings over a span of two centuries, and, finally, in 1066 and thereafter, the Normans of France. By the time of Plymouth Rock, all these genes, corpuscles and antibodies had congealed into that recognizable human package, the Englishman, who lost an empire but won America. Or so it seemed until recently.

Current tremors in WASPdom have yet to reach the panic stage, largely because the doom of the WASP has been sounded before in America without any breaking of the White Anglo-Saxon Protestant grip on the nation's economic power—and, after all, to update Calvin Coolidge, a Vermont WASP, the business of America is still business. Many years ago, the late iconoclast, Henry L. Mencken, tagged the 1920s as the decade "of the dying Anglo-Saxon," an obvious false alarm. Then, in the turbulent Franklin D. Roosevelt era, a wealthy WASP industrialist of Philadelphia gathered his family at the ancestral estate and took a vote on whether to defect to Canada. His theory, widely held among fellow clubmen, was that FDR, "a traitor to his class," was about to tax his kindred WASPs to the wall for the benefit of the downtrodden minorities. The family voted, narrowly, to hunker down and fight it out on the Main Line. Today, the aging industrialist is wealthier than ever.

More recently came the elevation to the U.S. Presidency of the first Roman Catholic in history, John F. Kennedy. Dire predictions of a WASP eclipse attended his rise. During the '60 campaign, a group composed chiefly of Protestant clergymen met to assess the state of the Union should Kennedy win. The eminent WASP inspirationalist, the Rev. Norman Vincent Peale, was overheard to say, "Our American culture is at stake. I don't say it won't survive, but it won't be what it was." As it turned out, Kennedy's election damaged the WASP community less than it did Dr. Peale, who was lampooned at the next Gridiron dinner as lamenting (to the tune of *Get Me to the Church on Time*), "Leave me in the church next time."

Still, this is an era of WASP anxiety. For the first time, WASP jokes are popping up at bars along with the Polish, Irish and Jewish jokes. Sample: Q. What do you call six WASPs sitting around a conference table? A. Price-fixing. Godfrey Cambridge, the Negro comedian, says that the petty Negro thief merely wants the same economic opportunity as the WASP crook—to flee to Brazil after embezzling $5,000,000. Many WASPs recall the adage: They can revile you, maul you or shoot you, but watch out when they start to make fun of you. There are other warning signs: WASP youth who drop out, become flower children and mock the suburban, Bermuda-shorts,

Scotch-on-the-rocks, get-ahead culture of their parents; the great Negro revolution; displacement of the WASP novelists, who described the illicit affairs and guilt complexes in WASPdom, by the Jewish, Negro and Catholic writers who tell about THEIR trials and alienations; the vanishing WASP in the theater, the art studios, the movies and the orchestra pits; and, most important of all, the hybrid assault on the largely WASP Establishment for the war against Asians in Vietnam.

The question of the hour for the apprehensive WASP is whether these flutterings are symptomatic of an irresistible movement that will sweep him from his seat of power. In a pluralistic society such as the American, power is a compound item—part political, part social, part economic. The last is by far the most pervasive: for in a thousand blunt and subtle ways, the dollar works its influence.

A series of LOOK research studies shows that the rulers of economic America—the producers, the financiers, the manufacturers, the bankers and the insurers—are still overwhelmingly WASP.

50 Largest Corporations. Of 790 directorships of these giants of business and industry, 88 percent are held by apparent WASPs. The word "apparent" is used because definite ethnic lineage cannot be determined in some cases. Boards of 31 of the corporations are exclusively WASP. Nine others have one or more Jews on the board, while nine have one or more Catholics. The executives, like the directors, are mostly WASPs.

10 Largest Commercial Banks. Of 241 directorships, about 200, or 83 percent, are held by WASPs. Of the remainder, Roman Catholics hold slightly more than Jews. An interesting case is that of the Bank of America, the nation's largest. It was founded by the late Amadeo Peter Giannini, son of Italian immigrants, under the name "Bank of Italy." By a combination of unorthodox retail methods and Italian flair, Giannini became the financial power of California. Today, the Bank of America is as heavily WASPish as its competitors.

5 Largest Life Insurance Companies. At least 100 of the 131 directorships are held by WASPs, and probably more. The WASP representation appears to be about 80 percent.

Other studies in recent years have shown the economic dominance of the WASP to have become but slightly dented since the 1920s, when Mencken thought the Anglo-Saxon to be moribund. While minority entrepreneurs have moved strongly into such fields as entertainment, construction, retailing and research laboratories, the big money generated by basic production remains in WASP hands. One survey showed that less than one percent of corporate executives in this country are Jewish, although Jews account for eight percent of all college graduates, the chief source for executive talent. Studies by the American Jewish Committee show but a sprinkling of Jews in the executive suites of such specific businesses as the auto industry, public utilities, banking, insurance and shipping. While Catholic organizations do not undertake such surveys, the movement of the Irish and Italian minorities into corporate management appears to be only slightly more ample than that of the Jews. The Negro executive remains a rarity, as does the Mexican-American and the Puerto Rican.

National government, despite potpourri political pressures and the brief tenure of a Catholic President, remains basically a WASP enterprise at the top. President Johnson is a WASP, as were all of his predecessors, save one, since the founding of the Republic. The Cabinet numbers ten WASPs, one Jew, one Negro. Of the 16 Senate committee chairmen, 15 are WASPs, one is a Catholic. Members of the National Security Council, where foreign and defense policies are shaped, are all WASPs. The ethnic mix is greater among chairmen of the House committees, but even there, WASPs hold 14 of the 21 chairmanships. The vast and powerful defense establishment is dominated by WASPs. While the enlisted military ranks, like the Federal Civil Service, are a blend of America's ethnic groups, the officer class is heavily WASP. Catholics are a small minority, and Jewish general officers are rare. Only one Negro holds high rank, Lt. Gen. Benjamin O. Davis, Jr. There is a greater mixture among junior officers, but Negroes still fare poorly, despite the large Negro GI contingent in Vietnam. Negro officers comprise but 3.6 percent of the Army, 1.7 percent of the Air Force and only 0.3 percent of the Navy, traditionally the most WASPish of the services.

The prestigious Council on Foreign Relations, a private organization with impact on the nation's foreign policy, is a WASPs' nest. Of 25 officers and directors, only one man is not solidly WASP. Eight of the officers are Episcopalians. The roster reads like a roll call of the WASP Establishment—Armstrong, Bundy, Dean, Dulles, Finletter, McCloy, Perkins, Reed, Rockefeller.

A survey of the five largest foundations, which also have an impact on national and foreign policy, shows that 83 percent of the directorships are held by WASPs, only a slight decline from 20 years ago, when the figure was 91 percent.

On the university campus, WASPs hold the presidencies, the purse strings and the top administrative posts that shape values and curricula. Of 775 leading public and nondenominational private universities surveyed in one study, less than one percent had Jewish presidents. Catholic administrators are as rare in the nonsectarian schools, for Catholic educators gravitate to the Catholic universities. Catholic intellectuals, in any event, have lagged behind Protestants and Jews in quantity. As Andrew M. Greeley, a Catholic priest at the University of Chicago, pointed out in a *Commonweal* article: ". . . even now half the Catholic adults in the country are immigrants or the children of immigrants. We are but a generation or two away from the peasant farms of Europe. . . . The development of a Catholic intellectual life in this country had to await the preparation of an adequate social and economic base, and such a base did not really come into existence until the late 1940s."

A LOOK study of the governing bodies of the ten universities with the largest endowments—Harvard, Texas, Yale, Chicago, Baylor, California, MIT, Princeton, Columbia and Stanford—shows that about 80 percent of the men who set policy on campus are WASPS. The remainder consists of two Jews for every Catholic. The study concentrated on the inner groups that directly affect policy, rather than on the larger trustee bodies. For instance, the nation's wealthiest and most influential university, Harvard, has a 30-member Board of Overseers elected by the alumni, but actual operating control is vested in a seven-member corporation, formally known as "The President and Fellows of Harvard College." This inner sanctum is all-WASP (including four Episcopalians), as it has been for decades, not to say timelessly. A Harvard spokesman thinks one of the corporation members in the early 1920s was a Catholic, but he won't stake his life on it.

The American male social club functions as an auxiliary to the executive suite. At the club, where fellowship mingles so intimately with commerce that many executives deduct club dues as business expenses on their income tax returns, the WASP reigns. One recent study showed that 67 percent of all downtown clubs in the United States practice discrimination against minorities. Membership bars to Catholics are relatively rare now, but hundreds of clubs exclude Jews, and there are many where no Negro, Puerto Rican or Mexican-American has ever entered except via the servants' entrance. It is remarkable that in a pluralistic society such as America's, the WASP has managed to barricade himself so securely against the freshness and the ferment of diversity.

In short, WASP dominance of the economic, political and social founts of America is as wide today as it was five years ago, when E. Digby Baltzell, a University of Pennsylvania sociologist, completed his brilliant book, *The Protestant Establishment*. Baltzell warned his fellow WASPS that they must move over or wither. "It is my central thesis," he wrote, "that in order for an upper class to maintain a continuity of power and authority, especially in an opportunarian and mobile society such as ours, its membership must, in the long run, be representative of the composition of society as a whole."

And it is the thesis of this article that just such an ethnically composite Establishment—from the executive suites of the corporations to the banks, the clubs, the university administrative halls and the Government-policy cloisters—is in prospect for America; not tomorrow, nor five years from now, but perhaps two decades hence, when the graduates of today's heterogeneous college campuses move into positions of leadership. There looms a requiem for WASPS not as individuals but as the unchallenged ruling class of America. Michael Young, a British sociologist, pointed out a fundamental truth in his delightful spoof, *The Rise of the Meritocracy*, when he said that "for hundreds of years society has been a battleground between two great principles—the principle of selection by family and the principle of selection by merit." The American WASP is no more prone to aid and abet his children than the Jew or the Catholic—we are all loving practitioners of nepotism—but because the WASP held the power reins so long, he was able to scatter his offspring through the Establishment.

Now, the family game is getting tougher. There are a variety of reasons. Among them: 1) The skyrocketing rise of the technocrats. The point is less whether a man is a WASP, Jew, Negro or Slovak, but can he program the computer, can he design that rocket engine, can he concoct that miracle drug? 2) "The coming scramble for executive talent," as Arch Patton terms it in a recent *Harvard Business Review* article. He points to the low birthrate of the 1930s, the recent huge corporate expansion, increasing complexity of management and the need for talent outside industry's traditional boundaries. The demand for brainy bosses, he forecasts, "could reach such boom proportions by 1975 that even the best-managed companies, which have executive talent in considerable depth today, would be unfavorably affected." 3) Political pressures for changes at the top. Voting minorities want "a piece of the action," as one Negro leader says. The law that bans discrimination in employment by companies holding Government contracts has had a tremendous influence. 4) Organized private drives to move ethnic minorities into the executive stream. 5) A belated recognition by many WASP businessmen that Baltzell was right—that they must make room at the top or fade into a powerless caste. David Rockefeller, president of the Chase Manhattan Bank, has become a symbol of the WASP executive who is recruiting and training future executive talent from minority ranks. So has John Howard Laeri of the First National City Bank of New York and president of the American Bankers Association, who is leading the ABA in a program to recruit and train thousands of bank employees and officers from minority groups. "There is no reason today," he says, "why a Negro can't go up the ladder to the top. And we're looking for the kind of men who want to." 6) The swiftly rising aspirations of minorities in a time of immense social flux.

Most important of all is the profound change that has taken place in the student bodies of the great prestige universities, which a few years ago resembled the lawns of WASP country clubs. Then came the hybrid stampede caused by the GI education law after World War II, plus soaring college-entrance rates and the shift of bedeviled admissions officers to selection by merit instead of family ties. The college-board exams became the chief fulcrum for admission. The high school senior and the private prep school senior had to score high or be content to enter Yazoo State instead of Yale. In one generation, student bodies altered drastically. Twenty-five percent of the recent graduates of Ivy League colleges are Jewish. Princeton, once called "the plantation" because of its Southern WASP complexion, now has about 60 Negro undergraduates. Harvard has 170 Negroes in an undergraduate population of 4,800, as against only 20 Negroes just four years ago. The Harvard Business School, elite training ground for future corporate bosses, is now graduating many Jews.

Dollar pressure is helping to crack barriers of the WASP social club. In Kansas City, Mo., last fall, the Kansas City Club admitted two Jews to membership after an organized drive had focused publicity on the exclusionary policies of three downtown clubs: the Kansas City, the River and the University. In the furor, Mayor Ilus Davis confirmed a rumor that Kansas City had been eliminated early as a site contender for a $250,000,000 proton accelerator of the Atomic Energy Commission. Jewish scientists connected with the project did not want to live in a city where they would be barred from the best clubs. In the last few years, Jews have been admitted, however sparingly, to social clubs in many cities, including three clubs in Los Angeles: the University, the Stock Exchange and the Chancery. The door opened at New York's University Club when a Jewish vice president of a corporation was sponsored by his nationally known WASP corporate superior. There was the fear of some members that the mighty corporation might withdraw its patronage should the bid fail. In Chicago, the exclusive Chicago Club now accepts Jewish members on a regular basis, following the cracking of the barrier several years ago. In New York, the boycott of athletic contests sponsored by the New York Athletic Club, which excludes Negroes from membership, became major sports-page news this winter. Our instant communications play subliminally but powerfully on our stereotypes. Thanks to television, millions of people have seen Negro athletes move into near-dominance of major professional sports in the span of a single decade. The magazines have chronicled the emergence of the "chic" Catholic, Jacqueline Bouvier Kennedy and William F. Buckley, Jr. The prototype Jew for the literate masses is the recently retired UN Ambassador, Arthur J. Goldberg.

Prophets, however, still cannot envision just how our predicted multiracial hierarchy will work. Personal trust is the fine glue of commerce and politics. WASP trusts WASP, Jew trusts Jew, etc. How does America operate when the first Jew occupies the White House; a Negro presides at General Motors; a Puerto Rican mayor guides New York City; a Mexican-American is the chief executive officer of Morgan Guaranty Trust Co., and a WASP graduate of Vassar runs the International Ladies' Garment Workers' Union? Nobody really knows.

Only one thing seems sure. "Squaredom," in the words of Digby Baltzell, "will always run the society—any society." By that, he means that tomorrow's leaders will be powered by the same bundle of drives—ambition, status, get-aheadism, success, thrift, progress—as those of today. The Black Nationalist, outnumbered ten to one in color, must don his tie and button-down shirt, or he'll never make it to the executive suite. Unless the hippie learns to handle the computer input, he'll wind up begging for his flower and pot money, and no industrialized nation can tolerate a society of beggars. Only the roaring steel furnaces of Pittsburgh, with their towers of white-collar clerks and executives, can make the land safe—and profitable—for Bob Dylan and Joan Baez. For every guitar, there must be a hot ingot.

And so, even as they sing a requiem for WASPs in the Catholic cathedral, the synagogue and the African M.E. church, they will be chanting the WASP litany—onward corporate soldiers, marching on to work. And a wry prospect it is too—all those free souls trapped forever in our WASP bag.

20. A Woman's Place
ANN DOUBILET

> One important aspect of the differentiation process is the variety of roles it imposes on particular people—roles that are often said to be ascribed (in contrast to those that are termed achieved). An obvious example of an ascribed role—defined as one which is assigned to people regardless of their interest or abilities—is the subordinate role demanded of women in most societies. That such subordination can no longer be tolerated is the central theme of this article by Ann Doubilet, a radical activist in the women's liberation movement.

Throughout the country young women like myself are coming together to fight for liberation. We are questioning our lack of self-fulfillment and are seeking to find the roots of our oppression. We have come to see that the basic problem lies in the roles we play—or are expected to play—as wives and mothers in the family system. It is not only the quality of the role that we question, but the fact that in spite of seemingly unlimited opportunities and new identities, the overwhelming majority of women are performing functional roles that have not changed in over five thousand years.

Even in the most elite of women's colleges where we are supposedly preparing to fulfill our potential, the insidious sex-role ideology is ever-present. We have been socialized to feel that we are not and cannot be whole unless and until we are married and have children. It is not that we feel we are half without a man; we feel less than half.

Advanced industrialized society is making old contradictions even harder to reconcile. Many young women are now educated sufficiently to be economically self-sustaining. In addition, many have become relatively independent of the restrictive values of the families they came from. The possibility of assuming a full and equal role in society seems to be available to increasing numbers of women. But, as it has been well put by

SOURCE: Ann Doubilet, "A Woman's Place," *New Generation* 51 (Fall 1969), 2–8. Reprinted by permission.

Myrna Wood and Cathy McAfee in *Leviathan,* precisely "because they have pushed the democratic myth to its limits, they know concretely how it limits them."

Because women like myself feel these contradictions very personally, we are not only exploring their psychological depths but are beginning to fight for concrete ways to overcome present constrictions in being wives and mothers. Many people in this country have gone far in questioning religious and cultural myths, but questioning the *family* system is still considered tremendously threatening to each of us and to the social order. That is not surprising, because the family plays a very specific economic role in a capitalist society, and questioning it *is* threatening.

First, it stabilizes the working force. In order to provide for his family, a man must "keep his nose to the grindstone." Since the wife is ostensibly denied the role of producer (although many married women work, it is generally considered to be supplementary, not "real" work), she must see to it that her husband stays on his job, no matter how alienating it is. Second, as part of the bargain, if he makes enough money, she can stay home and take good care of the house and serve as coordinator of the family unit's role as consumer. With its overproduction of goods and built-in obsolescence, our economy has a basic need to maintain a structural unit with a socialized need to consume. Third, the family is needed to socialize children to accept the harsh realities they will face in the competitive world, by teaching them to work hard, to "behave" and to conform.

Many young people are beginning to feel that the family doesn't meet their needs and that the historical conditions that gave rise to it no longer exist. The family, according to the classical definition, is a unit which fulfills reproductive, social, economic, emotional and sexual needs. But in an overpopulated world that no longer needs maximum reproduction of the species, where fewer and fewer people are needed to produce more and more goods, and where more and more men and women are breaking out of the family structure for satisfaction of their sexual and emotional needs, the old rationale becomes increasingly hard to justify. And so the "breakdown of the nuclear family" has become a commonplace subject in the mass media today.

And the evidence is quite compelling: One out of every three marriages today terminates in divorce. One out of every five American women, by the time they are 45, have had at least one abortion. With incredible rapidity, sexual relationships outside of marriage are becoming socially acceptable for younger men and women, who are insistent and outspoken about the need to change the existing hypocritical social mores. Older couples are not so outspoken, but the popularity of such dramas as *Peyton Place,* with their emphasis on clandestine adultery, wife-swapping, middle-aged swingers and frustrated, jealous spouses, attests to the universal nature of their discontent.

Single, independent, self-sustaining women do not, in the United

States, have the status of the most dependent woman who is married and has children. There are exceptions to this, but they are just that—exceptions. When people involved in women's liberation try to explain the movement to cynics they are shown sudden respect if they mention that they themselves are married and thus are not frustrated bitches. But other women in the movement, even if they are full professors respected in their fields, are often looked at skeptically by outsiders who wonder just what is wrong with them that they haven't married and had children and therefore "resolved" their lives.

In exploring the problems of women, it is impossible to separate cultural and psychological oppression from economic and material oppression. For example, even though I grew up in relative affluence and went to so-called good schools, I was made to believe that my life would not "really start" until I found the "right guy" and got married. It never occurred to me that I would ever have to define my own life by myself.

There are women, of course, who *are* encouraged to define themselves and perhaps acquire skills, but usually they are urged to do so in order to have something to do before marriage, to supplement their husband's income during marriage, or to have something to fall back on in case of divorce or widowhood or when the children grow up. Although in certain professions women are increasingly being acknowledged as people, they are still the exception. And the sex-role ideology is generally in full control, with "motherhood" at the pinnacle.

As Vicki Pollard wrote in the first issue of *Women: A Journal of Liberation:*

> One of the worst things that happens to a woman when she announces that she is pregnant is that she is congratulated and praised as if she has accomplished the most difficult task in the world. People suddenly look at her in a totally new way. She is seen as being of great worth, possibly for the first time in her life. Women who have been leading active, working lives are made to feel as if only *now* are they finally getting down to the real business of life.

If new economic and social conditions are making us question the roles of wives and mothers as they are still constituted, they are also making it possible for us to explore new possibilities for meaningful lives. (I define meaningful as that which is relevant in a given period.) Thus we are searching for new answers on two levels, in terms of current realities and future possibilities.

For the foreseeable future most of us will continue to get married and have children. Therefore we need to find the means right now that will enable us to do so without the oppressive nature of the typical family structure.

Many people are exploring new forms of living together both within and outside of marriage. In reaction to the isolation of most young couples, communes have sprung up within many ranges of ideology and practice. Increasing numbers of young people see the need to rid themselves of the overindividualistic and privatized nature of American life. They believe that groups of people working together can perhaps unravel the locked-in binds couples often find themselves in.

One possible outcome of group living is the breakdown of the traditional sexual division of labor in regard to housework. And this is also happening among couples not living in communes. Why, many in the women's liberation movement are asking, should the division of labor be such that when the man and woman both work all day, he reads while she cooks, after having rushed to do the shopping on the way home? Then over dinner they discuss the problems of the world and the important jobs they may hold in the liberal establishment or the left movement, fighting discrimination in the world and fighting for social and economic equality. And then *she* does the dishes while he reads. Or, as is beginning to happen more and more, if he shares the chores, why should both he and she feel that he is helping *her* to do *her* work and thus he is deserving of praise and appreciation?

Many men try to laugh off our concern with housework, calling it a trivial concern. But we know it is a very basic one and that full equality for women will not come until all tasks around the house, including child care, are not considered "women's work" and are shared equally by both sexes. Other alternatives that a number of people have recently suggested include the "industrialization of housework," payment to women for their labor in the house, and free and good child-care services. While these are all fine ideas, they are not going to be accomplished for a long time and, furthermore, they still would not eliminate the sex-role division of housework as woman's work; it would just be less time-consuming.

For some reason men in a number of other countries don't seem to resist housework and child care as strenuously as American men. In Sweden, for example, there is a movement to help women take jobs by having men share in all the tasks around the home. Some couples have even gone so far as to entirely reverse the typical roles: she works at a job she loves: he, after quitting a job that bored him, takes care of the house and child in his new role of *hemmaman,* or house-husband.

We are not, however, asking for role reversal but for complete equality. And we are finding ways to attain it. For example, a number of couples have rearranged their lives so that outside work and housework for each are equally divided. One such couple has worked out the following arrangement: he goes to work in the morning, while she takes care of their newborn baby; at noon he comes home and they switch—he cares for the baby and she goes to work. They share equally in the housework, food shopping, etc.

They have not had many problems with this division, although he gets hostile stares from other men in the street when he is shopping in midafternoon with the baby on his back, and he can see that his strange role is very threatening to them. But he feels very strongly that men are generally deprived of being able to take care of children and that there is often tremendous competition between the parents for the love of the child. (A man may feel left out when his child can be quieted only by its mother. He may be jealous of the child and resentful that it is taking up so much of the energy and love of the wife that was previously directed at him.)

The particular couple I have referred to are both professionals, and they emphasize that their arrangement is definitely a class privilege, as it is not often that both parents are sufficiently trained to be able to hold down fairly elite part-time jobs. But they feel that many couples could make similar arrangements if they were willing to give up the financial status that comes with either one or two full-time jobs in the house. However, for themselves, they feel that they have found the best possible interim arrangement until they are able to go on to their next goal—successful communal lives with other families.

Communal life is a long-term goal of many of us in the women's liberation movement. In the meantime if we want children but do not want to be enslaved by the role of mother, we feel we must develop cooperative forms of child care. Many mothers have come into the women's movement out of the sad isolation they have been forced into while taking care of their small children. They are wary of even considering cooperative child care because they have been so inculcated with the romanticism of motherhood that to admit they don't want to take care of their children themselves fills them with guilt.

We are convinced that such facilities would also be in the interests of the children. Our own experience has shown us that children are limited both by their dependence on their parents for love and security and learning experiences and by their parents' dependence on them. Parents hang on to their children as private property because they are often so unfulfilled and frustrated by their own lives that they have to live through their children, and so children grow up feeling guilty about achieving their own independence. Although people understand this well (and many of us have gone and are still going through this struggle), it is crucial to understand how it limits new generations from exploring new possibilities for human growth and development.

Now that we know the lessons of such countries as Sweden and Israel, many of us are working to establish child-care facilities that would involve men as well as women. We too need cooperative child-care facilities run by both men and women because of the enormous divorce rate, which leaves young mothers to bring up their children alone. Children need to be around both male and female adult models, and if there are many different grownups around, it is even better.

One of the problems with the few day-care cooperatives now existing is that they are often limited to women who work part-time. We would like to find ways to help women who work full-time and have to spend half their salaries on baby sitters.

There are also women who would like to work but cannot afford to or, again, feel guilty about not taking care of their babies as they are "supposed" to. In this regard, we have been thinking of ways to put pressure on corporations and factories to provide day-care facilities for the mother or father who works there or for the people in the surrounding community. These centers would be funded by the corporation but controlled by the people whose children are using them and by the people interested in working in them. It is important to emphasize that we want these centers to free women so that choices are opened up for them; we do not want to emulate, for example, the Olivetti Corporation in Italy, where everything is provided for the workers, including day care, in order to make it impractical and almost impossible for them to leave the corporation.

Cooperative child-care facilities would also make it possible for women who do not wish to get married to have children. We must have the right to decide if and when we will have babies. Birth control and abortion are complex questions because, again, it is impossible to separate the economic oppression of having children with no help to take care of them from the psychological brainwashing that women's only real fulfillment is having children. Thus we find many unmarried white women aborting babies they would like to have but can't because they can't afford to raise them alone or bear the psychological stigma, and many married women having children they don't want because they feel they must.

Nevertheless, it is clear that women must have the right to control their own bodies, and that means making free, safe and effective birth control available for those women who want it. At the same time, it should not be used—as it is now—as a form of genocide for black, Puerto Rican and Third World women. Free birth control is now much more readily available for black and brown women in New York City than it is for poor white women.

Free, safe and effective abortions must also be made available to all women who want them. It is possible for rich women to have expensive, safe legal or illegal abortions, but obviously it is not for the poor. Safe abortions are almost entirely ruled out for most black women; very few abortions are performed in city hospitals, although sterilization and forced tube tying is becoming a common practice. Abortion must not be used for population control and genocide.

Across the country, women's liberation groups are concerning themselves with these questions. In Washington, D.C., an alliance of Women's Liberation and welfare mothers has been fighting the unequal treatment under the abortion law and the lack of concern about the problem on the part of the health hierarchy. The two groups became allied through an abortion referral service started by Women's Liberation.

In New York a very large group of women has filed suit against the state to have the abortion law declared unconstitutional. We want this law repealed. [This law was repealed in 1970.—Ed.] We are fighting for our right as women to decide whether or not we will have children, and when. We know that this is our right and should not be decided by male legislators. (Indeed, almost all abortion laws on the books were made before women were given the vote!)

This is just a brief outline of some of the problems the women's movement is working on, but we have come to appreciate that they must be combined with a struggle to change our entire economic system to one which meets the needs of the majority of people, one in which the vast economic and technical resources available are allocated justly and where the control of the wealth of the country is not in the hands of a few.

When we begin to get rid of the superficial structures and mores that limit our lives, then the real problems of self-fulfillment and identity will be exposed. For example, marriage implies a certain ongoing commitment so that the partners don't continually have to ask for a reaffirmation of love. Many manners and structures of society exist so that we won't have to confront the deeper questions of identity. We should begin to explore the nature and content of our relationships and not hide behind the form. Although many of us see the limitations of marriage (formally contracted or not), we still persist in the myth that it will solve all our problems. It is not that marriage itself is necessarily unviable, but that the myth that it is one's salvation is wrong and stultifying. It is form without content. When we begin to look at the content of our relationships we come face to face with the ways in which society pushes us to form our identity.

Women are constantly being forced to please men and to be pleasant and charming and acquiescent. Our passivity is reinforced by men's need to be strong and have power over others in order to feel secure in their own masculinity. We believe that it is part of human nature to require love and that therefore we must discover new ways to give and receive love that let each of us develop our own potential and release our energies rather than being locked in by our needs. We must explore how these needs are developed; how society socializes us into crippling patterns that we then define as "feminine" or "masculine."

Many men, in turn, feel locked in by their masculine roles. They are socialized to keep up a strong front and to hide their feeings ("boys don't cry"), and in many ways they are prevented from exploring themselves and from reaching out to develop close relationships with each other for fear of exposing unallowed internal fears and doubts. Although they are not oppressed by the sex-role division in the same way as women are, and although they enjoy a certain sense of power from these divisions, they too are hampered by our distorted concepts of "masculine" and "feminine" and are not free. It will take strength and unity on the part of women to take away their monopoly on power, but we know that it will benefit both sexes.

Our involvement in the women's movement has given all of us great strength. As women, we hope to have a profound effect on the way in which people will be able to learn to work with each other in a world which is in great need of cooperative effort. In a nonoppressive way we are learning to work together and to help our sisters, and this strength has begun to change the nature of our needs for security and of our affirmation of ourselves as people. We have begun to be less dependent on our men to define us, and thus more able to begin to fight for equality; more able to challenge, confront and explore.

But individual relationships won't change overnight. And in that sense, the struggle is now becoming a political struggle to change the nature of society so that people can develop in a nonoppressive way. We cannot reach liberation in an oppressive society. We won't be able to break down the division of labor between man and woman until we achieve a society where all divisions between people—intellectual vs. laborer, professor vs. student, black vs. white, parent vs. child, farm vs. city, exploiter vs. exploited, those divisions which divide us all—are broken down.

We cannot predict at this point how relationships will look after this struggle, for we know that the history of mankind and womankind is the history of change. We do not imagine or project any ultimate static utopias; each new generation will have to decide for itself what is meaningful. The only constant we can project is permanent revolution.

21. Learning the Student Role: Kindergarten as Academic Boot Camp

HARRY L. GRACEY

A traditionally subordinate role is that ascribed to students. The student is "supposed" to defer to his "betters," i.e., teachers and school administrators. When do students learn this role? asks sociologist Harry Gracey. They learn it very early, he answers; they learn it in their first school experiences, where they quickly find that "knuckling under" to school routines is the efficient way to avoid trouble. Such learning, according to Gracey, is the prime purpose of kindergarten; all the talk about "self-development," "reading readiness," and the like is simply a cover for what amounts to a child's first basic training experience.

SOURCE: Harry L. Gracey, "Learning the Student Role: Kindergarten as Academic Boot Camp," in Dennis H. Wrong and Harry L. Gracey, eds., *Readings in Introductory Sociology* (New York: Macmillan Co., 1968), pp. 287–299. Copyright © 1972 by Macmillan Publishing Co., Inc. Reprinted with permission of Macmillan Publishing Co., Inc.

Kindergarten is generally conceived by educators as a year of preparation for school. It is thought of as a year in which small children, five or six years old, are prepared socially and emotionally for the academic learning which will take place over the next twelve years. It is expected that a foundation of behavior and attitudes will be laid in kindergarten on which the children can acquire the skills and knowledge they will be taught in the grades. A booklet prepared for parents by the staff of a suburban New York school system says that the kindergarten experience will stimulate the child's desire to learn and cultivate the skills he will need for learning in the rest of his school career. It claims that the child will find opportunities for physical growth, for satisfying his "need for self-expression," acquire some knowledge, and provide opportunities for creative activity. It concludes, "The most important benefit that your five-year-old will receive from kindergarten is the opportunity to live and grow happily and purposefully with others in a small society." The kindergarten teachers in one of the elementary schools in this community, one we shall call the Wilbur Wright School, said their goals were to see that the children "grew" in all ways: physically, of course, emotionally, socially, and academically. They said they wanted children to like school as a result of their kindergarten experiences and that they wanted them to learn to get along with others.

None of these goals, however, is unique to kindergarten; each of them is held to some extent by teachers in the other six grades at the Wright School. And growth would occur, but differently, even if the child did not attend school. The children already know how to get along with others, in their families and their play groups. The unique job of the kindergarten in the educational division of labor seems rather to be teaching children the student role. The student role is the repertoire of behavior and attitudes regarded by educators as appropriate to children in school. Observation in the kindergartens of the Wilbur Wright School revealed a great variety of activities through which children are shown and then drilled in the behavior and attitudes defined as appropriate for school and thereby induced to learn the role of student. Observations of the kindergartens and interviews with the teachers both pointed to the teaching and learning of classroom routines as the main element of the student role. The teachers expended most of their efforts, for the first half of the year at least, in training the children to follow the routines which teachers created. The children were, in a very real sense, *drilled* in tasks and activities created by the teachers for their own purposes and beginning and ending quite arbitrarily (from the child's point of view) at the command of the teacher. One teacher remarked that she hated September, because during the first month "everything has to be done rigidly, and repeatedly, until they know exactly what they're supposed to do." However, "by January," she said, "they know exactly what to do [during the day] and I don't have to be after them all the time." Classroom routines were introduced gradually from the beginning of the year in all the kindergartens, and the children were drilled in them as long as was necessary to achieve regular compliance. By the end of the school year, the successful kindergarten teacher has a well-organized group of children. They follow classroom routines automatically, having learned all the command signals and the expected responses to them. They have, in our terms, learned the student role. The following observation shows one such classroom operating at optimum organization on an afternoon late in May. It is the class of an experienced and respected kindergarten teacher.

AN AFTERNOON IN KINDERGARTEN

At about 12:20 in the afternoon on a day in the last week of May, Edith Kerr leaves the teachers' room where she has been having lunch and walks to her classroom at the far end of the primary wing of Wright School. A group of five- and six-year-olds peers at her through the glass doors leading from the hall cloakroom to the play area outside. Entering her room, she straightens some material in the "book corner" of the room, arranges music on the piano, takes colored paper from her closet and places it on one of the shelves under the window. Her room is divided into a number of activity areas through the arrangement of furniture and play equipment. Two easels and a paint table near the door create a kind of passageway inside the room. A wedge-shaped area just inside the front door is made into a teacher's area by the placing of "her" things there: her desk, file, and piano. To the left is the book corner, marked off from the rest of the room by a puppet stage and a movable chalkboard. In it are a display rack of picture books, a record player, and a stack of children's records. To the right of the entrance are the sink and clean-up area. Four large round tables with six chairs at each for the children are placed near the walls about halfway down the length of the room, two on each side, leaving a large open area in the center for group games, block building, and toy truck driving. Windows stretch down the length of both walls, starting about three feet from the floor and extending almost to the high ceilings. Under the windows are long shelves on which are kept all the toys, games, blocks, paper, paints and other equipment of the kindergarten. The left rear corner of the room is a play store with shelves, merchandise, and cash register; the right rear corner is a play kitchen with stove, sink, ironing board, and bassinet with baby dolls in it. This area is partly shielded from the rest of the room by a large standing display rack for posters and children's art work. A sandbox is found against the back wall between these two areas. The room is light, brightly colored and filled with things adults feel five- and six-year-olds will find interesting and pleasing.

At 12:25 Edith opens the outside door and admits the waiting children. They hang their sweaters on hooks outside the door and then go to the center of the room and arrange themselves in a semicircle on the floor, facing the teacher's chair which she has placed in the center of the floor.

Edith follows them in and sits in her chair checking attendance while waiting for the bell to ring. When she has finished attendance, which she takes by sight, she asks the children what the date is, what day and month it is, how many children are enrolled in the class, how many are present, and how many are absent.

The bell rings at 12:30 and the teacher puts away her attendance book. She introduces a visitor, who is sitting against the right wall taking notes, as someone who wants to learn about schools and children. She then goes to the back of the room and takes down a large chart labeled "Helping Hands." Bringing it to the center of the room, she tells the children it is time to change jobs. Each child is assigned some task on the chart by placing his name, lettered on a paper "hand," next to a picture signifying the task—e.g., a broom, a blackboard, a milk bottle, a flag, and a Bible. She asks the children who wants each of the jobs and rearranges their "hands" accordingly. Returning to her chair, Edith announces, "One person should tell us what happened to Mark." A girl raises her hand, and when called on says, "Mark fell and hit his head and had to go to the hospital." The teacher adds that Mark's mother had written saying he was in the hospital.

During this time the children have been interacting among themselves, as well as with Edith. Children have whispered to their neighbors, poked one another, made general comments to the group, waved to friends on the other side of the circle. None of this has been disruptive, and the teacher has ignored it for the most part. The children seem to know just how much of each kind of interaction is permitted—they may greet in a soft voice someone who sits next to them, for example, but may not shout greetings to a friend who sits across the circle, so they confine themselves to waving and remain well within understood limits.

At 12:35 two children arrive. Edith asks them why they are late and then sends them to join the circle on the floor. The other children vie with each other to tell the newcomers what happened to Mark. When this leads to a general disorder Edith asks, "Who has serious time?" The children become quiet and a girl raises her hand. Edith nods and the child gets a Bible and hands it to Edith. She reads the Twenty-third Psalm while the children sit quietly. Edith helps the child in charge begin reciting the Lord's Prayer, the other children follow along for the first unit of sounds, and then trail off as Edith finishes for them. Everyone stands and faces the American flag hung to the right of the door. Edith leads the pledge to the flag, with the children again following the familiar sounds as far as they remember them. Edith then asks the girl in charge what songs she wants and the child replies, "My Country." Edith goes to the piano and plays "America," singing as the children follow her words.

Edith returns to her chair in the center of the room and the children sit again in the semicircle on the floor. It is 12:40 when she tells the children, "Let's have boys' sharing time first." She calls the name of the first boy sitting on the end of the circle, and he comes up to her with a toy helicopter. He turns and holds it up for the other children to see. He says, "It's a helicopter." Edith asks, "What is it used for?" and he replies, "For the army. Carry men. For the war." Other children join in, "For shooting submarines." "To bring back men from space when they are in the ocean." Edith sends the boy back to the circle and asks the next boy if he has something. He replies "No" and she passes on to the next. He says "Yes" and brings a bird's nest to her. He holds it for the class to see, and the teacher asks, "What kind of bird made the nest?" The boy replies, "My friend says a rain bird made it." Edith asks what the nest is made of and different children reply, "mud," "leaves" and "sticks." There is also a bit of moss woven into the nest and Edith tries to describe it to the children. They, however, are more interested in seeing if anything is inside it, and Edith lets the boy carry it around the semicircle showing the children its insides. Edith tells the children of some baby robins in a nest in her yard, and some of the children tell about baby birds they have seen. Some children are asking about a small object in the nest which they say looks like an egg, but all have seen the nest now and Edith calls on the next boy. A number of children say, "I know what Michael has, but I'm not telling." Michael brings a book to the teacher and then goes back to his place in the circle of children. Edith reads the last page of the book to the class. Some children tell of books which they have at home. Edith calls the next boy, and three children call out, "I know what David has." "He always has the same thing." "It's a bang-bang." David goes to his table and gets a box which he brings to Edith. He opens it and shows the teacher a scale-model of an old-fashioned dueling pistol. When David does not turn around to the class, Edith tells him, "Show it to the children," and he does. One child says, "Mr. Johnson [the principal] said no guns." Edith replies, "Yes, how many of you know that?" Most of the children in the circle raise their hands. She continues, "That you aren't supposed to bring guns to school?" She calls the next boy on the circle and he brings two large toy soldiers to her which the children enthusiastically identify as being from "Babes in Toyland." The next boy brings an American flag to Edith and shows it to the class. She asks him what the stars and stripes stand for and admonishes him to treat it carefully. "Why should you treat it carefully?" she asks the boy. "Because it's our flag," he replies. She congratulates him, saying, "That's right."

"Show and Tell" lasted twenty minutes and during the last ten one girl in particular announced that she knew what each child called upon had to show. Edith asked her to be quiet each time she spoke out, but she was not content, continuing to offer her comment at each "show." Four children from other classes had come into the room to bring something from another teacher or to ask for something from Edith. Those with requests were asked to return later if the item wasn't readily available.

Edith now asks if any of the children told their mothers about their trip to the local zoo the previous day. Many children raise their hands. As Edith calls on them, they tell what they liked in the zoo. Some children cannot wait to be called on, and they call out things to the teacher, who asks them to be quiet. After a few of the animals are mentioned, one child says, "I liked the spooky house," and the others chime in to agree with him, some pantomiming fear and horror. Edith is puzzled, and asks what this was. When half the children try to tell her at once, she raises her hand for quiet, then calls on individual children. One says, "The house with nobody in it"; another, "The dark little house." Edith asks where it was in the zoo, but the children cannot describe its location in any way which she can understand. Edith makes some jokes but they involve adult abstractions which the children cannot grasp. The children have become quite noisy now, speaking out to make both relevant and irrelevant comments, and three little girls have become particularly assertive.

Edith gets up from her seat at 1:10 and goes to the book corner, where she puts a record on the player. As it begins a story about the trip to the zoo, she returns to the circle and asks the children to go sit at the tables. She divides them among the tables in such a way as to indicate that they don't have regular seats. When the children are all seated at the four tables, five or six to a table, the teacher asks, "Who wants to be the first one?" One of the noisy girls comes to the center of the room. The voice on the record is giving directions for imitating an ostrich and the girl follows them, walking around the center of the room holding her ankles with her hands. Edith replays the record, and all the children, table by table, imitate ostriches down the center of the room and back. Edith removes her shoes and shows that she can be an ostrich too. This is apparently a familiar game, for a number of children are calling out, "Can we have the crab?" Edith asks one of the children to do a crab "so we can all remember how," and then plays the part of the record with music for imitating crabs by. The children from the first table line up across the room, hands and feet on the floor and faces pointing toward the ceiling. After they have "walked" down the room and back in this posture they sit at their table and the children of the next table play "crab." The children love this; they run from their tables, dance about on the floor waiting for their turns and are generally exuberant. Children ask for the "inch worm" and the game is played again with the children squirming down the floor. As a conclusion Edith shows them a new animal imitation, the "lame dog." The children all hobble down the floor, table by table, to the accompaniment of the record.

At 1:30 Edith has the children line up in the center of the room; she says, "Table one, line up in front of me," and children ask, "What are we going to do?" Then she moves a few steps to the side and says, "Table two over here, line up next to table one," and more children ask, "What for?" She does this for table three and table four and each time the children ask, "Why, what are we going to do?" When the children are lined up in four lines of five each, spaced so that they are not touching one another, Edith puts on a new record and leads the class in calisthenics, to the accompaniment of the record. The children just jump around every which way in their places instead of doing the exercises, and by the time the record is finished, Edith, the only one following it, seems exhausted. She is apparently adopting the President's new "Physical Fitness" program in her classroom.

At 1:35 Edith pulls her chair to the easels and calls the children to sit on the floor in front of her, table by table. When they are all seated she asks, "What are you going to do for worktime today?" Different children raise their hands and tell Edith what they are going to draw. Most are going to make pictures of animals they saw in the zoo. Edith asks if they want to make pictures to send to Mark in the hospital, and the children agree to this. Edith gives drawing paper to the children, calling them to her one by one. After getting a piece of paper, the children go to the crayon box on the right-hand shelves, select a number of colors, and go to the tables, where they begin drawing. Edith is again trying to quiet the perpetually talking girls. She keeps two of them standing by her so they won't disrupt the others. She asks them, "Why do you feel you have to talk all the time," and then scolds them for not listening to her. Then she sends them to their tables to draw.

Most of the children are drawing at their tables, sitting or kneeling in their chairs. They are all working very industriously and, engrossed in their work, very quietly. Three girls have chosen to paint at the easels, and having donned their smocks, they are busily mixing colors and intently applying them to their pictures. If the children at the tables are primitives and neo-realists in their animal depictions, these girls at the easels are the class abstract-expressionists, with their broad-stroked, colorful paintings.

Edith asks of the children generally, "What color should I make the cover of Mark's book?" Brown and green are suggested by some children "because Mark likes them." The other children are puzzled as to just what is going on and ask, "What book?" or "What does she mean?" Edith explains what she thought was clear to them already, that they are all going to put their pictures together in a "book" to be sent to Mark. She goes to a small table in the play-kitchen corner and tells the children to bring her their pictures when they are finished and she will write their message for Mark on them.

By 1:50 most children have finished their pictures and given them to Edith. She talks with some of them as she ties the bundle of pictures together—answering questions, listening, carrying on conversations. The children are playing in various parts of the room with toys, games and blocks which they have taken off the shelves. They also move from table to table examining each other's pictures, offering compliments and suggestions. Three girls at a table are cutting up colored paper for a collage. Another girl is walking about the room in a pair of high heels with a woman's purse over her arm. Three boys are playing in the center of the room with the large block set, with which they are building walk-ways and walking on them. Edith is very much concerned about their safety and comes over a number of times to fuss over them. Two or three other boys are driving trucks around the center of the room, and mild altercations occur when they drive through the block constructions. Some boys and girls are playing at the toy store, two girls are serving "tea" in the play kitchen and one is washing a doll baby. Two boys have elected to clean the room, and with large sponges they wash the movable blackboard, the puppet stage, and then begin on the tables. They run into resistance from the children who are working with construction toys on the tables and do not want to dismantle their structures. The class is like a room full of bees, each intent on pursuing some activity, occasionally bumping into one another, but just veering off in another direction without serious altercation. At 2:05 the custodian arrives pushing a cart loaded with half-pint milk containers. He places a tray of cartons on the counter next to the sink, then leaves. His coming and going is unnoticed in the room (as, incidentally, is the presence of the observer, who is completely ignored by the children for the entire afternoon).

At 2:15 Edith walks to the entrance of the room, switches off the lights, and sits at the piano and plays. The children begin spontaneously singing the song, which is "Clean up, clean up. Everybody clean up." Edith walks around the room supervising the clean-up. Some children put their toys, the blocks, puzzles, games, and so on back on their shelves under the windows. The children making a collage keep right on working. A child from another class comes in to borrow the 45-rpm adaptor for the record player. At more urging from Edith the rest of the children shelve their toys and work. The children are sitting around their tables now and Edith asks, "What record would you like to hear while you have your milk?" There is some confusion and no general consensus, so Edith drops the subject and begins to call the children, table by table, to come get their milk. "Table one," she says, and the five children come to the sink, wash their hands and dry them, pick up a carton of milk and a straw, and take it back to their table. Two talking girls wander about the room interfering with the children getting their milk and Edith calls out to them to "settle down." As the children sit many of them call out to Edith the name of the record they want to hear. When all the children are seated at tables with milk, Edith plays one of these records called "Bozo and the Birds" and shows the children pictures in a book which go with the record. The record recites, and the book shows the adventures of a clown, Bozo, as he walks through a woods meeting many different kinds of birds who, of course, display the characteristics of many kinds of people or, more accurately, different stereotypes. As children finish their milk they take blankets or pads from the shelves under the windows and lie on them in the center of the room, where Edith sits on her chair showing the pictures. By 2:30 half the class is lying on the floor on their blankets, the record is still playing and the teacher is turning the pages of the book. The child who came in previously returns the 45-rpm adaptor, and one of the kindergarteners tells Edith what the boy's name is and where he lives.

The record ends at 2:40. Edith says, "Children, down on your blankets."

All the class is lying on blankets now. Edith refuses to answer the various questions individual children put to her because, she tells them, "it's rest time now." Instead she talks very softly about what they will do tomorrow. They are going to work with clay, she says. The children lie quietly and listen. One of the boys raises his hand and when called on tells Edith, "The animals in the zoo looked so hungry yesterday." Edith asks the children what they think about this and a number try to volunteer opinions, but Edith accepts only those offered in a "rest-time tone," that is, softly and quietly. After a brief discussion of animal feeding, Edith calls the names of the two children on milk detail and has them collect empty milk cartons from the tables and return them to the tray. She asks the two children on clean-up detail to clean up the room. Then she gets up from her chair and goes to the door to turn on the lights. At this signal the children all get up from the floor and return their blankets and pads to the shelf. It is raining (the reason for no outside play this afternoon) and cars driven by mothers clog the school drive and line up along the street. One of the talkative little girls comes over to Edith and pointing out the window says, "Mrs. Kerr, see my mother in the new Cadillac?"

At 2:50 Edith sits at the piano and plays. The children sit on the floor in the center of the room and sing. They have a repertoire of songs about animals, including one in which each child sings a refrain alone. They know these by heart and sing along through the ringing of the 2:55 bell. When the song is finished, Edith gets up and coming to the group says, "Okay, rhyming words to get your coats today." The children raise their hands and as Edith calls on them, they tell her two rhyming words, after which they are allowed to go into the hall to get their coats and sweaters. They return to the room with these and sit at their tables. At 2:59 Edith says, "When you have your coats on, you may line up at the door." Half of the children go to the door and stand in a long line. When the three o'clock bell rings, Edith returns to the piano and plays. The children sing a song called "Goodbye," after which Edith sends them out.

TRAINING FOR LEARNING AND FOR LIFE

The day in kindergarten at Wright School illustrates both the content of the student role as it has been learned by these children and the processes by which the teacher has brought about this learning, or, "taught" them the student role. The children have learned to go through routines and to follow orders with unquestioning obedience, even when these make no sense to them. They have been disciplined to do as they are told by an authoritative person without significant protest. Edith has developed this discipline in the children by creating and enforcing a rigid social structure in the classroom through which she effectively controls the behavior of most of the children for most of the school day. The "living with others in a small society" which the school pamphlet tells parents is the most important thing the children will learn in kindergarten can be seen now in its operational meaning, which is learning to live by the routines imposed by the school. This learning appears to be the principal content of the student role.

Children who submit to school-imposed discipline and come to identify with it, so that being a "good student" comes to be an important part of their developing identities, *become* the good students by the school's definitions. Those who submit to the routines of the school but do not come to identify with them will be adequate students who find the more important part of their identities elsewhere, such as in the play group outside school. Children who refuse to submit to the school routines are rebels, who become known as "bad students" and often "problem children" in the school, for they do not learn the academic curriculum and their behavior is often disruptive in the classroom. Today schools engage clinical psychologists in part to help teachers deal with such children.

In looking at Edith's kindergarten at Wright School, it is interesting to ask how the children learn this role of student—come to accept school-imposed routines—and what, exactly, it involves in terms of behavior and attitudes. The most prominent features of the classroom are its physical and social structures. The room is carefully furnished and arranged in ways adults feel will interest children. The play store and play kitchen in the back of the room, for example, imply that children are interested in mimicking these activities of the adult world. The only space left for the children to create something of their own is the empty center of the room, and the materials at their disposal are the blocks, whose use causes anxiety on the part of the teacher. The room, being carefully organized physically by the adults, leaves little room for the creation of physical organization on the part of the children.

The social structure created by Edith is a far more powerful and subtle force for fitting the children to the student role. This structure is established by the very rigid and tightly controlled set of rituals and routines through which the children are put during the day. There is first the rigid "locating procedure" in which the children are asked to find themselves in terms of the month, date, day of the week, and the number of the class who are present and absent. This puts them solidly in the real world as defined by adults. The day is then divided into six periods whose activities are for the most part determined by the teacher. In Edith's kindergarten the children went through Serious Time, which opens the school day, Sharing Time, Play Time (which in clear weather would be spent outside), Work Time, Clean-up Time, after which they have their milk, and Rest Time, after which they go home. The teacher has programmed activities for each of these Times.

Occasionally the class is allowed limited discretion to choose between proffered activities, such as stories or records, but original ideas for activities are never solicited from them. Opportunity for free individual action is open only once in the day, during the part of Work Time left after the general class assignment has been completed (on the day reported the class assignment was drawing animal pictures for the absent Mark). Spontaneous interests or observations from the children are never developed by the teacher. It seems that her schedule just does not allow room for developing such unplanned events. During Sharing Time, for example, the child who brought a bird's nest told Edith, in reply to her question of what kind of bird made it, "My friend says it's a rain bird." Edith does not think to ask about this bird, probably because the answer is "childish," that is, not given in accepted adult categories of birds. The children then express great interest in an object in the nest, but the teacher ignores this interest, probably because the object is uninteresting to her. The soldiers from "Babes in Toyland" strike a responsive note in the children, but this is not used for a discussion of any kind. The soldiers are treated in the same way as objects which bring little interest from the children. Finally, at the end of Sharing Time the child-world of perception literally erupts in the class with the recollection of "the spooky house" at the zoo. Apparently this made more of an impression on the children than did any of the animals, but Edith is unable to make any sense of it for herself. The tightly imposed order of the class begins to break down as the children discover a universe of discourse of their own and begin talking excitedly with one another. The teacher is effectively excluded from this child's world of perception and for a moment she fails to dominate the classroom situation. She reasserts control, however, by taking the children to the next activity she has planned for the day. It seems never to have occurred to Edith that there might be a meaningful learning experience for the children in re-creating the "spooky house" in the classroom. It seems fair to say that this would have offered an exercise in spontaneous self-expression and an opportunity for real creativity on the part of the children. Instead, they are taken through a canned animal imitation procedure, an activity which they apparently enjoy, but which is also imposed upon them rather than created by them.

While children's perceptions of the world and opportunities for genuine spontaneity and creativity are being systematically eliminated from the kindergarten, unquestioned obedience to authority and rote learning of meaningless material are being encouraged. When the children are called to line up in the center of the room they ask "Why?" and "What for?" as they are in the very process of complying. They have learned to go smoothly through a programmed day, regardless of whether parts of the program make any sense to them or not. Here the student role involves what might be called "doing what you're told and never mind why." Activities which might "make sense" to the children are effectively ruled out and they are forced or induced to participate in activities which may be "senseless," such as the calisthenics.

At the same time the children are being taught by rote meaningless sounds in the ritual oaths and songs, such as the Lord's Prayer, the Pledge to the Flag, and "America." As they go through the grades children learn more and more of the sounds of these ritual oaths, but the fact that they have often learned meaningless sounds rather than meaningful statements is shown when they are asked to write these out in the sixth grade; they write them as groups of sounds rather than as a series of words, according to the sixth-grade teachers at Wright School. Probably much learning in the elementary grades is of this character, that is, having no intrinsic meaning to the children, but rather being tasks inexplicably required of them by authoritative adults. Listening to sixth-grade children read social studies reports, for example, in which they have copied material from encyclopedias about a particular country, an observer often gets the feeling that he is watching an activity which has no intrinsic meaning for the child. The child who reads, "Switzerland grows wheat and cows and grass and makes a lot of cheese" knows the dictionary meaning of each of these words but may very well have no conception at all of this "thing" called Switzerland. He is simply carrying out a task assigned by the teacher *because* it is assigned, and this may be its only "meaning" for him.

Another type of learning which takes place in kindergarten is seen in children who take advantage of the "holes" in the adult social structure to create activities of their own, during Work Time or out-of-doors during Play Time. Here the children are learning to carve out a small world of their own within the world created by adults. They very quickly learn that if they keep within permissible limits of noise and action they can play much as they please. Small groups of children formed during the year in Edith's kindergarten who played together at these times, developing semi-independent little groups in which they created their own worlds in the interstices of the adult-imposed physical and social world. These groups remind the sociological observer very much of the so-called "informal groups" which adults develop in factories and offices of large bureaucracies.[1] Here too, within authoritatively imposed social organizations people find "holes" to create little sub-worlds which support informal, friendly, nonofficial behavior. Forming and participating in such groups seem to be as much part of the student role as it is of the role of bureaucrat.

The kindergarten has been conceived of here as the year in which children are prepared for their schooling by learning the role of student. In the classrooms of the rest of the school grades, the children will be asked to submit to systems and routines imposed by the teachers and the curriculum. The days will be much like those of kindergarten, except that academic subjects will be substituted for the activities of the kindergarten. Once out of the school system, young adults will more than likely find themselves working in large-scale bureaucratic organizations, perhaps on the assembly line in the factory, perhaps in the paper routines of the white collar occupations, where they will be required to submit to rigid routines imposed by "the company" which may make little sense to them. Those who can operate well in this situation will be successful bureaucratic functionaries. Kindergarten, therefore, can be seen as preparing children not only for participation in the bureaucratic organization of large modern school systems, but also for the large-scale occupational bureaucracies of modern society.

NOTES

1. See, for example, Peter M. Blau, *Bureaucracy in Modern Society* (New York: Random House, 1956), Chapter 3.

22. "The Lower Classes Smell"
GEORGE ORWELL

George Orwell is best known for his prophetic fictional works, Nineteen Eighty-Four *and* Animal Farm. *But he was also a noted essayist. The following selection is taken from a book that attempts to demonstrate the intolerable conditions under which British coal miners work and live. Incidental to this purpose, Orwell used the satiric part-title, "The Lower Classes Smell," to call attention to the elitist attitudes which are cultivated in their children by parents who want to believe they are superior to those whom they regard as "common as dirt."*

. . .

I was born into what you might describe as the lower-upper-middle class. The upper-middle class, which had its heyday in the 'eighties and 'nineties, with Kipling as its poet laureate, was a sort of mound of wreckage left behind when the tide of Victorian prosperity receded. Or perhaps it would be better to change the metaphor and describe it not as a mound but as a layer—the layer of society lying between £2,000 and £300 a year: my own family was not far from the bottom. You notice that I define it in terms of money, because that is always the quickest way of making yourself understood. Nevertheless, the essential point about the English class-system is that it is *not* entirely explicable in terms of money. Roughly speaking it is a money-stratification, but it is also interpenetrated by a sort of shadowy caste-system; rather like a jerry-built modern bungalow haunted by medieval ghosts. Hence the fact that the upper-middle class extends or extended to incomes as low as £300 a year—to incomes, that is,

SOURCE: George Orwell, *The Road to Wigan Pier* (New York: Harcourt, Brace and Company, 1958), pp. 153–163. Reprinted by permission of Harcourt Brace Jovanovich, Inc., Mrs. Sonia Brownell Orwell, and Secker & Warburg.

much lower than those of merely middle-class people with no social pretensions. Probably there are countries where you can predict a man's opinions from his income, but it is never quite safe to do so in England; you have always got to take his traditions into consideration as well. A naval officer and his grocer very likely have the same income, but they are not equivalent persons and they would only be on the same side in very large issues such as a war or a general strike—possibly not even then.

Of course it is obvious now that the upper-middle class is done for. In every country town in Southern England, not to mention the dreary wastes of Kensington and Earl's Court, those who knew it in the days of its glory, are dying, vaguely embittered by a world which has not behaved as it ought. I never open one of Kipling's books or go into one of the huge dull shops which were once the favourite haunt of the upper-middle class, without thinking "Change and decay in all around I see." But before the war [i.e. World War I—Ed.] the upper-middle class, though already none too prosperous, still felt sure of itself. Before the war you were either a gentleman or not a gentleman, and if you were a gentleman you struggled to behave as such, whatever your income might be. Between those with £400 a year and those with £2,000 or even £1,000 a year there was a great gulf fixed, but it was a gulf which those with £400 a year did their best to ignore. Probably the distinguishing mark of the upper-middle class was that its traditions were not to any extent commercial, but mainly military, official, and professional. People in this class owned no land, but they felt that they were landowners in the sight of God and kept up a semi-aristocratic outlook by going into the professions and the fighting services rather than into trade. Small boys used to count the plum stones on their plates and foretell their destiny by chanting "Army, Navy, Church, Medicine, Law"; and even of these "Medicine" was faintly inferior to the others and only put in for the sake of symmetry. To belong to this class when you were at the £400 a year level was a queer business, for it meant that your gentility was almost purely theoretical. You lived, so to speak, at two levels simultaneously. Theoretically you knew all about servants and how to tip them, although in practice you had one or, at most, two resident servants. Theoretically you knew how to wear your clothes and how to order a dinner, although in practice you could never afford to go to a decent tailor or a decent restaurant. Theoretically you knew how to shoot and ride, although in practice you had no horses to ride and not an inch of ground to shoot over. It was this that explained the attraction of India (more recently Kenya, Nigeria, etc.) for the lower-upper-middle class. The people who went there as soldiers and officials did not go there to make money, for a soldier or an official does not make money; they went there because in India, with cheap horses, free shooting, and hordes of black servants, it was so easy to play at being a gentleman.

In the kind of shabby-genteel family that I am talking about there is far more *consciousness* of poverty than in any working-class family above the level of the dole. Rent and clothes and school-bills are an unending nightmare, and every luxury, even a glass of beer, is an unwarrantable extravagance. Practically the whole family income goes in keeping up appearances. It is obvious that people of this kind are in an anomalous position, and one might be tempted to write them off as mere exceptions and therefore unimportant. Actually, however, they are or were fairly numerous. Most clergymen and schoolmasters, for instance, nearly all Anglo-Indian officials, a sprinkling of soldiers and sailors and a fair number of professional men and artists, fall into this category. But the real importance of this class is that they are the shock-absorbers of the bourgeoisie. The real bourgeoisie, those in the £2,000 a year class and over, have their money as a thick layer of padding between themselves and the class they plunder; in so far as they are aware of the Lower Orders at all they are aware of them as employees, servants and tradesmen. But it is quite different for the poor devils lower down who are struggling to live genteel lives on what are virtually working-class incomes. These last are forced into close and, in a sense, intimate contact with the working class, and I suspect it is from them that the traditional upper-class attitude towards "common" people is derived.

And what is this attitude? An attitude of sniggering superiority punctuated by bursts of vicious hatred. Look at any number of *Punch* during the past thirty years. You will find it everywhere taken for granted that a working-class person, as such, is a figure of fun, except at odd moments when he shows signs of being too prosperous, whereupon he ceases to be a figure of fun and become a demon. It is no use wasting breath in denouncing this attitude. It is better to consider how it has arisen, and to do that one has got to realise what the working classes look like to those who live among them but have different habits and traditions.

A shabby-genteel family is in much the same position as a family of "poor whites" living in a street where everyone else is a Negro. In such circumstances you have got to cling to your gentility because it is the only thing you have; and meanwhile you are hated for your stuck-up-ness and for the accent and manners which stamp you as one of the boss class. I was very young, not much more than six, when I first became aware of class-distinctions. Before that age my chief heroes had generally been working-class people, because they always seemed to do such interesting things, such as being fishermen and blacksmiths and bricklayers. I remember the farm hands on a farm in Cornwall who used to let me ride on the drill when they were sowing turnips and would sometimes catch the ewes and milk them to give me a drink; and the workmen building the new house next door, who let me play with the wet mortar and from whom I first learned the word "b———"; and the plumber up the road with whose children I used to go out birdnesting. But it was not long before I was forbidden to play with the plumber's children; they were "common" and I was told to keep away from them. This was snobbish, if you like, but it was also necessary, for middle-class people cannot afford to let their children grow up with vulgar accents. So, very early, the working class ceased to be a race of friendly and wonderful beings and became a race of enemies. We realised that they hated us, but we could never understand why, and we naturally set it down to pure, vicious malignity. To me in my early boyhood, to nearly all children of families like mine, "common" people seemed almost sub-human. They had coarse faces, hideous accents and gross manners, they hated everyone who was not like themselves, and if they got half a chance they would insult you in brutal ways. That was our view of them, and though it was false it was understandable. For one must remember that before the war there was much more *overt* class-hatred in England than there is now. In those days you were quite likely to be insulted simply for looking like a member of the upper classes; nowadays, on the other hand, you are more likely to be fawned upon. Anyone over thirty can remember the time when it was impossible for a well-dressed person to walk through a slum street without being hooted at. Whole quarters of big towns were considered unsafe because of "hooligans" (now almost an extinct type), and the London gutter-boy everywhere, with his loud voice and lack of intellectual scruples, could make life a misery for people who considered it beneath their dignity to answer back. A recurrent terror of my holidays, when I was a small boy, was the gangs of "cads" who were liable to set upon you five or ten to one. In term time, on the other hand, it was we who were in the majority and the "cads" who were oppressed; I remember a couple of savage mass-battles in the cold winter of 1916–17. And this tradition of open hostility between upper and lower class had apparently been the same for at least a century past. A typical joke in *Punch* in the 'sixties is a picture of a small, nervous-looking gentleman riding through a slum street and a crowd of street-boys closing in on him with shouts of " 'Ere comes a swell! Let's frighten 'is 'oss!" Just fancy the street boys trying to frighten his horse now! They would be much likelier to hang round him in vague hopes of a tip. During the past dozen years the English working class have grown servile with a rather horrifying rapidity. It was bound to happen, for the frightful weapon of unemployment has cowed them. Before the war their economic position was comparatively strong, for though there was no dole to fall back upon, there was not much unemployment, and the power of the boss class was not so obvious as it is now. A man did not see ruin staring him in the face every time he cheeked a "toff," and naturally he did cheek a "toff" whenever it seemed safe to do so. G. J. Renier, in his book on Oscar Wilde, points out that the strange, obscene bursts of popular fury which followed the Wilde trial was essentially social in character. The London mob had caught a member of the upper classes on the hop, and they took care to keep him hopping. All this was natural and even proper. If you treat people as the English working class have been treated during the past two centuries, you must expect them to resent it. On the other hand the children of shabby-genteel families could not be blamed if they grew up with a hatred of the working class, typified for them by prowling gangs of "cads."

But there was another and more serious difficulty. Here you come to the real secret of class distinctions in the West—the real reason why a European of bourgeois upbringing, even when he calls himself a Communist, cannot without a hard effort think of a working man as his equal. It is summed up in four frightful words which people nowadays are chary of uttering, but which were bandied about quite freely in my childhood. The words were: *The lower classes smell.*

That was what we were taught—*the lower classes smell.* And here, obviously, you are at an impassable barrier. For no feeling of like or dislike is quite so fundamental as a *physical* feeling. Race-hatred, religious hatred, differences of education, of temperament, of intellect, even differences of moral code, can be got over; but physical repulsion cannot. You can have an affection for a murderer or a sodomite, but you cannot have an affection for a man whose breath stinks—habitually stinks, I mean. However well you may wish him, however much you may admire his mind and character, if his breath stinks he is horrible and in your heart of hearts you will hate him. It may not greatly matter if the average middle-class person is brought up to believe that the working classes are ignorant, lazy, drunken, boorish and dishonest; it is when he is brought up to believe that they are dirty that the harm is done. And in my childhood we *were* brought up to believe that they were dirty. Very early in life you acquired the idea that there was something subtly repulsive about a working-class body; you would not get nearer to it than you could help. You watched a great sweaty navvy walking down the road with his pick over his shoulder; you looked at his discoloured shirt and his corduroy trousers stiff with the dirt of a decade; you thought of those nests and layers of greasy rags below, and, under all, the unwashed body, brown all over (that was how I used to imagine it), with its strong, bacon-like reek. You watched a tramp taking off his boots in a ditch—ugh! It did not seriously occur to you that the tramp might not enjoy having black feet. And even "lower-class" people whom you knew to be quite clean—servants, for instance—were faintly unappetising. The smell of their sweat, the very texture of their skins, were mysteriously different from yours.

Everyone who has grown up pronouncing his aitches and in a house with a bathroom and one servant is likely to have grown up with these feelings; hence the chasmic, impassable quality of class-distinctions in the West. It is queer how seldom this is admitted. At the moment I can think of only one book where it is set forth without humbug, and that is Mr. Somerset Maugham's *On a Chinese Screen.* Mr. Maugham describes a high Chinese official arriving at a wayside inn and blustering and calling everybody names in order to impress upon them that he is a supreme dignitary and they are only worms. Five minutes later, having asserted his dignity in the way he thinks proper, he is eating his dinner in perfect amity with the baggage coolies. As an official he feels that he has got to make his presence felt, but he has no feeling that the coolies are of different clay from himself. I have observed countless similar scenes in Burma.

Among Mongolians—among all Asiatics, for all I know—there is a sort of natural equality, an easy intimacy between man and man, which is simply unthinkable in the West. Mr. Maugham adds:

> In the West we are divided from our fellows by our sense of smell. The working man is our master, inclined to rule us with an iron hand, but it cannot be denied that he stinks: none can wonder at it, for a bath in the dawn when you have to hurry to your work before the factory bell rings is no pleasant thing, nor does heavy labour tend to sweetness; and you do not change your linen more than you can help when the week's washing must be done by a sharp-tongued wife. I do not blame the working man because he stinks, but stink he does. It makes social intercourse difficult to persons of sensitive nostril. The matutinal tub divides the classes more effectually than birth, wealth or education.

Meanwhile, *do* the "lower classes" smell? Of course, as a whole, they are dirtier than the upper classes. They are bound to be, considering the circumstances in which they live, for even at this late date less than half the houses in England have bathrooms. Besides, the habit of washing yourself all over every day is a very recent one in Europe, and the working classes are generally more conservative than the bourgeoisie. But the English are growing visibly cleaner, and we may hope that in a hundred years they will be almost as clean as the Japanese. It is a pity that those who idealise the working class so often think it necessary to praise every working-class characteristic and therefore to pretend that dirtiness is somehow meritorious in itself. Here, curiously enough, the Socialist and the sentimental democratic Catholic of the type of Chesterton sometimes join hands; both will tell you that dirtiness is healthy and "natural" and cleanliness is a mere fad or at best a luxury.[1] They seem not to see that they are merely giving colour to the notion that working-class people are dirty from choice and not from necessity. Actually, people who have access to a bath will generally use it. But the essential thing is that middle-class people *believe* that the working class are dirty—you see from the passage quoted above that Mr. Maugham himself believes it—and, what is worse, that they are somehow *inherently* dirty. As a child, one of the most dreadful things I could imagine was to drink out of a bottle after a navvy. Once when I was thirteen, I was in a train coming from a market town, and the third-class carriage was packed full of shepherds and pigmen who had been selling their beasts. Somebody produced a quart bottle of beer and passed it round; it travelled from mouth to mouth to mouth, everyone taking a swig. I cannot describe the horror I felt as that bottle worked its way towards me. If I drank from it after all those lower-class male mouths I felt certain I should vomit; on the other hand, if they offered it to me I dared not refuse for fear of offending them—you see here how the middle-class squeamishness works both ways. Nowadays, thank God, I have no feelings of that kind. A working-man's body, as such, is no more repulsive to me than a millionaire's. I still don't like drinking out of a cup or bottle after another person—another man, I mean: with women I don't mind—but at least the question of class does not enter. It was rubbing shoulders with the tramps that cured me of it. Tramps are not really very dirty as English people go, but they have the name for being dirty, and when you have shared a bed with a tramp and drunk tea out of the same snuff-tin, you feel that you have seen the worst and the worst has no terrors for you.

I have dwelt on these subjects because they are vitally important. To get rid of class-distinctions you have got to start by understanding how one class appears when seen through the eyes of another. It is useless to say that the middle classes are "snobbish" and leave it at that. You get no further if you do not realise that snobbishness is bound up with a species of idealism. It derives from the early training in which a middle-class child is taught almost simultaneously to wash his neck, to be ready to die for his country, and to despise the "lower classes."

. . .

NOTES

1. According to Chesterton, dirtiness is merely a kind of "discomfort" and therefore ranks as self-mortification. Unfortunately, the discomfort of dirtiness is chiefly suffered by other people. It is not really very uncomfortable to be dirty—not nearly so uncomfortable as having a cold bath on a winter morning.

Social Stratification in the United States

Part VI

The social classes resulting from the differentiation process, discussed in Part V, are the central structural elements of the social stratification system found in Western societies. The American stratification system is typical in the sense that it has produced dominant and subordinate groupings. At the same time, one prominent American value has been the commitment to equalitarianism. The contrast between these two features of the system—equalitarianism on one hand, and on the other, the various classes with sharply different access to power and privilege—leads to structural strain that probably cannot be endured indefinitely. Aspects of these features, and strains in the American stratification system, are explored in the four readings that follow.

23. A Flawed Humanism
RICHARD SENNETT AND JONATHAN COBB

Inspired by European humanists of the seventeenth- and eighteenth-century period of Enlightenment, American revolutionary leaders asserted in the Declaration of Independence that all persons are born equal. Idealistically, they believed that such essential equality must lead eventually to broad social equality. Obviously it has not. The reason, Sennett and Cobb believe, is that the humanism of the Enlightenment was a "flawed" phenomenon, and that which it spawned—the American value system, for example—has a fatal defect. The defect is as follows: Enlightenment humanists, and Americans since, believed that because all are born equal, inequality after birth must be due to a lack of personal drive; therefore, inequality among adults is not arbitrary. Such logic provides an elaborate defense of the established order for those who benefit from the differential distribution of the means to well-being. The answer, say Sennett and Cobb, is to cultivate the idea that all people should be respected simply for being human, rather than for what they do. As things stand now, in American society particularly, we stress accomplishment. "What do you do?" we ask new acquaintances, evidencing our commitment to a system that leads inevitably to injustice and exploitation.

In a letter to a friend, Madame de Sévigné writes about a hanging she witnessed one morning. It was striking, she records, to see the condemned man trembling during the preliminaries of the execution, when he was only a common peasant. He groaned and wailed incessantly, causing some amusement among the ladies and gentlemen come to see the spec-

SOURCE: Richard Sennett and Jonathan Cobb, *The Hidden Injuries of Class* (New York: Alfred A. Knopf, 1972), pp. 246–7, 251–6. Copyright © 1972 by Richard Sennett and Jonathan Cobb. Reprinted by permission of Alfred A. Knopf, Inc.

tacle; once hoisted up, his body wriggling in the noose, he presented, Madame de Sévigné remarked, a most remarkable sight.

The modern reader feels only horror at the callousness of this description. Yet Madame de Sévigné was not a vicious woman by the standards of the late seventeenth century. She, like other aristocrats of her circle, could view hangings with disinterested fascination, because the person being killed was a creature whose inner nature had little relation to her own. As good Christians, the highborn had of course to believe that all men were equal in the sight of God, but fortunately He had not gone to the extreme of demanding that they look at things among themselves in quite the same way. When the word "caste" is applied to the *ancien régime* in Europe, it refers, beyond all barriers of custom and hereditary right, to the notion that people of different social stations belong to different species, that the humanity or worthiness of a duchess has little relationship to the kind of humanity accessible to the common peasant. The corollary—explicitly stated in another letter of Madame de Sévigné's—is that the "humbling" of inferiors is necessary to the maintenance of social order.

At the end of Madame de Sévigné's generation, a small but influential group of writers were revolted by the human consequences of the old ideas of caste. Their rebellion took form as a defense of the most defenseless members of society, children in schools and adults in prisons. Cesare Beccaria examined the prisons of Italy and France in the 1720s and discovered that men were chained by the neck for twenty years as punishment for petty theft; no matter what their "civil condition," he wrote, this was unacceptable treatment. A long line of eighteenth-century humanists attacked the schools run by priests, Diderot for one being unable to understand why lashes of the whip enhanced the study of Latin or of Christian ethics. Within a short time, the condemnation of physical cruelty passed into a condemnation of all social situations where men were made vulnerable by arbitrary law or custom. Voltaire, for instance, attacked courts where a man could be thrown into prison not on the basis of what he had done, but on intimations that he might be a devil.

The outrage of these men was considered a strange aberration at the time. People of the greatest delicacy and refinement were accustomed to harsh measures directed at the mass below, whose brutish nature was thought to need strong reins. You accuse me of inhumanity and I ask you what you can possibly mean, when I treat my family with affection, my servants with firmness, and my rulers with loyal deference. In the face of this, it was a question for Diderot or Beccaria of finding a rationale for their own anger.

It was among this generation of reformers that a definite notion about the relationship between human dignity and compassion for men took form which has passed down into the public ideals of our time. The Enlightenment humanists came to believe that *caritas* in the world was demanded, not by the dictates of an unseen God, but by a common worldly power among men. The right to decent treatment came from a power of rational thinking that ran throughout the human species and in fact defined what it was to be a man. In Diderot's *Encylopedia,* for example, the section on "Art" excludes almost all discussion of court painting and sculpture and concentrates on the tools and products of manual laborers. Instead of people becoming more "noble" in the moral sense the higher their caste, he and his fellows saw the web of human merit running through all men in the society. Where the Renaissance philosopher Pico della Mirandola believed extraordinary men struggled to rise above the ordinary to produce the achievements of civilization, Enlightenment writers like Voltaire believed the capacity for civilized achievement to lie within the grasp of any member of the human race, if only he could develop the rational powers nature had instilled in him.

Most Enlightenment humanists never intended to preach a doctrine of equality in social conditions. They preached to the powerful of the old regime, arguing that bonds of respect must cut across the old castes. Indeed, we find one of the *Encyclopédistes* muttering as he is being led to the scaffold during the French Revolution, "Vicious, vicious levelers, you have betrayed reason in the name of equality."

The modern belief in social equality does, however, flow directly from the union of human compassion with the recognition of the potential power all men have to perform acts of reasoning and understanding. For if I am an ordinary man, and yet have within me a power of intellection like that of my lord, how do I make sense of the social separation between us? If I let the dream of a common dignity grow strong in me, then I want the barriers of privilege removed so that I can develop this potential.

This unintended consequence of Enlightenment humanism ought to be a standing rebuke to the inequities in the present industrial order. The ideal ought to provide those who are, or feel themselves to be, powerless with a simple, potent weapon with which to make sense of their condition: I am weak in the face of the Sirs of the world, they control my life, they make me feel ashamed as well as angry. But these things are *their* doing, their tricks. I know I have the potential within me to be as good as they; I won't take it. This is cause for anger, it demands joining together with others to rebel . . . And yet the belief alone is no comfort, under what appear to be very different conditions.

A Russian street-sweeper, an ardent believer in communism, tells an interviewer he does not personally "matter as much as a Party member"; German office workers are reported often to feel "humiliated" by their clothes; American construction workers tell a team of researchers they feel they have to give their sons cars in order to be respected as fathers. Without his possessions, every man walks with pride, preached the Abbé de Sieyès in 1790, but these workingmen and women of the modern world are not so sure. Just being a human being seems to them a state in which they are vulnerable; "I suppose I am not as dignified," the Russian remarks, "as people with more power and influence."

What these workers are saying is that the dignity of man is not *believable* as the Abbé de Sieyès preached it, even as they want to believe in themselves and have others respect them, even as they are outraged when others treat them like "part of the woodwork." Man alone, without making a demonstration of his worth, by just *being*, appears to them to be a vulnerable creature.

One of the reasons class makes the doctrine of the Abbé de Sieyès unbelievable is that his humanism, and that of the other Enlightenment writers of both Right and Left, has a flaw at its very center. The humanists banished the courts of appeal beyond the world, they banished higher authority whose power is unlike the powers of men—all these old notions are put away as enslaving superstition. The humanists effected a juncture between respect among men and a *potential* power all men had in the world. That is a fateful and risky step, as Nietzsche saw, for what happens to the mutual respect when men enact the potential within them? When the common potential is expressed in dissimilar ways? Surely those who are the most intelligent or able or competent have demonstrated more character in manifesting a potential that flows through all; don't they therefore deserve to be treated with more respect than others, or at least to be entrusted with more power? This would be only reasonable, after all; they showed themselves to be better in practice when all began the same.

If I believe that the man I call "Sir" and who calls me by my first name started with an equal fund of powers, do not our differences, do not all the signs of courtesy and attention given to him but denied me, do not his very feelings of being different in "taste" and understanding from me, show that somehow he has developed his insides more than I mine? How else can I explain inequalities? The institutions may be structured so that he wins and I lose, but this is my life, this is thirty or forty years of being alive that I am talking about, and what I have experienced in school, and at work, is that people are supposed to understand what happens to them in life in terms of what they make of themselves. I see this man, who I know is no better than I, being treated better by others—even I treat him that way. Much as I know it isn't right, much as I rebel against his putting on airs and trying to act superior, there is a secret self-accusation implanted in me by my very belief in our basic equality. Even though we might have been born in different stations, the fact that he is getting more means that somehow he had the power in him, the character, to "realize himself," to earn his superiority.

It is in this way that a system of unequal classes is actually reinforced by the ideas of equality and charity formulated in the past. The idea of potential equality of power has been given a form peculiarly fitted to a competitive society where *in*equality of power is the rule and expectation. If all men start on some basis of equal potential ability, then the inequalities they experience in their lives are *not* arbitrary, they are the logical consequence of different personal drives to use those powers—in other words, social differences can now appear as questions of character, of moral resolve, will, and competence.

The lesson of this historic flaw is that once respect is made the reward for human ability, no matter if the ability is seen potentially in all, the stage is set for all the dangers of individualism: loneliness for those who are called the possessors, a feeling of individual guilt for those who do not come off as well.

24. The Forgotten American
PETER SCHRAG

One of the conspicuous results of the nonequalitarian features of American society is the life style of "ethnics," who are, in general, the lower status Catholic descendants of Irish and eastern European immigrants. As Peter Schrag—editor of Change *magazine—points out, these people typically get the "short end of the stick." They are the classic victims caught in the middle: too well off to get welfare aid, but too poor to help and fend for themselves adequately. Furthermore, when it comes to sacrifices—as in providing soldiers for war, or taxes for welfare projects—they are "first in the hearts of their countrymen." The result is anger that prompts many American ethnics to respond favorably to political extremists who promise to put down both "the privileged rich" and "welfare bums." Schrag's discussion of these matters includes a number of dated observations, but his basic points are even more apropos today than when they were penned.*

There is hardly a language to describe him, or even a set of social statistics. Just names: racist-bigot-redneck-ethnic-Irish-Italian-Pole-Hunkie-Yahoo. The lower middle class. A blank. The man under whose hat lies the great American desert. Who watches the tube, plays the horses, and keeps the niggers out of his union and his neighborhood. Who might vote for Wallace (but didn't). Who cheers when the cops beat up on demonstrators. Who is free, white, and twenty-one, has a job, a home, a family, and is up to his eyeballs in credit. In the guise of the working class—or

SOURCE: Peter Schrag, *Out of Place in America* (New York: Random House, 1969). Copyright © 1969 by Peter Schrag. Reprinted by permission of Random House, Inc.

the American yeoman or John Smith—he was once the hero of the civics book, the man that Andrew Jackson called "the bone and sinew of the country." Now he is "the forgotten man," perhaps the most alienated person in America.

Nothing quite fits, except perhaps omission and semi-invisibility. America is supposed to be divided between affluence and poverty, between slums and suburbs. John Kenneth Galbraith begins the foreword to *The Affluent Society* with the phrase, "Since I sailed for Switzerland in the early summer of 1955 to begin work on this book . . ." But *between* slums and suburbs, between Scarsdale and Harlem, between Wellesley and Roxbury, between Shaker Heights and Hough, there are some eighty million people (depending on how you count them) who didn't sail for Switzerland in the summer of 1955, or at any other time, and who never expect to. Between slums and suburbs: South Boston and South San Francisco, Bell and Parma, Astoria and Bay Ridge, Newark, Cicero, Downey, Daly City, Charlestown, Flatbush. Union halls, American Legion posts, neighborhood bars and bowling leagues, the Ukrainian Club and the Holy Name. Main Street. To try to describe all this is like trying to describe America itself. If you look for it, you find it everywhere: the rows of frame houses overlooking the belching steel mills in Bethlehem, Pennsylvania, two-family brick houses in Canarsie (where the most common slogan, even in the middle of a political campaign, is "curb your dog"); the Fords and Chevies with a decal American flag on the rear window (usually a cut-out from the *Reader's Digest*, and displayed in counter-protest against peaceniks and "those bastards who carry Vietcong flags in demonstrations"); the bunting on the porch rail with the inscription, "Welcome Home, Pete." The gold star in the window.

When he was Under Secretary of Housing and Urban Development, Robert C. Wood tried a definition. It is not good, but it's the best we have:

> He is a white employed male . . . earning between $5,000 and $10,000. He works regularly, steadily, dependably, wearing a blue collar or white collar. Yet the frontiers of his career expectations have been fixed since he reached the age of thirty-five, when he found that he had too many obligations, too much family, and too few skills to match opportunities with aspirations.
>
> This definition of the "working American" involves almost 23-million American families.
>
> The working American lives in the gray area fringes of a central city or in a close-in or very far-out cheaper suburban subdivision of a large metropolitan area. He is likely to own a home and a car, especially as his income begins to rise. Of those earning between $6,000 and $7,500, 70 per cent own their own homes and 94 per cent drive their own cars.
>
> 94 per cent have no education beyond high school and 43 per cent have only completed the eighth grade.

He does all the right things, obeys the law, goes to church and insists—usually—that his kids get a better education than he had. But the right things don't seem to be paying off. While he is making more than he ever made—perhaps more than he'd ever dreamed—he's still struggling while a lot of others—"them" (on welfare, in demonstrations, in the ghettos) are getting most of the attention. "I'm working my ass off," a guy tells you on a stoop in South Boston. "My kids don't have a place to swim, my parks are full of glass, and I'm supposed to bleed for a bunch of people on relief." In New York a man who drives a Post Office trailer truck at night (4:00 P.M. to midnight) and a cab during the day (7:00 A.M. to 2:00 P.M.), and who hustles radios for his Post Office buddies on the side, is ready, as he says, to "knock somebody's ass." "The colored guys work when they feel like it. Sometimes they show up and sometimes they don't. One guy tore up all the time cards. I'd like to see a white guy do that and get away with it."

WHAT COUNTS

Nobody knows how many people in America moonlight (half of the eighteen million families in the $5,000 to $10,000 bracket have two or more wage earners) or how many have to hustle on the side. "I don't think anybody has a single job anymore," said Nicholas Kisburg, the research director for a Teamsters Union Council in New York. "All the cops are moonlighting, and the teachers; and there's a million guys who are hustling, guys with phony social-security numbers who are hiding part of what they make so they don't get kicked out of a housing project, or guys who work as guards at sports events and get free meals that they don't want to pay taxes on. Every one of them is cheating. They are underground people—*Untermenschen*. . . . We really have no systematic data on any of this. We have no ideas of the attitudes of the white worker. (We've been too busy studying the black worker.) And yet he's the source of most of the reaction in this country."

The reaction is directed at almost every visible target: at integration and welfare, taxes and sex education, at the rich and the poor, the foundations and students, at the "smart people in the suburbs." In New York State the legislature cuts the welfare budget; in Los Angeles, the voters reelect Yorty after a whispered racial campaign against the Negro favorite. In Minneapolis a police detective named Charles Stenvig, promising "to take the handcuffs off the police," wins by a margin stunning even to his supporters: in Massachusetts the voters mail tea bags to their representatives in protest against new taxes, and in state after state legislatures are passing bills to punish student demonstrators. ("We keep talking about permissiveness in training kids," said a Los Angeles labor offical, "but we forget that these are our kids.")

And yet all these things are side manifestations of a malaise that lacks a language. Whatever law and order means, for example, to a man who feels his wife is unsafe on the street after dark or in the park at any time, or whose kids get shaken down in the school yard, it also means something like normality—the demand that everybody play it by the book, that cultural and social standards be somehow restored to their civics-book simplicity, that things shouldn't be as they are but as they were supposed to be. If there is a revolution in this country—a revolt in manners, standards of dress and obscenity, and, more importantly, in our official sense of what America is—there is also a counter-revolt. Sometimes it is inarticulate, and sometimes (perhaps most of the time) people are either too confused or apathetic—or simply too polite and too decent—to declare themselves. In Astoria, Queens, a white working-class district of New York, people who make $7,000 or $8,000 a year (sometimes in two jobs) call themselves affluent, even though the Bureau of Labor Statistics regards an income of less than $9,500 in New York inadequate to a moderate standard of living. And in a similar neighborhood in Brooklyn a truck driver who earns $151 a week tells you he's doing well, living in a two-story frame house separated by a narrow driveway from similar houses, thousands of them in block after block. This year, for the first time, he will go on a cruise—he and his wife and two other couples—two weeks in the Caribbean. He went to work after World War II ($57 a week) and he has lived in the same house for twenty years, accumulating two television sets, wall-to-wall carpeting in a small living room, and a basement that he recently remodeled into a recreation room with the help of two moonlighting firemen. "We get fairly good salaries, and this is a good neighborhood, one of the few good ones left. We have no smoked Irishmen around."

Stability is what counts, stability in job and home and neighborhood, stability in the church and in friends. At night you watch television and sometimes on a weekend you go to a nice place—maybe a downtown hotel—for dinner with another couple. (Or maybe your sister, or maybe bowling, or maybe, if you're defeated, a night at the track.) The wife has the necessary appliances, often still being paid off, and the money you save goes for your daughter's orthodontist, and later for her wedding. The smoked Irishmen—the colored (no one says black; few even say Negro)—represent change and instability, kids who cause trouble in school, who get treatment that your kids never got, that you never got. ("Those fucking kids," they tell you in South Boston, "raising hell, and not one of 'em paying his own way. Their fucking mothers are all on welfare.") The black kids mean a change in the rules, a double standard in grades and discipline, and—vaguely—a challenge to all you believed right. Law and order is the stability and predictability of established ways. Law and order is equal treatment—in school, in jobs, in the courts—even if you're cheating a little yourself. The Forgotten Man is Jackson's man. He is the vestigial American democrat of 1840: "They all know that their success depends upon their own industry and economy and that they must not expect to become suddenly rich by the fruits of their toil." He is also Franklin Roosevelt's man—the man whose vote (or whose father's vote) sustained the New Deal.

There are other considerations, other styles, other problems. A postman in a Charlestown (Boston) housing project: eight children and a ninth on the way. Last year, by working overtime, his income went over $7,000. This year, because he reported it, the Housing Authority is raising his rent from $78 to $106 a month, a catastrophe for a family that pays $2.20 a day for milk, has never had a vacation, and for which an excursion is "going out for ice cream." "You try and save for something better; we hope to get out of here to someplace where the kids can play, where there's no broken glass, and then something always comes along that knocks you right back. It's like being at the bottom of the well waiting for a guy to throw you a rope." The description becomes almost Chaplinesque. Life is humble but not simple; the terrors of insolent bureaucracies and contemptuous officials produce a demonology that loses little of its horror for being partly misunderstood. You want to get a sink fixed but don't want to offend the manager; want to get an eye operation that may (or may not) have been necessitated by a military injury five years earlier, "but the Veterans Administration says I signed away my benefits"; want to complain to someone about the teen-agers who run around breaking windows and harassing women but get no response either from the management or the police. "You're afraid to complain because if they don't get you during the day they'll get you at night." Automobiles, windows, children, all become hostages to the vague terrors of everyday life; everything is vulnerable. Liabilities that began long ago cannot possibly be liquidated: "I never learned anything in that school except how to fight. I got tired of being caned by the teachers so at sixteen I quit and joined the Marines. I still don't know anything."

AT THE BOTTOM OF THE WELL

American culture? Wealth is visible, and so, now, is poverty. Both have become intimidating clichés. But the rest? A vast, complex, and disregarded world that was once—in belief, and in fact—the American middle: Greyhound and Trailways bus terminals in little cities at midnight, each of them with its neon lights and its cardboard hamburgers; acres of tarpaper beach bungalows in places like Revere and Rockaway; the hair curlers in the supermarket on Saturday, and the little girls in the communion dresses the next morning; pinball machines and the *Daily News*, the *Reader's Digest* and Ed Sullivan; houses with tiny front lawns (or even large ones) adorned with statues of the Virgin or of Sambo welcomin' de folks home; Clint Eastwood or Julie Andrews at the Palace; the trotting tracks and the dog tracks—Aurora Downs, Connaught Park, Roosevelt, Yonkers, Rockingham, and forty others—where gray men come not for sport and beauty, but to read numbers, to study and dope. (If you win you have figured something, have in a small way controlled your world, have surmounted your impotence. If you lose, bad luck, shit. "I'll break his goddamned head.") Baseball is not the national pastime; racing is. For every man who goes to a major-league baseball game there are four who go to the track and probably four more who go to the candy store or the barbershop to make their bets. (Total track attendance in 1965: 62 million plus another 10 million who went to the dogs.)

There are places, and styles, and attitudes. If there are neighborhoods of aspiration, suburban enclaves for the mobile young executive and the aspiring worker, there are also places of limited expectation and dead-end districts where mobility is finished. But even there you can often find, however vestigial, a sense of place, the roots of old ethnic loyalties, and a passionate, if often futile, battle against intrusion and change. "Everybody around here," you are told, "pays his own way." In this world the problems are not the ABM or air pollution (have they heard of Biafra?) or the international population crisis; the problem is to get your street cleaned, your garbage collected, to get your husband home from Vietnam alive; to negotiate installment payments and to keep the schools orderly. Ask anyone in Scarsdale or Winnetka about the schools and they'll tell you about new programs, or about how many are getting into Harvard, or about the teachers; ask in Oakland or the North Side of Chicago, and they'll tell you that they have (or haven't) had trouble. Somewhere in his gut the man in those communities knows that mobility and choice in this society are limited. He cannot imagine any major change for the better; but he can imagine change for the worse. And yet for a decade he is the one who has been asked to carry the burden of social reform, to integrate his schools and his neighborhood, has been asked by comfortable people to pay the social debts due to the poor and the black. In Boston, in San Francisco, in Chicago (not to mention Newark or Oakland) he has been telling the reformers to go to hell. The Jewish schoolteachers of New York and the Irish parents of Dorchester have asked the same question: "What the hell did Lindsay (or the Beacon Hill Establishment) ever do for us?"

The ambiguities and changes in American life that occupy discussions in university seminars and policy debates in Washington, and that form the backbone of contemporary popular sociology, become increasingly the conditions of trauma and frustration in the middle. Although the New Frontier and Great Society contained some programs for those not already on the rolls of social pathology—federal aid for higher education, for example—the public priorities and the rhetoric contained little. The emphasis, properly, was on the poor, on the inner cities (*e.g.*, Negroes) and the unemployed. But in Chicago a widow with three children who earns $7,000 a year can't get them college loans because she makes too much: the money is reserved for people on relief. New schools are built in the ghetto but not in the white working-class neighborhoods where they are just as dilapidated. In Newark the head of a white vigilante group (now a city councilman) runs, among other things, on a platform opposing pro-Negro discrimination. "When pools are being built in the Central Ward —don't they think white kids have got frustration? The white can't get a job; we have to hire Negroes first." The middle class, said Congressman Roman Pucinski of Illinois, who represents a lot of it, "is in revolt. Everyone has been generous in supporting anti-poverty. Now the middle-class American is disqualified from most of the programs."

"SOMEBODY HAS TO SAY NO..."

The frustrated middle. The liberal wisdom about welfare, ghettos, student revolt, and Vietnam has only a marginal place, if any, for the values and life of the working man. It flies in the face of most of what he was taught to cherish and respect: hard work, order, authority, self-reliance. He fought, either alone or through labor organizations, to establish the precincts he now considers his own. Union seniority, the civil-service bureaucracy, and the petty professionalism established by the merit system in the public schools become sinecures of particular ethnic groups or of those who have learned to negotiate and master the system. A man who worked all his life to accumulate the points and grades and paraphernalia to become an assistant school principal (no matter how silly the requirements) is not likely to relinquish his position with equanimity. Nor is a dock worker whose only estate is his longshoreman's card. The job, the points, the credits become property:

> Some men leave their sons money [wrote a union member to the *New York Times*], some large investments, some business connections, and some a profession. I have only one worthwhile thing to give: my trade. I hope to follow a centuries-old tradition and sponsor my sons for an apprenticeship. For this simple father's wish it is said that I discriminate against Negroes. Don't all of us discriminate? Which of us . . . will not choose a son over all others?

Suddenly the rules are changing—all the rules. If you protect your job for your own you may be called a bigot. At the same time it's perfectly acceptable to shout black power and to endorse it. What does it take to be a good American? *Give the black man a position because he is black, not because he necessarily works harder or does the job better.* What does it take to be a good American? Dress nicely, hold a job, be clean-cut, don't judge a man by the color of his skin or the country of his origin. What about the demands of Negroes, the long hair of the students, the dirty movies, the people who burn draft cards and American flags? Do you have to go out in the street with picket signs, do you have to burn the place down to get what you want? What does it take to be a good American? *This is a sick society, a racist society, we are fighting an immoral war.* ("I'm against the Vietnam war, too," says the truck driver in Brooklyn. "I see a good kid come home with half an arm and a leg in a brace up to here, and what's it all for? I was glad to see *my kid* flunk the Army physical. Still, somebody has to say no to these demonstrators and enforce the law.") What does it take to be a good American?

The conditions of trauma and frustration in the middle. What does it take to be a good American? Suddenly there are demands for Italian power and Polish power and Ukrainian power. In Cleveland the Poles demand a seat on the school board, and get it, and in Pittsburgh John Pankuch, the seventy-three-year-old president of the National Slovak Society demands "action, plenty of it to make up for lost time." Black power is supposed to be nothing but emulation of the ways in which other ethnic groups made it. But have they made it? In Reardon's Bar on East Eighth Street in South Boston, where the workmen come for their fish-chowder lunch and for their rye and ginger, they still identify themselves as Galway men and Kilkenny men; in the newsstand in Astoria you can buy *Il Progresso, El Tiempo,* the *Staats-Zeitung,* the *Irish World,* plus papers in Greek, Hungarian, and Polish. At the parish of Our Lady of Mount Carmel the priests hear confession in English, Italian, and Spanish and, nearby, the biggest attraction is not the stickball game, but the *bocce* court. Some of the poorest people in America are white, native, and have lived all of their lives in the same place as their fathers and grandfathers. The problems that were presumably solved in some distant past, in that prehistoric era before the textbooks were written—problems of assimilation, of upward mobility—now turn out to be very much unsolved. The melting pot and all: millions made it, millions moved to the affluent suburbs; several million—no one knows how many—did not. The median income in Irish South Boston is $5,100 a year but the community-action workers have a hard time convincing the local citizens that any white man who is not stupid or irresponsible can be poor. Pride still keeps them from applying for income supplements or Medicaid, but it does not keep them from resenting those who do. In Pittsburgh, where the members of Polish-American organizations earn an estimated $5,000 to $6,000 (and some fall below the poverty line), the Poverty Programs are nonetheless directed primarily to Negroes, and almost everywhere the thing called urban backlash associates itself in some fashion with ethnic groups whose members have themselves only a precarious hold on the security of affluence. Almost everywhere in the old cities, tribal neighborhoods and their styles are under assault by masscult. The Italian grocery gives way to the supermarket, the ma-and-pa store and the walk-up are attacked by urban renewal. And almost everywhere, that assault tends to depersonalize and to alienate. It has always been this way, but with time the brave new world that replaces old patterns becomes increasingly bureaucratized, distant, and hard to control.

Yet beyond the problems of ethnic identity, beyond the problems of Poles and Irishmen left behind, there are others more pervasive and more dangerous. For every Greek or Hungarian there are a dozen American-Americans who are past ethnic consciousness and who are as alienated, as confused, and as angry as the rest. The obvious manifestations are the same everywhere—race, taxes, welfare, students—but the threat seems invariably more cultural and psychological than economic or social. What upset the police at the Chicago convention most was not so much the politics of the demonstrators as their manners and their hair. (The barbershops in their neighborhoods don't advertise Beatle Cuts but the Flat Top and the Chicago Box.) The affront comes from middle-class people —and their children—who had been cast in the role of social exemplars (and from those cast as unfortunates worthy of public charity) who offend all the things on which working-class identity is built: "hippies [said a San Francisco longshoreman] who fart around the streets and don't work"; welfare recipients who strike and march for better treatment; "all those [said a California labor official] who challenge the precepts that these people live on." If ethnic groups are beginning to organize to get theirs, so are others: police and firemen ("The cop is the new nigger"); schoolteachers; lower-middle-class housewives fighting sex education and bussing; small property owners who have no ethnic communion but a passionate interest in lower taxes, more policemen, and stiffer penalties for criminals. In San Francisco the Teamsters, who had never been known for such interests before, recently demonstrated in support of the police, and law enforcement and, on another occasion, joined a group called Mothers Support Neighborhood Schools at a schoolboard meeting to oppose—with their presence and later, apparently, with their fists—a proposal to integrate the schools through bussing. ("These people," someone said at the meeting, "do not look like mothers.")

Which is not to say that all is frustration and anger, that anybody is ready "to burn the country down." They are not even ready to elect standard model demagogues. "A lot of labor people who thought of voting for Wallace were ashamed of themselves when they realized what they were about to do," said Morris Iushewitz, an officer of New York's Central Labor Council. Because of a massive last-minute union compaign, and perhaps for other reasons, the blue-collar vote for Wallace fell far below the figures predicted by the early polls last fall. Any number of people, moreover, who are not doing well by any set of official statistics, who are earning well below the national mean ($8,000 a year), or who hold two jobs to stay above it, think of themselves as affluent, and often use that word. It is almost as if not to be affluent is to be un-American. People who can't use the word tend to be angry; people who come too close to those who can't become frightened. The definition of affluence is generally pinned to what comes in, not to the quality of life as it's lived. The $8,000 son of a man who never earned more than $4,500 may, for that reason alone, believe that he's "doing all right." If life is not all right, if he can't get his curbs fixed, or his streets patrolled, if the highways are crowded and the beaches polluted, if the schools are ineffectual he is still able to call himself affluent, feels, perhaps, a social compulsion to do so. His anger, if he is angry, is not that of the wage earner resenting management—and certainly not that of the socialist ideologue asking for redistribution of wealth—but that of the consumer, the taxpayer, and the family man. (Inflation and taxes are wiping out most of the wage gains made in labor contracts signed during the past three years.) Thus he will vote for a Louise Day Hicks in Boston who promises to hold the color line in the schools or for a Charles Stenvig calling for law enforcement in Minneapolis but reject a George Wallace who seems to threaten his pocketbook. The danger is that he will identify with the politics of the Birchers and other middle-class reactionaries (who often pretend to speak for him) even though his income and style of life are far removed from theirs; that taxes, for example, will be identified with welfare rather than war, and that he will blame his limited means on the small slice of the poor rather than the fat slice of the rich.

If you sit and talk to people like Marjorie Lemlow, who heads Mothers Support Neighborhood Schools in San Francisco, or Joe Owens, a house painter who is president of a community-action organization in Boston, you quickly discover that the roots of reaction and the roots of reform are often identical, and that the response to particular situations is more often contingent on the politics of the politicians and leaders who appear to care than on the conditions of life or the ideology of the victims. Mrs. Lemlow wants to return the schools to some virtuous past; she worries about disintegration of the family and she speaks vaguely about something that she can't bring herself to call a conspiracy against Americanism. She has been accused of leading a bunch of Birchers, and she sometimes talks Birch language. But whatever the form, her sense of things comes from a small-town vision of national virtues, and her unhappiness from the assaults of urban sophistication. It just so happens that a lot of reactionaries now sing that tune, and that the liberals are indifferent.

Joe Owens—probably because of his experience as a Head Start parent, and because of his association with an effective community-action program—talks a different language. He knows, somehow, that no simple past can be restored. In his world the villains are not conspirators but bureaucrats and politicians, and he is beginning to discover that in a struggle with officials the black man in the ghetto and the working man (black or white) have the same problems. "Every time you ask for something from the politicians they treat you like a beggar, like you ought to be grateful for what you have. They try to make you feel ashamed."

WHEN HOPE BECOMES A THREAT

The imponderables are youth and tradition and change. The civics book and the institution it celebrates—however passé—still hold the world together. The revolt is in their name, not against them. And there is simple decency, the language and practice of the folksy cliché, the small town, the Boy Scout virtues, the neighborhood charity, the obligation to support the church, the rhetoric of open opportunity: "They can keep Wallace and they can keep Alabama. We didn't fight a dictator for four years so we could elect one over here." What happens when all that becomes Mickey Mouse? Is there an urban ethnic to replace the values of the small town? Is there a coherent public philosophy, a consistent set of beliefs to replace family, home, and hard work? What happens when the hang-ups of upper-middle-class kids are in fashion and those of blue-collar kids are not? What happens when Doing Your Own Thing becomes not the slogan of the solitary deviant but the norm? Is it possible that as the institutions and beliefs of tradition are fashionably denigrated a blue-collar generation gap will open to the Right as well as to the Left? (There is statistical evidence, for example, that Wallace's greatest support within the unions came from people who are between twenty-one and twenty-nine, those, that is, who have the most tenuous association with the liberalism of labor.) Most are politically silent; although SDS has been trying to organize blue-collar high-school students, there are no Mario Savios or Mark Rudds—either of the Right or the Left—among them. At the same time the union leaders, some of them old hands from the Thirties, aren't sure that the kids are following them either. Who speaks for the son of the longshoreman or the Detroit auto worker? What happens if he doesn't get to college? What, indeed, happens when he does?

Vaguely but unmistakably the hopes that a youth-worshiping nation historically invested in its young are becoming threats. We have never been unequivocal about the symbolic patricide of Americanization and upward mobility, but if at one time mobility meant rejection of older (or European) styles it was, at least, done in the name of America. Now the labels are blurred and the objectives indistinct. Just at the moment when a tradition-bound Italian father is persuaded that he should send his sons to college—that education is the only future—the college blows up. At the moment when a parsimonious taxpayer begins to shell out for what he considers an extravagant state university system the students go on strike. Marijuana, sexual liberation, dress styles, draft resistance, even the rhetoric of change become monsters and demons in a world that appears to turn old virtues upside down. The paranoia that fastened on Communism twenty years ago (and sometimes still does) is increasingly directed to vague conspiracies undermining the schools, the family, order and discipline. "They're feeding the kids this generation-gap business," says a Chicago housewife who grinds out a campaign against sex education on a duplicating machine in her living room. "The kids are told to make their own decisions. They're all mixed up by situation ethics and open-ended questions. They're alienating children from their own parents." They? The churches, the schools, even the YMCA and the Girl Scouts, are implicated. But a major share of the villainy is now also attributed to "the social science centers," to the apostles of sensitivity training, and to what one California lady, with some embarrassment, called "nude therapy." "People with sane minds are being altered by psychological methods." The current major campaign of the John Birch Society is not directed against Communists in government or the Supreme Court, but against sex education.

(There is, of course, also sympathy with the young, especially in poorer areas where kids have no place to play. "Everybody's got to have a hobby," a South Boston adolescent told a youth worker. "Ours is throwing rocks." If people will join reactionary organizations to protect their children, they will also support others: community-action agencies which help kids get jobs; Head Start parent groups, Boys Clubs. "Getting this place cleaned up" sometimes refers to a fear of young hoods; sometimes it points to the day when there is a park or a playground or when the existing park can be used. "I want to see them grow up to have a little fun.")

CAN THE COMMON MAN COME BACK?

Beneath it all there is a more fundamental ambivalence, not only about the young, but about institutions—the schools, the churches, the Establishment—and about the future itself. In the major cities of the East (though perhaps not in the West) there is a sense that time is against you, that one is living "in one of the few decent neighborhoods left," that "if I can get $125 a week upstate (or downstate) I'll move." The institutions that were supposed to mediate social change and which, more than ever, are becoming priesthoods of information and conglomerates of social engineers, are increasingly suspect. To attack the Ford Foundation (as Wright Patman has done) is not only to fan the embers of historic populism against concentrations of wealth and power, but also to arouse those who feel that they are trapped by an alliance of upper-class Wasps and lower-class Negroes. If the foundations have done anything for the blue-collar worker he doesn't seem to be aware of it. At the same time the distrust of professional educators that characterizes the black militants is becoming increasingly prevalent among a minority of lower-middle-class whites who are beginning to discover that the schools aren't working for them either. ("Are all those new programs just a cover-up for failure?") And if the Catholic Church is under attack from its liberal members (on birth control, for example) it is also alienating the traditionalists who liked their minor saints (even if they didn't actually exist) and were perfectly content with the Latin Mass. For the alienated Catholic liberal there are other places to go; for the lower-middle-class parishioner in Chicago or Boston there are none.

Perhaps, in some measure, it has always been this way. Perhaps none of this is new. And perhaps it is also true that the American lower middle has never had it so good. And yet surely there is a difference, and that is that the common man has lost his visibility and, somehow, his claim on public attention. There are old liberals and socialists—men like Michael Harrington—who believe that a new alliance can be forged for progressive social action:

> From Marx to Mills, the Left has regarded the middle class as a stratum of hypocritical, vacillating rear-guarders. There was often sound reason for this contempt. But is it not possible that a new class is coming into being? It is not the old middle class of small property owners and

entrepreneurs, nor the new middle class of managers. It is composed of scientists, technicians, teachers, and professionals in the public sector of the society. By education and work experience it is predisposed toward planning. It could be an ally of the poor and the organized workers—or their sophisticated enemy. In other words, an unprecedented social and political variable seems to be taking shape in America.

The American worker, even when he waits on a table or holds open a door, is not servile; he does not carry himself like an inferior. The openness, frankness, and democratic manner which Tocqueville described in the last century persists to this very day. They have been a source of rudeness, contemptuous ignorance, violence—and of a creative self-confidence among great masses of people. It was in this latter spirit that the CIO was organized and the black freedom movement marched.

There are recent indications that the white lower middle class is coming back on the roster of public priorities. Pucinski tells you that liberals in Congress are privately discussing the pressure from the middle class. There are proposals now to increase personal income-tax exemptions from $600 to $1,000 (or $1,200) for each dependent, to protect all Americans with a national insurance system covering catastrophic medical expenses, and to put a floor under all incomes. Yet these things by themselves are insufficient. Nothing is sufficient without a national sense of restoration. What Pucinski means by the middle class has, in some measure, always been represented. A physician earning $75,000 a year is also a working man but he is hardly a victim of the welfare system. Nor, by and large, are the stockholders of the Standard Oil Company or U.S. Steel. The fact that American ideals have often been corrupted in the cause of self-aggrandizement does not make them any less important for the cause of social reform and justice. "As a movement with the conviction that there is more to people than greed and fear," Harrington said, "the Left must . . . also speak in the name of the historic idealism of the United States."

The issue, finally, is not *the program* but the vision, the angle of view. A huge constituency may be coming up for grabs, and there is considerable evidence that its political mobility is more sensitive than anyone can imagine, that all the sociological determinants are not as significant as the simple facts of concern and leadership. When Robert Kennedy was killed last year, thousands of working-class people who had expected to vote for him—if not hundreds of thousands—shifted their loyalties to Wallace. A man who can change from a progressive democrat into a bigot overnight deserves attention.

25. "I'm the True Southerner"
ROBERT COLES

Robert Coles, M.D., is a psychiatrist who teaches at Harvard University. (He is also coauthor of selection 42.) If it were possible, more of his work would be included here, because Dr. Coles is beyond doubt one of the most sensitive observer-interviewers whose writings have been published in recent years. His trilogy, The Children of Crisis, *a study of poor farmers and migrants, has achieved near-classic status. In the following piece Dr. Coles interviews Mrs. Trumbull, a southern gentlewoman whose entire background could have led her to become a thoughtlessly prejudiced, exploitive adult. Instead, she has emerged as a quietly outspoken liberal, a fighter for progressive change. What Mrs. Trumbull has done, and what she stands for, may not seem like much to radical youth, but in a relative sense, her stance—given her era and environment—is roughly comparable to those present-day Russians who, in brave defiance of their totalitarian central government, have called openly for freedom of expression.*

In many respects she is the most explicitly Southern person I know. Her name is Southern, Flora (Searcy) Trumbull. Her speech is as soft, her accent as honeyed as any in the South. In her bones—they are slight and she is a thin and small woman—she is the delicate Southern lady the region continues to venerate and make a show of defending. Her family background is unblemished: in the early eighteenth century her ancestors came to Virginia, then moved down to South Carolina, to Charleston. "That's where they were during the American Revolution," she once told me. In that same conversation she rather quietly and wryly reminded me that she was a daughter of both that revolution and a later one: "Sometimes I tell my own daughters they're going to have to choose when they're twenty-one—either they'll be a Daughter of the American Revolution or a Daughter of the Confederacy."

Mrs. Trumbull lives in Mississippi on a plantation, "a smaller one," she apologetically says. Her husband was a lawyer as well as a farmer, and his death, in 1957, revealed to her how very much she had become a Mississippian, and a planter's wife.

"I was born in South Carolina, and I expected to die there. Do you know that both my parents made a point of telling my brother and me that they never had put a foot out of that state. They claimed distinction for that, and even said that their parents hadn't either—though I think each of them had something on the other in that respect. I later found out

SOURCE: Robert Coles, *The Children of Crisis: A Study of Courage and Fear* (Boston: Atlantic-Little, Brown, 1967), pp. 248–259. Copyright © 1964, 1965, 1966, 1967 by Robert Coles. Reprinted by permission of Little, Brown and Co. in association with the Atlantic Monthly Press.

what: both sets of grandparents had traveled out West, and my father's father had gone to Washington, even to New York—'on business,' he insisted when I confronted him with what I had discovered."

She knew that laughable as the determined and boastful parochialism of her parents was, they were living quite intimately with history, with the temper and style of their generation's South. "It was fashionable for Southerners to stay home then, or travel only to Europe. They would even justify their travel to London or Paris by reminding themselves of the great sympathy felt for the Confederacy in London or Paris. It may seem absurd to you, but that's the way many of our present-day leaders were brought up to think. I don't frankly know how I managed to free myself of such blindness. In a way, it was coming to Mississippi with my husband that did it. I realized that after he died. I went back to Charleston on a visit—alone this time, and so more exposed to people and their views. I found old friends of my age still talking about the wonderful, mystical South, unblemished by Negroes except in the cotton fields or our kitchens. Those friends are young, too, if you think being forty-five is young.

"One evening I went to a party, filled with youthful conservative segregationists. They knew the South they wanted was gone forever. (I don't believe it ever existed.) Four years after 1954 they must have known history was moving in the opposite direction. Yet, there they were, talking like my parents, only sounding harsher and more absurd. Suddenly I understood what had happened to me. When, as my mother put it, I went 'West' to Mississippi I went from the frying pan to the fire; but I also went away, to a different state with different customs, even if staunchly segregationist ones. (People forget how very different each Southern state's history is.) It was geographic distance and a new social situation that gave me a real chance to see what nonsense and cruelty I had overlooked all my life—indeed even accepted as fair and honorable."

I first met her in 1958, shortly after her husband had died. I was living in Mississippi at the time, and a doctor I knew told me I should go see her: "Mrs. Trumbull is the most outspoken integrationist who has ever managed to stay alive in this state. She's a well-to-do white lady, unquestionably a Southern lady, and the mother of four daughters. She has gray hair, and she's a churchwoman, a devout Methodist. Maybe for all those reasons no one has shot her yet. One thing I know, there isn't anyone else in the state—white or Negro—who would dare talk the way she does—without expecting to die in twenty-four hours."

When I approached her house I felt disrespectful for doing so in a car. The home, the trees, shrubbery and flowerbeds around it, the cotton fields nearby all suggested an earlier, quieter age: columns in front of the fine, white plantation manor; high ceilings and antique furniture bought in the shops of Royal Street in New Orleans; delicately scented rooms where one is sent to be "refreshed"; warm air that must not be cooled, as Mrs. Trumbull puts it derisively, "artificially"; fragile china and carefully brewed tea served by the strong hands of a tall, confident young Negro servant; a sense of timelessness. We sometimes take authors to task for being "romantics" when in fact they do literal justice in describing people like Mrs. Trumbull and homes like hers.

During the two years I lived in Mississippi I gradually came to appreciate how astonishing her leadership was. In subsequent years, while living in Louisiana and Georgia, I continued to visit her, or watch her in action at a committee organized to insure peaceful desegregation of schools, or at meetings of human relations councils—groups dedicated to what Mrs. Trumbull delicately called "improvement for all the people of the South." Her voice would ever so gently yet firmly emphasize the word "all." As she put it once: "You have to pay respect to the possibilities in language. Perhaps we in the South have produced so many writers because everyone, from the intellectuals to the ungifted, has to learn the subtleties and indirections of what my husband used to call 'race talk.' Even outspoken segregationists who seem capable of nothing that is refined so far as the Negro is concerned will resort to euphemisms and pretense under certain circumstances.

"I remember a friend of ours who screamed 'treason' just because I used the word 'Negro' instead of 'nigger.' (I think I was probably the first friend he ever heard do so; and he took a long time to get used to it.) Yet, when he went hunting he wanted company, and the company he most wanted and enjoyed was that of his 'nigger boy,' James. They were friends, anyone who cared to look closely could see that. They enjoyed talking about work to be done on the plantation, about everything from the weather and the state of the crops to hunting. They hunted together, too; only the Negro had to go as 'help.'

"Well, I saw them going and coming back, and they were companions. They even drank together. The Negro was his boss's age, and they had known one another since they were both children. They had grown up together. For a while when boys they called one another Jimmie and Ted; but soon Jimmie becames James, and Ted had to be called Mr. Theodore, which still makes James privileged, a 'house nigger,' as men like him are called—in 1960, mind you. The others, field hands or more remote servants, have to say Mr. Stanton.

"Anyway, one Sunday I saw Ted Stanton and James coming back; half drunk they were, and happy and familiar with one another as could be. I asked my husband how Ted could do it, do it in his mind so that James and he got along the way they did. I'll never forget what he said: 'There's not very much logic to human emotions. People do contradictory things, and there's no explaining why. It's just in their nature to do so.'

"I disagreed with him then, and I do now. It's the one thing we never agreed on, to his last day. I believe that when Ted Stanton talks about needing 'help' from James he is behaving in a very logical, predictable way. When I first asked my husband how Ted could do it, I meant that I was surprised at the man's ability to miss the logic of his own behavior.

Ted wants a friend's company, but he has to call for his 'help.' That means Ted, despite all his money and influence in our community, follows the rules rather than makes them. He thinks of himself as a leader, but he talks like a follower. It's not that his actions are illogical, it's that he protects himself from the truth that would explain them."

Mrs. Trumbull willingly talked with me about her reasons for being extraordinarily committed to so unpopular a cause. She, like Ted Stanton, had grown up close to Negroes, had been cared for and "helped" by them. Her mother had been a sick woman, intermittently confined to bed with tuberculosis while her three children were growing up. Mrs. Trumbull has two older brothers, both lawyers, both in Charleston, both in her words "conservative and segregationist, but not indecorously so."

"Why you and not them?" I asked her—and, as we got to know one another, she asked herself out loud. If she had been a boy she would now have the same social and political attitudes her brothers have, or so she was inclined to speculate: "I've thought about all this vaguely. You have to think about what you're doing when it's so unpopular. It's hard to do it though. You don't want to discuss your motives too much with those who are taking the same risks you are—if you start doing that, you'll soon stop doing anything else. So you talk to yourself sometimes, in front of the mirror while dressing; or when you should be reading and your mind drifts; or after one of those calls, telling you your life is about to end.

"I never come up with a real answer. Right now I'm 'too far gone,' as my friends tell me rather angrily at times. To them I'm sick, mentally ill. They wouldn't even believe *you* if you told them I was sane. They would say you're crazy, too. That's how they dismiss anyone whose thinking they don't like, or they fear. They call the person insane, or they say the ideas he advocates are crazy ideas. Sometimes I find myself going along with them, thinking just as they do—about myself. I'll remember the quiet life I lived as a child in South Carolina, and ask myself what in those years ever made me the way I am now. (Isn't that what you're trying to find out?)"

"To some extent," I replied. "Though I don't think we can fully 'explain' someone's contemporary behavior on the basis of specific childhood experiences. I think we can look back at a life and see trends in it—of cruelty or kindness, of concern for others or self-absorption, of indifference or continuing involvement in one or another problem or activity. Yet, such trends—they are patterns of thinking or acting—come about for many reasons, some of them apparently innocuous, or inconsistent with one another. There may have been a cruel parent who inspired compassion in a suffering son; or a kind parent whose child for one or another cause grew to confuse easygoing toleration with indifference, or gentleness with weakness. Then, as you know, events in the world, and in one's later life, bring out things in people, or for that matter, prevent people from being the kind of people they perfectly well might have been. So, I think a lot happens in childhood that either helps make us what we are, or prevents us from becoming what others are; but each person's life—entire life—has to be considered very carefully before 'explanations' are offered for his or her willingness to take an unpopular, a very dangerously unpopular stand in full public."

Once she gave me a long letter she had written to herself. She had been told by the sheriff of the county that he could not be responsible for her safety, for her life, if she continued her advocacy of "race-mixing." This time he not only said so, but wrote her a letter telling her so. She started her letter of reply in direct response to his, but soon felt impelled to wander through her past.

"Of course I have always known that one day a vulgar threat on my life, or my family's safety, might become much more, a nightmare become real. I have discussed the dangers with my daughters, and though they are more fearful than I—they have more living ahead of them, more to lose—they support my position.

"What is my position, according to you so likely to cause me 'serious harm'? I simply believe in the law of the land, in the obligation that every American citizen must assume to obey the courts and the decisions of Congress.

"You, sir, may find me simple-minded for insisting that Mississippi is one state in the United States, and as much subject to the Constitution and its spirit as any other state. You address me as if I were in peril. You write to me as if I were a confused outcast, causing trouble, but also deeply in trouble with herself, and in need of what you call 'wise counsel' before it is too late. My 'eccentric position,' you tell me, will 'ruin' me and my children. We might very well die, you say; or at a minimum, we will be destroyed socially and psychologically. Fortunately I have enough money to resist economic pressure. If I didn't have enough I am sure you would have mentioned the likelihood of *that* ruin, too.

"I want you to know why I'm doing what I am; why I am 'risking my life,' as you have described it, 'in order to get a few niggers into a school, and change everything around against the will of the people.' Until you understand that fellow Southerners, and not simply 'outside agitators,' want to abandon segregation as both criminal and wrong, you will be as confused about me as your letter was insulting to me.

"As you know, I am from South Carolina, and I dare say as Southern as you or anyone else in this town. Perhaps it is because I am a woman that I feel the way I do, a woman who grew up with two brothers who constantly made light of what I could do or be. Instead of being their pet younger sister, I became someone they could bully, and call weak. My mother and I were close, though, and in her eyes she was weak, too. She believed that all women were weak because she believed my father, and he said so—often. He was a rich man, partly through money he inherited and partly through money he made in law and investments. My brothers worshiped him, and my mother obeyed him. She was the 'Southern woman' you sheriffs are always talking about; the one who is so wonderful and beautiful and fragile and delicate and in need of your brute force to protect her against—of all things—the nigger-lust in every Negro's body and soul.

"Actually my mother was silently strong; and my father was noisily weak, so weak that he had to scare everyone around him to compliance, submission, agreement, or at least a pretense of such behavior. Thus, neither of my brothers ever had a chance to be anything but lawyers, and anything but intolerant—about the poor, the North, Negroes, foreigners, and in a way, women.

"My mother and I were supposed to mind the house, the garden, and ourselves. I remember my mother waiting until my father left the house to read his newspapers and magazines. She used to go to the library to read books—there. 'Your father wants us to breed and decorate the world, but when someone is lynched I feel a child of God has been killed against His will, and my instinct as a mother is aroused.' She told me that when I was about ten or twelve. I suppose I must remember that women then had only recently been able to vote, let alone object to murder.

"When I was a teen-ager my mother wanted to join a group of Southern churchwomen who had organized to protest the wave of lynchings that periodically took place over the South. My father absolutely forbade it, and she gave in immediately to his decision. At least she pretended to do so. That's where she and I have always differed. I believe that women and men have to respect one another. When I was engaged to my husband he promised me that he would never treat me as a child because I was a woman. He never did, and I will never be able to forget his kindness and fairness. To my mind, the Negro is treated like a child by nervous white people, who feel safe so long as they have someone to step on and generally abuse—women and Negroes, not to mention children! When I was fifteen I told my mother that—long before I read books by historians or psychologists. She smiled at me and told me not to get too 'thoughtful,' as she put it. That was her way of admitting how impossible it was sometimes to look at certain problems. Of course, I think my mother would be different now. Women have become much more independent, even among the sheltered rich or middle class.

"I came here to Mississippi because it was my husband's home. His family has been here for a long time, and they are fine people. They are now troubled and frightened by my stand. They worry for my life and even for their own, since the Klan does not discriminate in its hate; a family is a family to them. I don't say my in-laws go as far as I do, even when we talk in the privacy of our own homes. They try to make up for the historical record, for the cruelty that the Negro race as a whole has suffered in the South, by being unusually generous with their tenant farmers and household help. They have even offered to help them go North, and pay them a yearly wage *there* until they feel settled. None of the Negroes want to leave though; they are as devoted to my husband's family as they were ten or twenty years ago.

"I argue that it's still paternalism. My sister-in-law and my two brothers-in-law say that *their* generosity is not paternalistic. It's hard to settle the point, but I think we all agree that the *system*, apart from exceptions, is paternalistic, at best. I would rather have a few favored Negroes on their own but poorer, and the rest finally free. My husband always agreed, but he never would say so out loud, and his brothers and sister are like him today, silent about what they think.

"Since he died I've been the one who has taken the risks, gone out on a limb by writing letters and helping form committees, in order to *declare* what some know in their hearts is right—and others feel is dead wrong. For doing that, speaking my mind, I have been ostracized and threatened as if I were a murderer, or a foreign agent. Even those who agree with me think I am crazy—'emotionally disturbed,' one of them told me after two martinis. Those who disagree with me are trying to find out how much I'm paid by Northern emissaries, or government people. It would all be funny if it weren't done at the expense of a whole race of people, who have about lost their patience with such antics all over the world.

"People have asked me to wait. 'This thing will take generations. Why do you want to take the whole burden on yourself—and your children?' (They always wait before they add the last few words; and they smile, so as to conceal their nastiness with a veneer of friendliness.) Of course I thank them for their concern—especially for my children—and tell them the simple truth: they want nothing done; I want to do something; that is that.

"'Are you afraid?' they ask. There would be something wrong with me if I weren't. But I'm no more afraid than they are. At least I know why I'm afraid, and what I fear. They're so frightened and suspicious they've lost their common sense. They talk of 'conspiracies' and the like. They get nervous at every whisper, every news story, every rumor, every hate-mongering voice they meet up with. Yes, I'm afraid that one day I'll be shot at. I've settled my affairs in case it happens, and I'm ready to go. Meanwhile, I live every day as my conscience tells me to do, and as a result I feel content with myself, if scared at times. What about my friends, who wish me so well and keep on telling me to talk with a doctor or minister for 'counsel'? They're angry, distrustful, shrill and hateful—and getting worse in all those respects every day. Most of all, they're guilty, and they don't know it. Who needs the 'counsel,' I ask you?

"There is one more matter I would like to bring up. I have been asked by everyone from the police to members of my family why I have 'chosen' (as they put it) to be so 'different.' The truth is that I was brought up to feel as I do. My mother taught me most of what I say. She may have feared saying it in public—and sometimes even at home when my father was present—but if she were alive today she would be proud of me for doing so. My husband might have disagreed with me, but he never would have tried to silence me. We would have talked it all out—and perhaps changed one another a bit in doing so. Now he is gone, and I must do what I feel is right, without his advice or views. I miss him when some of those threatening calls come, but I can't dishonor his memory by buckling under to those calls because he isn't here to protect us. I told my daughter the other day that we owe it to his memory to be strong—to prove that he truly *gave* us his strength, that we have it in us, to use and rely upon. So long as I can think back and see my mother and my husband, I think I'll be able to keep my courage up. I know they would be happy for what I'm doing. They would be afraid, too; I know that. If they were alive they might be so afraid that they wouldn't do what I'm doing. I know that, too. But they are gone, and I am here. Perhaps I'm too loyal to them—still—but I feel somehow I can make the best of them live on, in honor."

Mrs. Trumbull never mailed that letter to the sheriff. Instead she sent him yet another curt note, reproving him for his "illegal, unconstitutional manner of law enforcement." She had kept a diary for years, and told me she intended to make the letter a part of it.

I felt lucky to have a chance to read the letter, but at a loss to answer her question after I had finished. "Does this explain anything to you, about why I've taken the stand I have?" I said yes, it did; as much as such things could be explained. Her reply to that was quick in coming and a surprise to me: "I think explanations don't settle an issue, they only make way for more questions. I've asked myself a lot of the questions you've asked me, directly or indirectly, these past years. After I answer them I still don't feel at rest. There are other women who have had mothers like mine, and have lost husbands like mine. I could have done other things with my memories, or my loneliness. It seems that I couldn't though. That's the only explanation I've ever been able to find for myself that sets my mind to rest."

26. The Making of a Black Muslim
JOHN R. HOWARD

This selection is analogous to selection 2, which described how and why Mao Tse-tung became a rebel. In like fashion, exploitive, discriminatory American society has inevitably produced black rebels. Some of this rebellion expresses itself as "deviant" religious commitment, as described here by John Howard. As a black American,

SOURCE: John R. Howard, "The Making of a Black Muslim," *Trans-action*, vol. 4, no. 2 (December 1966): 15–21. Copyright ©1966 by Transaction, Inc. and reprinted by permission.

Professor Howard possesses a special insight into those he describes. His success in the academic world evidently has not undermined the kind of keen understanding that graces the insider alone. His work, as represented in this article, brings to mind this assertion: The wonder is not that American society produces a number of Black Muslims who are alienated from the society at large; the wonder is that countless more black Americans, given their tragic history and present state of mind, have not totally rejected the society that has so long given them, at best, "the back of the hand."

You were black enough to get in here. You had the courage to stay. Now be man enough to follow the honorable Elijah Muhammad. You have tried the devil's way. Now try the way of the Messenger.
Minister William X, in a West Coast Black Muslim mosque

The Lost-Found Nation of Islam in the Wilderness of North America, commonly known as the Black Muslim movement, claims a small but fanatically devoted membership among the Negroes of our major cities. The way of the "Messenger" is rigorous for those who follow it. The man or woman who becomes a Muslim accepts not only an ideology but an all-encompassing code that amounts to a way of life.

A good Muslim does a full day's work on an empty stomach. When he finally has his one meal of the day in the evening, it can include no pork, nor can he have drink before or a cigarette after; strict dietary rules are standard procedure, and liquor and smoking are forbidden under any circumstances. His recreation is likely to consist of reading the Koran or participating in a demanding round of temple-centered activities, running public meetings or aggressively proselytizing on the streets by selling the Muslim newspaper, *Muhammad Speaks*.

Despite allegations of Muslim violence (adverse publicity from the slaying of Malcolm X supports the erroneous notion that Muslims preach violence), the member's life is basically ascetic. Why then in a non-ascetic, hedonistically-oriented society do people become Muslims? What is the life of a Muslim like? These are questions I asked in research among West Coast members. Specifically, I wanted to know:

What perspective on life makes membership in such an organization attractive?

Under what conditions does the potential recruit develop those perspectives?

How does he happen to come to the door of the temple for his first meeting?

The Black Muslims are a deviant organization even within the Negro community: the parents or friends of many members strongly objected to their joining. So how does the recruit handle pressures that might erode his allegiance to the organization and its beliefs?

Presenting my questions as an effort to "learn the truth" about the organization, I was able to conduct depth interviews with 19 West Coast recruits, following them through the process of their commitment to the Nation of Islam.

Two main points of appeal emerged—black nationalism and an emphasis on self-help. Some recruits were attracted primarily by the first, and some by the second. The 14 interviewees who joined the organization for its aggressive black nationalism will be called "Muslim militants." The remaining five, who were attracted more by its emphasis on hard work and rigid personal morality, may be aptly termed "Protestant Ethic Muslims."

MUSLIM MILITANTS: BEATING THE DEVIL

Of the 14 Muslim militants, some came from the South, some from border states, and some from the North. All lived in California at the time of the interviews: some migrated to the state as adults, others were brought out by their families as children. They varied in age from 24 to 46, and in education from a few years of grade school to four years of college. Regardless of these substantial differences in background, there were certain broad similarities among them.

At some point, each one had experiences that led away from the institutionally-bound ties and commitments that lend stability to most people's lives. Nine had been engaged in semi-legal or criminal activities. Two had been in the military, not as a career but as a way of postponing the decision of what to do for a living. None had a stable marital history. All of them were acutely aware of being outsiders by the standards of the larger society—and all had come to focus on race bias as the factor which denied them more conventional alternatives.

Leroy X came to California in his late teens, just before World War II:

> I grew up in Kansas City, Missouri, and Missouri was a segregated state. Negroes in Kansas City were always restricted to the menial jobs. I came out here in 1940 and tried to get a job as a waiter. I was a trained waiter, but they weren't hiring any Negroes as waiters in any of the downtown hotels or restaurants. The best I could do was busboy, and they fired me from that when they found out I wasn't Filipino.

Leroy X was drafted, and after a short but stormy career was given a discharge as being psychologically unfit.

> I tried to get a job, but I couldn't so I started stealing. There was nothing else to do—I couldn't live on air. The peckerwoods didn't seem to give a damn whether I lived or died. They wouldn't hire me and didn't seem to worry how I was going to stay alive. I started stealing.
>
> I could get you anything you wanted—a car, drugs, women, jewelry. Crime is a business like any other. I started off stealing myself. I wound

up filling orders and getting rid of stuff. I did that for fifteen years. In between I did a little time. I did time for things I never thought of doing and went free for things I really did.

In my business you had no friends, only associates, and not very close ones at that.... I had plenty of money. I could get anything I wanted without working for it. It wasn't enough, though.

Bernard X grew up in New York City:

As a kid ... you always have dreams—fantasies—of yourself doing something later—being a big name singer or something that makes you outstanding. But you never draw the connection between where you are and how you're going to get there. I had to—I can't say exactly when, 13, 14, 15, 16. I saw I was nowhere and had no way of getting anywhere.

Race feeling is always with you. You always know about The Man, but I don't think it is real, really real, until you have to deal with it in terms of what you are going to do with your own life. That's when you feel it. If you just disliked him before—you begin to hate him when you see him blocking you in your life. I think then a sense of inevitability hits you and you see you're not going to make it out—up—away—anywhere—and you see The Man's part in the whole thing, that's when you begin to think thoughts about him.

Frederick 2X became involved fairly early in a criminal subculture. His father obtained a "poor man's divorce" by deserting the family. His mother had children by other men. Only a tenuous sense of belonging to a family existed. He was picked up by the police for various offenses several times before reaching his teens. The police patrolling his neighborhood eventually restricted him to a two-block area. There was, of course, no legal basis for this, but he was manhandled if seen outside that area by any policeman who knew him. He graduated in his late teens from "pot" to "shooting shit" and eventually spent time in Lexington.

William 2X, formerly a shoeshine boy, related the development of his perspective this way:

You know how they always talk about us running after white women. There have always been a lot of [white] servicemen in this town—half of them would get around to asking me to get a woman for them. Some of them right out, some of them backing into it, laughing and joking and letting me know how much they were my friend, building up to asking me where they could find some woman. After a while I began to get them for them. I ran women—both black and white. . . . What I hated was they wanted me to do something for them [find women] and hated me for doing it. They figure "any nigger must know where to find it. . . ."

THINGS BEGIN TO ADD UP

Amos X grew up in an all-Negro town in Oklahoma and attended a Negro college. Because of this, he had almost no contact with whites during his formative years.

One of my aunts lived in Tulsa. I went to see her once when I was in college. I walked up to the front door of the house where she worked. She really got excited and told me if I came to see her anymore to come around to the back. But that didn't mean much to me at the time. It is only in looking back on it that all these things begin to add up.

After graduating from college, Amos joined the Marines. There he began to "see how they [the whites] really felt" about him; by the end of his tour, he had concluded that "the white man is the greatest liar, the greatest cheat, the greatest hypocrite on earth." Alienated and disillusioned, he turned to professional gambling. Then, in an attempt at a more conventional way of life, he married and took a job teaching school.

I taught English. Now I'm no expert in the slave masters' language, but I knew the way those kids talked after being in school eight and nine years was ridiculous. They said things like "mens" for "men." I drilled them and pretty soon some of them at least in class began to sound like they had been inside a school. Now the principal taught a senior class in English and his kids talked as bad as mine. When I began to straighten out his kids he felt I was criticizing him. . . . That little black man was afraid of the [white] superintendent and all those teachers were afraid. They had a little more than other so-called Negroes and didn't give a damn about those black children they were teaching. Those were the wages of honesty. It's one thing to want to do an honest job and another to be able to. . . .

With the collapse of his career as a public school teacher and the break-up of his marriage, Amos went to California, where he was introduced to the Muslim movement.

I first heard about them [the Muslims] in 1961. There was a debate here between a Muslim and a Christian minister. The Muslim said all the things about Christianity which I had been thinking but which I had never heard anyone say before. He tore the minister up.

Finding an organization that aggressively rejected the white man and the white man's religion, Amos found his own point of view crystallized. He joined without hesitation.

Norman Maghid first heard of the Muslims while he was in prison.

I ran into one of the Brothers selling the paper about two weeks after I got out and asked him about the meetings. Whether a guy could just go and walk in. He told me about the meetings so I made it around on a Wednesday evening. I wasn't even bugged when they searched me. When they asked me about taking out my letter [joining the organization] I took one out. They seemed to know what they were talking about. I never believed in nonviolence and love my enemies, especially when my enemies don't love me.

Muhammad Soule Kabah, born into a family of debt-ridden Texas sharecroppers, was recruited into the Nation of Islam after moving to California.

> I read a series of articles in the Los Angeles *Herald Dispatch*, an exchange between Minister Henry and a Christian minister. It confirmed what my grandfather had told me about my African heritage, that I had nothing to be ashamed of, that there were six thousand books on mathematics in the Library of the University of Timbucktoo while Europeans were still wearing skins. Also my father had taught me never to kow-tow to whites. My own father had fallen away. My parents didn't want me to join the Nation. They said they taught hate. That's funny isn't it? The white man can blow up a church and kill four children and the black man worries that an organization which tells you not to just take it is teaching hate.

PROTESTANT ETHIC MUSLIMS: UP BY BLACK BOOTSTRAPS

The Protestant Ethic Muslims all came from backgrounds with a strong tradition of Negro self-help. In two cases, the recruit's parents had been followers of Marcus Garvey; another recruit explicitly endorsed the beliefs of Booker T. Washington, and the remaining two, coming from upwardly mobile families, were firm in the belief that Negroes could achieve higher status if they were willing to work for it.

When asked what had appealed to him about the Muslims, Norman X replied:

> They thought that black people should do something for themselves. I was running this small place [a photography shop] and trying to get by. I've stuck with this place even when it was paying me barely enough to eat. Things always improve and I don't have to go to the white man for anything.

Ernestine X stressed similar reasons for joining the Muslims.

> You learned to stand up straight and do something for yourself. You learn to be a lady at all times—to keep your house clean—to teach your children good manners. There is not a girl in the M-G-T [Muslim Girls' Training.—Ed.] who does not know how to cook and sew. The children are very respectful: they speak only when they are spoken to. There is no such thing as letting your children talk back to you the way some people believe. The one thing they feel is the Negroes' downfall is men and sex for the women, and women and sex for the men, and they frown on sex completely unless you are married.

Despite their middle-class attitudes in many areas, Protestant Ethic Muslims denounced moderate, traditional civil rights organizations such as the NAACP, just as vigorously as the militant Muslims did. Norman X said that he had once belonged to the NAACP but had dropped out.

> They spent most of their time planning the annual brotherhood dinner.

Besides it was mostly whites—whites and the colored doctors and lawyers who wanted to be white. As far as most Negroes were concerned they might as well not have existed.

Lindsey X, who had owned and run his own upholstery shop for more than 30 years, viewed the conventional black bourgeoisie with equal resentment.

I never belonged to the NAACP. What they wanted never seemed real to me. I think Negroes should create jobs for themselves rather than going begging for them. That's why I never supported CORE.

In this respect Norman and Lindsey were in full accord with the more militant Amos X, who asserted:

They [the NAACP and CORE] help just one class of people. . . . Let something happen to a doctor and they are right there; but if something happens to Old Mose on the corner, you can't find them.

The interviews made it clear that most of the Protestant Ethic Muslims had joined the Nation because, at some point, they began to feel the need of organizational support for their personal systems of value. For Norman and Lindsey, it was an attempt to stop what they considered their own backsliding after coming to California. Both mentioned drinking to excess and indulging in what they regarded as a profligate way of life. Guilt feelings apparently led them to seek Muslim support in returning to more enterprising habits.

COMMITMENT TO DEVIANCE

The Nation of Islam is a deviant organization. As such it is subject to public scorn and ridicule. Thus it faces the problem of consolidating the recruit's allegiance in an environment where substantial pressures operate to erode this allegiance. How does it deal with this problem?

The structural characteristics of the Nation tend to insulate the member from the hostility of the larger society and thus contribute to the organization's survival. To begin with, the ritual of joining the organization itself stresses commitment without questions.

At the end of the general address at a temple meeting, the minister asks those nonmembers present who are "interested in learning more about Islam" to step to the back of the temple. There they are given three blank sheets of ordinary stationery and a form letter addressed to Elijah Muhammad in Chicago:

Dear Savior Allah, Our Deliverer:
I have attended the Teachings of Islam, two or three times, as taught by one of your ministers. I believe in it. I bear witness that there is no God but Thee. And, that Muhammad is Thy Servant and Apostle. I

desire to reclaim my Own. Please give me my Original name. My slave name is as follows:

The applicant is instructed to copy this letter verbatim on each of the three sheets of paper, giving his own name and address unabbreviated at the bottom. If he fails to copy the letter perfectly, he must repeat the whole task. No explanation is given for any of these requirements.

Formal acceptance of his letter makes the new member a Muslim, but in name only. Real commitment to the Nation of Islam comes gradually—for example, the personal commitment expressed when a chain smoker gives up cigarettes in accordance with the Muslim rules even though he knows that he could smoke unobserved. "It's not that easy to do these things," Stanley X said of the various forms of abstinence practiced by Muslims. "It takes will and discipline and time . . . but you're a much better person after you do." Calvin X told of periodic backsliding in the beginning, but added, "Once I got into the thing deep, then I stuck with it."

This commitment and the new regimen that goes with it have been credited with effecting dramatic personality changes in many members, freeing alcoholics from the bottle and drug addicts from the needle. It can be argued, however, that the organization does not change the member's fundamental orientation. To put it somewhat differently, given needs and impulses can be expressed in a variety of ways; thus, a man may give vent to his sadism by beating up strangers in an alley or by joining the police force and beating them up in the back room of the station.

"Getting into the thing deep" for a Muslim usually comes in three stages:

Participation in organizational activities—selling the Muslim newspaper, dining at the Muslim restaurant, attending and helping run Muslim meetings.

Isolation from non-Muslim social contacts—drifting away from former friends and associates because of divergent attitudes or simply because of the time consumed in Muslim activities.

Assimilation of the ideology—marking full commitment, when a Muslim has so absorbed the organization's doctrines that he automatically uses them to guide his own behavior and to interpret what happens in the world around him.

The fact that the organization can provide a full social life furthers isolation from non-Muslims. Participation is not wholly a matter of drudgery, of tramping the streets to sell the paper and studying the ideology. The organization presents programs of entertainment for its members and for the public. For example, in two West Coast cities a Negro theatrical troupe called the Touring Artists put on two plays, "Jubilee Day" and "Don't You Want to Be Free." Although there was a high element of humor in both plays, the basic themes—white brutality and hypocrisy and the necessity of developing Negro self-respect and courage—were consonant with the organization's perspective. Thus the organization makes it possible for a member to satisfy his need for diversion without going outside to do so. At the same time, it continually reaches him with its message through the didactic element in such entertainment.

Carl X's experiences were typical of the recruit's growing commitment to the Nation. When asked what his friends had thought when he first joined, he replied: "They thought I was crazy. They said, 'Man, how can you believe all that stuff?'" He then commented that he no longer saw much of them, and added:

> When you start going to the temple four or five times a week and selling the newspaper you do not have time for people who are not doing these things. We drifted—the friends I had—we drifted apart. . . . All the friends I have now are in the Nation. Another Brother and I get together regularly and read the Koran and other books, then ask each other questions on them like, "What is Allah's greatest weapon? The truth. What is the devil's greatest weapon? The truth. The devil keeps it hidden from men. Allah reveals it to man." We read and talk about the things we read and try to sharpen our thinking. I couldn't do that with my old friends.

Spelled out, the "stuff" that Carl X had come to believe, the official Muslim ideology, is this:

The so-called Negro, the American black man, is lost in ignorance. He is unaware of his own past history and the future role which history has destined him to play.

Elijah Muhammad has come as the Messenger of Allah to awaken the American black man.

The American black man finds himself now in a lowly state, but that was not always his condition.

The Original Man, the first men to populate the earth, were non-white. They enjoyed a high level of culture and reached high peaks of achievement.

A little over 6,000 years ago a black scientist named Yakub, after considerable work, produced a mutant, a new race, the white race.

This new race was inferior mentally, physically, and morally to the black race. Their very whiteness, the very mark of their difference from the black race, was an indication of their physical degeneracy and moral depravity.

Allah, in anger at Yakub's work, ordained that the white race should rule for a fixed amount of time and that the black man should suffer and by his suffering gain a greater appreciation of his own spiritual worth by comparing himself to the whites.

The time of white dominance is drawing near its end. It is foreordained that this race shall perish, and with its destruction the havoc, terror, and brutality which it has spread throughout the world shall disappear.

The major task facing the Nation of Islam is to awaken the American black man to his destiny, to acquaint him with the course of history.

The Nation of Islam in pursuing this task must battle against false prophets, in particular those who call for integration. Integration is a plot of the white race to forestall its own doom. The black bourgeoisie, bought off by a few paltry favors and attempting to ingratiate themselves with the whites, seek to spread this pernicious doctrine among so-called Negroes.

The Nation of Islam must encourage the American black man to begin now to assume his proper role by wresting economic control from the whites. The American black man must gain control over his own economic fortunes by going into business for himself and becoming economically strong.

The Nation of Islam must encourage the so-called Negro to give up those habits which have been spread among them by the whites as part of the effort to keep them weak, diseased, and demoralized. The so-called Negro must give up such white-fostered dissolute habits as drinking, smoking, and eating improper food. The so-called Negro must prepare himself in mind and body for the task of wresting control from the whites.

The Nation of Islam must encourage the so-called Negro to seek now his own land within the continental United States. This is due him and frees him from the pernicious influence of the whites.

THE PROBLEM OF DEFECTION

Commitment to the Nation can diminish as well as grow. Four of the members I interviewed later defected. Why?

These four cases can be explained in terms of a weak point in the structure of the Nation. The organization has no effective mechanisms for handling grievances among the rank and file. Its logic accounts for this. Muslim doctrine assumes that there is a single, ultimate system of truth. Elijah Muhammad and, by delegation, his ministers are in possession of this truth. Thus only Elijah Muhammad himself can say whether a minister is doing an adequate job. The result is the implicit view that there is nothing to be adjudicated between the hierarchy and its rank and file.

Grievances arise, however. The four defectors were, for various reasons, all dissatisfied with Minister Gerard X. Since there were no formal mechanisms within the organization for expressing their dissatisfaction, the only solution was to withdraw.

For most members, however, the pattern is one of steadily growing involvement. And once the ideology is fully absorbed, there is virtually no such thing as dispute or counterevidence. If a civil rights bill is not passed, this proves the viciousness of whites in refusing to recognize Negro rights. If the same bill *is* passed, it merely proves the duplicity of whites in trying to hide their viciousness.

The ideology also provides a coherent theory of causation, provided one is willing to accept its basic assumptions. Norman X interpreted his victory over his wife in a court case as a sign of Allah's favor. Morris X used it to account for the day-to-day fortunes of his associates.

> Minister X had some trouble. He was sick for a long time. He almost died. I think Allah was punishing him. He didn't run the temple right. Now the Brothers make mistakes. Everyone does—but Minister X used to abuse them at the meetings. It was more a personal thing. He had a little power and it went to his head. Allah struck him down and I think he learned a little humility.

When a man reasons in this fashion, he has become a fully committed member of the Nation of Islam. His life revolves around temple-centered activities, his friends are all fellow Muslims, and he sees his own world—usually the world of an urban slum dweller—through the framework of a very powerful myth. He is still doing penance for the sins of Yakub, but the millennium is at hand. He has only to prepare.

The Nation of Islam does not in any real sense convert members. Rather it attracts Negroes who have already, through their own experiences in white America, developed a perspective congruent with that of the Muslim movement. The recruit comes to the door of the temple with the essence of his ideas already formed. The Black Muslims only give this disaffection a voice.

Social Institutions

Part VII

In all societies there are formalized and relatively stable phenomena that are generally termed *institutions*. However, there is lack of agreement on just which phenomena are properly denoted as such. Some sociologists apply the term solely to highly organized, systematized, long-term procedures; others assert that *groups* of a similar nature should also be called institutions. The present editor agrees with the latter practice —that is, it seems logical to conclude that any procedure or group is properly termed "institutionalized" if it is to a considerable degree organized, systematized, and stable. At any rate, it is clear that although institutions are often vital, they frequently develop inhumane and inefficient features. Some of these are explored in the following selections.

27. Four- or Five-Minute Speech for a Symposium on American Institutions and Do They Need Changing or What?
JAMES HERNDON

James Herndon, young father of two children, expresses here his total disillusionment with institutions. He did not always feel this way. These convictions arose when, as an elementary school teacher, he learned that established procedures and entrenched forces make it almost impossible for the truly creative school employee to survive. It would be unwise, however, to take Herndon's pronouncements completely at face value. No doubt there is much truth in them, but on the other hand, a large-scale society would become chaotic if it were permeated with spontaneity to the degree that Herndon appears to favor.

. . .

The first characteristic of any institution is that no matter what the inevitable purpose for which it was intended, it must devote all its energy to doing the exact opposite. Thus, a Savings Bank must encourage the people to borrow money at Interest, and a School must inspire its students toward Stupidity.

The second characteristic is that an institution must continue to exist. Every action must be undertaken with respect to eternity. This second characteristic is the reason for the first. For unless a Savings Bank can persuade the people not to Save, the Savings Bank will go broke. But the

SOURCE: James Herndon, *How to Survive in Your Native Land* (New York: Simon & Schuster, 1971), pp. 109–111. Copyright © 1971 by James Herndon. Reprinted by permission of Simon & Schuster, Inc.

Savings Bank must continue to exist, since otherwise the people would have No Place To Save. Just so, the School must encourage its students not to learn. For if the students learned quickly, most of them could soon leave the school, having Learned. But if the students left the school it would cease to exist as an institution and then the students would have No Place In Which To Learn.

Following that argument, we can arrive at a description of an institution: An Institution Is A Place To Do Things Where Those Things Will Not Be Done.

If the institutions are reproached forcefully enough, they will admit it. Thus the Savings Bank will say, You want to Save? So hide your bread under the mattress! Bury it in the back yard, you bastard!

And the School: You want to Learn? Hire a tutor! Watch TV. Get your parents to teach you! Fuck you!

An institution and its arguments are both circular. Change it? Better change the music of the spheres instead!

Change! An institution is like an English middle-class audience going to see a play by George Bernard Shaw.

Change! An institution loves change and criticism. It adapts. It endures. It is hip to the warp and woof of the nation. It perns in the gyres, if necessary. For example, if the parents of America, realizing that their child has already learned all he needs from the school, namely how to write his name, read C-A-T and recite the Preamble, wish to send him out to be apprenticed or to a job in the garment district where the child can learn about the ways of the world and at the same time make a little bread for the family, the school incites the Institution of Congress to respond with a law about Universal Education, to wit, every parent must send his child to the School until age x. (Fuck you, says the school.) A hundred years later when things have changed—the kids want to work, the Union don't want them children, the nation would rather the kid went to Junior College—the school pretends that the Law was made to *make the children* go to school until age x.

Change! An old conservative general once rose to complain that the Youth had lost all respect for its Elders, that it had lost interest in the Games, that it had no Character. He did not think it would do well at another Thermopylae. He thought it had to do with the Schools. The Schools, he said, rob Youth of its Imagination, which is the only important Quality it has! In saying that, he implied that imagination and character were somehow associated, an idea which we find ludicrous.

Change! An institution can only be changed in the same way that a mountain is changed by highway engineers into a pile of dust. No institution, once invented, has ever ceased to exist. Nor has any institution ever changed, except according to the exigencies of time as above. Not changed, only adapted. Its fundamental purpose remains, namely to provide a place to do things where these things won't be done.

28. The Tyranny of Qwerty
CHARLES LEKBERG

The cynicism expressed in selection 27 is here given substance by "The Tyranny of Qwerty." The author, Charles Lekberg, is a freelance writer and former editor of Chicago *magazine. As he indicates, sheer inertia sometimes plays a large part in maintaining institutionalized procedures that become outmoded. Beyond that, typically there are vested interests in the established order. Think of the number of those who may be inconvenienced at least initially, or even lose heavily, if "Qwerty" is supplanted: authors and publishers of standard typing manuals; typewriter manufacturers, distributors, and repairers; secretarial schools; secretarial firms and services; school typing teachers; individual typists who would have to alter long-term habits. And, if typists became twice as productive, what would that do to the labor market and its suppliers? Further, if it is difficult to change an institutionalized procedure such as typing, how incredibly more complex are the implications of changing more vital institutions! Little wonder, then, that desirable social changes so often come slowly, painfully, reluctantly.*

What can you say about a valuable, desperately needed skill that:

—takes up to twice as long as it should to learn;
—takes up to twice as long as it should to use;
—makes you work perhaps twenty times harder than necessary;
—uses equipment booby-trapped to ensure errors;
—has persisted out of sheer inertia since 1872;
—is still being taught to millions of unsuspecting people?

Well, you can't say much.

The skill in question is typing, typing on qwerty. Qwerty—in case you've been using it for so long that you have forgotten what it is—is the name for the standard typewriter keyboard. Q, w, e, r, t, and y are the first six keys in the upper row of letters. Together they make up the traditional name for the keyboard. Qwerty even sounds faintly contemptible, and, after you learn the facts, it is.

Briefly, qwerty came about this way. The first commercially practical typewriter was put together in Milwaukee through the work of C. Latham Sholes, Carlos Glidden, Samuel Soule, James Densmore, Matthias Schwalbach, and a few others. Sholes and his associates began with a device to number the pages of a book and by 1867 created a rather crude

SOURCE: Charles Lekberg, "The Tyranny of Qwerty," *Saturday Review* 55 (September 30, 1972), 37–40. Reprinted by permission.

machine that could make every man his own typesetter. This working model was first patented in 1868, went through many refinements, and was then turned over to E. Remington and Sons, gun makers, of Ilion, New York, for manufacture, in 1873.

In their innocence Sholes and his partners first arranged the letters of the typewriter's keyboard in alphabetical order, but the uselessness of this system soon became apparent. Also, that particular model had mechanical problems. Type was suspended by wires in a small, circular nest inside the machine. You didn't have to type very fast for the letters to rise up and jam at the platen (the roller of a typewriter), the very place where they were supposed to print.

To end that annoyance, James Densmore asked his son-in-law, a Pennsylvania school superintendent (who surely should have known), what letters and combinations of letters appeared most often in the English language. Then, in 1872, Densmore and Sholes put what they believed to be the most used characters as far apart as possible in the type basket and ended up with the horror of qwerty.

Since that time typewriters have become so refined mechanically that they almost operate themselves; the keyboard designed in 1872, however, remains basically the same. Today you and I and about fifty million other people in the English-speaking world still use qwerty. Touch typing, in use almost from the very start, still has beginners thumping away, mumbling to themselves, "a, s, d, f, space . . . semicolon, l, k, j, space."

Will it last forever? It could, for all we typers seem to care. And yet for forty years—since 1932—a logical alternative has been available but almost totally ignored. The world has hardly beaten a path to his door, but in 1932, after twenty years of study financed by two grants from the Carnegie Corporation, August Dvorak came forth with a new typewriter keyboard. It was a dream.

On this keyboard you could type more than 3,000 words on the familiar home row compared with perhaps only fifty on qwerty's home row.

Dvorak put all the vowels in his home row, under the fingers of the left hand. The right hand rested atop h, t, n, and s, with d just to the left of the right index finger. Qwerty's j and k, occupying the most prominent place, were banished to just about the least prominent on Dvorak's keyboard. And so on.

Dvorak rearranged things so that 70 per cent of the work could be done in the home row, 22 per cent in the row above, and 8 per cent below. Numbers remained at the top, though in a different lineup. With qwerty, 32 per cent of the work is done in the home row, 52 per cent above, and 16 per cent below.

Dvorak also made the right hand work harder, giving it 56 per cent of the load, the left hand 44 per cent. On qwerty, the left hand had to handle 57 per cent of the work, the right hand 43 per cent. Dvorak also straightened out the work load of the separate fingers and greatly reduced the clumsy stroking that almost guaranteed fatigue and errors.

In his 538-page book *Typewriter Behavior,* Dvorak, then professor of education and director of research at the University of Washington in Seattle, described his work. He had studied thousands of words to discover the frequency of letters and letter combinations. He scrutinized finger movements with slow-motion films of typists. And he tested more than 250 possible keyboards.

One of his early conclusions was that you could come up with a better keyboard simply by arranging the letters at random—a pretty strong condemnation of qwerty.

Dvorak, of course, was not the first, or the last, to try to improve the old Sholes keyboard. As far back as 1893, for example, J. G. Hammond came up with what he believed was a better arrangement. And in the 1940s Roy T. Griffith of Pittsburgh introduced his Minimotion keyboard, which also allowed more words to be typed on the home row. But Dvorak's arrangement seems to have been the best researched and, in the opinion of many, by far the best.

True, there was a certain flurry of interest when Dvorak came out with his keyboard, but no one could figure out how to change. Everybody—typists, industries, schools—was committed to another system.

Dvorak persisted. One of his most impressive demonstrations took place during World War II when he retrained fourteen navy women to use his keyboard. After a month the women were turning out 74 per cent more work and were 68 per cent more accurate. After only ten days, in fact, the change had paid for itself.

Using the Dvorak simplified keyboard, or DSK, as it came to be called, the women's fingertips were moving little more than one mile on an average day, compared with twelve or twenty miles a day for typists using the standard keyboard.

Test after test was conducted—so many in fact that by 1965 the U.S. Bureau of Standards felt compelled to say that "there is little need to demonstrate further the superiority of the Dvorak keyboard in experimental tests. Plenty of well-documented evidence exists."

Part of that evidence was accumulated during the 1940s, when typing competitions were the vogue. Between 1933 and 1941 DSK typists captured twenty-six international speed records, forty-five first places, and four grand championships.

The outstanding virtuoso on DSK was one of Dvorak's own pupils, Lenore Fenton MacClain, who won eight world records in typing and transcription. Mrs. MacClain typed 70 words a minute pre-DSK, then switched and reached a zippy 182 words a minute, net, in one unofficial test. A net score is computed by subtracting ten words typed for each error. You could say that Mrs. MacClain's achievement is unusual, and you would be right. But many DSK typists do double their former speeds and break the 100-word-a-minute barrier.

Looking at such results, Robert L. McCauley, a former computer man and now promoter of instructional literature for DSK, asks: "Is the DSK that good, or is the standard keyboard just that bad?" To these questions his answers are "Yes!" and "Yes!" McCauley, now based in Burbank, California, turned to DSK a few years ago. He maintains that:

—anyone, including children, can begin to master DSK in less than two weeks;
—speeds of forty to fifty words a minute can be attained in two to three months;
—superspeeds of more than 100 words a minute are possible for many in less than a year;
—fatigue and mistakes are greatly lessened.

But McCauley doesn't believe DSK is for everyone, even though it is obviously hands-down superior. Like power steering and automatic transmissions for automobiles, it should, he feels, be available for those who want it. He believes the "let's-all-change-to-DSK" talk turns a lot of people off and is actually slowing down acceptance of a new keyboard.

Such fears, however, don't seem to bother the other main advocate of DSK, Philip Davis of Irvington, New Jersey.

Davis, a journeyman printer and former teacher, became seriously interested in DSK in 1964 and now heads a company that offers typewriters with the new keyboard. (Davis recently delivered a DSK typewriter to Ralph Nader at the Center for Auto Safety in Washington, D.C. Interestingly, Nader requested a manual machine rather than an electric one. He believes, it seems, that electric typewriters add to the nation's energy crisis.)

Davis wants DSK adopted by individual typists and, especially, by the printing industry for its composing machines, many of which are now the so-called cold-type perforators that use qwerty instead of the old linotype keyboard, itself a special monster. A perforator is a sort of minicomputer with typewriter keyboard that produces holes in a tape. After typing up a tape, the operator feeds it back into the machine and out comes column after column of justified type.

Unlike Bob McCauley, Davis looks for total conversion to DSK eventually. "But a switch to Dvorak keyboarding is not like changing the rules about which side of the street you drive on," he says, attacking what he calls the "clean-sweep" theory.

"The change can be made perfectly well," he says, "one person at a time, one operator at a time. Any office manager can rearrange work loads to fit his schedule."

According to Davis, "present-day typing classes fail to bring seventy per cent of the students up to a forty-word-a-minute competence. The Dvorak record, on the other hand, is virtually one hundred per cent successful in imparting sixty-word-a-minute excellence in about the same training time that would have led to thirty words a minute on old qwerty."

But couldn't computers come up with something even better than Dvorak, which was, after all, developed some forty years ago?

Davis doesn't think so. "Every newcomer thinks he'll get different and better answers if he rounds up new data and runs it through a computer," he says. "Dvorak took the utmost pains to get the ultimate keyboard. Of course, there are thousands of ways to arrange a typewriter keyboard. But few of these are even plausible, and all the plausible ones were analyzed down to the last detail. Dvorak is the outcome."

And how about the equipment problem?

Davis says: "For every alphanumerically keyboarded device, except most of the old models of linotype and intertype, there is some conversion method well within the range of economic practicability. An attachment to convert a rather wide variety of machines could be provided at about the cost of a good office-model typewriter. For the flexible, more expensive electronic devices, not even this is required.

"You can make the change by attrition," he adds. "It takes about the same time to train an operator as it does to get equipment. The life of a typewriter in a big bank is eight years. Most office careers last longer than that. When the time comes to get a new machine, the time to retrain the operator has come, too."

Davis cites a two-year experiment (1966–1968) when DSK was tested in the composing room of the Western Publishing Company printing plant in Cambridge, Maryland. A woman employee was retrained for two full weeks on a DSK keyboard. Then she was put to work on a perforator.

The woman, previously the slowest operator in the plant, rose from 12,000 strokes an hour to 16,000, the plant record being 18,000. But then Western had a change in management, and that was about as far as it all went.

More recently Blaine Hiscock, head machinist at the Toronto *Globe and Mail*, trained two composing room operators on DSK. Hiscock reports: "We found we were able to move the two people involved to the perforating machines after about a month of practicing one to three hours a day on a DSK typewriter."

Hiscock emphasizes that the *Globe and Mail* doesn't have a concentrated training program for DSK perforation, but he says, "We would consider the results of our experimentation quite encouraging if we decided to expand with DSK."

He adds that he converted two of his own typewriters to DSK, one manual and one electric portable, by resoldering the type slugs to the type bars.

Suppose you want to introduce DSK in your home or office. Can you easily get the equipment and retrain yourself and your staff? The equipment is easy enough to get, as is the instructional material. And you can retrain yourself or others if you can spare the time or persuade people to relearn on machines that they will find almost nowhere else. It takes a minimum of six weeks to switch, preferably after you take a rest from qwerty. Unlike being bilingual, however, you can't be bidigital to the extent that you can switch from one multikeyed machine to another with a different setup.

How do you get a DSK? Any typewriter company will sell you one. Like any company, typewriter firms are first interested in profits—revolution comes second, if at all. So they don't push DSK.

Remington makes no additional charge for the keyboard if it is ordered with pica type. Smith-Corona Marchant makes a "slight additional charge," depending on the model ordered. It adds that "the demand is increasing as people learn of the advantages of DSK."

Royal reveals that it sells "fewer than twenty-five machines a year" with DSK, adding that there is a fixed charge of $20 extra for DSK and "all nonstandard keyboards."

IBM offers DSK on one model only, at an additional charge of $40.

So there it is—perhaps the perfect keyboard. Supporters like Phil Davis believe the arrival of the computer will hasten its adoption. You talk to a computer by keyboard, he says, and it doesn't make much sense to use the 1872 arrangement to slow down a lightning-swift machine.

Others aren't so sure. They think electronics may find other ways of transferring information into machine language. Also, critics say, if Dvorak's keyboard were going to be adopted, it would have happened before this.

Still, it's hard for an observer to plow through all the history, consider all the facts, think of all the wasted time and effort and failure connected with qwerty, and then conclude that DSK is doomed. August Dvorak, now eighty years old and living in Seattle, certainly doesn't think so, even though his patent rights ran out in 1962 and he can no longer profit financially from his creation.

Inquiries about, and individual conversion to, DSK are constant even if adoption by industry and schools is not. As the years go by, in fact, DSK looks more and more like some sleeping beauty waiting for a handsome, efficiency-conscious prince to awaken her with a kiss. It may be a long, long time before the world stops thinking of "Humoresque" every time it hears the name Dvorak, but it can happen. There must, after all, be a better way for that silly, quick brown fox to jump over that lazy dog.

29. NATAPROBU*

NATAPROBU, The National Association of Professional Bureaucrats, was formed recently by a man named James Borden. He puts out an occasional publication called "Inaction Line" and has written the official Association song, "Let's Fingertap Together." The Association is built around three laws: (1) When in charge, ponder; (2) When in trouble, delegate; (3) When in doubt, mumble.

*Source unknown

30. Serc: A Dizzying Story of Vertigo in the FDA
CONSUMER REPORTS

The prototype of the institutionalized group is the formal organization known as a bureaucracy. This type of organization can be simultaneously the epitome of efficiency and the essence of ineptitude. The latter aspect of bureaucracy is emphasized by the anonymous observer who penned the description of NATAPROBU *in selection 29. A related story is presented in the following reading in which* Consumer Reports *reveals some disheartening facts about the Federal Drug Administration.*

Serc is a prescription drug first marketed in 1966 by Unimed, Inc., of Morristown, N.J. It was intended to be used by physicians for symptomatic treatment of Ménière's Syndrome. That's an affliction of the inner ear that causes intermittent episodes of vertigo, progressive hearing loss and tinnitus (a sensation of buzzing and other noises). An estimated 100,000 to 300,000 persons in the United States suffer from it.

Serc—betahistine hydrochloride—has finally been ordered off the market by the U.S. Food and Drug Administration, the Federal agency charged by the law with the responsibilities of protecting the public against contaminated food products and hazardous or ineffective drugs.

At the beginning of the six-year-long Serc episode, there were serious questions within the FDA itself about the drug's efficacy, or effectiveness. At the end, although there was no allegation that Serc presented a hazard, there was some evidence that it might actually *aggravate* the symptoms of Ménière's Syndrome in some patients. In between the beginning and the end of the Serc saga was a succession of about-faces on the part of the FDA. That chain of events is yet another case example of the systemic problems within the agency. . . . The dizzying chronology of Serc suggests that the FDA, itself, might have a touch of Ménière's Syndrome within its own bureaucratic inner ear.

OVERRULING THE EXPERTS

Serc went on sale in 1966 when Dr. James Goddard, then FDA commissioner, overruled the objections of FDA medical officers and approved Serc marketing. The FDA medical officers had contended that Unimed's studies failed to prove the drug worked and that therefore Serc did not meet the so-called efficacy requirement formulated by Congress in 1962. That amendment to the Food, Drug, and Cosmetic Act added to the

SOURCE: "Serc: *A Dizzying Story of Vertigo in the FDA,*" *Consumer Reports* 38 (March 1973), 155–156. Copyright © 1973 by Consumers Union of United States, Inc., Mount Vernon, N.Y. 10550. Excerpted by permission of *Consumer Reports.*

responsibilities of the FDA the provision that a new drug must be proven effective prior to its approval for public sale. Although the FDA's standard for approval calls for two controlled studies, *Serc* was approved on the strength of only one study. The label Goddard ordered for the drug was far from reassuring: "There is some evidence suggesting that *Serc*—betahistine hydrochloride—may reduce the frequency of episodes of vertigo associated with Ménière's Syndrome in some patients." The law requires "substantial," not "some" evidence of effectiveness and a top FDA official later conceded that the label was ". . . not consistent with the wording of the law." Before Goddard approved *Serc* he heard intercessions on the drug's behalf from several prominent political figures, most notably the then Senator Lister Hill, of Alabama. Hill was chairman of two Senate subcommittees that controlled the FDA's appropriations and its rulemaking authority.

THE FDA IS CHALLENGED

Six months after *Serc's* approval, the single study underpinning the FDA's action was challenged. *The Medical Letter,* a nonprofit publication respected by physicians, contended that the controls employed by *Serc's* investigator, Dr. Joseph C. Elia, were "seriousy inadequate." Dr. Elia had conducted the clinical studies of the drug under sponsorship of Unimed.

The FDA did nothing, however, until it was prodded by a letter from Representative L. H. Fountain, chairman of the watchdog House Intergovernmental Relations Subcommittee, who asked the FDA to take another look at the Elia study. The FDA's "second look" tended to confirm *The Medical Letter's* findings. It found further that Elia had not mentioned that six of the 16 subjects in his study had received other medications concurrently with *Serc*. The Elia study did not establish whether the favorable findings Elia attributed to *Serc* resulted from *Serc* or from the other medications. At this point, the FDA's episode of vertigo seemed to have passed. But then the FDA dropped the *Serc* matter with no further action.

Six months later, prodded by another letter from Fountain, this time expressing an intention to hold hearings of his subcommittee about the *Serc* approval, the FDA initiated action to withdraw *Serc's* approval. In July, 1968, the agency issued a notice of hearing—a prescribed step in the FDA procedure for revising drug approval. In its notice, the FDA called Elia's study "defective" and "inadequate" and said the original application contained "untrue statements of material facts about the status of some of the patients involved in the clinical trials, the drugs they were given and the results obtained."

The FDA's vertigo had receded again. But then two new players appeared on stage. They were Martin Sweig, later convicted of criminal misuse of his post as chief administrative aid to then House Speaker John W. McCormack, and Nathan M. Voloshen, a lobbyist who later pleaded guilty to being Sweig's partner in influence peddling. Sweig asked Fountain to grant an interview to Voloshen. Voloshen implied to Fountain that he had new evidence of the wonders of *Serc,* suggesting that Fountain's hearings were not needed. Fountain says he told Voloshen to give his evidence to the FDA, not to him.

ALMOST, BUT NOT QUITE

The FDA, in the typically slow pace of agency rulemaking, eventually held a revocation hearing for *Serc,* and finally ruled in November, 1970, that proof of efficacy was lacking and that the drug should be withdrawn from sale. Unimed appealed to the U.S. Court of Appeals. The FDA stayed its withdrawal order pending the outcome of the court appeal. The Food, Drug and Cosmetic Act contains the provision that "The commencement of proceedings ... shall not, unless specifically ordered by the court to the contrary, operate as a stay of the Secretary's order."

Fifteen months later, in February, 1972, the court upheld the FDA withdrawal order. At last, it appeared, *Serc* would be taken off the market. But Ménière's Syndrome set in at the FDA again. In a letter to Unimed that was not made public at the time, the FDA ordered its removal order stayed a second time, and gave Unimed until 1973 to complete new studies on *Serc's* effectiveness.

The FDA offered this explanation for its unprecedented action in staying its own formal withdrawal ruling upheld in court: "This action was taken bearing in mind that no safety question is involved, and that there is no proven alternative therapy for those who suffer from Ménière's Syndrome. The studies could not be financed unless marketing of the drug was permitted to continue." Unimed, in other words, was given an official blessing to continue to sell *Serc*—a drug already found ineffective—in hopes that it could disprove the finding. Consumers were, in effect, given the opportunity to pay Unimed's research bill to the tune of about a million dollars worth of *Serc* sales a year.

QUESTION OF DISCRETION

The FDA's general counsel, Peter B. Hutt, defended this decision with the argument that the agency has discretionary power to stay, delay, or otherwise set the time of withdrawal after a finding of lack of efficacy. Hutt's position was contrary to his predecessor's view that withdrawal should be automatic after a formal finding. The Comptroller General of the United States also contends that withdrawal should be automatic and said in an advisory opinion last fall that the FDA's stay of its withdrawal notice in the *Serc* case "was clearly contrary to law" and an abdication by FDA of its functions and responsibilities...."

The 1962 amendment to the Food, Drug, and Cosmetic Act states that the FDA "shall" withdraw marketing approval after determining "... that there is a lack of substantial evidence that the drug will have the effect it purports or is represented to have ... or that the application contains any untrue statement of a material fact. ..." Hutt's predecessor and the Comptroller General interpret "shall" to mean "must." CU [Consumers Union.—Ed.] agrees with the Comptroller General, and last December 15 filed a complaint in U.S. District Court against Elliot L. Richardson, then secretary of the Department of Health, Education and Welfare, and against Dr. Charles C. Edwards, FDA commissioner. The suit asked the court to order the defendants to implement the existing FDA withdrawal notice for *Serc*.

Quiety, in what CU hopes is FDA's final recovery from bureaucratic vertigo, the FDA made an interim evaluation of Unimed's ongoing *Serc* studies. The FDA said it found that some patients on a placebo (an inert substance that looks like the medication being tested) did considerably better than those receiving *Serc*. "*Serc* does something to the modification of Ménière's Syndrome," concluded Dr. Philip R. Jacoby, an FDA medical officer. "This something is to alter the course of Ménière's Syndrome in such a way as to result in increased episodes of vertigo."

A QUIET WITHDRAWAL

Six days after the CU suit was filed, and without public fanfare, the FDA withdrew its approval of *Serc* in a letter to Unimed. The withdrawal order got little attention outside the drug trade press. After a further CU inquiry, the FDA ordered Unimed to recall *Serc* from all channels of commerce. At that point CU withdrew its suit.

Despite this commendable FDA action at last, which CU hopes will end the *Serc* saga, there remains an unsettled and potentially dangerous precedent, in CU's opinion. The *Serc* case did not resolve the important question of whether the FDA does, in fact, have the right to stay a court-upheld withdrawal order. If the FDA still considers that it does, there's little to stop the *Serc* script from being restaged again and again with a succession of new casts of characters while consumers pay their money for and put their hopes in medications whose worth is unproved.

. . .

31. The Dusty Outskirts of Hope
MARY WRIGHT

Here we have the second of social worker Mary Wright's contributions to this volume (see selection 3). She tells a sad story about what happens when passive persons attempt to deal with bureaucratic personnel. Those who can deal adequately with such personnel typically don't need to! Wright's tale has another moral: Certain aspects of the American social system produce people who are so beaten they cannot benefit from the programs which are specially designed to help just such people. No doubt this same situation prevails in other large societies. When such societies grind their Buddy Banks, "they grind exceeding small."

I know a man, I'll call him Buddy Banks. He lives in a ravine in a little one-room pole-and-cardboard house he built himself, with his wife, their six children, and baby granddaughter. Mr. Banks, 45 years old, is a sober man, a kindly man, and a passive man. He can read and write a little, has worked in the coal mines and on farms, but over the years he's been pretty badly battered up and today is "none too stout." Last fall, when he could no longer pay the rent where he was staying, his mother-in-law gave him a small piece of ground, and he hastened to put up this little shack in the woods before the snow came. If, as you ride by, you happened to glance down and see where he lives, and see his children playing among the stones, you would say, "White trash." You would say, "Welfare bums."

When the newspaper announced the new ADC program for unemployed fathers, I thought of Buddy Banks. There is not much farm work to be done in the wintertime, and Mr. Banks has been without a job since summer. Here in their ravine they can dig their coal from a hole in the hill, and dip their water from the creek, and each month he scratches together $2 for his food stamps by doing odd jobs for his neighbors, who are very nearly as poor as he is. Other than this there is nothing coming in. I thought, maybe here is some help for Buddy Banks.

Mr. Banks does not get a newspaper, nor does he have a radio, and so he had not heard about the new program. He said, yes, he would be interested. I offered to take him to town right then, but he said no, he would have to clean up first, he couldn't go to town looking like this. So I agreed to come back Friday.

On Friday he told me he'd heard today was the last day for signing up. We were lucky, eh? It wasn't true, but it's what he had heard and I won-

SOURCE: Mary Wright, "The Dusty Outskirts of Hope," *Mountain Life and Work* 15 (Spring 1964), 10–15. Reprinted by permission of author and publisher.

dered, suppose he'd been told last Tuesday was the last day for signing up, and I hadn't been there to say, well, let's go find out anyway.

Buddy Banks was all fixed up and looked nice as he stepped out of his cabin. His jacket was clean, and he had big rubber boots on and a cap on his head. I felt proud walking along with him, and he walked proud. (Later, in town, I noticed how the hair curled over his collar, and the gray look about him, and the stoop of his shoulders. If you saw him you'd have said, "Country boy, come to get his check.")

When we reached the Welfare Office it was full of people, a crowd of slouchy, shuffly men, standing around and looking vaguely in different directions. I followed Buddy Banks and his brother-in-law, who had asked to come with us, into the lobby, and they too stood in the middle of the floor. Just stood. It was not the momentary hesitation that comes before decision. It was the paralysis of strangeness, of lostness, of not knowing what to do. A girl was sitting at a table, and after a number of minutes of nothing, I quietly suggested they ask her. No, they told me, that was the food stamp girl. But there was no other. So finally, when I suggested, well, ask her anyway, they nodded their heads, moved over, and asked her. I wondered how long they might have gone on standing there, if I'd kept my mouth shut. I wondered how long the others all around us had been standing there. I had an idea that if I hadn't been right in the way, Buddy Banks just might have turned around and gone out the door when he saw the crowd, the lines, and that smartly-dressed food stamp girl bending over her desk.

Yes, he was told, and after waiting a few minutes, he was shown behind the rail to a chair beside a desk, and a man with a necktie and a big typewriter began to talk with him. They talked a long long time, while the brother-in-law and I waited in the lobby. (They had asked the brother-in-law if he had brought the birth certificates. No, he hadn't, and so they said there wasn't anything they could do, to come back next Tuesday. He said nothing, stared at them a moment, then walked away. He stood around waiting for us all day long and never asked them another question. He said he would tend to it some other time. Fortunately, they got Mr. Banks sitting down before they inquired about the birth certificates.)

I knew what they were talking about: I have talked long times with Mr. Banks myself, and they were going over it again, and again, and I could imagine Mr. Banks nodding his head to the question he didn't quite understand, because he wanted to make a good impression, and it would be a little while before the worker realized that he hadn't understood, and so they would go back and try again, and then Mr. Banks would explain as best he could, but he would leave something out, and then the worker wouldn't understand, so that, in all, their heads were bent together for almost an hour and a half. It seemed a long time to take to discover Buddy Banks' need—a visit to his home would have revealed it in a very few minutes, but of course twelve miles out and twelve miles back takes time too, and there are all those eligibility rules to be checked out, lest somebody slip them a lie and the editorials start hollering "Fraud! Fraud!" Actually, I was impressed that the worker would give him that much time. It takes time to be sympathetic, to listen, to hear—to understand a human condition.

At last he came out, and with an apologetic grin he said he must return on Tuesday, he must go home and get the birth certificates. Then they would let him apply. (How will you come back, Mr. Banks? Where will you get the $3 for taxi fare by next Tuesday? Perhaps you could scrape it up by Monday week, but suppose you come on Monday week and your worker isn't here? Then perhaps you won't come back at all . . .)

While Mr. Banks was busy talking, I was chatting with one of the other workers. Because I am a social worker too, I can come and go through the little iron gate, and they smile at me and say, "Well, hello there!" We talked about all the work she has to do, and one of the things she told me was how, often, to save time, they send people down to the Health Department to get their own birth records. Then they can come back and apply the same day. I wondered why Mr. Banks' worker never suggested this. Maybe he never thought of it. (Maybe he doesn't live twelve miles out with no car, and the nearest bus eight miles from home. And no bus fare at that.) Or perhaps he did mention it, and Mr. Banks never heard him, because his head was already filled up with the words that went before: "I'm sorry, there's nothing we can do until you bring us the birth certificates," and he was trying to think in which box, under which bed, had the children been into them . . . ?

So I tried to suggest to him that we go now to the Health Department, but he didn't hear me either. He said, and he persisted, I'm going to the Court House, I'll be right back, will you wait for me? I tried to stop him: let's plan something, what we're going to do next, it's almost lunchtime and things will close up—until suddenly I realized that after the time and the tension of the morning, this was no doubt a call of nature that could not wait for reasonable planning, nor could a proud man come out and ask if there might not be a more accessible solution. And so, as he headed quickly away for the one sure place he knew, I stood mute and waited while he walked the three blocks there and the three blocks back. I wonder if that's something anybody ever thinks about when they're interviewing clients.

Mr. Banks and I had talked earlier about the Manpower Redevelopment Vocational Training Programs, and he had seemed interested. "I'd sure rather work and look after my family than mess with all this stuff, but what can I do? I have no education." I told him about the courses and he said, yes, I'd like that. And so we planned to look into this too, while we were in town. But by now Mr. Banks was ready to go home. "I hate all this standing around. I'd work two days rather than stand around like this." It wasn't really the standing around he minded. It was the circumstances of the standing around. It took some persuading to get him back into the building, only to be told—at 11:30—to come back at ten to one. (Suppose his ride, I thought, had been with somebody busier than I. Suppose they couldn't wait till ten to one and kept badgering him, "Come on, Buddy, hurry up, will you? We ain't got all day!")

I tried to suggest some lunch while we waited, but they didn't want lunch. "We had breakfast late; I'm not hungry, really." So instead, I took him around to the Health Department and the Circuit Court and the County Court, and we verified everything, although he needed some help to figure which years the children were born in.

At ten to one he was again outside the Welfare Office, and he drew me aside and said that he'd been thinking: maybe he should go home and talk this whole thing over a little more. He felt that before jumping into something, he should know better what it was all about. This startled me, for I wondered what that hour and a half had been for, if now, after everything, he felt he must return to his cronies up the creek to find out what it all meant. So we stood aside, and I interpreted the program as best I could, whom it was for and what it required, and what it would do for him and his family, while he stood, nodding his head and staring at the sidewalk. Finally, cautiously, almost grimly, he once again pushed his way into that crowded, smoke-filled lobby.

"Those who are to report at one o'clock, stand in this line. Others in that line." Mr. Banks stood in the one o'clock line. At 1:15 he reached the counter. I don't know what he asked, but I saw the man behind the desk point over toward the other side of the building, the Public Assistance side, where Mr. Banks had already spent all morning. Mr. Banks nodded his head and turned away as he was told to do. At that point I butted in. "Assistance for the unemployed is over there," the man said, and pointed again. So I mentioned training. "He wants training? Why didn't he say so? He's in the wrong line." I don't know what Mr. Banks had said, but what **does** a person say when he's anxious, and tired and confused, and a crowd of others, equally anxious, are pushing from behind and the man at the counter says, "Yes?" I butted in and Mr. Banks went to stand in the right line, but I wondered what the man behind us did, who didn't have anybody to butt in for him.

While Mr. Banks was waiting, to save time, I took the birth certificates to his worker on the other side. I walked right in, because I was a social worker and could do that, and he talked to me right away and said, "Yes, yes, this is good. This will save time. No, he won't have to come back on Tuesday. Yes, he can apply today. Just have him come back over here when he is through over there. Very good."

At 1:30 Buddy Banks reached the counter again, was given a card and told to go sit on a chair until his name was called. I had business at 2:00 and returned at 3:00, and there he was, sitting on the same chair. But I learned as I sat beside him that things had been happening. He had talked with the training counsellor, returned to his welfare worker, and was sent back to the unemployment counsellor, after which he was to return once more to his welfare worker. I asked what he had learned about the training. "There's nothing right now, maybe later." Auto mechanics? Bench work? Need too much education. There may be something about washing cars, changing oil, things like that. Later on. Did you sign up for anything? No. Did they say they'd let you know? No. How will you know? I don't know.

At last his ADC (Unemployed) application was signed, his cards were registered, his name was in the file. Come back in two weeks and we'll see if you're eligible. (How will you get back, Buddy? I'll find a way.)

It was four o'clock. "Well, that's over." And he said, "I suppose a fellow's got to go through all that, but I'd sure rather be a-working than a-fooling around with all that mess." We went out to the car, and I took him home. "I sure do thank you, though," he said.

While I'd been waiting there in the lobby, I saw another man come up to the counter. He was small and middle-aged, with a wedding band on his finger, and his face was creased with lines of care. I saw him speak quietly to the man across the desk. I don't know what he said or what the problem was, but they talked a moment and the official told him, "Well, if you're disabled for work, then there's no use asking about training," and he put up his hands and turned away to the papers on his desk. The man waited there a moment, then slowly turned around and stood in the middle of the floor. He lifted his head to stare up at the wall, the blank wall, and his blue eyes were held wide open to keep the tears from coming. I couldn't help watching him, and when suddenly he looked at me, his eyes straight into mine, I couldn't help asking him—across the wide distance of the crowd that for just an instant vanished into the intimacy of human communion—I asked, "Trouble?" Almost as if he were reaching out his hands, he answered me and said, "I just got the news from Washington and come to sign up, and . . ." but then, embarrassed to be talking to a stranger, he mumbled something else I couldn't understand, turned his back to me, stood another long moment in the middle of the crowd, and then walked out the door.

Disabled or not disabled. Employed or not employed. In need or not in need. Yes or no. Black or white. Answer the question. Stand in line.

It is not the program's fault. You have to have questionnaires, and questionnaires require a yes or no. There is no space for a maybe, but . . .

Nor is it the people-who-work-there's fault, for who can see—or take time to see—the whole constellation of people and pressures, needs and perplexities, desires and dreads that walk into an office in the person of one shuffling, bedraggled man—especially when there are a hundred other bedraggled men waiting behind him? You ask the questions and await the answers. What else can you do?

Then perhaps it is the fault of the man himself, the man who asks—or doesn't quite know how to ask—for help. Indeed, he's called a lazy cheat if he does, and an unmotivated ignorant fool if he doesn't. It must be his own fault.

Or maybe it's nobody's fault. It's just the way things are . . .

Three Major Institutions: Religion, Marriage and the Family, Education

Part VIII

The next seven readings describe central aspects of three institutions that are prominent in all societies—religion, marriage and family life, and education. In no known society are these matters left solely to chance or spontaneous events. The important procedures and groupings associated with them are always highly organized, systematized, and stabilized. They change, yes—but usually only very slowly, in an evolutionary fashion. When there is occasionally a precipitate change—as in the appearance of a new religious sect—the fresh phenomenon typically becomes institutionalized very swiftly even though, ironically, it may have arisen as an expression of protest against institutionalization.

32. Children of Yearning
PETER MARIN

Peter Marin has been described by Saturday Review, *where this article first appeared, as a "radical educator." As such, he has been involved in the free school movement and in student protests against the meaningless "education" so often foisted on the unsuspecting young. Mr. Marin quite evidently speaks as an outsider when he describes those attracted to the mystical aspects of religion. But he seems quite sympathetic to those who seek, sometimes with an air of desperation, a scheme or answer that will make sense out of a chaotic world or personal life. Cynics will no doubt want to make light of the religious enthusiasts described by Marin. But the ecological and political state of the world is such that, perhaps, a critically needed aspect of effective long-term answers is to be found in the more ennobling features of religion—those features that encourage adherents to be unselfish, courageous, kind, gentle, and at one with all their fellow humans.*

These days I keep pinned to my wall a note from a friend. "Ah, Peter, the distances are so great, my paralysis so nearly complete. I feel like a grim, weary animal on the banks of a river as it is moving on." Though my friend is Jewish, as am I, and still unmoved by the revivalism of the times, his note is as good a place as any to begin talking of the New Christians. He has been through it all: the free-speech movement, civil rights, hash and acid, traditional and communal marriage, fatherhood and a book, and even a hint of fame. What he has learned from it all is summed up by one of his favorite phrases: the long march. What he means by that is simply that we have barely begun a journey it will take us decades to complete. Our "new" consciousness has not released us

SOURCE: Peter Marin, "Children of Yearning," *Saturday Review* 55 (May 6, 1972), 58–63. Reprinted by permission.

from the demons of the age, but has simply brought us face to face with them.

In his exhaustion, vision, and hope, he is one of those souls the Zohar, the Jewish *Book of Splendor,* calls "children from the chamber of yearning"—those compelled to suffer in their privacies and nightmares the confusion of the age. I understand, as do some of my comrades and most of the young, the loneliness and exhaustion he feels, for the condition is not his alone. It is a natural one. The age itself is a chamber of yearning; what disappears in the midst of it is the sense of any hold on life, any touch with the physical world, any feeling of ease or belonging.

The new "millennialism" of the young is a desperate response to this mixture of public chaos and private isolation. What moves the young is only in part the desire for the simple life, religious ecstasy, and justification. There is a more desolate and organic need, the need to reduce the nightmare complexity of things to a manageable form. The Jesus revolution is simply the most recent, popular, and obvious expression of that need. One can find among the young dozens of other disciplines and creeds—Krishna-consciousness, Subud, Zen, Yoga, transcendental meditation—and, beyond those, the whole hazy landscape of pop therapies and enthusiasms. Every passing idea is turned zealously into a faith. The *I Ching,* the Tarot cards, the *Whole Earth Catalog,* and the ephemerides become fundamentalist texts.

In all these zealotries the driving need is for certainty and purity, for a transcendence of the self. The Jesus-cults are more popular than others have been because they offer the young what other faiths do not—an instantaneous and push-button forgiveness, an apparent and abrupt end to guilt and self-disgust. They are familial, offer an authoritative Father, brothers, and sisters for company. Though ultimately triumphant, they can explain and justify present suffering. Though ultimately millennial, they are comfortably regressive, a denial of the probable future and its crises. One becomes a child again. The world is defused, depoliticized. *Jesus is coming.* First the necessary catastrophe, then the New World. There is little one can do save render the State its due and prepare oneself for the Second Coming.

Much of the need for refuge is, of course, the direct result of civic terror and individual impotence. Perhaps the cruelest legacy of the past decade has been the steady demoralization of the young. Whatever private avenues have opened for them—sex, drugs, mobility—have all been overshadowed by the growing sense that men and women are not really free in America, if they ever have been. In face of that realization, the young were driven first to protest and then to violence. But on the furthest edge of things, they found the State ready to murder them. Those unwilling to resist with comparable violence were forced to withdraw, not into the "system," but into a disconsolate quietism that has become boredom for some and despair for others. Terrorized, some were radicalized and deepened by it all. Others have become, for the moment, members of a middle-class version of what the radical South American educator, Paolo Freire, calls the "silent culture"—a class that is so disheartened by its victimization that it retreats into passivity and silence.

But that is not all there is to their retreat. Deeper down something else is going on, something that cannot be explained in simple sociological terms. It is a kind of cultural involution occurring in many young people at the deepest levels of private experience. They have entered an internal evolutionary maelstrom in which they undergo radical changes and trials. They are surrounded by adults who seem unable to live passionately or effectively in the world, unable to understand or aid them. The adult hopes they hear voiced around them—"reformation of the system," "social engineering," "human potential"—must seem to the young both desperate and self-delusive, shrill tunes whistled in the dark. The young are left in their own gravid darkness to fabricate little myths and fancies. The poignant result is what one sees among the young—brittle, innocent, and millennial fantasies, a mixture of half-truths and insights garbled by fear. They salvage shreds of past beliefs and patch them together to give to the age an ostensible purpose and end.

One evening I talk to a newly converted Christian. "I'd just got outta jail. Met a girl on the beach, and we started for the New Mexican communes but ended up here. When I first saw the house, I said, *O Christ, Jesus freaks*, but after a while I saw they'd gotten it together, and nobody else I knew had done it. Now I been here six months, baptized and everything."

"And before?"

"I hustled and dealt. Lived on the street. Got into some shit that was wrong."

"Wrong?"

"Yeah, shit I know was wrong. I mean, I was hanging out with a black dude, and one of his friends got killed by the pigs. So we went out one night with this shotgun and found a pig sitting alone in his squad car. Stuck the gun through the window and blew him wide open."

His face is open and scrubbed, and he says all this casually in a weedy southern drawl. We are standing on a leafy, suburban street, late on a quiet American night, but you can hear in his words the disorder that lies beneath them. He is a member of a new marginal class, the lumpen-young. They drift across immense internal and external distances, seeking solace, meaning, and contact, all dispossessed, mobile, and pained, all without ways to feel useful, potent, or good. They have come in their own lives to an edge of the world, and they have come to it crippled by isolation. Though the surface taboos have apparently been broken, there remains in their lives an undertow of doubt and self-disgust. There is an inability to find any pleasure in sensation, any satisfaction in experience.

They are both the victims and products of one of the century's many botched revolutions—the partial release of libido, of Lawrence's "dark gods," and our fumbled attempts to confront those gods. Under our surface *yes* to sensation, we have not yet learned how to stop saying *no* to life. Our new patterns of behavior allow us increased experience. We are driven toward sensation by a shrill mental need. But we also suffer in the flesh a contaminating guilt, a fear and detachment that empty whatever we do of significance. If there is among the young a slant toward ecstasy or carnal delight, it is riddled at the moment with more hysteria and fear than one finds in their parents. In this no man's land of the psyche, the young experience an inexplicable hurt. There is a sense of bewilderment, betrayal, and humiliation.

That is where salvation comes in—and the divine and resurrected Christ. Conversion means a new life for these children, not merely a deepening of an integration of feeling, but a new beginning altogether. It is not the exemplary Jesus they follow, not Jesus the man in and of the world. It is instead the miraculous, sacrificing, risen Son of God whose death and divine resurrection mean forgiveness for our sins. Their faith is a Pauline faith in a Christ devoid of mystery and human ambiguity, a Christ denied his manhood. Paul wrote to the Romans, "If thou shalt confess with thy mouth the Lord Jesus and shall believe in thine heart that God has raised him from the dead, thou shalt be saved."

In this rawly fundamentalist approach to Christ, one professes and converts, and the past is left behind. Many of the new Christians were at one time deeply involved with drugs, destructively into a passive and pleasureless sexuality. Others were merely adrift and purposeless. Conversion offers them an alternative to those pasts, an absolute therapy. The past is neither explored nor analyzed. It is simply left behind, forgiven and forgotten, at the very moment one embraces Jesus.

Trying to come to terms with it all, I visit with some local Christians at their weekly prayer meeting. The participants are all in their teens and twenties, some in couples, a few married, all clean and smiling. As they arrive, they are greeted by exclamations of thanksgiving. "O praise Jesus, brother. O praise the Lord." There is no leader. There is no service. In other groups there is sometimes a leader or a sermon of sorts or speaking in tongues. But here it is simpler—testimony and singing. Someone hands out a hymnbook. A few of the hymns are traditional, but most of them are newly written to familiar tunes. One of the tunes is "Lend an Ear." Another is "Chopsticks." A third is "Dixie." Its refrain is *look within, look within, look within for Jesus Christ*. The hymns are interspersed with spontaneous outbursts of enthusiasm and testimony. Most of the members testify about their daily lives—how Jesus has found them a job, or has settled a fight between roommates, or has improved a floundering marriage. There is a continuous round of exhortation and praise, all of it colored by a curious and heady mixture of the humility of the meek and the smugness of the redeemed.

Someone cries out: "Gonna join you, Lord. We're knocking at the gate."
Another: "You're our master, Jesus, our only King."

Another: "Gonna rise right up out of slavery, Jesus, gonna sit on God's throne."

And another: "Thank you, Jesus, thank you. We're no longer under the thumb of the world."

It is all so antiseptic, so hygienic, so humorless, so innocent and distressing at the same time—a roomful of shiny pennies stamped with the same date. But one can hear underneath all the snuffling and scuttling of small animals seeking a place to hide. There is a kind of nostalgia to the meeting, an old-fashioned boosterism and a curious oscillation between zeal and fear. It is as if the last night of summer camp were being held in the hold of the sinking *Titanic*.

These are the "good" children, those who do not want to burn or smash the world but merely desire to shut their eyes and wish it out of existence.

I remember talking to a recently converted friend of mine about a man I thought had learned, by the end of his days, to face life bravely and with gentleness. "Maybe so," she shrugged, "but he wasn't, after all, a true Christian." What she meant was that his warmth, courage, and tenderness could mean nothing unless it fell within the limits of her world. This is America after all, and these are middle-class American children, as ready as ever to diminish whatever fails to fit their dream of things.

I remember, too, watching a friend argue with a few evangelical young Christians. In a patient way he insisted that Buddha and Muhammad were also adequate models and gods and that most religions could bring one to a sense of the divine. But the new Christians would have none of it. Christ, they insisted, was the only way. Those who chose other paths were damned. In the face of my friend's quiet persistence they began to rage, and finally one of them shouted: "No! No! Jesus is the way. Compared to him what you believe is nothing. Nothing!"

What moves these children is fright. What terrifies them is what seems to bewilder us all these days: something beneath political disorder and social chaos, a peculiar kind of psychic event occurring at the center of the soul, an event for which we have no precedents, theories, or laws. We have only the sense of boundaries given way, of a kind of nakedness, of distances shrinking and yet increasing at the same speeds—as if we have lost all sense of privacy but are still absolutely isolated from the world.

Somewhere at the heart of it all lies the end of the Renaissance "person," of the whole structure and experience of the self as we have known it. From the Renaissance onward, we have held, in one form or another, a hard-edged image of man fundamentally independent and self-contained. Now our ladderlike image of self as superego, ego, and id—a skeletal but a highly charged model—has become something else altogether, a kind of porous sieve, less of a structure and more of a field, a curious, hybrid puddle of sensation. The self lacks hard edges and melts into the world around it, is easily swept by the world's currents and waves.

What I am talking about is a fundamental change in the way we experience our relation to the world. What is occurring now is a process of psychic collectivization that comes close to what some have called a "retribalization." But it is actually radically different. What tribes share is a visceral world view, a physical sense of the shared sources of communal power and physical reality—a connection of *flesh and blood*. What we share is something else altogether: a loss of touch with physical nature and a connection of *consciousness,* something far more electric and mental, a soup of inexplicable and contagious sensations and moods in which the physical world is somehow forgotten—and with it the primacy and value of the *person.*

What the collectivization produces is not the state of ecstasy Norman Brown envisioned in *Love's Body,* but the kind of condition Blake described in *Milton:* "No human form but only a fibrous vegetation, a polypus of soft affections without Vision or Thought." The self becomes a vast and vulnerable suggestibility. Nothing is generated from within. Instead, impulses flow in from the outside in a kind of perpetual "imprinting" at odds with all ripening.

What one often sees, working or living with the young, is a peculiar condition of personality, an expansiveness and release at the surface, but beneath, a self held in suspension and closed defensively against the world like a fist or a fetus, struggling to maintain some sort of identity. Though there is, in general, an ache for transcendence, there is in many of the young little sense of, or love for, the reality to be transcended. There is an impatience with both ego and thought, but there is no fully developed ego to be set aside. Usually, what takes the place of thought is neither ecstasy nor imagination, but merely superstition. There is a sweet hollowness, an undercurrent of anger, a gentle impulse toward potency and touch, but not yet the hard daring and resilience it takes to survive in the world.

All of that is probably transitional, a direct result of the confusions of the age, but for the time being many young persons are struggling to survive. Sex, drugs, and motion are all seemingly expansive and liberating, but only if one is at home in the world or whole enough to make use of their ambiguous lessons. Survival depends upon a resonance and depth of self, the existence at the center of experience of *someone,* a self strong enough to absorb the strains. But too often a center seems to be missing. Unable to deal adequately with the unceasing rush of experience, the young are forced to armor themselves against it with abstract systems and beliefs.

The irony, of course, is that the systems they choose to bring them closer to life are inevitably those that divorce them from it. The "new" Christianity is merely another shape of our habitual cultural rejection of the truth of our own lives. To reject the State and its institutions and choose instead the dogma of the Resurrected Christ is merely to replace one web of evasions with another. As Erich Gutkind argued in *The Absolute Collective,* mysticism and nationalism are forms of the same panicked impulse. Of course, there are always men and women who live their lives in the "white heat of God," but for most of us creedal mysticism and idealism are simply refined forms of spiritual jingoism—the same old American refrain set to a different tune. They leave men and women in the same closed box, clinging to abstraction and evasion for the sense of contact or meaning that it would be too painful to wrest from the world.

The Jesus-cults are in reality an ironic extension of what Henry Miller once called the "universe of Death," the grid of compulsive moral abstractions that separates us from experience. They are the latest resurgence of a recurrent theme in Western and American experience: the compulsive search for a transcendental consciousness; a disembodied and pure awareness, a "love" to lift us beyond the physicality we cannot tolerate or love. We use our spirituality in much the same way we use our technology, as a defense against life. It is no accident that we are drawn to both, for they offer us the same gifts: an end not only to pain, age, and death but also to the complexities of "personhood." In both realms we struggle to escape or subdue whatever seems to us mysterious, alien, or wild; we are driven to control or transcend because we are afraid to enter or inhabit. "We are like balloons held down by strings of ego," says one of my Sufi friends. "We can cut ourselves loose. We can be high *all* the time."

A knowledgeable friend of mine calls our new faiths the "emerging schizoid ethic"—an attempt to rationalize dis-ease into a system of values. For we still suffer the grievous condition we have inherited from the past, not simply the split between body and mind, but the more awful separation between being and meaning. The history of Western religion is the history of that separation, a record of the monopolization of meaning by religion, the substitution of a divine and distant significance for an earthly one. The world and the flesh are denied; there is a sacred and a profane, and the profane is always the world, always the flesh—unless redeemed from above. Meaning, once separated from the world, must be begged back or earned from Heaven.

But that won't work. What we need is not a new or higher "consciousness" but a renewal of the raw stuff that moves beneath consciousness, of the substance of things, of the underpinnings of life, of our ability as fleshed creatures to come warmly and fully to the world. Only such great renegade Christians as Blake and Lawrence understood that meaning is nothing "spiritual," nothing transcendent. It is instead a kind of heat and light, the natural result of felt contact with life, of a passionate receptivity to the world. What we forget in our zeal and belief is that meaning and value are incarnate. "Love, Mercy, Pity, Peace," as Blake said, "have a human form divine." They reside in each of us as the meaning released when we make real contact with the world. All we are, all self is, is life in touch with life. But when we fail to make that touch, we are prey to both a feeling of deadness and the dream of salvation.

But why bother to rage about it all? As I sit here writing, making it all so important, it suddenly seems unimportant. The sun is hot this afternoon. The sky is clear. A warm breeze moves through these mountains, and the eucalyptus leaves brush against one another. The physical world is still here. It has not disappeared. My daughter, sitting nude on the table, smiles a gap-toothed, Gatsby-like smile and pastes blue-chip stamps to her feet in a rite of some kind of magic. These are hard times, and why begrudge to anyone the fancies and extremes he needs to save himself? Some of us take consolation in independence, others have the university or the corporation, and some cling still to possessions, or professions, or an idealized dream of the future.

These days I keep muttering to myself: "How great a need." Like all of us, the new Christians seek and improvise what they need, and the hard truth is that many of them can find no consolation elsewhere. If they have left behind the flag, the university, and the two parties, only to replace them with astrology, yoga, and Jesus, well, that is the way we progress from age to age.

The trouble, of course, is that we may not progress at all, but merely mark time and substitute one set of delusions for another. There is a change in values but no deepening of life. The world stays flat. These days offer nothing less than the chance for a resignification of being, a chance to recreate some kind of meaning in the world. But it is a turbulent task, and it will be decades before we emerge on the other side of this chaos with any sense of belonging or ease in the world. The young will cling, before we are through, to dozens of millennial enthusiasms. They will seek meaning in new systems and creeds, forgetting, as we always do, that meaning is never assigned to the world, is never found. It is created by the depth of imagination and feeling we bring to the world.

What matters after all, especially in times such as ours, is never how saved or whole one is, but the extent to which one restores to others, through presence and passion, a sense of possibility and independence. As for myself, what I prize among my comrades these days has nothing to do with enlightenment or heightened consciousness. It is instead a fierceness, an animal tenacity, a sense one sometimes gets from others of a complex, evolving person, of a rare and lusty insistence on a complex, honest, solitary privacy that protects life in the flesh against abstractions, ideals, and even salvation itself. The most difficult task of all is to steer between exhaustion and illusion, between resignation and an escape into dogma.

Those who try it will find—like my friend from the chamber of learning—a kind of grimness and weariness, a kind of loneliness. But if they are lucky, they will also get a glimpse here and there of light and depth, an occasional sense of freedom and potency, a few good comrades to hold in their thoughts or arms.

33. What Kind of People Does a Religious Cult Attract?
WILLIAM R. CATTON, JR.

The type of religious enthusiasts discussed by Peter Marin in the preceding selection are more systematically studied by William Catton in the following piece. Dr. Catton, professor of sociology at Washington State University, presents us with a classic sociological research project. It is classic in two senses: it typifies a prominent type of sociological research, and it represents the best of such research. Critics of this kind of research stress the externality of the findings—we do not know what the enthusiasts really felt. But we certainly know some of the relevant things they did *pertaining to their "Christ," and we learn these things systematically and thoroughly.*

On the basis of existing theory of institutional behavior, is it possible to predict what classes of people may be attracted to a new religious cult? Consider the following propositions about religion:

(1) Religion is a spontaneously appearing, perennial, and universal attribute of man. . . . The element of chance, here and hereafter, everlastingly must be contended with. (2) From earliest known times, religion has assumed institutionalized forms. Apparently it . . . cannot exist without social expression and social organization. (3) Organized religions tend to become over-organized, from the very fact of their organization as "going concerns". . . . They become ends in themselves rather than means. (4) . . . it is easier to administer the affairs of an organization than it is to keep creeds flexible, codes of conduct clear and uncompromised, and the life of the spirit immanent. Historically this has meant either the eventual disappearance of the particular religious organization, or more commonly, reform or schism, especially in the form of new sects or cults.[1]

From these propositions we may deduce that any sufficiently large and varied population is likely to contain a number of individuals whose religious interests are intense but are not adequately served by existing religious institutions. These would include persons we should predict might be attracted to a new religious cult. But can such persons be identified in terms of objective characteristics observable prior to their actual

SOURCE: William R. Catton, Jr., "What Kind of People Does a Religious Cult Attract?" *American Sociological Review* 22 (October 1957), 561–566. Reprinted by permission of the author and the American Sociological Association.

affiliation with the cultist movement? The study reported here suggests an affirmative answer.

A RESEARCH OPPORTUNITY

An opportunity to study public reaction to a man whose small band of followers regarded him as Christ (and who himself acknowledged that status) arose when such a group visited Seattle, Washington, in the winter of 1952. Their presence was first announced by a two-column 8-inch advertisement in both Seattle newspapers. The ad contained a photograph of a bearded man in a long robe, resembling the traditional portraits of Christ. Beside the picture were the words: "We Believe THIS IS CHRIST The Begotten Son of God. What MORE can we say! ! ! Listen to the words of Christ." The time, place, and auspices for a public appearance were specified in smaller print at the bottom.

The writer and a friend[2] attended the meeting. The audience numbered about 300. We watched and listened, but asked no questions of anyone. At subsequent meetings our investigation included direct personal conversation with the "Christ," Krishna Venta. We were able to establish sufficient rapport to facilitate fairly systematic study of this embryonic cult with tape recorder and questionnaires.[3]

THE MEETINGS

The first meeting, on January 20, was quietly conducted by several "disciples" dressed in plain robes, moving about on bare feet, wearing beards and long hair, and embracing each member of the audience upon entrance. One of them, called "Peter," gave a quiet, lengthy introduction of the "Master" who made a dramatic entrance. In an hour-long lecture he reprimanded the crowd for having paid him so little heed 1,900 years before, and stated his present mission as the "gathering of the elect," disclaiming any present intent to "save souls." During an ensuing question session, several members of the audience sought to ridicule the speaker, but the majority of the audience seemed content to enjoy the show.

At the second meeting the following evening Krishna's entry was unexpectedly interrupted by the minister of the liberal church in which the meeting was being held. He disclaimed all personal connection with the affair by announcing his discovery since the previous meeting that Krishna had a criminal record. Krishna was, however, permitted to speak. His lecture was defiant, referring repeatedly to persecutions inflicted on him by so-called Christians. The audience, containing many people who had attended the first meeting, reacted very differently on this occasion. In addition to those who had come just to see a show and the few who sought to ridicule the "Master," as at the first meeting, there now appeared to be a highly motivated and articulate minority who saw him as a serious threat to their own orthodox Christian beliefs. They fought him aggressively, armed with Bible verses. Their questions were of the type: "If you're really the Christ, show us the scars of your crucifixion!" In short, they seemed exclusively concerned with *reassuring* themselves that Krishna was an imposter.[4]

A different meeting place was obtained for the third and subsequent meetings. The third meeting (on January 27, Sunday) dealt with prophecy.

At the fourth meeting (Wednesday evening, January 30) Krishna lectured on "Hypnotism and Mental Telepathy" in rather abstract terms.

In his fifth lecture (Sunday, February 3) Krishna informed the audience that Christ and Jesus were two different people; that Christ assisted God in the creation of the universe, has been with men since their beginning, and that Christ, not Jesus, was crucified. Krishna reasserted that he himself was Christ: "I am Christ, the son of the living God. The eternal Christ. The one that was crucified 1,900 years ago, died and was buried and on the third day rose again."

In addition, the speaker devoted himself to a lament for the current state of freedom of the press in the United States. Both Seattle newspapers had refused to carry further advertising about his group, due, Krishna asserted, to pressure from interests that were afraid of his power.

At the sixth and last meeting on Sunday, February 10, Krishna discussed his criminal record,[5] describing himself as a martyr for humanity at the hands of a cruel and selfish society. His remarks were tape-recorded, and included the following words spoken in a quiet tone, weary from long suffering:

> It is true, children, I have served time for committing that bad check. I served . . . nine months, in a road gang, three years on probation. It is true, children, that I . . . was convicted for a so-called burglary. . . . The truth cannot be in someone like that because that person is bad, and society says he is bad, and condemns him for everything he has done. And yet it has not stopped me from my mission, and my work. As much as society has said that I was guilty of those crimes, I say I was not guilty. —Why?—It's good for all of you. You know why I'm telling you this today? I want you to condemn me too and show your true "Christian" spirit. I want to see how much Christian you are and how much Hypocrite you are.

Several members of the audience wept throughout Krishna's talk. At the close of this last meeting, a member of the audience once again challenged Krishna: "Are you the embodiment of Christ?" Krishna answered:

> If I were to say "no" to you, you would be pleased because you are not willing to accept. If I were to say "yes" that I am, you would be very highly displeased and say "No, it isn't possible!" So I have to make my choice between you and God. I fear not what man might say about me. In all of his rejections I do not fear; but I do fear God. Therefore, I cannot lie to you to please you. I must tell the truth in the sight of God. I *am* the Son of God.

A woman in the audience cried out ecstatically, "I knew it!" Shortly afterward Krishna and his disciples departed in their Buick station wagon for their home base, a utopian colony in southern California.

THE AUDIENCES

From our informal observations at the first two meetings, it seemed that while many people attended as mere spectators, others were genuinely concerned whether or not this man was really Christ.[6] The degree to which persons accepted Krishna's claim seemed to depend more on their own predilections than on what he said. Our first questionnaire, therefore, was designed to measure *degree of acceptance* of his claim, and to obtain some indication of *predispositions*.

The audiences appeared to range from middle to lower socioeconomic status, with men and women about equally represented. Very few nonwhite persons were present at any of the meetings. Questionnaire responses showed that collectively the audiences included one or more adherents of each of the following faiths: Baptist, Catholic, Christian, Christian Scientist, Church of the People, Congregational, Episcopal, Greek Orthodox, Jehovah's Witnesses, Latter Day Saints, Lutheran, Mental Science, Methodist, Open Bible Standard, Pentecostal Assembly of God, Presbyterian, Quaker, Rosicrucian, Seventh Day Adventist, Spiritualist, The Church, United Brethren, and Unity. In size the audiences ranged as shown in Table 1.

Each questionnaire included the open-ended query: "What was your main interest in coming to this meeting?" With very few exceptions[7] it was possible to divide the respondents into two rather clear-cut categories: those who said "To learn," "To seek the truth," or "To gain an understanding of God," etc. were classified as *seekers;* those who said "To see a show," or "I was curious," etc. were designated *observers*.

What kind of people were these seekers and observers? Other questions showed that seekers were less likely to be church members, attended church less often than did observers, more frequently read the Bible, were more inclined to believe in the possibility of a second coming, devoted somewhat more of their idle thoughts to questions of where and

Table 1. Size of Audience and Number of Questionnaires Returned by Date of Meeting

	Size of Audience	Questionnaires Returned
Sunday, Jan. 20	About 300	...
Monday, Jan. 21	No count taken	...
Sunday, Jan. 27	420	125
Wednesday, Jan. 30	132	70
Sunday, Feb. 3	120	58
Sunday, Feb. 10	84	37

how they would spend eternity, were lonelier, were slightly more apprehensive about war and depression. In short, seekers tended to be those who had strong religious interests that were not being satisfied through normal institutional channels. These were the people, as identified by questionnaire items, whom we would predict as most likely to become followers of Krishna, according to the theoretical position stated at the beginning of this paper.

THE QUESTIONNAIRE FINDINGS

Did any of these people in fact become "followers" of Krishna? A total of 129 names and addresses were obtained from the questionnaires, and each individual's questionnaires were assembled into a single unit. The number of meetings attended by seekers and observers is shown in Table 2.

If the nine "no responses" are eliminated and the table is condensed into a four-fold contingency table (seekers vs. observers, and one meeting vs. more-than-one-meeting attended), this condensed table yields a Chi-square of 12.05, which for one degree of freedom is significant beyond the .001 level. This indicates that seekers were more prone to return to subsequent meetings after first exposure to "the Master" than were observers. Returnees can be regarded, in a limited sense, as "followers."

Despite the greater proneness of seekers to return to Krishna's lectures, the proportion of *new observers* in successive audiences appears to have increased, as shown by Table 3.

Based on the same "voluntary sample" as Table 2, Table 3 indicates that successive audiences included proportionately fewer *new* seekers, and proportionately more *new* observers. Since the later meetings were held without benefit of newspaper advertising, it may be hypothesized that word-of-mouth recruiting of new audience members was more effective in bringing in additonal observers than seekers. This hypothesis is supported by responses in the mailed follow-up questionnaire to the item: "I *first* found out about Krishna by (a) hearing about him from another person, (b) reading his ad in the papers" (see Table 4).

By eliminating the N.R. row and column, Table 5 can be reduced to a four-fold contingency table that yields a Chi-square of 4.71, which is

Table 2. Predisposition of Respondents by Frequency of Attendance*

No. of meetings attended	Seekers	Observers	N.R.	Totals
1	61	37	9	107
2	10	—	—	10
3	11	—	—	11
4	1	—	—	1
Totals	83	37	9	129

* Includes only those who gave their names.

Table 3. Predisposition of Respondents by Date of First Attendance*

First Attendance	Seekers No.	%	Observers No.	%	N.R. No.	%	Totals No.	%
Sunday, Jan. 27	(56)	71	(17)	22	(5)	6	(78)	100
Wednesday, Jan. 30	(14)	61	(9)	39	—	—	(23)	100
Sunday, Feb. 3	(10)	53	(7)	37	(2)	11	(19)	100
Sunday, Feb. 10	(3)	33	(4)	44	(2)	22	(9)	100
Totals	(83)		(37)		(9)		(129)	

* Restricted to those who gave their names.

significant for one degree of freedom at the .05 level. Thus Table 4 indicates a significant tendency for seekers to learn of Krishna predominantly via newspaper advertising and for observers to learn principally via word-of-mouth.

For both categories, however, the median number of persons *told* was two, and if we compare telling versus not telling by seekers and observers we obtain Table 5.

The first four cells of this table, taken as a four-fold contingency table, yield a Chi-square of .032, which is far from significant. Therefore, we cannot argue that seekers were any more, or less, talkative than observers.

It was hypothesized that once present in the audience, *seekers would be more inclined to accept Krishna's claim to be Christ than would observers.* The degree of acceptance of this claim was measured by an item involving a thermometer-like diagram. The top of its column was labeled "Absolutely certain," and the bottom, where it joined the ther-

Table 4. Sources of Information for Seekers and Observers

	Word-of-Mouth	Advertisement	N.R.	Totals
Seekers	13	32	7	52
Observers	10	7	2	19
N.R.	1	3	—	4
Totals	24	42	9	75

Table 5. Comparison of Seekers with Observers as Oral Communicators

	Told Nobody	Told Somebody	N.R.	Totals
Seekers	17	28	7	52
Observers	6	11	2	19
N.R.	2	2	—	4
Totals	25	41	9	75

mometer bulb, was labeled "Absolutely impossible." Above the thermometer diagram were the words, "Degrees of likelihood." Respondents were asked to blacken the tube up to a height that would indicate "how likely you think it is that Krishna is Christ." While this constituted a very unsophisticated attitude-scale it had the merit of being clearly meaningful to the respondents.

This item appeared twice on each questionnaire, and respondents were instructed to indicate their degree of belief boh *before* and *after* the meeting. The markings were converted later to a numerical index ranging from 0, "Absolutely impossible," to 1.0, "Absolutely certain."

The signed questionnaires enabled us to observe individual opinions before and after *one or more* exposures to Krishna. For the 51 seekers and 29 observers who put their names on their questionnaires *and* gave at least two responses on the likelihood (thermometer) question, definite shifts of opinion occurred, as shown in Table 6.

The initial level of belief differed significantly between seekers and observers (C.R.=12.09) in the direction one would expect. More than this, the initially favorable seekers became more favorable (C.R.=2.25) through exposure to Krishna's lectures, while the initially skeptical observers became still more skeptical (C.R.=2.85) in response to "the same" stimuli.

In response to the questionnaire item, "What do you think was the main thing you got out of coming [to the meeting]?" one respondent—a non-church member—wrote, "Satisfaction of Krishna being the Christ." Another said, "A lovely friendly feeling and a light heart." Still another—a church member—wrote, "Satisfaction that he is a fraud. . . ." Several respondents indignantly called him "anti-Christ."

SUMMARY AND CONCLUSION

When a man who claimed to be Christ gave a series of public lectures in Seattle, his audiences consisted largely of two kinds of persons: *seekers*, persons who wanted to consider him seriously as a religious leader and many of whom were not affiliated with a church, and *observers* who came because of curiosity. Seekers were more inclined than observers to return to subsequent meetings. Initial announcement of the meetings was by newspaper advertisement, but audience members could later be recruited only by word-of-mouth. The latter means of communication was more

Table 6. Opinion Shifts Among Identified Respondents

	Likelihood Krishna is Christ	
	Mean First Response	Mean Last Response
Seekers (N=51)	.44	.51
Observers (N=29)	.10	.04

effective in bringing in observers to the lectures, while seekers were mainly brought in by the printed advertising, so successive audiences contained increasing proportions of observers. The acceptance of his claim to be Christ was initially higher among seekers than among observers, and increased among seekers upon exposure to the lectures, whereas the lectures decreased acceptance among observers.

It can be argued theoretically that any religious organization that is "successful" institutionally must "fail" religiously for at least some of its constituents. These people will be more prone than others to accept the claims (at least temporarily, until institutionalization sets in) of a cultist leader. The present research has indicated that it is possible, even with relatively unsophisticated techniques, to identify these persons in the larger population, and to predict their responses to religious stimuli. Often, of course, there are a number of different cults "on the market" at the same time. It is plausible that important differences exist between the sort of person who was attracted to Krishna Venta and those who find themselves aroused by a different sort of appeal.[8] The evidence reported in this paper would not enable us to predict which of several competing cults might be selected by a cult-prone (institutionally alienated but religiously intense) person. Much further research would be required before such specific prediction could be attempted.

NOTES

1. J. O. Hertzler, "Religious Institutions," *Annals of the American Academy of Political and Social Science*, 256 (March, 1948), pp. 1, 3, 12.
2. The author wishes to acknowledge the cooperation of Lynn B. Lucky in the execution of this study, from the original decision to attend the first of this unusual series of meetings, to the analysis of the questionnaire data. Acknowledgement is also due the Washington Public Opinion Laboratory, by which both the author and Lucky were then employed, for the use of its facilities. The criticism of Melvin L. DeFleur, Indiana University, was of great help in preparing this report.
3. This rapport was close enough, in fact, to be slightly embarrassing, and may have influenced some of the responses to our questionnaires. Some audience members regarded us as followers of Krishna. Weeks after the last meeting, when this group had left Seattle, the irate husband of one woman (whose attendance at several meetings had convinced her Krishna was really Christ) threatened us by telephone: "I'll have the law on you."
4. Elizabeth K. Nottingham, *Religion and Society*, New York: Doubleday, 1954, p. 5, points out that the unholy is often closely associated with the holy in religious thought. The devout persons who thought Krishna was a wicked imposter seemed especially anxious to obtain proof that he was not the genuine Christ.
5. Krishna was fond of the Book of Revelation, which attributes to Christ the following words: "...I will come like a thief, and you will not know at what hour I will come upon you." Rev. 3:3.
6. This was true also of the "secondary audience"—persons who heard of the affair second-hand through us. Many of them were chiefly concerned to know whether *we* thought Krishna really was Christ.
7. The exceptions probably included a small group of relatives and friends of two

of Krishna's robed followers who happened to be from Seattle. Responses: "I came on account of a friend," or "To see Brother Gene," etc. These appear under "N.R." in the tables.
8. The possibility that some persons may have a generalized cult-proneness seems implied by the previous involvement with Dianetics of several of the members of the cult studied by Leon Festinger, Henry W. Riecken, and Stanley Schachter, in *When Prophecy Fails,* Minneapolis: University of Minnesota Press, 1956. There are seekers, apparently, who move from cult to cult in a never-ending quest.

34. The Universality of the Family: A Conceptual Analysis
IRA L. REISS

A professor at the University of Minnesota, Dr. Reiss specializes in studying family life and sex behavior. In the present instance, Professor Reiss uses a great variety of cross-cultural and other data in an attempt to specify carefully what is, and is not, universal about family life. One of his major findings is that, in every known society, the family is a small kinship group whose prime function is to care for the young, especially in an emotional sense. How long such care is provided, and what other functions the family has, vary greatly with the society and with time. But when it comes to "nurturant socialization," families in all societies are essentially alike.

During the last few decades, a revived interest in the question of the universality of the family has occurred. One key reason for this was the 1949 publication of George Peter Murdock's book *Social Structure*.[1] In that book, Murdock postulated that the nuclear family was universal and that it had four essential functions which it always and everywhere fulfilled. These four functions were: (1) socialization, (2) economic cooperation, (3) reproduction, and (4) sexual relations. Even in polygamous and extended family systems, the nuclear families within these larger family types were viewed as separate entities which each performed these four functions.

The simplicity and specificity of Murdock's position makes it an excellent starting point for an investigation of the universal functions of the human family. Since Murdock's position has gained support in many

SOURCE: Ira L. Reiss, "The Universality of the Family: A Conceptual Analysis," *Journal of Marriage and the Family* 27 (November 1965), 443–453. Reprinted by permission of the author and the National Council on Family Relations.

quarters, it should be examined carefully.[2] Brief comments on Murdock's position appear in the literature, and some authors, such as Levy and Fallers, have elaborated their opposition.[3] The present paper attempts to go somewhat further, not only in testing Murdock's notion but in proposing and giving evidence for a substitute position. However, it should be clear that Murdock's position is being used merely as an illustration; our main concern is with delineating what, if anything, is universal about the human family.

The four functions of the nuclear family are "functional prerequisites" of human society, to use David Aberle's term from his classic article on the topic.[4] This means that these functions must somehow occur for human society to exist. If the nuclear family everywhere fulfills these functions, it follows that this family should be a "structural prerequisite" of human society, i.e., a universally necessary part of society.[5] The basic question being investigated is not whether these four functions are functional prerequisites of human society—almost all social scientists would accept this—but whether these four functions are necessarily carried out by the nuclear family. If these functions are not everywhere carried out by the nuclear family, then are there any functional prerequisites of society which the nuclear family or any family form does fulfill? Is the family a universal institution in the sense that it always fulfills some functional prerequisite of society? Also, what, if any, are the universal structural features of the family? These are the ultimate questions of importance that this examination of Murdock's position is moving toward.

Murdock's contention that the nuclear family is a structural prerequisite of human society since it fulfills four functional prerequisites of human society is relatively easy to test. If a structure is essential, then finding one society where the structure does not exist or where one or more of the four functions are not fulfilled by this structure is sufficient to refute the theory. Thus, a crucial test could best be made by focusing on societies with rather atypical family systems to see whether the nuclear family was present and was fulfilling these four functions. The more typical family systems will also be discussed. A proper test can be made by using only groups which are societies. This limitation is necessary so as not to test Murdock unfairly with such subsocietal groups as celibate priests. For purposes of this paper, the author accepts the definition of society developed by Aberle and his associates:

> A society is a group of human beings sharing a self-sufficient system of action which is capable of existing longer than the life-span of an individual, the group being recruited at least in part by the sexual reproduction of the members.[6]

A TEST OF MURDOCK'S THESIS

One of the cultures chosen for the test of Murdock's thesis is from his own original sample of 250 cultures—the Nayar of the Malabar Coast of India. In his book, Murdock rejected Ralph Linton's view that the Nayar lacked the nuclear family.[7] Since that time, the work of Kathleen Gough has supported Linton's position, and Murdock has accordingly changed his own position.[8] In letters to the author dated April 3, 1963 and January 20, 1964, Murdock took the position that the Nayar are merely the old Warrior Caste of the Kerala Society and thus not a total society and are more comparable to a celibate group of priests. No such doubt about the societal status of the Nayar can be found in his book. Murdock rejects the Nayar only after he is forced to admit that they lack the nuclear family. In terms of the definition of society adopted above, the Nayar seem to be a society even if they, like many other societies, do have close connections with other groups.

The matrilineage is particularly strong among the Nayar, and a mother with the help of her matrilineage brings up her children. Her husband and "lovers" do not assist her in the raising of her children. Her brother typically assists her when male assistance is needed. Assistance from the linked lineages where most of her lovers come from also substitutes for the weak husband role. Since many Nayar women change lovers rather frequently, there may not even be any very stable male-female relation present. The male is frequently away fighting. The male makes it physiologically possible for the female to have offspring, but he is not an essential part of the family unit that will raise his biological children. In this sense, sex and reproduction are somewhat external to the family unit among the Nayar. Very little in the way of economic cooperation between husband and wife occurs. Thus, virtually all of Murdock's functions are outside of the nuclear family. However, it should be noted that the socialization of offspring function is present in the maternal extended family system. Here, then, is a society that seems to lack the nuclear family and, of necessity, therefore, the four functions of this unit. Even if we accept Gough's view that the "lovers" are husbands and that there really is a form of group marriage, it is still apparent that the separate husband-wife-child units formed by such a group marriage do not here comprise separately functioning nuclear families.

One does not have to rely on just the Nayar as a test of Murdock. Harold E. Driver, in his study of North American Indians, concludes that in matrilocal extended family systems with matrilineal descent, the husband role and the nuclear family are often insignificant.[9] It therefore seems that the relative absence of the nuclear family in the Nayar is approached particularly in other similar matrilineal societies. Thus, the Nayar do not seem to be so unique. They apparently demonstrate a type of family system that is common in lesser degree.

A somewhat similar situation seems to occur in many parts of the Caribbean. Judith Blake described a matrifocal family structure in which the husband and father role are quite often absent or seriously modified.[10] Sexual relations are often performed with transitory males who have little relation to raising of the resultant offspring. Thus, in Jamaica one can also question whether the nuclear family exists and performs the four functions Murdock ascribed to it. Socialization of offspring is often performed by the mother's family without any husband, common law or legal, being present. Naturally, if the husband is absent, the economic cooperation between husband and wife cannot occur. Also, if the male involved is not the husband but a short-term partner, sex and reproduction are also occurring outside the nuclear family.

The above societies are all "mother-centered" systems. A family system which is not mother-centered is the Israeli Kibbutz family system as described by Melford Spiro.[11] Here the husband and wife live together in a communal agricultural society. The children are raised communally and do not live with their parents. Although the Kibbutzim are only a small part of the total Israeli culture, they have a distinct culture and can be considered a separate society by the Aberle definition cited above. They have been in existence since 1909 and thus have shown that they can survive for several generations and that they have a self-sufficient system of action. The function which is most clearly missing in the Kibbutz family is that of economic cooperation between husband and wife. In this communal society, almost all work is done for the total Kibbutz, and the rewards are relatively equally distributed regardless of whether one is married or not. There is practically no division of labor between husbands and wives as such. Meals are eaten communally, and residence is in one room which requires little in the way of housekeeping.

Here, too, Murdock denies that this is a real exception and, in the letters to the author referred to above, contends that the Kibbutzim could not be considered a society. Murdock's objection notwithstanding, a group which has existed for over half a century and has developed a self-sufficient system of action covering all major aspects of existence indeed seems to be a society by almost all definitions. There is nothing in the experience of the Kibbutzim that makes it difficult to conceive of such groups existing in many regions of the world or, for that matter, existing by themselves in a world devoid of other people. They are analogous to some of the Indian groups living in American society in the sense that they have a coherent way of life that differs considerably from the dominant culture. Thus, they are not the same as an average community which is merely a part of the dominant culture.

Melford Spiro concludes that Murdock's nuclear family is not present in the Kibbutz he and his wife studied. He suggests several alterations in Murdock's definition which would be required to make it better fit the Kibbutz. The alterations are rather drastic and would still not fit the Nayar and other cultures discussed above.[12]

There are other societies that are less extreme but which still create some difficulty with Murdock's definition of the nuclear family. Malinowski, in his study of the Trobriand Islanders, reports that except for perhaps nurturant socialization, the mother's brother rather than the father is the male who teaches the offspring much of the necessary way of life of the group.[13] Such a situation is certainly common in a matrilineal society, and it does place limits on the socialization function of the nuclear family per se. Further, one must at least qualify the economic function in the Trobriand case. The mother's brother here takes a large share of the economic burden and supplies his sister's family with half the food they require. The rigidity of Murdock's definition in light of such instances is apparent. These examples also make it reasonable that other societies may well exist which carry a little further such modifications of the nuclear family. For example, we find such more extreme societies when we look at the Nayar and the Kibbutz.

Some writers, like Nicholas Timasheff, have argued that the Russian experience with the family evidences the universality of the nuclear family.[14] While it is true that the Communists in Russia failed to abolish as much of the old family system as they wanted to, it does not follow that this demonstrates the impossibility of abolishing the family.[15] In point of fact, the family system of the Israeli Kibbutz is virtually identical with the system the Russian Communists desired, and thus we must admit that it is possible for at least some groups to achieve such a system. Also, the Communists did not want to do away with the family *in toto*. Rather, they wanted to do away with the patriarchal aspects of the family, to have marriage based on love, easy divorce, and communal upbringing of children. They ceased in much of this effort during the 1930's when a falling birth rate, rising delinquency and divorce rates, and the depression caused them to question the wisdom of their endeavors. However, it has never been demonstrated that these symptoms were consequences of the efforts to change the family. They may well have simply been results of a rapidly changing social order that would have occurred regardless of the family program. Therefore, the Russian experience is really not evidence pro or con Murdock's position.

The Chinese society deserves some brief mention here. Marion Levy contends that this is an exception to Murdock's thesis because in the extended Chinese family, the nuclear family was a rather unimportant unit, and it was the patrilineal extended family which performed the key functions of which Murdock speaks.[16] Regarding present day Communist China, it should be noted that the popular reports to the effect that the Chinese Communes either aimed at or actually did do away with the nuclear family are not supported by evidence. The best information indicates that the Chinese Communists never intended to do away with the nuclear family as such; rather, what they wanted was the typical communist family system which the Israeli Kibbutzim possess.[17] The Communists in China did not intend to do away with the identification of a child with a particular set of parents or vice-versa. If the Israeli Kibbutz is any indication, it would seem that a communal upbringing system goes quite well with a strong emphasis on affectionate ties between parent and child.[18] However, it is well to note that the type of communal family system toward which the Chinese are striving and have to some extent already achieved, clashes with Murdock's conception of the nuclear family and its functions in just the same way as the Kibbutz family does.

Overall, it appears that a reasonable man looking at the evidence presented above would conclude that Murdock's position is seriously in doubt. As Levy and Fallers have said, Murdock's approach is too simplistic in viewing a particular structure such as the nuclear family as always, in all cultural contexts, having the same four functions.[19] Robert Merton has said that such a view of a very specific structure as indispensable involves the erroneous "postulate of indispensability."[20] Certainly it seems rather rash to say that one very specific social structure such as the nuclear family will always have the same consequences regardless of the context in which it is placed. Surely this is not true of specific structures in other institutions such as the political, religious, or economic. The consequences of a particular social structure vary with the sociocultural context of that structure. Accordingly, a democratic bicameral legislative structure in a new African nation will function differently than in America; the Reform Jewish Denomination has different consequences in Israel than in America; government control of the economy functions differently in England than in Russia.

The remarkable thing about the family institution is that in so many diverse contexts, one can find such similar structures and functions. To this extent, Murdock has made his point and has demonstrated that the nuclear family with these four functions is a surprisingly common social fact. But this is quite different from demonstrating that this is always the case or necessarily the case. It should be perfectly clear that the author feels Murdock's work has contributed greatly to the advancement of our knowledge of the family. Murdock is used here because he is the best known proponent of the view being examined, not because he should be particularly criticized.

A safer approach to take toward the family is to look for functional prerequisites of society which the family fulfills and search for the full range of structures which may fulfill these functional prerequisites. At this stage of our knowledge, it seems more valuable to talk of the whole range of family structures and to seek for a common function that is performed and that may be essential to human society. What we need now is a broad, basic, parsimonious definition that would have utility in both single and cross-cultural comparisons.[21] We have a good deal of empirical data on family systems and a variety of definitions—it is time we strove for a universal definition that would clarify the essential features of this institution and help us locate the family in any cultural setting.

Looking over the four functions that Murdock associates with the nuclear family, one sees that three of them can be found to be absent in some cultures. The Nayar perhaps best illustrate the possibility of placing sex and reproduction outside the nuclear family. Also, it certainly seems within the realm of possibility that a "Brave New World" type of society could operate by scientifically mating sperm and egg and presenting married couples with state-produced offspring of certain types when they desired children.[22] Furthermore, the raising of children by other than their biological parents is widespread in many societies where adoption and rearing by friends and relatives is common.[23] Thus, it seems that sex and reproduction may not be inexorably tied to the nuclear family.[24]

The third function of Murdock's which seems possible to take out of the nuclear family is that of economic cooperation. The Kibbutz is the prime example of this. Furthermore, it seems that many other communal-type societies approximate the situation in the Kibbutz.

The fourth function is that of socialization. Many aspects of this function have been taken away from the family in various societies. For example, the Kibbutz parents, according to Spiro, are not so heavily involved in the inculcation of values or the disciplinary and caretaking aspects of socialization. Nevertheless, the Kibbutz parents are heavily involved in nurturant socialization, i.e., the giving of positive emotional response to infants and young children. A recent book by Stephens also reports a seemingly universal presence of nurturance of infants.[25] It should be emphasized that this paper uses "nurturance" to mean not the physical, but the emotional care of the infant. Clearly, the two are not fully separable. This use of the term "nurturant" is similar to what is meant by "expressive" role.[26] Interestingly enough, in the Kibbutz both the mother and father are equally involved in giving their children nurturant socialization. All of the societies referred to above have a family institution with the function of nurturant socialization of children. This was true even for the extreme case of the Nayar.

The conception of the family institution being developed here has in common with some other family definitions an emphasis on socialization of offspring. The difference is that all other functions have been ruled out as unessential and that only the nurturant type of socialization is the universal function of the family institution. This paper presents empirical evidence to support its contention. It is important to be more specific than were Levy and Fallers regarding the type of socialization the family achieves since all societies have socialization occurring outside the family as well as within. It should be noted that this author, unlike Murdock, is talking of *any* form of family institution and not just the nuclear family.

As far as a universal structure of the family to fulfill the function of nurturant socialization is concerned, it seems possible to set only very broad limits, and even these involve some speculation. First, it may be said that the structure of the family will always be that of a primary group. Basically, this position rests on the assumption that nurturant socialization is a process which cannot be adequately carried out in an impersonal setting and which thus requires a primary type of relation.[27] The author would not specify the biological mother as the socializer or even a female, or even more than one person or the age of the person. If one is trying to state what the family must be like in a minimal sense in any society—what its universally required structure and function is—one cannot be too specific. However, we can go one step farther in specifying the structure of the family group we are defining. The family is here viewed as an institution, as an integrated set of norms and relationships which are socially defined and internalized by the members of a society. In every society in the world, the institutional structure which contains the roles related to the nurturant function is a small kinship structured group.[28] Thus, we can say that the primary group which fulfills the nurturant function is a kinship structure. Kinship refers to descent—it involves rights of possession among those who are kin. It is a genealogical reckoning, and people with real or fictive biological connections are kin.[29]

This specification of structure helps to distinguish from the family institution those nonkin primary groups that may in a few instances perform nurturant functions. For example, a nurse-child relation or a governess-child relation could, if carried far enough, involve the bulk of nurturant socialization for that child. But such a relationship would be a quasi-family at best, for it clearly is not part of the kinship structure. There are no rights of "possession" given to the nurse or the child in such cases, and there is no socially accepted, institutionalized, system of child-rearing involving nurses and children. In addition, such supervisory help usually assumes more of a caretaking and disciplinary aspect, with the parents themselves still maintaining the nurturant relation.

Talcott Parsons has argued, in agreement with the author's position, that on a societal level, only kinship groups can perform the socialization function.[30] He believes that socialization in a kin group predisposes the child to assume marital and parental roles himself when he matures and affords a needed stable setting for socialization. Clearly other groups may at times perform part of the nurturant function. No institution in human society has an exclusive franchise on its characteristic function. However, no society exists in which any group other than a kinship group performs the dominant share of the nurturant function. Even in the Israeli Kibbutz with communal upbringing, it is the parents who dominate in this area.

Should a society develop wherein nonkin primary groups became the predominant means of raising children, the author would argue that these nonkin groups would tend to evolve in the direction of becoming kin groups. The primary quality of the adult-child relation would encourage the notion of descent and possession. Kin groups would evolve as roles and statuses in the nonkin system became defined in terms of accepted male-female and adult-child relationships and thereby became institutionalized. Once these nonkin groups had institutionalized their sex roles and adult-child (descent) roles, we would in effect have a kinship-type system, for kinship results from the recognition of a social relationship between "parents" and children. It seems that there would be much pressure toward institutionalization of roles in any primary group child-rearing system, if for no other reason than clarity and efficiency. The failure of any one generation to supply adequate role models and adequate nurturance means that the next generation will not know these skills, and persistence of such a society is questionable. The importance of this task makes institutionalizaton quite likely and kinship groups quite essential. To avoid kinship groups, it seems that children would have to be nurtured in a formal secondary group setting. The author will present evidence below for his belief that the raising of children in a secondary group setting is unworkable.

In summation then, following is the universal definition of the family institution: *The family institution is a small kinship structured group with the key function of nurturant socialization of the newborn.* How many years such nurturant socialization must last is hard to specify. There are numerous societies in which children six or seven years old are given a good deal of responsibility in terms of care of other children and other tasks. It seems that childhood in the West has been greatly extended to older ages in recent centuries.[31] The proposed definition focuses on what are assumed to be the structural and functional prerequisites of society which the family institution fulfills. The precise structure of the kinship group can vary quite radically among societies, and even within one society it may well be that more than one small kinship group will be involved in nurturant socialization. The definition seeks to avoid the "error" of positing the indispensability of any *particular* family form by this approach. Rather, it says that any type of kinship group can achieve this function and that the limitation is merely that it be a kinship group. This degree of specification helps one delimit and identify the institution which one is describing. Some writers have spelled out more specifically the key structural forms in this area.[32] Adams has posited two key dyads: the maternal dyad and the conjugal dyad. When these two join, a nuclear family is formed, but these dyads are, Adams believes, more fundamental than the nuclear family.

There are always other functions besides nurturant socialization performed by the kinship group. Murdock's four functions are certainly quite frequently performed by some type of family group, although often not by the nuclear family. In addition, there are some linkages between the family kinship group and a larger kinship system. But this is not the place to pursue these interconnections. Instead, an examination follows of evidence relevant to this proposed universal definition of the family institution.

EVIDENCE ON REVISED CONCEPTION

The evidence to be examined here relates to the question of whether the definition proposed actually fits all human family institutions. Three types of evidence are relevant to test the universality of the proposed definition of the family. The first source of evidence comes from a cross-cultural examination such as that of this article. All of the cultures that were discussed were fulfilling the proposed functional prerequisite of nurturant socialization, and they all had some sort of small kinship group structure to accomplish nurturant socialization. The author also examined numerous reports on other cultures and found no exception to the proposed definition. Of course, other functions of these family groups were present in all instances, but no other specific universally present functions appeared. However, the author hesitates to say that these data confirm his position because it is quite possible that such a cross-cultural examination will reveal some function or structure to be universally *present* but still not universally *required*. Rather, it could merely be universally present by chance or because it is difficult but not impossible to do away with. As an example of this, one may cite the incest taboo. The evidence recently presented by Russell Middleton on incest among commoners in Ptolemaic Egypt throws doubt on the thesis that incest taboos are functional prerequisites of human society.[33] We need some concept of functional "importance," for surely the incest taboo has great functional importance even if it is not a prerequisite of society. The same may be true of the functional importance of Murdock's view of the nuclear family.

If being universally present is but a necessary and not a sufficient condition for a functional prerequisite of society, then it is important to present other evidence. One source of such evidence lies in the studies of rhesus monkeys done by Harry Harlow.[34] Harlow separated monkeys from their natural mothers and raised them with surrogate "cloth" and "wire" mother dolls. In some trials, the wire mother surrogate was equipped with milk while the cloth mother was not. Even so, the monkeys preferred the cloth mother to the wire mother in several ways. The monkeys showed their preference by running more to the cloth mother when threatened and by exerting themselves more to press a lever to see her. Thus, it seemed that the monkeys "loved" the cloth mother more than the wire mother. This was supposedly due to the softer contact and comfort afforded by the cloth mother. One might speculatively argue that the contact desire of the monkeys is indicative of at least a passive, rudimentary nurturance need. Yerkes has also reported similar "needs" in his study of chimpanzees.[35]

Further investigation of these monkeys revealed some important findings. The monkeys raised by the surrogate mothers became emotionally disturbed and were unable to relate to other monkeys or to have sexual relations. This result was produced irreversibly in about six months. One could interpret this to mean that the surrogate mothers, both cloth and wire, were inadequate in that they gave no emotional response to the infant monkeys. Although contact with the cloth mother seemed important, response seemingly was even more important. Those laboratory-raised females who did become pregnant became very ineffective mothers and were lacking in ability to give nurturance.

Harlow found that when monkeys were raised without mothers but with siblings present, the results were quite different. To date, these monkeys have shown emotional stability and sexual competence. In growing up, they clung to each other just as the other monkeys had clung to the cloth mother, but in addition they were able to obtain the type of emotional response or nurturance from each other which they needed.

Harlow's evidence on monkeys is surely not conclusive evidence for the thesis that nurturant socialization is a fundamental prerequisite of human society. There is need for much more precise testing and evidence on both human and nonhuman groups. Despite the fact that human beings and monkeys are both primates, there is quite a bit of difference in human and monkey infants. For one thing, the human infant is far more helpless and far less aware of its environment during the first few months of its life. Thus, it is doubtful if placing a group of helpless, relatively unaware human infants together would produce the same results as occurred when monkeys were raised with siblings. The human infant requires someone older and more aware of the environment to be present. In a very real sense, it seems that the existence of human society is testimony to the concern of humans for each other. Unless older humans care for the newborn, the society will cease to exist. Every adult member of society is alive only because some other member of society took the time and effort to raise him. One may argue that this care need be only minimal and of a physical nature, e.g., food, clothing, and shelter. The author believes that such minimal care is insufficient for social survival and will try to present additional evidence here to bear this out.

One type of evidence that is relevant concerns the effect of maternal separation or institutional upbringing on human infants. To afford a precise test, we should look for a situation in which nurturant socialization was quite low or absent. Although the Kibbutzim have institutional upbringing, the Kibbutz parents and children are very much emotionally attached to each other. In fact, both the mother and father have expressive roles in the Kibbutz family, and there is a strong emphasis on parent-child relations of a nurturant sort in the few hours a day the family is together.

A better place to look would be at studies of children who were raised in formal institutions or who were in other ways separated from their mothers. Leon J. Yarrow has recently published an excellent summary of over one hundred such studies.[36] For over 50 years now, there have been reports supporting the view that maternal separation has deleterious effects on the child. The first such reports came from pediatricians pointing out physical and psychological deterioration in hospitalized infants. In 1951, Bowlby reviewed the literature in this area for the World Health Organization and arrived at similar conclusions.[37] More recent and careful studies have made us aware of the importance of distinguishing the effects of maternal separation from the effects of institutionalization. Certainly the type of institutional care afforded the child is quite important. Further, the previous relation of the child with the mother before institutionalization and the age of the child are important variables. In addition, one must look at the length of time separation endured and whether there were reunions with the mother at a later date. Yarrow's view is that while there is this tendency toward disturbance in mother separation, the occurrence can best be understood when we learn more about the precise conditions under which it occurs and cease to think of it as inevitable under any conditions. In this regard, recent evidence shows that children separated from mothers with whom they had poor relationships displayed less disturbance than other children. Further, infants who were provided with adequate mother-substitutes of a personal sort showed much less severe reactions. In line with the findings on the Kibbutz, children who were in an all-day nursery gave no evidence of serious disturbance.

Many studies in the area of institutionalization show the importance of the structural characteristics of the institutional environment. When care is impersonal and inadequate, there is evidence of language retardation, impairment of motor functions, and limited emotional responses toward other people and objects.[38] Interestingly, the same types of characteristics are found among children living in deprived family environments.[39] One of the key factors in avoiding such negative results is the presence of a stable mother-figure in the institution for the child. Individualized care and attention seem to be capable of reversing or preventing the impairments mentioned. Without such care, there is evidence that ability to form close interpersonal relations later in life is greatly weakened.[40] As Yarrow concludes in his review of this area:

> It is clear from the studies on institutionalization that permanent intellectual and personality damage may be avoided if following separation there is a substitute mother-figure who develops a personalized relationship with the child and who responds sensitively to his individualized needs.[41]

The evidence in this area indicates that some sort of emotionally nurturant relationship between the child in the first few years of life and some other individual is rather vital in the child's development. Disease and death rates have been reported to rise sharply in children deprived of nurturance. The author is not rash enough to take this evidence as conclusive support for his contention that nurturant socialization is a functional prerequisite of human society which the family performs. Nevertheless, he does believe that this evidence lends some support to this thesis and throws doubt on the survival of a society that rears its children without nurturance. In addition, it seems to support the position that some sort of kin-type group relationship is the structural prerequisite of the nurturant function. Indeed, it seemed that the closer the institution approximated a stable, personal kinship type of relationship of the child and a nurse, the more successful it was in achieving emotional nurturance and avoiding impairments of functions.

SUMMARY AND CONCLUSIONS

A check of several cultures revealed that the four nuclear family functions that Murdock states are universally present were often missing. The nuclear family itself seems either absent or unimportant in some cultures.

An alternate definition of the family in terms of one functional prerequisite of human society and in terms of a broad structural prerequisite was put forth. The family was defined as a small kinship structured group with the key function of nurturant socialization of the newborn. The nurturant function directly supports the personality system and enables the individual to become a contributing member of society. Thus, by making adult role performance possible, nurturant socialization becomes a functional prerequisite of society.

Three sources of evidence were examined: (1) cross-cultural data, (2) studies of other primates, and (3) studies of effects on children of maternal separation. Although the evidence did tend to fit with and support the universality of the new definition, it must be noted that much more support is needed before any firm conclusion can be reached.

There is both a structural and a functional part to the definition. It is theoretically possible that a society could bring up its entire newborn population in a formal institutional setting and give them nurturance through mechanical devices that would reassure the child, afford contact, and perhaps even verbally respond to the child. In such a case, the family as defined here would cease to exist, and an alternate structure for fulfilling the functional requirement of nurturant socialization would be established. Although it is dubious whether humans could ever tolerate or achieve such a means of bringing up their children, this logical possibility must be recognized. In fact, since the evidence is not conclusive, one would also have to say that it is possible that a society could bring up its offspring without nurturance, and in such a case also, the family institution as defined here would cease to exist. The author has argued against this possibility by contending that nurturance of the newborn is a functional prerequisite of human society and therefore could never be done away with. However, despite a strong conviction to the contrary, he must also admit that this position may be in error and that it is possible that the family as defined here is not a universally required institution. There are those, like Barrington Moore, Jr., who feel that it is largely a middle-class sentimentality that makes social scientists believe that the family is universal.[42] It is certainly crucial to test further the universality of both the structural and functional parts of this definition and their interrelation.

The definition proposed seems to fit the existing data somewhat more closely than Murdock's definition. It also has the advantage of simplicity. It affords one a definition that can be used in comparative studies of human society. Further, it helps make one aware of the possibilities of change in a society or an institution if we know which functions and structures can or cannot be done away with. In this way, we come closer to the knowledge of what Goldenweiser called the "limited possibilities" of human society.[43] If nurturance in kin groups is a functional and structural prerequisite of society, we have deepened our knowledge of the nature of human society for we can see how, despite our constant warfare with each other, our conflicts and internal strife, each human society persists only so long as it meets the minimal nurturant requirements of its new members. This is not to deny the functions of social conflict that Coser and others have pointed out, but merely to assert the importance of nurturance.[44]

In terms of substantive theory, such a definition as the one proposed can be of considerable utility. If one views the marital institution, as Malinowski, Gough, Davis, Radcliffe-Brown, and others did, as having the key function of legitimization of offspring, then the tie between the marital and family institution becomes clear.[45] The marital institution affords a social definition of who is eligible to perform the nurturant function of the family institution. However, it is conceivable that a family system could exist without a marital system. This could be done by the state scientifically producing and distributing infants or, as Blake believes occurs in Jamaica, by the absence of socially acceptable marriage for most people until childbirth is over.[46]

There may be other universally required functions of the family institution. Dorothy Blitsten suggests universal family contributions to the social order.[47] Kingsley Davis posits several universal functions, such as social placement, which are worth investigating further.[48]

One major value of the approach of this paper is that it has the potentiality of contributing to our ability to deal cross-culturally with the family. Surely it is useful to theory building to ascertain the essential or more essential features of an institution. Such work enables us to locate, identify, and compare this institution in various cultural settings and to discover its fundamental characteristics. In this respect, Murdock has contributed to the search for a cross-cultural view of the family by his work in this area, even though the author has taken issue with some of his conclusions. It should be clear that this "universal, cross-cultural" approach is not at all presented as the only approach to an understanding of the family. Rather, it is viewed as but one essential approach. Research dealing with important but not universal functions is just as vital, as is empirical work within one culture.

Also of crucial importance is the relation of the family institution to the general kinship structure. It does seem that every society has other people linked by affinal or consanguineal ties to the nurturant person or persons. It remains for these aspects to be further tested. The family typologies now in existence are adequate to cover the proposed definition of the family, although a new typology built around the nurturant function and the type of kin who perform it could be quite useful.

The interrelations of the marital, family, and courtship institutions with such institutions as the political, economic, and religious in terms of both important and essential functions and structures is another vital avenue of exploration. One way that such exploration can be made is in terms of what, if any, are the functional and structural prerequisites of these institutions and how they interrelate. It is hoped that such comparative research and theory may be aided by a universal definition of the family such as that proposed in this paper.

NOTES

* The author is grateful to his colleagues David Andrews, June Helm, and David Plath, all of whom read this article and gave the benefits of their comments.
** Ira L. Reiss, Ph.D., is Professor of Sociology, Department of Sociology and Anthropology, University of Iowa, Iowa City. [This was Professor Reiss' affiliation when the article was written—Ed.]
1. George P. Murdock, *Social Structure*, New York: Macmillan, 1949.
2. Many of the textbooks in the family field fail to really cope with this issue and either ignore the question or accept a position arbitrarily. The Census definition also ignores this issue: "A group of two persons or more related by blood, marriage, or adoption and residing together." The recently published *Dictionary of the Social Sciences*, ed. by Julius Gould and William Kolb, Glencoe, Ill.: Free Press, 1964, defines the nuclear family as universal. See pp. 257–259. Parsons, Bales, Bell and Vogel are among those who also seem to accept Murdock's position. See: Talcott Parsons and Robert F. Bales, *Family, Socialization and Interaction Process*, Glencoe, Ill.: Free Press, 1955; Talcott Parsons, "The Incest Taboo in Relation to Social Structure and the Socialization of the Child," *British Journal of Sociology*, 5 (January 1954), pp. 101–117; *A Modern Introduction to the Family*, ed. by Norman Bell and Ezra Vogel, Glencoe, Ill.: Free Press, 1960.
3. Marion J. Levy, Jr. and L. A. Fallers, "The Family: Some Comparative Considerations," *American Anthropologist*, 61 (August 1959), pp. 647–651.
4. David F. Aberle *et al.*, "The Functional Prerequisites of a Society," *Ethics*, 60 (January 1950), pp. 100–111.
5. *Ibid.*
6. *Ibid.*, p. 101.
7. Murdock, *op. cit.*, p. 3.
8. For a brief account of the Nayar, see: E. Kathleen Gough, "Is the Family Universal: The Nayar Case," pp. 76–92 in *A Modern Introduction to the Family, op. cit.* It is interesting to note that Bell and Vogel, in their preface to Gough's article on the Nayar, contend that she supports Murdock's position on the universality of the nuclear family. In point of fact, Gough on page 84 rejects Murdock and actually deals primarily with the marital and not the family institution. See also: *Matrilineal Kinship*, ed. by David M. Schneider and Kathleen Gough, Berkeley: U. of California Press, 1961, Chaps. 6 and 7. A. R. Radcliffe-Brown was one of the first to note that the Nayar lacked the nuclear family. See his: *African Systems of Kinship and Marriage*, New York: Oxford U. Press, 1959, p. 73.
9. Harold H. Driver, *Indians of North America*, Chicago: U. of Chicago Press, 1961, pp. 291–292.
10. Judith Blake, *Family Structure in Jamaica*, Glencoe, Ill.: Free Press, 1961. Whether Jamaicans actually prefer to marry and have a more typical family system is a controversial point.
11. Melford E. Spiro, *Kibbutz: Venture in Utopia*, Cambridge, Mass.: Harvard U. Press, 1956; and Melford E. Spiro, *Children of the Kibbutz*, Cambridge, Mass.: Harvard U. Press, 1958.
12. Spiro suggests that "reference residence" be used in place of actual common residence. The Kibbutz children do speak of their parents' room as "home." He suggests further that responsibility for education and economic cooperation be substituted for the actual doing of these functions by the parents. The parents could be viewed as responsible for the education of their children, but since nothing changes in economic terms when one marries, it is difficult to understand

just what Spiro means by responsibility for economic cooperation being part of the family. Spiro also would alter Murdock's definition of marriage so as to make emotional intimacy the key element.

13. Bronislaw Malinowski, *The Sexual Life of Savages in North-Western Melanesia*, New York: Harvest Books, 1929.
14. Nicholas S. Timasheff, "The Attempt to Abolish the Family in Russia," pp. 55–63 in Bell and Vogel, *op. cit.*
15. Timasheff refers to the family as "that pillar of society." But nothing in the way of convincing evidence is presented to support this view. The argument is largely that since disorganization followed the attempt to do away with the family, it was a result of that attempt. This may well be an example of a *post hoc ergo propter hoc* fallacy. Also, it should be noted that the love-based union of parents that the early Communists wanted might well be called a family, and thus that the very title of Timasheff's article implies a rather narrow image of the family. For a recent account of the Soviet family see: David and Vera Mace, *The Soviet Family*, New York: Doubleday, 1963; and Ray Bauer *et al.*, *How the Soviet System Works*, Cambridge, Mass.: Harvard U. Press, 1950.
16. Levy and Fallers, *op. cit.*, pp. 649–650.
17. Felix Greene, *Awakened China*, New York: Doubleday, 1961, esp. pp. 142–144. Philip Jones and Thomas Poleman, "Communes and the Agricultural Crises in Communist China," *Food Research Institute Studies*, 3 (February 1962), pp. 1–22. Maurice Freedman, "The Family in China, Past and Present," *Pacific Affairs*, 34 (Winter 1961–2), pp. 323–336.
18. Spiro, *op. cit.*
19. Levy and Fallers, *op. cit.*
20. Robert K. Merton, *Social Theory and Social Structure*, Glencoe, Ill.: Free Press, 1957, p. 32.
21. Zelditch attempted to see if the husband-wife roles would be differentiated in the same way in all cultures, with males being instrumental and females expressive. He found general support, but some exceptions were noted, particularly in societies wherein the nuclear family was embedded in a larger kinship system. Morris Zelditch, Jr., "Role Differentiation in the Nuclear Family: A Comparative Study," in Parsons and Bales, *op. cit.* The Kibbutz would represent another exception since both mother and father play expressive roles in relation to their offspring.
22. Aldous Huxley, *Brave New World*, New York: Harper & Bros., 1950.
23. See: *Six Cultures: Studies in Child Rearing*, ed. by Beatrice B. Whiting, New York: John Wiley, 1963. Margaret Mead reports exchange of children in *Coming of Age in Samoa*, New York: Mentor Books, 1949. Similar customs in Puerto Rico are reported in David Landy, *Tropical Childhood*, Chapel Hill: U. of North Carolina Press, 1959.
24. Robert Winch, in his recent textbook, defines the family as a nuclear family with the basic function of "the replacement of dying members." In line with the present author's arguments, it seems that the actual biological production of infants can be removed from the family. In fact, Winch agrees that the Nayar lack the family as he defined it because they lack a permanent father role in the nuclear family. See: *The Modern Family*, New York: Holt, 1963, pp. 16, 31, and 750.
25. William N. Stephens, *The Family in Cross Cultural Perspective*, New York: Holt, Rinehart & Winston, 1963, p. 357. Stephens discusses the universality of the family in this book but does not take a definite position on the issue. See Chapter 1.
26. Zelditch, *op. cit.*, pp. 307–353.
27. The key importance of primary groups was long ago pointed out by Charles Horton Cooley, *Social Organization*, New York: Scribners, 1929.
28. The structural definition is similar to Levy and Fallers, *op cit.*

29. Radcliffe-Brown, *op. cit.*
30. Parsons, *op. cit.*
31. Phillippe Aries, *Centuries of Childhood*, New York: Alfred A. Knopf, 1962.
32. Richard N. Adams, "An Inquiry into the Nature of the Family," pp. 30–49 in *Essays in the Science of Culture in Honor of Leslie A. White*, ed. by Gertrude E. Dole and Robert L. Carneiro, New York: Thomas Y. Crowell, 1960.
33. Russell Middleton, "Brother-Sister and Father-Daughter Marriage in Ancient Egypt," *American Sociological Review*, 27 (October 1962), pp. 603–611.
34. See the following articles, all by Harry F. Harlow: "The Nature of Love," *American Psychologist*, 13 (December 1958), pp. 673–685; "The Heterosexual Affection System in Monkeys," *American Psychologist*, 17 (January 1962), pp. 1–9; (with Margaret K. Harlow), "Social Deprivation in Monkeys," *Scientific American*, 206 (November 1962), pp. 1–10.
35. Robert M. Yerkes, *Chimpanzees*, New Haven: Yale U. Press, 1943, esp. pp. 43, 68, 257–258; and Robert M. Yerkes and Ada W. Yerkes, *The Great Apes*, New Haven: Yale U. Press, 1929, passim.
36. Leon J. Yarrow, "Separation from Parents During Early Childhood," pp. 89–136 in *Review of Child Development*, ed. by Martin L. Hoffman and Lois W. Hoffman, New York: Russell Sage Foundation, 1964, Vol. 1.
37. John Bowlby, *Maternal Care and Mental Health*, Geneva: World Health Organization, 1951.
38. Yarrow, *op. cit.*, p. 100.
39. *Ibid.*, p. 101–102.
40. *Ibid.*, p. 106.
41. *Ibid.*, pp. 124–125.
42. Barrington Moore, Jr., *Political Power and Social Theory*, Cambridge, Mass.: Harvard U. Press, 1958, Chap. 5.
43. Alexander A. Goldenweiser, *History, Psychology, and Culture*, New York: Alfred A. Knopf, 1933, esp. pp. 45–49.
44. Lewis Coser, *The Functions of Social Conflict*, Glencoe, Ill.: Free Press, 1956.
45. See Gough, *op. cit.*, Kingsley Davis, "Illegitimacy and the Social Structure," *American Journal of Sociology*, 45 (September 1939), pp. 215–233 A. R. Radcliffe-Brown, *op. cit.*, p. 5. The structure of the marital institution is not specified in terms of number or sex, for there are cultures in which two women may marry and raise a family. See: B. E. Evans Pritchard, *Kinship and Marriage Among the Nuer*, London: Oxford U. Press, 1951, pp. 108–109. It is well to note here that Murdock stressed a somewhat different view of marriage. He focused on sexual and economic functions, and the woman-woman marriage found in the Nuer would not fit this definition. Morris Zelditch recently has used this legitimacy function as the key aspect of his definition of the family rather than marriage. Such a usage would, it seems, confuse the traditional distinction between these two institutions. See p. 682 in *Handbook of Modern Sociology*, ed. by Robert Faris, New York: Rand-McNally, 1964.
46. Blake, *op. cit.*
47. Dorothy R. Blitsten, *The World of the Family*, New York: Random House, 1963, esp. Chap. 1.
48. Kingsley Davis, *Human Society*, New York: Macmillan, 1950, p. 395. Davis lists reproduction, maintenance, placement, and socialization of the young as universal family functions. Social placement is the only function that differs from Murdock's list. One could conceive of this function as part of the marital rather than the family institution.

35. Sex as Work
LIONEL S. LEWIS AND DENNIS BRISSETT

In the original version of this article sociologists Lewis and Brissett pay considerable attention to "avocational counselors," specialists consulted by Americans in doubt about how to play "properly." In this cut version, we focus solely on the sex advice given by such counselors. This advice, considered in the abstract, seems almost hilarious. At the very least, it suggests that the Puritan heritage, which extolled work above all, still has a powerful grip upon Americans in general. Puritanical sex counsel seems to be this: If you must play this way, then for heaven's sake work at it so you do it correctly and efficiently! Playing just for the hell of it would not occur to a Puritan.

. . . .

WORKING AT SEX

Marital sex, as depicted by the marriage manuals, is an activity permeated with qualities of work. One need not even read these books, but need only look at the titles or the chapter headings to draw this conclusion. Thus, we have books titled *The Sex Technique in Marriage* (10), *Modern Sex Techniques* (14), *Ideal Marriage: Its Physiology and Technique* (15). There are also chapters titled "How to Manage the Sex Act (3)," "Principles and Techniques of Intercourse (7)," "The Fourth Key to Soundly Satisfying Sex: A Controlled Sexual Crescendo (5)." [Numbers in parentheses refer to the reference list at the end of this article.—Ed.]

From the outset, as we begin to read the books, we are warned not to treat sex frivolously, indeed not to play at sex:

> An ardent spur-of-the-moment tumble sounds very romantic. . . . However, ineptly arranged intercourse leaves the clothes you had no chance to shed in a shambles, your plans for the evening shot, your birth control program incomplete, and your future sex play under considerable better-be-careful-or-we'll-wind-up-in-bed-again restraint (5, pp. 34–35).

In other words, marital sex should not be an impromptu performance.

Moreover, sex should not be approached with a casual mien. Rather, we are counseled, sexual relations, at least good sexual relations, are a goal to be laboriously achieved. It is agreed that "satisfactory intercourse is the basis for happy marriage." However, it is added, "It does not occur automatically but must be striven for (12, p. 39)." In the plain talk of the avocational counselor, "Sexual relations are something to be worked at and developed (7, p. 6)."

This work and its development are portrayed as a taxing kind of en-

SOURCE: Lionel S. Lewis and Dennis Brissett, "Sex as Work: A Study of Avocational Counseling," *Social Problems* 15 (Summer 1967), 8–18. Reprinted by permission of the authors and The Society for the Study of Social Problems.

deavor; as behavior involving, indeed requiring, a good deal of effort. That sex involves effort is a pervasive theme in the 15 manuals. From the start one is advised to direct his effort to satisfying his or her mate so that mutual climax is achieved, sexual activity is continual, and one's partner is not ignored after climax. Thus, we are told:

> Remember, *couple* effort for *couple* satisfaction! That's the key to well-paced, harmonious sex play (5, p. 62).

Certain positions of intercourse are also seen as particularly taxing, in fact so taxing that certain categories of people are advised not to use them. One author, in discussing a particularly laborious position, remarks that "This is no position for a couple of grandparents, no matter how healthy and vigorous they are for their age, for it takes both effort and determination (4, p. 201)." Quite obviously, certain kinds of marital sex are reserved only for those persons who are "in condition."

The female is particularly cautioned to work at sex, for being naturally sexual seems a trait ascribed only to the male. The affinity of sex to her other work activities is here made clear: "Sex is too important for any wife to give it less call upon her energy than cooking, laundry, and a dozen other activities (5, p. 36)." To the housewife's burden is added yet another chore.

Even the one manual that takes great pains to depict sex as sport, injects the work theme. It is pointed out that

> You certainly can [strive and strain at having a climax]—just as you can ... help yourself to focus on a complex musical symphony. ... Just as you strive to enjoy a party, when you begin by having a dull time at it. Sex is often something to be worked and strained at—as an artist works and strains at his painting or sculpture (6, p. 122).

Sex, then, is considered a kind of work; moreover, a very essential form of labor. Regular sexual activity is said, for instance, to contribute to "physical and mental health (7, p. 27)," and to lead to "*spiritual unity* (14, frontispiece)." In the majestic functionalist tradition, "A happy, healthy sex life is vital to wholesome family life, which in turn is fundamental to the welfare of the community and of society (1, XIII)." Marital sex, most assuredly, is the cornerstone of humanity, but not any kind of marital sex—only that which leads to orgasm. "It is the orgasm that is so essential to the health and happiness of the couple ... (10, p. 80)."

Indeed it is the orgasm which may be said to be the *product* of marital sexual relations. It is the *raison d'être* for sexual contact, and this orgasm is no mean achievement. In fact,

> Orgasm occasionally may be the movement of ecstasy when two people together soar along a Milky Way among stars all their own. This moment is the high mountaintop of love of which the poets sing, on which the two together become a full orchestra playing a fortissimo of a glorious symphony (4, pp. 182–183).

In masculine, and somewhat more antiseptic terms, "ejaculation is the aim, the summit and the end of the sexual act (15, 133)." Woe be to the couple who fail to produce this state as there are dire consequences for the unsuccessful, particularly for the woman.

> When the wife does not secure an orgasm, she is left at a high peak of sexual tension. If this failure to release tension becomes a regular thing, she may develop an aversion to starting any sex play that might lead to such frustrations. . . . Repeated disappointments may lead to headaches, nervousness, sleeplessness, and other unhappy symptoms of maladjustment (1, p. 65).

So important is it to reach orgasm, to have a product, that all the other sexual activities of marriage are seen as merely prosaic ingredients or decorative packaging of the product.

In fact, orgasm as a product is so essential that its occasion is not necessarily confined to the actual act of intercourse, at least for the women. Numerous counselors indicate that it may be necessary for the man to induce orgasm in the woman during afterplay. "A woman who has built up a head of passion which her husband was unable to requite deserves a further push to climax through intensive genital caress . . . (5, p. 111)." Particularly in the early years of marriage, before the husband has learned to pace his orgasm, he may have to rely on the knack of digital manipulation. In one author's imagery, "Sometimes it may be necessary for the husband to withdraw and continue the stimulation of his wife by a rhythmic fondling of clitoris and vulva until orgasm is attained (1, p. 66)."

The central importance of experiencing orgasm has led many of the authors to de-emphasize the traditional organs of intercourse. The male penis (member) is particularly belittled. It is considered "only one of the instruments creating sensation in the female, and its greatest value lies as a mental stimulant and organ of reproduction, not as a necessary medium of her sexual pleasure." The same author adds, ". . . the disillusioning fact remains that the forefinger is a most useful asset in man's contact with the opposite sex . . . (14, p. 71)." Furthermore, this useful phallic symbol should be directed primarily to the woman's seat of sensation, the clitoris. Only a man who is ignorant of his job directs his digital attention to the vulva, the female organ that permits conventional union.

One must often deny himself immediate pleasure when manufacturing the orgasm. One author, in referring to an efficient technique to attain orgasm, states that: "Unfortunately, some men do not care for this position. This, however, should be of little importance to an adequate lover, since his emotions are the less important of the two (14, p. 122)." Likewise, the woman may have to force herself in order to reach orgasm, even though she may not desire the activity which precedes it. It is specified that "If you conscientiously work at being available, you may ultimately find the feminine role quite satisfying even in the absence of ardor or desire (5, p. 38)." The work ethic of the sexual side of marriage, then, is one resting quite elaborately on what has been referred to as the "cult of the orgasm."

Still, one cannot easily perform one's job; its intricacies must first be mastered. After all, "... there is considerably more in the sexual relationship than ... at first thought (8, p. 136)." "Remember that complete development of couple skills and adaptations takes literally years (5, p. 206)." There is a great deal to be learned. One author talks of eight steps "in order to facilitate sexual arousal and lead, finally, to satisfactory orgasm" and of seven "techniques which she and her mate may employ to help her attain full climax (6, pp. 124–126)."

All of this requires a good deal of mastery, a mastery that is necessary if the sex relationship is not to undergo "job turnover." Firstly, in the face of incompetence, the marriage partner may, at times, turn to autoeroticism. One author stipulates that "There cannot be a shadow of a doubt that faulty technique, or a total lack of it on the man's part, drives thousands of wives to masturbation as their sole means of gratification (3, p. 140)." Moreover, if sexual skills are not acquired, the husband or wife may seek out new partners for sexual activity. The woman is admonished that adequate sexual relations will keep a man from "The Other Woman ... (4, pp. 264–265)." The male also must be proficient in sexual encounters for "it is the male's habit of treating ... [sexual relationships] as such [mechanically] which causes much dissatisfaction and may ultimately drive the wife to someone who takes it more seriously (14, p. 77)."

LEARNING SEX: PASSIVE AND ACTIVE

Marital sex is said to necessitate a good deal of preparation if it is to be efficiently performed. In one author's words: "This [complete satisfaction] cannot be achieved without study, practice, frank and open discussion ... (12, p. 45)." This overall preparation seems to involve both a passive and an active phase. The passive phase seems most related to an acquisition of information previous to engaging in sexual, at least marital sexual, relations. The active phase best refers to the training, one might say on-the-job training, that the married couple receive in the sexual conduct of wedlock.

The matter of passive preparation receives a great deal of attention from the avocational counselors. Thirteen of the fifteen books call attention to the necessity of reading, studying and discussing the various facets of sexual relationships. After listing a number of these activities, one author advises that "If the two of them have through reading acquired a decent vocabulary and a general understanding of the fundamental facts listed above, they will in all likelihood be able to find their way to happiness (1, p. 20)." Another counselor cites the extreme importance of reciprocal communication by noting that "... the vital problem ... must be solved through intelligent, practical, codified, and instructive discussion ... (14, p. 7)." The general purpose of all this learning is, of course, to dispel ignorance, as ignorance is said to lead to "mistakes at work," and such cannot be tolerated. The learning of the other partner's physiology is particularly emphasized, most counselors devoting at least one chapter and a profusion of illustrations to relieve the ignorance of the marriage partners. One author, however, quite obviously feels that words and pictures are insufficient. Presenting a sketch of the woman's genitals, he asserts that "It should be studied; on the bridal night ... the husband should compare the diagram with the wife's genital region ... (14, p. 18)."

Together with learning physiology, the various manuals also stress the critical importance of learning the methodology of marital sex. Sexual compatibility seems not a matter of following one's natural proclivities, but rather "The technique of the sexual relation has to be learned in order to develop a satisfactory sex life (13, p. 172)." One must know one's job if one is to be successful at it. Not surprisingly, to like one's job also requires a learning experience, particularly for the woman. As one book scientifically asserts:

> There is a striking consensus of opinion among serious specialists (both men and women) that the average woman of our time and clime must *learn* to develop specific sexual enjoyment, and only gradually attains to the orgasm in coitus. ... they [women] have to *learn how* to feel both voluptuous pleasure and actual orgasm (15, p. 262).

In summary, then, passive learning involves the mastering of physiology and techniques. By the desexualized female of the marriage manuals, the fine art of emotional experience and expression is also acquired. And the naturally inept male must learn, for

> If the husband understands in even a general way the sexual nature and equipment of his wife, he need not give the slightest offense to her through ignorant blundering (1, p. 20).

This learning process, according to most of the manuals, eventually becomes subject to the actual experience of matrimonial sex. The marriage bed here becomes a "training" and "proving" ground. Again, wives seem particularly disadvantaged: "Their husbands have to be their guides (3, p. 108)." However, generally the training experience is a mutual activity. As one author suggests in his discussion of the various positions for coitus,

> In brief, the position to be used is not dictated by a code of behavior but should be selected as the one most acceptable to you and your mate. To find this you will examine your own tastes and physical conformation. By deliberate application of the trial and error method you will discover for yourselves which is most desirable for you both (11, p. 11).

In training, rigorous testing and practice is a must. In the words of one manual "experimentation will be required to learn the various responses within one's own body as well as those to be expected from one's beloved ... (9, p. 7)," and also, "After a variable time of practice, husband and wife may both reach climax, and may do so at the same time (11, p. 10)."

Both the husband and wife must engage in a kind of "muscular control" training if the sex act is to be efficiently performed. The woman's plight during intercourse is picturesquely portrayed with the following advice. "You can generally contract these muscles by trying to squeeze with the vagina itself ... perhaps by pretending that you are trying to pick up marbles with it (5, p. 97)." Fortunately, the man is able to practice muscular control at times other than during intercourse. Indeed, the man, unlike the woman, is permitted to engage in activities not normally related to sexual behavior while he is training. It is advised that "You can snap the muscles [at the base of the penile shaft] a few times while you are driving your car or sitting in an office or any place you happen to think of it ... (5, p. 96)." The practice field, at least for the male, is enlarged.

In general, then, a careful learning and a studied training program are necessary conditions for the proper performance of marital sex. As seems abundantly true of all sectors of work, "'Nature' is not enough.... Man must pay for a higher and more complex nervous system by study, training, and conscious effort ... (7, p. 34)."

THE JOB SCHEDULE

As in most work activities, the activity of marital sex is a highly scheduled kind of performance. There is first of all a specification of phases or stages in the actual conduct of the sex act. Although there is disagreement here, some authors indicating four or five distinct phases (15, p. 1), the consensus of the counselors seems to be that "Sexual intercourse, when satisfactorily performed, consists of three stages, only one of which is the sex act proper (11, p. 7)."

The sexual act therefore is a scheduled act and the participants are instructed to follow this schedule. "All three stages have to be fitted into this time. None of them must be missed and none prolonged to the exclusion of others (8, p. 155)." Practice and study is said to insure the proper passage from one phase to another (12, p. 42). Moreover, to guarantee that none of the phases will be excluded, it is necessary to engage in relations only when the sexual partners have a sizable amount of time during which they will not be distracted: "... husbands and wives should rarely presume to begin love-play that may lead to coitus unless they can have an hour free from interruptions (1, p. 51)." Even then, however, the couple must be careful, for there is an optimal time to spend on each particular phase. For instance, "Foreplay should never last less than fifteen minutes even though a woman may be sufficiently aroused in five

(14, p. 43)." Likewise, the epilogue to orgasm should be of sufficient duration to permit the proper recession of passion.

Given this schedule of activity, the marriage manuals take great pains to describe the various activities required at each particular phase. It is cautioned, for instance, that "all contact with the female genital region . . . should be kept at an absolute minimum (14, pp. 42:–43)" during foreplay. The man is warned furthermore to "refrain from any excessive activity involving the penis (14, p. 77)" if he wishes to sustain foreplay. Regarding afterplay, the advice is the same; the partners must not permit themselves "any further genital stimulation (15, p. 25)."

The "job specification" is most explicit, however, when describing the actual act of intercoure. It is particularly during this stage that the sexual partners must strain to maintain control over their emotions. Innumerable lists of "necessary activities" are found in the various manuals. The adequate lovers should not permit themselves to deviate from these activities. Sometimes, in fact, the male is instructed to pause in midaction, in order to ascertain his relative progress:

> After the penis has been inserted to its full length into the vagina, it is usually best for the husband to rest a bit before allowing himself to make the instinctive in-and-out movements which usually follow. He needs first to make sure that his wife is comfortable, that the penis is not pushing too hard against the rear wall of the vagina, and that she is as ready as he to proceed with these movements (1, p. 61).

TECHNIQUES

The "labor of love" espoused by the avocational counselors is one whose culmination is importantly based on the proper use of sexual technique. In fact, ". . . *miserable failure results from ignorance of technique* (3, p. 49)." Indeed "no sex relationship will have permanent value unless technique is mastered . . . (8, p. 177)." Thirteen of the fifteen books devote considerable space to familiarizing the reader with the techniques of sexual activity. These discussions for the most part involve enumerating the various positions of intercourse, but also include techniques to induce, to prolong, to elevate, and to minimize passion. Many times the depiction of particular coital positions takes on a bizarre, almost geometric, aura. In one such position, "The woman lies on her back, lifts her legs at right angles to her body from the hips, and rests them on the man's shoulders; thus she is, so to speak, doubly cleft by the man who lies upon her and inserts his phallus; she enfolds both his genital member and his neck and head. At the same time the woman's spine in the lumbar region is flexed at a sharp angle . . . (15, p. 218)." Often, however, the mastery of sexual technique seems to involve little more than being able to keep one's legs untangled, ". . . when the woman straightens her right leg the man, leaving his right leg between both of hers, puts his left one outside her right, and rolls over onto his left side facing her (1, p. 58)."

At times, in order to make love adequately, it is required of the participants that they supplement their technique with special equipment. Some of this equipment, such as lubricating jellies, pillows, and birth control paraphernalia, is simple and commonplace. Others are as simple but not as common, such as chairs, foot-high stools, and beds with footboards or footrails. Some, like aphrodisiacs, hot cushions, medicated (carbonic acid) baths, and sitz baths, border on the exotic. Still others actually seem to detract from the pleasure of intercourse. In this vein would be the rings of sponge rubber which are slipped over the penis to control depth of penetration and the various devices which make the male less sensitive, such as condoms and a local anesthetic applied to the glans.

This equipment that minimizes stimulation, while not particularly inviting, might be said to give greater pleasure than still other techniques that are suggested to add variety to the sex life. The latter, in fact, seem cruelly painful. For instance,

> . . . both partners tend to use their teeth, and in so doing there is naught abnormal, morbid or perverse. Can the same be said of the real love-bite that breaks the skin and draws blood? Up to a certain degree—yes (15, p. 157).

Indeed, a certain amount of aggression should be commonplace.

> . . . both of them can and do exult in a certain degree of male aggression and dominance. . . . Hence, the sharp gripping and pinching of the woman's arms and nates (15, p. 159).

At times, the authors seem to go so far as to indicate that the proper performance of the sex act almost requires the use of techniques that create discomfort. The element of irksomeness becomes an almost necessary ingredient of the conduct of marital sex.

CONCLUDING REMARKS

The kinds of impressions assembled here seem to support the notion that play, at least sexual play in marriage, has indeed been permeated with dimensions of a work ethic. The play of marital sex is presented by the counselors quite definitely as work.

This paradox, play as work, may be said to be an almost logical outcome of the peculiar condition of American society. First of all, it seems that in America, most individuals are faced with the problems of justifying and dignifying their play. In times past, leisure was something earned, a prize that was achieved through work. In the present era, it might be said that leisure is something ascribed or assumed. Indeed, as Riesman and Bloomberg have noted, "leisure, which was once a residual compensation for the tribulations of work, may become what workers recover from at work." [1]

The American must justify his play. It is our thesis that he has done this by transforming his play into work. This is not to say that he has disguised his play as work; it is instead to propose that his play has become work.[2] To consume is, in most cases, to produce. Through this transformation of play, the dignity of consumption is seemingly established; it is now work, and work is felt to carry with it a certain inherent dignity. The individual now is morally free to consume, and moreover free to seek out persons to teach him how to consume, for learning how to play is simply learning how to do one's job in society.

This transformation of play into work has been attended by another phenomenon that is also quite unique to contemporary American society. Given the fact that work has always been valued in American society, a cult of efficiency has developed. As a consequence, the productive forces in America have become very efficient, and an abundance of consumer goods have been created. So that such goods will be consumed, Americans have been socialized into being extremely consumption oriented. As Jules Henry[3] has noted, the impulse controls of most Americans have been destroyed. The achievement of a state of general satisfaction has become a societal goal. To experience pleasure is almost a societal dictum.

Thus there seem to be two antagonistic forces operating in American society. On the one hand, there is an emphasis on work and, on the other hand, there is an emphasis on attaining maximum pleasure. These two themes were recurrent in the fifteen manuals which we read, and as one writer put it:

> . . . it may well be that the whole level of sexual enjoyment for both partners can be stepped up and greatly enriched if the man is able to exercise a greater degree of deliberation and management (1, p. 33).

It was as if the avocational counselors were trying to solve a dilemma for their audience by reminding them to both "let themselves go" while cautioning them that they should "work at this." If sex be play, it most assuredly is a peculiar kind of play.

NOTES

1. David Riesman and Warner Bloomberg, Jr., "Work and Leisure: Tension or Polarity," in Sigmund Nosow and William H. Form, editors, *Man, Work, and Society*, New York: Basic Books, Inc., 1962, p. 39.
2. Many investigators have observed the intertwining of work and play. We are here only interested in one aspect of admixture, the labor of play.
3. Jules Henry, *Culture Against Man*, New York: Random House, 1963, pp. 20–21.

REFERENCES

1. Oliver M. Butterfield, Ph.D., *Sexual Harmony in Marriage*, New York: Emerson Books, 1964 (sixth printing).
2. Mary Steichen Calderone, M.D., M.S.P.H., and Phyllis and Robert P. Goldman, *Release from Sexual Tensions*, New York: Random House, 1960.
3. Eustace Chesser, M.D., *Love Without Fear*, New York: The New American Library, 1947 (twenty-ninth printing).
4. Maxine Davis, *Sexual Responsibility in Marriage*, New York: Dial Press, 1963.

5. John E. Eichenlaub, M.D., *The Marriage Art*, New York: Dell Publishing Co., 1961 (fourteenth printing).
6. Albert Ellis, Ph.D., and Robert A. Harper, Ph.D., *The Marriage Bed*, New York: Tower Publications, 1961.
7. Bernard R. Greenblat, B.S., M.D., *A Doctor's Marital Guide for Patients*, Chicago: Budlong Press, 1964.
8. Edward F. Griffith, *A Sex Guide to Happy Marriage*, New York: Emerson Books, 1956.
9. Robert E. Hall, M.D., *Sex and Marriage*, New York: Planned Parenthood-World Population, 1965.
10. Isabel Emslie Hutton, M.D., *The Sex Technique in Marriage*, New York: Emerson Books, 1961 (revised, enlarged, and reset edition following thirty-fifth printing in 1959).
11. Lena Levine, M.D., *The Doctor Talks with the Bride and Groom*, New York: Planned Parenthood Federation, 1950 (reprinted, February 1964).
12. S. A. Lewin, M.D., and John Gilmore, Ph.D., *Sex Without Fear*, New York: Medical Research Press, 1957 (fifteenth printing).
13. Hannah M. Stone, M.D., and Abraham Stone, M.D., *A Marriage Manual*, New York: Simon and Schuster, 1953.
14. Robert Street, *Modern Sex Techniques*, New York: Lancer Books, 1959.
15. Th. H. Van de Velde, M.D., *Ideal Marriage: Its Physiology and Technique*, New York: Random House, 1961.

36. Weddings, Old and New
MARCIA SELIGSON

The persistence of marriage and the family, despite superficial changes, is illustrated in the accompanying excerpts from a book by free-lance journalist Marcia Seligson. As indicated by Ms. Seligson, the "wedding industry" is large and flourishing. Further, although young people today very often prefer an informal, nontraditional wedding, they still do marry eventually and they do celebrate their marriages ceremonially. An example "close to home" was recently provided your editor when his son married Robin, the young lady who had been sharing his life. The total ceremony consisted of their own wording of vows made to one another. These vows were read to a small circle of fond relatives gathered on a pine-shrouded knoll in northern Arizona.

The wedding, they say, is a dodo bird. Extinct.
They say that America's children are abandoning established American

SOURCE: Marcia Seligson, *The Eternal Bliss Machine: America's Way of Wedding* (New York: William Morrow & Company, 1973), pp. 1–3, 264–276, 287–288. Copyright © 1973 by Marcia Seligson. Abridged by permission of William Morrow & Company, Inc.

values with the speed and ferocity of a cat bolting from the garden hose. Marriage, we are told, is in its terminal stages, gasping for its dying breath as the new breed of youth shuns wedlock for cohabiting, or one-to-oneness for the communal clan. Those few who are still choosing to get married, everybody insists, are certainly not doing it the way their parents or even older sisters and brothers did—that is, in the traditional, conventional fashion of flowing white lace, "Oh, Promise Me" and a week in Bermuda. Garish, extravagant wingdings of the doves-soaring-from-cakes school are dead; bridal showers, engagement diamonds, trousseaus, a frippery of the past; the "Dearly-beloved-we-are-gathered-together" litany, meaningless, obsolete. That's what everybody says about weddings in America.

They are dead wrong.

Consider these facts:

—In 1971, there were 2,196,000 marriages in America, 648,000 more than in 1961. In those ten years the steady increase paralleled the population growth, that is, 1 percent of the population got married every year.

—Seven out of eight first-time couples are married in a church or synagogue.

—Seven out of eight first-time brides receive an engagement ring.

—In 1971, 80 percent of all first-time weddings were formal; in 1967, that figure was 73 percent.

—In 1971, 96 percent of marrying couples held a reception; in 1967, 85 percent.

—84.5 percent of first-time brides wear a formal bridal gown.

—The wedding industry represents $7 billion a year to the American economy.

Said "wedding industry"—that is, those products and services involved with the first marriage itself and with the formation of a new family household—boasts a staggering bank of statistics to prove its glowing health. Two billion dollars last year spent on wedding receptions; 40 percent of the total jewelry industry; $1 out of every $8 spent on home furnishings and appliances, $640,000,000 in honeymoon travel—all are being joyously shelled out by America's youth. We have come to believe that *most* of this youth now embraces a substantial chunk of counterculture ideology beginning with hair and ending with rejection of the classic American dreams. We've known that they are avid consumers (not yet immune to that invincible strain of national virus), but we thought their purchases confined to rock albums and marijuana. We would assume —if the rumors be true about youthful shunning of the acquisitiveness of their elders—that if and when married they would build their own furniture or do the orange-crate routine. We are, then, startled to learn that 84 percent of all American newlyweds begin their life together as the proud owners of a basic set of establishment fine china dinnerware. That is, incidentally, 17 percent more than ten years ago.

Making generalizations about American youth has of late become a thorny dilemma. Woodstock makes headlines, as do campus demonstrations, marijuana busts, freaky outfits, Mick Jagger and the wedding on a Big Sur cliff where the bride and groom arrived on horseback—nude—and all the guests peeled off their jeans and tie-dyed shirts in a whooping tribal celebratory dance. One makes vast assumptions based on *Time* magazine covers and the seven o'clock news, but the question always remains: How many? How many kids are dropping out, dropping acid, dropping their drawers at their weddings? Many, many fewer, I believe, than we think.

Hair, not too many years ago, was considered an apt yardstick for measuring a stranger; you knew a guy's politics by its length. But our culture has a way of absorbing external aberrations without a ripple disturbing the fabric, and now one can attend a Rotary Club convention and be hand-shook to death by hirsute hail-fellows. Clothes, too, no longer peg the man, as our Hollywood moguls and sky-blue-blooded aristocrats today parade about town in hand-sewn couturier dungarees. And scruffy rock stars drive gleaming Bentleys. So where are we, who's who and what's really going on "Out There"?

. . .

Radical chic in action? Another cutesy-poo idea for a party when we've "done" the mariachi bit and the omelet maker and the whole lambs roasted on the spit and the soul food? Certainly, but let's not be confused. The New Wedding, in its pure form, is a very real—if still infant—metaphor of change in this country. It speaks of a "greening of America," of a journey among certain pockets of youth away from fraudulence and toward a new humanism.

"Some of our ancient language simply doesn't express the meaning these kids want to express to each other when they take marriage vows," says the Reverend A. Myrvin DeLapp of Philadelphia. "Their great concern is for the honesty of the human relationship; the sense of personhood is to be honored and respected. They don't view the marriage as simply entering into a contract, nor the wedding as a performance. They want their marriage to have the fullest possible meaning, validity and integrity."

Distaste for the way one's elders do things is a classic youthful pattern. You see the failure of their dreams so you simply discard those dreams and replace them with the polar opposite. Theirs didn't work, ours will. The kids of the upwardly striving middle class, especially, have seen the hunger for The American Dream burning in their parents' eyes, have felt the heavy price they paid to reach it and, having reached it, its ultimate unsatisfactoriness. Even its destructiveness.

The New Wedding, like the counter-culture itself, is, in the main, a syndrome of children from the successful middle class. (One Boston minister reports most of his offbeat "cases" are kids from Ivy League schools who are in psychoanalysis.) The offspring of folks who have "made it" in our traditional American terms and in whose bosom bloodless revolution is tacitly permissible, and small rejections are understood not to rend the family fabric. The rebellion is against what the kids consider a dearth of values and values of the wrong kind. It is a rejection of plastic, of false emotion, of obsession with material things to validate who we are, of sterility, of hollow forms, of competitiveness, of white bread, of supertechnology, of isolation. In theory, the New Wedding is spontaneous, without artifice and "personally relevant" (an expression that is used as often in this crowd as is "dearly beloved" in the black-tie set). Sometimes even in practice. It is often, this sort of pageant, moving and irresistible and indeed "personally relevant." Sometimes it is self-conscious and ludicrous. I have seen both.

There is a myth afoot in the land that youngsters of the new consciousness have no sense of romantic love, that their relationships mostly consist of leaping from bed to bed with the capricious speed of fleas hopping from one dog to another. "Doing your own thing," it is believed, implies living only for the moment, for the peak experience, eschewing concepts like "future" and "commitment" and "responsibility." Couples move in with each other easily, swiftly, moving out with the same ease, only to be replaced before the mattress is yet cool. Musical sheets. Those few who stay together surely do not do anything as mundane as getting married.

But, according to a Manhattan rabbi who has performed over five hundred weddings, all of them of the "new" species, every one of his couples has been living together previously, but still—to smash the mythology—opt for marriage. For all the reasons that people want to get married. "The new wedding is more a ceremony to confirm what a couple has found by living together rather than to make promises about what they hope will happen," says Rev. William Glenesk, the Brooklyn clergyman who joined Tiny Tim to Miss Vicki. A celebration of what is already there, a public reaffirmation of the commitment and continuity, rather than a beginning. "We don't believe that our wedding is going to be the most important event in our life together," quoted one bride in the *Los Angeles Times*, "and we don't believe that a wedding makes you a married couple."

Does it seem paradoxical then that the loveliest of the new weddings are extremely romantic, poignant in a way that the American matrimonial machinery has otherwise demolished? To the degree that today's traditional American weddings are fixated on a thousand concerns other than the relationship of two people, that the issue of should the chopped liver be beef or chicken transcends—no, obliterates—the issue of the vows, that is the degree of our dehumanization.

So the key word in the new wedding is "meaningful." "I had never been to a wedding that had any meaning at all until the past year or so," says one girl who has recently gotten married on a beach in Virginia. "When Tom and I planned our wedding, we talked about all the formal church and hotel affairs we'd been to—those of friends and relatives—and realized how empty they were. Phony, with all that etiquette junk and everything done for the parents who just wanted to show off for their friends. You never knew what the couple was like and you never cared. And there was no real joy at all. We knew we wanted to have something that would be more than just another drunken party, something uniquely ours."

What seems to be most "meaningful" to the new breed is the beauty of an outdoor setting. Beaches, hilltops, meadows, parks, in caves, on rocks. Free space. Serenity. (Anyway, few kids attend church in their daily lives, and nobody's been inside a synagogue since his bar mitzvah, so that environment would seem as false as a catering hall.) The *Goodbye, Columbus* revelers spend $5000 transforming the Plaza ballroom into a forest; these kids simply use the forest. And the setting naturally dictates the tone of the fete. One cannot quite summon up visions of haughty white-gloved waiters trooping through the sand dunes with silver trays of miniature quiche lorraine, or a trumpety band blasting out the strains of a bossa nova through the Grand Canyon. Or a bride in Piccione lace and satin greeting her chiffoned guests in a receiving line—on top of a rock. The setting indeed sets the tone and thus the new weddings are natural and informal.

So is the food. Wine or even milk has killed off Jack Daniels, and the vittles are so virtuous as to make one pant for a lead-filled ravioli. Organic everything is the order of the day. Goat cheese, homemade yogurt, soybean concoctions, stone-ground bread, health-food brownies. One would kill for a knish. "The hardest thing for me to get used to in these new weddings," says one minister in San Francisco, "is how lousy the food is. The kids may like all this organic stuff, and I'm sure it's good for you, but I just can't face honey on *everything*. As a matter of fact, everything they serve is just like what I eat when I have the flu!"

(At a wedding on a hilltop outside Denver, an array of various salads was created and we guests commanded to eat with our fingers, right from the huge communal bowls. The only liquid available was a tragic blend of wine and beer.)

The most graphic departure from the conventional American wedding scheme is that the new frontier has usurped control from their parents. Normally the event is unquestionably in Mother's hands, or perhaps really in the caterer's. Surely there is no space in a multimillion-dollar spectacle for self-expression and spontaneity, so the bride bows out under the tidal pressures of money and minutiae. That's the unspoken bargain between mama and daughter. But the conventional wedding is not "personally relevant," so it is said—at least not to the two people who are being married. And the new wedding is, in spirit, a statement about who the bride and groom are. Mother is but another guest.

Self-expression and spontaneity. Who ever heard of it at the Beverly Hills Hotel or the Houston Country Club or even on the grounds of

Daddy's Connecticut estate with the tennis courts tented for the dancing? (Footnote: Weddings on Daddies' estates *do not* qualify as New Weddings, even though they are outdoors.) But the theme of this wedding as an expression of who the couple is permeates the day. Dress, for example, is of the anything-goes school, and men—as a FIRST in wedding history—are encouraged to groove, the rebel grooms looking easily as zingy as their brides. I attended one dune-top frolic where the boy, clad in the smashingest getup of white satin bell-bottoms, white boots and a balloon-sleeved silk shirt that didn't omit one color in the entire spectrum, received the awed gasps classically reserved for the bride. She, you see, was bedecked only in your ordinary white suede hooded monk's robe and was completely overshadowed.

A new wedding is an exercise in Do-It-Yourself. And not just for the bride, but also the guests, who are thought of as significant participants, instead of passive audience. One doesn't invite fringe people to this intimate day—none of Father's business accounts or Mother's bowling team will clutter *this* hilltop with indifference. Only true loved ones to share and care. And join in, not merely on the dance floor or in polishing off the prime ribs remnants, but in the essence of the wedding.

—A prominent New York psychiatrist's son married the girl he had been living with for three years and the wedding consisted of an encounter group where the twenty-odd guests all sat on the floor in a circle and shared anecdotes from their own relationship with the couple, as a gift in understanding. Much hugging and crying and primal kissing took place, and everybody remembers it as "a beautiful ceremony."

—At one wedding the bride and groom walked through the assemblage, handing out flowers to everybody, then passed their rings around while they and the rabbi sat on the grass and held a breezy chat (which turned out to be the only vows) about marriage and air pollution.

—On a beach in New Hampshire the minister encouraged the guests to express anything they felt about the bride and groom during the ceremony. The response was spontaneous, to be sure—one young woman burst forth with the news that she had always, until this moment, believed her dearest friend had made a terrible choice and that the groom was in fact a jerk, but that she was beginning to change her mind.

The notion of Do-It-Yourself (with a little help from your friends) begins from the beginning—with the invitations. Sometimes they are in the form of a scroll, sometimes a mobile, even a message written on hard-boiled eggs. They are generally original, handmade and highly personal. "We have found ourselves in each other and want you to share the ceremony of commitment to our love," stated the hand-printed prelude to a classic new wedding held in Los Angeles' rustic Topanga Canyon. Linda, the bride, made her own white peasant dress and her groom's white pants festooned with yellow ribbons; she composed a song for the ceremony and together they wrote their vows; each of their friends contributed some organic tidbit to the feast (including a wheat-flour wedding cake), and folk dancing to the music of an Autoharp continued long into the night. "All the work that went into it," reminisces Linda, "was a true labor of love and we felt that the wedding expressed the feelings that all of us have for each other."

The new gifts are as far afield of the rococo silver samovar as the commune from a condominium. If they are not yet the manure spreaders advocated by the *Whole Earth Catalog*, they are at least as contemporary and utilitarian—like the delicate glass hashish pipe. And often they are handmade—quilts, candles, pottery, jewelry. A California group called the Los Altos Neighborhood Conservationists published a mimeographed sheet called "For a New Life, a New Life-Style Wedding Plans"—a sort of renegade Amy Vanderbilt adviser—with hints for gifts that include a wicker basket filled with biodegradable cleaning agents, or "soul gifts"— season concert tickets, gift certificate to a plant nursery, a course at a university. They recommend not giving the mechanical gadgetry that overkills our lives and makes every newlywed's kitchen resemble a Sears, Roebuck warehouse—the electric bread warmers, the fondue pots, those frills that alienate us in small but cumulative ways from our hands and the sources of our satisfactions. Instead, in this spirit of self-help, they suggest gifts of garden tools and seed packets, ice cream makers, a supply of various flours and pans for baking bread.

The conventional middle-class American wedding serves as a reconciliation—at least for one day—of disparate elements within the family. The two brothers who have loathed each other for twenty years because each insists the other screwed him in business bury their hatchets in the veal Parmesan; octogenarian great-aunts are invited to waltz by young lads who can't even remember the Korean War. Folks who in normal life have nothing much to say to one another today somehow find a commonality. And the inevitable, inexorable war of the generations is called to a temporary cease-fire on this meeting ground where for once everybody's needs seem to jibe.

But the New Wedding stretches the parental/offspring generation gap into a continental divide. When I was in college the most defiant gesture I could make, the apex of rebellion against my background, was to date a black boy (who was then called a Negro). Today, I am told, what with liberal guilt, that act is no longer guaranteed to send a white Mother to the Nembutal. The announcement, however, that you are abandoning her lifetime plans for The Wedding and having a barefoot gypsy fest on a Big Sur rock surely will. She does not, cannot, understand; you are stamping on her sand castle of dreams and, in truth, challenging everything in which she believes. You are also demolishing tradition, and that is frightening.

In *Fiddler on the Roof,* each of Tevye's three daughters defies the established nuptial customs—the first by marrying the boy she loves instead of the arranged match, the second by not asking her father's permission, the third by marrying a Gentile. "Because of our tradition," Tevye says, "everyone knows who he is and what God expects of him," and each time he is sorely threatened by the collapse of the rules by which he lives.

But his misery and that of the mother described above also emanate from the inescapable message that they have lost power over their children. The wedding is the rite of passage that symbolizes the end of their child's childhood and dependence. Unconsciously they prepare themselves for the inevitable, just as we unconsciously prepare ourselves for pain before an operation. But parents *do* see the wedding as their day, the final chapter that *they* are the authors of, and to disrupt these ingrained assumptions is to cause an earthquake of major proportions.

Usually the quake takes the form of Mama summoning up the old head-in-the-oven number, and if that doesn't work (as it generally doesn't anymore—the new species of youth does not seem to have guilt as its prime mover), Daddy threatens withdrawal of the purse. Then several things may happen: (1) as in the story of the New England society lass who announced that she and boyfriend intended to consummate the marriage in front of the assembled guests, Mother fainted, Daddy made the classic threat, lass reconsidered and got married in the Episcopal church in a $600 Priscilla frock, saving the lust for later; (2) the parents do not come to the wedding, so disgraced are they and so unthinkable is it for them to accept the horror; (3) a compromise is made, as in the Long Island two-ceremony wedding—the first in the woods, with flutes, Indian drums and original poetry, followed instantly by a standard service and reception within the gilded confines of Leonard's of Great Neck. Or the one in a Japanese restaurant in L.A. where the bride's psychiatrist (who was also a mail-order minister) performed the ceremony, and the ensuing reception feast of tongue and pastrami was served by mincing ladies in kimonos.

The most commonly seen denouement of the drama is that the folks relinquish, bitterly, and finally attend this peculiar happening over which they had had no dominion. I would like to tell you that they get caught up in the spirit, groove on the jubilation and freedom and ultimately understand and accept. Mostly, I am sorry to say, they do not. Mostly they hate every moment.

Not too long ago I attend a New Wedding in the woods of Malibu Canyon, just north of Los Angeles. The setting is lovely, utterly removed from any vestiges of city life, and the day is sunny, balmy. Virginia and Ken, the couple, are in their early twenties and have lived together for about a year; he is a film editor and she works in a plant store; they are both from L.A. and Jewish. Although Virginia's family knows that she has been living with Ken, they still expected her to have a veritable Barnum and Bailey spectacular at one of the local hotels, and a great rift followed her declaration of wedding intentions. But tempers eased and now both sets of parents are present, along with a dozen or so close relations and fifty of the couple's friends.

One has to park the car at the bottom of a rolling grassy hill and walk for about half a mile, the hill changing to woods, then back to hill. Lining the path and sitting poised in several trees are young friends playing soft rock tunes on flutes, guitars and harmonicas. The scene is idyllically beautiful and the aura of open friendliness and joy is pure, untrammeled by the robot presence of banquet-managers or the rigor mortis of etiquette edicts. I saunter up the hill, feeling the magic of the day, and almost immediately have my first confrontation of many with the generation chasm. It seems that behind me the bride's aunt Florence, wearing a pink brocade Hadassah gown, has caught the heel of her pink satin shoe in a tree root and now she wants to go home. I don't know whether I feel like laughing or sympathizing, so terror-stricken is she about this wedding, so incapable of bending to it, flowing with it, even seeing how inescapably pretty and sweet it is.

But then, nothing that occurs this day bears any familiarity for Aunt Florence. The bride does not march down an aisle, enveloped in trick lighting; she is standing on the hill when we arrive, wearing a long peasanty dress made of patchwork tablecloths, no shoes and a coronet of daffodils. Ken is splendid in orange-and-yellow-striped bell-bottoms and a fringed Apache vest and a matching daffodil headpiece. All the friends are dressed flamboyantly, exuberantly, as if for a fabulous costume revelry. Bare midriffs, leather shorts, gypsy wildnesses. The clothes of the counter-culture have become—as they say in the world of *Vogue*—"a fashion story."

The elders, of course, are in their spiffiest wedding finery—except for one or two chic matrons in peasant frocks from Beverly Hills boutiques, who are urgently "With It."

People are talking, drinking wine, joints are being passed with some discretion (I cannot tell whether the older generation detects, but certainly nobody hands one to Aunt Florence), and both sets of parents are trying, they are really trying—desperately, with smiles frozen like the masks of comedy. Soon a rabbi appears—one of the "hippie rabbis," as they are known around L.A., not because they themselves are hippies, mind you, but because they do this kind of wedding—and the joints are extinguished. (This cleric has insisted ahead of time that no pot smoking take place while he is on the premises; Rabbi Bruce Goldman in New York prefers the presence of marijuana to cigarettes or alcohol.)

At some point everybody casually sits down on the grass (chairs have been provided for Aunt Florence, et al.) in a circle around Ken and Virginia and the rabbi, and easy rapping just sort of flows into the "ceremony." A young girl carrying an infant (which she periodically nurses in front of everybody during the day) hands the child to somebody, picks up a guitar and sings a Joni Mitchell ballad in a clear soprano. The rabbi then recites some familiar lines from *The Prophet* that begin "Love one another but make not a bond of love . . ."

Virginia speaks a Carl Sandburg poem, looking lovingly into Ken's eyes: "But leave me a little love/A voice to speak to me in the day's end/A hand to touch me in the dark room/Breaking the long long loneliness." Now, so far everything is terribly romantic and touching and even the elders, poised stiffly in wooden chairs, their regal hairdos and garbs successfully defying the strong breeze to make them budge—even they are moved. After all, Ali and Ryan in *Love Story* read Elizabeth Barrett Browning to each other in their nuptials, so it must be sort of okay.

But then the recitation takes a turn away from the schmaltzy, a bizarre turn with Ken and Virginia together reciting the Fritz Perls "Gestalt Prayer": "I do my thing, and you do your thing./I am not in this world to live up to your expectations/And you are not in this world to live up to mine./You are you and I am I, and if by chance we find each other, it's beautiful." (The last line, "If not, it can't be helped," was tactfully omitted from the reading.) The families start to twitch nervously and glance around at each other over their shoulders in unspoken *you-see-I-knew-it* looks of anger.

Then something incredible happens, something awful, the coalescence of everybody's terrors of how this debauchery would turn out. Okay, maybe all these hippies aren't screwing on the grass or going berserk on LSD or all those other things that these kids do, but suddenly this strange ceremony—not even a word of Hebrew, or a "for better or worse"—suddenly it gets POLITICAL. Virginia stands up and reads from Emma Goldman on Woman's Suffrage, all about "asserting herself as a personality and not as a sex commodity" and "refusing the right to anyone over her body" and "refusing to bear children, unless she wants them" and "refusing to be a servant to God, the State, society, the husband, the family . . ." And the kids shout *"Right on, sister,"* and the family drops dead.

In ancient Jewish lore, when a girl marries a Gentile, she is declared dead by the father and, in effect, is treated as such forever. Virginia—I see by the faces of the judges on the chairs, faces at once iced and terrified—has just been pronounced a corpse. When, at the end, the couple shatters the traditional glass, adding the hope that the noise will drive away the repressive forces in our society like Nixon and Agnew—well, hardly anybody even notices. They are all comatose.

The party following is jolly, with lots of group singing and folk dancing and the playing of games like Spin the Bottle and Pin the Tail on the Donkey, and an organic feast which includes fruit salad, homemade breads, the invariable honey-in-the-comb. The only incongruous note is the presence of a whole roast suckling pig, which reclines dead-center in the mélange of food—like a gigantic middle finger pointed upward.

The pig is just one more stab to the older generation, who has not yet recovered from Emma Goldman, and their rage and confusion suffuses the otherwise joyful ambiance. I am saddened by the real depths of the breach—they cannot step down off their chairs and the kids cannot understand or lessen their pain. As a final event, Ken and Virginia open the gifts—a gesture hopefully meant to involve both planets—but even there the barriers prevail. One present is a garish cut-crystal something—a bowl, or a decanter, or a lamp, it's hard to tell which—and the next is a membership in Zero Population Growth.

Mother tries hard throughout the day but finally falls apart, goes limp. I go over to her as she is sipping some rose-petal soup and it is as if she is in shock. "This has nothing to do with anything I've come to associate with a wedding," she mourns. "I don't know what to do here and to tell you the truth, I don't really believe they're even married."

(What the lady doesn't realize, of course, is that the New Wedding is nothing if not a direct throwback to the past, to the style in which *everybody* got married before the entrance of the church and the caterer. All weddings took place outdoors, were cooperative ventures with the whole tribe or village sharing in the experience, the feast and gifts and decorations hand-wrought. The rebel youth, it appears, in their rejection of their parents' vision of The Good Life, have instinctively turned back to pure folklore, to a sense of the communal and a way that seems to them richer, more natural.)

. . .

The bedrock of society shifts slowly, imperceptibly. But it does shift. What the homosexual wedding and the New Wedding express in common is the budding claim for Self, for dignity and autonomy, for alternatives and for change. Some lovers are dispensing with the marriage institution entirely and drawing up short-term renewable contracts, specifying who will do what and what are the arrangements in case of "divorce." Others, finding fulfillment in numbers, are entering group marriages ("Do you, Martha and Irving and Emily and Benjamin and Rosemary and Avery, take . . ."). And who can tell what is waiting in the wings?

The one constant, in all of this, is our undying hunger for the wedding ritual, with all of its apparently crucial qualities and ingredients. Even the New Wedding in its insistence—sometimes poignant, sometimes strident—on "personal relevance" is beginning already to fall into the predictable, repetitive mold of its conventional cousins and to become Kitsch: ho-hum, another sunrise ceremony in a cow pasture, yet another crunchy granola soufflé, yawn, those same old weary passages from *The Prophet* that we've heard at the last three weddings. In ten years will every white leather photo album entitled "My Wedding" close with the New Cliché—Susie and Jimmy, framed in a heart, lovingly passing a joint to one another? Will we have to reserve cow pastures six months in advance? And are the different drummers ultimately just banging out the same old beat?

That, as they say, remains to be seen.

37. Unequal Education and the Reproduction of the Class Structure
SAMUEL BOWLES

In this and in the next article, the point is made that schools are major instruments whereby ruling classes maintain their control over society. Here we focus attention on primary and secondary schools. Knowledgeable people will not be surprised at the general tenor of Bowles' revelations. In truth, all the major institutions of a society, and not merely its schools, are typically used by the powerful to consolidate and preserve their special privileges. It has always been this way, but the major question is, must it continue to be?

Education has long been the chosen instrument of American social reformers. Whatever the ills that beset our society, education is thought to be the cure. Most Americans share the faith—voiced by Horace Mann over a century ago—that education is the "great equalizer." With access to public schools, the children of every class and condition have an equal chance to develop their talents and make a success of themselves. It is our public system of education—so the conventional wisdom goes—that guarantees an open society where any citizen can rise from the lowliest background to high social position according to his ability and efforts.

The record of educational history in the United States and scrutiny of the present state of our colleges and schools lend little support to this comforting optimism. Rather, the available data suggest an alternative interpretation. Apparently our schools have evolved not as part of a pursuit of equality but rather to meet the needs of capitalist employers for a disciplined and skilled labor force and to provide a mechanism for social control in the interests of political stability. As the economic importance of skilled and well-educated labor has grown, inequalities in the school system have become increasingly important in reproducing the class structure from one generation to the next. In fact, the United States school system is pervaded by class inequalities which have shown little sign of diminishing over the last half-century. The evidently unequal control over school boards and other decision-making bodies in education does not provide a sufficient explanation of the persistence and pervasiveness of these inequalities. Although the unequal distribution of political power serves to maintain inequalities in education, their origins are to be

SOURCE: Samuel Bowles, "Getting Nowhere: Programmed Class Stagnation," *Society* vol. 9, no. 8 (June 1972), 42–45, 47–49. Copyright © 1972, from Transaction, Inc. Published by permission of Transaction, Inc.

found outside the political sphere in the class structure itself and in the class subcultures typical of capitalist societies. Thus unequal education has its roots in the very class structure which it serves to legitimize and reproduce.

In colonial America, as in most pre-capitalist societies of the past, the basic productive unit was the family. For the vast majority of male adults, work was self-directed and was performed without direct supervision. Though constrained by poverty, ill health, the low level of technological development and occasional interferences by the political authorities, a man had considerable leeway in choosing his working hours, what to produce and how to produce it. While great inequalities in wealth, political power and other aspects of status normally existed, differences in the degree of autonomy in work were relatively minor, particularly when compared with what was to come.

PARENTS AS TEACHERS

Transmitting the necessary productive skills to the children as they grew up proved to be a simple task, not because the work was devoid of skill, but because the quite substantial skills required were virtually unchanging from generation to generation, and because the transition to the world of work did not require that the child adapt to a wholly new set of social relationships. The child learned the concrete skills and adapted to the social relations of production through learning by doing within the family.

All of this changed with the advent of the capitalist economy in which the vast majority of economically active individuals relinquished control over their labor power in return for wages or salaries and in which the non-labor means of production were privately owned. The extension of capitalist production (particularly the factory system) undermined the role of the family as the major unit of both socialization and production. Small farmers were driven off the land or competed out of business. Cottage industry was destroyed. Ownership of the means of production became heavily concentrated in the hands of the owners of capital and land. Increasingly, production was carried on in large organizations in which a small management group directed the work activities of the entire labor force. The social relations of production—the authority structure, the prescribed types of behavior and response characteristic of the workplace—became increasingly distinct from those of the family.

The divorce of the worker from control over production—from control over his own labor—is particularly important in understanding the role of schooling in capitalist societies. The resulting social division of labor between controllers and the controlled is a crucial aspect of the class structure and will be seen as an important barrier to the achievement of social-class equality in schooling.

While undermining both family and church—the main institutions of socialization—the development of the capitalist system created at the same time an environment which would ultimately challenge the political order. Workers were thrown together in oppressive factories, and the isolation which had helped to maintain quiescence in earlier, widely dispersed peasant populations was broken down. With an increasing number of families uprooted from the land, the workers' search for a living resulted in large-scale labor migrations. Transient (and even foreign) elements came to constitute a major segment of the population and began to pose seemingly insurmountable problems of assimilation, integration and control. Inequalities of wealth became more apparent and were less easily justified and less readily accepted. The simple legitimizing ideologies of the earlier period—for example, the divine right of kings and the divine origin of social rank—fell under the capitalist attack on the royalty and the traditional landed interests. The broadening of the electorate, first sought by the capitalist class in the struggle against the entrenched interests of the pre-capitalist period, soon threatened to become an instrument for the growing power of the working class. Having risen to political power, the capitalist class sought a mechanism to insure social control and political stability.

An institutional crisis was at hand. The outcome, in virtually all capitalist countries, was the rise of mass education. In the United States, the many advantages of schooling as a socialization process were quickly perceived. The early proponents of the rapid expansion of schooling argued that education could perform many of the socialization functions which earlier had been centered in the family and to a lesser extent in the church.

An ideal preparation for factory work was found in the social relations of the school, specifically in its emphasis on discipline, punctuality, acceptance of authority outside the family and individual accountability for one's work. A manufacturer writing to the Massachusetts State Board of Education from Lowell in 1841 commented:

> I have never considered mere knowledge . . . as the only advantage derived from a good education. . . . [Workers with more education possess] a higher and better state of morals, are more orderly and respectful in their deportment, and more ready to comply with the wholesome and necessary regulations of an establishment. . . . In times of agitation, on account of some change in regulations or wages, I have always looked to the most intelligent, best educated and the most moral for support. The ignorant and uneducated I have generally found the most turbulent and troublesome, acting under the impulse of excited passion and jealousy.

The social relations of the school would replicate the social relations of the workplace and thus help young people adapt to the social division of labor. Schools would further lead people to accept the authority of the state and its agents—the teachers—at a young age, in part by fostering the illusion of the benevolence of the government in its relations with citizens. Moreover, because schooling would ostensibly be open to all, one's position in the social division of labor could be portrayed as the result not of birth, but of one's own efforts and talents. And if the children's everyday experiences with the structure of schooling were insufficient to inculcate the correct views and attitudes, the curriculum itself would be made to embody the bourgeois ideology. Thomas Cooper, an American economist, wrote in 1828:

> Education universally extended throughout the community will tend to disabuse the working class of people in respect of a notion that has crept into the minds of our mechanics and is gradually prevailing, that manual labor is at present very inadequately rewarded, owing to combinations of the rich against the poor; that mere mental labor is comparatively worthless; that property or wealth ought not to be accumulated or transmitted; that to take interest on money lent or profit on capital employed is unjust. . . . The mistaken and ignorant people who entertain these fallacies as truths will learn, when they have the opportunity of learning, that the institution of political society originated in the protection of property.

The movement for public elementary and secondary education in the United States originated in the nineteenth century in states dominated by the burgeoning industrial capitalist class, most notably in Massachusetts. It spread rapidly to all parts of the country except the South. In Massachusetts the extension of elementary education was in large measure a response to industrialization and to the need for social control of the Irish and other non-Yankee workers recruited to work in the mills. The fact that some working people's movements had demanded free instruction should not obscure the basically coercive nature of the extension of schooling. In many parts of the country, schools were literally imposed upon the workers.

A system of class stratification developed within this rapidly expanding educational system. Children of the social elite normally attended private schools. Because working-class children tended to leave school early, the class composition of the public high schools was distinctly more elite than that of the public primary schools. And as a university education ceased to be merely training for teaching or the divinity and became important in gaining access to the pinnacles of the business world, upper-class families increasingly used their money and influence to get their children into the best universities, often at the expense of the children of less elite families.

Around the turn of the century, large numbers of working-class (and particularly immigrant) children began attending high schools. At the same time, a system of class stratification developed within secondary education.

The older democratic ideology of the common school—that the same curriculum should be offered to all children—gave way to the "progressive" insistence that education should be tailored to the "needs of the child." The superintendent of the Boston schools summed up the change in 1908:

> Until very recently [the schools] have offered equal opportunity for all to receive *one kind* of education, but what will make them democratic is to provide opportunity for all to receive such education as will fit them *equally well* for their particular life work.

In the interests of providing an education relevant to the later life of the students, vocational schools and tracks were developed for the children of working families. The academic curriculum was preserved for those who would later have the opportunity to make use of book learning either in college or in white-collar employment. This and other educational reforms of the progressive education movement reflected an implicit assumption of the immutability of the class structure.

TRACKING BY SOCIAL CLASS

The frankness with which students were channeled into curriculum tracks on the basis of their social-class background raised serious doubts concerning the openness of the class structure. The apparent unfairness of the selection and tracking procedures was disguised (though not mitigated much) by another "progressive" reform—"objective" educational testing. Particularly after World War I, the capitulation of the schools to business values and the cult of efficiency led to the increased use of intelligence and scholastic achievement testing as an ostensibly unbiased means of measuring school outputs and classifying students. The complementary growth of the guidance counseling profession allowed much of the channeling to proceed from the students' own well-counselled choices, thus adding an apparent element of voluntarism to the mechanisms perpetuating the class structure.

As schooling became the standard for assigning children positions in the class structure, it played a major part in legitimizing the structure itself. But at the same time it undermined the simple processes by which the upper class had preserved its position from one generation to the next—the inheritance of physical capital. When education and skills play an important role in the hierarchy of production, the inheritance of capital from one generation to the next is not enough to reproduce the social division of labor. Rather skills broadly defined and educational credentials must somehow be passed on within the family. It is in furthering this modern form of class structure that the school plays a fundamental role. Children whose parents occupy positions at the top of the occupational hierarchy receive more and better schooling than working-class children. Inequalities in years of schooling are particularly evident. My analysis of United States Census data indicate that if we define social-class standing by the income, occupation and educational level of the parents, a child from the 90th percentile in the class distribution may expect on the average to achieve over four-and-a-half more years of schooling than a child from the tenth percentile. Even among those who had graduated from high school, children of families earning less than $3,000 per year were over six times as likely not to attend college as were the children of families earning over $15,000.

Because schooling is heavily subsidized by the general taxpayer, the longer a child attends school, the more public resources he has access to. Further, public expenditure per student in four-year colleges greatly exceeds that in elementary schools; those who stay in school longer receive an inceasingly large *annual* public subsidy. In the school year 1969-70, per-pupil expenditures of federal, state and local funds were $1490 for colleges and universities and $747 for primary and secondary schools. Even at the elementary level, schools in low-income neighborhoods tend to be less well endowed with equipment, books, teachers and other inputs into the educational process.

The inequalities in schooling go deeper than these simple measures. Differences in rules, expected modes of behavior and opportunities for choice are most glaring when we compare levels of schooling. Note the wide range of choice over curriculum, life style and allocation of time afforded to college students compared with the obedience and respect for authority expected in high school. Differentiation also occurs within each level of schooling. One needs only to compare the social relations of a junior college with those of an elite four-year college, or those of a working-class high school with those of a wealthy suburban high school, for verification of this point. It is consistent with this pattern that the play-oriented, child-centered pedagogy of the progressive movement found little acceptance outside of private schools and public schools in wealthy communities.

MIRROR OF THE FACTORY

These differences in socialization patterns do not arise by accident. Rather, they are the product of class differences in educational objectives and expectations held by parents and educators alike and of differences in student responsiveness to various patterns of teaching and control. Further, a teacher in an understaffed, ill-equipped school may be compelled to resort to authoritarian tactics whether she wants to or not. Lack of resources precludes having small intimate classes, a multiplicity of elective courses, specialized teachers (except disciplinary personnel), free time for the teachers and the free space required for a more open, flexible educational environment. Socialization in such a school comes to mirror that of the factory; students are treated as raw materials on a production line. There is a high premium on obedience and punctuality and there are few opportunities for independent, creative work or individualized attention by teachers.

Even where working-class children attend a well-financed school they do not receive the same treatment as the children of the rich. Class stratification within a given school is achieved through tracking and differential participation in extracurricular activities; it is reinforced by attitudes of teachers and particularly guidance personnel who expect working-class children to do poorly, to terminate school early and to end up in jobs similar to their parents'.

Not surprisingly, the results of schooling differ greatly for children of different social classes. On nationally standardized achievement tests, children whose parents were themselves highly educated outperform by a wide margin the children of parents with less education. A recent study revealed, for example, that among white high school seniors, those whose parents were in the top education decile were on the average well over three grade levels ahead of those whose parents were in the bottom decile.

Given class differences in scholastic achievement, class inequalities in college attendance are to be expected. Thus one might be tempted to argue that the data in Table 1 are simply a reflection of unequal scholastic achievement in high school and do not reflect any additional social-class inequalities peculiar to the process of college admission. This view, so comforting to the admissions personnel in our elite universities, is unsupported by the available data, some of which is presented in Table 2. Access to a college education is highly unequal, even for students of the same measured academic ability.

And inequalities of educational opportunity show no signs of abatement. In fact, data from a recent United States Census survey reported in Table 3 indicate that graduation from college is at least as dependent on one's class background now as it was 50 years ago. Considering access to all levels of education, the data suggest that the number of years of schooling attained by a child depends upon the social-class standing of the father slightly more in the recent period than it did at the beginning of the century.

The pervasive and persistent inequalities in the United States system of education pose serious problems of interpretation. If the costs of education borne by students and their families were very high, or if nepotism

Table 1. College Attendance in 1967 among High School Graduates, by Family Income

Family income	Percent who did not attend college
Total	53.1
under $3,000	80.2
$3,000 to $3,999	67.7
$4,000 to $5,999	63.7
$6,000 to $7,499	58.9
$7,500 to $9,999	49.0
$10,000 to $14,999	38.7
$15,000 and over	13.3

Refers to high school seniors in October 1965 who subsequently graduated. Bureau of the Census, *Current Population Report,* 1969. College attendance refers to both two- and four-year institutions.

Table 2. Probability of College Entry for a Male Who Has Reached Grade 11

		Socioeconomic quartiles			
		Low 1	2	3	High 4
Ability quartiles	1 Low	.06	.12	.13	.26
	2	.13	.15	.29	.36
	3	.25	.34	.45	.65
	4 High	.48	.70	.73	.87

Based on a large sample of U.S. high school students studied by Project Talent at the University of Pittsburgh, 1966.
The socioeconomic index is a composite measure including family income, father's occupation and education, mother's education and so forth. The ability scale is a composite of tests measuring general academic aptitude.

were rampant, or if formal segregation of pupils by social class were practiced, or educational decisions were made by a select few whom we might call the power elite, it would not be difficult to explain the continued inequalities in the system. The problem is to reconcile the above empirical findings with the facts of our society as we perceive them: public and virtually tuition-free education at all levels, few legal instruments for the direct implementation of class segregation, a limited role for contacts or nepotism in the achievement of high status or income, a commitment (at the rhetorical level at least) to equality of educational opportunity and a system of control of education which if not particularly democratic extends far beyond anything resembling a power elite. The attempt to reconcile these apparently discrepant facts leads us back to a consideration of the social division of labor, the associated class cultures and the exercise of class power.

The social division of labor—based on the hierarchical structure of production—gives rise to distinct class subcultures, each of which has its own values, personality traits and expectations. The social relations of production characteristic of advanced capitalist societies (and many socialist societies) are most clearly illustrated in the bureaucracy and hierarchy of the modern corporation. Occupational roles in the capitalist economy may be grouped according to the degree of independence and control exercised by the person holding the job. The personality attributes associated with the adequate performance of jobs in occupational categories defined in this broad way differ considerably, some apparently requiring independence and internal discipline, and others emphasizing such traits as obedience, predictability and willingness to subject oneself to external controls.

These personality attributes are developed primarily at a young age, both in the family and to a lesser extent in secondary socialization institutions such as schools. Daily experience in the workplace reinforces these traits in adults. Because people tend to marry within their own

Table 3. Among Sons Who Had Reached High School, Percentage Who Graduated from College, By Son's Age and Father's Level of Education

Son's age in 1962	Likely dates of college graduation	Less than 8 years
25–34	1950–1959	07.6
35–44	1940–1949	08.6
45–54	1930–1939	07.7
55–64	1920–1929	08.9

Based on U.S. Census data for 1962 as reported in William G. Spady, "Educational Mobility and Access: Growth and Paradoxes," *American Journal of Sociology*, November 1967. Assumes college graduation at age 22.

class, both parents are likely to have a similar set of these fundamental personality traits. Thus children of parents occupying a given position in the occupational hierarchy grow up in homes where child-rearing methods and perhaps even the physical surroundings tend to develop personality characteristics appropriate to adequate job performance in the occupational roles of the parents. The children of managers and professionals are taught self-reliance within a broad set of constraints; the children of production-line workers are taught conformity and obedience.

Melvin Kohn summarizes his extensive empirical work on class structure and parental values as follows:

> Whether consciously or not, parents tend to impart to their children lessons derived from the condition of life of their own class—and thus help to prepare their children for a similar class position. . . . The conformist values and orientation of lower- and working-class parents are inappropriate for training children to deal with the problems of middle-class and professional life. . . . The family, then, functions as a mechanism for perpetuating inequality.

This relation between parents' class position and child's personality attributes is reinforced by schools and other social institutions. Teachers, guidance counselors and school administrators ordinarily encourage students to develop aspirations and expectations typical of their social class, even if the child tends to have deviant aspirations.

It is true that schools introduce some common elements of socialization for all students. Discipline, respect for property, competition and punctuality are part of implicit curricula. Yet the ability of a school to appreciably change a child's future is severely limited. However, the responsiveness of children to different types of schooling seems highly dependent upon the personality traits, values and expectations which have been developed through the family. Furthermore, since children spend a small amount of time in school—less than a quarter of their waking hours over the course of a year—schools are probably more effective

	Father's Education				
Some high school		High school graduate		Some college or more	
Percent graduating	Ratio to less than 8 years	Percent graduating	Ratio to less than 8 years	Percent graduating	Ratio to less than 8 years
17.4	2.29	25.6	3.37	51.9	6.83
11.9	1.38	25.3	2.94	53.9	6.27
09.8	1.27	15.1	1.96	36.9	4.79
09.8	1.10	19.2	2.16	29.8	3.35

where they complement and reinforce rather than oppose the socialization processes of the home and neighborhood. Not surprisingly, this relationship between family socialization and that of the schools reproduces patterns of class culture from generation to generation.

Among adults the differing daily work experiences of people reinforce these patterns of class culture. The reward structure of the workplace favors the continued development of traits such as obedience and acceptance of authority among workers. Conversely, those occupying directing roles in production are rewarded for the capacity to make decisions and exert authority. Thus the operation of the incentive structure of the job stabilizes and reproduces patterns of class culture. The operation of the labor market translates these differences in class culture into income inequalities and occupational hierarchies. Recent work by Herbert Gintis and other economists shows that the relation between schooling and economic success cannot be explained by the effect of schooling on intellectual capacity. Rather, the economic success of individuals with higher educational attainments is explained by their highly rewarded personality characteristics which facilitate entry into the upper echelons of the production hierarchy. These personality characteristics, originating in the work experiences of one's parents, transmitted in turn to children through early socialization practices and reinforced in school and on the job are an important vehicle for the reproduction of the social division of labor.

But the argument thus far is incomplete. The perpetuation of inequality through the schooling system has been represented as an almost automatic, self-enforcing mechanism, operating through the medium of class culture. An important further dimension is added to this interpretation if we note that positions of control in the productive hierarchy tend to be associated with positions of political influence. Given the disproportionate share of political power held by the upper classes and their capacity for determining the accepted patterns of behavior and procedures, to define the national interest and to control the ideological and institutional context in which educational decisions are made, it is not surprising to find that resources are allocated unequally among school tracks, between schools serving different classes and between levels of schooling. The same configuration of power results in curricula, methods of instruction and criteria which, though often seemingly innocuous and ostensibly even egalitarian, serves to maintain the unequal system.

ILLUSION OF FAIR TREATMENT

Take the operation of one of these rules of the game—the principle that excellence in schooling should be rewarded. The upper class defines excellence in terms on which upper-class children tend to excel (for example, scholastic achievement). Adherence to this principle yields inegalitarian outcomes (for example, unequal access to higher education) while maintaining the appearance of fair treatment. Those who would defend the "reward excellence" principle on the grounds of efficient selection to ensure the most efficient use of educational resources might ask themselves this: why should colleges admit those with the highest college entrance examination board scores? Why not the lowest or the middle? According to conventional standards of efficiency, the rational social objective of the college is to render the greatest increment in individual capacities ("value added," to the economist), not to produce the most illustrious graduating class ("gross output"). Thus the principle of rewarding excellence does not appear to be motivated by a concern for the efficient use of educational resources. Rather it serves to legitimize the unequal consequences of schooling.

Though cognitive capacities are relatively unimportant in the determination of income and occupational success, the reward of intellectual ability in school plays an important role. The "objective" testing of scholastic achievement and relatively meritocratic system of grading encourages the illusion that promotion and rewards are distributed fairly. The close relationship between educational attainments and later occupational success further masks the paramount importance of race and social-class background for getting ahead.

At the same time, the institution of objectively administered tests of performance serves to allow a limited amount of upward mobility among exceptional children of the lower class, thus providing further legitimation of the operations of the social system by giving some credence to the myth of widespread mobility.

The operation of the "reward excellence" rule illustrates the symbiosis between the political and economic power of the upper class. Adherence to the rule has the effect of generating unequal consequences via a mechanism which operates largely outside the political system. As long as one adheres to the reward (academic) excellence principle, the responsibility for unequal results in schooling appears to rest outside the upper class, often in some fault of the poor—such as their class culture—which is viewed as lying beyond the reach of political action or criticism.

Thus it appears that the consequences of an unequal distribution of political power among classes complement the results of class culture in maintaining an educational system which has thus far been capable of transmitting status from generation to generation, and capable in addition of political survival in the formally democratic and egalitarian environment of the contemporary United States.

The role of the schools in reproducing and legitimizing the social division of labor has recently been challenged by popular egalitarian movements. At the same time, the educational system is showing signs of internal structural weakness. I have argued elsewhere that overproduction of highly educated workers by universities and graduate schools and a breakdown of authority at all levels of schooling are not passing phenomena, but deeply rooted in the pattern of growth and structural change in the advanced capitalist economy. These two developments suggest that fundamental change in the schooling process may soon be possible.

But it should be clear that educational equality cannot be achieved through changes in the school system alone. Attempts at educational reform may move us closer to that objective (if, in their failure, they lay bare the unequal nature of our school system and destroy the illusion of unimpeded mobility through education). Yet if the record of the last century and a half of educational reforms is any guide, we should not expect radical change in education to result from the efforts of reformers who confine their attention to the schools. My interpretation of the educational consequences of class culture and class power suggests that past educational reform movements failed because they sought to eliminate educational inequalities without challenging the basic institutions of capitalism.

Efforts to equalize education through changes in school finance, compensatory education and similar programs will at best scratch the surface of inequality. As long as jobs are structured so that some have power over many and others have power over nothing—as long as the social division of labor persists—educational inequality will be built into U.S. society.

38. Our Kept Universities
LEE STEPHENSON

In this selection we see some of the ways in which universities become instruments whereby the ruling forces of society guarantee their own continued preeminence. The author, Lee Stephenson, was formerly on the staff of the Nader Project on Corporate Responsibil-

SOURCE: Lee Stephenson, "Our Kept Universities," *The Progressive* 37 (March 1973), 46–49. Reprinted by permission.

ity, where he conducted the study described below. He is currently Washington correspondent for the Council on Economic Priorities, a nonprofit, public-interest organization headquartered in New York City.

It is a peculiar irony, amid growing public opinion that American universities have become all too liberal, that the majority of trustees who run colleges politically identify most with Nelson Rockefeller and Richard Nixon and believe that faculty members should sign loyalty oaths.

This comes as no great surprise to those familiar with university operations. Boards of governors, regents, or trustees have ultimate policy-making power on campuses, but most trustees are selected for political services rendered or for their ability to generate money for the school. Thus, statistics show that the average trustee is a conservative, white, male, high-income business executive. Various university constituencies—women, minority groups, students, and faculty—have protested in the past that trustees selected on this basis may be good at raising money, but that their views on policy do not always adequately represent other university groups, and that such a narrow view may not be healthy or in the best interest of higher education.

Students have been the most vocal and active of the unrepresented university constituencies but have met limited success in their efforts. In an unprecedented boost for a student voice last year, former Senator Fred R. Harris, Oklahoma Democrat, took the debate to Congress by sponsoring a "sense-of-the-Congress" measure which would have urged colleges to place at least one student with full voting rights on the board of trustees.

Passed by the Senate as an amendment to the omnibus Higher Education Act, the Harris proviso was virtually killed in conference committee before the entire measure passed both houses last year. Now all that remains of the amendment is the simple statement that ". . . governing boards of institutions of higher education should give careful consideration to student participation . . ."

Senator Harris and the National Student Lobby, a year-old Washington-based student interest group which fought hard for the measure, expressed disappointment with the changes but say the amendment will still be an asset. "It will become a license" to legitimatize student drives to obtain board seats, according to Layton Olson, executive director of the student lobby.

Research on the composition of university governing boards, although sketchy and somewhat outdated, confirms that students and other groups have little participation or power in the educational process and suggests that some serious problems may develop if the old patterns persist.

A nationwide study by the highly respected Educational Testing Service (ETS) of Princeton, New Jersey, attempted to define the actual makeup of governing boards, including the occupations and attitudes of members.

The study drew this profile of the average trustee: male (eighty-seven per cent); white (more than ninety-eight per cent); aging (seventy-five per cent over fifty, only five per cent under forty); and high income (more than half above $30,000 yearly). The occupations of the 5,180 trustees were "frequently in medicine, law, and education, but more often . . . business . . ." In fact, thirty-five per cent of the total were executives of manufacturing, merchandising, or investment firms. When combined with other professional categories (attorneys, physicians, engineers) the total reached a majority of fifty-nine per cent. In contrast, only thirteen per cent of the trustees in the sample were educators of any type.

Some colleges have yielded to increasing pressure to broaden their ruling base and have added more women, young alumni, minority representatives, and students to their boards, but the trend is not developing fast enough to suit critics like Senator Harris or the National Student Lobby. The Educational Testing Service found some evidence of this broadening trend when it updated its original 1969 study one year later. Fourteen per cent of the non-black schools reported that they had added "one or more" blacks to their boards, seventeen per cent of the non-women's institutions (coeducational or all-male) added one or more women, and nearly a third of the schools added one or more persons under forty years of age. However, only three per cent reported adding students with voting rights (seven per cent added non-voting students).

Moreover, the real impact on board representation in 1970 was minimal because most of the "one or more" increases reported were, in fact, one. Incredibly, of the more than 5,000 trustees covered by the study there were still only sixteen black trustees on boards of integrated or predominantly white schools. Although figures for 1971 and 1972 are not yet available, ETS found in 1970 that less than ten per cent of the colleges had plans for 1971 to add more young people, minority representatives, or women to their boards.

With the knowledge that the majority of college trustees come from business and professional circles, it is a reasonable guess that the "average" trustee has basically conservative attitudes. ETS research confirmed this assumption and, in addition to the belief of fifty-three per cent of the trustees that it was reasonable to require a loyalty oath from faculty members, the study also found that:

Seventy per cent thought only administrators and trustees—no students or faculty—should participate in the selection of a new president.

Forty per cent thought the administration should control the contents of the student newspaper.

Sixty-four per cent thought only administrators and trustees should rule on tenure decisions.

Eighty-one per cent thought students who "actively disrupt the functioning of a college by demonstrating . . . or otherwise refusing to obey the rules should be expelled or suspended."

Sixty-three per cent thought the faculty should *not* have major authority in the appointment of their dean.

Twenty-seven per cent of the trustees *disagreed* that faculty members should have the right to express freely their opinions.

Forty-nine per cent of those trustees identifying themselves as businessmen said running a college is "basically like running a business" and regarded experience in high-level management as an important quality for a new president.

ETS said the majority of the trustees were Protestant and Republican (fifty-eight per cent). In one other curious finding, ETS reported, "Trustees do not read—indeed, have generally never even heard of—the more relevant higher education books and journals."

All of this is meaningless if, as many trustees maintain, governing boards really do not have much power and do not exercise what little they do have. However, ETS data contradict this theory. The ETS study indicates that trustees generally exercise great authority primarily in two areas—finance and selection of the institution's president. Having chosen a president based on their opinions of how the university should be run, the trustees normally allow him to handle daily affairs.

College governing boards vary widely in structure. Private universities generally self-perpetuate their governing board majority by selection of new trustees by the board. In some cases a minority of the board may be elected by alumni of the university. Thus, new trustees of private schools tend to mirror the opinions, lifestyle, and goals of the current board majority.

Most public university boards are appointed by the state governor, and often confirmation by the state senate is required. Most such appointments are political rewards, although it must be noted that students have gained more board representation by governor appointment than by any other means. Governors of Maine (Kenneth M. Curtis), Alabama (George C. Wallace), Pennsylvania (Milton J. Shapp), and Montana (Forrest H. Anderson) all appointed one or more students. However, only the Maine appointee is a voting member. It will take years by this method for students to gain even token representation in a majority of states.

A second and less common way of selecting state university trustees is election at large by the voters of the state. This is hailed by many reformers as the most equitable means of ruling a state-supported school, although officials who work under such a system report with disappointment and some cynicism that the candidates listed on the top of the ballot almost always win.

Only one state (Nevada) has elected trustees for the entire state higher education system, but five other states (Alabama, Colorado, Illinois, Michigan, and Nebraska) elect trustees for one or more schools in their systems. In each of these states most of the colleges have boards appointed by the governor. At those few schools where trustees are elected at large, the system dates back to the original charters of the schools, in which the founders preferred public election.

With the eighteen-year-old vote, such an at-large system should allow students or any other group the opportunity to elect its representatives. To date, however, publicly elected boards have not been much different from appointed ones.

Thus, although governing boards are selected by a variety of processes, there is currently little difference in the result. No studies have been made to determine the impact of such narrowly representative boards of trustees on curricula, faculty hiring, political orientation, or long-range goals of the university. However, some examples are available which suggest that the makeup and attitudes of boards can create serious decision conflicts.

For instance, in the wake of the U.S. invasion of Cambodia in 1970, President Robert Morse of Case Western Reserve University in Cleveland, Ohio, was fired in a suspected ideological clash with the college's board of trustees. The board claimed it had released Morse because of his allegedly poor handling of university financial matters. However, to Case students and faculty, who generally supported Morse, the dismissal was clearly the result of the president's liberal handling of the highly successful local student strike in protest of the Cambodian incursion. Morse, in his resignation statement, said: "There has developed an explicit impasse between me and the executive committee of the trustees... a conflict between their perceptions of the university and mine."

In a later speech, Morse added: "I love universities; I did not want to leave my university . . . I had my perspectives. The trustees had theirs . . . A university with a balanced budget and no moral stance is a bankrupt university . . . There is something seriously wrong in the conditions for leadership of America's colleges and universities . . . I do not believe that management consultants, with corporate techniques, will ever do more than rearrange the numbers."

Another example of decision conflict has occurred in the growing controversy over corporate stock ownership by universities, which has become increasingly important for university finance. Concerned students and faculty have found trustees uncooperative in revealing information about stocks held in corporations which may be serious polluters, lawbreakers, employment discriminators, or war weapons producers.

One group which solicited stock proxies from universities to attempt to add minority representatives and women to the board of directors of the General Motors Corporation found fierce resistance from trustees. The Washington-based group, Campaign GM, subsequently studied the business affiliations of trustees and the stock portfolios at fifty-five public and private four-year colleges in an attempt to find causes for poor trustee cooperation.

The most important finding of the unpublished 1971 study, covering more than 1,500 trustees, was that nearly twenty per cent of all the trustees in the sample were either executives or directors of corporations in which their university owned stock. Thus, in many cases, students and faculty found themselves proposing the vote of college stock proxies against the management of a corporation which had its own representative on the college board. Most of these "interlocked" stocks were those of large corporations listed on the New York Stock Exchange.

Campaign GM found that many of the interlocks were the result of gifts to a university from a trustee or his company. Such gifts are important to the colleges, which now find funding more desperately needed than ever, but the Campaign GM study concluded that some caution should be exercised in the amount of influence gained by appointing large numbers of businessmen and cultivating multi-million-dollar stock gifts.

For example, the largest single "interlocked" stock holding identified in the Campaign GM study was Emory University's (Atlanta, Georgia) ownership in the Coca-Cola Company—238,076 shares of common stock worth some $60 million and comprising 56.7 per cent of the school's total endowment, according to a 1970 securities listing by the school. Two Emory trustees are Coca-Cola directors—C. Howard Candler, Jr., and George W. Woodruff. In addition, the Woodruff family (a major stockholder of Coca-Cola) is estimated to have contributed $50 million to the university through various family foundations. Robert W. Woodruff is the chief benefactor of Emory's Medical Center, which bears his name.

At Northwestern University, the Campaign GM study data showed that 24.8 per cent of the college's $236 million endowment was invested in corporations served by Northwestern trustees as executives or directors.

The most dramatic example of business and corporate representation revealed in the Campaign GM study was the University of Pittsburgh and Carnegie-Mellon University in Mellon-family dominated Pittsburgh. The three flagships of the Mellon portfolio of corporations are Gulf Oil Corporation, Aluminum Corporation of America (Alcoa), and the Mellon National Bank and Trust Company, which are also the largest holdings of the two universities.

Carnegie-Mellon and the University of Pittsburgh each held roughly 280,000 shares of Gulf common stock in 1970; each holding was worth about $6.5 million. Carnegie-Mellon also held 103,331 shares of Alcoa worth about $5 million. Three trustees at each school were Gulf directors, and four Carnegie-Mellon trustees were directors of Alcoa. The family bank had the greatest representation on the two boards, with ten directors as Carnegie-Mellon trustees and eight as University of Pittsburgh trustees.

No matter how lofty the motives of any trustee, reliance on businessmen and corporate gifts for fund raising to the degree of excluding other balancing views in general policy-making can logically lead only to the slanting of presidential appointments, curricula, faculty hiring, and long-range goals of the university toward the wishes of the business community.

An example of the individual who is recruited as a college trustee because of his fund-raising capabilities is Felix G. Rohatyn. A trustee of Middlebury College in Vermont, Rohatyn is the consummate example of what colleges are looking for—young, ambitious, interested in university policy, moderately liberal, and a man with his fingers in many pies. He is a governor of the New York Stock Exchange, a partner in a large brokerage firm (Lazard Freres and Company), and an influential director of one of the largest conglomerates in the world, International Telephone and Telegraph.

None of this is to say Rohatyn and his contemporaries should not be represented on college boards or that they are not needed; the point is that it is not in the best interests of higher education to have a majority of any like-thinking group controlling universities. Private colleges, especially, are growing so dependent on the contributions and assistance of powerful individuals that they may soon find that they are both economically and ideologically bankrupt.

However, what is just as important as analysis of how the course of higher education is being influenced from the top is consideration of how students and faculties are feeling about their universities from the bottom. Having little to say about the course of universities at present, these groups have increasingly expressed their alienation and loss of respect for education by adopting confrontation tactics.

Concern over these matters has begun to have an impact on college administrators and trustees. With the passage of the Harris amendment, pressure on campuses will likely increase. Some suggestions have been offered in academic circles to solve representation and conflict of interest problems while retaining the benefit of business fund-raising capability. One proposal would create a two-board system on each campus to separate decision-making and fund-raising functions. The first board would carry out all legally defined decision duties of the board. The second (probably much larger) would be composed of contributors and fund-raisers for the school and would meet only to coordinate and evaluate this activity. The proposed policy board would broadly represent those groups with an interest in the future of the university—campus constituencies as well as younger and women alumni, minority representatives, and traditional trustees. A number of colleges are operating under a two-board concept, but there has been little distinction between the two boards except in degree of activity. No school has taken extensive steps to divorce policy and purse.

The prevailing system has tactical as well as ideological considerations as boards of trustees increasingly are confronted with contemporary social problems. The Educational Testing Service study concluded that "willing or otherwise, trustees are becoming the pivotal force" which must deal with the complicated decisions being forced on universities.

The ETS study predicted that as long as the verbal and ideological gap remains between the governors and the governed on college campuses, "we expect greater conflict and disruption of the academic program, a deeper entrenchment of the ideas of competing factions, and, worst of all, an aimless, confusing collegiate experience, where the students' program is the result of arbitration rather than mutual determination of goals and purposes."

The potential benefits of widening board representation are many. First, and most important, modification of board majorities would give unrepresented constituencies a genuine voice in selecting their university president, the institution's most powerful voice. An important measure of confidence and cooperation could be gained by actual participation—rather than the current practice of allowing these groups to join in preliminary presidential selection, only to be shut out of final closed-door sessions. In addition, participation by unrepresented groups could add important perspective to other issues, including faculty tenure rights, hiring and promotion, long-range curriculum, and general administrative policy.

Perhaps the greatest damage in the current inability of the governors and governed to talk to each other is the lack of understanding of divergent points of view. Just as most college trustees and many administrators did not really understand the honest but intense reaction of many students and faculty to the Vietnam war, many campus groups are ignorant of the complexity and difficulty of funding and operating a university.

If the killings at Kent State, Jackson State, and Southern University have proven anything, it should be that closed doors and confrontation are not consistent with the goals of higher education. In addition to being a place to digest facts, college communities should be a laboratory of understanding, negotiation, and self-determination to prepare young people to act as concerned citizens in days to come. The governing boards of colleges and universities should be a forum where all segments of the campus can, with equal representation, discuss their common problems and goals.

Politico-Economic Institutions

Part IX

Politico-economic institutions are particularly pervasive: they affect the lives of all members of a society. It is in the political realm that ultimate power lies; and it is in terms of economic reality that all persons must conduct their daily lives. Given the importance of politico-economic institutions, this section of readings is the longest and most varied. Even so, we can only sample the views of a limited number of observers as they comment on political and economic conditions and trends of the day.

39. "Power Elite" or "Veto Groups"?
WILLIAM KORNHAUSER

Despite the central importance of political and economic institutions, social scientists have varying conceptions about their basic character. Two of the most influential ideas are compared and contrasted in this article by sociologist William Kornhauser. Professor Kornhauser teaches at the Berkeley campus of the University of California. He is the author of The Politics of Mass Society, *an influential study of the fragility of social bonds in the large-scale, secularized, industrial nation.*

In the 50's two books appeared purporting to describe the structure of power in present-day America. They reached opposite conclusions: where C. Wright Mills found a "power elite," David Riesman found "veto groups." Both books have enjoyed a wide response, which has tended to divide along ideological lines. It would appear that *The Power Elite* has been most favorably received by radical intellectuals, and *The Lonely Crowd* has found its main response among liberals. Mills and Riesman have not been oblivious to their differences. Mills is quite explicit on the matter: Riesman is a "romantic pluralist" who refuses to see the forest of American power inequalities for the trees of short-run and discrete balances of power among diverse groups. [244][1] Riesman has been less explicitly polemical, but he might have had Mills in mind when he spoke of those intellectuals "who feel themselves very much out of power and who are frightened of those who they think have the power," and who "prefer

SOURCE: William Kornhauser, "'Power Elite' or 'Veto Groups'?" in Seymour Martin Lipset and Leo Lowenthal, eds., *Culture and Social Character* (The Free Press of Glencoe, 1961), pp. 252–267. Copyright © 1961 by The Free Press. Reprinted with permission of Macmillan Publishing Co., Inc.

to be scared by the power structures they conjure up than to face the possibility that the power structure they believe exists has largely evaporated." [257–258][2]

I wish to intervene in this controversy just long enough to do two things: (1) locate as precisely as possible the items upon which Riesman and Mills disagree; and (2) formulate certain underlying issues in the analysis of power that have to be met before such specific disagreements as those between Riesman and Mills can profitably be resolved.

We may compare Mills and Riesman on power in America along five dimensions:

1. structure of power: how power is distributed among the major segments of present-day American society;

2. changes in the structure of power: how the distribution of power has changed in the course of American history;

3. operation of the structure of power: the means whereby power is exercised in American society;

4. bases of the structure of power: how social and psychological factors shape and sustain the existing distribution of power;

5. consequences of the structure of power: how the existing distribution of power affects American society.

1. STRUCTURE OF POWER

It is symptomatic of their underlying differences that Mills entitles his major consideration of power simply "the power elite," whereas Riesman has entitled one of his discussions "who has the power?" Mills is quite certain about the location of power, and so indicates by the assertive form of his title. Riesman perceives a much more amorphous and indeterminate power situation, and conveys this view in the interrogative form of his title. These contrasting images of American power may be diagrammed as two different pyramids of power. Mills' pyramid of power contains three levels:

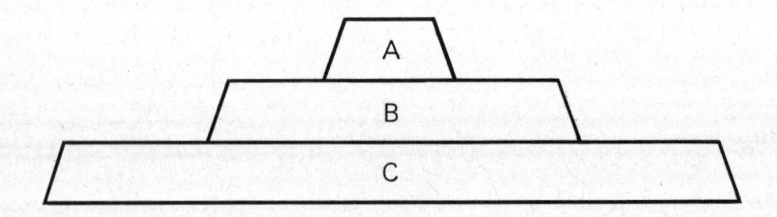

The apex of the pyramid (A) is the "power elite": a unified power group composed of the top government executives, military officials, and corporation directors. The second level (B) comprises the "middle levels of power": a diversified and balanced plurality of interest groups, perhaps most visibly at work in the halls of Congress. The third level (C) is the "mass society": the powerless mass of unorganized and atomized people who are controlled from above.

Riesman's pyramid of power contains only two major levels:

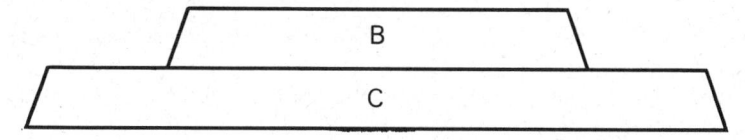

```
   /          B          \
  /─────────────────────────\
 /            C              \
```

The two levels roughly correspond to Mills' second and third levels, and have been labeled accordingly. The obvious difference between the two pyramids is the presence of a peak in the one case and its absence in the other. Riesman sees no "power elite," in the sense of a single unified power group at the top of the structure, and this in the simplest terms contrasts his image of power in America with that of Mills. The upper level of Riesman's pyramid (B) consists of "veto groups": a diversified and balanced plurality of interest groups, each of which is primarily concerned with protecting its jurisdiction by blocking efforts of other groups that seem to threaten that jurisdiction. There is no decisive ruling group here, but rather an amorphous structure of power centering in the interplay among these interest groups. The lower level of the pyramid (C) comprises the more or less unorganized public, which is sought as an ally (rather than dominated) by the interest groups in their maneuvers against actual or threatened encroachments on the jurisdiction each claims for itself.

2. CHANGES IN THE STRUCTURE OF POWER

Riesman and Mills agree that the American power structure has gone through four major epochs. They disagree on the present and prospective future in the following historical terms: Mills judges the present to represent a fifth epoch, whereas Riesman judges it to be a continuation of the fourth.

The first period, according to Mills and Riesman, extended roughly from the founding of the republic to the Jacksonian era. During this period, Riesman believes America possessed a clearly demarcated ruling group, composed of a "landed-gentry and mercantilist-money leadership." [239] According to Mills, "the important fact about these early days is that social life, economic institutions, military establishment, and political order coincided, and men who were high politicians also played key roles in the economy and, with their families, were among those of the reputable who made up local society." [270]

The second period extended roughly from the decline of Federalist leadership to the Civil War. During this period power became more widely dispersed, and it was no longer possible to identify a sharply defined ruling group. "In this society," Mills writes, "the 'elite' became a plurality of top groups, each in turn quite loosely made up." [270] Riesman notes that farmer and artisan groups became influential, and "occasionally, as with Jackson, moved into a more positive command." [240]

The third period began after the Civil War and extended through McKinley's administration in Riesman's view [240] and until the New Deal according to Mills. [271] They agree that the era of McKinley marked the high point of the unilateral supremacy of corporate economic power. During this period, power once more became concentrated, but unlike the Federalist period and also unlike subsequent periods, the higher circles of economic institutions were dominant.

The fourth period took definite shape in the 1930's. In Riesman's view this period marked the ascendancy of the "veto groups," and rule by coalitions rather than by a unified power group. Mills judges it to have been so only in the early and middle Roosevelt administrations: "In these years, the New Deal as a system of power was essentially a balance of pressure groups and interest blocs." [273]

Up to World War II, then, Mills and Riesman view the historical development of power relations in America along strikingly similar lines. Their sharply contrasting portrayal of present-day American power relations begins with their diverging assessments of the period beginning about 1940. Mills envisions World War II and its aftermath as marking a new era in American power relations. With war as the major problem, there arises a new power group composed of corporate, governmental, and military directors.

> The formation of the power elite, as we may now know it, occurred during World War II and its aftermath. In the course of the organization of the nation for that war, and the consequent stabilization of the warlike posture, certain types of man have been selected and formed, and in the course of these institutional and psychological developments, new opportunities and intentions have arisen among them.[3]

Where Mills sees the ascendancy of a power elite, Riesman sees the opposite tendency toward the dispersal of power among a plurality of organized interests:

> There has been in the last fifty years a change in the configuration of power in America, in which a single hierarchy with a ruling class at its head has been replaced by a number of "veto groups" among which power is dispersed [239].
>
> The shifting nature of the lobby provides us with an important clue as to the difference between the present American political scene and that of the age of McKinley. The ruling class of businessmen could relatively easily (though perhaps mistakenly) decide where their interests lay and what editors, lawyers, and legislators might be paid to advance them. The lobby ministered to the clear leadership, privilege, and imperative of the business ruling class. Today we have substituted for that leadership a series of groups, each of which has struggled for and finally attained a power to stop things conceivably inimical to its interests and, within far narrower limits, to start things. [246–247]

In short, both Mills and Riesman view the current scene from an historical perspective; but where one finds a hitherto unknown *concentration* of power, the other finds an emerging *indeterminacy* of power.

3. OPERATION OF THE STRUCTURE OF POWER

Mills believes the power elite sets all important public policies, especially foreign policy. Riesman, on the other hand, does not believe that the same group or coalition of groups sets all major policies, but rather that the question of who exercises power varies with the issue at stake: most groups are inoperative on most issues, and all groups are operative primarily on those issues that vitally impinge on their central interests. This is to say that there are as many power structures as there are distinctive spheres of policy. [256]

As to the modes of operation, both Mills and Riesman point to increasing *manipulation*, rather than command or persuasion, as the favored form of power play. Mills emphasizes the secrecy behind which important policy-determination occurs. Riesman stresses not so much manipulation under the guise of secrecy as manipulation under the guise of mutual tolerance for one another's interests and beliefs. Manipulation occurs, according to Riesman, because each group is trying to hide its concern with power in order not to antagonize other groups. Power relations tend to take the form of "monopolistic competition": "rules of fairness and fellowship [rather than the impersonal forces of competition] dictate how far one can go." [247] Thus both believe the play of power takes place to a considerable extent backstage; but Mills judges this power play to be under the direction of one group, while Riesman sees it as controlled by a mood and structure of accommodation among many groups.

Mills maintains that the mass media of communication are important instruments of manipulation: the media lull people to sleep, so to speak, by suppressing political topics and by emphasizing "entertainment." Riesman alleges that the mass media give more attention to politics and problems of public policy than their audiences actually want, and thereby convey the false impression that there is more interest in public affairs than really exists in America at the present time. Where Mills judges the mass media of communication to be powerful political instruments in American society [315–316], Riesman argues that they have relatively little significance in this respect. [228–231]

4. BASES OF THE STRUCTURE OF POWER

Power tends to be patterned according to the structure of interests in a society. Power is shared among those whose interests coincide, and divides along lines where interests diverge. To Mills, the power elite is a reflection and solidification of a *coincidence of interests* among the ascendant institutional orders. The power elite rests on the "many interconnections and points of coinciding interests" of the corporations, political institutions, and military services. [19] For Riesman, on the other hand, there is an amorphous power structure, which reflects a *diversity of interests* among the major organized groups. The power structure of veto groups rests on the divergent interests of political parties, business groups, labor organizations, farm blocs, and a myriad of other organized groups. [247]

But power is not a simple reflex of interests alone. It also rests on the capabilities and opportunities for cooperation among those who have similar interests, and for confrontation among those with opposing interests. Mills argues in some detail that the power elite rests not merely on the coincidences of interests among major institutions but also on the "psychological similarity and social intermingling" of their higher circles. [19] By virtue of similar social origins (old family, upper-class background), religious affiliations (Episcopalian and Presbyterian), education (Ivy League college or military academy), and the like, those who head up the major institutions share codes and values as well as material interests. This makes for easy communication, especially when many of these people already know one another, or at least know many people in common. They share a common way of life, and therefore possess both the will and the opportunity to integrate their lines of action as representatives of key institutions. At times this integration involves "explicit coordination," as during war. [19–20] So much for the bases of power at the apex of the structure.

At the middle and lower levels of power, Mills emphasizes the lack of independence and concerted purpose among those who occupy similar social positions. In his book on the middle classes,[4] Mills purports to show the weakness of white-collar people that results from their lack of economic independence and political direction. The white-collar worker simply follows the more powerful group of the moment. In his book on labor leaders,[5] Mills located the alleged political impotence of organized labor in its dependence on government. Finally, the public is conceived as composed of atomized and submissive individuals who are incapable of engaging in effective communication and political action. [302 ff.]

Riesman believes that power "is founded, in large measure, on interpersonal expectations and attitudes." [253] He asserts that in addition to the diversity of interest underlying the pattern of power in America there is the psycho-cultural fact of widespread feelings of weakness and dependence at the top as well as at the bottom of the power structure: "If businessmen feel weak and dependent they do in actuality become weaker and more dependent, no matter what material resources may be ascribed to them." [253] In other words, the amorphousness of power in America rests in part on widespread feelings of weakness and dependence. These feelings are found among those whose position in the social structure provides resources that they could exploit, as well as among those whose position provides less access to the means of power. In fact, Riesman is concerned to show that people at all levels of the social structure tend to feel weaker than their objective position warrants.

The theory of types of conformity that provides the foundation of so much of Riesman's writings enters into his analysis of power at this point. The "other-directed" orientation in culture and character helps to sustain the amorphousness of power. The other-directed person in politics is the "inside-dopester," the person who possesses political competence but avoids political commitment. This is the dominant type in the veto groups, since other-direction is prevalent in the strata from which their leaders are drawn. "Both within the [veto] groups and in the situation created by their presence, the political mood tends to become one of other-directed tolerance." [248] However, Riesman does not make the basis of power solely psychological:

> This does not mean, however, that the veto groups are formed along the lines of character structure. As in a business corporation there is room for extreme inner-directed and other-directed types, and all mixtures between, so in a veto group there can exist complex "symbiotic" relationships among people of different political styles. . . . Despite these complications I think it fair to say that the veto groups, even when they are set up to protect a clearcut moralizing interest, are generally forced to adopt the political manners of the other-directed. [249]

Riesman and Mills agree that there is widespread apathy in American society, but they disagree on the social distribution of political apathy. Mills locates the apathetic primarily among the lower social strata, whereas Riesman finds extensive apathy in higher as well as lower strata.[5] Part of the difference may rest on what criteria of apathy are used. Mills conceives of apathy as the lack of political meaning in one's life, the failure to think of personal interests in political terms, so that what happens in politics does not appear to be related to personal troubles.[6] Riesman extends the notion of apathy to include the politically uninformed as well as the politically uncommitted.[7] Thus political indignation undisciplined by political understanding is not a genuine political orientation. Riesman judges political apathy to be an important *basis* for amorphous power relations. Mills, on the other hand, treats political apathy primarily as a *result* of the concentration of power.

5. CONSEQUENCES OF THE STRUCTURE OF POWER

Four parallel sets of consequences of the structure of power for American society may be inferred from the writings of Mills and Riesman. The first concerns the impact of the power structure on the interests of certain groups or classes in American society. Mills asserts that the existing power arrangements enhance the interests of the major institutions whose directors constitute the power elite. [276 ff.] Riesman asserts the contrary: no one group or class is decisively favored over others by the culminated decisions on public issues. [257]

The second set of consequences concerns the impact of the structure of power on the quality of politics in American society. Here Mills and Riesman are in closer agreement. Mills maintains that the concentration of power in a small circle, and the use of manipulation as the favored manner of exercising power, lead to the decline of politics as public debate. People are decreasingly capable of grasping political issues, and of relating them to personal interests.[8] Riesman also believes that politics has declined in meaning for large numbers of people. This is not due simply to the ascendancy of "veto groups," although they do foster "the tolerant mood of other-direction and hasten the retreat of the inner-directed indignants." [251] More important, the increasing complexity and remoteness of politics make political self-interest obscure and aggravate feelings of impotence even when self-interest is clear.[9]

The third set of consequences of the American power structure concerns its impact on the quality of power relations themselves. Mills contends that the concentration of power has taken place without a corresponding shift in the bases of legitimacy of power: power is still supposed to reside in the public and its elected representatives, whereas in reality it resides in the hands of those who direct the key bureaucracies. As a consequence, men of power are neither responsible nor accountable for their power. [316–317] Riesman also implies that there is a growing discrepancy between the facts of power and the images of power, but for the opposite reason from Mills: power is more widely dispersed than is generally believed. [257–258]

Finally, a fourth set of consequences concerns the impact of the power structure on democratic leadership. If power tends to be lodged in a small group that is not accountable for its power, and if politics no longer involves genuine public debate, then there will be a *severe weakening of democratic institutions*, if not of leadership (the power elite exercises leadership in one sense of the term, in that it makes decisions on basic policy for the nation). Mills claims that power in America has become so concentrated that it increasingly resembles the Soviet system of power:

> Official commentators like to contrast the ascendancy in totalitarian countries of a tightly organized clique with the American system of power. Such comments, however, are easier to sustain if one compares mid-twentieth-century Russia with mid-nineteenth-century America, which is what is often done by Tocqueville-quoting Americans making the contrast. But that was an America of a century ago, and in the century that has passed, the American elite have not remained as patrioteer essayists have described them to us. The "loose cliques" now head institutions of a scale and power not then existing and, especially since World War I, the loose cliques have tightened up. [271]

If, on the other hand, power tends to be dispersed among groups that are primarily concerned to protect and defend their interests rather than to advance general policies and their own leadership, and if at the same time politics has declined as a sphere of duty and self-interest, then there will be a *severe weakening of leadership*. Thus Riesman believes that "power in America seems to [be] situational and mercurial; it resists attempts to locate it." [257] This "indeterminacy and amorphousness" of power inhibits the development of leadership: "Where the issue involves the country as a whole, no individual or group leadership is likely to be very effective, because the entrenched veto groups cannot be budged." [257] "Veto groups exist as defense groups, not as leadership groups." [248] Yet Riesman does not claim that the decline of leadership directly threatens American democracy, at least in the short run: the dispersion of power among a diversity of balancing "veto groups" operates to support democratic institutions even as it inhibits effective leadership. The long run prospects of a leaderless democracy are of course less promising.

Two Portraits of the American Power Structure

	Mills	Riesman
Levels	a. Unified power elite b. Diversified and balanced plurality of interest groups c. Mass of unorganized people who have practically no power over elite	a. No dominant power elite b. Diversified and balanced plurality of interest groups c. Mass of unorganized people who have some power over interest groups
Changes	a. Increasing concentration of power	a. Increasing dispersion of power
Operation	a. One group determines all major policies b. Manipulation of people at the bottom by group at the top	a. Who determines policy shifts with the issue b. Monopolistic competition among organized groups
Bases	a. Coincidence of interest among major institutions (economic, military, governmental)	a. Diversity of interests among major organized groups b. Sense of weakness and dependence among those in higher as well as lower status
Consequences	a. Enhancement of interests of corporations, armed forces, and executive branch of government b. Decline of politics as public debate c. Decline of responsible and accountable power—loss of democracy	a. No one group or class is favored significantly over others b. Decline of politics as duty and self-interest c. Decline of capacity for effective leadership

II

In the second part of this paper, I wish to raise certain critical questions about Riesman's and Mills' images of power. One set of questions seeks to probe more deeply the basic area of disagreement in their views. A second set of questions concerns their major areas of agreement.

Power usually is analyzed according to its distribution among the several units of a system. Most power analysts construe the structure of power as a *hierarchy*—a rank-order of units according to their amount of power. The assumption often is made that there is only one such structure, and that all units may be ranked vis-à-vis one another. Units higher in the hierarchy have power over units lower in the structure, so there is a one-way flow of power. Mills tends to adopt this image of the structure of power.

Riesman rejects this conception of the power structure as mere hierarchy:

> The determination of who [has more power] has to be made all over again for our time: we cannot be satisfied with the answers given by Marx, Mosca, Michels, Pareto, Weber, Veblen, or Burnham. [255]

> The image of power in contemporary America presented [in *The Lonely Crowd*] departs from current discussions of power which are usually based on a search for a ruling class. [260]

Riesman is not just denying the existence of a power elite in contemporary American society; he is also affirming the need to consider other aspects of power than only its unequal distribution. He is especially concerned to analyze common responses to power:

> If the leaders have lost the power, why have the led not gained it? What is there about the other-directed man and his life situation which prevents the transfer? In terms of situation, it seems that the pattern of monopolistic competition of the veto groups resists individual attempts at power aggrandizement. In terms of character, the other-directed man simply does not seek power; perhaps, rather, he avoids and evades it. [275]

Whereas Mills emphasizes the *differences* between units according to their power, Riesman emphasizes their *similarities* in this respect. In the first view, some units are seen as dominated by other units, while in the second view, all units are seen as subject to constraints that shape and limit their use of power *in similar directions*.

The problem of power is not simply the differential capacity to make decisions, so that those who have power bind those who do not. Constraints also operate on those who are in decision-making positions, for if these are the places where acts of great consequence occur, so are they the targets for social pressures. These pressures become translated into restrictions on the alternatives among which decision-makers can choose.

Power may be meaningfully measured by ascertaining the range of alternatives that decision-makers can realistically consider. To identify those who make decisions is not to say how many lines of action are open to them, or how much freedom of choice they enjoy.

A major advance in the study of power is made by going beyond a formal conception of power, in which those who have the authority to make decisions are assumed to possess the effective means of power and the will to use it. Nor can it be assumed that those not in authority lack the power to determine public policy. The identification of effective sources of power requires analysis of how *decision-makers are themselves subject to various kinds of constraint.* Major sources of constraint include (1) opposing elites and active publics; and (2) cultural values and associated psychological receptivities and resistances to power. A comparison of Mills and Riesman with respect to these categories of constraint reveals the major area of disagreement between them.

Mills implies that both sources of constraint are by and large inoperative on the highest levels of power. (1) There is little opposition among the top power-holders. Since they are not in opposition to one another, they do not constrain one another. Instead, they are unified and mutually supportive. Furthermore, there are few publics to constrain the elite. Groups capable of effective participation in broad policy determination have been replaced by atomized masses that are powerless to affect policy, since they lack the social bases for association and communication. Instead, people in large numbers are manipulated through organizations and media controlled by the elite. (2) Older values and codes no longer grip elites, nor have they been replaced by new values and codes that could regulate the exercise of power. Top men of power are not constrained either by an inner moral sense or by feelings of dependence on others. The widespread permissiveness toward the use of expedient means to achieve success produces "the higher immorality," that is to say, elites that are irresponsible in the use of power.

In sharp contrast to Mills, Riesman attaches great importance to both kinds of constraints on decision-makers. (1) There is a plethora of organized groups, "each of which has struggled for and finally attained a power to stop things conceivably inimical to its interests." [247] Furthermore, there is extensive opportunity for large numbers of people to influence decision-makers, because the latter are constrained by their competitive relations with one another to bid for support in the electoral arena and more diffusely in the realm of public relations. (2) The cultural emphasis on "mutual tolerance" and social conformity places a premium on "getting along" with others at the expense of taking strong stands. People are psychologically disposed to avoid long-term commitments as a result of their strong feelings of dependence on their immediate peers. "Other-directed" persons seek approval rather than power.

In general, the decisive consideration in respect to the restraint of power is the presence of multiple centers of power. Where there are many power groups, not only are they mutually constrained; they also are dependent on popular support, and therefore responsive to public demands. Now, there are many readily observable cases of institutionalized opposition among power groups in American society. In the economic sphere, collective bargaining between management and labor is conflict of this kind; and to the extent that "countervailing power" among a few large firms has been replacing competition among many small firms in the market place, there is a *de facto* situation of opposition among economic elites. In the political sphere, there is a strong two-party system and more or less stable factionalism within both parties, opposition among interest blocs in state and national legislatures, rivalry among executive agencies of government and the military services, and so forth.

Mills relegates these conflicting groups to the middle levels of power. Political parties and interest groups, both inside and outside of government, are not important units in the structure of power, according to Mills. It would seem that he takes this position primarily with an eye to the sphere of foreign policy, where only a few people finally make the big decisions. But he fails to put his argument to a decisive or meaningful test: he does not examine the pattern of decisions to show that foreign policy not only is made *by* a few people (this, after all, is a constitutional fact), but that it is made *for their particular interests.* Mills' major premise seems to be that all decisions are taken by and for special interests; there is no action oriented toward the general interests of the whole community. Furthermore, Mills seems to argue that because only a very few people occupy key decision-making *positions*, they are free to decide on whatever best suits their particular interests. But the degree of *autonomy* of decision-makers cannot be inferred from the *number* of decision-makers, nor from the *scope* of their decisions. It is determined by the character of decision-making, especially the dependence of decision-makers on certain kinds of *procedure* and *support.*

Just as Mills is presenting a distorted image of power in America when he fails to consider the pressures on those in high positions, so Riesman presents a biased picture by not giving sufficient attention to *power differentials* among the various groups in society. When Riesman implies that if power is dispersed, then it must be relatively equal among groups and interests, with no points of concentration, he is making an unwarranted inference. The following statement conjures up an image of power in America that is as misleading on its side as anything Mills has written in defense of his idea of a power elite.

> One might ask whether one would not find, over a long period of time, that decisions in America favored one group or class . . . over others. Does not wealth exert its pull in the long run? In the past this has been so; for the future I doubt it. The future seems to be in the hands of the small business and professional men who control Congress, such as realtors, lawyers, car salesmen, undertakers, and so on; of the military men who

control defense and, in part, foreign policy; of the big business managers and their lawyers, finance-committee men, and other counselors who decide on plant investment and influence the rate of technological change; of the labor leaders who control worker productivity and worker votes; of the black belt whites who have the greatest stake in southern politics; of the Poles, Italians, Jews, and Irishmen who have stakes in foreign policy, city jobs, and ethnic, religious and cultural organizations; of the editorializers and storytellers who help socialize the young, tease and train the adult, and amuse and annoy the aged; of the farmers—themselves a warring congeries of cattlemen, corn men, dairymen, cotton men, and so on—who control key departments and committees and who, as the living representatives of our inner-directed past, control many of our memories; of the Russians and, to a lesser degree, other foreign powers who control much of our agenda of attention; and so on. [257]

It appears that Riesman is asking us to believe that power differentials do not exist, but only differences in the spheres within which groups exercise control.

If Riesman greatly exaggerates the extent to which organized interests possess equal power, nevertheless he poses an important problem that Mills brushes aside. For Riesman goes beyond merely noting the existence of opposition among "veto groups" to suggest that they operate to smother one another's initiative and leadership. It is one thing for interest groups to constrain one another; it is something else again when they produce stalemate. Riesman has pointed to a critical problem for pluralist society: the danger that power may become fragmented among so many competing groups that effective general leadership cannot emerge.

On Mills' side, it is indisputable that American political institutions have undergone extensive centralization and bureaucratization. This is above all an *institutional* change wrought by the greatly expanded scale of events and decisions in the contemporary world. But centralization cannot be equated with a power elite. There can be highly centralized institutions and at the same time a fragmentation of power among a multiplicity of relatively independent public and private agencies. Thus Riesman would appear to be correct that the substance of power lies in the hands of many large organizations, and these organizations are not unified or coordinated in any firm fashion. If they were, surely Mills would have been able to identify the major mechanisms that could produce this result. That he has failed to do so is the most convincing evidence for their nonexistence.

To complete this analysis, we need only remind ourselves of the fundamental area of agreement between our two critics of American power relations. Both stress *the absence of effective political action* at all levels of the political order, in particular among the citizenry. For all of their differences, Mills and Riesman agree that there has been a decline in effective political participation, or at least a failure of political participation to measure up to the requirements of contemporary events and decisions. This failure has not been compensated by an increase in effective political action at the center: certainly Riesman's "veto groups" are not capable of defining and realizing the community's general aspirations; nor is Mills' "power elite" such a political agency. Both are asserting the inadequacy of political associations, including public opinion, party leadership, Congress, and the Presidency, even as they see the slippage of power in different directions. In consequence, neither is sanguine about the capacity of the American political system to provide responsible leadership, especially in international affairs.

If there is truth in this indictment, it also may have its sources in the very images of power that pervade Mills' and Riesman's thought. They are both inclined toward a negative response to power; and neither shows a willingness to confront the idea of a political system and the ends of power in it. Riesman reflects the liberal suspicion of power, as when he writes "we have come to realize that men who compete primarily for wealth are relatively harmless as compared with men who compete primarily for power." That such assertions as this may very well be true is beside the point. For certainly negative consequences of power can subsist alongside of positive ones. At times Riesman seems to recognize the need for people to seek and use power if they as individuals and the society as a whole are to develop to the fullest of their capacities. But his dominant orientation toward power remains highly individualistic and negative.

Mills is more extreme than Riesman on this matter, since he never asks what is socially required in the way of resources of power and uses of power, but instead is preoccupied with the magnitude of those resources and the (allegedly) destructive expropriation of them by and for the higher circles of major institutions. It is a very limited notion of power that construes it only in terms of coercion and conflict among particular interests. Societies require arrangements whereby resources of power can be effectively used and supplemented for public goals. This is a requirement for government, but the use of this term should not obscure that fact that government either commands power or lacks effectiveness. Mills does not concern himself with the *ends* of power, nor with the conditions for their attainment. He has no conception of the bases of political order, and no theory of the functions of government and politics. He suggests nothing that could prevent his "power elite" from developing into a full-blown totalitarianism. The logic of Mills' position finally reduces to a contest between anarchy and tyranny.

The problem of power seems to bring out the clinician in each of us. We quickly fasten on the pathology of power, whether we label the symptoms as "inside-dopesterism" (Riesman) or as "the higher immorality" (Mills). As a result, we often lose sight of the ends of power in the political system under review. It is important to understand that pivotal decisions increasingly are made at the national level, and that this poses genuine difficulties for the maintenance of democratic control. It is also important to understand that a multiplicity of public and private agencies increasingly pressure decision-makers, and that this poses genuine difficulties for the maintenance of effective political leadership. But the fact remains that there have been periods of centralized decision-making *and* democratic control, multiple constraints on power *and* effective leadership. There is no simple relationship between the extent to which power is equally distributed and the stability of democratic order. For a democratic order requires strong government as well as public consent by an informed citizenry. Unless current tendencies are measured against both sets of needs, there will be little progress in understanding how either one is frustrated or fulfilled. Finally, in the absence of more disciplined historical and comparative analysis, we shall continue to lack a firm basis for evaluating such widely divergent diagnoses of political malaise as those given us by Mills and Riesman.

NOTES

1. Page references in the text for remarks by C. Wright Mills refer to *The Power Elite* (New York: Oxford University Press, 1956).
2. Page references in the text for remarks by David Riesman refer to *The Lonely Crowd* (New York: Doubleday Anchor, 1953).
3. C. Wright Mills, "The Power Elite," in A. Kornhauser (ed.), *Problems of Power in American Society* (Detroit: Wayne University Press, 1957), p. 161.
4. C. Wright Mills, *White Collar* (New York: Oxford University Press, 1951).
5. C. Wright Mills, *The New Men of Power* (New York: Harcourt, Brace and Company, 1948).
6. *White Collar*, p. 327.
7. David Riesman and Nathan Glazer, "Criteria for Political Apathy," in Alvin W. Gouldner (ed.), *Studies in Leadership* (New York: Harper & Brothers, 1950).
8. *White Collar*, pp. 342–350.
9. "Criteria for Political Apathy," p. 520.

40. Like Marrying a Rich Woman
JAMES BOYD

"A good merger is like marrying a rich woman and taking her money. It's as sweet as that, sweeter even, because you can have as many of these brides as you want and you don't have to live with them any longer

SOURCE: James Boyd, introduction to "Men of Distinction" in Robert L. Heilbroner, et al., *In the Name of Profit* (Garden City, New York: Doubleday and Company, 1972), pp. 156–157. Copyright © 1972 by Doubleday & Company, Inc., and reprinted by permission.

than you want to. Or it's like politics. You can often get control and speak for the majority with only 10 percent of the voting stock, because you're organized while the mass of stockholders are strung out and don't pay much attention. Best of all, you do it with borrowed money. Never use your own.

"You start out with control of a little fleabag company that's ready for the receivers. Then you find a fat corporation that's been selling its assets and is sitting on lots of cash. You send in a spy to find out where the 'control stock' is; usually it's held by directors of the company. You bribe them, in a manner of speaking, by offering to buy the company stock they hold at a price much higher than it's worth; in return, they agree to resign and appoint your men in their places. Then you go to your bank, let them in on the deal, offer their key men personal stock options and other side deals—and they'll loan you all you need to buy out the directors. Once you're in control of the new company, you use some of its assets to pay off your bank and divvy up what's left with your insiders. The only way you can do that legally, of course, is to merge your new company with the old one you've just about bankrupted. That way the new entity assumes all your old debts.

"Stockholders? They don't know anything about it, really. You've already bought out their leaders. All they see is what's on the proxy statement—and you're the fellow who puts it out, because you're the management now. Hide your old company's debts, doctor up the figures, hire one of those New York evaluating firms to back you up, and always promise the exact opposite of what you plan to do. Like I said, it's just like politics. And don't waste your time worrying about the courts or the SEC. Don't they always take the side of management? Only one thing —you have to keep mergerin' or it will catch up with you."

—Confession of an Anonymous Mergerer

41. The Concentration of Corporate Power
GABRIEL KOLKO

Professor Kolko, a historian at the University of Pennsylvania, has become a controversial figure in the academic world. To some, he is

SOURCE: Gabriel Kolko, *Wealth and Power in America: An Analysis of Social Class and Income Distribution* (New York: Praeger Publishers, 1962), pp. 55–69. Copyright © 1962 by Frederick A. Praeger, Inc., New York. Excerpted and reprinted by permission.

a hero who has helped to expose the hypocrisy of a system that is touted as a model of equalitarian democracy; to others, his work is a living example of how research should not be done, since, they say, he gathers selected data solely to shore up his preconceived notions about "alleged injustices" in American society. Let the reader judge for himself, both on the basis of this selection and on the basis of the book from which it is taken.

The distribution of power over corporations, the dominant sector of the economy, is of major consequence in determining the extent to which America has attained a democratic economic structure.

Most recent theoretical discussions of the role of the corporation in American life have ignored the facts about the actual distribution of corporate power in favor of theories about the relationship of the corporation to the rest of society and the nature of the corporate executive as an individual.

The dominant image of the corporate leadership today is that of the responsible trustee. This concept has its roots in a basic proposition set forth by Berle and Gardiner Means as long ago as 1932, in *The Modern Corporation and Private Property*. They contended that stock ownership had been widely dispersed and that corporate management had been separated from stock ownership and from stock owners and now operated independently of the profit motive.

Although it is granted by practically all that corporate power is still very great, current theory suggests that it is self-restrained and socially responsible, a power in equilibrium with the state and the labor union. For many, it is an article of faith that its potential for social harm will not and could not be exercised.

There is a notion that corporate power is held in trust for the community. The corporate leadership, writes David Riesman in *The Lonely Crowd*, is "coming more and more to think of themselves as trustees for their beneficiaries."[1] The corporation, writes Berle, "has been compelled to assume in appreciable part the role of conscience-carrier of twentieth-century American society."[2] Further, he says, "the corporation is now, essentially, a nonstatist political institution, and its directors are in the same boat with public officeholders."[3]

Such assertions assume that the power of the stockholder is no longer a factor of major significance. They further assume that the corporate leadership has no interests that are in conflict with the "public's"—and that it shares none with the amorphous and presumably constantly expanding ranks of stockholders. In this view, the operating executives— the men who make the short- and intermediate-range decisions for the large corporations—have displaced the directors as architects of fundamental, long-range policies. "Corporate control," writes David E. Lilienthal, "far from being a virtual absolute in the majority of directors or stockholders, is now divided and diffused."[4] And so, it is suggested, the corporate managers, freed from responsibility to those whose only incentive is profit, have brought new motives to business leadership.

But the real question, the heart of the matter, is whether there is in fact a small group of persons in a position to exercise control over the corporate structure. If there is such a group, the matter of whether they actually utilize this power is secondary—the overriding consideration is, Do they have such power? It doesn't matter how they exercise this power, whether for their particular interests or for those of society as a whole. The philosophy of their views may be debatable; the anatomy of their power is not.

The facts, in brief, are these: In 1955 the 200 top nonfinancial companies—most of which dominated their respective industries as price and policy leaders—directly owned 43.0 per cent of the total assets of 435,000 nonfinancial corporations; this amounted to at least 18.3 per cent of the total national reproducible tangible assets of $891 billion.[5]

These corporations were controlled by approximately 2,500 men—and probably even fewer.

These men, in both direct ownership of economic assets and control over the corporate structure, are the most important single group in the American economic elite.

INTERLOCKING DIRECTORATES

Interlocking directorates, whereby a director of one corporation also sits on the board of one or more corporations, are a key device for concentrating corporate power, since they enable one corporation to wield influence over one or more others. The director representing Company A can, by sitting on the board of Company B, exert influence over it to increase its financial cooperation with Company A or make purchases from it. He can also act to prevent Company B from manufacturing a competing product or diversifying into a field occupied by Company A.

The Temporary National Economic Committee discovered that in 1939, within the top 200 corporations, there were 3,511 directorships held by about 2,500 persons.[6] Offhand, this would seem to suggest that interlocking directorships were not very significant.

But let us look at corporations that rank below the top 200 in size. It is, after all, much more likely that a giant corporation would attempt to influence a corporation smaller than itself than one larger or the same size. When one tabulates the number of directorships in corporations of every size held by the directors of the top 200 corporations, a pattern of extensive interlocking directorships emerges, involving a very large percentage of the top directors. Here, then, is the dominant fact of economic control: the top 200 corporations cooperate with each other and exert influence within innumerable smaller companies. Generally, of course, the larger corporation sends its representatives to the board of the smaller firm.

In 1957, Sidney J. Weinberg, of the investment house of Goldman, Sachs, sat on not only five boards among the top 200 corporations, but six boards of smaller companies; T. W. Collins, an officer-director of Crown-Zellerbach, was on seven boards below the top 200; and James Bruce, a director of National Dairy, sat on three boards among the top 200 and 13 lesser ones.

Interlocking directorates are classified by the Federal Trade Commission into seven major forms:

1. Between competing firms—whether direct (one company's director sits on another company's board) or indirect (two companies share a director whose primary tie is with a third company)—and thereby control or eliminate competition. In 1946, five of the 12 big meat packers were indirectly interlocked, 16 of the 23 largest sugar companies were directly and indirectly interlocked, and 17 of the 20 largest petroleum companies were interlocked.[7]

2. Between companies in related industries that are interested in preventing diversification into directly competitive products. Such interlocking exists in the glass industry, for example, so that bottle and sheet-glass makers will not encroach on each other.

3. Between companies in a single industry that face similar problems and share a community of interests, whether direct or indirect. Thus, the four largest electrical-machinery corporations were indirectly interlocked in 1946.

4. Between purchasing company and supplier, whose relationship generally involves a strategic advantage to the purchasing company. The food industry is heavily interlocked with the container industry, the automobile companies with the parts manufacturers. This is the most important form of interlocking.

5. Between producer and distributor, for the purpose of gaining preferential markets. Thus Westinghouse Air Brake Company is linked with most of the major manufacturers of railroad cars and locomotives, and the glass-making companies with the distilleries and drug companies.

6. Between corporation and financial institution, to provide adequate credit for the corporation and possible denial of credit to competitors. Myriad examples of this exist.

7. Between companies with common ownership. The General Motors–Du Pont–U.S. Rubber–Ethyl group is an excellent case in point.

The annual proxy statement rarely gives details of a company's contacts and transactions with the firms with which it has common directors. Among the proxy statements of the 100 top industrials for 1957, I was able to find only one significant policy statement on intercorporate relations. Republic Steel, in a statement that innumerable other corporations could have made just as well, frankly declared, "In accordance with the policy of the Corporation Messrs. White, Patton, Foy, and Hancock, as well as other officers of the Corporation, serve as officers and directors of certain companies in which the Corporation has a substantial (but not controlling) stock interest, from which it purchases raw materials and/or to which it has advanced funds for construction or exploration programs." The directors and major officers of Republic Steel each sit on an average of six other boards. No corporation in a position of dependency on one of the top 200 corporations can refuse the giant a seat on its board, and thus a potent voice in the guidance of its affairs, without risking the loss of an important, if not decisive, segment of its sales.

THE DIRECTORS

Now let us undertake to discover if the corporate director is, in fact, the passive yet statesmanlike creature that is portrayed by modern theories. To accomplish this, we shall examine in some detail the nature of power and control in the 100 largest industrial corporations, as ranked by assets, in 1957. (Of these, 72 were also in the top 100 in 1937.) These 100 corporations accounted for 54 per cent of the assets of the 200 largest nonfinancial corporations in 1957—compared to only 37 per cent in 1937—or about one-quarter of all nonfinancial corporation assets and one-tenth of total national assets.[8] The form and extent of control within these 100 corporations is significant, both in measuring the concentration of wealth within the very small elite and in evaluating the dominant theories on the nature of corporate power in America.

In the largest industrial corporations, the directors are neither a passive group nor at odds with the basic policies and interests of management. The reason is simple: Most company directors are also members of management. The trend in this direction has been decisive. In 1937–39, 36 per cent of the directors of the top industrials were also key officers in their respective companies. By 1957, that figure was 50 per cent. This meant, taking into account interlocking directorates, that the majority of the 1,477 directors of the 100 top companies were active officers in some of those companies. In 47 of the top 100, officer-directors held absolute majorities.[9] So with most directors, it is obvious how they exert power: They are actively engaged in the management of the largest corporations.

A National Industrial Conference Board study of directors of 638 manufacturing corporations of varied sizes in 1959, found that 46 per cent were officers as well as directors of their companies. Another 17 per cent were "substantial stockholders" who were not officers, and 10 per cent represented interested financial institutions.[10]

There remains the problem of how power is exercised by directors who are not also officers.

Some directors, as we have seen in our discussion of interlocking directorates, exert influence because they represent other, and usually larger, corporations. Backed by their primary company, they are in a position to demand conformity to certain policies. Whether or not they exert this power is immaterial. The fact is that they can.

For a director of one firm, obtaining a connection as director in other firms—and preferably a large number of them—is motivated by the realization that this power in reverse may be useful to his primary firm or himself. General Motors, for example, was helped in monopolizing the bus-manufacturing industry by the fact that a number of bankers sat on transit-company boards of directors. Eager for GM accounts, these bankers intervened with transit managers on behalf of GM buses.[11]

In 1939, the top officers and directors of each of the 97 largest manufacturing corporations collectively owned an average of 7.0 per cent of the *total* number of shares in their own company. This is a conservative estimate based on far more abundant data than are available for the present period.

Now let us investigate the stock ownership of directors. From the annual proxy statements and documents filed with the Securities and Exchange Commission, we can arrive at a *minimum* percentage for the ownership of *voting* stock by the directors of the 100 largest industrial corporations. In 1957, the board of directors of these corporations owned or represented an average of 9.9 per cent of its shares. That figure would probably be increased by several percentage points if it were possible to include the stock ownership in several closely owned giants that do not issue proxy statements. In only 23 of these 100 companies are directors listed as owning more than 10 per cent of the voting stock; in 36, they are listed as owning less than 1 per cent. As in 1937, the vast majority of stock owned by directors is held by no more than 300 men.[12]

The matter of stock ownership by directors only begins with the figure of 10 per cent. We know that large holdings are synonymous with power; however, their absence does not necessarily rule out the presence of power in some subtler or more complex form. It is much more likely that we are ignorant of crucial information. It is important to press the matter further, to persevere in the search for the location of such power by assuming that it is not necessarily diffused.

Let us first look back a generation, and examine the 1937–39 directorates of the 72 of 1957's 100 top industrials for which we have information. It is quite clear that many of the important stockholding groups of the late 1930's are still in the same controlling positions. In board after board, the same family names appear in 1957 and in 1937–39—even when these people are no longer listed as having significant stock holdings. It is especially intriguing to find that the family pattern is very noticeable in 22 of the 72 corporations, and that in 1957, these 22 had an average stock ownership by directors of only 3.1 per cent, which very substantially pulled down the overall average.

The splitting of blocks of stocks among family members for tax purposes, or the placing of the stocks in professionally managed trusts and investment companies, where identities can be obscured, may have practical value for the corporate elite. But these moves can hardly be regarded as significant changes in stock ownership.

In 1937-39 the Phipps family, via Bessemer Securities Corporation, owned 9.7 per cent of the stock of International Paper. In 1957, Ogden Phipps, chairman of Bessemer, sat on the International Paper board and was listed as owning 0.1 per cent of its stock. The Mellon family owned more than 50 per cent of Gulf Oil in 1937–39, but the two Mellons who sat on Gulf's board in 1957 were listed as owning a mere 6.5 per cent. The Mathers owned 9.3 per cent of Youngstown Sheet and Tube in 1937–39, but were listed, through their one director, as owning only 0.5 per cent in 1957.

The Du Ponts owned 15 per cent of U.S. Rubber in 1937–39, but in 1957, their representative, G. P. Edwards, who sat on the board was listed as owning virtually nothing. The Jones, Laughlin, and Robinson families owned about one-third of the Jones & Laughlin stock in 1937–39, but in 1957, their three board seats derived from their combined ownership of 0.5 per cent. The McCormick family owned about one-third of International Harvester in 1937–39, but the two family members on the board in 1957 owned a mere 1.2 per cent. The Levis family owned 16.8 per cent of Owens-Illinois Glass in 1937–39; they had two board members but less than 1.5 per cent of the stock in 1957. The Root family held 3.6 per cent of this company's stock in 1937–39, but in 1957, its one director was listed for about 0.3 per cent.

In search of some definition of the top elite, Robert A. Gordon, in *Business Leadership in the Large Corporation* (1945), took the 20 largest shareholders—including banks, trusts, foundations, insurance, and other corporations, as well as individuals—of each of the 200 largest corporations in 1937–39 (as determined by the TNEC), which he pruned to 176 by eliminating subsidiaries. He found that the cumulative top 20 stockholders owned an average of 28.6 per cent of the market value of common stock. In 101 out of 183 stock issues, they owned at least 20 per cent, or what is for all practical purposes a controlling share. Individuals or their legal devices, such as trusts and personal holding companies, owned half of the stock held by this tiny group of no more than 4,000 shareholders. In effect, they were the dominant shareholder influence in corporate affairs.[13]

Here the concentration of stock ownership in a small group is plainly seen. But what it means in terms of economic power is less clear. It is debatable how much this group can do toward obtaining control, if they do not already have it, over the corporations they own. However, the large increase in the number of corporate proxy fights in recent years and the success of insurgents in about one-third of these indicate that the power of key stockholders is no myth.[14]

In many corporations whose stock is highly concentrated in a very small group, key stockholders choose not to exert power through direct representation on the board of directors and in top officer groups. Obviously their major concern as stockholders is profits and investment security, which, as indicated by the consistently high net corporate income and the restricted distribution of dividends to lower personal taxes, has been well served by the existing officers and directors. Since no major American corporation has ever sought to pursue a policy of enlightened public activities at the cost of basic profit margins, stockholders have never been forced to exert power for this reason.

The power of both stockholders and managers, however, exists within a small elite whose relation to society is rarely changed by disputes within its own ranks. In 1937–39, there was no visible center of control through ownership in only 58 of the top 176 corporations. In 83 corporations, ultimate power rested with family stockholding groups, some owning as little as 4 per cent and actively involved in management, most owning much more and inactive. Thirty-five companies were dominated by corporate groups who were in turn owned by large shareholders.[15]

Because of the continued, if not intensified, concentration of shares in a very small proportion of the stockholders, it must be concluded that the most powerful corporate giants still remain within the control of a small group of men. This was at least as true in 1957 as in the late 1930's, since the means of control have become more centralized in the intervening years.

MANAGEMENT

Berle and Means have alleged that the top officers of the giant corporations no longer own any significant percentage of the stock and that, as professional managers, they do not have the same interests as the stockholders. The new managers, it is claimed, are oriented toward rationalizing and consolidating the position of the corporation, are more sensitive to public opinion, and are concerned with avoiding risk ventures that might maximize profits but would endanger the basic security of the corporation.

Whether the "great faceless corporations [are] 'owned' by no one and run by self-designated 'managers'" can be settled by the answers to two crucial questions that have been ignored by the theorists: (1) How much stock do the key managers own in the top corporations they run? (2) How much stock does management, as a class, own in all corporations, and thus to what extent do they share the profit motive of stockholders? Is it true, as corporation lawyer David T. Bazelon put it, that the manager of the giant corporation is "not a capitalist at all; he is a new fish?"[16]

The issue here is not the concentration of economic power but the motivation of managerial actions by tangible incentives. However small their percentage of the stock may be, it is exceedingly important to their personal fortunes and, therefore, a crucial motivating factor in their corporate role. In early 1957, 25 General Motors officers owned an average of 11,500 shares each.[17] Collectively, their holdings would have been inconsequential if they had chosen to try to obtain control of GM through their stocks. Yet each of these men had a personal stake of roughly a half million dollars in the company—plus the tantalizing prospect that over the next decade or two the corporation's growth and profits might double or treble the value of his stock and make him an exceptionally wealthy man.

The corporate executive is tied to the profit performance of the corporate system in many tangible ways. But the discussions by Berle, Riesman, and others of the separation of management from the profit incentive, and from stock in particular, is based on a failure to appreciate the nature of the executive compensation system. Most serious of all, they have ignored the major, and potentially revolutionary, impact of the stock option on the corporate executive.

The stock option, originated in 1950, has committed top management more strongly than ever before to the corporation's profit position, because without profits, the options are largely worthless. By 1957, option plans had been instituted by 77 per cent of the manufacturing corporations listed on the New York or American Stock Exchanges. Of the 100 largest industrials, only 13 did not have option plans in 1959, and in most of these corporations, there was heavy stock ownership by directors. Of the 87 with option plans, the 83 for which public data was available had granted key officers options on an average of 1.9 per cent of their outstanding voting stock by 1959.[18]

Suggestive of future trends is the percentage of outstanding stock reserved for executive options. By 1960, Inland Steel had assigned the equivalent of 11 per cent of its outstanding voting stock for options. Ford, in 1960, reserved 6.7 per cent of its outstanding shares for future options. If this trend continues, it will further strengthen the tie between management and stock, especially in companies whose management holdings are now comparatively small.

Top corporation executives are very well-paid men. In 1958, the median income for the highest-paid 1,700 was $73,600.[19] But Berle and the others assume that they, unlike most others in this income class, will not buy stock. The fact is that the corporate executive *does* buy stock. Thus his personal fortunes are bound not only to the money-making success of his own company but also to that of the larger corporate structure in which he has invested. Theoretically, it would not make a great deal of difference if the managers had, in fact, no personal interest in the dividend performance or market value of stocks, since it has never been shown how the managers differ, in practice and theory, from the stockholding elite.

In fact, the managerial class is the largest single group in the stockholding population, and a greater proportion of this class owns stock than any other. The statistics: 44.8 per cent of all administrative officials —top company officials and managers in corporations, banks, and the like

—own stock. For operating supervisory officials—managers of medium-size and small companies, department heads of these companies or larger organizations, and kindred types—the figure was 19.4 per cent. These are the results of the Brookings Institution's 1952 census of stockholders, which also showed that 6.3 per cent of all shareholders were administrative executives and 13.1 per cent were operating supervisory officials.[20]

How much stock does the managerial class own? We know that spending units owning $100,000 or more in marketable stock in 1949 accounted for at least 65 to 71 per cent of the total individual ownership, and we can reasonably assume that this figure is valid after 1949, since stock concentration has been fairly stable. Of all the spending units in that category in 1957, nearly half—47.4 per cent to be precise—were from the managerial class. Also, one-fifth of the managerial spending units owning stock in 1957 possessed more than $100,000 worth.[21]

It is impossible to give a precise figure on the percentage of stock owned by the managerial class, but these figures indicate that the managers own a very large proportion, if not well over the majority, of shares in the United States.

Management, then, is the class most interested in the highest dividends, in both their own firms and others. And taking into account the greater prevalence of stock ownership among top management shown by the Brookings study, as well as the high incomes and stock options in this group, it becomes clear that the interest of top executives in stock is undoubtedly the most important among those in the managerial class.

To talk of a separation between management and major stockholders in the United States is obviously quite impossible; they are virtually one and the same.

The concentration of economic power in a very small elite is an indisputable fact. This power is a function of both their direct ownership in the corporate structure and their ability to control it. Their possession of savings and wealth is possible because of the continuing basic inequality of income that is simply a part of a larger pattern of inequality in the United States.

The implications of this intense centralization of economic power are twofold. First, the concentration of income allocates a large share of the consumption of goods to a small proportion of the population. For a public policy directed toward maintenance of full employment through full consumption, this fact raises major obstacles for working within the existing income distribution structure. Second, and more important for this study, a social theory assuming a democratized economic system—or even a trend in this direction—is quite obviously not in accord with social reality. Whether the men who control industry are socially responsive or trustees of the social welfare is quite another matter; it is one thing to speculate about their motivations, another to generalize about economic facts. And even if we assume that these men act benevolently toward their workers and the larger community, their actions still would not be the result of social control through a formal democratic structure and group participation, which are the essentials for democracy; they would be an arbitrary *noblesse oblige* by the economic elite. When discussing the existing corporate system, it would be more realistic to drop all references to democracy.

The real questions are: (1) Do a small group of very wealthy men have the power to guide industry, and thereby much of the total economy, toward ends that they decide upon as compatible with their own interests? (2) Do they own and control the major corporations?

The answers must inevitably be affirmative.

NOTES

1. David Riesman *et al.*, *The Lonely Crowd* (Garden City, N.Y.: Doubleday & Company, 1953), p. 252.
2. Adolf A. Berle, Jr., *The 20th Century Capitalist Revolution* (New York: Harcourt, Brace & Company, 1954), p. 182.
3. *Ibid.*, p. 60.
4. David E. Lilienthal, *Big Business: A New Era* (New York: Harper & Brothers, 1953), p. 28.
5. Data for 1937 are calculated from TNEC Monograph No. 29, pp. 23, 350–54; data for 1955 are calculated from "The *Fortune* Directory of the 500 Largest U.S. Industrial Corporations," *Fortune*, June, 1956; Internal Revenue Service, *Statistics of Income, 1955—Corporation Income Tax Returns* (Washington, D.C.: Government Printing Office, 1958), pp. 70–71; Bureau of the Census, *Statistical Abstract—1957*, p. 320. Data for 1937, and especially 1955, underestimate the degree of concentration by including in the top 200 corporations some that are in reality part of another corporation's empire; e.g., Western Electric should be counted as a wholly-owned subsidiary of American Telephone and Telegraph. Certain of these adjustments were made for 1955, but these figures must be regarded as conservative estimates.
6. TNEC Monograph No. 29, p. 59; also National Resources Committee, "Basic Characteristics," *The Structure of the American Economy*, Part I (Washington, D.C.: Government Printing Office, 1939), p. 158.
7. Data on these seven types of interlocks are taken from *Report of the Federal Trade Commission on Interlocking Directorates* (Washington, D.C.: Government Printing Office, 1951), pp. 22–36.
8. Relevant data for 1957 calculated from "The *Fortune* Directory," *Fortune*, July and August, 1958. I excluded from the *Fortune* list Western Electric, a subsidiary of a utility, and Joseph E. Seagram & Sons and Shell Oil, both foreign-controlled firms. Richfield Oil was excluded since the majority of its stock is owned by Cities Service and Sinclair Oil. Weyerhaeuser Timber and Singer Manufacturing were excluded since neither is listed on stock exchanges and therefore neither issues any data on internal control, though both are known to be closely owned by the founding families. The Henry J. Kaiser corporations were treated here as one firm.
9. Data for 1937–39 were calculated from TNEC Monograph No. 29, pp. 350–531; 1957 data were calculated from proxy statements and *Moody's Industrials—1957*. A National Industrial Conference Board study of 638 large manufacturing companies, published after my research was completed, applies the line of analysis I used in its examination of companies not in the top 100. In 45 per cent of these

corporations, officers held majorities on boards of directors, and they occupied 46 per cent of the board seats. See NICB, *Corporate Directorship Practices*, "Studies in Business Policy," No. 90 (New York: National Industrial Conference Board, 1959).
10. NICB, *Corporate Directorship Practices*, pp. 17–18.
11. *Ibid.*, p. 52; U.S. Senate, Committee on the Judiciary, *Bigness and the Concentration of Economic Power—A Case Study of General Motors Corporation*, Report of the Committee, 84th Cong., 2nd Sess. (Washington, D.C.: Government Printing Office, 1956), p. 55.
12. All data on these and the 100 corporations discussed in this chapter were calculated from proxy statements for 1957 in the Corporate Records Division, Baker Library, Harvard Business School, and from Forms 4, 5, and 6 on file in the Public Reference Room, Securities and Exchange Commission, Washington, D.C. Forms S-1 and 10-K were also used. Only voting stock, common or preferred, is calculated, though preferred is of very little consequence. Stock options held but not exercised were excluded. Included is stock managed by professional representatives sitting on boards—either for personal trusts or holding companies—and directors' beneficial interests in partnerships, trusts, and estates, including the known holdings of their direct families.
13. Robert A. Gordon, *Business Leadership in the Large Corporation* (Washington, D.C.: Brookings Institution, 1945), pp. 32–34.
14. For a discussion of proxy fights, see *Wall Street Journal*, April 30, 1958, p. 1; *New York Times*, March 22, 1959, p. 1 F.
15. Gordon, *op. cit.*, pp. 40–41 ff.
16. David T. Bazelon, "Facts and Fictions of U.S. Capitalism," *The Reporter*, September 17, 1959, pp. 43, 45; John K. Galbraith in *New York Times Book Review*, September 6, 1959, p. 3.
17. Securities and Exchange Commission, *Official Summary of Security Transactions and Holdings*, February, 1957, p. 11.
18. NICB, *Compensation of Top Executives*; and calculations from *Moody's Industrial Manual—1960*.
19. "1,700 Top Executives," *Fortune*, November, 1959, p. 138.
20. Louis H. Kimmel, *Share Ownership in the U.S.* (Washington, D.C.: Brookings Institution, 1952), pp. 98–99. Kimmel provides very detailed information on the occupational-class affiliations of individual shareholders. The major shortcoming of his survey is the inclusion of an additional 2.13 million unemployed housewives and 130,000 students and preschool children in its figure of 6.49 million shareholders. Housewives and children do not form a socioeconomic class, however, and since only 4.75 million separate families and individuals own stock, it is obvious they must be sharply reduced in number to 520,000 living units if an accurate, noninflated occupational distribution is to be obtained.
21. J. Keith Butters *et al.*, *Effects of Taxation—Investment by Individuals* (Boston: Harvard Business School, 1953), p. 382; and calculations from "Study 650" (Unpublished data: Survey Research Center, 1957), Table LA-156.

42. Peonage in Florida
ROBERT COLES AND HARRY HUGE

With this piece, we have the second of Robert Coles' contributions to this volume (see selection 25). His coauthor, Harry Huge, is a lawyer especially interested in the legal problems faced by the poor.

Around October, cold spells begin to reach up North and into the Midwest, and thousands of Americans remind themselves that in a nation as large as ours, spread out over so many latitudes, a willing traveller can find summer anytime. So the trek to Florida begins. The southern part of the state begins to bulge with the rich and the not-so-rich, the owners of winter homes and the one-week guests who fill up thousands of hotels, motels and rooming houses.

Others also manage a return to Florida in October, though to get there they don't use jets or toll roads. Often they even shun our new and free interstate roads, and if asked why, they demur, or quickly assert their wish to move quietly, to attract nobody's attention. Yet, they do get attention. When they arrive at a state line, they may be met by the police and told to go right through, fast and with no stops at all; if they should try to pause here and there, to use a restroom or enter a restaurant, they are quickly singled out and shouted at and pushed away. The owner of one gas station in Collier County, Florida told us who these other winter visitors are: "They're dirty, the migrants. They'll come by, and I tell them to scram. They'll ruin your restrooms for good, inside an hour. Sure, we need them here, to pick the crops, but that's all they're good for, if you ask me, and I've lived here all my life and seen them come and go each year. I'll tell you—I don't even want to sell them gas. You know why? We're a first-class station, and if tourists or the regular people here drove up and saw those migrants around, they'd go somewhere else with their business, and I wouldn't blame them. You don't come from up North all the way to Collier County, only to find yourself standing next to—the likes of them."

What *are* they like? Where do they come from and how do they live, the some one-hundred-thousand migrant farmers who each year harvest Florida's vegetables and fruit, worth millions of dollars?

Actually we don't know all there is to know, because the migrants commonly slip by census-takers or local officials charged with recording births and deaths. Nomads, itinerants, wanderers, they live everywhere and nowhere. Each county of each state calls them someone else's responsibility, though in all places the terribly hard and demanding work

SOURCE: Robert Coles and Harry Huge, "Peonage in Florida," *The New Republic* 161 (July 26, 1969), 17–21. Reprinted by permission of *The New Republic*, © 1969 Harrison-Blaine of New Jersey, Inc.

they do is considered essential. Nor has the federal government ever seen fit to step in and say, yes they will in a sense belong to all of us, for whose benefit, after all, so much of that travelling and stopping and cutting and picking is done. On the contrary, migrant farmers are denied just about every benefit that 30 years of struggle achieved for other workers—such as the right to organize into labor unions without harassment and bargain collectively with employers, and the right to get unemployment insurance or a degree of compensation for injuries sustained at work. Most migrants can't vote, are ineligible for any kind of welfare or other advantages and services that towns or countries offer their residents.

Here is how one migrant worker talked to us about his life as a virtual peon: "Well sir, I was born in Louisiana, I was; my daddy worked there on shares, and before him my granddaddy, and I guess it goes back to slavery. (My granddaddy, he'd tell us about all the slaves he used to know, and how one by one they died, and when the last slave died—I mean that was a slave before they was all set free—well my granddaddy, he said his mother said she hated to see him die, but it was just as well we tried to forget about slavery.) I guess I thought I was going to stay there, in Louisiana, but I sure didn't, I'll tell you. I was thirteen or fourteen, I think it was, and my daddy was telling us that we were in real bad trouble, because the government up in Washington was giving the bossman a lot of money, and in return he wasn't doing as much planting as before; and what he was planting, he was going to do it all by machine and he didn't need us anymore to pick the crops. So, he told us we could stay there in the cabins, but that was all, and the sooner we went up to Chicago the better, he said, and my daddy was all set to go with us, but we got the message that his sister up there had died all of a sudden, and he got scared to go.

"I remember him saying that if we went up there, we'd all die like his sister, and if we stayed down on that plantation, we'd not last long, and so there wasn't anything to choose—except that one day a man came along, and he was going door to door, he said, and signing people up for work, to pick the crops he said, over in Florida. And he told us, I remember, that all our worries was over, and all we had to do was go on over there with him and the others and do what we knew to do, pick some beans and some tomatoes and like that, and it wasn't any different from working on cotton, and maybe easier, he said. So daddy told us he thought we should go, and there was, I think, five or six families he got, just from our bossman's place; and of course he got others. And would you believe it that they had these buses, four of them I recall, and they put us on them, and they looked like the school buses, only they were older, much older, and soon we were on the road, yes sir; and I'll tell you, it's been a lot of that ever since, moving here and there and everywhere, until you don't know where you're at and how you'll ever stop. Believe me, sir, we wants to stop and find us a place to live, all year round, like other folks do. But if you're trying to eat, and you owe them all that money, and you have to eat while you try to get even and not be owing them, well then, you just have to go up North and come back, or else they'll have you in jail. I'll tell you that, or worse than that, much worse, they'll just go and pull the trigger, I believe some of them might, if you tried to run free of them. And I'd like to know where you could go even if they let you, and they didn't call the sheriff, and they even drove you where you wanted to go. We wouldn't know where to go, because the people, they just don't want us, to use their restrooms or even buy from them. They'll tell you to 'git,' and they sure mean it, you can tell on their face by the way they looks down on you."

His story is not unusual. Thousands of sharecroppers and tenant farmers have gone North to our cities, where they frequently found no work and went on welfare. Thousands of other field hands have given their lives to constant travel and the hardest, most menial jobs, for which they are called "lazy" and "shiftless" and paid the lowest possible wages. (Only recently did farm workers come under the protection of the minimum-wage law, and their minimum wage just moved up from $1.15 to $1.30 per hour, whereas other workers are guaranteed $1.60 per hour.) Worse, migrants like the man just quoted fall victim to a kind of peonage that seals not only their fate but that of their children. They are brought to Florida, whole families or single men or single women or groups of teen-aged children. The men who bring them are called "contractors" or "crew leaders," and are paid, say, "50 dollars a head," (their words) by growers. The frightened, confused former sharecroppers and their children are housed in camps and put to work, but soon they discover that in return for long hours on their knees out in the fields they will get very little cash. For one thing, in the course of a year there are days, even weeks, when there is no work to be had. The migrants move from one camp to another, and become part of a world few outsiders know anything about. The camps have their own stores and vendors, and are often guarded by "camp boys" who walk around with guns. Migrants are told they cannot leave unless all their debts are paid; the ledgers are tallied by the men who own and run the camps.

"There's always something you owe them," we kept on hearing as we talked with one migrant after another. From Rodolfo Juarez, a new and young leader of Mexican-American migrants in Florida (they make up about half the state's agricultural workers), we heard it spelled out: "I was born in South Texas, in San Benito, and when I was about fifteen I was sold, that's right. They came and got a whole group of us and told us there was a lot of money to make up North and over in Florida, if we just went along with them, and they'll take us, and even feed us. I now know they got so much money from the growers for each body they brought up from Texas. Well, we were living like animals where we were, and getting practically nothing for doing crop work in south Texas, so we thought: why not? why not? I was taken up to Indiana and Ohio, to work on farms there, and then we tried to break out, but it's hard.

They tell you that you owe them for the food and the transportation and the mattress on the floor you use for sleeping, and they tell you that if you try to leave, they'll get you thrown in jail and you'll never get out until you pay your bills. How else can you pay them but by going back to work for them, and when you do that, you have to eat and you have to sleep somewhere and a lot of the time there's no work, until it's time to harvest, and so you're their property, that's what it amounts to with some of those contractors. They own people, that's what, unless they escape, like I did; but I'll tell you the truth, a lot of migrants —you know, they're Mexican-Americans like me, or black people, and a few are white, yes, but not many—they're not aware of their rights, and they're scared, and they should be. Have you seen them patrolling some of those camps? The men will ride around with guns, and the crew leaders will herd the people into the trucks to go picking. They stand them up and they look like cattle going to the market, and that's no exaggerating."

We visited the camps and the fields all through Collier County and Palm Beach County. We saw the same sites that recently shocked Senator McGovern's Select Committee on Nutrition and Human Needs: broken-down shacks, some without even windows, some nothing more than enlarged outhouses without running water or heat, a few even without electricity, all of which rent for $10, $15, even $20 a *week*. The drinking water is often contaminated, taken as it is from superficial wells located near garbage-filled swamps. Children are supposed to walk a quarter of a mile or more to unspeakably inadequate outdoor privies. There are no showers, no baths, no stoves and often no refrigerators. Entire families live in one room, sleep, if lucky, on mattresses, live on soda pop and bread and grits and fat-back and cheap candy. Yet, Collier County has no food-stamp program, no commodity food program, and no welfare program for migrants, who have been called by local officials "federal people," or "not our people." In Collier County's Immokalee, an Indian word which ironically means "my home," we saw children not only hungry and malnourished, but obviously and seriously ill, yet never seen by physicians. Born "on the road," brought up on buses and trucks, or carried from farm to farm in cars, left to themselves in the fields and, when twelve or thirteen, quietly put to work in the fields, they nevertheless have to be considered fortunate if they are still alive, since the infant mortality rate for such children in places like Collier County is estimated to be about five times that of other American children. The children are badly frightened and confused. They live unstable, chaotic lives and feel at loose ends, worthless, virtually dead.

One of us spent two years studying migrant children in Belle Glade and Pahokee, Florida, and we recently went to see some of those children, a little older now but still to be found (through a minister) in one of the camps: "Yes, we're soon to be going north again," a ten-year-old boy told us. "I'm afraid each time that we won't get back here, but we do."

How did school go for him this year: "Well, I didn't get there much. We moved from place to place, and I helped with the picking a lot, and the schools, when you go to them, they don't seem to want you, and they'll say that you're only going to be there a few weeks anyway, so what's the use." What does he want to do when he gets older? "I don't know. I'd like to stay someplace, I guess, and never have to leave there for the rest of my life, that's what. I could have a job—maybe it would be where they make cars and trucks and planes. I could make plenty of money, and bring it home, and we'd all live on it, my brothers and my sister. But my mother says someone has to pick the crops, and we don't know what else there is to do, and they'll come and beat you and throw you in the canal, the crew leaders, if you cross them; and then you'd be dead in one minute. So, we'd better stay with the crops; because my mother is probably right. I hope I never fall in one of those canals. You can never get out. They're deeper than the ocean I hear. I've never seen the ocean, but I know it's not far away."

The ocean is indeed nearby—Palm Beach and all its glitter to the east, and to the west the more sedate but no less wealthy Naples, the seat of Collier County's government. One can drive the major roads of Palm Beach County or Collier County and get no idea what is happening down those dusty pathways that lead to fields and camps and "loading zones" where human beings are picked up and left off. "There's no end to it," a migrant mother said to us in Immokalee, "you just hope you'll die in between picking-time, so you're resting. I'd hate to die on the road, yes sir; my children, they'd never find their way back to Florida. I guess that's our home, yes sir. We spend more time there than in the other states; but I'll say this, they're not very good to us there, if you ask for anything."

What has she asked for? What does she need that Collier County might supply, particularly since the county's officials have publicly acknowledged that without migrant workers like her its huge farms and its dozens of well-equipped packing houses would be worthless? She is, of course, rather modest when she talks about her needs. She'd like good food for her children, particularly during those weeks when she is waiting for work. (The migrant's average annual income is $1,700 a year.) She would like to be paid in full for her work. (Migrants repeatedly claim they are short-changed—given, say, five dollars at the end of a day and told that for "meals and transportation" they have been charged another five.) She would like to find decent housing and pay a reasonable amount of rent: "In Immokalee a few white men own everything. They push us into those little rooms, one for each family, and you pay $20 a week. If you go to the camps, after they deduct the rent you've got no money left, and they tell you that you owe them some, on top of it."

She is not about to fight things out with Collier County's officials. We saw a little of what frightens her—those "camp boys" and labor contractors driving pickup trucks fitted with gun racks that hold three or four rifles. We saw a jail in Immokalee, only recently abandoned, whose cramped and primitive quarters must rival anything that ever was or is in Siberia. On the other hand, we met up with a fine group of lawyers who are fighting hard for that woman and others like her under a program called the South Florida Migrant Legal Services, begun in April, 1967 under an OEO grant. Lawyers cannot by their exertions alone bring social and economic justice to a group of people variously called in the last two or three years, not a half century ago, "the slaves we rent" or "serfs upon the land" or "America's wretched of the earth." Yet, every day migrants feel themselves victimized, cheated, deceived; and they have no past experience with lawyers, no money for them, and no belief that a lawsuit will lead to anything. Now, for the first time, some of those Florida migrants have found out that there are intelligent and compassionate men who know the law and are ready to represent the interests of people who haven't a cent to offer for legal fees. No social revolution has occurred in Florida, but at least a few complaints on behalf of the migrants are being made—and as a result the growers and crew leaders and labor contractors and real estate groups that employ migrants and herd them about and rent shacks to them have become convinced that the South Florida Migrant Legal Services must be brought to an end very soon, when the OEO grant runs out. Florida's political leaders are putting strong pressure on OEO to refuse another grant, and though the agency's staff reportedly has high praise for the program, the real test will come not only when (and if) refunding takes place, but after Governor Kirk exercises his expected veto, and OEO's new chief, Donald Rumsfeld, decides either to stand firm and override the veto or allow one of the agency's best programs to be killed. It is, too, a program that aims to change things through legal action, through reliance on court orders and "due process," those quiet, slow, patient maneuvers we are daily urged to respect.

Meanwhile, Senators come and are horrified and ashamed. Tourists drive by and if they see anything, shake their heads and wonder how many miles to the next Holiday Inn. People like us quickly find ourselves out of Collier County's Immokalee and safely in Collier County's Naples —where we can eat well and take a swim, and give vent to our confusion and sadness and most galling, our frustration: how can our words do justice to the misery and heartache we have seen, and how can we describe and make unforgettable the worried, pained faces of boys and girls whose bodies are thin and covered with sores and bites and covered also with Florida's rich muckland, whose crops those children have harvested? Back in Immokalee we were offended, disgusted; later in Naples there was the tropical green water and the soft sand and a long, long pier where we could stand and discuss things with Michael Foster and Michael Kantor, two resourceful young lawyers who work for the South Florida Migrant Legal Services in Collier County and every day try to get housing codes enforced, and money paid to people who have bent and stooped from dawn to dusk, only to be denied their rightful earnings, or who have gone for weeks without work, without unemployment compensation, without relief payments.

We stood on the pier for a long time and looked at sworn affidavits that had been taken six months ago and sent up to the Justice Department, affidavits that spell out the details of peonage: "From October 17, 1968 until late in November, 1968, I was only paid wages of $5.50. I went to the camp authorities to ask why I had been paid so little and they merely responded they had paid three doctors bills for me and that I was not due any money at this time. To the best of my knowledge I did not have three doctor bills while I was at Camp Happy." During her stay she "had many problems" with the camp guards. She was beaten, thrown across a room, told she might be killed. When she asked to leave, one of the camp's guards said "I could not go because I owed $25 to the company." What is more, others kept on arriving to share her fate: "On January 11, 1969, a bus with forty-two people arrived from the state of Mississippi. . . . Around half of these persons were under sixteen years of age and were not accompanied by adults. The man who brought the children to the camp was paid $15 for each person he brought." And finally, so that everybody at Camp Happy was kept happy, "persons also used to come from Fort Myers and sell narcotics at the camp. I did not know the names of these persons. They carried on their activities with the full consent of those who operated the camp."

What is to be done? The two lawyers told us they could only keep trying, keep pressing matters through the courts—though even that method has caused an uproar among Florida's political leaders. We said we could report on what we had seen and learned, even though we know that in past decades reports have been written and written—and the evident futility of all those words must haunt those who wrote them. Perhaps, we speculated, the only answer to the problem is one suggested by a tough, angry "community organizer"—an "outside agitator," no doubt about it, we met near Immokalee: "Look, you people can do your lawyering and your doctoring and your writing, but a lot of good it will do these people. They're in bondage, don't you see that? They're treated like animals—in a country that's the richest, fattest country in the world. They have no constituency, that's the problem. They don't even have the kind of constituency the blacks do in Mississippi—you know, the Northern liberals, with the voting laws they've put through, and like that. These people have nothing to fall back on but the conscience of the nation, and a lot of good that's done for them. I'll tell you, there's only one way to change things here in Florida, in Collier County. Over there in Naples there's Roger Blough of United States Steel, and there's the president of Grant's department store, and there's the president of Eli Lilly, and all the rest. They have it nice here in Florida. There's no personal income tax, and no tax on the corporations. I'll bet if the migrants started marching down that highway 846 to Naples, and fought their way to that Gulf Shore

Boulevard there—well, I'll bet the people who live there would call in those sheriffs and county commissioners, and they'd call in the politicians who do what they're told to do, and say to all of them: boys, give them a bigger slice, because we don't want any more trouble here. You hear that! And then the migrants would be a little better off and you guys, you'd praise yourselves and all your attitudes and say like you always do: democracy, it's wonderful!"

We are in no danger of the kind of middle-class self-congratulations he scornfully described—the kind that follows a successful uprising of the poor. For there's no danger the migrants will be causing anyone much trouble. They will roam the land, follow the sun and the crops, harvest our food, and go on getting just about nothing.

43. The Starbird Memorandum
J. W. FULBRIGHT

The author of this selection was long the well-known senator from Arkansas. Since he is hardly a flaming radical (nor even a consistent liberal), Mr. Fulbright lends a special credibility to his critique of Pentagon personnel and practices. He shows with devastating clarity that Americans at large have become victims of the Pentagon. We are victims in very realistic terms because the Pentagon is so powerful and prestigious, and has access to such enormous resources, that it can manipulate the American Congress and public almost at will. The result, says Fulbright, is that violence is now our most important product.

In September, 1968, Secretary of the Army Stanley R. Resor sent to the then Secretary of Defense Clark M. Clifford two "classified" memoranda. One was Resor's own; the other, a detailed, fifteen-page document, had been put together by Lieutenant General Alfred D. Starbird, "manager" of the Sentinel System, the Johnson Administration's version of the ABM. Together the papers spelled out a coordinated high-pressure propaganda and public relations program, to be undertaken by various branches of the armed forces, designed to sell the ABM to the American public.

At the time, the Johnson Administration was running into trouble with

SOURCE: J. W. Fulbright, *The Pentagon Propaganda Machine* (New York: Liveright Publishing Corporation, 1970), pp. 1–4, 9–10, 12–15. Copyright © 1970 by Liveright Publishing Corporation and reprinted by permission.

its proposal to deploy fifteen to twenty missile sites around the country to protect major American cities against possible Communist Chinese attack. Pentagon officials were getting worried about public reaction. Army Secretary Resor's memorandum reflected that concern, saying there was "public confusion" about the need for such a missile defense system. "I feel it essential," he wrote, "that the Army undertake a time-phased public affairs program to provide information to dispel this public confusion."

General Starbird noted that there was opposition to ABM "in certain segments of Congress, in scientific circles, and in citizen-public official interest groups." His list of reasons for congressional and scientific opposition—reasons as valid today as they were then—included "technical and operational feasibility, cost, disarmament, the international arms race, and national priorities." He was less exact in describing the reasons for community opposition, but what he said acknowledged the understandable displeasure a large number of citizens were voicing over having nuclear warheads virtually in their backyards.

Although designed initially to persuade the public that billions of dollars should be spent on a particular weapon, its long-term aim was to intervene in the decision-making process at the congressional level where complex questions of foreign and domestic priorities compete in an area outside the competence of the military. General Starbird's memorandum recognized that the basic wisdom of the ABM proposal was doubted by many honest and technically competent people. Nearly a year after the Army set up the Sentinel publicity program, forty-nine members of the Senate expressed that doubt when they voted against Safeguard, the Nixon Administration's diluted version of the Sentinel System.

In size and intensity, the Sentinel publicity program rivaled anything the military had tried in recent years in support of one specific weapons program. Since the battle over unification in the late 1940s when the services vigorously competed for status there have been a series of similar efforts. Each impinged on the traditional system for making general public policy. The ABM campaign, for example, directly affected the national welfare and national interests, and security. Its details were kept secret from the public and parts of its operation were so designed that the Army's hand would not be visible even after the campaign was in full swing.

Five months passed from the time the Resor and Starbird memoranda went to Secretary Clifford before their existence became known to the public. Even then, the information did not come from the Pentagon but from a newspaper, the *Washington Post*. On February 16, 1969, the *Post* carried a front-page story by Philip Geyelin about the memoranda, saying high Army officials were conducting "an extraordinarily intricate and comprehensive campaign" to persuade the American people and their representatives in the Congress of the need for the ABM. The newspaper, in an editorial the following day, labeled the campaign "The Big ABM Brainwash."

There were indeed many elements of "brainwashing" in the campaign. Congressional and scientific criticism had been voiced and opposition developed in the two cities first selected as Sentinel sites.

In September 1968, however, a true national discussion of the desirability of the ABM deployment and the far-reaching implications of that decision had not fully developed. The public as a whole was relatively uninformed. The Pentagon timing, from a public relations man's point of view, was good. But its aim—to manipulate public opinion using all the weapons in the Pentagon PR arsenal, so that ultimately Congress might be influenced in a matter of such importance—was not good. . . .

. . .

The word "propaganda" in current usage implies some degree of subterfuge. And there certainly was subterfuge involved in the Army's promotion campaign for Sentinel. The attempt to get scientists to support the program and the alliance with military contractors, along with other elements of the project, had been hidden from public view. Though the Resor and Starbird memoranda were not classified documents in the strict security sense, they were labeled "For Official Use Only." This label is stamped on papers to keep them privy to the bureaucracy, and once the label is affixed the chances of anyone outside seeing them—unless they are specifically asked for—are nil. Such papers are said to be "administratively controlled."

. . .

Violence is our most important product. We have been spending nearly $80 billion a year on the military, which is more than the profits of all American business, or, to make another comparison, is almost as much as the total spending of the federal, state, and local governments for health, education, old age and retirement benefits, housing, and agriculture. Until the past session of the Congress, these billions have been provided to the military with virtually no questions asked.

The military has been operating for years in that Elysium of the public relations man, a seller's market. Take the climate into which the Sentinel ABM program was introduced. Many people looked on it, as they now look on Safeguard, not as a weapon but as a means of prosperity. For the industrialist it meant profits; for the worker new jobs and the prospect of higher wages; for the politician a new installation or defense order with which to ingratiate himself with his constituents. Military expenditures today provide the livelihood of some ten percent of our work force. There are 22,000 major corporate defense contractors and another 100,000 subcontractors. Defense plants or installations are located in 363 of the country's 435 congressional districts. Even before it turns its attention to the public-at-large, the military has a large and sympathetic audience for its message.

These millions of Americans who have a vested interest in the expensive weapons systems spawned by our global military involvements are as much a part of the military-industrial complex as the generals and the corporation heads. In turn they have become a powerful force for the perpetuation of those involvements, and have had an indirect influence on a weapons development policy that has driven the United States into a spiraling arms race with the Soviet Union and made us the world's major salesman of armaments.

A Marine war hero and former Commandant of the Corps, General David M. Shoup, has said, "America has become a militaristic and aggressive nation." He could be right. Militarism has been creeping up on us during the past thirty years. Prior to World War II, we never maintained more than a token peacetime army. Even in 1940, with Nazi Germany sweeping over Europe, there were fewer than half a million men in all of the armed services. The Army, which then included the Air Corps, had one general and four lieutenant generals. In October 1941, six weeks before Pearl Harbor, the extension of the draft law was passed by but a single vote. Many of those who voted no did so for partisan political reasons, but antimilitarism certainly was a consideration for some. Today we have more than 3.5 million men in uniform and nearly 28 million veterans of the armed forces in the civilian population. The Air Force alone has twelve four-star generals and forty-two lieutenant generals. The American public has become so conditioned by crises, by warnings, by words that there are few, other than the young, who protest against what is happening.

The situation is such that last year Senator Allen J. Ellender of Louisiana, hardly an apostle of the New Left, felt constrained to say:

"For almost twenty years now, many of us in the Congress have more or less blindly followed our military spokesmen. Some have become captives of the military. We are on the verge of turning into a military nation."

This militarism that has crept up on us is bringing about profound changes in the character of our society and government—changes that are slowly undermining democratic procedure and values.

Confronted in the past generation with a series of challenges from dynamic totalitarian powers, we have felt ourselves compelled to imitate some of the methods of our adversaries. I do not share the view that American fears of Soviet and Chinese aggressiveness have been universally paranoiac, although I think there have been a fair number of neurotic anxieties expressed. The point is that the very objective we pursue—the preservation of a free society—proscribes certain kinds of policies even though they might be tactically expedient. We cannot, without doing ourselves the very injury that we seek to secure ourselves against from foreign adversaries, pursue policies which rely primarily on the threat or use of force, because policies of force and the preeminence given to the wielders of force—the military—are inevitably disruptive of democratic values. Alexis de Tocqueville, that wisest of observers of American democracy, put it this way:

War does not always give democratic societies over to military government, but it must invariably and immeasurably increase the powers of civil government; it must almost automatically concentrate the direction of all men and the control of all things in the hands of the government. If that does not lead to despotism by sudden violence, it leads men gently in that direction by their habits.[1]

During the twenty years Senator Ellender cited we have not only been infected by militarism but by another virus as virulent—an ideological obsession about communism. The head of steam built up in the country by the late Joe McCarthy has never really been blown off, and the extremists of the right utilize it to keep the hatreds that have developed over the years as hot as possible. This heat and the ideas espoused by these extremists produce such deceptively quick and simple solutions as "Bomb Hanoi!" Or "Overthrow Castro!" Or "America: Love It or Leave It!" If we would only proclaim and pursue our dedication to total victory over world communism, they say, root out the subversives—real and imaginary—at home, make our allies follow our lead in world affairs, all of our troubles would soon be solved.

This heated climate makes militarism luxuriate, for the military solution is also the simple solution. I am not, of course, implying that the men of our military forces are of the extreme right. They are in the main patriotic, hard-working, worried men, but their parochial talents have been given too much scope in our topsy-turvy world. There is little in the education, training, or experience of most soldiers to equip them with the balance of judgment needed to play the political role they now hold in our society.

NOTES

1. Alexis de Tocqueville, *Democracy in America*, vol. 2 (New York: Harper & Row, 1965), p. 625.

44. The Vietnam Quagmire—How It All Began
DAVID HALBERSTAM

Journalist David Halberstam shows persuasively, both in this article and in his recent book, The Best and the Brightest, *how men of reason and exalted purpose made such drastic errors that the nation became bogged down in the Vietnam war, to the sorrow of Viet-*

SOURCE: David Halberstam, "How It All Began," *The Progressive*, 37 (April 1973), 15–18. Reprinted by permission of the author.

namese and American alike. Here he concentrates on the social conditions that prompted good men to make gross errors. Although our forces have returned from Vietnam, we have left there an evil legacy in the form of the mandarins, whom the French once used as a cover for exploiting the peasants, and whom we also used as our local agents. These mandarins now constitute the "democratic" government of South Vietnam.

Where, then, are the roots of it? How did it happen? How in fact could it happen? Did the roots invisibly grow while we still slept, watched the more visible crises mount at Berlin, in the Congo, in the Middle East? It did not, after all, just happen in February, 1965, when Lyndon Johnson, with the consent of those around him, began the bombing, or in July, 1965, when he first sent combat troops. Too much had been prepared long in advance. And why, if there was no great chorus of enthusiasm for what he was doing, was there such a mute acceptance of his course from the Congress, the press, the business community—indeed, the State Department itself?

Could we really have a country in the sixth enlightened decade of an enlightened and rational Twentieth Century, the United States, anti-colonial in its origins and traditions, pick up a colonial war where the French had left off without a single officer from the Department of State resigning? The answer is yes, we could. Why had the men who might have doubted been winnowed out, how had the course been set? Where had the damage been done? Why did intelligent, rational men go against the course of history, against, finally, common sense, so that the United States would end up in Vietnam, in the words of the late Bernard Fall, "walking in the same footsteps as the French, although dreaming different dreams"?

The answers, it seems to me, lie in the damage done to the Government, the Democratic Party, and the press as well by the Joseph McCarthy period, and by the general tensions created in the domestic reaction to the Cold War. To blame it all on McCarthy is far too simple, he was merely a crude symptom of the time, an accident looking for a place to happen, a name grafted on an era. Indeed, the fears that his name evokes had existed even before his famous speech in Wheeling, West Virginia, in February, 1950, and the foreign policy accommodations to those fears had already begun to take place.

I write of invisible decisions—that is, decisions made in another time, under other conditions, which seem so minor, so on the periphery of great events as to have no import in our lives. In Vietnam one of the most crucial of these decisions took place in May, 1950, before McCarthy was a household word, before the Korean war broke out: the decision to supply military aid to the French in Indochina. Secretary of State Dean Acheson's decision, not his successor, John Foster Dulles'. It was a fateful moment, for until then we had not supported the French cause. We had resisted the French claim that this was part of the great global struggle against world Communism, that the French were fighting for freedom in Vietnam, that their enemy was our enemy. From the very start, in 1945, we had refused French requests for troop ships to return the white colonial troops to Vietnam. Other requests for military aid had followed, and we had always rejected them. Acheson himself in the past had referred to the French cause as a colonial war, loath though he was to pressure the French to do anything about it. (The French, after all, were a serious European nation and Europe was a serious place; Asians were not serious enough to merit the tensions caused if the United States pressured the French over such a nasty little war.)

May, 1950, changed all that. Acheson threw the switch, deciding to give the French military support and therefore—even more important as far as American history was concerned—moral support. (One does not give military aid without legitimizing the cause as well.) His reasons were twofold. The first was his abiding concern to stop the Communists in Europe: Acheson felt that a strong Europe required a strong West Germany, and increasing German steel production was the best means of reviving that economy. The French had been recalcitrant, uneasy about mounting German strength; yet they desperately needed economic aid for Indochina. A deal was made, what Acheson later would call a simple *quid pro quo*: West German steel production could go up, and the United States would give major military assistance to the French in Vietnam. On May 8, after making his deal with Robert Schuman, Acheson announced:

> The United States Government, convinced that neither national independence nor democratic evolution exists in any area dominated by Soviet imperialism, considers the situation to be such as to warrant its according economic aid and military equipment to the Associated States of Indochina and France in order to assist them in restoring stability and permitting these states to pursue their peaceful and democratic development.

What would follow was two billion dollars in American aid, and growing American support; by 1954 we who had once doubted the cause were more enthusiastic for the French to continue than they were. It was no longer a colonial war but a just war, a war for freedom: the West against the Communists.

The second reason behind Acheson's decision was dictated to a large extent by American political terms. The storm against the Administration's Asia policies was already brewing; the Republicans, hungry after eighteen years out of office, were willing to exploit the fall of China, and to accuse the Administration of betraying American interests there. The word they used was "treason." China had gone Communist, not because of the fickle quality of history, but because the Democrats had harbored Communists in the State Department. Acheson was already on the defensive; he was trying to protect as best he could his favorites among the Asia people (John Carter Vincent, G. Walton Butterworth) from the head hunters. The smell of witch hunt was in the air. The first of the China security cases would be heard under Acheson, involving the brilliant John Service. Now Acheson was trimming; he had been charged with losing one country, and he did not want to endanger his President and his party by losing another. There was some foreign aid money left over after the fall of China, and Acheson would send a special commission to Vietnam in late 1949 to see if the French needed weapons and aid. Not surprisingly, the French said they did. By sending the mission, Acheson was a man asking the question in order to give his own answer.

This was an easy time to sell fear and demagoguery: The country had moved head first from isolationism into super-power status. The normal tensions between great powers were made more intense first by the addition of *ism* to the struggle—Communism versus capitalism—a factor which gave it a moral-religious distinction, and then by the added threat of the atomic bomb. It was a particularly dark chapter in American life: our foreign policy had become locked into an all-encompassing blind and total anti-Communism. Intelligence, enlightened self-interest, traditional anti-colonialism, and old-fashioned common sense—our guidelines in the past—had been supplanted by ideological purity and domestic fear. And if Acheson had accommodated to a certain degree, Dulles, who followed him, was far worse; he made peace quickly with the right, and his peace offering was the Asian experts and Asian office of the State Department. He did not want trouble with Congress and Asia was the price: in a move of historic proportion and appalling consequences, he opened the doors of his department to the loyalty and security people. Thus would American policy-making on Vietnam by poisoned by the McCarthy period, and vital organs—the Democratic Party and the Department of State—damaged beyond easy repair.

How do you estimate the damage done to the Democrats in the 1950s and 1960s? Can you calibrate the damage done to a party hiding from its past? How much was the political center moved from the liberal-left to the right, to what extent were a generation of leaders of the party forced to offer their own pledges toward the greater cause of anti-Communism? It became a party forced to demonstrate its credentials in foreign affairs instead of concentrating on domestic reform. Men like Chester Bowles and Adlai Stevenson were edged from the center of the party, too scarred by the struggles of the 1950s and the charges of the Republicans, no matter how erroneous those charges might be. By 1960 John Kennedy attained the nomination and the office by straddling the two main camps within the party and matching Nixon's Quemoy with his own Matsu. (This, despite earlier pledges to Bowles that the most important business in American life was reversing the madness of the China policy.)

So the Democrats, when they came to power in 1961, came pledged, if anything, to be more hard line than the Republicans in foreign policy, and they were nervous about any sign which might be seized upon by Nixon or Goldwater as a mark of weakness. Could Kennedy appoint a Secretary of State who might be charged with softness? No, he felt he could not; he chose the centrist Dean Rusk, who arrived with the imprimatur of Henry Luce, Foster Dulles, and Dean Acheson. Had Rusk, who had worked on China during the postwar years, ever been touched by the China business? Dick Goodwin asked a China hand while checking Rusk out for Kennedy. No, they never laid a glove on him, the China hand replied, and Goodwin was relieved. After the election, whenever Bowles or Stevenson talked to Kennedy about changing the China policy, the President would agree that it was in fact all madness, but there was nothing he could do right then, perhaps in the second term . . . It was all very disarming. The Kennedy Administration, so flashy, so sophisticated, accepted the norms of the Dulles years, norms set in the McCarthy period, though the world was vastly different. Kennedy, whose perceptions were better than most of those around him, did not intend to take any premature heat on Asia. He would do all these good things in the second term.

There was no second term, there was an assassination, and Lyndon Johnson became President. Even more than Kennedy, Johnson was a man affected by the McCarthy period. Though the official rationale for intervening in Vietnam was the domino theory, the fear of what had happened after the fall of China was far more immediate, and he was terrified of losing a country and seeing his Administration besieged from the right. Younger White House staff members discussing disengagement from Vietnam were told by Johnson that they were simply too young, they did not understand the emotional effect Asia had upon the Congress, how it could tear a Presidency apart. Again and again, to those in his inner circle questioning the course of the policy, he came back to the 1950s and the damage it had done. Truman and Acheson, he said, had lost China, and in losing China they had lost the Congress, and he, Lyndon Johnson, was not going to be the President who lost Vietnam and thus the Great Society.

There were others who seemed to share Johnson's fear. McGeorge Bundy, for instance (picked by Kennedy because he represented foreign policy excellence, but excellence which had not been damaged during the McCarthy period and was thus not soft), could rationalize his own support of a bombing campaign against the North on the grounds that even if it failed, the President would be able to say he had done all he could to save South Vietnam. John McNaughton, Secretary of Defense Robert McNamara's most trusted deputy, acting with McNamara's approval, asked Daniel Ellsberg to work on a paper discussing the possibilities for withdrawal. It was a paper, McNaughton insisted, that must be absolutely secret, and could not even be typed by a secretary. "You should be clear," he told Ellsberg in a particularly revealing conversation, "that you could be signing the death warrant to your career by having anything to do with calculations like these. A lot of people were ruined for less."

If this, then, was the atmosphere at the very top, what was it like for the men at the working level, and particularly for those Asia experts working for the State Department? Because that particular organ had been ravaged by the McCarthy years. The best of a generation—Service, Davies, Clubb, Vincent, Ludden, Emmerson—had been driven out, and now the younger Asia officers, having seen their superiors ruined, had only two courses open to them: either leave the foreign service, which many of them did, or stay at State but work in other areas, Latin America or Western Europe. So Asia was cleared of expertise; but if these men were out, who had taken their place? An altogether different breed: men willing to serve under the worst political and intellectual conditions, the hardest line anti-Communists in an area where anti-Communism as a basic precept of judgment was most dangerous. China, the most important nation in the area, was seen as a major international villain, a demonic yellow monster with blood dripping off its teeth, still working at Moscow's command. The smaller nations were not to follow their own development, to find their own place in the world, they were to become pawns of American foreign policy, extensions of Europe, bastions of anti-Communism. Vietnam was to become France; Laos, Italy. The split between Moscow and Peking simply could not be recognized, nor could its impact for U.S. foreign policy. Nationalism in the area could be recognized only under U.S. conditions and terms—our kind of nationalism.

The Kennedy choice of Ambassador Frederick Nolting for what was clearly one of the two or three most sensitive ambassadorial appointments of that era is revealing of the limits of the period. Nolting was not a bad man, he was simply uniquely unsuited for the job. He had never served in Asia, his experience was entirely European (NATO); he was chosen because he was good at getting along with the military. He was not by the wildest stretch of the imagination a man you would choose because he was sensitive to stirrings below the surface; rather, he was a man you chose because somehow he reassured you about what you were already doing. He seemed to symbolize the change that had come over American diplomacy in the decade after the McCarthy period, the career diplomat, who, instead of being able to listen, think, and evaluate a country on its terms, is replaced by a man who (a) will not cause trouble and become disputatious; (b) is there to make sure that the country can evolve to an American definition of itself and will not go Communist— the ambassador as doer, activist, team player. His entire embassy reflected him; there was an almost total unwillingness to try to define Vietnamese feelings in terms of Vietnamese nationalism, for fear of where it might take us and of the larger doubts that this might involve. Those on his staff who knew something about Vietnam and whose doubts were growing were extremely covert; Nolting made it clear early in his tour that he did not want to hear doubts, he wanted positive information; he would not sign on to critical reporting. This was discouragement enough, particularly since, for many of the middle-rank officials, the dangers of pessimism were already implicit; if the government fell, if the country went Communist, someone might trace through and in the reams of boring paper find a soft report, one doubting Diem and the anti-Communist cause.

Thus, in the State Department in the field there was an instinct not to look for reality, not to challenge myths which had been set in the Dulles years. And this was equally true back at home in State. The one issue that could not be mentioned was China, not even at Policy Planning, where officers were supposed to think in terms of the future. Rusk himself had seen many of his colleagues and friends destroyed by the McCarthy period and he was particularly sensitive to any mention of China from his subordinates. Kennedy did, through Averell Harriman, begin to unleash some new forces and new thinking in State's Far East office, but even here the limits were considerable. The only speech on China was given by Roger Hilsman *after* Kennedy was dead, the Secretary of State refused to let Harriman meet covertly with the Chinese in Geneva, and on Vietnam, one could criticize Diem, but that was as far as it went. The larger questions had to go unasked because the President did not want them asked. These were the root questions: Whether we should be there at all, whether under any conditions it could work, whether Ho was really a threat in terms of American national interest, and whether an anti-Communist government in Saigon was that much of an asset. A Democratic President still on the defensive did not want even interior dialogue on the question within his Government; in a town as gossipy as Washington, interior dialogue meant eventually press reports that the Government might be thinking the unthinkable on China.

And so it went. No one wanted to see, and no one wanted to listen. The poison injected in the political bloodstream in the early 1950s remained. No one in all those intervening years had really tried to combat the lies of our policy in Asia; there was a hope that if no one said anything, time would pass and these aberrations would simply go away. The Democratic Party leaders, themselves on the defensive, had merely avoided the issues left behind by McCarthy. Whether in fact the nation was the same country it had been in the mid-1950s is another question; but, in the minds of the Administration, the risks involved in finding out were simply too great. Decision-making in the 1960s was handled by men fearful of losing a country, fearful of being accused of being soft. The State Department was a badly damaged instrument, filled with fear and ignorance, devoted largely to the preservation of myths. Yet no one could admit this, could admit that the policy-making in this stylish and modern Administration was still mired down in a darker past. No wonder, then, that seemingly intelligent men made such unwise choices. It was all a Greek thing: as a nation we had stood by during the McCarthy period and allowed, with a kind of national consent, a group of witch hunters to destroy good men who had performed honorable public services. No one had challenged it then, nor challenged the legacy of what had happened. Now, a decade later, with the war in Vietnam, we got what we deserved.

45. Terror Makes No Fine Distinctions
THE NEW YORKER

This selection is the first of four concerned with various aspects of relatively recent frightening events that indicate the United States is in danger of becoming a police state. One of the features of the typical police state is that it "makes no fine distinctions." Therefore, those who fancy that they will escape the attention of malevolent officials very often fool only themselves. In a police state safety is not assured even by allying oneself with the authorities—when it suits their purpose, they don't hesitate to dispose of even their closest "friends."

Some observers, after getting over their shock at discovering that something called an enemy list was being kept at the White House, have taken comfort in the list's evident sloppiness. A number of friends of the President were on it, and the name of former Secretary of Defense Clark Clifford was misspelled ("Gifford"). The nation may have been heading in the direction of a police state, these observers argue, but at least it would have been an inefficient police state. They should take no comfort in that thought. Though the absence of any clear distinctions in the selection of people placed on the enemy list has some amusing aspects at first glance, it is in reality one more of the frightening things about the list. It is a great mistake to think that totalitarian regimes attack only their foes. Inefficiency, particularly in the form of indiscrimination in punishing political enemies, has been a virtual hallmark of twentieth-century totalitarianism. Totalitarian terror may begin with the singling out of a handful of supposed "subversives" (or "wreckers," as they were originally called in the Soviet Union), but it expands by degrees into every sphere of the lives of ordinary people, and soon reaches into the circles of the terrorizers themselves, who end by putting each other's names down on

SOURCE: "Notes and Comment," *The New Yorker* 44 (July 16, 1973), 21. Copyright © 1973 by The New Yorker Magazine, Inc. Reprinted by permission.

their enemy lists and shooting each other. In the purges in the Soviet Union during the nineteen-thirties, for example, the Communist Party, in whose name they were being carried out, was more heavily purged, perhaps, than any other group in the society; indeed, it very nearly succeeded in wiping itself out altogether. And now it is interesting to note that the Nixon men, as they made their first exploratory steps down the path toward totalitarian rule, began to wiretap each other almost as soon as they began to wiretap the opposition. One official rationalized Henry Kissinger's decision to wiretap his own aides with a pretty little piece of totalitarian logic: Kissinger had them bugged not because he mistrusted them, the official suggested, but because he *trusted* them and being so certain of their loyalty, knew that their trustworthiness would be reaffirmed when it was put to the test of the taps. In President Nixon's White House, then, to be tapped was a favor, since the tangible proofs of your loyalty provided by wiretap logs would increase your stature with the President and his most important aides. Of course, in a world in which you are tapped because you are trusted and tapped because you are mistrusted, no one escapes tapping.

Totalitarian indiscrimination, flowing, as it does, from an irrational and blinding fear, which knows no boundaries, is indeed "inefficient" in the narrow sense that it leads to the wholesale punishment of "innocent" people, including people who are completely uninvolved with politics. But this inefficiency is highly efficient in a broader sense, for by punishing people virtually at random a totalitarian regime keeps everyone, and not just its enemies, in a state of fear. Totalitarian indiscrimination gives the regime a reputation for an inhuman, godlike ruthlessness that ignores not only ordinary human moral distinctions but even the twisted distinctions put forward in the regime's own propaganda. That is why, when a police state is forming, anyone who fancies that he can win safety by allying himself with the regime is fooling himself. In many cases, it is the friends of the regime who turn out to be in the greatest danger of all, as the Nixon loyalists who have had their phones tapped or have discovered their names on the enemy list are beginning to learn. They are finding out what the Southeast Asian peasantry has known for a long time now: that American terror, like all other outbreaks of terror in our time, does not make fine distinctions. In our country, as elsewhere, once the police break down your door and start shooting, it isn't of any help that they can't spell your name.

46. The Watergate Putsch
SEYMOUR MELMAN

In this reprint of a pamphlet distributed by SANE *(officially called A Citizen's Organization for a Sane World), Seymour Melman shows how similar the Watergate participants were to those who have taken part in the classic political* Putsch. *Another observer has remarked that the Watergate revelations, despite their ugliness, may well have saved us from the evil designs of a regime that was marching steadily to the far Right. Because of Watergate, even the most politically naive have become less credulous, less willing to believe the claims of those "on high." Mr. Melman, co-chairman of* SANE, *is a Columbia University professor of industrial engineering; he authored the book* Pentagon Capitalism *in 1970.*

Watergate is the name of a political *putsch* that stalled, following a series of major successes. The known successes include: a secret war operated against Cambodia and Laos; the 1972 elections strongly manipulated; selling off the grain reserve of the U.S. to obtain electorally helpful favors from the Soviets (no objection to the Haiphong mining, a Moscow preelection welcome).

A *putsch* is a conspiratorial effort to seize total control of a government, using illegal methods and force if necessary. Behind the dramatic play of Watergate personalities featured in the media there has unfolded, at this writing, sufficient data to define the structure of a classical *putsch*. The facts are virtually undisputed. What remains unclear is the precise role of particular persons and the full scope of the operation.

While there is no space here for presenting the historical detail, I underscore the fact that, apart from the special features of each national history, every putschist feature identified here was present in the fascist takeovers in Germany and Italy. The point of this analysis is to inform and not to frighten, to enable us to identify without delay the crucial actions that must be taken to reverse the course of this *putsch* and to preclude another one from succeeding. It is simply not prudent to expect that the organizational, personal and technical failures of the Watergate *putsch* would be repeated. Here are twenty characteristics of the Watergate *putsch*:

1. Recruitment of a cadre of true believers who abdicate personal responsibility and place commitment to the leader's success and his orders at the top of their scale of values.

SOURCE: Seymour Melman, "The Watergate *Putsch*," *Sane World* 12 (September 1973), 1, 3. Reprinted by permission.

2. Organization of a secret police to handle political opponents in and out of government.
3. Infiltrating government departments with members of the putschist cadre to obtain the compliance of the older bureaucracies with the main goals of the putschist group.
4. Illegal uses of existing government police organizations in the service of the *putsch*.
5. Use of military organizations for carrying out covert operations that are in violation of law.
6. Illegal uses of various security agencies of government.
7. Exempting members of the putschist cadre and their agents from normal police and due process controls—using illegal methods including perjury and destruction of evidence.
8. Extortion of secret funds from businessmen for the operation of the *putsch*.
9. Threats to businessmen for non-compliance with money demands.
10. Business favors and special privileges to businessmen who cooperate with the *putsch*.
11. Agents provocateurs placed among opposing political groups.
12. Preparation of falsfied personal and political histories of opponents to mislead and confuse the general public.
13. Co-opting a part of the organized labor movement to give allegiance to the *putsch* and its leaders, and help create the facade of a "national front."
14. The use of government agencies to harass individuals and organizations that are actual or potential opponents.
15. Infiltration and disruption of organizations of political opponents to confuse and block their ordinary activities and thereby render them ineffectual.
16. Organization of a centralized government within the government to give the putschist leaders parallel machinery which can be used to control the regular departments and agencies of the government.
17. Repeated and confident affirmation of the existence of a threat to the security of the nation as a whole that justifies the elements of conspiracy and illegality in the *putsch*. In the absence of actual threats the actions of agents provocateurs are used to create necessary evidence.
18. Attempted manipulation of the courts to serve the *putsch* and its people.

19. Manipulation of the legislature to bend the law-making process to the goals of the *putsch*.

20. Organization of a conspiracy to do all the above while maintaining a facade of performing the ordinary, legal functions of government.

NAZIS TOOK OVER LEGALLY

It should be recalled that the Nazis came into office early in 1933 by proper constitutional means. Once having taken over the formal legal powers of the German Executive, they proceeded to grant themselves extraordinary powers which they used to centralize and concentrate power and implement the rest of the putschist operation. This was done with the help of a willing parliament, backed by a middle-class mass movement, most big business, and part of the working class.

The Nazis, unlike the Watergaters, had declared their political purposes and principal methods quite openly. It was all laid out for the public to read in Adolph Hitler's *Mein Kampf*. Richard Nixon's putschists also came into office by proper constitutional means, but by contrast with the Nazis our putschists carried with them a secret agenda. The contents of that political agenda began coming to light only as the press, Senate hearings, and court cases exposed the putschist process, including the operation of secret wars.

The Watergate *putsch* was facilitated by the already existing centralization of government power in the White House, including concentration of peak military, political, and economic authority. The Nazis, by contrast, had the problem of effecting concentration of power after they were named to office by President Hindenburg.

Since the consequence of a successful *putsch* would very likely be a militarized society along the lines of George Orwell's *1984*, it is prudent to regard the stalling of the Watergate putsch as a narrow escape that gave us a reprieve, an unknown length of time in which to try to see to it that a *putsch* cannot be undertaken once again.

What are some of the crucial requirements for this result? The critical target requirements for precluding a future *putsch* must be the dismantling and reduction of the massive centralization of military, political, and economic decision power that is now located in the White House and in the giant bureaucracy that it commands in the Pentagon.

The White House now includes a great array of agencies and sections that constitute a government within a government. The White House staff should be drastically reduced to a size appropriate to the President's personal secretariat. Other functions should be transferred to the various government departments or terminated altogether. The staff of several thousands should be cut to a few hundred.

The deflation of the military and allied security agencies requires reformulation of their missions with removal of capability for military takeovers—abroad or at home—and appropriate reductions in the tax funds made available to them. These actions, with collateral demystification of the pro-centralist and pro-war economy ideologies in American life, are key parts of the political movement away from authoritarianism and sustained war-making.

The Bill of Rights is still operative. There is no fascist mass movement in the U.S. Big Business is not unified behind the *putsch*. . . . There is a fighting chance.

47. Civil Liberties: The Crucial Issue
WILLIAM O. DOUGLAS

As indicated below, this article by Supreme Court Justice William O. Douglas originally appeared in Playboy. *Justice Douglas' willingness to have his words appear in such a publication has led to widespread criticism among those who, disliking what he stands for, hope to find some excuse for deriding him. But* Playboy *is not really an inappropriate place for a discussion of civil liberties. It is a prime function of such liberties, Justice Douglas points out, to ensure equality before the law. Like the poor, those who subscribe to the "Playboy philosophy" are often denied such equality. The philosophy asserts that all private, consensual sex acts between adults should be free of legal restraints, but officials repeatedly demonstrate a special prejudice against those accused of "perversion." More important, when those so accused are brought to trial, they are in no real sense "equal before the law"—again, as with the poor in general. The legal vulnerability of the powerless—if not adequately countered—will eventually play a prominent part in bringing about a total breakdown of the system, Justice Douglas concludes.*

Most modern constitutions contain promises of things that government must do for people. Our Constitution, an 18th Century product, guarantees no one such benefits as an education, social security or the right to work. It is not a welfare-state document. To the contrary, it specifies in some detail what government may *not* do to the individual. In other

SOURCE: William O. Douglas, "Civil Liberties: The Crucial Issue," *Playboy* 16 (January 1969), 93–4, 120, 223. Copyright © 1958 by William O. Douglas. Reprinted by permission.

words, it was designed to take government off the backs of people and majorities off the backs of minorities.

It stakes out boundaries that no executive, no legislature, no judiciary may violate. The "law and order" advocates never seem to understand that simple constitutional principle. An example will illustrate what I mean. The First Amendment says that government may not abridge the free exercise of religion. Suppose a city enacts an ordinance that provides that no minister may deliver a sermon without first obtaining a permit from the Department of Safety. To exact a license before the citizen may exercise a constitutional right is to abridge that right. No minister worth his salt would knuckle under. If he defied the ordinance, he would be acting in the best American tradition. If he were prosecuted, the unconstitutionality of the ordinance would be a complete defense. The person who concludes that a law is unconstitutional and defies it runs the risk, of course, that he guessed wrong. Yet his punishment is not thereby compounded. Law and order is the guiding star of totalitarians, not of free men.

This principle of civil disobedience can be appreciated only if the antecedents of our Constitution and Bill of Rights are understood.

The ideas of freedom, liberty and sovereignty of the individual reflected in the two documents come from a long stream of history. The ideas of political freedom trace at least as far back as the Athenian model. But the political freedom of classical Greece did not guarantee private freedom, which was first emphasized by the Romans through the development of natural law. The church added the tradition of a divine order and a set of precepts based on the integrity of the individual before God: the Reformation gave the individual a choice of religio-political orders. The divine right of kings—one form of the social contract—was successfully challenged by the end of the 17th Century. Rousseau's *Social Cotract* was a frontal assault.

But the single thinker who had the most direct impact on the framers of the Constitution was John Locke. Locke taught that morality, religion and politics should conform to God's will as revealed in the essential nature of man. God gave man reason and conscience as natural guides to distinguish between good and bad; and they were not to be restrained by an established church or by a king or a dynasty. Isaac Newton, who in 1687 published *Principia*, his great work, seemed to abolish mystery from the world and enable a rational mind to uncover the secrets of nature and nature's God. This parallel thought gave wings to Locke, who wrote:

> Men being . . . all free, equal and independent, no one can be put out of his estate, and subjected to the political power of another, without his consent. The only way whereby any one divests himself of his liberty and puts on the bonds of civil society is by agreeing with other men to join and unite into a community, for their comfortable, safe and peaceable living one amongst another, in a secure enjoyment of their properties and a greater security against any that are not of it. . . . When any

number of men have so consented to make one community or government, they are thereby presently incorporated and make one body politic, wherein the majority have a right to act and conclude the rest.

These ideas were well-known to our Colonists through the church as well as through Locke, Newton and many other writers. God, nature and reason were the foundations of politics and government; they were extolled in the Declaration of Independence and further distilled in constitutional precepts.

The foregoing is but an outline of the history of ideas behind the Constitution. They were translated into the body of Anglo-American law in a series of crucial test cases over a period of at least 400 years.

The political counterpart of heresy in the 16th Century was treason. The law of England allowed a man to be tried for treason if he "doth compass or imagine the death" of the king. This was called "constructive treason," for the accused did not have to lift his hand against the king to be guilty; all he need do was wish the king were dead. As a result, treason is narrowly defined in our Constitution: "Treason against the United States shall consist only in levying war against them, or in adhering to their enemies . . ." and the proof required is very strict. That clause is the product of the philosophy of Madison and Jefferson. Madison wanted treason narrowly defined, because history showed that "new-fangled and artificial treasons" were the "great engines" by which partisan factions "wreaked their alternate malignity on each other." Jefferson had the like view, pointing out that the definitions of treason often failed to distinguish between "acts against government" and "acts against the oppressions of the government." Madison and Jefferson are strangers to our law-and-order school, whose spokesmen go so far these days as to call dissent to our Vietnam policy "treason."

In the 17th Century, it was the practice to force citizens to make loans to the British crown, failing which the citizen would be jailed and languish there without bail. Thomas Darnel met that fate in 1627. From his prison, he applied for a writ of habeas corpus, the conventional way in those days of testing the legality of a confinement. The case was argued before judges who were appointees of the king, serving at his pleasure. They ruled that they were required to "walk in the steps of our forefathers," that the word of the king was sufficient to hold a man, saying, "We trust him in great matters." This case resulted in the petition of Right of 1628, which led to vesting in Parliament, rather than in the king, the authority to levy taxes; and it also established the prisoner's *right to bail*.

The legislative branch was also a source of oppression. A bill of attainder is an act of the legislature punishing individuals or members of a group without a *judicial trial*. Its vice is that it condemns a person by legislative fiat without the benefit of a trial having all the safeguards of due process of law. English history, as well as our own history between 1776 and 1787, is replete with instances where the legislature, by its own fiat, subjected men to penalties and punishments. The Constitution abolishes bills of attainder outright, both at the state and at the Federal level.

The foregoing are merely examples of how the sovereignty of the individual was, historically speaking, jeopardized by acts of all branches of Government—the Executive, the Legislative and the Judicial.

The fear of our forefathers was also a fear of the majority of the people who from time to time might crush a minority that did not conform to the dominant religious creed or who in other ways were ideological strays.

One episode that occurred in this nation just before the 1787 Philadelphia Convenion is illustrative. Times were hard in 1786. A post-War depression had hit the country. The state legislatures were swept by agrarian influences. Debtors wanted relief. There was no strong central government. Only Congress, under the feeble Articles of Confederation, had national authority, and it was not in a position to act decisively.

Up at Northampton, Massachusetts, in August 1786, Daniel Shays moved into action. His armed group seized the courthouse in order to put an end to legal proceedings for the collection of debts. The example at Northampton was followed in other parts of the state, about 2000 armed men joining Shays. Courts were paralyzed. In September, Shays' men moved on Springfield and overawed the court with their claims that their leaders should not be indicted and that there should be a moratorium on the collection of debts. They also insisted that the militia be disbanded. The stakes were high, because at Springfield there was a Federal arsenal filled with artillery, guns and ammunition, which Shays planned to take. The decisive engagement took place on January 25, 1787, the Shays group being routed by militia equipped with Federal cannon.

Shays' Rebellion gave impetus not only to a strong central Government but also to checks and restraints on populism. The mercantile, financial and large landed interests were getting tired of talk of the rights of man; they were becoming concerned with the protection of their property. Too much democracy in the state governments, it was argued, was bringing bad times on the country. Massachusetts, New Hampshire and Rhode Island were said to be disintegrating. General Henry Knox, in the mood of our modern law-and-order men, wrote Washington from Massachusetts in the fall of 1786: "This dreadful situation, for which our Government has made no adequate provision, has alarmed every man of principle and property in New England."

Though Shays' Rebellion was shortly put down, the populist or agrarian forces remained in control of some state legislatures and repudiation of debts remained a threat. Majorities in state legislatures ruled without restraint. The commercial, financial and landed interests moved to Philadelphia for the Constitutional Convention in an antidemocratic mood. A republican form of government emerged that, to use the words of Madison, was designed "to protect the minority of the opulent against the majority." This majority, Madison said on another occasion, might well be the landless proletariat.

Numerous barriers were written into the Constitution designed to thwart the will of majorities. As Charles A. Beard said in his monumental work *An Economic Interpretation of the Constitution of the United States,* those who campaigned for ratification of the Constitution made "their most cogent arguments" to the owners of property "anxious to find a foil against the attacks of leveling democracy."

While the House was to be elected for a short term by the people, Senators (until the 17th Amendment) were selected by the state legislatures; and the President was picked for a fixed term by electors chosen by the people. Thus, a measure of assurance was granted that *majority* groups would not be able to unite against the *minority* propertied interests. Moreover, amendment of the Constitution was made laborious: Two thirds of both the Senate and the House were to propose amendments; three fourths of the states were to ratify them. A final check or balance was an independent judiciary named by the President, approved by the Senate and serving for life.

The "minority of the opulent" were also protected when it came to the Bill of Rights, as in the provisions in the Fifth Amendment that "private property" could not be taken for a "public purpose" without payment of "just compensation."

But the Bill of Rights went much, much further. It was concerned with all minorities, not only the minority of the opulent. Government was taken off the backs of all people and the individual was made *sovereign* when it came to making speeches and publishing papers, tracts and books. Those domains had "no trespassing" signs that government must heed.

Great battles have raged over those guarantees. Peaceful and orderly opposition to the Government—even by Communists—is, of course, constitutionally protected. Chief Justice Charles Evans Hughes said: "The maintenance of the opportunity for free political discussion to the end that government may be responsive to the will of the people and that changes may be obtained by lawful means, an opportunity essential to the security of the republic, is a fundamental principle of our constitutional system."

American law also honors protests, whether they are in the form of letters to the editor, picketing, marches on the statehouse or rallies to whip up action. As already noted, police historically have arrested dissenters for "disorderly conduct" and "breach of the peace," often using these devices to suppress an unpopular minority. But such charges are no longer permissible at either the state or Federal level, though the law-and-order men often try to use "vagrancy" or other misdemeanors to suppress dissent or to promote racism.

Government is also constrained against interfering with one's free exercise of religion. A man can worship how and where he pleases. Government at times has preferred one religion over another, giving it privileges as respects marriages, baptisms and the like, and even putting some prelates on the public payroll. The Bill of Rights bans this practice by prohibiting the "establishment" of any religion by the Government.

It was the pride of British tradition that a man's home was his castle. Even the king could not enter without legal process. On this side of the Atlantic, British officers had ransacked homes (and offices as well) under search warrants that were good for all time and for all kinds of evidence. This led to the Fourth Amendment, which, in general, requires an officer making a search to have a warrant issued by a judge on a showing of probable cause that a crime has been committed. And the warrant must describe with particularity the scope of the search and the articles or person to be seized. Modern technology has developed electronic devices that can record what goes on in the sanctuary of a home without entering the home in any conventional sense. They, too, have now been included within the Fourth Amendment. Yet the law-and-order propagandists would brush aside the Fourth Amendment and use any short cut to convict any unpopular person.

The much misunderstood self-incrimination clause of the Fifth Amendment had a similar history: "No person . . . shall be compelled in any criminal case to be a witness against himself." At one time in England, the oath that one takes to tell the truth was used against the accused with devastating effect. If he refused to take the oath, he was held in contempt and punished. If he took the oath and then refused to answer a question, the refusal was taken as a confession of the thing charged in the question. Thus were men compelled to testify against themselves.

A widely heralded defiance of this practice was that of John Lilburne, who was charged with sending scandalous books into England. He refused to be examined under oath, saying that the oath was "both against the law of God and the law of the land." He announced that he would never take it, "though I be pulled to pieces by wild horses." Lilburne was held in contempt, publicly whipped, fined and placed in solitary confinement. That was in 1638. On February 13, 1645, the House of Lords set aside that judgment as "against the liberty of the subject and law of the land and Magna Charta." And in 1648, Lilburne was granted damages for his imprisonment.

The idea spread to this country. The Puritans who came here knew of the detested oath that Lilburne refused to take. They, too, had been its victims. *The Body of Liberties,* adopted in 1641 by Massachusetts, afforded protection against self-incrimination either through torture or through the oath. The high-handed practices of the royal governors who believed in law and order and who sought to compel citizens to accuse themselves of crimes also whipped up sentiment for the immunity. A majority of the colonists, therefore, as part of their programs for independence, adopted bills of rights that included the immunity against self-incrimination. Later, it was written into the Fifth Amendment and into most state constitutions.

The immunity has been broadly interpreted. It extends to all manner of proceedings in which testimony is taken, including legislative committees. It was early held by the Supreme Court to give immunity from testifying not only to acts or events that themselves constitute a crime or that are elements of a crime but also to things that "will tend to criminate him" or subject him to fines, penalties or forfeitures. As Chief Justice John Marshall put it at the beginning, immunity protects the witness from supplying any "link" in a chain of testimony that would convict him. Yet in spite of this long history, the law-and-order propagandists denounce the decisions that forbid the police from using coercion to obtain confessions from people in custody.

The protection against double jeopardy, the right to counsel, the right to confront the person who accuses one, the guarantee against cruel and unusual punishment—these all have a similar specific and detailed history of abuse by government. Each reflects a clear and calculated design to prevent government from meddling with individual lives.

The law-and-order people say that "criminals" and "Communists" deserve no such protection. But the Constitution draws no line between the good and the bad, the popular and the unpopular. The word is "person," which, of course, includes "aliens." *Every* person is under the umbrella of the Constitution and the Bill of Rights. The Bill of Rights purposely makes it difficult for police, prosecutors, investigating committees, judges and even juries to convict anyone. We know that the net that often closes around an accused man is a flimsy one. Circumstantial evidence often implicates the innocent as well as the guilty. Some countries have the inquisitorial system, in which the criminal case is normally made out from the lips of the accused. But our system is different; it is accusatorial. Those who make the charge must prove it. They carry the burden. The sovereignty of the individual is honored by a presumption of innocence.

The principle of *equality* entered our constitutional system with the Civil War amendments, which banned discrimination based on race, creed, color or poverty. So today we stand for both *liberty* and *equality*. The Russians who protested the 1966 Ukrainian trials came out strong for *liberty*: "The highest saturation of material goods, without free thought and will," creates "a great prison in which the food rations of prisoners are increased." Whatever continent one visits, he finds man asserting his sovereignty—and usually receiving punishment for doing so. There are few places in the world where man can think and speak as he chooses and walk with his chin held high. Yet in spite of our commitment to both, we are confronted with tremendous internal discontent. Some are in rebellion only to obtain control over existing institutions so that they may use them for their own special or selfish ends. But most of the discontent, I think, comes from individuals who clamor for sovereign rights—not rights expressed in laws but rights expressed in jobs and in other dignified positions in our society. We face civil disobedience on a massive scale.

Civil disobedience, though at times abused, has an honored place in our traditions. Some people refuse to pay taxes because the money raised is for a purpose they disapprove. That is *not* a permissible course of conduct; for, by and large, the legislative branch has carte blanche to prepare budgets and levy taxes. It would paralyze government to let each taxpayer exercise the sovereign right to pay or not to pay, depending on whether he approves of the social, economic or political program of those in power. The same is true, in general, of most other laws imposed on the citizen, whether it be observing a speed law or obeying a zoning ordinance or a littering regulation.

Gandhi's much-publicized civil disobedience was quite different. It expressed a universal principle. Gandhi had no political remedy to right a wrong. Disobedience of the law embodying the wrong was his only recourse. Colonial India, like Colonial America, was under a foreign yoke. Regulations were often imposed from overseas or taxes exacted by the fiat of the colonial ruler. The subject had to submit *or else*. "Taxation without representation" was one of the complaints of both Sam Adams and Mahatma Gandhi. Our Declaration of Independence stated the philosophy—all men are created equal; they are endowed by their Creator with certain "inalienable rights." Governments derive their just powers from "the consent of the governed"; and whenever a form of government becomes "destructive to those ends, it is the right of the people to alter or abolish it." Thus, the right of revolution is deep in our heritage. Nat Turner did not get the benefit of our Declaration of Independence. But he moved to the measure of its philosophy. These days, some people are caught in a pot of glue and have no chance to escape through use of a political remedy. Civil disobedience, therefore, evolves into revolution and is used as a means of escape.

Revolution is therefore basic in the rights of man. Where problems and oppression pile high and citizens are denied all recourse to political remedies, only revolution is left. Sometimes revolution with violence is the only remedy. Violence often erupts these days in Latin America and Southeast Asia, where feudal and military regimes hold people in a vise, making it impossible for them to be freed from oppression by the political processes. In some nations, a trade-union organizer is considered an enemy and is shot. So is a person who tries to organize the peasants into cooperatives. In those extreme situations, there is no machinery for change, except violence.

We have had civil disobedience accompanied by violence, the bloodiest one being the Civil War. Prior to that, there was the widespread rebellion under John Adams against the Alien and Sedition Acts, which made it a crime to utter any false or malicious statement about the nation, the President or Congress. The Virginia and Kentucky Resolutions called them a "nullity," because—by reason of the First Amendment—Congress may pass no law abridging freedom of speech or press. Those laws expired under Jefferson and for years the country reimbursed the victims for the wrongs done.

The Embargo Act was a self-blockade, in the sense that it forbade the departure of any ships from American ports to foreign countries. Jefferson tried in vain to enforce it, and it was repealed in 1809.

In World War One, there were about 300,000 draft dodgers, in spite of the fact that Congress passed a declaration of war.

Some of those episodes were accompanied by violence and many people were fined or imprisoned for their misdeeds. During those crises, the majority clamored for conformity. The minority, impatient at the existence of laws they deemed unjust, took matters into their own hands and did not wait until the power to correct the abuse at the polls could be exercised.

Today the dissenters, both black and white, claim that the changes needed to admit the lower fourth of our people into an honored place in our society are being thwarted. There is a growing feeling that the existing political parties are not likely instruments of change. The colleges' and universities' administrations, in general, walk more and more to the measure of traditional thought and have lost their revolutionary influence. The Cold War flourishes, diminishing our overseas potential and making the military the most potent force in our lives and in our economy. The Puritan ethic—hard work and industry will guarantee success—is not valid in a system of private enterprise that is less and less dependent on labor. For many, the only recourse for employment is in the public sector; yet blueprints for an expanding public sector are hardly ever in the public view. Racial discrimination takes an awful toll, as partially evidenced by the fact that the average annual income of whites who go to work at the end of the eighth grade tends to be higher than the average annual income of blacks who go on to college and enter the professions.

The crises these days are compounded because the *real* dissenters from the principle of equality in our laws and in the Constitution are often the establishment itself—sometimes a municipal, county or state government; sometimes slumlords allied with corrupt local machines; sometimes finance companies or great corporations or even labor unions. That is to say, these existing institutions often ask minorities to conform to practices and customs that are unconstitutional. People are apt to overlook the fact that those who make such a request are the offenders, not the vociferous minorities who demand their rights.

Rebellion by members of the establishment against full equality cannot be met with apathy and inaction, for that is the stuff out of which violent revolutions are made. Blacks and whites must join hands in momentous programs of political action. Those who put law and order above liberty and equality are architects of a new fascism that would muzzle all dissenters and pay the individuals in our lower strata to remain poor, obedient and subservient.

Unprecedented civic action is needed. When my friend Luis Muñoz Marín first ran for governor of Puerto Rico, he actually drafted and had printed and circulated the precise laws he would have enacted when elected. He was elected and the laws were passed. Those who march need specific proposals in their hands—proposals to put an end to a particular injustice. India, when dealing with the explosive problem of the untouchables, required about 15 percent of all matriculating students and about 15 percent of all government employees to be drawn from those ranks. While the maximum age for taking examinations for government service was generally 24 years, it was increased to 27 years in the case of the untouchables. And this once-abhorred group also has a certain minimum number of seats reserved for it in the national parliament and in the state legislatures.

We need to think in terms as specific as those in dealing with our own minorities, whether black or white. No one today is on the side lines. We are all caught up in a tremendous revolutionary movement. It starts with a demand for equality in educational and employment opportunities. It extends to a removal from our laws of all bias against the poor. It embraces a host of other specifics that will, if faced frankly and adopted, make a viable and decent society out of our multiracial, multireligious, multiideological communities—and both preserve the sovereignty and honor the dignity of each and every individual.

48. The American Myth is Dead
DAVID McREYNOLDS

The author of this selection is a journalist. He works full time for War Resisters International and writes regularly for WIN *magazine. The book from which both this and selection 55 are taken is composed of McReynolds' columns from* WIN. *Judging from his writings, David McReynolds is a marvelously gentle, humane person, but he is not sloppily sentimental. As in the following piece, and in his other selection, he writes with vigor, calling the proverbial spade a spade, dammit, a spade.*

... The American myth is dead.

Those under thirty may not realize the extent to which America, from the time of its inception, fascinated and radicalized the rest of the world. Students see America through the dark glass of war and racism. But, in

SOURCE: David McReynolds, *We Have Been Invaded by the 21st Century* (New York: Praeger Publishers, 1970), pp. 15–18. Copyright © 1970 by Praeger Publishers, Inc., New York. Excerpted and reprinted by permission.

1776, our Declaration of Independence and, later, our Bill of Rights helped shape the politics of Latin America, Asia, and Europe. We were, then, as much a "revolutionary fact" as Cuba is today to Latin America. We were an open society, without rigid classes, and with mobility between classes (always excepting the black American, who was part of a *caste* system from the beginning, never a part of a class structure). We were noninterventionist regarding other nations (simply because we were too weak to do anything else—the doctrine of nonintervention being invariably the doctrine of shrewd but weak powers).

To a Europe rigidly bound by classes, the United States was a door into Utopia. Even in the twentieth century, American history influenced African and Asian radicals. The constitution of North Vietnam was patterned after the American Declaration of Independence. I know that America was not so benevolent as it seemed to others. I know that Tom Jefferson kept slaves, that we slaughtered tens of thousands in the Philippines, that we meddled in Cuba, and "invented" the nation of Panama. One could go on. The point here is not what the facts were, but what the myth was. And the American myth had an extraordinary power that every nation envied. Only one other nation in recent history has drawn so deeply on the loyalty and faith of men and women distant from her borders, and that is the Soviet Union. Stalin, Hungary, and, finally, Czechoslovakia did for the Soviet Union what racism, assassination, and Vietnam did for us.

Europe watched Southern cops club down women and then found, in the mid-1960's, that the liberal North was no better, as tanks cruised the streets of the nation's capital and troops moved into Detroit. Racism was no longer a hidden issue, something everyone knew was there and about which we all felt badly. Suddenly, racism was Molotov cocktails, machine guns, snipers, broken windows, and kids running with radios, shoes, TV sets. And black bodies, lying in pools of blood, in Watts, Detroit, Newark, Washington.

More important, I think, were the assassinations. I do not think most Americans realize that our "level of violence" has always been unusually high. If we lump together murder and suicide and count that as the "violence index" we find the United States to be a world leader. There is a strange quirk of murder in America's head, like some spider in the darkness, and that quirk broke through in the 1960's. Medgar Evers, John F. Kennedy, Malcolm X, Martin Luther King, Jr., Robert Kennedy. And, in an eerie finish to the decade, the murder of Joseph Yablonski, on New Year's Eve, ushered the 1970's in with blood.

No other democratic society has a record of political murder that can equal ours in the 1960's. If no one else was killed, if all our wars ended, and if racism vanished—if all this happened tomorrow—it would be twenty years before the world would trust us again. But our murders are not done; they breed on one another.

Vietnam is the third factor that destroyed world confidence in us.

Youth in America feel this is a war of unique evil. They feel this because they are ignorant of history, having disdained its study. German slaughter of the Jews exceeded by many times our murder of Vietnamese. Soviet Russia, it is generally agreed, killed millions of her own people during the Stalinist period. England watched without any great concern while hundreds of thousands of Irish perished in the famines that hit Ireland in 1848. And even in the 1960's, the death toll in Biafra exceeded that in Vietnam.

. . .

The problem is not that Vietnam is unique, but that, in the eyes of the world, America is no longer unique. We are able to be as brutal as the Soviets, as murderous as the Nazis, as complacent as the British. We are just another empire, murdering, oppressing, imprisoning.

But, if our image has changed for the world, it has also changed for ourselves, and the 1960's were the decade when unquestioning patriotism died. In the bars of Middle America, one can see this sign: "If your heart is not in America, get your ass out." Or sometimes the sign above the bar, in slowly fading red, white, and blue, says, "America—Love It or Leave It." The response of our youth is to say, "America—Fix It or Forget It."

. . .

If there is any special decency to America, it is demonstrated by the disloyalty of our youth. The German youth under Hitler obeyed orders to the end, killing Jews, Communists, and civilians, with the pride of our own Special Forces. Every country can find men for the Green Berets, but Hitler found a nation of Green Berets, unquestioningly loyal and patriotic. Our youth, confronted by a murderous war, resisted. By their very disloyalty to the state, our youth demonstrated, unwittingly and against their will, the force of a national tradition that included slavery, but also Thoreau; Teddy Roosevelt, but also Eugene Victor Debs.

Demography and Ecology

Part X

The next four readings illustrate some important factors that concern those interested in the two sociological subfields known as **demography** and **human ecology**. These specialties are often grouped together because both concentrate on the conditions and trends affecting humans in their environment. Demographers focus on population, with particular reference to birth, death, and migration rates; while the center of interest for human ecologists is the relationship between people and their physical surroundings.

49. Malthus in Retrospect: The Stork Visits Dorking—1766
ROBERT C. COOK

Nearly two centuries ago, the British clergyman Thomas Malthus predicted an inevitable, fatal collision between population growth and available food supplies. Although incorrect as to precise timing, his gloomy forecast is apparently coming true before our eyes. The energy crisis and world-wide food shortages are only two of many indications that humankind is caught in a trap from which there seems to be no escape. If this message came from prophets of doom alone, there would be grounds for discounting it. But now it also comes from cautious scientists such as Robert Cook, the author of the accompanying article. Mr. Cook, who has broad training in genetics and demography, is the editor of Population Bulletin, *which is published by the Population Reference Bureau, Inc.*

Thomas Robert Malthus, often regarded as an anti-Cupid, was born on St. Valentine's Day, February 14, 1766. (Sources differ: some give his date of birth as February 13.) Outside the circle of his family and their friends, his appearance as a new member of the human race went unnoticed. But 32 years later, Malthus's growing interest in the proliferation of mankind, as set forth in his *Essay on the Principle of Population,* wrenched him from comfortable obscurity and set off a tumultuous controversy which has continued even to this day, two hundred years after his birth.

This debate centers around a simple enough proposition: that there exists a tendency for population to press on the means of subsistence.

SOURCE: Robert C. Cook, "Malthus in Retrospect: The Stork Visits Dorking—1766," *Population Bulletin* 22 (February 1966), 1–5. Reprinted by permission.

Malthus formulated this concept: if unchecked, populations had a built-in tendency to increase geometrically—as does money at compound interest.

Malthus equated this to the ascending powers of 2: 1, 2, 4, 8, 16, 32, etc. The "doubling time" for human populations he set at every 25 years —an oversimplification, but no exaggeration, for all that.

The means of subsistence—the primary element being food—had no such built-in multiplier. That the quantity of food could be doubled was certainly not beyond the realm of possibility. That it could be doubled again—and as quickly—appeared to him to be well-nigh impossible.

Malthus's basic premise was elementary to the point of being axiomatic. Obviously, no population of living organisms—be they men or mice—can exist beyond its "means of subsistence." The primary limiting factor is food: the ultimate limit is space. This is the case on occasion in the periodic population explosions experienced by certain species of rodents. Even though food is adequate, the unbearable crowding of a growing multitude triggers compulsive migrations into the sea.

Malthus's "principle of population" grew out of concern with a problem as old as time. "For ye have the poor always with you," Christ said. They were a multitude in Malthus's day. Now, a century and a half later, President Johnson is in the midst of a gargantuan "war on poverty" dedicated to accomplishing what neither prayer nor good works nor legislative fiat has ever managed before.

Poverty was very much in the minds of Englishmen by the end of the 18th Century. The poor laws and the corn laws, dating back to the time of the first Queen Elizabeth attempted to deal with poverty symptomatically. In a shifting and urbanizing world on the threshold of a new era, they were increasingly inadequate.

That something had to be done about poverty was generally agreed. The Establishment was concerned that growing misery could ignite fires of revolution, sparked by a France in turmoil only 21 miles away. Liberal reformers—among them Godwin, Bentham, Hume, and Owen—were busy elaborating roseate plans to establish a new Utopia.

Malthus was concerned with the roots rather than with the branches of this perennial evil: *"How to provide for those who are in want, in such a manner as to prevent a continual increase of their numbers, and of the proportion which they bear to the whole society."* [The italics are Malthus's.]

Malthus took up his pen to warn that high-flown idealism in the hands of reformers, bemused with alluring theories, was not calculated to decrease the numbers of the poor nor to improve their condition. That hunger had been endemic in England during much of the 18th Century provided a somber backdrop for the controversy generated by Malthus.

By reason of his background and the rigid theology which was his heritage, Malthus was able to accept, apparently with minor humanitarian qualms, the action of direct and ruthless "positive checks," famine, disease, and war as the ultimate and irrevocable and divinely ordained determinants of population growth.

Malthus was quite aware that an alternative solution existed, but this he looked upon with aversion akin to horror. This was the possibility that fertility could be checked by human action. The prudential checks—still seen as a solution by the Roman Catholic Church—he fully approved of, namely, delayed marriage and rigid premarital continence He recognized "vice" as a significant factor in reducing the rate of population growth. In a deep moral penumbra, he alluded to certain "improper arts"—quite clearly contraception—which he considered to be no better than "vice"; perhaps even worse.

In a variety of ways, the "affair Malthus" is rich in paradoxes. As Victor Hugo said, nothing can check an idea whose time has come. Malthus's "principle of population" is a notable example of a badly timed idea. It aggravated and infuriated. It challenged men's minds. Its axiomatic base was bolstered with a rickety supporting structure. And the rigid feudalistic frame of reference in which most of Malthus's discourse was cast repelled acceptance of the very important and significant and relevant parts of his writings.

He expected England and her neighbors to be plagued with mounting hunger. Famine had been endemic in Europe for centuries. Populations were growing, and a grim day of reckoning seemed close at hand. In the 19th Century, the countries of the Western industrial world were to witness a multiplication of people, the like of which Malthus could not have imagined. This was accompanied by an unprecedented improvement in the level of living of the population. A wave of vast and varied technological improvisation badly upset Malthus's schedule.

The substitution of heat-energy for muscle and water power quickly brought about an industrial revolution, and greatly increased productivity. The iron horse and iron ships shrank the continents and made millponds of the oceans. For a time the problem of on-the-spot subsistence was bypassed. Europe could beg the question of multiplying mouths and of the food to fill them by turning to other continents for sustenance.

Now, 168 years after the publication of the famous *Essay*, a new day of reckoning seems parlously near at hand. Recent developments in Asia, Africa, and Latin America strongly suggest that in the century and a half since Malthus took pen in hand, mankind has gone full circle. The collision between geometrical multiplication of people and arithmetical increase in means of subsistence was averted for a time. But the basic problem of those in want—and acutely in want—for the essentials of survival has not been resolved.

There was a time—and not very long ago—when the cornucopia philosophy of indefinite abundance was quite generally accepted. The Food and Agriculture Organization of the United Nations (FAO), established in 1945, rode the crest of the wave of abundance in its early years. Its first Director-General, Sir John Boyd-Orr, wrote in 1952:

> Can the earth provide food on a health standard for this increased number? The author gives well-authenticated facts to show that there is no

physical difficulty in doubling or redoubling the world food supply. If the farmers fail us, the chemist has already shown the way to synthetic food. The only practical limitations to food production are the amount of capital and labor human society is willing to devote to it.

But in the last hundred years the rather brutal mercantile age fighting for profits at whatever expense to their fellow men has been with increasing rapidity changing to a social age in which both political and economic freedom are beginning to be regarded as the inalienable rights of every human being. If, by some miracle, there could be an absolute guarantee that there would be no war for fifty years, the next generation would see human society well on the way to a world of peace and plenty, with hunger, poverty and preventable disease, which have always afflicted the majority of mankind, banished forever from the earth.

The food inventories of the U.S. Department of Agriculture, published about that time, and in the face of a crisis of local over-production and primitive distribution, took a hopeful view of the future. For a time, per capita food production, world-wide, actually showed a hopeful improvement.

This rosy optimism has collapsed since 1960. A recent Department of Agriculture report sees very little prospect of a quick increase in world agricultural yield:

> Given the projected high population growth rates of nearly all countries in Asia, Africa, and Latin America, the limited possibilities for expanding the cultivated area in most of the densely populated countries, and the lack of success in generating a yield takeoff, it does not appear likely that the downward trends in per capita food output now in evidence in these regions can be easily arrested. Barring a rise in the death rate due to widespread malnutrition in these regions, projections show the fastest population increase in history over the next 10 years. Failure to arrest the downward trend in per capita food output in these regions will leave two alternatives: (1) a continuing decline in consumption levels (narrowing the already thin margin between current consumption levels and survival levels); or (2) growing dependence on food imports—if imports are available.

The futility of attempting to provide for open-ended population growth is now recognized by Lord Boyd-Orr's successor, the present Director-General of FAO, Dr. Bimay R. Sen. He recently called the next 35 years "a most critical period in man's history." He warned, "Either we take the fullest measures both to raise productivity and to stabilize population growth, or we will face disaster of an unprecedented magnitude."

FAO data show that, for the world as a whole, population is increasing faster than food. There has been no gain in per capita food production since 1958–59. Dr. Sen reported that between 1959 and 1964 population in Latin America increased by 11.5 percent, while food production rose by only 6.5 percent. In the Far East, population grew by nearly 10 percent during the same period; food production went up by only 8.5 percent.

Before World War II, the less-developed nations exported 11 million tons of grain annually to the developed nations. As their populations grew, developing countries ceased to export. By 1964, they were *importing* an estimated 25 million tons of grain. The only large pool of excess food in the world today is in the United States and Canada.

A National Seminar on the world food outlook with special reference to the role of the United States was held in July 1965. The report of this conference states:

> ... Some countries of Latin America, for example Brazil, are also food importers, but Argentina, Uruguay and Mexico are net exporters; for Latin America as a whole, imports and exports are just about in balance, but serious imbalances exist locally ...
>
> Roughly half the total food imports of the developing countries in 1965 will come from the U.S. on more or less concessional terms under the Food for Peace program. Thus, in thinking about the future of this program, one basic consideration must be an estimate of the future food needs of the developing countries, and the extent to which their needs may have to be met by food exports from developed countries.
>
> Overall net food imports supply 4% of food consumed in the developing countries. While the percentage seems small, these imports are critically important in supplying food to the cities, to areas of more than average shortage, and to the extremely poor, and in stabilizing food prices in the recipient countries.
>
> There are two reasons why the world food deficit could not be made up entirely by imports: (1) the needed increase per capita in the developing countries could only be obtained by a large increase in agricultural production, since agriculture is the basis of their economics; (2) neither the farm capacity of the developed nations nor the world's shipping and distribution facilities are adequate for the large international food transfers that would be needed.

What these words say is that two hundred years after Malthus's birth, the problem he addressed himself to has not been solved: "to provide for those in want"—and acutely in want. The new powers which "proved Malthus wrong" have been exploited without understanding their limitations, and with no real appreciation of the impact of the reproductive urge in an era of declining mortality and increasing life expectancy.

To evoke science-fiction solutions to solve the crisis is not helpful. Great gains can unquestionably be made in increasing food production, worldwide. At best this will be a slow process involving education, the development of adapted varieties of animals and plants and very large capital expenditures for fertilizers, insecticides, agricultural machinery, food storage facilities, etc.

Malthus's approach—identifying the basic elements essential to a solution and adopting practical steps to implement them—is badly needed in a world where 1.7 billion men, women and children are perilously close to starvation.

50. Are Capitalism and the Conservation of a Decent Environment Compatible?

HARRY M. CAUDILL

It has become almost commonplace to observe that humankind is confronted with an environmental crisis. Many have heard the warnings so often they have become almost blasé about them. Perhaps they would be less so if they were fully aware that some of the causes of the crisis may not be reformable in the time left to us. One of the prime causes, for example, is the capitalistic economic system that is the bedrock of major segments of the industrialized world. The essence of capitalism is profit, which is defined as the excess of income over expense. One of the requirements of a profit-making system is constant growth, expansion, and ever more efficient exploitation of resources. In contrast, the preservation of nature depends on harmony and stability. Thus, as explained by Harry M. Caudill in the accompanying article, our economic system and the forces of nature are on a fatal collision course. Mr. Caudill's assertions are particularly impressive, since he has gained a national reputation for his book Night Comes to the Cumberlands. *In this work, and as a Kentucky legislator, Caudill has striven to prevent the destruction of the earth by surface mining.*

I am addressing these remarks to my fellow students of this intriguing planet and to those voiceless unborn millions who must some day inhabit the wastelands this century is creating.

Symptoms of serious illness in our ecosystem abound on every hand. All who can discern the signs of our times must occasionally be depressed to melancholia and despair by the encroaching horror.

We are inflicting a doleful list of disasters on the only life-supporting planet known to astronomy:

Noxious emissions from automobile exhaust pipes, power plants, and factory stacks have buried our cities at the bottom of vast and oppressive atmospheric sewers.

SOURCE: Harry M. Caudill, "Are Capitalism and the Conservation of a Decent Environment Possible?" in Harold W. Helfrich, Jr., ed. *Agenda for Survival: The Environmental Crisis*—2. (New Haven and London: Yale University Press, 1970), pp. 165–183. Copyright © 1970 by Yale University and reprinted by permission.

Innumerable mills drain highly toxic acids and sludge into rivers and lakes.

Many municipalities pour sewage into rivers, compelling their neighbors downstream to drink chlorinated essence of urine.

These same municipalities too often dump mountains of trash into swamps or bury it in stinking mounds on every hand.

Tankers pump oily bilge into the oceans.

Petroleum escaping from undersea wells blackens beaches and kills marine life, as well as many birds.

Gigantic tankers are floating ecological disasters traveling about in quest of a place to happen.

Lumber corporations "harvesting" trees with bulldozers sometimes ruin the ecology of whole forests and destroy their capacity to regenerate the kind of timber resources the land once produced.

Agri-businessmen frequently drench their land with insecticides, pesticides, and fertilizers until the soil is dependent upon them, the ground water is rank with deadly concentrations of nitrates and phosphates, and new and ever more voracious strains of insects emerge to plague us.

Gargantuan feed lots, great pens where staggering numbers of cattle and hogs are kept for intensive feeding before slaughter, generate enormous quantities of manure—the sewage equivalent of large cities —that wastes into rivers to the ruinous deprivation of the land.

Manufacturers of automobiles, tin cans, glass bottles, and thousands of other products spew them out with no provision for recycling the scrap, thus cluttering the landscape with unimaginable quantities of junk.

Unsealed mines in a dozen states sluice sulfuric acid into streams on which strings of towns and cities are totally dependent for water.

Actually, the United States' massive degradation is only part of a worldwide debasement by which all the continents are systematically being robbed of the nutrients essential to the continuance of life, while the oceans simultaneously are choking with an accelerated flow of nutrients so vast that they cannot be assimilated. Thus man has become time's most traumatic geological force—a force that threatens to reduce the continents to deserts and the oceans to algae-ridden sumps.

The common theme running through this tapestry of ruin is an unbridled quest for economic advantage, a quest that becomes increasingly absurd because there can be no preeminence in the worldwide charnel house we are creating.

In the United States and throughout most of the world the economic system is impelled in a classic five-point cycle: *greed* produces *exploitation of other people* and *destruction of the land for its resources, pollution of the environment,* and finally, *monetary profit.* This system worked tolerably well for generations because the number of people was relatively small and the space and natural resources appeared to be inexhaustible. Now, however, the whole concept is losing validity with the twin realizations that the earth's natural resources are finite and that the procreative instinct, combined with modern medicine, can swamp the world with uncountable multitudes of human beings.

Under the prevailing ethics of the market place each corporation strives to manufacture its products at the lowest attainable cost and unload them on the public at the highest obtainable price. This inevitably results in a flow of unneeded—and frequently little tested—products into our homes and stomachs. The products are accompanied by seemingly endless misinformation, deceptions, and subtle suggestions of need, so that the consumer has scant basis for judgment as to what is safe or dangerous, desirable or pernicious.

The dominant attitude toward our mother earth continues to reflect the traditional savage frontier impulse to "gut, gouge, and git out!" From giant metal-mining companies down to small quarries, corporations routinely plunder the land and the communities dependent upon it, while making the smallest possible investment in social institutions. After pillaging the earth for resources to create products for sale to an unwitting public, the same corporations rid themselves of undesirable and dangerous residues by casting them onto or among their customers.

With a population of 205 million, we in the United States are much like the lady with the five suitors in Sir Richard Francis Burton's delightful nineteenth-century translation from *The Arabian Nights.* Everybody is defecating on everyone else and, despite the wails of protest, the practice continues. When hit, we emulate the outraged suitors and yell, "What nastiness is this?" Then we fling the odious substance onto someone else.

The situation was funny in Burton's fable, and generations have laughed at it; but we can see no mirth in it in the United States today. Indeed, if one insists on being amused, he may find himself laughing amid the skulls.

The madness that has brought us to our present untenable situation raises questions about man's fitness for survival. The technology of production expands constantly and, because production generates profits, the technology is vigorously applied. Simultaneously a huge reservoir of unused technology accumulates in the fields of air and water sanitation, waste abatement, and land regeneration. Such technology languishes because its application consumes profits. These dynamics are so potent that they threaten our very existence.

The issue thus posed transcends by far the conventional arguments for "conservation" and the "preservation of a decent environment." It brings us to a grim choice between survival and extinction. Survivalists believe that, regardless of costs, the insights of science must be employed to save the world's eco-system as a functioning machine. The extinctionists murmur that there is no really serious problem and that, in any event, the contemplated costs are unthinkable. The contest between these points of view will dominate the next decade or two, and the outcome will determine whether life will continue into the twenty-first century.

We are led quite inevitably to consider whether capitalism and the conservation of a decent environment are compatible. Is the one impossible where the other holds sway?

To survive the sea of junk beneath which the capitalistic system is inundating us, will we be compelled to junk the system itself?

Because this symposium and book are originating in the Yale School of Forestry, I want to comment at length on the huge hardwood forest of the Cumberlands in the central Appalachian Mountains. It is so rich in flora, so varied in its life forms, so majestic in its natural beauty that its worth to mankind is inestimable. But our corporate system treats this marvelous forest and the minerals beneath its roots with a soulless rapacity that is unsurpassed in the annals of greed. Here capitalism has demonstrated its total contempt for the good earth, for the green that cloaks it, and for the creatures that dwell upon its face; it has achieved the supreme pollution of utter destruction. Unless our economic and political overlords change their attitudes toward it, the entire heart of this vast woodland will have been lost to the United States and the world long before the 1970s are gone.

When Europeans first viewed eastern Kentucky, it was a land of primordial splendor. Its web of life constituted an ecology of marvelous complexity and interdependency; it was indescribably ancient and, in some respects, remarkably frail.

Millions of visitors have reveled in the beauty and majesty of the Great Smokies, and most of the scientific attention that has been devoted to the Appalachians has centered in these high domes with their plunging streams, dense "laurel hells," and stately groves. Other than professional botanists and foresters, few are aware that the richest expression of the great eastern deciduous forest of North America was found in the Cumberland Plateau region in eastern Kentucky, rather than in the loftier and more venerable Smokies. Indeed, the finest forest in the world's temperate zones was found there, exceeding all other areas in the variety of trees, in age and size attained, and in the almost limitless quantity and diversity of the low-growing ground cover above their roots.

This vast and remarkable woodland is of a character known to ecologists as "mixed mesophytic forest"—that is, midway between wet and dry, and implying a moderate climate and a rich vegetation in a well-drained habitat that is protected from excessive exposure to burning sun and drying wind.

All of these environmental characteristics are found in full measure in the Kentucky Cumberlands. In July the thermometer rarely climbs above 90 degrees; in January it seldom sinks to zero. Rainfall amounts to nearly

50 inches annually, more than in any other part of the United States except the rain forest of Oregon and Washington. The ridges are gentle, and ages-long erosion by wind and water has carved their slopes into deep coves and capped their crests with picturesque crags of sandstone. They reach their highest elevation on the southern border in the Big Black Mountain, but even here, at 4,400 feet above sea level, they fall short of the arctic air that produces the balds that dot the Smokies. In the moist, warm, protected coves a benevolent nature set the stage for the highest development of that type of vegetation botanists have termed "the deciduous forest of the Northern Temperate Climatic Zone."

In no other forest in the Northern Hemisphere can we count so many kinds of trees; the total number of species exceeds a hundred. Nowhere else on earth do the hillsides blaze with such a rich tapestry of color in the autumn, each specie assuming its own particular shade of scarlet or gold or plum, of mahogany, rose, orange or yellow—all glowing against the deep, dark evergreen of the pines, hemlocks, rhododendrons, and laurels. Nowhere else on our planet is the spring so fragrant and gay from March to June as one tree and shrub after another comes into bloom.

Geologic upheaval occurred there long before our modern forest evolved. And long before that upheaval the land was covered by shallow seas fringed with a rank growth of tree-size club mosses and gigantic ferns. In those remote ages litter from the swampy forests accumulated in the shallow waters and formed the organic deposits that were to be turned, by time and the weight of later sediments, into the potent mineral we call coal. Finally the weight of accumulating sediments became too great for the crust to bear. The earth buckled, rearing the Appalachians far above the continental floor. The long ridges that form the backbone of the Cumberlands and Alleghanies were a part of this vast Appalachian uplift. Later and more gentle uplifts perpetuated the mountainous character of the land, which otherwise would long ago have been worn down by the incessant action of water.

For more than 200 million years this land has been here above the seas, relatively unchanged except for alternating cycles of erosion and uplift. In this immense era of stability nature perfected the forest that astounded the first white explorers, a woodland so venerable that if one could enter a time machine and explore time's abyss he would find growing here trees closely resembling those we can see today—but 70 million years before man stood erect anywhere on the planet.

During the early part of the geologic period known as the Tertiary the Rocky Mountains were low hills, and even the arctic regions were blessed with mild temperatures. The trees of the Cumberlands grew far westward across North America. They put down their roots along the shores of Greenland and northward into Alaska. Then, over land bridges that have long since vanished, they reached northeastern Asia and advanced southward into China.

Rock fossils tell us the story of these trees and of the fragile ground cover that grew in their ancient shade. The imprint of sycamore and maple leaves has been found along the front of the Rockies in Montana, Colorado, and the Dakotas; their track remains in Greenland and northern Canada. As impressive as these stone traces of forests that rose and died are the forest survivals that have persisted to our own time. In central Appalachia and in eastern China the tulip tree grows beside sassafras, sweet gum, spicewood, and magnolias. Nowhere else in today's world, except in eastern North America and eastern China, are these species found. Many of the flowers and ferns beneath them are common to both regions.

But there were forces at work to reduce the forest in the same eons when it reached its greatest magnitude and splendor. Twenty or thirty million years ago, and again only a million or so years ago, the land rose from northwestern Canada to New Mexico and the Rockies of today were thrust up to their towering heights. They acted as a barrier to the moisture-laden winds from the Pacific, and the rain and snow fell on the western slopes of the ragged new ridges. The central stretches of the continent became too dry to support trees; they became a grassland, and the forest retreated to the east where rain from the Atlantic provided moisture for its perpetuation.

Slowly the north turned cold. The deciduous trees retreated southward for thousands of miles and were replaced by firs and spruces moving down from frigid mountaintops. The deciduous forest was restricted to eastern America south of Canada and north of the subtropics. Similar changes in Asia restricted that portion of the forest to eastern China.

Then came the frigid Pleistocene, with its continental glaciers that began grinding down from the north about a million years ago. At their greatest extent the glaciers covered all of New England, reached the southern tip of Illinois, spread across Indiana and Ohio and most of Pennsylvania. The gargantuan shields of sliding ice destroyed all vegetation in their path, but they inched forward so slowly that northern species of trees managed to survive by seeding ever southward in front of the glacial margin. Thus spruce and fir came to stand beside magnolia and paw-paw, and to this day they are found as "glacial relics" on the highest peaks of the Smokies.

At last the glaciers retreated northward, leaving in their wake a bleak, shattered land. Everywhere the glaciers had dumped immense loads of pulverized rock—in drifts, in heaps, and in ground sheets. No "soil" remained in the path of the glaciers. The paper-thin sheet of nutrient-rich, humus-filled material that had been built up through millions of years had been completely dissipated in the rubble heaps. Not until the arrival of modern "civilized" man with his diesel engines and bulldozers would the North American continent again experience such thoroughgoing devastation.

Climates were much colder south of the ice sheet than they are now, but they were not frigid enough to kill vegetation far beyond the glacial rim. In the protected valleys and deep coves of Appalachia and the Ozarks the deciduous forest survived, to serve as a huge storehouse of seeds to reclothe the naked land.

Some plants are exceedingly adaptable and, as the ice withdrew, they followed closely in its wake. The first to pursue the receding ice shield were those plants of northern origin: the spruce and fir, the bunchberry and bead lilly. These hardy pioneers began the infinitely slow process of rebuilding soil in the rubble heaps and on the bare rocks, preparing the way for other plants that must have a more luxuriant environment for their survival. As temperatures climbed, white pine, sugar maple, and yellow birch crept out of the hills to replace the spruce and fir. Then the oaks, the beeches and tulip trees could also move northward again.

Throughout the long, bleak millennia of the Ice Age the ancient forest of the Cumberland plateau survived in all its infinite variety. Protected by a labyrinth of coves and valleys, its trees were ready to seed northward and northwestward to establish new woodlands. However, not all of the species could tolerate pioneer environment—the drought, the alternating extremes of heat and cold, and the raw abrasive characteristics of the deeply scarred land. Some, especially the white basswood and the yellow buckeye, demand rich humus and the protection of a long-established forest; so they remained in the Cumberlands and in the lessening hills to the south. Others could endure cold but not drought; so the beech, sugar maple, hemlock, and yellow birch spread northward into New England, then across Canada and into Wisconsin. Others could tolerate drought as well as cold; so the oaks and hickories moved both northwestward and northward.

Not all of them could make it to the western limits of the deciduous forest, where the prairies begin. The chestnut oaks dropped out in Indiana. The tulip poplar demanded rich soil and much moisture when it left its ancient home; it could travel as far as Indiana, southern Michigan, and the eastern limits of Illinois, where it survives today in only the most luxuriant habitats. The forest that reached the northwestern limits of the deciduous preserves contains fewer than a fifth of the species found in the Cumberland heartland.

A new geologic force has obtruded upon the forest—mechanized man. His efforts at "development" threaten to eradicate that which the glaciers spared. Unlike the great ice sheets, man can go anywhere; no flower or fern or tree, or any creature that shelters in their shade, can escape him. He is a living cataclysm. The question now is not whether the age-old forest can ever again spread to new regions, but simply whether it can manage to survive, even in its ancient mountain fastnesses.

The Indians treated the forest of the Cumberlands with supreme reverence. It was frequented by the Cherokee and numerous lesser tribes, who harmed it as little as shadows cast by the clouds.

The white men who drove them out decimated the forest, clearing huge areas for cattle pastures and the endless "new grounds" on which their agriculture depended. After the turn of this century coal mining began, and tunnels were thrust into hundreds of hillsides. At one time 55,000 men were boring into the Cumberlands, propping up countless miles of sagging sandstone with timbers from the hills above their heads.

However, the wounded forest—with the exception of the chestnut tree—survived in all its multitudinous forms down to our own time. (The noble chestnut perished from an imported blight that swept the nation in 1929.) The almost endless catalogue of plants that made the hills and valleys so distinctive were there, ready to reconstitute the forest in all its magnificence when time and the prudence of man could combine to permit it.

In the 1950s a vast human exodus flowed out of the hills into northern cities. The old mining industry, with its dependence on thousands of laborers, collapsed. Machines replaced men in the tunnels, and strip mining developed on a large scale. The deserted areas quickly reverted to new forests. The open fields disappeared under a choking growth of young trees. In a strange silence amid vacant, decaying houses along hundreds of creeks the old grandeur of the Cumberlands began to return.

But this forest, which had passed through so many trials during the vast span of its history, was to face its most devastating crisis at the hands of men digging coal with explosives, bulldozers, and power shovels. At this hour the mountains and their vegetation are under the most deadly and systematic assault any portion of the North American land ever has suffered.

In the Cumberlands three to five veins of coal run through each hill, and the demand for it appears to be insatiable. It generates our electric power, smelts our metals, and provides medicines and fertilizers. The cheapest way to get it out of the ground is by surface mining. Behind the rumble of exploding dynamite the bulldozers shove their way along the contours of the hills, spreading a wake of devastation that can scarcely be believed. The mind boggles at the immensity and completeness of the ruin.

Generally the first coal seam to be worked is the one nearest the base of the hill. The contour cut produces a great notch or flat bench at the level of the vein. The earth and its living organisms are simply thrust aside by the massive machines and the shattering blasts. The rock and dirt above the coal are pushed down the slope, and an abrupt man-made cliff rears sheer and sullen from thirty to ninety feet in height. A serpentine expanse of glittering carbon stretches behind the roaring Euclids and Caterpillars, and after the coal is loosened by new explosions, the power shovels lift it into trucks that speed their twenty-five-ton cargoes to the railroads.

After the base of the hill has been reduced in this manner, the process is repeated at the next level. Sometimes the top of a mountain is blasted away, and the ancient crags and their oaks are rolled into the hollows. Sharp weather-carved mountains become man-made mesas.

In Breathitt County, Kentucky, a whole range is being dismembered. Layer by layer the mountains are being cut down and the spoil pushed into the valleys. The labyrinth of hills and valleys is being reduced to a jumble of broken rock, slate, shale, and yellow subsoil. Under all this ruin lies the corpse of a forest.

Kentucky has a reclamation law; after the last of the hardwoods, ferns, and flowers has been rooted out and buried, men walk over the dead acidulous earth scattering fescue and lespedeza seeds. In a few instances hydro-seeders spray water, straw, fertilizer, and seeds across the rock-strewn jumble. Later a few hundred pine seedlings are planted on each acre. Then the land is certified as "reclaimed" and, with awesome finality, is forgotten.

In the meantime the inhabitants of the valleys take flight. Massive erosion from spoil banks sends thick sheets of mud onto their lawns and croplands and into the channels of creeks. Wells go dry or become highly mineralized. Ugliness marks their communities, and people refuse to stay in such hideous surroundings. A million Kentuckians have fled the hills since 1950. Strip mining has been one of the prime causes of their exodus.

Much of the land is owned by coal companies, who bought it cheaply in the 1880s. The mineral rights on practically all the remaining land are owned by the same companies under deeds that sever the title to the minerals from that of the surface. Kentucky's highest court has ruled that the owner of the minerals may "recover" them by any means he deems necessary or convenient, including stripping [*Martin v. Kentucky Oak Mining Co.*, 429 SW 2d (Ky.), p. 395]. The court of justice has declared that, although stripping totally destroys the land, the mining company has no obligation to make restitution to the farmer who owns the trees and topsoil.

Can there be any wonder that the region is synonymous with poverty and dejection?

Thus the destruction of a broad territory has been given lawful sanction, and while men talk of saving the environment, the ruin spreads like an obscene cancer. Two hundred thousand acres of eastern Kentucky forest land have already been ruined. In all of Appalachia a million acres have been similarly devastated, and the coal market is now so strong that the giant machines seldom rest by day or night.

Who are these destroyers of this ancient part of our terrestrial heritage? Are they madmen turned out of insane asylums? Are they Bolsheviks who have found a way of destroying the United States by plundering her land?

They are, in fact, some of the nation's most respected names. They include U.S. Steel, Bethlehem Steel, Ford Motor Company, Continental Oil, Occidental Petroleum, Republic Steel, Georgia Power, American Electric Power, and Uncle Sam himself operating through the Tennessee Valley Authority (TVA). Many of the great interests that mine, transport, and consume coal are engaged in this gigantic rape.

According to Ferdinand Lunberg's noteworthy study of the United States power structure, *The Rich and the Super-Rich*, the fantastically wealthy Mellon family holds billions in their coffers. He says that the family controls Bethlehem Steel, and a subsidiary of Bethlehem Steel owns about 40,000 acres in four eastern Kentucky counties. This land is dark with second-growth hardwoods, and much of it has been deep-mined. But 8 million tons of high-grade metallurgical coal remain in the outcrop, the narrow border of coal at the outside of the hill that subterranean mining procedures cannot "recover." Bethlehem Steel has ignored the protests of the National Audubon Society, the World Wildlife Fund, the Izaak Walton League, the Sierra Club, and the pleas of hundreds of just plain Americans. Those 8 million tons will have a market worth of $44 million when fed into Bethlehem's furnaces. The cost of those dollars to the nation will be desolate wastelands stretching across the middle of Appalachia. The Mellons will have added a few more unneeded millions to their hoard. Bethlehem will continue its massive shipments of cheap steel to foreign countries (among them the Soviet Union), and several thousand new Appalachian migrants will have fled into the slums of Cleveland and Chicago.

Bethlehem's operation began on Millstone Creek in a week when Mrs. Paul Mellon was interviewed at Upperville, Virginia, at one of her five spacious homes. Her husband and his kinsmen had given away $700 million, including much largesse to Yale. She conducted the reporter through her lovely garden, speaking with pride of its flowers and shrubs.

Since then Mrs. Mellon's garden has passed through another season of growth and bloom, but Millstone Valley will bloom no more. As the local newspaper has reported, "Millstone Creek is dead."

Thus there are two kinds of gardens that our rich masters create. The one is truly beautiful, with its precious plants and blooms surrounding stately houses and shaded drives. The other will be inhabited by people like you and me, and by those who will carry our genes in the aftertime, and consists of tumbled wastes like those described in the opening verses of Genesis.

Corporations headquartered in New York and Philadelphia hold the destiny of the Cumberlands in their hands. I have no doubt that—despite the golden rhetoric emanating from Washington's federal cave of winds —this forest and other mineral-bearing lands in the nation are doomed. You and I will protest, but the destruction will continue. We have voices, but the corporate directors have power. We are serfs; they are the masters.

The attitude of our capitalist overlords was clearly expressed by James D. Reilly, a vice president of Consolidated Coal Company, in a speech at Pittsburgh on May 8, 1969:

> The conservationists who want stripminers to restore land are stupid idiots, Socialists, and Commies who don't know what they are talking

about. I think it is our bounden duty to knock them down and subject them to the ridicule they deserve.

It is remarkable how much times have changed since the year 1000, and yet how much they have remained the same. In that distant era the barons and their ladies lived in moated castles, surrounded by retainers and supported by multitudes of toiling serfs. The countries were run by their feudal elites. No one consulted the serfs or listened to their occasional entreaties.

A millennium of advancing technology has elevated living standards for all, and the lords of the land now live in different surroundings. But the barons are still with us, and they exercise most of the prerogatives of a royal class. The new royalty consists of the corporate power structure, and the serfs are the people who work for them and pay the taxes that keep the system going.

Sometimes the serfs strike or march in protest. They petition lawmakers and write letters to editors; but make no mistake, the power is in the board rooms. A telephone call from S. S. Corts, president of Bethlehem Steel, to a governor or the president of the United States is likely to achieve more than an entreaty signed by many thousands of ordinary one-vote citizens. The thing that distinguishes serfs and masters in the modern U.S.A. is the power to make decisions, and that power is where the weight of unlimited millions of dollars focuses. It is not with the individual citizens, no matter how concerned, intelligent, and vocal they may be.

For this reason the Fords continue to pollute the River Rouge as they have for sixty years. The Ford family fortune is gigantic, as befits a tribe which has poured gigantic quantities of wastes into our air and water. To date they have polluted with impunity.

However, no polluters can exceed the Rockefellers. They have turned the Garden State into a sink of nauseous gases from the refineries of Rockefeller-dominated Standard Oil of New Jersey. But Rockefellers are clever as well as rich. They distribute largesse among the serfs and hire clever propagandists to cozen and mislead them. Consequently, Rockefellers govern a growing list of states. From the top of Rockefeller Center they can gaze down into the filthy canyons of a city that their companies have done much to render squalid and hideous. They can yacht in oceans that their tankers have helped to turn rancid with their wastes.

And, of course, the exploits of the $7 billion Dupont clan are worthy of note. Their grip on once lovely Delaware is sure, and their chemical wastes have damned land, air, and water alike.

These examples illustrate the awesome power of the polluters. They would like to see the country clean and lovely; but making it that way will cost immense sums, and the polluters are in the business of accumulating—not expending—money. They will be happy to see the United States cleaned up, if the serfs will pay the bill.

Keep in mind that Richard Nixon and the fifty governors are merely foremen who run the economic ranch for such polluters and destroyers as General Motors, Ford, Occidental Petroleum, Continental Oil, Gulf Oil, Standard Oil of New Jersey, U.S. Steel, and practically the whole roster of United States industrial might. Such foremen are carried into office on cash gifts from their economic masters who exercise their subtle but effective control over both parties. Almost every truly powerful "establishment" figure in Congress is a steadfast servant of the rich.

Our masters—like the barons of feudal England before them—are too big to restrain. When Lyndon Johnson talked of a war on poverty or Richard Nixon spoke of a campaign against environmental decline, each had to resort to broad generalities. The dynamics of the power structure prevent the singling out of culprits who create poverty and ugliness. To do so would spark an uprising among the barons, while the serfs would remain quiescent or unresponsive. Under three United States presidents I have tried to entice a secretary of the interior into eastern Kentucky to look at the devastation of strip mining, but none has dared to come. I thought his high office would dramatize a national concern for the desperate plight of Appalachia's expiring hills. Each secretary expressed a sincere personal concern, but none would brave the wrath of the barons. So the hills died friendless, and the ruin widened, as it still does.

Brave to foolhardiness is the politician who will beard a Mellon, a Rockefeller, or a Dupont. Prisons are made for serfs; mansions are constructed for lords. Every day Americans go to penitentiaries for petty thefts. But when a roomful of belted knights from General Electric and Westinghouse fixed prices and defrauded the government of hundreds of millions of dollars, they were fined and given short jail sentences—most of which are suspended.

In my opinion our present system of government can never cope with the horrendous problems of our deteriorating environment. It has come down to us as a Rube Goldberg contraption consisting of one federal government, fifty states, 3,500 counties, and an indescribable tangle of 76,000 other governmental units. This jungle can absorb—and waste—tax money as sand soaks up water, but its very complexity and immensity induce near paralysis. At every turn opponents of change baffle and retard undertakings that deserve the highest priority. In such a swamp implementation of reform programs is an exhausting nightmare experience. Huge undertakings generally accomplish little and, out of bewilderment and frustration, the public loses interest and withdraws its support. Thus, at a time when we must strive to save ourselves, our principal instrument of survival is archaic, overgrown, inefficient, and uninspired. I can think of no major problem of war or peace with which this governmental monstrosity is able to deal successfully.

If the needs of our whole society could be served, if we could escape the baronial restraints that reduce our democratic system to near immobility, we could enact and strictly enforce a federal law to save the

Appalachians and the other mineral fields of the United States. It would:

1. Outlaw strip mining where prompt and total restoration of the land and its water and vegetation is impossible. This would stop the practice altogether in Appalachia.

2. Permit stripping only where prompt and total restoration of the land to its original contour and natural utility can be accomplished. Topsoil on the plains can be scraped back and saved. The underlying strata can be dug out and segregated. After the mineral is lifted out, the strata can go back to their natural order. The surface can be smoothed and treated with limestone and fertilizers and can be made useful again. Such procedures are routine in England, Germany, and Czechoslovakia, but they are rarely employed in America the Beautiful.

3. Levy a substantial severance tax on the extraction of all minerals. This money would be devoted to reclamation—insofar as reclamation is possible—of the 4 million acres of strip-mined land and the 10,000 miles of ruined streams that are making much of the United States as hideous as the pockmarked face of a corpse.

We have or can acquire the capacity to restore our land and air, to preserve our rivers and seas, to safeguard our mountains, to limit our numbers—in short, to assure the survival of our planet. But my optimism about the likelihood that we will do so is restrained.

I fear that greed and indifference will continue to hold sway in the nation's boardrooms, where not even life will outweigh the lust for profits. I am afraid we are headed into a new politics of pious gesture and bold rhetoric, dramatized by occasional visits to stinking lakes, the planting of a few trees, and the dedication now and then of a new sewage treatment plant. As one who was born during the Return to Normalcy, grew up under the New Deal, went to war for the Four Freedoms, was mustered out under the Fair Deal, marched in the Great Crusade, fared forth to the New Frontier, and enlisted in the Great Society, I have developed certain reservations about the sincerity of officials who proclaim grand new goals.

I come from eastern Kentucky, one of the world's richest resource regions and certainly a primary ecological disaster area of the United States. I have seen capitalism at work there through many painful years. I have seen one of the richest lands on earth acrawl with the poorest people in the nation, where illiteracy runs to one-fourth of the adults, and the very name of the region equates with poverty. I have seen pipelines lacing the land to carry out rivers of oil and gas, and since infancy my sleep has been disturbed by the rumbling of endless coal drags and lumber trains. I have seen hordes of people lining up for food stamps and the dole, and swarms of school children in tattered clothes trudging past the offices of the United States' richest corporations on their way to tumbledown schoolhouses perched above junk-choked streams.

In addition to the poorest white people in this country, my neighbors have long included the two most prosperous investor-owned corporations in the United States—The Penn-Virginia Company and Kentucky River Coal. Each clears, after taxes, sixty-one cents out of every dollar, and pays out as dividends 45 percent of its gross receipts. I have seen legislators and presidents tax meager salaries and bread, clothing, and medicine while granting an astonishing tax immunity to these same corporations. And I have read the proud boast of the president of Penn-Virginia, "We carry practically all of our income down to net."

Here we have the reality that looms up like a dark mountain—the reality of a multitude of uncertain and crisis-ridden governments, and virtually all of them dependent upon and subservient to the economic barons; a reality of ever-darkening cities, reeking rivers, putrefying lakes, dying mountains and burgeoning populations.

Albert Schweitzer once wrote, "Man has lost the capacity to foresee and to forestall. He will end by destroying the earth." His grim prophecy is certain to occur unless this generation of serfs finds some way of rising against their overlords, the globe-girdling corporate litter kings, and instituting somehow and quickly an international land ethic for the nurture, enhancement, and conservation of the earth. In short, a whole generation must become militant and vocal advocates—not only for themselves but for the unborn multitudes who have a right to be heard but cannot speak. This is the urgent necessity of survival. Without such a land ethic, without a regeneration of the spirit in matters relating to the land, beginning here and spreading across the world, there will be no future.

Such a regeneration would be truly revolutionary, and revolutions are extremely hard to bring off. The earth is a generous mother and will provide for all her children, if they will populate her with prudence and treat her with restraint. The capitalistic system has yet to demonstrate that it is capable of such restraint. Nor, for that matter has any other system. For example, the Russians under Communism have devastated and polluted on a scale approaching our own.

As I listen to murmurings of concern, I like to suppose that I hear the faint beginning of a revolt and of a new politics of survival, a politics that will say frankly to capitalism: "You claim to live by the motto 'produce or perish.' Now we demand that you produce a decent environment in the lands you dominate or make way for a new system of economics and a new order of values. Goods alone are not enough!"

If such a revolt comes, it will fight entrenched institutions of great age and wealth, institutions that now wield practically every instrument of power—economic, political, and social. All of these weapons will be exercised with cunning and tenacity to delay change and to preserve the doomed and polluted present.

And so I leave you to ponder a paraphrase from the Right—from Barry Goldwater's 1964 presidential nomination acceptance speech: Moderation in the cause of survival is no virtue! Extremism in the cause of survival is no vice!

NOTES

1. Goldwater said: "Moderation in defense of liberty is no virtue. Extremism in defense of liberty is no vice."

51. Is Main Street Still There?
PETER SCHRAG

In this, the second of his articles included here (see selection 24), Peter Schrag expresses his interest in small-town life. He concludes that despite the surface attractions of such towns, they are fragile phenomena far removed from the truly vital aspects of modern life. Ever since Schrag's article appeared in 1970, the energy crisis and food shortages have prompted some people to consider moving out of metropolitan areas and back to "the country." It remains to be seen whether or not such moves will involve a truly substantial number of people.

It is hard to stay in any small American town for more than a few days and remain an outsider. There seems to be a common feeling that anyone —even a writer from New York—is, somewhere in his heart, a small-town boy come home. The light but increasing stream of traffic that moves through Main Street— Federal Avenue in Mason City—north to Minneapolis and beyond, south to Des Moines, reinforces the belief that this flat, open place is part of a great American continuity extending through other Main Streets, across the fields of corn and beets, past tractor depots and filling stations, past grain elevators and loading pens to the very limits of the national imagination. Such a belief must make it difficult to conceive of anyone as a total stranger, for being here—local pride notwithstanding—cannot seem very different from being anywhere else.

They take you in, absorb you, soak you up; they know where you've been, whom you've seen, what you've done. In Mississippi hamlets, the

SOURCE: Peter Schrag, "Is Main Street Still There?" *Saturday Review* 53 (January 17, 1970), 20–25. Reprinted by permission.

sheriff follows you around; here it is The Word. *Small towns co-opt* (you tell yourself), *and nice small towns co-opt absolutely*. But it is not just them, it's you. The things that you bring with you—your sense of yourself as a friendly sort, the wish to believe that the claims of small-town virtue are valid, your particular kind of chauvinism—all these things make you a willing collaborator. So maybe they're right. *Maybe we're all just small-town boys come home.* Yes, you're willing to come to dinner, to visit the Club, to suspend the suspicion that all this is some sort of do-it-yourself Chamber of Commerce trick. Later perhaps (says the Inner Voice of Reason) you will be able to sort things out, to distinguish Main Street from the fantasies that you and a lot of other people from New York have invented for it. Later.

You have come here to see what is happening to the heart of this country, to ask how the great flat democracy responds to Vietnam and Black Power, to marijuana and SDS, to see how it is taking technology and the Bomb—all the things that overwhelm the visible spectrum of public concern. Is there something here that can survive in New York and Chicago? Is there an Americanism that will endure, or will it perish with the farm and the small town? What, you ask, is happening to Main Street? Later. For the moment you are simply in it, listening to them worry about a proposed civic center, about the construction of a mall, about taxes and industrial development, and about something they call "the traffic problem," which seems, by even the more placid standards of New York, more imagined than real.

There are ghosts in this country—local ghosts, and ghosts that you bring with you, that refuse to stay behind: shades of brawling railroad workers and dispossessed farmers; frontiersmen and Babbitts; the old remembered tales of reaction and America First, of capital "R" Republicanism and the Ku Klux Klan; the romance of Jefferson and Frederick Jackson Turner, the yeoman farmer and the self-made man. As a place of literary irony, Middle America is celebrating its golden anniversary. "Main Street," wrote Sinclair Lewis in 1920, "is the climax of civilization. That this Ford car might stand in front of the Bon Ton Store, Hannibal invaded Rome and Erasumus wrote in Oxford cloisters. What Ole Jensen the grocer says to Ezra Stowbody the banker is the new law for London, Prague, and the unprofitable isles of the sea; whatsoever Ezra does not know and sanction, that thing is heresy, worthless for knowing and wicked to consider." But such irony, too, may be a ghost—now as much myth, perhaps, as the self-flattering cultural propositions invented to answer it. ("Right here in Mason City," someone tells you, "we sell 300 tickets each year for the Metropolitan Opera tour performances in Minneapolis.") The life of Babbittry, you tell yourself, follows the life (and art) of others. But the models are no longer clear. Main Street once insisted on rising from Perfection (rural) to Progress (urban): Sauk Centre and Zenith were trying to do Chicago's "thing," but what does Chicago have to offer now? The Main Street boosters are still there, hanging signs across the road proclaiming "A Community on the March," but their days are numbered. How would Lewis have portrayed the three hundred marchers of the Vietnam Moratorium in Mason City? How would he deal with the growing number of long-haired, pot-smoking kids? Here, too, Mason City follows New York and Chicago. (The Mafia, you are told, controls the floating dice games that occasionally rumble through the back rooms of a local saloon.) The certainty of Lewis's kind of irony was directed to the provincial insularity that war, technology, and television are rendering obsolete. Main Street lives modern not in its dishwashers and combines—not even in Huntley-Brinkley and Walter Cronkite—but in its growing ambivalence about the America that creates them, the America that crosses the seas of beets and corn, and therefore about Main Street itself.

It is not a simple place, and perhaps never was. You see what you expect, and then begin to see (or imagine) what you did not. Standard America, yes; the Civil War monument in the square; the First National Bank; Osco's Self-Service Drugs; the shoe store and movie theaters; Damon's and Younkers' ("Satisfaction Always"); Maizes' and Penney's; Sears and Monkey Ward. Middle America the way it was supposed to be: the farmers coming to shop on Saturday afternoon; the hunting and fishing; the high school football game Friday night; the swimming and sailing at Clear Lake, a small resort nine miles to the west. You cannot pass through town without being told that Mason City is a good place to raise a family, without hearing praise for the schools, and without incessant reminders that Meredith Willson's musical play *The Music Man* was *about* Mason city, that Willson was born here, and that the town was almost renamed River City because of it. (There *is* a river, the Winnebago, which makes itself known only at times of flood.) Mr. Toot, the figure of a trombone-blowing bandsman (says a man at the Chamber of Commerce) is now the town symbol. We hope, says the man, "that we can make our band festival into a major event." Someday, you imagine, this could be the band capital of the nation, the world, and maybe the whole wicked universe.

Mason City, they tell you, is a stable community: steady population, little unemployment, no race problem (there are, at most, 300 Negroes in town), clean water, and—with some huffy qualifications (dust from one of the cement plants, odor from the packing house)—clean air. A cliché. In the *Globe Gazette*, the editor, Bob Spiegel, suggests that the problems and resources of the large cities be dispersed to all the Mason Cities in America. A Jeffersonian, Mr. Spiegel, and a nice guy: "The smaller communities need the plants and the people that are polluting the urban centers—not in large doses, but steadily, surely. . . . The small communities are geared up. They have comprehensive plans. They know they can't stand still or they will be passed by." Stable, perhaps, but what is stable in a relativistic universe? The very thing that Spiegel proposes seems to be happening in reverse. The community is becoming less pluralistic; it has fewer Negroes, fewer Jews, and fewer members of other minorities than it had twenty years ago. "After the war," said Nate Levinson, an attorney, who is president of the synagogue, "we had eighty Jewish families. Now we have forty. We can't afford a rabbi anymore." On the few occasions that Mason City has tried to attract Negro professionals, they refused to come or to stay. There is nobody to keep them company, and the subtle forms of discrimination—in housing and employment—are pervasive enough to discourage pioneers. ("My maid says if she hears any more about Black Power she'll scream. . . . I wouldn't mind one living next door, if he mowed the grass and kept the place neat.") The brighter kids—black and white—move away, off to college, off to the cities, and beneath that migration one can sense the fear that the city's declining agricultural base will not be replaced by enough industrial jobs to maintain even the stability that now exists.

Mason City is not a depressed town, although in its stagnating downtown shopping area it often looks like one. (Shopping centers are thriving on the periphery; the farmers come in to shop, but not all the way.) The city shares many of the attributes of other small Middle Western communities, competing with them for industry, counting, each week, another farm family that is selling out or giving up, counting the abandoned houses around the county, counting the number of acres (now exceeding 200) required for an efficient agricultural operation. An acre of land costs $500, a four-row combine $24,000. If you stop in such places as Plymouth, a town of 400, nine miles from Mason City, you hear the cadences of compromise and decline: men who have become part-time farmers and make ends meet, at $2.25 an hour, by working in the sugar mill in Mason City. Independence becomes, ever more, a hopeful illusion belied by abandoned shops and boarded windows, and by tales of success set in other places—an engineer in California, a chemist in Detroit, a teacher in Oregon.

Iowa, you realize, not just from statistics, but from faces, is a state of old people: "What do the kids here want to do? What do the kids in Mason City want to do? What do the kids in Iowa want to do? They want to get out. I'd get out, go to California if I could." There is a double migration, from farms into towns, from towns into cities, and out of the state. More than 10 per cent of Mason City's work force is employed at the Decker packing plant on the north side of town. (The plant is a division of Armour and Company.) At the moment the plant is prosperous; it pays good wages. (A hamboner—who does piece work—can make $6 to $7 an hour.) But what would happen, asked one of the city's corporate managers, if the place should succumb to the increasing efficiency of newer plants? "What'll we do the day—and don't quote me—when the place has to shut down?"

It is the fashion to worry slow, worry with a drawl. Urgency and crisis are not the style. Through most of its history, Mason City was dominated by a few families, and to some extent it still is—not because they are so powerful, but because Federal Avenue once thought they were. Small towns create their own patriarchs, tall men who look even taller against the flatness of history, producing—inevitably—a belief that civic motion and inertia are the subtle work of Big Men: bankers, real estate operators, and corporate managers. Mason City still talks about the General, Hanford MacNider (banking, cement, real estate), who was an Assistant Secretary of War under Coolidge, ambassador to Canada, an aspirant for the 1940 Republican nomination for President, and, for a time, a supporter of America First. (In Mason City, MacNider was *Secretary* of War and barely missed becoming President.) The MacNiders gave the city land for parks, for the public library, and for a museum. (The General was also a founder of the Euchre and Cycle Club, a lunch-and-dinner club—all the best people—which still has no Jewish members, and he is remembered, among other things, as the man who did not lower his flag for thirty days after John F. Kennedy was killed.) "My father," said Jack MacNider, now president of the Northwestern States Portland Cement Company, "was quite a guy. Some people thought he was tough. To some he was a patron saint. You should have known him."

The General's shadow has survived him, and there are still people who are persuaded that nothing of major consequence can be accomplished in Mason City against the opposition of the MacNider family. Is that true, you ask Jack, sitting in his second-story office overlooking Federal Avenue. (There is a picture of the General, in full uniform, behind Jack's desk.) "I'm flattered," he answers, not defensively, but with some amusement, saying more between the lines than on the record, telling you—you imagine—that the MacNiders take the rap for a lot of small-town inertia they can't control, and that they suffer (or enjoy) a visibility for which they haven't asked. At this very moment a young lawyer named Tom Jolas, a second generation Greek, is challenging the Establishment (such as it is) in his campaign for mayor; you both know that Jolas is likely to win (on November 4 he did win, handily) and that the city's style and mood are now determined as much by younger businessmen and professionals—and by hundreds of packing house workers and cement workers —as they are by the old families. "This must be a fish bowl for the MacNiders," you say, and Jack offers no argument. And when you speak about prejudice in Mason City, Jack agrees—yes, there is—but you can't be sure whether he means only against Catholics, Jews, and Negroes (or Greeks, and Chicanos), or also against the MacNiders. The shadow is still there, but the General is dead.

Mason City's traditional style of politics and political behavior was nicely represented by sixty-five-year-old George Mendoń, who was mayor for sixteen years until Jolas beat him. Small towns always create the illusion of responsiveness—you can call any public official, any corporate manager, with little interference from secretaries who ask your business, your name, and your pedigree—and you thus can walk into Mendon's office unannounced and receive an audience. But you are never sure that, once in, you have really arrived anywhere. The action must be someplace else. The room is almost bare, the desk virtually clean, the man without visible passion. Yes, jobs and industrial development are a problem, and Mason City has done pretty well, but there are 20,000 other towns trying to attract industry, and, you know, these things take time. Yes, they would like to hire some Negroes for the police force, but none has qualified. Yes, the MacNiders had been good to the city—all that land they'd given (and all those tax deductions?) but . . . When Mendon was challenged during the campaign about operating an underpaid and undertrained police force, he answered that the city had the most modern equipment, including riot guns, Mace, and bulletproof vests. What are they for, you ask, and Mendon, rattling the change in his pockets, identifies himself. "Our colored population is peaceful," he said. "They wouldn't riot. But you never know when people from the outside might come in and try to start something." Mason City is prepared for Watts and Newark, and somewhere in its open heart there lurks an edge of apprehension that the fire next time might burn even here. But when Mendon spoke about his riot guns at an open meeting, the general response was tempered by considerable facetious amusement, and the people who were amused went out to vote against him, and beat him.

There is no single current running against the old style of politics, or against the Mendons and the Establishment they are supposed to represent. In 1968, Mason City voted for Nixon, for the conservative Congressman H. R. Gross, and for Harold Hughes, a liberal Democrat, for the U.S. Senate. ("We helped elect Gross the first time he ran," said a union official, "and we've been sorry ever since.") Sociology and political calculations don't help much. "The issue here," said Bud Stewart, who runs a music store and worked for Jolas, "is generational," implying that whatever was young and progressive supported the challenger against the older Establishment. Jolas campaigned under the slogan "Time for a Change," including, among other things, concern for public housing (which the city does not have, but desperately needs), more attention to the problems of youth, and the creation of a modern police force that could meet what he called the rising rate of crime. (And which meant, I was told, getting rid of the reactionary police chief who had bought all the riot junk). But what Jolas said was clearly not as important as what he is: young, energetic, and, beneath it all, ambiguously liberal, and unambiguously decent. "I had my hair long and wore sideburns," he tells you (two years ago, he managed a teen-age rock band), "but my friends said I couldn't win with it; so I cut it short. But maybe after the election I might get a notion and let it grow again."

Jolas's great political achievement before he ran for mayor was to force the state to reroute a projected interstate highway, so that it would pass within a few miles of Mason City, but it was undoubtedly personality rather than politics that elected him. ("You know what they're saying about me?" he mused one day toward the end of the campaign. "They're saying that, if I'm elected, the Greeks and the niggers are going to take over Mason City. I even had someone charge that I belong to the Mafia—the Greek Mafia.") More than anything else, Jolas seems to have a sense of concern about youth—not a program—but an awakening awareness of how kids are shortchanged by schools, politicians, by adults. ("He knows," I wrote in my notes, "that the world screws kids.")

What Jolas can achieve is doubtful. He will not have a sympathetic city council nor perhaps even a sympathetic community, and his commitment to a downtown civic center and mall as a means of restoring the vitality of the central business area may be more the token of modernism than the substance of progress; yet it is clear that Jolas received the support, and represented the aspirations of whatever liberalism (black, labor, professional) the city could muster. If you sit in his storefront headquarters long enough, you learn how far Main Street has come from Babbittry. You meet Marie Dresser, the recently widowed wife of a physician, who, as president of the Iowa League of Women Voters, carried a reapportionment fight through the legislature and who speaks of how, when their son decided to grow a mustache, she and her husband decided to back him against the school authorities and how, eventually, they won; Jean Beatty, the wife of a psychologist, answering phone calls and stuffing Jolas campaign envelopes, and shuttling between meetings of the league and the local branch of the NAACP, knowing that the organization should be run by black people, but knowing also that its precariously weak membership cannot sustain it without help; or Jim Shannon, the county Democratic chairman, who has worked for the Milwaukee Railroad all his life, and who has gone back to the local community college (working nights, studying economics during the day), speaking in his soft, laconic, infinitely American cadences about the campaign for Bobby Kennedy in 1968, about a decade of legislative fights, reminding you, without meaning to, or even mentioning it, that liberalism wasn't invented in New York, that the Phil Harts, the Frank Churches, the Fred Harrises, and the George McGoverns weren't elected by professors.

If that were all—if one could merely say that Mason City and Middle America are going modern—it would be easy, but it is not. (What, after all, is modern—uniquely modern—after technology has been dispensed with?) The national culture is there—mass cult, high, middle, and low, mod and trad: Bud Steward in the Edwardian doublebreasted suits that he orders from advertisements through the local stores; the elite trooping off to Minneapolis to hear the Met when it comes on tour, or to Ames to catch the New York Philharmonic (mostly, say the cynics, to be conspicuous, not for love of music); the rock on the radio and in the jukes (the Fifth Dimension, Blood, Sweat and Tears, new Dylan and old Baez, plus some leavening from the likes of Johnny Cash); the long hair and the short skirts, the drugs and the booze. (At the same time, beer, rather than pot, seems still to be the preponderant, though not the exclusive, form of adolescent sin.) But somehow what Mason City receives through the box and the tube—and from trips to Minneapolis and Des Moines, where some of the ladies do almost weekly shopping—Mason City seems to shape and reshape into its own forms. There is a tendency to mute the decibels of public controversy and social friction, perhaps because people are more tolerant and relaxed, perhaps because they are simply less crowded. There is talk about crime and violence, but the most common examples seem usually to involve the theft of bicycles and the destruction of Halloween pumpkins. (Another way of staking a claim on the modern?) If you ask long enough, you can get some of the blue-collar workers to speak about their resentment against welfare, taxes, and student demonstrators (not at Harvard, mind you, but at the State University of Iowa), but it is commonly only television and the newspapers that produce the talk. And so it tends to be dispassionate, distant, and somewhat abstract. Bumper stickers and decals are scarce; American flags are rarely seen on the rear windows of automobiles because, one might assume, there aren't many people at whom to wave them, not many devils to exorcise. The silent majority here is an abstraction, a collage of minorities, except when it comes to the normalcy of the ladies' study clubs and bridge clubs, the football, the hunting and fishing, and the trip to the lake. And every two years they go back, most of them, and vote for H. R. Gross.

And yet, here are the kids, high school students and students at the Community College, organizing a Moratorium march, running a little newspaper semi-underground within the high school, and with the blessing of the school authorities; here are the clergymen, not all, but a few, giving their support for the march from the pulpit (when she heard her minister that Sunday, one prominent parishioner promptly resigned from the church); and here are ordinary people responding to the critics of dissent with their own protest. In a letter to the *Globe Gazette*:

> We supported the Moratorium Day demonstration. We have a son in Vietnam. We love our country. We fly the American flag.
> But we do not believe in blindly following our leader as the Germans did when their leader decided to exterminate the Jews, or as some Americans would do if our leader should decide to exterminate the Indians.
> We feel our country was wrong to send 40,000 of our boys to their death, not defending their own shores.
> Supporting the Moratorium was our way of saying we love our country right or wrong, and this time it was wrong.

Given the reputation of the average small town in America, the greatest surprise is the school system, which, under Rod Bickert, the superintendent, and John Patzwald, the high school principal, has managed to move well beyond the expected, even in the conventional modern suburb. Mason City has abandoned dress codes in its high school, has instituted flexible-modular scheduling (meaning that students have only a limited number of formal lecture classes, and can do their own thing—in "skill" and study centers, in the library, or in the cafeteria—as they will), and has begun to experiment, in the high school, with an "open mike" on which a student can talk to the entire school on anything he pleases. There are no bells, no monitors. As you walk through the halls (modern, sprawling, corporate style) with Patzwald, a Minnesotan, he explains that he first came to the school as a disciplinarian. "It was a conservative school, and I ran a tight ship." When he became principal, he turned things around. "We're something of an island, and when some of the parents first heard about it, they thought it was chaos. We had an open meeting—parents and students—to explain the flex-mod schedule, but most of the parents wanted to know about dress. You know, we have everything here, including girls in miniskirts and pants suits. The students helped us carry it. They know that some sort of uproar could blow this thing right out of the water, but I think they can do the job."

Every day Patzwald spends a couple of hours visiting classes, asking students irreverent questions that are, at least tangentially, directed to the teachers. "I ask them why they're doing what they're doing. What's the significance of this? Why study it at all? Sure we have some weak teachers, but now when I hire people I role-play with them a little. I want to see how they take pressure. In the classroom it's too easy for the teachers always to be the last resort and to put the screws down. That's no way to improve the climate of learning." The conversation is frequently interrupted while Patzwald stops to talk with students (he knows many by name), and later he tells you about them. "Kids are my life," he says, rounding a corner after a brief encounter with two boys. "The whole point is to get them to appreciate the worth of an individual. We have to reach the ones who are overlooked, like one boy they were taunting and who talked about himself as 'a ball that they always kick around.' Those are the ones we have to reach. But I think we're coming."

The militant students seek you out. Mason City is still a confining place, and they find The Man from *Saturday Review,* the outsider, walking through the hall alone. The organizers of the Moratorium, the editors of the mimeographed paper the *Bitter End* (not quite underground, not quite official), the activists are sons and daughters of affluent lawyers and doctors, all local people, not carpetbaggers from the East. The school, they say, is divided between "pointy heads like us" and "the animals." (A group passes through the hall after school, and the pointy heads, through a glass door, follow the herd with "moo-moo," "oink-oink.") The radicals still see the school as a fraud. "There is no way to get a decent education in a public school. Everybody's too up-tight." Like what? "Like being allowed to leave school during your unstructured time to make a movie. You can get a release to dish hamburgers at McDonald's; so why not to make movies?" One of them gets threatening letters for his part in the peace movement, another loses his allowance because he won't cut his hair. Their lives are no different—nor are their parents'—from those of similar people in Scarsdale or Shaker Heights or Winnetka. (Some of them, said Patzwald, "have told their parents to go to hell.") What is surprising is that, although they are a lonely minority, they can be found in this community at all.

For the majority of the young, the concerns are universal: cars, dances, sports. You hear them in Vic's ("Real Dago Pizza"): "It's a '65 Chevy. I traded it for that car that was sitting in the grass by the Hub." "Paid $350 and put a new engine in it, and it runs great." They want to go to college, to get jobs; more than half the high school students work, so they can maintain those automobiles, and get married. The modest dream is to become an airline stewardess—"If I'm not too clumsy"—to enlist in the Army, to learn a trade. On Friday nights they cruise up and down Federal, shuttling from a root beer stand at the south end to a drive-in at the other. There is some talk about establishing a teen center, a Place Where Kids Can Go, but the proposal draws little enthusiasm from adults and less from the kids. And yet, even among the majority, the animals, the apathetic, something may be happening. The war perhaps, or television, or the music. There was a time, said a school administrator, "when the war seemed very distant." Mason City's enlistment rate was always high; the college students were exempt anyway, and the draft wasn't much of an issue. But in the past year eight recent graduates of Mason City High were killed in Vietnam, making death and change more personal. Nearly a hundred turned out to hear discussions about the war inside the school, and, while the patriotic speakers still come to address the assembly, other messages are being heard as well. The hair gets longer, the music a little harder, and the news is on everybody's set.

The young are slowly becoming mediators of the culture; they receive the signals from the outside and interpret the messages for the adults. And that's new for all America, not just for Mason City. "The kids are having an effect on their parents," said a mental health worker, apparently one of the few clinicians in town whom the adolescents are willing to trust. "People here are friendly and uptight at the same time. Many of them take the attitude that the children should have their fun, that eventually they'll come around to their parents' view. But people have been jarred—by TV and by their own children—and they know, some of them at least, that they've got to listen. They're trying to become looser."

But becoming looser is still a struggle and, given the conditions of life, an imperative that can be deferred. ("I'm *not* going to send my son to Harvard," says a Harvard graduate. "An eighteen-year-old is not mature enough to handle SDS and all that other garbage.") The space, the land, the weather, the incessant reminders of physical normalcy make it possible to defer almost anything. Church on Sunday, football on Friday, and the cycle of parties, dinners, and cookouts remain more visible (not to say comprehensible) than the subtleties of cultural change or social injustice. If the churches and their ministers are losing some of their influence among the young (and if the call for psychiatrists is increasing), they are still holding their members, and if the Catholic monsignor, Arthur Breen, has to schedule a folk mass at Holy Family every Sunday (in addition to four other masses) he nonetheless continues to pack them in.

What you see most of all (see is not a good word; feel, maybe) is a faith in the capacity of people and institutions to be responsive, the belief that, finally, things are pretty much what they seem, that Things Work. "This is just a big farm town," said a Mason City businessman. "You don't check people's credit here. You just assume they'll pay their bills. In Waterloo, which is really an industrial city, even though it isn't very big, you check everybody out." The answer to an economic problem is to work harder, to take a second job, or to send your wife to work, usually as a clerk or a waitress. (Wages for women are extremely low.) On the radio, *Junior Achievement* makes its peace with modernism by setting its jingle to "Get With It" to a rock beat, but the message of adolescent enterprise (Babbittry?) is the same, and around the lunch tables at the Green Mill Restaurant or the bar at Tom MacNider's Chart House it is difficult to convince anyone that sometimes even people with the normal quota of ambition can't make it.

The advantages of that faith are obvious, but the price is high. "This is a nice town as long as you don't rock the boat," said Willis Haddix, a meat packer, who is president of the struggling Mason City chapter of NAACP. "What's wrong here is in the secret places": in subtle discrimination in housing and jobs; in the out-of-sight, dilapidated frame houses at the north and south ends of town, buildings surrounded with little piles of lumber, rusting metal chairs, decaying junk cars once slated for repair; in the lingering aroma of personal defeat; and in the cross between arrogance and apathy that declares "there are no poor people in this area." On Sundays, while most people are packing their campers for the trip home, or making the transition between church and television football, the old, who have little to do, wander into the Park Inn for lunch—hot roast beef sandwiches for $1.25—and to talk about Medicare. And against theirs you hear other voices: Murray Lawson, for example, a civilized, compassionate man, who represents Mason City in the legislature, saying, "We've been generous with education, but not so generous with the old. We've had a rough time with nursing homes"; Jim Shannon, who supports his wife and seven children on the salary of a railroad clerk and janitor, describing the effects of a regressive sales tax that victimizes the small man but makes little impact on the rich: the official of the local OEO poverty agency talking about the county's third welfare generation and reflecting that "an admission of poverty is an admission of failure, and people here don't do that"; Tom Jolas describing Mason City's enthusiasm for the New York Mets when they won the World Series after a ninth place finish in 1968, because "people believe in coming off the bottom."

And then you learn something else—about yourself, and about the phenomenon you choose to call Main Street. You hear them complain about Eastern urban provincialism, about those people who cannot believe that Mason City has television ("You must get it from the West Coast"), let alone an art museum, a decent library, or a couple of go-go joints (or that you can buy Philip Roth, Malcolm X, and Henry Miller in the bookstore), and you begin to understand, almost by suggestion, what the barriers of comprehension are all about. Is it really surprising that Main Street cannot fully comprehend talk about police brutality, police rigidity, or social disillusionment? If the system works here, why doesn't it work everywhere else? Main Street's uniquely provincial vice lies in its excessive, unquestioning belief (in the Protestant ethic, hard work, honesty, and conventional politics); New York's in the conviction that most of the time nothing may make much difference, that institutions and public life are by their very nature unresponsive. And if New York has come to doubt the values and the beliefs of tradition, it still hasn't invented anything to replace them. The anger of the blue-collar worker —at welfare, students, Negroes—is rooted in the frustrated ethic of Main Street, frustrated in not only its encounters with urban problems and technology, but in the growing doubt of the Best people—Wallace's pointy heads, Agnew's effete impudent snobs—that it still has merit. Among the characteristic excesses of rural populism (whether expressed by William Jennings Bryan, Joe McCarthy, or Spiro Agnew) was a paranoia about Them: the bankers, the railroads, the Communists in government, the Eastern Establishment. But paranoia is surely also one of the characteristic defenses of almost every other inhabitant of New York. (If you try to explain the vicissitudes of dealing with Con Edison or the New York Telephone Company, most people in Mason City stare at you in disbelief; if you speak about rents and housing, they're certain you've gone mad.) Every rural or small-town vote against some proposal for the alleviation of a problem in New York or Chicago or Cleveland is not merely an act of self-interest (keeping taxes low, protecting the farmers) but a gesture of disbelief that Main Street's ethic and tactics—if they really applied— would be ineffective in the Big City.

At the end, sitting in the waiting room at the Municipal Airport (all flights from Chicago, naturally, are late), you detach yourself. You hear, still, one of the Federal Avenue lawyers saying, "This town is solid. It's solid as a commercial center, and as a medical and cultural center for a large region." You see his nearly bare office, the brown wood furniture, the linoleum floors, and the fluorescent lights, see his partner in a sleeveless, gray pullover walking through the outer office (Clarence Darrow?), and hear the trucks stopping for the red light at the intersection below. You hear Jack MacNider speaking about the gradual movement of the "iron triangle"—the Midwestern industrial region—into north central Iowa, speaking about the ultimate industrialization of the area around the city. You see the high school homecoming queen, fragile and uncomfortable in the back of an open convertible in the wind-chilled stadium; see the wide residential streets with their maples and time-threatened elms, the section of magnificent houses by Prairie School architects (one of them by Frank Lloyd Wright) and the crumbling streets at the south end, near the Brick and Tile; and you hear, in that same neighborhood, two NAACP ladies, one white, one Negro, discussing the phrasing of a letter to the school board politely protesting the use of *Little Black Sambo* in the elementary grades. And then, finally, you hear again all those people speaking about how good Mason City is for raising a family, and you wonder what kind of society it is that must separate growing up and the rearing of children from the places where most of its business is transacted, its ideas discussed, and its policies determined. And then you wonder, too, what would happen if something ever came seriously to disturb Main Street's normalcy, if direct demands were ever made, if the letters ceased being polite, if the dark places—the discrimination and disregard—were probed and, for the first time, tested. Small towns do co-opt, you think, not by what they do, not by their hospitality, but by what we wish they were—because all of us, big city boys and small, *want* to believe. And yet, when Ozark 974 rises from the runway, off to Dubuque, over the corn and beets, over the Mississippi, off to Chicago, you know that you can't go home again, that the world is elsewhere, and that every moment the distances grow not smaller but greater. Main Street is far away.

52. Strategies for Survival
BARBARA WARD AND RENÉ DUBOS

Among scientific scholars, the authors of this selection are known as two of the most prestigious. Their respective accomplishments are deeply impressive. Mrs. Ward is a native of Britain. Dubos, born in France but now a naturalized American, has won numerous awards for his work in bacteriology. The selection that follows is the concluding chapter in the Ward/Dubos volume describing the precarious condition of the earth as a closed ecosystem. But, knowing that those without hope give up any pretense at attempting reform, Ward and Dubos counsel that there are strategies we can use to save humanity's home. These strategies must be international in

SOURCE: Barbara Ward and René Dubos, *Only One Earth: The Care and Maintenance of a Small Planet* (New York: W. W. Norton Co., 1972), pp. 213–220. Copyright © 1972 by Report on the Human Environment, Inc. Reprinted by permission.

scope, they warn. To those who say it is useless to think that nationalism can be surmounted by internationalism, they answer that self-interest alone is leading people to the realization that our planet has ". . . totally continuous and interdependent systems of air, land, and water . . ." They go on to say:

> It is even possible that recognition of our environmental interdependence can do more than save us, negatively, from the final folly of war. It could, positively, give us that sense of community, of belonging and living together, without which no human society can be built up, survive, and prosper.

THE NEED FOR KNOWLEDGE

. . . We are not sleepwalkers or sheep. If men have not hitherto realized the extent of their planetary interdependence it was in part at least because, in clear, precise physical and scientific fact, it did not yet exist. The new insights of our fundamental condition can also become the insights of our survival. We may be learning just in time.

There are three clear fields in which we can already begin to perceive the direction in which our planetary policies have to go. They match the three separate, powerful and divisive thrusts—of science, of markets, of nations—which have brought us, with such tremendous force, to our present predicament. And they point in the opposite direction—to a deeper and more widely shared knowledge of our environmental unity, to a new sense of partnership and sharing in our sovereign economics and politics, to a wider loyalty which transcends the traditional limited allegiance of tribes and peoples. There are already pointers to these necessities. We have now to make them the new drives and imperatives of our planetary existence.

We can begin with knowledge.

The first step toward devising a strategy for planet Earth is for the nation to accept a *collective* responsibility for discovering more—much more—about the natural system and how it is affected by man's activities and vice versa. This implies cooperative monitoring, research, and study on an unprecedented scale. It implies an intensive world-wide network for the systematic exchange of knowledge and experience. It implies a quite new readiness to take research wherever it is needed, with the backing of international financing. It means the fullest cooperation in converting knowledge into action—whether it be placing research satellites in orbit or reaching agreements on fishing, or introducing a new control for snail-borne disease.

But it is important not to make so much of our state of ignorance that we are inhibited from vigorous action now. For while there is much that we do not yet understand, there are fundamental things that we *do* know. Above all, we know that there are limits to the burdens that the natural system and its components can bear, limits to the levels of toxic substances the human body can tolerate, limits to the amount of manipulation that man can exert upon natural balances without causing a breakdown in the system, limits to the psychic shock that men and societies can absorb from relentlessly accelerating social change—or social degradation. In many cases we cannot yet define these limits. But wherever the danger signals are appearing—inland seas losing oxygen, pesticides producing resistant strains of pests, laterite replacing tropical forests, carbon dioxide in the air, poisons in the ocean, the ills of the inner cities—we must be ready to set in motion the cooperative international efforts of directed research which make available, with all possible speed, solutions for those most intimately concerned with the immediate problem and wider knowledge for all men of how our natural systems actually work. To go blindly on, sharing, inadvertently, the risks and keeping to ourselves the knowledge needed for solutions can only mean more agonies than we can cope with and more danger than future generations deserve.

A full and open sharing of new knowledge about the interdependence of the planetary systems on which we all depend can also help us, as it were, to creep up on the infinitely sensitive issues of divisive economic and political sovereignty.

SOVEREIGNTY AND DECISION-MAKING

Given our millennial habits of separate decision-making and the recent tremendous explosion of *national* power, how can any perception of the biosphere's essential unity and interdependence be combined with the acutely self-conscious separate sovereignty of more than 130 national governments?

Yet, in fact, for at least a century, some habits of cooperation have been accepted by states simply through recognition of their own self-interests. Ever since the world economy began to increase in extent and interdependence in the eighteenth and nineteenth centuries, sovereign states have shared some of their authority either by binding themselves to certain forms of cooperative behavior or by delegating limited power to other bodies. Despite rhetorical insistence on absolute sovereignty, governments have recognized in practice that this is impossible in some cases and inordinately foolish in many more. It is no use claiming the sovereign right not to deliver other people's letters if they use their sovereign right to refuse yours. The alternative to international allocation of radio frequencies would be chaos in world communications to the disadvantage and danger of all states. In brief, when governments are faced with such realities, they have exercised their inherent sovereign right to share voluntarily their sovereignty with others in limited and agreed areas of activity.

In the twentieth century, as a consequence of an ever greater overlap between supposedly sovereign national interests, the number of international treaties, conventions, organizations, consultative forums, and cooperative programs has multiplied rapidly. The growth of an intergovernmental community finds its most concrete expression in the United Nations and its family of specialized functional agencies and regional commissions. Outside the United Nations system, there has been an analagous growth of international organizations, governmental and nongovernmental, especially on the regional level.

All intergovernmental institutions are still, ultimately, creatures of national governments, but a large amount of their day-to-day work is sufficiently and obviously useful that a measure of authority and initiative comes to rest with them. They acquire support within national governments from the relevant ministries and agencies which, in turn, find useful constituencies within the ranks of international organizations. This is, none of it, a formal departure from sovereignty. But a strict, literal definition of sovereignty gets blurred in practice and the existence of continuous forums for debate and bargaining helps instill the habit of cooperation into the affairs of reluctant governments.

It is on to this scene of ultimate national sovereignty and proliferating intermediate institutions that the new environmental imperatives have broken in the last few years. The first effect has undoubtedly been to complicate still further a very complicated situation. Quite suddenly, for a whole variety of reasons, a very wide range of institutions have added an environmental concern to their other interests. In some cases, traditional programs and activities have been renamed to qualify them under the environmental rubric. In others a number of agencies have taken up the same environmental topic, though mainly from differing points of view. There has been some genuine innovation, and there is much ferment and groping as international organizations, to a greater or lesser degree, seek to comprehend and to adapt to the environmental imperative.

One example of combined good will and overlap can be taken from air pollution. The industrialized nations are the main polluters. So regional groupings are starting to respond. The Organization for Economic Cooperation and Development—the successor to the old Marshall Plan bureaucracy, linking North America with Western Europe and, more recently, Japan—is setting up an Environment Committee to coordinate a number of its existing research activities, for instance, its Air Management Research Group. The regional commissions of the United Nations are also beginning to move and the Economic Commission for Europe also has a Committee of Experts on Air Pollution. So has the North Atlantic Treaty Organization, which includes air pollution among a number of other research activities such as open waters and inland waters pollution, disaster relief, and regional decision-making for environmental issues.

This picture of somewhat uncoordinated and hence not fully focused activity, however, largely reflects the recentness of the environmental awareness. National governments, too, are trying to find means of adding an environmental angle of vision to institutions which have hitherto followed the traditional one-track approach to specialized problems through separate and usually uncoordinated administration. A rash of environmental councils and commissions is now appearing round the world to coordinate the activities of hitherto separate ministries. Several countries have taken the bolder step of bringing relevant ministries—housing, transport, technology—together in single Departments of the Environment. The various experiments are mostly not yet two years old, and it is too soon to say how well they may succeed in introducing an integrative view of man-environment relations into the national decision-making process. Certainly it will not be easy.

And certainly it will be still more difficult at the international than at national levels of decision-making. So locked are we within our tribal units, so possessive over national rights, so suspicious of any extension of international authority that we may fail to sense the need for dedicated and committed action over the whole field of planetary necessities. Nonetheless there are jobs to be done which perhaps require at this stage no more than a limited, special, and basically self-interested application of the global point of view. For instance, it is only by forthright cooperation and action at the global level that nations can protect mankind from inadvertent and potentially disastrous modification in the planetary weather system, over which no nation can assert sovereignty. Again, no sovereignty can hold sway over the single, interconnected global ocean system which is nature's ultimate sink and man's favorite sewer.

Where pretensions to national sovereignty have no relevance to perceived problems, nations have no choice but to follow the course of common policy and coordinated action. In three vital, related areas this is now the undeniable case—the global atmosphere, the global oceans, and the global weather system. All require the adoption of a planetary approach by the leaders of nations, no matter how parochial their point of view toward matters that lie within national jurisdiction. A strategy for planet Earth, undergirded by a sense of collective responsibility to discover more about man-environment relations, could well move, then, into operation on these three fronts: atmosphere, oceans, and climate. It is no small undertaking, but quite possibly the very minimum required in defense of the future of the human race.

But it is not only the pollutions and degradations of the atmosphere and the oceans that threaten the quality of life at the planetary level. There are threats, too, of disease spreading among undernourished children, of protein deficiency maiming the intelligence of millions, of spreading illiteracy combined with rising numbers of unemployed intellectuals, of landless workers streaming to the squalid cities, and worklessness growing there to engulf a quarter of the working force. An acceptable strategy for planet Earth must, then, explicitly take account of the fact that the natural resource most threatened with pollution, most exposed to degradation, most liable to irreversible damage is not this or that species, not this or that plant or biome or habitat, not even the free airs or the great oceans. It is man himself.

THE SURVIVAL OF MAN

Here again, no one nation, not even groups of nations, can, acting separately, avoid the tragedy of increasing divisions between wealthy north and poverty-striken south in our planet. No nations, on their own, can offset the risk of deepening disorder. No nations, acting singly or only with their own kind, rich or poor, can stave off the risks of unacceptable paternalism on the one hand or resentful rejection on the other. International policies are, in fact, within sight of the point reached by *internal* development in the mid-nineteenth century. Either they will move on to a community based upon a more systematic sharing of wealth—through progressive income tax, through general policies for education, shelter, health, and housing—or they break down in revolt and anarchy. Many of today's proposals for development aid, through international channels, are a first sketch of such a system.

But at this point, if gloom is the psychological risk of all too many ecological forecasts, may we not go to the opposite extreme of Pollyanna optimism in forecasting any such growth of a sense of community in our troubled and divided planet? With war as mankind's oldest habit and divided sovereignty as his most treasured inheritance, where are the energies, the psychic force, the profound commitment needed for a wider loyalty?

Loyalty may, however, be the key. It is the view of many modern psychologists that man is a killer not because of any biological imperative but because of his capacity for misplaced loyalty. He will do in the name of a wider allegiance what he would shrink to do in his own nature. His massive, organized killings—the kind that distinguishes him from all other animals—are invariably done in the name of faith or ideology, of people or clan. Here, it is not wholly irrational to hope that the full realization of planetary interdependence—in biosphere and technosphere alike—may begin to affect man in the depths of his capacity for psychic commitment. All loyalty is based on two elements—the hope of protection and the hope of enhancement. On either count, the new ecological imperative can give a new vision of where man belongs in his final security and his final sense of dignity and identity.

At the most down-to-earth level of self-interest, it is the realization of the planet's totally continuous and interdependent systems of air, land, and water that helps to keep a check on the ultimate lunacies of nuclear weaponry. When after the nuclear testing conducted in 1960, the air above Britain was found to contain 20 per cent more strontium 90 and cesium 137, it is not a very sophisticated guess that the air of the testing states contained no less. It is the force of such recognitions that lay behind the first global environmental agreement—the Test-Ban Treaty negotiated in 1963—which has kept earlier nuclear powers out of competitive air testing and saved unnumbered children from leukemia. Similar calculations of enlightened self-interest underlie the treaty to keep nuclear weapons out of space, off the seabeds, and away from Antarctica.

Where negotiations continue—as in the Treaty to prevent the spread of nuclear weapons, or the Soviet-American talks on a mutual limitation of strategic arms—the underlying rationale is still the same. As the airs and oceans flow round our little planet, there is not much difference between your strontium 90 and my strontium 90. They are lethal to us both.

It is even possible that recognition of our environmental interdependence can do more than save us, negatively, from the final folly of war. It could, positively, give us that sense of community, of belonging and living together, without which no human society can be built up, survive, and prosper. Our links of blood and history, our sense of shared culture and achievement, our traditions, our faiths are all precious and enrich the world with the variety of scale and function required for every vital ecosystem. But we have lacked a wider rationale of unity. Our prophets have sought it. Our poets have dreamed of it. But it is only in our own day that astronomers, physicists, geologists, chemists, biologists, anthropologists, ethnologists, and archaeologists have all combined in a single witness of advanced science to tell us that, in every alphabet of our being, we do indeed belong to a single system, powered by a single energy, manifesting a fundamental unity under all its variations, depending for its survival on the balance and health of the total system.

If this vision of unity—which is not a vision only but a hard and inescapable scientific fact—can become part of the common insight of all the inhabitants of planet Earth, then we may find that, beyond all our inevitable pluralisms, we can achieve just enough unity of purpose to build a human world.

In such a world, the practices and institutions with which we are familiar inside our domestic societies would become, suitably modified, the basis of planetary order. In fact, in many of our present international institutions the sketch of such a system already exists. A part of the process would be the nonviolent settlement of disputes with legal, arbitral, and policing procedures on an international basis. Part of it would be the transfer of resources from rich to poor through progressive world sharing—the system of which a 1 per cent standard of gross national product for aid-giving is the first faint sign. World plans for health and education, world investment in progressive farming, a world strategy for better cities, world action for pollution control and an enhanced environment would simply be seen as logical extensions of the practice of limited intergovernmental cooperation, already imposed by mutual functional needs and interests.

Our new knowledge of our planetary interdependence demands that the functions are now seen to be world-wide and supported with as rational a concept of self-interest. Governments have already paid lip service to such a view of the world by setting up a whole variety of United Nations agencies whose duty it is to elaborate world-wide strategies. But the idea of authority and energy and resources to support their policies seems strange, visionary, and Utopian at present, simply because world institutions are not backed by any sense of planetary community and commitment. Indeed, the whole idea of operating effectively at the world level still seems in some way peculiar and unlikely. The planet is not yet a center of rational loyalty for all mankind.

But possibly it is precisely this shift of loyalty that a profound and deepening sense of our shared and interdependent biosphere can stir to life in us. That men can experience such transformations is not in doubt. From family to clan, from clan to nation, from nation to federation—such enlargements of allegiance have occurred without wiping out the earlier loves. Today, in human society, we can perhaps hope to survive in all our prized diversity provided we can achieve an ultimate loyalty to our single, beautiful, and vulnerable planet Earth.

Alone in space, alone in its life-supporting systems, powered by inconceivable energies, mediating them to us through the most delicate adjustments, wayward, unlikely, unpredictable, but nourishing, enlivening, and enriching in the largest degree—is this not a precious home for all of us earthlings? Is it not worth our love? Does it not deserve all the inventiveness and courage and generosity of which we are capable to preserve it from degradation and destruction and, by doing so, to secure our own survival?

Collective Behavior–Sociocultural Change

Part XI

In this final section we have four articles illustrating some of the factors in what are termed *collective behavior* and *sociocultural change*. The sociological speciality known as collective behavior deals with such phenomena as riots, fashion, and social movements. Sociocultural change, as the term clearly indicates, is concerned with the various things that lead to significant alterations in society and culture. Since collective behavior results from, and causes, change, and vice versa, the two phenomena are conveniently studied together.

53. Prohibition: A Case Study of Societal Misguidance

MARGARET NELSON

Among the phenomena involved in collective behavior, social movements are the most important because they are so often significant for sociocultural change. All such change is not necessarily for the good, as Margaret Nelson contends in this study of the factors leading to the adoption of the Eighteenth Amendment to the Constitution. At the time of writing her article, Ms. Nelson was a sociology graduate student at Columbia University. She manages to throw new light on a subject that is perennially the best example sociologists cite to illustrate the point that legal enactments can be truly effective only to the degree that they are compatible with the sociocultural system of which they are a part.

The ratification of the Eighteenth Amendment seems in retrospect a social and political anomaly. In a country where the "social drink" is a widely accepted custom, attacked only by small groups on the fringes of society (Gusfield, 1955: 232), the idea of prohibition has an unfamiliar ring. Similarly, to Americans who have watched countless half-hearted governmental attempts at solving social problems, only to see them left in the end to non-governmental agencies or to state control, the early-twentieth-century decision to write into the Constitution a broad national reform is astonishing, particularly since a decentralized, inertial government is regarded favorably by a large proportion of the population.

Such an occurrence, then, as the vote for the Eighteenth Amendment is not easily explained. (Other social movements have come and gone, leaving no more trace than a few sentences buried in history textbooks; social

SOURCE: Margaret Nelson, "Prohibition: A Case Study of Societal Misguidance," *American Behavioral Scientist*, vol. 12, no. 2 (November/December 1968): 37–43. Reprinted by permission of the Publisher, Sage Publications, Inc., and the author.

problems have been brought to public attention only to be ignored a short while later; powerful pressure groups have lobbied furiously before Congress without attaining their goals. To say, as Frederick Lewis Allen (1964: 205), that "The country accepted it [prohibition] not only willingly, but almost absentmindedly," or, as many historians (i.e., Clark, 1965: 114) claim, that it was the declining rural areas wreaking their final revenge on the growing cities, is inadequate. Nor are there simple answers to why prohibition rather than temperance, or why at that particular point in history. Regulative measures concerning the use of alcohol had existed as early as the colonial period (Krout, 1925: 2), and the fifty years preceding the passage of the Eighteenth Amendment had seen two great waves of prohibition sentiment. What was it, then, in this particular movement coming at this particular time which allowed it such great success at one point and such deep failure several years later?

Few societies accomplish radical changes easily. By and large, people find it simpler to adapt to ongoing processes: to control or guide these processes requires money, energy, and often great sacrifices on the part of the population at large. The tendency toward inaction or compromise is particularly strong if, as in America in the early 1900's suggested controls run counter to social customs:[1] to traditional ideas of individualism, states' rights, and laissez-faire; and to opposition from big business. Against such strong forces, neither vague sentiment nor a widely popular idea can make much headway—as was evidenced, in part, by the failures of two earlier prohibition movements.

A successful social movement, then, needs more than a favorable climate of opinion. First, groups supporting the change must be organized. Second, as many potential adherents as possible must be mobilized into political activity. For this, funds must be raised, and propaganda produced and distributed. Third, politically powerful men must be educated in the same manner as the public at large and pressured through lobbies and the fear of losing votes. Finally, the group favoring change must be able to take advantage of any unforeseen occurrences: it must be able to prevent important national events from obscuring the "cause" or swinging public opinion against it.[2]

In the case of Prohibition, the Anti-Saloon League performed these four activities of organization, mobilization, pressure politics, and careful exploitation of fortuitous events. However, the Anti-Saloon League was not operating in a vacuum: it had a powerful and rich enemy in the liquor interests and in their mouthpiece, the United States Brewers' Association. In the first round, culminating with the ratification of the Eighteenth Amendment, the Brewers were easily defeated. That the second round began so quickly, however, was an indication that something had gone wrong. The public consensus which had seemed so solid when the Eighteenth Amendment was ratified showed itself to be hollow almost immediately: National Prohibition was questioned as soon as it began through the actions of countless individuals who found it less satisfactory in their daily lives than they had in the voting booths. When the question was brought to a vote for a second time, the pro-liquor forces, using many of the same tactics as before ratification, but with much less effort and expense, were able to bring about repeal.[3]

In this paper I will analyze the actions of the Anti-Saloon League in creating necessary conditions for the ratification of the Eighteenth Amendment, from its inception in 1895 through its victory in 1920. The emphasis is on this early period because it was then that the battle was both won and lost. That the Eighteenth Amendment would either be repealed or ignored became apparent quickly enough. The problem is to examine how it happened that the society accepted so drastic and unrealistic a solution to the social problem of drinking in the first place.

ORIGINAL SUPPORT

In his book, *Symbolic Crusade: Status Politics and the American Temperance Movement,* Joseph Gusfield draws a useful distinction between the earlier nineteenth-century temperance movements and the post-Civil War, primarily twentieth-century, prohibition movements. Basically he asserts that the temperance movement took the form of "assimilative reform": the middle class advocated abstinence as a distinct symbol of its way of life and offered temperance to the lower class as a means by which its members could raise themselves to a higher level of economic wellbeing. The middle class viewed temperance as "a sign of life-style commitment and status group membership" (Gusfield, 1963: 29), and temperance activities provided it with a way of reacting to the increasing number of underprivileged, low-status persons in the society. "Within this context total abstinence was a doctrine of change and assimilation of the non-conformer into middle-class life, an expression of the terms by which social and economic success had been gained by temperance adherents and could be gained by the reformed drinker" (Gusfield, 1963: 71).

In the period following the Civil War, the status and values of the middle class were no longer so certain. From above it was threatened by a rising industrial plutocracy, of which the growing liquor industry was an important element; from below, by a rapidly increasing immigrant class, which in the nineteenth century had received the franchise. As these changes became more apparent, "coercive reform," whose object was seen as "an intractable defender of another culture" (Gusfield, 1963: 6) came to dominate the temperance movement. "Armed with the response of indignation at their declining social position, the adherents of temperance sought a . . . victory through legislation" (Gusfield, 1963: 141). Assimilation was no longer enough. The middle class felt it necessary to make sure that all other members of the society would accept its morality.

The Prohibition Movement, therefore, can be partially identified as a middle-class movement. However, it is important to recognize that it contained within it a "status movement" as well. As Gusfield points out, "class movements are oriented toward the 'interests' of particular groups in the economic system of production and distribution and are instrumental in their goals. Status movements are oriented toward the enhancement of the prestige of groups" (Gusfield, 1963: 20). Both these elements played a vital part.

There were important religious and ethnic strands as well. First, the movement was strengthened by the support of the Protestant Church. During the nineteenth century, evangelical Protestantism had moved into the temperance reform movement for moral, social, economic, and political reasons. Intemperance ran counter to the church emphasis on piety and asceticism; it destroyed self-discipline and social morality; it "struck at the well-being of the individual and prevented him from achieving success" (Timberlake, 1963: 8); and "by attacking man's reason and paralyzing his moral nature, [it] was believed to strike at the very foundation of political democracy" (Timberlake, 1963: 9).

In addition to attempts to bring about a general religious revival, the church promoted young people's societies and the interdenominational United Society of Christian Endeavor. In 1912, the Federal Council of the Churches of Christ in America organized a Commission on Temperance which in 1915 was working on a nationwide campaign for total abstinence (Timberlake, 1963: 21).

Although the ethnic strain is rarely stressed in books dealing with the Prohibition Movement, there is always at least passing reference to the fact that the main supporters of the movement were *Anglo-Saxon* middle-class Protestants. Fears of the lower classes were intensified not only because of the threat they were thought to pose to a middle-class way of life or religion, but because of their differing racial or ethnic origins. In the North, particularly in the cities, Prohibition supporters were constantly exposed to large groups of people whose appearance, language, and habits differed from their own. In the South, the movement rapidly caught the imagination of those who saw prohibition as a means of controlling the activities of the Negro. It is little surprise, then, that many of the areas which contained strong prohibitionist elements were also areas where Methodists, Baptists, and Ku Klux Klan members were in a majority (Sinclair, 1963: 25).

These three sources of support for the prohibition movement include much that is commonly referred to as the basic values of traditional rural America, i.e., the faith in "a fusion of free enterprise, capitalism, evangelical Protestantism, and political democracy" (Timberlake, 1963: 29). Advocates of this constellation of values located its source in the West and Midwest. Because the East was dotted with cities in which one found lower-class immigrants of all races and religions, it did not take much for the prohibitionists to view the East, as William Jennings Bryan did, as "the enemy's country" (Sinclair, 1963: 14). The Anti-Saloon League simply adopted the symbols of its supporters when it self-consciously presented itself as a "champion of rural America in its struggle against city corruption" (Clark, 1965: 114).

ORGANIZATION

That the leaders of the Anti-Saloon League were aware of the predominant groups behind them is apparent from the structure of their organization. Formed in 1895, the Anti-Saloon League was modeled after the successful "Ohio Idea" of political action originating in the churches. The church was to be the basic unit, supervised by a hierarchical structure of executive boards at the local, state, and national levels. This had two immediate advantages: (1) the federal framework allowed room for state initiative as well as unitary control, and (2) "with its roots in the local churches, the League had access to a large and sympathetic constituency willing to provide the money necessary for its support" (Timberlake, 1963: 135).

Federalism meant, on the one hand, that if one state produced a novel idea which ultimately proved successful, other states could follow suit. On the other hand, power was centered in the hands of a few men at the national level to the extent that directives sent down were obeyed and the rank and file were prevented from having much say (Odegard, 1928: 15). Internal splintering was thus avoided. Although there were many groups working across the country (some of which were not affiliated with the Anti-Saloon League), the League leaders, by using the threat of cutting off resources, ensured unity of action.

By 1913, when it adopted a new constitution, the League, through its closely coordinated state branches, could "reach down into thousands of local churches and mobilize at almost a moment's notice a large body of Protestant voters" (Timberlake, 1963: 135). In 1915, 40,000 churches were participating in League activities (Timberlake, 1963: 138).

MOBILIZATION

The task of converting a basic fund of prohibition sentiment "into a sustained demand for Prohibition, rather than an appeal for Temperance ... required the expenditure of a vast amount of money and the unrelenting efforts of many salaried men" (Merz, 1932: 8). It was a touchy business as well: the leaders had to calculate how quickly public opinion could be changed.

The League recognized the inevitable mercurial pattern of support for a social movement and appropriately viewed its task of mobilizing the concerned public opinion as an almost endless one, "for once an election was over, a large part of the public promptly lost its interest and the campaign had to start afresh. Mr. Wheeler himself once testified that even in 1917, following the most critical election in the history of the

League, at a time when the crusading spirit of this movement had theoretically reached its height, the problem which faced the Anti-Saloon League was how to maintain public interest in Prohibition until the new Congress should convene" (Merz, 1932: 11).

From the beginning the leaders showed considerable tactical skill in their methods for minimizing counter-mobilization. In the early years of the Prohibition campaign, the ASL concentrated on the abolition of the saloons themselves, rather than on the entire liquor traffic, and emphasized the liquor business rather than private consumption, in this way they were able to maintain the support of those who drank in the privacy of their homes but were opposed to the saloons (Timberlake, 1963: 145) and to avoid mention of coercive power until the last possible moment. Similarly, the leaders showed their awareness of the predominant rural support by speaking mainly about city drinks—hard liquor, rum, and beer—rather than the farmers' hard cider and corn whiskey (Sinclair, 1963: 18).

Two other general tactics were singleness of purpose and the refusal to enter into politics as a separate political party. By not allying itself with other current reform movements, the League was able to direct its total energy in a single direction and thus avoid antagonizing possible supporters who might be put off by the connotations of a general reform movement. By working through existing party structure, the ASL avoided competition with the voters' usual political allegiances.

Funds. The League's church affiliations and middle-class roots provided it with potentially great financial assets. The problem was to release these resources and employ them to generate power. The original mechanism was the "custom in cooperating churches to set aside each year one regular Sunday service for the presentation of the League's work, by a trained representative" (Odegard, 1928: 191). Although these field days, as they were called, allowed the League to carry on its propaganda as well, the main function was the raising of funds. When the subscription privilege did not accompany an invitation to speak, the League uniformly declined it: "Let no church open its doors merely for the sake of having a League speaker come in and preach a temperance sermon. That is the least and most insignificant element involved."

Following the sermon, "pledge envelopes" were distributed: a new subscriber could pledge anywhere from 35 cents to $500 per month, to be collected regularly for either one or five years. Once the pledges were in, the subscription department of the state or national League would see to it that they were actually paid.

The success of such a method is shown by the income of the ASL. Between 1903 and 1914, the yearly income rose from $125,000 to $1,000,000. In the final drive years, when the prohibition amendment was before Congress, this figure rose to $2,500,000 (Odegard, 1928: 200).

Of course, not all of this money came from pledge subscriptions alone: there was a fair amount of business support. John D. Rockefeller and S. S.

Kresge were commonly known to be contributing impressive sums. The League's refusal to divulge the names of its principal contributers laid it open to charges of being a corrupt, corporation-controlled political lobby.[4] But there is evidence to support the assertion that "during the years 1911 to 1919, the years of the League's greatest prosperity, between 80 and 90 per cent of the national League's income came from pledges secured in its own field days in the churches" (Odegard, 1928: 195).

As the income of the League grew, so did its professional staff. Increasingly the ASL was able to attract better men to its service and to select them with greater care. These men were carefully trained and then put to work directing agitation activities which took up nine-tenths of the League's yearly income (Timberlake, 1963: 132).

Political Loyalties. The most important aspect of this agitation was the mobilization of political loyalties through propaganda—the production and dissemination of arguments favoring the dry cause. The League set out to turn the floodlight of publicity on the saloon and the liquor traffic, and it found many quasi-scientific, social, and economic arguments to support its assertions.

The scientific argument ran along lines uncovered by contemporaneous research and was directed at a generation of Americans that was placing more and more of its faith in science. The research underscored the vulnerability of the brain and nervous system to alcohol and indicated that inebriety in parents was a cause of physical, mental, and moral degeneracy in children (Timberlake, 1963: 44). A few scientists even declared that alcohol, when taken in small quantities, was not only not a food (as had previously been supposed) but was a narcotic poison. Other scientists estimated the maximum safe amount of drinking as equal to the alcoholic content of two to four beers a day. "What had once been considered moderate drinking, therefore, was now regarded as excessive. Science, in short, had made out a practical case for almost total abstinence" (Timberlake, 1963: 46). The scientific argument against moderate drinking ultimately proved to be of decisive importance in changing the public attitude toward liquor, for as the statistical and scientific argument filtered down into the public consciousness, a marked change occurred in the drinking habits of many Americans (Timberlake, 1963: 55).

The Anti-Saloon newsheets were responsible for spreading social arguments as well. They exploited the findings of an investigation by the Committee of Fifty which found poverty traceable to liquor in a quarter of the cases studied. Other surveys traced the role of alcohol as the primary cause of crime in some 50% of cases. The fact that liquor was a source of crime was "proved" by citing the decrease of crime in prohibition states (Odegard, 1928: 76). Many studies were quick to find a relationship between liquor and prostitution, underlining the fact that if alcohol stimulated social vice it also led to venereal disease. And, finally, under the impetus of the doctrine of environmentalism, the ASL spread the fear of corrupting children.

The League was also ready with economic arguments to swing big business to its side. In this effort, too, the timing was propitious. After the enactment of the first Workmen's Compensation laws in 1911, employers became more concerned with the safety of their plants. With a little prodding they were able to see the connection between sobriety and the prevention of accidents. At the same time, as scientific management became the vogue in industry, employers became vitally concerned with efficiency, and, subsequently, aware of its inverse relation to drink.

The hard-headed economic reasons that justified temperance worked even more strongly for statewide prohibition: (1) prohibition would give industry in dry territory the advantage over competitors in wet territory; (2) prohibition would mean the transfer of 1.8 billion dollars spent on liquor to other industry (it was well-known at the time that those who ran the Coca-Cola Company and Welch's Grape Juice were strongly behind prohibition); (3) prohibition would mean lowered taxes, since the middle class would no longer have to support asylums and jails filled with drunkards; and (4) prohibition would mean greater order and well-being during labor strikes (Timberlake, 1963: 76). In addition, these sensible businessmen were, by and large, members of the middle class, which had its own reasons for supporting prohibition. All the ASL had to do was present the case.

The arguments were varied and ingenious. Luther, Goethe, Bismarck, Kaiser Wilhelm, Lincoln, and Grant were cited as enemies of liquor (Odegard, 1928: 60). In the South, the menace of the drunken Negro was exploited. A connection between Presidential assassinations and inebrity was "discovered." And, on the theory that "nothing succeeds like success, the League made extensive use of maps showing the rapid spread of Prohibition" (Odegard, 1928: 67). Under this barrage, the public came to view the saloon as the enemy of the child, the ruination of the home, the rendezvous of the criminal, the office of the political manipulator, and the purveyor of drugs.

This literature was disseminated in vast quantities. By 1912 the League's eight presses were printing more than forty tons of temperance literature a month, including thirty-one state editions of the newspaper *The American Issue*, with an aggregate monthly circulation of approximately 500,000. By 1916, the main plant in Westerville, Ohio, was printing six different temperance journals, including four monthlies with an aggregate circulation of about 420,000; one weekly with a circulation of over 130,000 each week; and a daily with a circulation of approximately 15,000 (Odegard, 1928: 74). In addition, the large middle-class journals provided space for pro-temperance articles, editorials, and stories (Timberlake, 1963: 156).

POWER

As mobilization progressed, the power of the ASL grew and manifested itself in the political arena. Of course, figures showing the progress of the

Prohibition campaign do not prove that the League mobilization alone produced its successes. Other factors could have been involved.[5] It is noteworthy, however, that the Prohibition Movement closely followed the lines set down by the ASL and won its major victories in those places where the League was most active and most widely supported.

Between 1900 and 1913, the tactic favored by the leaders of the ASL was to induce state legislatures to enact a "local option" law giving the citizens of local units of government the right to grant or withhold licenses for the sale of liquor during a specific period. Largely as a result of these local options, the number of people living in saloonless territory increased by 16% between 1900 and 1907 alone (Timberlake, 1963: 154). By 1913, more than half the nation's cities, towns, and counties were saloonless.

Following the passage of the Webb-Kenyon Act in 1913, which restricted the import of liquor into dry states, the League shifted its efforts toward statewide prohibition. But it was also convinced that state prohibition would succeed only in a dry nation. The campaign for National Prohibition was formally launched at the 1913 national convention. Following the convention, "Grand Committees" composed of all the leading temperance forces marched in Washington and, at the steps of the Capitol, entrusted their petitions to Senator Sheppard and Congressman Hobson. Simultaneously, local leagues spurred on the church folks: within a year Congress had received petitions which contained the names of over 9,296 organizations with a total membership of 3,358,586 (Odegard, 1928: 153).

The League decision not to form a separate political party continued to serve it in good stead. Since it would endorse candidates of either major party who promised to vote dry, in elections where the populations was evenly split, an ASL endorsement could swing the vote. The League did not insist that a candidate be a personal abstainer: if his vote was dry, he could drink all he wanted.

Efforts were made in primaries and conventions to secure the nomination of drys. Where no legislative record was available for a candidate, a strong written pledge was required for League support. Its questionnaire left little room for misunderstanding or ambiguity. "Politicians who liked to carry water on both shoulders were loath to make definite declarations on public questions. To such the Anti-Saloon League questionnaire was a source of embarrassment" (Odegard, 1928: 92).

Once the attitude of the candidate had been determined, it was handed on to the voters. "Elaborate indexes of politicians and their records were kept in Washington and in most of the states, and professions of sympathy were matched with deeds. When a man had kept faith with the League, it did not desert him" (Odegard, 1928: 91). On the other hand, the League did not hesitate to wreak vengeance on a recalcitrant legislator.

The League made steady progress in placing its men in Congress. However, it staked its main hopes on the elections of 1916, for Wheeler had insisted that the amendment be passed in that session of Congress.

"We have got to win it now because when 1920 comes and reapportionment is here, 40 new Congressmen will come in from the great wet centers with their rapidly increasing population" (Odegard, 1928: 173).

WAR

The ASL was well aware that the time was running out: it could control Congress only so long as the rural areas were over-represented. Reapportionment would mean defeat, both in Congress and in many of the state legislatures. At this critical juncture the war began, offering three major changes which the drys were quick to exploit: (1) it centralized authority in Washington; (2) it stressed the importance of saving food and of general self-sacrifice on the part of the population; and (3) it stigmatized all things German (Odegard, 1928: 97).

> The first of these three changes was inevitable. The war brushed aside the restraints normally imposed on Congress. In rapid succession laws were adopted authorizing the government to do things which it had never done when the nation was at peace: seize railways, requisition factories, take over mines. . . . draft men for an army, and send that army to war in France. With such drastic legislation as a pattern, the proposal for one more drastic law seemed commonplace [Merz, 1932: 25].

Second, food and fuel supplies became limited. The friends of Prohibition were quick to point out what great quantities of food could be saved if brewing and distilling were put to an end. Figures were cited to prove that by shutting off the grain from the breweries and distilleries, the country would save the equivalent of 11,000,000 loaves of bread a day—"enough to supply the bread needs of the English, French, and Italian armies, and much more than enough to supply the entire bread relief of Belgium," Congress was told. At the same time, the ASL newspaper, *The American Issue* (Jan. 5, 12, 19, and 26, 1918), carried articles stressing the wasteful use of coal by the breweries.

Self-sacrifice was another theme enunciated by the government, and picked up by the League as well. With the "boys" doing their share "over there," it was only fair that those at home offer support in every way.

Finally, there was the obvious opportunity the war afforded the drys in and out of Congress to point out the close association between the brewers and the German-American Alliance (Merz, 1932: 27). The Anti-Saloon League made sure that its friends would keep this association in mind at all times in articles with such titles as: "What Brewery Money Has Aided German-American Alliance To Do Since Beginning of War in 1914: Despicable and Seditious Activities Furthered With Brewery Knowledge and Brewery Coin" (*American Issue*, July 6, 1918: 221).

There was no room for moderation. As the antagonism toward the Germans grew, beer was declared unpatriotic and pretzels were banned from bars. And the sentiment was generalized: in some quarters it was suggested that advocating drink was tantamount to advocating defeat of the United States Army. And when the ASL asserted that the bombing of Attorney General A. Mitchell Palmer's home was "inspired by Germans with wet tendencies" (Leuchtenberg, 1958: 76), people were willing to accept the relevance.

This, then, was the mood during the war. Politicians, like other citizens, were thinking in extremes. Other sacrifices were being made by the population. Why not prohibition, if it could help the war effort? And why stop with war-time prohibition, when the problem could be solved for all time? Moreover, Congressmen knew that their decision would not be final. If they accepted an amendment, it would still need ratification by the states.

One can regard the war as acting as a "trigger event." Brzezinski and Huntington (1963: 76), who introduce the concept in their book, explain how such events operate:

> Decision is always difficult, and in any political system it tends to be delayed. . . . The proposal drifts in limbo. In such circumstances eventual approval may depend upon a trigger event to alter the political balance of forces. In the United States the trigger event is usually external to the political system. . . . Such stimuli produce a momentary crystallization of opinion which, if expeditiously taken advantage of by the proponents of a measure, can result in its formal approval.

This exactly describes the procedures of the ASL. It applied the final pressure and gained Congressional approval of a Constitutional amendment requiring state ratification. And state ratification, the drys knew, would not pose an insuperable problem. It was on the state level that the League had been functioning most effectively for two decades.

COUNTER-MOBILIZATION

At this point it is necessary to ask what happened to the resistance to the Eighteenth Amendment. Notwithstanding efforts to minimize opposition, there *were* groups who supported the saloons. Why could they not stop the drys?

Insofar as we can claim that the ASL was successful because of its ability to organize, mobilize, and pressure, we must assert that the liquor interests were defeated because they performed none of these tasks with equal facility. Perhaps the war tipped the scale: that is, the brewers might have lost no matter how well they carried on their fight. However, the war period could be exploited by the ASL only because of its powerful and influential position when it began. The liquor interests, on the other hand, miscalculated the strength of the drys, and by the time they began to play the game with any earnestness, they were already hopelessly behind.

The liquor interests had strong public support. The great majority of

American laborers was opposed to Prohibition. These men believed that the destruction of the liquor industry would deprive millions of workers of jobs and that Prohibition smacked of paternalism and class exploitation (Timberlake, 1963: 93). And they had other reasons for opposing the movement. Whereas the middle and upper classes did most of their drinking in the privacy of their homes, the working class frequented the saloons (which were the main target of attack). There, in addition to drink, they found companions, warmth, and an occasional free meal.

Two factors made this public a less useful one to the brewers than the middle class was to the ASL. First, the working class was located primarily in the great urban-industrial centers and therefore too concentrated to provide effective opposition, particularly since the urban areas were extremely underrepresented at this time. Second, it could scarcely offer as much financial support as could the middle class, except through direct patronage of the saloons.

On the other hand, the Brewers had some useful cards in their hands. A barrelage tax imposed on all members of their association provided finances. The saloons allowed it easy access to its "constituents." And, page for page, it attempted to match the propaganda output of the ASL. The Brewers' monthly magazine, *The Hearth-Stone,* had a circulation of 301,000 in 1915, and in the same year, it was estimated that 431,600,000 pieces of literature were sent out by the brewers or the foreign language press in the cities (Odegard, 1928: 217).

The prohibition forces had learned quickly that united action was essential. Brewers spent much of their time and energy in solving internal disputes. This was, perhaps, inevitable in view of their business interests: there was almost as much reason for each brewer to work against, as with, his competitors. It was not until 1916, when they realized the earnestness and effectiveness of the Anti-Saloon League attack, that they decided to work together.

At this late stage, the brewers promised to clean up the saloons and to promote temperance. However, the brewers were too tied up with the operation of the saloons to put through any true clean-up. The failure of this attempt led to more desperate measures. The brewers organized a blacklist system which threatened to withhold trade from a long list of businesses regarded as unfriendly, and they also attempted to buy elections.

Whatever was accomplished by these defensive activities, however, was more than offset by the exposés of liquor corruption of elections in Texas and Pennsylvania. And the publicized link between the brewers and the German-American Alliance convinced many Americans that "the only way to mend the liquor industry was to end it" (Odegard, 1928: 217).

A number of other factors worked to the disadvantage of the Brewers. While those who argued against the liquor trade could cite massive evidence of the harmfulness of liquor, there was very little that the wets could use as arguments for their side. States rights and protection of private property might have been powerful arguments in some periods, but they carried little weight during a national crisis. Similarly, while a man could prove his moral rectitude by speaking against the liquor trade, he could show little by speaking wet. Finally, the wets were unlucky. The war added to the dry lead on them. Once the Prohibitionists had gained so much headway, little could be done to reverse the tide.

CONCLUSION

The Prohibition Movement failed in its attempt to transform the United States into a dry country. What success it had was short-lived. On January 16, 1920, National Prohibition went into effect. Fourteen years later, on December 5, 1933, the Eighteenth Amendment was repealed. The story of those years is well known. The ubiquitous speakeasies; gangsters, racketeers, and bootleggers; 15,000 cases of "jake paralysis"; the report of the Wickersham Commission; and Harding's "Ohio Gang" are just a few of the highlights. All of them testify to the fact that the Eighteenth Amendment had not put an end to liquor consumption in the United States.

The Prohibition Movement, then, shows an unusual pattern. It is rare in the history of the country that a law has been passed (and never a Constitutional amendment) as the culmination of a movement, only to be rejected a short time later. How is this occurrence explained, then, and what do we learn from it about societal guidance?

When studying history one is limited by unalterable facts. One cannot recreate the situation and apply controls. No logical proof of the necessity of any one element can emerge from such a study. It is entirely conceivable, for example, that World War I alone would have been sufficient to bring about Prohibition and that the ASL's activities were not necessary. The events of the Prohibition Movement, therefore, cannot be said to vindicate the theory of societal guidance sketched in this paper. But the theory does provide an extremely useful tool with which to analyze the events.

On the basis of the facts we have presented, the hypothesis with which we began still stands. The failure of earlier movements and the failure of the brewers are characterized by insufficient organization and mobilization, and inept use of power—the very functions at which the Anti-Saloon League proved most adept.

The ultimate failure of the Prohibition Movement is more easily explained than is its short-lived success. It is fair to say that the history of the movement illustrates the danger of a preponderance of downward mobilization without commensurate upward consensus formation.

Under the Eighteenth Amendment, the United States was an "overmanaged society": two prominent features of the Prohibition years were sporadic high-control and consistent low-consensus with respect to liquor consumption (Etzioni, 1967: 184). For a time some consensus did exist. However, it was an ignorant, and therefore inauthentic, consensus which disappeared when it became known.

NOTES

1. Between 1850 and 1913 the consumption of intoxicating liquor increased steadily. In 1850 the per capita consumption was 4.08 gallons a year. By 1860 it had risen to 6.43 gallons; 1880, to 8.78 gallons; 1890, to 13.20 gallons; 1900, to 16.68 gallons; 1910, to 20.53 gallons; and in 1913 (when the Anti-Saloon League was asserting that "two-thirds of the territory of the country is now dry"), consumption had risen to 22.80 gallons a year. Figures quoted in Merz (1932: 12).
2. This analysis follows the general theoretical lines presented by Amitai Etzioni (1967, 1968).
3. "It was the dry Wayne B. Wheeler who had calculated that the Eighteenth Amendment cost $50,000,000 to secure; another $15,000,000 was spent during the life of the amendment, making a total of $65,000,000; yet repeal had cost only $20,000,000" (Sinclair, 1963: 398).
4. Wayne B. Wheeler gave as his reason for refusing to divulge the names the annoyance which beset persons known to have made large contributions to any cause, and more particularly, to the Prohibition cause: there was considerable evidence that the Brewers systematically made war on businessmen who supported the Anti-Saloon League. A further discussion of this can be found in Odegard (1928: 184).
5. One other factor, for instance, could have been the general reform movement which was apparent in the country at the same time that the ASL was working for its liquor reforms.

REFERENCES

Allen, F. L. (1964) *Only Yesterday*. New York: Harper and Row. *American Issue* (1918) Vol. 14; Nos. 1 (Jan. 5), 2 (Jan. 12), 3 (Jan. 19), 4 (Jan. 26), and 27 (July 6).

Brzezinski, Z. and S. Huntington (1963) *Political Power USA/USSR*. New York: Viking.

Clark, N. (1965) *The Dry Years: Prohibition and Social Change in Washington*. Seattle: Univ. of Washington Press.

Etzioni, A. (1967) "Toward a theory of societal guidance." *Am. J. Sociol.* 73, No. 2 (Sept.): 173–187.

——— (1968) *The Active Society*. New York: Free Press.

Gusfield, J. (1955) "Social structure and moral reform: a study of the Women's Christian Temperance Union." *Am. J. Sociol.* 61, No. 3 (Nov.): 221–232.

——— (1963) *Symbolic Crusade: Status Politics and the American Temperance Movement*. Urbana: Univ. of Illinois Press.

Krout, J. (1925) *The Origins of Prohibition*. New York: Knopf.

Leuchtenburg, W. (1958) *The Perils of Prosperity: 1914–1932*. Chicago: Univ. of Chicago Press.

Merz, C. (1932) *The Dry Decade*. New York: Doubleday, Doran, and Co.

Odegard, P. (1928) *Pressure Politics*. New York: Columbia Univ. Press.

Sinclair, A. (1963) *Era of Excess*. Boston: Little, Brown.

Timberlake, J. (1963) *Prohibition and the Progressive Movement*. Cambridge: Harvard Univ. Press.

54. A Police Riot
DANIEL WALKER

After the riots that occurred during the summer of 1968, particularly those associated with the Democratic party's national convention in Chicago, the federal government formed a National Commission on the Causes and Prevention of Violence. Members of the commission inaugurated a number of appropriate studies, including one that concentrated on the Chicago convention disorders. The director of the Chicago study team was Daniel Walker. His report to the commission is summarized in the article that follows. The report is significant on several levels, but its most notable feature is its clear finding that rioting is not confined to the poor and disadvantaged; government officials—police officers, for example—also riot on occasion. Mr. Walker's report was so well done—it was based on 3,437 statements of eyewitnesses and 20,000 pages of witness statements—that it is said to have been a most significant factor in his later political success. In November 1972, after walking throughout the entire state, Mr. Walker was elected governor of Illinois, despite the opposition of the political machine that traditionally controls the state's electoral process.

During the week of the Democratic National Convention, the Chicago police were the targets of mounting provocation by both word and act. It took the form of obscene epithets, and of rocks, sticks, bathroom tiles and even human feces hurled at police by demonstrators. Some of these acts had been planned; others were spontaneous or were themselves provoked by police action. Furthermore, the police had been put on edge by widely published threats of attempts to disrupt both the city and the Convention.

That was the nature of the provocation. The nature of the response was unrestrained and indiscriminate police violence on many occasions, particularly at night.

That violence was made all the more shocking by the fact that it was often inflicted upon persons who had broken no law, disobeyed no order, made no threat. These included peaceful demonstrators, onlookers, and large numbers of residents who were simply passing through, or happened to live in, the areas where confrontations were occurring.

Newsmen and photographers were singled out for assault, and their equipment deliberately damaged. Fundamental police training was ignored; and officers, when on the scene, were often unable to control their

SOURCE: Daniel Walker, *Rights in Conflict* (New York: Bantam Books, 1968), pp. 1–11.

men. As one police officer put it: "What happened didn't have anything to do with police work."

The violence reached its culmination on Wednesday night.

A report prepared by an inspector from the Los Angeles Police Department, present as an official observer, while generally praising the police restraint he had observed in the parks during the week, said this about the events that night:

> There is no question but that many officers acted without restraint and exerted force beyond that necessary under the circumstances. The leadership at the point of conflict did little to prevent such conduct and the direct control of officers by first line supervisors was virtually nonexistent.

He is referring to the police-crowd confrontation in front of the Conrad Hilton Hotel. Most Americans know about it, having seen the 17-minute sequence played and replayed on their television screens.

But most Americans do not know that the confrontation was followed by even more brutal incidents in the Loop side streets. Or that it had been preceded by comparable instances of indiscriminate police attacks on the North Side a few nights earlier when demonstrators were cleared from Lincoln Park and pushed into the streets and alleys of Old Town.

How did it start? With the emergence long before convention week of three factors which figured significantly in the outbreak of violence. These were: threats to the city; the city's response; and the conditioning of Chicago police to expect that violence against demonstrators, as against rioters, would be condoned by city officials.

The threats to the city were varied. Provocative and inflammatory statements, made in connection with activities planned for convention week, were published and widely disseminated. There were also intelligence reports from informants.

Some of this information was absurd, like the reported plan to contaminate the city's water supply with LSD. But some were serious; and both were strengthened by the authorities' lack of any mechanism for distinguishing one from the other.

The second factor, the city's response—matched, in numbers and logistics at least, the demonstrators' threats.

The city, fearful that the "leaders" would not be able to control their followers, attempted to discourage an inundation of demonstrators by not granting permits for marches and rallies and by making it quite clear that the "law" would be enforced.

Government—federal, state and local—moved to defend itself from the threats, both imaginary and real. The preparations were detailed and far ranging: from stationing firemen at each alarm box within a six block radius of the Amphitheatre to staging U.S. Army armored personnel carriers in Soldier Field under Secret Service control. Six thousand Regular

Army troops in full field gear, equipped with rifles, flame throwers, and bazookas were airlifted to Chicago on Monday, August 26. About 6,000 Illinois National Guard troops had already been activated to assist the 12,000 member Chicago Police Force.

Of course, the Secret Service could never afford to ignore threats of assassination of Presidential candidates. Neither could the city, against the background of riots in 1967 and 1968, ignore the ever-present threat of ghetto riots, possibly sparked by large numbers of demonstrators, during convention week.

The third factor emerged in the city's position regarding the riots following the death of Dr. Martin Luther King and the April 27th peace march to the Civic Center in Chicago.

The police were generally credited with restraint in handling the first riots—but Mayor Daley rebuked the Superintendent of Police. While it was later modified, his widely disseminated "shoot to kill arsonists and shoot to maim looters" order undoubtedly had an effect.

The effect on police became apparent several weeks later, when they attacked demonstrators, bystanders and media representatives at a Civic Center peace march. There were published criticisms—but the city's response was to ignore the police violence.

That was the background. On August 18, 1968, the advance contingent of demonstrators arrived in Chicago and established their base, as planned, in Lincoln Park on the city's Near North Side. Throughout the week, they were joined by others—some from the Chicago area, some from states as far away as New York and California. On the weekend before the convention began, there were about 2,000 demonstrators in Lincoln Park; the crowd grew to about 10,000 by Wednesday.

There were, of course, the hippies—the long hair and love beads, the calculated unwashedness, the flagrant banners, the open lovemaking and disdain for the constraints of conventional society. In dramatic effect, both visual and vocal, these dominated a crowd whose members actually differed widely in physical appearance, in motivation, in political affiliation, in philosophy. The crowd included Yippies come to "do their thing," youngsters working for a political candidate, professional people with dissenting political views, anarchists and determined revolutionaries, motorcycle gangs, black activists, young thugs, police and Secret Service undercover agents. There were demonstrators waving the Viet Cong flag and the red flag of revolution and there were the simply curious who came to watch and, in many cases, became willing or unwilling participants.

To characterize the crowd, then, as entirely hippy-Yippie, entirely "New Left," entirely anarchist, or entirely youthful political dissenters is both wrong and dangerous. The stereotyping that did occur helps to explain the emotional reaction of both police and public during and after the violence that occurred.

Despite the presence of some revolutionaries, the vast majority of the demonstrators were intent on expressing by peaceful means their dissent either from society generally or from the administration's policies in Vietnam.

Most of those intending to join the major protest demonstrations scheduled during convention week did not plan to enter the Amphitheatre and disrupt the proceedings of the Democratic convention, did not plan aggressive acts of physical provocation against the authorities, and did not plan to use rallies of demonstrators to stage an assault against any person, institution, or place of business. But while it is clear that most of the protesters in Chicago had no intention of initiating violence, this is not to say that they did not expect it to develop.

It was the clearing of the demonstrators from Lincoln Park that led directly to the violence: symbolically, it expressed the city's opposition to the protesters; literally, it forced the protesters into confrontation with police in Old Town and the adjacent residential neighborhoods.

The Old Town area near Lincoln Park was a scene of police ferocity exceeding that shown on television on Wednesday night. From Sunday night through Tuesday night, incidents of intense and indiscriminate violence occurred in the streets after police had swept the park clear of demonstrators.

Demonstrators attacked too. And they posed difficult problems for police as they persisted in marching through the streets, blocking traffic and intersections. But it was the police who forced them out of the park and into the neighborhood. And on the part of the police there was enough wild club swinging, enough cries of hatred, enough gratuitous beating to make the conclusion inescapable that individual policemen, and lots of them, committed violent acts far in excess of the requisite force for crowd dispersal or arrest. To read dispassionately the hundreds of statements describing at firsthand the events of Sunday and Monday nights is to become convinced of the presence of what can only be called a police riot.

Here is an eyewitness talking about Monday night:

> The demonstrators were forced out onto Clark Street and once again a traffic jam developed. Cars were stopped, the horns began to honk, people couldn't move, people got gassed inside their cars, people got stoned inside their cars, police were the objects of stones, and taunts, mostly taunts. As you must understand, most of the taunting of the police was verbal. There were stones thrown of course, but for the most part it was verbal. But there were stones being thrown and of course the police were responding with tear gas and clubs and everytime they could get near enough to a demonstrator they hit him.
>
> But again you had this police problem within—this really turned into a police problem. They pushed everybody out of the park, but this night there were a lot more people in the park than there had been during the previous night and Clark Street was just full of people and in addition now was full of gas because the police were using gas on a much larger scale this night. So the police were faced with the task, which took them about an hour or so, of hitting people over the head and gassing them enough to get them out of Clark Street, which they did.

But police action was not confined to the necessary force, even in clearing the park:

A young man and his girl friend were both grabbed by officers. He screamed "We're going, we're going," but they threw him into the pond. The officers grabbed the girl, knocked her to the ground, dragged her along the embankment and hit her with their batons on her head, arms, back and legs. The boy tried to scramble up the embankment to her, but police shoved him back in the water at least twice. He finally got to her and tried to pull her in the water, away from the police. He was clubbed on the head five or six times. An officer shouted, "Let's get the fucking bastards!" but the boy pulled her in the water and the police left.

Like the incident described above, much of the violence witnessed in Old Town that night seems malicious or mindless:

> There were pedestrians. People who were not part of the demonstration were coming out of a tavern to see what the demonstration was . . . and the officers indiscriminately started beating everybody on the street who was not a policeman.

Another scene:

> There was a group of about six police officers that moved in and started beating two youths. When one of the officers pulled back his nightstick to swing, one of the youths grabbed it from behind and started beating on the officer. At this point about ten officers left everybody else and ran after this youth, who turned down Wells and ran to the left.
>
> But the officers went to the right, picked up another youth, assuming he was the one they were chasing, and took him into an empty lot and beat him. And when they got him to the ground, they just kicked him ten times—the wrong youth, the innocent youth who had been standing there.

A federal legal official relates an experience of Tuesday evening.

> I then walked one block north where I met a group of 12-15 policemen. I showed them my identification and they permitted me to walk with them. The police walked one block west. Numerous people were watching us from their windows and balconies. The police yelled profanities at them, taunting them to come down where the police would beat them up. The police stopped a number of people on the street demanding identification. They verbally abused each pedestrian and pushed one or two without hurting them. We walked back to Clark Street and began to walk north where the police stopped a number of people who appeared to be protesters, and ordered them out of the area in a very abusive way. One protester who was walking in the opposite direction was kneed in the groin by a policeman who was walking towards him. The boy fell to the ground and swore at the policeman who picked him up and threw him to the ground. We continued to walk toward the command post. A derelict who appeared to be very intoxicated, walked up to the policeman and mumbled something that was incoherent. The policeman pulled from his belt a tin container and sprayed its contents into the eyes of the derelict, who stumbled around and fell on his face.

It was on these nights that the police violence against media representatives reached its peak. Much of it was plainly deliberate. A newsman was pulled aside on Monday by a detective acquaintance of his who said: "The word is being passed to get newsmen." Individual newsmen were warned, "You take my picture tonight and I'm going to get you." Cries of "get the camera" preceded individual attacks on photographers.

A newspaper photographer describes Old Town on Monday at about 9:00 P.M.:

> When the people arrived at the intersection of Wells and Division, they were not standing in the streets. Suddenly a column of policemen ran out from the alley. They were reinforcements. They were under control but there seemed to be no direction. One man was yelling, "Get them up on the sidewalks, turn them around." Very suddenly the police charged the people on the sidewalks and began beating their heads. A line of cameramen was "trapped" along with the crowd along the sidewalks, and the police went down the line chopping away at the cameras.

A network cameraman reports that on the same night:

> I just saw this guy coming at me with his nightstick and I had the camera up. The tip of his stick hit me right in the mouth, then I put my tongue up there and I noticed that my tooth was gone. I turned around then to try to leave and then this cop came up behind me with his stick and he jabbed me in the back.
>
> All of a sudden these cops jumped out of the police cars and started just beating the hell out of people. And before anything else happened to me, I saw a man holding a Bell & Howell camera with big wide letters on it, saying 'CBS.' He apparently had been hit by a cop. And cops were standing around and there was blood streaming down his face. Another policeman was running after me and saying, "Get the fuck out of here." And I head another guy scream, "Get their fucking cameras." And the next thing I know I was being hit on the head, and I think on the back, and I was just forced down on the ground at the corner of Division and Wells.

If the intent was to discourage coverage, it was successful in at least one case. A photographer from a news magazine says that finally, "I just stopped shooting, because every time you push the flash, they look at you and they are screaming about, 'Get the fucking photographers and get the film.'"

There is some explanation for the media-directed violence. Camera crews on at least two occasions did stage violence and fake injuries. Demonstrators did sometimes step up their activities for the benefit of TV cameras. Newsmen and photographers' blinding lights did get in the way of police clearing streets, sweeping the park and dispersing demonstrators. Newsmen did, on occasion, disobey legitimate police orders to "move" or "clear the streets." News reporting of events did seem to the police to be an anti-Chicago and anti-police.

But was the response appropriate to the provocation?

Out of 300 newsmen assigned to cover the parks and streets of Chicago during convention week, more than 60 (about 20%) were involved in incidents resulting in injury to themselves, damage to their equipment, or their arrest. Sixty-three newsmen were physically attacked by police; in 13 of these instances, photographic or recording equipment was intentionally damaged.

The violence did not end with either demonstrators or newsmen on the North Side on Sunday, Monday and Tuesday. It continued in Grant Park on Wednesday. It occurred on Michigan Avenue in front of the Conrad Hilton Hotel, as already described. A high-ranking Chicago police commander admits that on that occasion the police "got out of control." This same commander appears in one of the most vivid scenes of the entire week, trying desperately to keep individual policemen from beating demonstrators as he screams, "For Christ's sake, stop it!"

Thereafter, the violence continued on Michigan Avenue and on the side streets running into Chicago's Loop. A federal official describes how it began:

> I heard a 10-1 call [policeman in trouble] on either my radio or one of the other hand sets carried by men with me and then heard 'Car 100—sweep.' With a roar of motors, squads, vans and three-wheelers came from east, west and north into the block north of Jackson. The crowd scattered. A big group ran west on Jackson, with a group of blue shirted policemen in pursuit, beating at them with clubs. Some of the crowd would jump into doorways and the police would rout them out. The action was very tough. In my judgment, unnecessarily so. The police were hitting with a vengeance and quite obviously with relish. . . .

What followed was a club-swinging melee. Police ranged the streets striking anyone they could catch. To be sure, demonstrators threw things at policemen and at police cars; but the weight of violence was overwhelmingly on the side of the police. A few examples will give the flavor of that night in Chicago.

> "At the corner of Congress Plaza and Michigan," states a doctor, "was gathered a group of people, numbering between thirty and forty. They were trapped against a railing [along a ramp leading down from Michigan Avenue to an underground parking garage] by several policemen on motorcycles. The police charged the people on motorcycles and struck about a dozen of them, knocking several of them down. About twenty standing there jumped over the railing. On the other side of the railing was a three-to-four-foot drop. None of the people who were struck by the motorcycles appeared to be seriously injured. However, several of them were limping as if they had been run over on their feet."

A UPI reporter witnessed these attacks, too. He relates in his statement that one officer, "with a smile on his face and a fanatical look in his eyes, was standing on a three-wheel cycle, shouting, 'Wahoo, wahoo,' and trying to run down people on the sidewalk." The reporter says he was chased thirty feet by the cycle.

A priest who was in the crowd says he saw a "boy, about fourteen or fifteen, white, standing on top of an automobile yelling something which was unidentifiable. Suddenly a policeman pulled him down from the car and beat him to the ground by striking him three or four times with a nightstick. Other police joined in . . . and they eventually shoved him to a police van.

"A well-dressed woman saw this incident and spoke angrily to a nearby police captain. As she spoke, another policeman came up from behind her and sprayed something in her face with an aerosol can. He then clubbed her to the ground. He and two other policemen then dragged her along the ground to the same paddy wagon and threw her in."

"I ran west on Jackson," a witness states. "West of Wabash, a line of police stretching across both sidewalks and the street charged after a small group I was in. Many people were clubbed and maced as they ran. Some weren't demonstrators at all, but were just pedestrians who didn't know how to react to the charging officers yelling 'Police!' "

"A wave of police charged down Jackson," another witness relates. "Fleeing demonstrators were beaten indiscriminately and a temporary, makeshift first aid station was set up on the corner of State and Jackson. Two men lay in pools of blood, their heads severely cut by clubs. A minister moved amongst the crowd, quieting them, brushing aside curious onlookers, and finally asked a policeman to call an ambulance, which he agreed to do. . . ."

An Assistant U.S. Attorney later reported that "the demonstrators were running as fast as they could but were unable to get out of the way because of the crowds in front of them. I observed the police striking numerous individuals, perhaps 20 to 30. I saw three fall down and then overrun by the police. I observed two demonstrators who had multiple cuts on their heads. We assisted one who was in shock into a passer-by's car."

Police violence was a fact of convention week. Were the policemen who committed it a minority? It appears certain that they were—but one which has imposed some of the consequences of its actions on the majority, and certainly on their commanders. There has been no public condemnation of these violators of sound police procedures and common decency by either their commanding officers or city officials. Nor (at the time this Report is being completed—almost three months after the convention) has any disciplinary action been taken against most of them. That some policemen lost control of themselves under exceedingly provocative circumstances can perhaps be understood; but not condoned. If no action is taken against them, the effect can only be to discourage the majority of policemen who acted responsibly, and further weaken the bond between police and community.

Although the crowds were finally dispelled on the nights of violence in Chicago, the problems they represent have not been. Surely this is not the last time that a violent dissenting group will clash head-on with those whose duty it is to enforce the law. And the next time the whole world will still be watching.

55. We Have Been Invaded by the 21st Century
DAVID McREYNOLDS

This is the second piece by David McReynolds included in these readings (see selection 48). Here McReynolds makes the point that technological change occurs with disturbing speed. This point may seem too obvious to need explication, but McReynolds has a knack of illustrating such an "obvious" point in a way that clarifies its vast importance.

The world has changed with increasing speed. Two hundred years ago, we could travel only as fast as our horses could run. Today, we walk on the moon. Five hundred years ago, the American continents were still undiscovered. Now, we are mapping the solar system.

Perhaps 2 million years ago, the human race became a biological fact, having evolved at last from the dust and the sea: life, drawn by cosmic tides to move from water to land, to creep, to crawl, and, at last, to stand, cunning, fearful, and loving. Perhaps fifty thousand years ago, we entered upon a period of savage splendor, with tools and pottery and a fear of the gods. Not more than seven thousand years ago, civilization began along the Indus Valley, the Nile, the Yellow River of China (and, inexplicably, in the high Andes of Peru and the mountain-rimmed region of Mexico). Man is not new, but his civilization is. It is recent and fragile. The discovery of the wheel and the taming of fire were much more important to us than the first landing on the moon.

Then, when we had not yet integrated "civilization" into our psyche, along came the Industrial Revolution, followed, in the last fifty years,

SOURCE: David McReynolds, *We Have Been Invaded by the 21st Century* (New York: Praeger Publishers, 1970), pp. 19–23. Copyright © 1970 by Praeger Publishers, Inc., New York. Excerpted and reprinted by permission.

by the Technological Revolution and, now by the Cybernetics Revolution. These things are "invasions" from our future, and whatever the future may be—whether it be a planet laid to waste by nuclear war, devastated slowly by shifts in the ecology, or blossoming forth with abundance for all—that future will be determined by our technology.

In the recent past, man lived with the forces of nature, both as a constant companion and an occasional enemy. Today, it is not nature that impinges on our lives, dictating our behavior, but, rather, it is our own machines. They are, at present, as much a threat to us as any raging storm, because we have invented them without knowing how to control them. The future has invaded us.

Tick off, in your own mind, the major problems we face. They do not include fires, floods, hurricanes, tidal waves, or earthquakes. Within limits, we have learned how to deal with these. It is air pollution that burdens our lungs and water pollution that makes it risky to swim in our rivers.

Chemical miracles, such as DDT, now haunt us. We build freeways to speed the flow of traffic and find this only encourages more people to drive more cars, requiring more freeways to speed the flow of traffic, and freeways become a blight creeping across our major cities.

We found the chemicals that will control pain, but, now, we see heroin, a plague as cold as ice, as deadly as poisoned snow, drifting through the slums. We exist in a world infiltrated by nuclear bombs, missiles, germ- and chemical-warfare devices. The science-fiction writers in the 1930's saw a future that glistened with little air-cars flitting through vast clean cities, a world where man, having dealt with his physical problems, could at last explore his own meaning. But we don't have that: Our hospitals are overcrowded; the noise level of city life is hard to tolerate; our transporation is worse now than twenty years ago; we are all coughing from cigarettes or smog and depressed to learn that some of the food additives we've been using may be giving us cancer. More people live to an old age and find themselves without friends or employment or social meaning, driven into the ghettos of the aged, where, rejected by a society of the young, they can find no meaning in remaining alive. We have Telstar for instant communication, but little of value has been thus communicated.

We are losing control to the machines, the computers, the electronic brains. We shape our society—and own lives—around the needs of the machinery, rather than shaping the machinery around the human needs of our lives. We are becoming mechanized rather than finding ways to humanize and gentle the technology.

New York in the 1960's was a frightening example of battles lost to the invading forces. In November, 1965, our power failed. I was leaving the WRL [War Resisters' League—Ed.] office for a TV show in midtown when the lights flickered, dimmed, and went out. Using my cigarette lighter, I walked down ten flights and caught a bus, assuming, all the while, that the failure extended only into lower Manhattan. But the bus, roaring up Second Avenue that night, oblivious of the fact the signals were no longer working, carried us into the darkness of midtown Manhattan. There was a strange, frightening beauty to the canyons of central Manhattan, darkened streets caught between black towers, only skylight for a guide. My own mind was sick with tension, because I had burned my draft card on November 5th and, the next morning, Roger LaPorte of the Catholic Worker had immolated himself at the United Nations and lay dying in the hospital. Tom Cornell and I both felt that LaPorte, aware of the tremendous public antagonism directed toward the five of us who had burned our cards, was trying to "draw the violence to himself" by the act of immolation. When the power failed, three days after LaPorte had incurred the burns that proved fatal, I could only think of the New Testament with its statement that, as Jesus was crucified, "from the sixth hour there was darkness over all the land." (The power failure came about 5:30 P.M., and LaPorte did, in fact, die during the time of darkness.)

I got to the TV studio, still assuming the power failure was local and temporary, and asked one of the men how serious the failure was. "All the way from New Jersey to Canada," he replied. I walked home from Times Square, stopping for drinks at some little bar on Third Avenue. When I go home, I found Peter and Ernesto there. We all lit candles and drank, and I relaxed, and then, much later, Peter and I wandered downstairs in the darkness and out onto the streets, filled with people curious at the disaster. We walked from the Bowery and Fourth Street up to Sixth Avenue and Eighth Street and, there, peered in the window of Bigelow's Pharmacy, realizing we were looking into another century—for Bigelow's had never dismantled their gas lamps from the last century and, with the failure of electricity, they lit the old lamps, leaving their store in a warm glow.

A couple of years later, we had a subway strike, and we all walked to work, or cadged rides from strangers: the weather, bitter cold and very January: a city under siege. When the subways started again, we had a garbage strike, and grateful we were it came in winter, for the garbage piled high on every street, would have made Manhattan smell like the Orient, if the strike had come in July. By the end of the decade, our phones phased out and became a problem and a joke. The efficiency of the New York Telephone Company hardly matched that of some obscure newly emerged African or Asian state. And, all the while, the crime rate went up. To Middle America, the phrase "law and order" may mask anti-Negro attitudes. In Manhattan, it just means we are all afraid, with statistically verified reason, of being mugged, as we walk the streets. The city was becoming feudalized, as New Yorkers moved into those buildings that offered the best protection. We imprisoned ourselves with bars across our windows, double locks on every door.

The 1960s also saw a major water shortage, which could not be alleviated by drawing on the Hudson River because of its pollution. Joking signs like "Save Water—Shower With a Friend" went on sale in head shops, while serious signs like "Don't Flush After Every Use" went up in the subway rest rooms. The lawns in Queens and Brooklyn dried and went brown. City fountains were turned off. We held our breath, prayed for rain, and survived.

All of these troubles hit us within five years, reminding us how vulnerable the great cities are.

The invasion we endure has not left us joyous, healthy, cheerful, but, instead, frightened, gasping, and cautious. Technology has not liberated us but, rather, has constricted us. The imperatives of American power have taken our youth off to war, killing them even as they kill Vietnamese. We do not live in peace but in terror. Nuclear energy has not ended hard labor but only left us fearful of radiation.

56. Change for Survival
ANDREI D. SAKHAROV

In this final selection, Andrei Sakharov, the famous physicist who created the Soviet hydrogen bomb, indicates the social conditions that must prevail—those we must, therefore, seek to establish— if we are to have any chance at all to save humanity from total destruction. Sakharov's plea is particularly impressive, since, in making it, he has opened himself to Russian charges that he is "subversive," "anti-Soviet," "in league with foreign ideologists." But Sakharov's conviction is so deeply felt that he has continued to issue his warnings even in the face of open threats by Soviet government officials either to silence him forcibly or to exile him, as they have novelist Aleksandr Solzhenitsyn.

In this essay, advanced for discussion, the author has set himself the goal to present, with the greatest conviction and frankness, two theses that are supported by many people in the world. The theses relate to the destruction threatened by the division of mankind and the need for intellectual freedom.

SOURCE: Andrei D. Sakharov, *Progress, Coexistence, and Intellectual Freedom*, translated by *The New York Times*, with an Introduction, Afterword and Notes by Harrison E. Salisbury (New York: W. W. Norton & Company, Inc., 1968), pp. 27–30. Copyright © 1968, 1970 by *The New York Times*. Reprinted by permission of W. W. Norton & Company, Inc.

1

The division of mankind threatens it with destruction. Civilization is imperiled by: a universal thermonuclear war, catastrophic hunger for most of mankind, stupefaction from the narcotic of "mass culture," and bureaucratized dogmatism, a spreading of mass myths that put entire peoples and continents under the power of cruel and treacherous demagogues, and destruction or degeneration from the unforeseeable consequences of swift changes in the conditions of life on our planet.

In the face of these perils, any action increasing the division of mankind, any preaching of the incompatibility of world ideologies and nations is madness and a crime. Only universal cooperation under conditions of intellectual freedom and the lofty moral ideals of socialism and labor, accompanied by the elimination of dogmatism and pressures of the concealed interests of ruling classes, will preserve civilization.

The reader will understand that ideological collaboration cannot apply to those fanatical, sectarian, and extremist ideologies that reject all possibility of rapprochement, discussion, and compromise, for example, and ideologies of Fascist, racist, militaristic, and Maoist demagogy.

Millions of people throughout the world are striving to put an end to poverty. They despise oppression, dogmatism, and demagogy (and their more extreme manifestations—racism, Fascism, Stalinism, and Maoism). They believe in progress based on the use, under conditions of social justice and intellectual freedom, of all the positive experience accumulated by mankind.

2

The second basic thesis is that intellectual freedom is essential to human society—freedom to obtain and distribute information, freedom for open-minded and unfearing debate and freedom from pressure by officialdom and prejudices. Such a trinity of freedom of thought is the only guarantee against an infection of people by mass myths, which, in the hands of treacherous hypocrites and demagogues, can be transformed into bloody dictatorship. Freedom of thought is the only guarantee of the feasibility of a scientific democratic approach to politics, economy, and culture.

But freedom of thought is under a triple threat in modern society—from the opium of mass culture, from cowardly, egotistic and narrow-minded ideologies, and from the ossified dogmatism of a bureaucratic oligarchy and its favorite weapon, ideological censorship. Therefore, freedom of thought requires the defense of all thinking and honest people. This is a mission not only for the intelligentsia but for all strata of society, particularly its most active and organized stratum, the working class. The worldwide dangers of war, famine, cults of personality, and bureaucracy—these are perils for all of mankind.